Supporting resources

Visit **www.pearsoned.co.uk/sloman** to access all the supporting resources available. Click on the *Essentials of Economics*, fifth edition cover at the top of the page for both student and lecturer resources

MyEconlab for students

MyEconLab for *Essentials of Economics*, fifth edition enables you to assess your learning, and provides you with a personalised Study Plan which identifies areas you need to concentrate on to improve your grades. Specific tools are provided to direct your study in the most efficient way. Access to MyEconLab is provided with every new purchase of the main text.

MyEconLab contains the following resources:

- a customisable Study Plan, with extensive self testing and homework that can be set by your tutor;
- a complete online workbook for use alongside the textbook as you learn;
- multiple choice questions to test your learning;
- over 170 extra case studies with questions;
- answers to all pause for thought questions and odd-numbered end-of-chapter questions;
- an economics news blog updated several times per month. Each news item has an introduction, links to a range of news articles, questions and references to the relevant chapter of the book;
- animations of all key models with audio explanations. These can be downloaded to your iPod or MP3 player;
- extensive annotated Hotlinks to relevant sites on the Internet, regularly updated;
- an online glossary to explain key terms with flashcards to test your knowledge;
- detailed explanations of each of the 15 Threshold Concepts.

MyEconLab for lecturers

- MyEconLab's gradebook automatically records each student's time spent and performance on the tests and Study Plan and generates reports you can organise by student or chapter.
- Lecturers can use MyEconLab to build their own tests, quizzes and homework assignments from the question base provided.
- Questions are generated algorithmically so that they use different values each time they are used.
- If you want to devote the time you can create your own exercises by using the econ exercise builder.

For lecturers wanting more information about the MyEconLab product please contact your local Pearson Education sales representative at **www.pearsoned.co.uk/replocator** or visit **www.myeconlab.com**

Additional lecturer resources:

- customisable testbank of question material;
- customisable lecture plans in PowerPoint with questions for use in lectures with or without an audience response system;
- key models animated as full-colour PowerPoint slide shows;
- downloadable PowerPoint slides of all figures and tables from the book;
- a range of teaching and learning case studies;
- workshops with answers – one workshop for each chapter;
- answers to all questions in the book: end-of-chapter, pause for thought and box questions;
- answers to all questions in the case studies and Web appendices found in MyEconLab.

These lecturer resources can be downloaded from the lecturer website at **www.pearsoned.co.uk/sloman**. Sample resources are available on open access. Adopters of the book can obtain a password for the remaining resources from their Pearson Education sales representative (see above).

We work with leading authors to develop the strongest educational materials in economics, bringing cutting-edge thinking and best learning practice to a global market.

Under a range of well-known imprints, including Financial Times Prentice Hall we craft high quality print and electronic publications which help readers to understand and apply their content, whether studying or at work.

To find out more about the complete range of our publishing, please visit us on the World Wide Web at: www.pearsoned.co.uk

ESSENTIALS OF ECONOMICS

Fifth edition

John Sloman
The Economics Network, University of Bristol

Dean Garratt
Nottingham Trent University

**Financial Times
Prentice Hall
is an imprint of**

Harlow, England • London • New York • Boston • San Francisco • Toronto • Sydney • Singapore • Hong Kong
Tokyo • Seoul • Taipei • New Delhi • Cape Town • Madrid • Mexico City • Amsterdam • Munich • Paris • Milan

Pearson Education Limited

Edinburgh Gate
Harlow
Essex CM20 2JE
England

and Associated Companies throughout the world

Visit us on the World Wide Web at:
www.pearsoned.co.uk

First published 1998
Second edition 2001
Third edition 2004
Fourth edition 2007
Fifth edition 2010

ISBN: 978-0-273-72241-0

British Library Cataloguing-in-Publication Data
A catalogue record for this book is available from the British Library

Library of Congress Cataloging-in-Publication Data
Sloman, John, 1947–
 Essentials of economics / John Sloman, Dean Garratt. – 5th ed.
  p. cm.
 ISBN 978-0-273-72241-0 (pbk.)
1. Economics. I. Garratt, Dean, 1970– II. Title.
HB171.S59 2010
330–dc22

                    2009038939

10 9 8 7 6 5 4 3 2
13 12 11 10

Typeset in 9/12.5pt Stone Serif by 35
Printed and bound by Rotolito Lombarda, Italy

About the authors

John Sloman is Director of the Economics Network (www.economicsnetwork.ac.uk) of the UK Higher Education Academy. The Economics Network is based at the University of Bristol and provides a range of services designed to promote and share good practice in learning and teaching economics. The Network is one of 24 subject centres covering the range of disciplines taught in UK Higher Education. The HE Academy is backed by grants from the four UK higher education funding councils.

John is also visiting professor at the University of the West of England, Bristol where, from 1992 to 1999, he was Head of School of Economics. He taught at UWE until 2007.

John has taught a range of courses, including economic principles on social science and business studies degrees, development economics, comparative economic systems, intermediate macroeconomics and managerial economics. He has also taught economics on various professional courses.

John is also the author of *Economics* (Pearson Education, 7th edition 2009) and *Economics and the Business Environment* (2nd edition 2008). He is co-author, with Kevin Hinde from the University of Durham and Dean Garratt, of *Economics for Business* (Pearson Education, 5th edition 2010) and with Peter Smith from the University of Southampton of the *Economics Workbook* designed to accompany *Economics* 7th edition. Translations or editions of the various books are available for a number of different countries with the help of co-authors around the world.

John is very interested in promoting new methods of teaching economics, including group exercises, experiments, role playing, computer-aided learning and use of audience response systems and podcasting in teaching. He has organised and spoken at conferences for both lecturers and students of economics throughout the UK and in many other countries.

As part of his work with the Economics Network he has contributed to its two sites for students and prospective students of economics: Studying Economics (www.studyingeconomics.ac.uk) and Why Study Economics? (www.whystudyeconomics.ac.uk)

From March to June 1997, John was a visiting lecturer at the University of Western Australia. In July and August 2000, he was again a visiting lecturer at the University of Western Australia and also at Murdoch University in Perth.

In 2007, John received a Lifetime Achievement Award as 'outstanding teacher and ambassador of economics' presented jointly by the Higher Education Academy, the Government Economic Service and the Scottish Economic Society.

Dean Garratt is senior lecturer in economics at Nottingham Trent University. Dean joined Nottingham Trent after a spell working as an economic assistant at both HM Treasury and then at the Council of Mortgage Lenders. While at these institutions Dean was briefing on a variety of issues relating to the household sector and to the housing and mortgage markets.

His time as an economic assistant has significantly influenced Dean's approach towards the teaching of economics. This has seen Dean increasingly adopt a problem- or issues-based approach in his teaching of economics. He believes that this approach can help to cultivate amongst students the same interest and fascination that Dean has for economics. He believes that a deeper understanding of what it means to think like an economist can be achieved when students can clearly see the relevance and application of economic ideas and principles

In 2006 Dean received an Outstanding Teaching Award from the Economics Network of the Higher Education Academy. The award is given to an academic who demonstrates excellence in course structure, delivery, student response, student performance and peer recognition.

Subsequently, Dean has become an Associate of the Economics Network helping to promote quality teaching practices through presentations and workshops. He has been involved in projects to develop issues-based learning and teaching resources for economists, including resources for use on level 1 quantitative methods and data analysis modules.

Dean teaches economics at a variety of levels both to students on economics programmes and to those taking economics as part of non-economics programmes. In 2008/9 he was the learning and teaching co-ordinator for the Nottingham Business School.

Brief contents

Part A: INTRODUCTION

Part B: MICROECONOMICS

Part C: MACROECONOMICS

Part D: **INTERNATIONAL ECONOMICS**

Detailed contents

Part A:	INTRODUCTION

Part D: INTERNATIONAL ECONOMICS

Custom publishing

Custom publishing allows academics to pick and choose content from one or more textbooks for their course and combine it into a definitive course text.

Here are some common examples of custom solutions which have helped over 1000 courses across Europe:

- different chapters from across our publishing imprints combined into one book;
- lecturer's own material combined together with textbook chapters or published in a separate booklet;
- third-party cases and articles that you are keen for your students to read as part of the course;
- any combination of the above.

The Pearson Education custom text published for your course is professionally produced and bound – just as you would expect from any Pearson Education text. Since many of our titles have online resources accompanying them we can even build a Custom website that matches your course text.

If you are teaching a first year Economics course you may have a large teaching team with different lecturers teaching the micro and macroeconomics sections. Do you find that it can be difficult to agree on one textbook? If you do, you might find combining the macro and micro halves from different Pearson textbooks a useful solution. You may teach a mixed ability class and would like to be able to provide some advanced material from Sloman's larger economics text or perhaps you take more of a business focus where chapters from Sloman's *Economics for Business* might be useful.

Custom publishing has enabled adopters of this text to employ these different solutions.

If, once you have had time to review this title, you feel Custom publishing might benefit you and your course, please do get in contact. However minor, or major the change – we can help you out.

For more details on how to make your chapter selection for your course please go to www.pearsoned.co.uk/sloman and select the custom publishing link.

You can contact us at: **www.pearsoncustom.co.uk** or via your local representative at: **www.pearsoned.co.uk/replocator**.

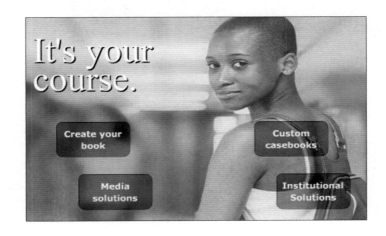

Guided tour

The book is divided into four **parts,** each with a part map to help you navigate around the book. **Chapter maps** located at the start of each chapter indicate each chapter's topics. **Chapter openers** provide an overview of the topics to be covered in each chapter and learning objectives in the form of questions.

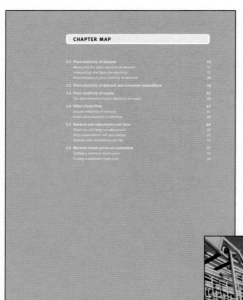

Markets in action

In this chapter we explore the working of markets in more detail. We start by examining one of the most important concepts in the whole of economics – that of elasticity (Sections 3.1–3.4).

A bumper harvest may seem like good news for farmers: after all, they will be able to sell more. But is it good news? Although they will sell more, the effect of the increased supply will be to drive down the price – and that's bad news for farmers! So will the increased sales (the good news) be enough to compensate for the reduction in price (the bad news)? Will farmers end up earning more or less from their bumper harvest? It all depends on just how much the price falls, and this depends on the *price elasticity of demand* for their produce. This is a measure of how *responsive* demand is to a change in price.

It is not just the responsiveness of *demand* that is important in determining the functioning of markets. It is also the responsiveness of *supply.* Why, do you think, do some firms respond to a rise in price by producing a lot more, whereas others only produce a little more? Is it simply because of different technologies? We will discover just what influences the price elasticity of supply in Section 3.3.

The chapter closes by looking at what happens if governments set about *controlling* prices. Why will shortages occur if the government sets the price too low, or surpluses if it sets it too high? When might governments feel that it is a good idea to fix prices?

PRACTISING AND TESTING YOUR LEARNING

Pause for thought questions throughout the text enable you to test your understanding of what you have just read. **Answers appear in MyEconLab**.

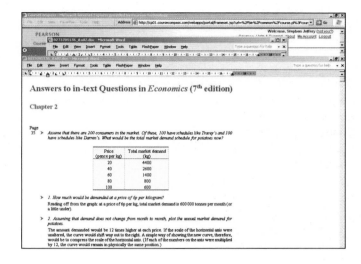

End-of-chapter questions can be used for self-testing or in class.

AIDING YOUR UNDERSTANDING

All key terms are highlighted where they first appear in the text, and **definitions** are provided in boxes nearby. The **Key Ideas** in an economist's toolkit are highlighted and explained where they first appear. Again, an icon appears in the margin whenever they recur later in the book. All terms also appear in the comprehensive glossary that appears at the back of the book and in MyEconlab.

Fifteen of the key ideas have been given **Threshold Concept** status to highlight their importance in helping us to think like an economist. These are explained in detail in MyEconlab.

Recap section summaries at the end of each section allow you to check up on your understanding at frequent intervals and provide an important revision tool.

You can use your personalised **MyEconLab Study Plan** to assess how well you are doing, and identify areas you need to concentrate on to improve.

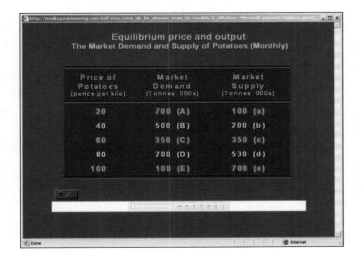

Extra resources such as animated graphs with audio explanations are provided to further explain the topics you need to focus on to improve your grades. For details on how to access MyEconLab, see the access card that is packaged with every new copy of this book.

APPLYING ECONOMICS TO THE REAL WORD

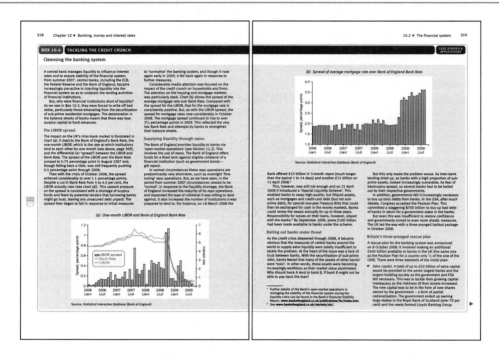

Case studies and applications boxes include examples, data and scenarios from the real world to show you why this subject really matters in everyday life.

Websites relevant to each chapter are listed at the end of the chapter, and are linked to from the chapter resources area of MyEconLab.

Additional case studies relevant for each chapter can be found in MyEconLab. These cases are listed at the end of each chapter.

FLEXIBLE LEARNING

Exploring economics boxes consider economic applications or elaborate on themes or theories covered in the text.

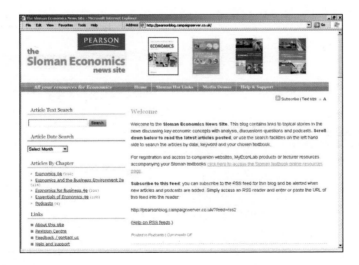

A news blog site. New items are added several times per month. These link to articles in the press and there are questions on each news item and references to the book. There is also a powerful search feature that lets you search for articles by chapter of the book, by topic or by month.

Getting started with MyEconLab

The fifth edition of *Essentials of Economics* comes with a new improved and updated version of MyEconLab. MyEconLab is a personalised and innovative online study and testing resource which provides a variety of tools to enable you to assess and progress your own learning. In addition to the exercises interspersed in the text that you are encouraged to tackle as you go along you should log on to this new online tool and practise further.

To get started, take out your **access kit** included inside this book to register online.

Registration and login

Go to www.myeconlab.com and click on student register. Enter your course ID if you have already been given this by your lecturer. If not, choose don't have a course id and search for the author and book title to register and login and follow the instructions on screen using the code inside your access kit, which will look like this:

> **Example**
> SIMPLE-FRILL-TONLE-WEIRS-CHOIR-FLEES

The login screen will look like this:

Now you should be registered with your own password ready to log directly into your own course.

When you log in to your course for the first time, the course home page will look like this:

Now follow the steps below for the chapter you are studying.

Step 1 – Take a sample test

Sample tests (two for each chapter) enable you to test yourself to see how much you already know about a particular topic and identify the areas in which you need more practice. Click on the Study Plan button in the menu and take **sample test a** for the chapter you are studying. Once you have completed a chapter, go back and take **sample test b** and see how much you have learned.

Step 2 – Review your study plan

The results of the sample tests you have taken will be incorporated into your study plan showing you what sections you have mastered and what sections you need to study further helping you make the most efficient use of your self-study time.

Step 3 – Have a go at an exercise

From the study plan, click on the section of the book you are studying and have a go at the series of interactive **Exercises. Exercises with page references are based on end of chapter questions in the book.** When required, use the **Grapher** on the right hand side to select the graphing tools you need to complete the question. For help using the grapher click on the question icon. Additional study tools such as **Guided Solutions** and **Examples** break the question down step-by-step for you, helping you to complete the exercises successfully. You can try the same exercises over and over again, and each time the values will change, giving you unlimited practice.

Step 4 – Use the E-book and additional multimedia tools found in Textbook Resources to help you further.

Use the online workbook for an interactive way to review what you have learned in the text and practise further here with additional support, before you attempt the questions in MyEconlab.

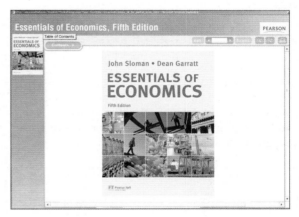

If you are struggling with a question, you can click on the textbook icon to read the relevant part of your text book again.

You can also click on the animation icon to help you visualise and improve your understanding of key concepts.

Good luck getting started with *MyEconLab*.

For an online tour go to **www.myeconlab.com**.

For any help and advice contact the 24 online support at **www.myeconlab.com** and click on student support.

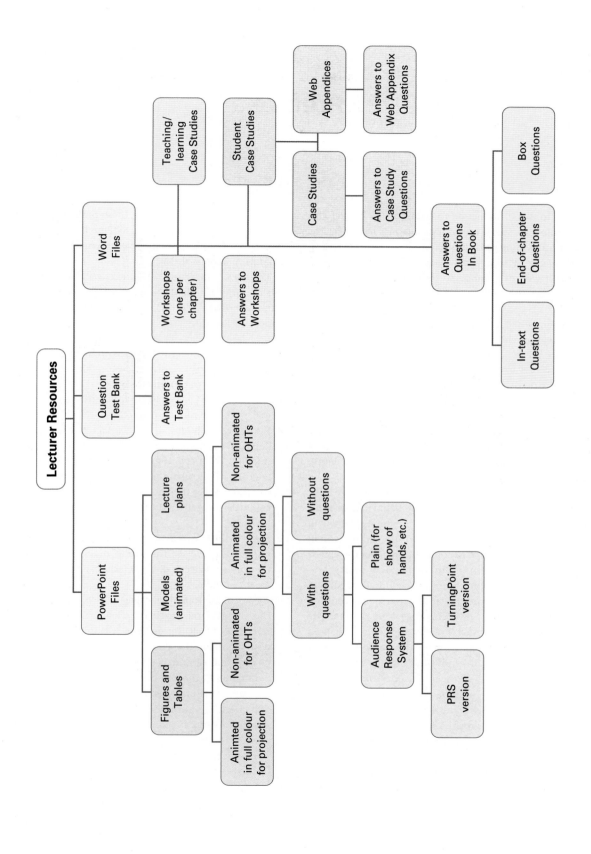

Preface

Welcome to this introduction to economics. Whether you are planning to study economics beyond this level, or whether this will be your only exposure to this fascinating subject, we hope that you will find the book enjoyable and that it will give you some insight into the economy in which you live and the economic forces that shape all our lives.

Although you have probably never studied the subject before, you will almost certainly know quite a lot of economics already. After all, you make economic decisions virtually every day of your life. Every time you go shopping, you are acting as an 'economist': deciding what to buy with your limited amount of money. And it is not just with decisions about buying that we act as economists. How much to work (something that students are increasingly forced to do nowadays), how much to study, even how much time to devote to various activities during the course of the day, are all, in a way, *economic* choices.

To satisfy us as consumers, goods and services have to be produced. We will therefore study the behaviour of firms and what governs the decisions that they make. How will the decisions of big businesses differ from those of small firms? How will the degree of competition affect the extent to which we gain or lose from the activities of firms?

We will also look at some of the big economic issues that face us all as members of society in the twenty-first century. Despite huge advances in technology, and despite the comfortable lives led by many people in the industrialised world, we continue to suffer from the consequences of volatile economic growth, industrial change and unemployment and, of course, all the uncertainty and insecurity that these bring. We continue to witness poverty and inequality, and in many countries the gap between rich and poor has actually grown wider; our environment is polluted; our growing affluence as consumers is increasingly bought at the expense of longer hours at work and growing levels of stress. In an increasingly interdependent world, actions have implications elsewhere; economic problems like the banking crisis of 2008/9 can spread like a contagion.

So what can be done about these problems? This book seeks not only to analyse these problems but also to examine the sorts of policies that governments pursue in their attempt to address them.

The book is designed with one overriding aim: to make this exciting and highly relevant subject as clear to understand as possible. To this end, the book has a number of important features:

- A direct and straightforward written style; short paragraphs to aid rapid comprehension. The aim all the time is to provide maximum clarity.
- A careful use of colour to guide you through the text and make the structure easy to follow.
- Key ideas highlighted and explained where they first appear. These ideas are key elements in the economist's 'toolkit'. Whenever they recur later in the book, an icon appears in the margin and you are referred back to the page where they are defined and explained. All the key ideas are gathered together at the beginning of the Glossary.
- Some of the key ideas are particularly important in affecting the way we see the world: they help us think like economists. We call these 'threshold concepts' and there are 15 of these.
- Clear chapter-opening pages, which set the scene for the chapter and provide a 'chapter map', giving page references of all the sections within the chapter. They also highlight the issues that will be covered in the chapter and can thus be seen as 'learning objectives'.
- Summaries at the end of each section (rather than each chapter). This provides a very useful means of revising and checking your understanding as you progress.
- Definitions of all technical terms placed in the margin close to the position in the text where the term is used. The term itself is highlighted in the text.
- 'Pause for thought' questions integrated in the text. These are designed to help you reflect on what you have just read and to check on your understanding. Answers to all 'pause for thought' questions are given in MyEconLab.

- A comprehensive index, including reference to all defined terms. This enables you to look up a definition as required and to see it used in context.
- An alphabetical glossary at the end of the book. This gathers together all the defined terms.
- Plentiful use of up-to-date examples to illustrate the arguments. This helps to bring the subject alive and puts it in context.
- Review questions at the end of each chapter for either individual or class use.
- Answers to all odd-numbered questions are given in MyEconLab. These questions will be helpful for self-testing, while the even-numbered ones can be used for class testing.
- Many boxes (typically four per chapter) providing case studies, news items, applications, or elaborations of the text. The boxes are of two types: Case Studies and Applications; and Exploring Economics.

- A comprehensive set of web references at the end of each chapter. Each reference is numbered to match those in the Web Appendix at the end of the book. You can easily access any of these sites from MyEconLab. When you enter the site (at http://www. pearsoned.co.uk/sloman), click on **Hot Links**. You will find all the sites from the Web Appendix listed. Click on the one you want and the 'hot link' will take you straight to it.
- Appendices for most chapters appear in MyEconLab. These Web Appendices take the argument further than in the text and look at some more advanced theories. Whilst none of these is necessary for studying this book, and many courses will not refer to them, they provide the necessary additional material for more advanced courses that still require a short textbook.

Good luck with your studies, and have fun. Perhaps this will be just the beginning for you of a lifelong interest in economic issues and the economy.

TO LECTURERS AND TUTORS

This fifth edition of *Essentials of Economics* is an abridged version of *Economics*, 7th edition (John Sloman and Alison Wride). Some passages have been directly transcribed, while others have been extensively rewritten in order to provide a consistent coverage of the 'essentials' of economics.

The book is designed specifically for one-semester courses in introductory economics. There are 14 chapters (an introductory chapter, 6 micro, 5 macro and 2 international), each providing about a week's worth of reading. The book is also ideal for year-long courses that are designed for those not going on to specialise in economics, or where economics is only a subsidiary component at level 2.

Naturally, in a one-semester course, or in courses for non-specialists, tutors cannot hope to cover all the principles of economics. Thus some things have had to go. The book does not cover indifference curves or isoquants. The analysis of costs is developed with only an informal reference to production functions. Distribution theory is confined to the determination of wage rates. In macroeconomics, ISLM analysis has been left out, as have some of the more advanced debates in monetary and exchange rate theory. In addition, many passages have been simplified to reflect the nature of courses on which the book is likely to be used. The result is a book that is approximately half the length of *Economics*, 7th edition.

Suggestions for longer or more advanced courses

If you want to use this book on more rigorous courses, most chapters have one or more Web Appendices. These

introduce students to more advanced models, such as indifference analysis, isoquant analysis, general equilibrium in both a closed and an open economy, ISLM, the full money multiplier, and trade creation and diversion. You can use any or all of them to fit your course.

The book is also ideal for the new economics AS/A2 syllabuses of the various boards.

The book is also highly suitable for courses, such as HND, where the economic environment component is part of a larger module.

Extensive revision

Essentials of Economics (fifth edition) uses a lot of applied material both to illustrate theory and policy and to bring the subject alive for students. This has meant considerable revisions to reflect contemporary issues. In particular, the macroeconomic chapters have been extensively rewritten. Specifically, this means that:

- Many of the boxes are new or extensively revised.
- There are many new examples given in the text.
- The impact of the extensive turmoil experienced in the financial markets and the banking sector in 2008/9 has been covered, as has been the subsequent recession, allowing us to consider fully the implications for monetary and fiscal policy, particularly in Chapter 12.
- All tables and charts have been updated, as have factual references in the text.
- A revised introductory chapter to the macroeconomics section with a fuller coverage of the components of aggregate demand and their relevance.

- The materials relating to the issue of economic growth – both in the short run and long run – have been brought together in a new macroeconomics chapter
- Theoretical coverage has been strengthened at various points of the books. For example, there is an expanded section on game theory in Chapter 5, which now includes discussion of the multiple move games. The chapter on banking, money and interest rates has been expanded and strengthened in the light of the collapse of the banking system in 2008/9. Particular attention has been paid to the role of securitisation and the issues of liquidity and risk.

The book also contains 34 'Key Ideas' and these are highlighted and explained when they first appear. These fundamental concepts provide a 'toolkit' for students. Students can see them recurring throughout the book, and an icon appears in the margin to refer back to the page where the idea first appears. Showing how these ideas can be used in a variety of contexts helps students to relate the different parts of the subject to each other. Fifteen of these concepts are given the special status of 'Threshold Concepts'. Understanding and being able to use these concepts, such as opportunity cost, help students to 'think like an economist'. Each of these concepts is explained in detail in MyEconLab.

We hope that your students will find this an exciting and interesting text that is relevant to today's issues.

SUPPLEMENTS

MyEconLab (for students)

MyEconLab provides a comprehensive set of online resources. Access is provided with every new purchase of this text. MyEconLab provides a variety of tools to enable students to assess their own learning. A personalised Study Plan identifies areas to concentrate on to improve grades, and specific tools are provided to each student to direct their studies in the most efficient way.

In addition, a large range of additional resources are available in MyEconLab, including:

- A highly interactive online workbook
- Animations of key models with audio explanations
- A news blog with news items added several times each month
- A comprehensive glossary with flashcards to check students' knowledge
- 179 case studies with questions for self-study, ordered chapter by chapter and referred to in the text
- 20 self-test questions per chapter
- Updated list of over 250 hotlinks to sites of use for economics
- Answers to all in-chapter questions
- Answers to odd-numbered end-of-chapter questions
- Learning objectives for each chapter written in 'student-friendly' language

Note that the news blog and hotlinks can also be accessed directly from www.pearsoned.co.uk/sloman

See Guided Tour (pages xx–xxviii) for more details.

For lecturers and tutors

MyEconlab

MyEconLab can be set up by you as a complete virtual learning environment for your course or embedded into Blackboard, WebCT or Moodle. You can customise its look and feel and its availability to students. You can use it to provide support to your students in the following ways:

- MyEconLab's gradebook automatically records each student's time spent and performance on the tests and Study Plan. It also generates reports you can use to monitor your students' progress.
- You can use MyEconLab to build your own test, quizzes and homework assignments from the question base provided to set for your own students' assessment.
- Questions are generated algorithmically so they use different values each time they are used.
- You can create your own exercises by using the econ exercise builder.

Memory stick (also available to download from the lecturer website – password protected)

A memory stick is available free of charge from Pearson Education to tutors using the book as a course text. It contains the following:

- PowerPoint® slide shows in full colour for use with a data projector in lectures and classes. These can also be made available to students by loading them on to a local network. The memory stick contains several types of these slide shows:

- All figures from the book and most of the tables. Each figure is built up in a logical sequence, thereby allowing tutors to show them in lectures in an animated form. They are also available in a simple version suitable for printing onto acetate for OHPs or for handouts.
- A range of models. Each file contains one of the key models from the book, developed in an animated sequence of between 20 and 80 screens.
- Customisable lecture plans. These are a series of bullet-point lecture plans. There is one for each chapter of the book. Each one can be easily edited, with points added, deleted or moved, so as to suit particular lectures. A consistent use of colour is made to show how the points tie together. They come in various versions:
  - Lecture plans with integrated diagrams. These lecture plans include animated diagrams and charts at the appropriate points.
  - Lecture plans with integrated diagrams and questions. These allow lectures to become more interactive and can be used with or without an audience response system (ARS). ARS versions are available for InterWrite PRS® and for TurningPoint®.

- Lecture plans are also available without the diagrams so that you can construct your own on the blackboard or whiteboard or use an OHP.
- Multiple-choice questions. This test bank has been revised and contains many new questions. It is flexible and easy to use.
- Case studies. These, also available on the book's website, can be reproduced and used for classroom exercises or for student assignments. Answers are also provided.
- Workshops. There are 14 of these – one for each chapter. They are in Word® and can be reproduced for use with large groups of students (up to 200). In A-level classes, they can be used as worksheets, either for use in class or for homework. Suggestions for use are given on the memory stick. Answers to all workshop questions are given in separate Word® files.
- Teaching/learning case studies. These examine various ways to improve student learning of introductory economics.
- Answers to all end-of-chapter questions, pause for thought questions, questions in boxes, questions in Web Cases and Web Appendices and to all 14 workshops.

WINECON: SLOMAN – ESSENTIALS OF ECONOMICS VERSION

The widely acclaimed, award-winning WinEcon software, produced and authored by the Economics Consortium of the Teaching and Learning Technology Programme (TLP) and designed to support introductory economics, is now available to download in a version specifically designed for *Essentials of Economics* (5th edition).

There is a separate chapter in this Sloman version of WinEcon to correspond to the relevant chapter in the book. The software is highly interactive and is attractive to use and is regularly updated. It has been redesigned in a new attractive format.

For more information on downloading this software, please go to http//:www.winecon.com/sloman-essentials.

ACKNOWLEDGEMENTS

As with previous editions, we owe a debt to various people. Thanks to the team at Pearson Education, and especially to Ellen Morgan, who has been a tremendous help and support at every stage of revising the book. Thanks also to Mary Lince and Melanie Beard for all the work they have put in. Thanks too to the many users of the book who have given us feedback. We always value their comments. Thanks to Rob Ackrill of Nottingham Trent University for his contribution to Box 3.4 on the Common Agricultural Policy.

John: First, a huge thank you to Dean who has put a lot of effort into this new edition, especially the macro chapters.

It's been great working together and I'm really pleased with what he's done. Then, as always, a massive thanks to my family, and especially to my wife Alison for her love and encouragement in both this and previous editions. Without her support, the book would probably never have been written in the first place, and certainly not got to five editions.

Dean: I am deeply appreciative of the love and support given by my family. A special mention must go to Pat who has been incredibly important in helping me to truly understand the things that matter in life. She has been a real rock – thank you.

Publisher's acknowledgements

We are grateful to the following for permission to reproduce copyright material:

Figures

Figure on page 48 from Coffee Production and Prices, www.ico.org, source: the International Coffee Organization; Figure 6.1 adapted from *European Historical Statistics 1750–1970* (Mitchell, B.R. 1978), Palgrave Macmillan; Figure on page 161 based on time series data from *Economic and Labour Market Review*, National Statistics website: www.statistics.gov.uk, Crown Copyright material is reproduced with the permission of the Controller, Office of Public Sector Information (OPSI); Figure on page 161 from *Economic and Labour Market Review* (National Statistics), National Statistics website: www.statistics.gov.uk; Figures 6.8 and 6.10 based on data in *Family Spending*, National Statistics website: www.statistics.gov.uk; Figure 6.9 based on data in *Annual Survey of Hours and Earnings*, National Statistics website: www.statistics.gov.uk; Figures page 279 from European Commission, *Japanese Nominal and Real GDP* © European Communities 2009; Figures on page 279 from European Commission, from *Output Gaps in UK and France* © European Communities 2009; Figure on page 295 from National Statistics website: www.statistics.gov.uk; Figures 9.2, 9.6, 11.18, 12.1, 12.6, 14.2 and 14.3 based on time series data, National Statistics website: www.statistics.gov.uk; Figure 9.5 from http://ec.europa.eu/economy, from Annual growth in French and UK real GDP © European Communities 2009; Figure 11.9 based on data in *OECD StatExtracts*, National Statistics website: www.statistics.gov.uk; Figure 12.5 from *Inflation Report May 2009*, Bank of England with permission; Figures 13.1 and 13.2 from Statistics Database, World Trade Organization.

Tables

Tables 3.1, 3.2 from Table 4.4, page 132 *Intermediate Microeconomics and Its Application (with Economics Applications Card and InfoTrac)*, 10E. © 2007 South-Western, a part of Cengage Learning, Inc. Reproduced by permission. www.cengage.com/permissions, 10th ed., South-Western Publishers (Nicholson, W & Snyder C, 2007); Table on page 101 from *Research on the Costs of Non-Europe*, 2; Table on page 101 from *The Single Market Review (Sub-series V)*, Vol. 4 (1997); Table on page 161 from *Labour Force Survey*, National Statistics website: www.statistics.gov.uk, Crown Copyright material is reproduced with the permission of the Controller, Office of Public Sector Information (OPSI); Tables on page 176, page 177 from *Annual Survey of Hours and Earnings*, Office of National Statistics, National Statistics website: www.statistics.gov.uk; Table 6.1 from *Economic and Labour Market Review*, National Statistics website: www.statistics.gov.uk; Table on page 246 based on data in *UK Economic Accounts*, National Statistics website: www.statistics.gov.uk; Table on page 278 from AMECO, *Potential and Actual Output in France and the UK* © European Communities 2009; Table on page 294 based on data from *Capital Stocks Tables for Publication and UK Output, Income and Expenditure*, National Statistics website: www.statistics.gov.uk; Table on page 431 adapted from data in the annual macro-economic of the European Commission's Directorate General for Economic and Financial Affairs, AMECO, from the AMECO database managed by the European Commission's Directorate General for Economic and Financial Affairs, with permission; Table on page 431 from Statistics Database, World Trade Organization.

In some instances we have been unable to trace the owners of copyright material, and we would appreciate any information that would enable us to do so.

Part A

Introduction

CHAPTER MAP

Economic issues

You may never have studied economics before, and yet when you open a newspaper what do you read? – a report from 'our economics correspondent'. Turn on the television news and what do you see? – an item on the state of the economy. Talk to friends and often the topic will turn to the price of this or that product, or whether you have got enough money to afford to do this or that.

The fact is that economics affects our daily lives. Continually we are being made aware of local, national and international economic issues: whether it be price increases, interest rate changes, fluctuations in exchange rates, unemployment, economic recessions or the effects of globalisation.

We are also continually faced with economic problems and decisions of our own. What should I buy in the supermarket? Should I save up for a summer holiday, or spend more on day-to-day living? Should I go to university, or should I try to find a job now?

So just what is economics about? In this introduction we will attempt to answer this question and to give you some insights into the subject you will be studying by using this book.

We will also see how the subject is divided up, and in particular we will distinguish between the two major branches of economics: microeconomics and macroeconomics.

We conclude by considering alternative ways in which societies can address the key economic problem of scarcity: an excess of human wants over what can be produced. How would economies work if they were run totally by the government or, at the other extreme, if they relied totally on the decisions of households and firms?

After studying this chapter, you should be able to answer the following questions:

- What is economics about?
- What is the central economic problem faced by all individuals and societies?
- How can people set about making the best of their limited resources?
- What is meant by 'opportunity cost'? How is it relevant when people make economic choices?
- What is the difference between microeconomics and macroeconomics?
- How can you represent simply economic relationships in a graph?
- How do different economic systems tackle the problem of scarcity?

1.1 THE ECONOMIC PROBLEM

What is economics all about?

Many people think that economics is about *money*. Well, to some extent this is true. Economics has a lot to do with money: with how much money people are paid; how much they spend; what it costs to buy various items; how much money firms earn; how much money there is in total in the economy. But economics is more than just the study of money.

It is concerned with the following:

■ The **production** of goods and services: how much the economy produces; what particular combination of goods and services; how much each firm produces; what techniques of production it uses; how many people it employs.

■ The **consumption** of goods and services: how much the population as a whole spends (and how much it saves); what the pattern of consumption is in the economy; how much people buy of particular items; what particular individuals choose to buy; how people's consumption is affected by prices, advertising, fashion and other factors.

But we still have not quite got to the bottom of what economics is about. What is the crucial ingredient that makes a problem an *economic* one? The answer is that there is one central problem faced by all individuals and all societies. From this one problem stem all the other economic problems we shall be looking at throughout this book.

This central economic problem is *scarcity*. This applies not only in Ethiopia and Sudan, but also in the UK, the USA, Japan, France and all other countries of the world. For an economist, scarcity has a very specific definition. Let us examine that definition.

The problem of scarcity

Ask people if they would like more money, and the vast majority would answer 'yes'. They want more money so that they can buy more goods and services; and this applies not only to poor people but also to most wealthy people too. The point is that human wants are virtually unlimited.

Yet the means of fulfilling human wants are limited. At any one time the world can produce only a limited amount of goods and services. This is because the world has only a limited amount of resources. These resources, or **factors of production** as they are often called, are of three broad types:

■ Human resources: **labour**. The labour force is limited both in number and in skills.
■ Natural resources: **land and raw materials**. The world's land area is limited, as are its raw materials.
■ Manufactured resources: **capital**. Capital consists of all those inputs that have themselves been produced in the first place. The world has a limited stock of capital: a limited supply of factories, machines, transportation and other equipment. The productivity of capital is limited by the state of technology.

So here is the reason for scarcity: human wants are virtually unlimited, whereas the resources available to satisfy these wants are limited. We can thus define **scarcity** as follows:

Definitions

Production
The transformation of inputs into outputs by firms in order to earn profit (or meet some other objective).

Consumption
The act of using goods and services to satisfy wants. This will normally involve purchasing the goods and services.

Factors of production (or resources)
The inputs into the production of goods and services: labour, land and raw materials, and capital.

Labour
All forms of human input, both physical and mental, into current production.

Land (and raw materials)
Inputs into production that are provided by nature: e.g. unimproved land and mineral deposits in the ground.

Capital
All inputs into production that have themselves been produced: e.g. factories, machines and tools.

Scarcity
The excess of human wants over what can actually be produced to fulfil these wants.

KEY IDEA 1

Scarcity is the excess of human wants over what can actually be produced. Because of scarcity, various choices have to be made between alternatives.

Of course, we do not all face the problem of scarcity to the same degree. A poor person unable to afford enough to eat or a decent place to live will hardly see it as a 'problem' that a rich person cannot afford a second Ferrari. But economists do not claim that we all face an *equal* problem of scarcity. In fact this is one of the major issues economists study: how resources and products are *distributed*, whether between different individuals, different regions of a country or different countries of the world.

But given that people, both rich and poor, want more than they can have, this makes them behave in certain ways. Economics studies that behaviour. It studies people at work, producing the goods that people want. It studies people as consumers buying the goods they themselves want. It studies governments influencing the level and pattern of production and consumption. In short, it studies anything to do with the process of satisfying human wants.

> **Pause for thought**
>
> *If we would all like more money, why doesn't the government simply print a lot more?*

Demand and supply

We said that economics is concerned with consumption and production. Another way of looking at this is in terms of *demand* and *supply*. In fact, demand and supply and the relationship between them lie at the very centre of economics. But what do we mean by the terms, and what is their relationship with the problem of scarcity?

Demand is related to wants. If goods and services were free, people would simply demand whatever they wanted. Such wants are virtually boundless: perhaps limited only by people's imagination. *Supply*, on the other hand, is limited. It is related to resources. The amount firms can supply depends on the resources and technology available.

KI 1
p 5

Given the problem of scarcity, given that human wants exceed what can actually be produced, *potential* demands will exceed *potential* supplies. Society therefore has to find some way of dealing with this problem. Somehow it has to try to match demand and supply. This applies at the level of the economy overall: *aggregate* demand will need to be balanced against *aggregate* supply. In other words, total spending in the economy must balance total production. It also applies at the level of individual goods and services. The demand and supply of cabbages must balance, and so must the demand and supply of DVD recorders, cars, houses and package holidays.

But if potential demand exceeds potential supply, how are *actual* demand and supply to be made equal? Either demand has to be curtailed, or supply has to be increased, or a combination of the two. Economics studies this process. It studies how demand adjusts to available supplies, and how supply adjusts to consumer demands.

Recap

1. The central economic problem is that of scarcity.
2. Given that there is a limited supply of factors of production (labour, land and capital), it is impossible to provide everybody with everything they want.
3. Potential demands exceed potential supplies.

1.2   DIVIDING UP THE SUBJECT

What's meant by 'macroeconomics' and 'microeconomics'?

Economics is traditionally divided into two main branches – *macroeconomics* and *microeconomics*, where 'macro' means big and 'micro' means small.

Macroeconomics is concerned with the economy as a whole. It is thus concerned with **aggregate demand** and **aggregate supply**. By 'aggregate demand' we mean the total amount of spending in the economy, whether by consumers, by customers outside the country for our exports, by the government, or by firms when they buy capital equipment or stock up on raw materials. By 'aggregate supply' we mean the total national output of goods and services.

Microeconomics is concerned with the individual parts of the economy. It is concerned with the demand and supply of *particular* goods and services and resources: cars, butter, clothes and haircuts; electricians, shop assistants, blast furnaces, computers and oil.

Macroeconomics

Because things are scarce, societies are concerned that their resources should be used as *fully as possible*, and that over time their national output should *grow*.

The achievement of growth and the full use of resources is not easy, however, as demonstrated by the periods of high unemployment and stagnation that have occurred from time to time throughout the world (for example, in the 1930s, the early 1980s, the early 1990s and the late 2000s). Furthermore, attempts by government to stimulate growth and employment have often resulted in inflation and a large rise in imports. Even when societies do achieve growth, it can be short-lived. Economies are inherently unstable and display what are known as business cycles: periods of high growth followed by periods of low or even negative growth.

Macroeconomics, then, studies the determination of national output and its growth over time. It also studies the problems of recession, unemployment, inflation, the balance of international payments and cyclical instability, and the policies adopted by governments to deal with these problems.

Macroeconomic problems are closely related to the balance between aggregate demand and aggregate supply.

If aggregate demand is *too high* relative to aggregate supply, inflation and balance of trade deficits are likely to result.

- **Inflation** refers to a general rise in the level of prices throughout the economy. If aggregate demand rises substantially, firms are likely to respond by raising their prices. After all, if demand is high they can probably still sell as much as before (if not more) even at the higher prices, and thus make more profit. If firms in general put up their prices, inflation results.
- **Balance of trade deficits** are the excess of imports over exports. If aggregate demand rises, people are likely to buy more imports. In other words, part of the extra expenditure will go on Japanese MP3 players, German cars, Chilean wine, and so on. Also if inflation is high, home-produced goods will become uncompetitive with foreign goods. We are likely, therefore, to buy more foreign imports, and people abroad are likely to buy fewer of our exports.

If aggregate demand is *too low* relative to aggregate supply, unemployment and recession may well result.

■ **Recession** occurs when output in the economy declines: in other words, growth becomes negative. A recession is associated with a low level of consumer spending. If people spend less, shops are likely to find themselves with unsold stocks. As a result they will buy less from the manufacturers, which in turn will cut down on production.

■ **Unemployment** is likely to result from cutbacks in production. If firms are producing less, they will need to employ fewer people.

Government macroeconomic *policy*, therefore, tends to focus on the balance of aggregate demand and aggregate supply. It can be **demand-side policy**, which seeks to influence the level of spending in the economy. This in turn will affect the level of production, prices and employment. Or it can be **supply-side policy**. This is designed to influence the level of production directly: for example, by trying to create more incentives for firms to innovate.

Microeconomics

Microeconomics and choice

Because resources are scarce, choices have to be made. There are three main categories of choice that must be made in any society.

■ *What* goods and services are going to be produced and in what quantities, given that there are not enough resources to produce all the things people desire? How many cars, how much wheat, how much insurance, how many rock concerts, etc. will be produced?

■ *How* are things going to be produced, given that there is normally more than one way of producing things? What resources are going to be used and in what quantities? What techniques of production are going to be adopted? Will cars be produced by robots or by assembly-line workers? Will electricity be produced from coal, oil, gas, nuclear fission, renewable resources or a mixture of these?

■ *For whom* are things going to be produced? In other words, how will the nation's income be distributed? After all, the higher your income, the more you can consume of the nation's output. What will be the wages of farm workers, printers, cleaners and accountants? How much will pensioners receive? How much of the nation's income will go to shareholders or landowners?

All societies have to make these choices, whether they be made by individuals, by groups or by the government. These choices can be seen as *micro*economic choices, since they are concerned not with the *total* amount of national output, but with the *individual* goods and services that make it up: what they are, how they are made, and who gets the incomes to buy them.

Choice and opportunity cost

Choice involves sacrifice. The more food you choose to buy, the less money you will have to spend on other goods. The more food a nation produces, the less resources there will be for producing other goods. In other words, the production or consumption of one thing involves the sacrifice of alternatives. This sacrifice of alternatives in the production (or consumption) of a good is known as its **opportunity cost**.

 The *opportunity cost* of something is what you give up to get it or do it.

If the workers on a farm can produce either 1000 tonnes of wheat or 2000 tonnes of barley, then the opportunity cost of producing 1 tonne of wheat is the 2 tonnes of barley forgone. The opportunity cost of buying a textbook is the new pair of jeans you also wanted that you have had to go without. The opportunity cost of working overtime is the leisure you have sacrificed.

Opportunity cost as the basis for choice is a key idea. But it is more than that. It is also the first of our 'Threshold Concepts' (click on the Threshold Concepts link in MyEconLab for a detailed explanation of each one). There are 15 of these threshold concepts, which we shall be exploring throughout the book. Each of them keeps recurring in a variety of different contexts. Each time one recurs, there is a green numbered TC icon in the magin.

Once you have grasped these concepts and seen their significance, they will affect the way that you understand and analyse economic problems. They help you to 'think like an economist'.

Rational choices

Economists often refer to **rational choices**. This simply means the weighing-up of the *costs* and *benefits* of any activity, whether it be firms choosing what and how much to produce, workers choosing whether to take a particular job or to work extra hours, or consumers choosing what to buy.

Imagine you are doing your shopping in a supermarket and you want to buy a bottle of wine. Do you spend a lot of money and buy a top-quality French wine, or do you buy a cheap eastern European one instead? To make a rational (i.e. sensible) decision, you will need to weigh up the costs and benefits of each alternative. The top-quality wine may give you a lot of enjoyment, but it has a high opportunity cost: because it is expensive, you will need to sacrifice quite a lot of consumption of other goods if you decide to buy it. If you buy the cheap bottle, however, although you will not enjoy it so much, you will have more money left over to buy other things: it has a lower opportunity cost.

Thus rational decision making, as far as consumers are concerned, involves choosing those items that give you the best value for money: i.e. the *greatest benefit relative to cost*.

The same principles apply to firms when deciding what to produce. For example, should a car manufacturer open up another production line? A rational decision will again involve weighing up the benefits and costs. The benefits are the revenues that the firm will earn from selling the extra cars. The costs will include the extra labour costs, raw material costs, costs of component parts, etc. It will be profitable to open up the new production line only if the revenues earned exceed the costs entailed: in other words, if it adds to profit.

Marginal costs and benefits

In economics we argue that rational choices involve weighing up **marginal costs** and **marginal benefits**. These are the costs and benefits of doing a little bit more or a little bit less of a specific activity. They can be contrasted with the *total* costs and benefits of the activity.

Take a familiar example. What time will you set the alarm clock to go off tomorrow morning? Let us say that you have to leave home at 8.30. Perhaps you will set the alarm for 7.00. That will give you plenty of time to get up and get ready, but it will mean a relatively short night's sleep. Perhaps then you will decide to set it for 7.30 or even 8.00. That will give you a longer night's sleep, but much more of a rush in the morning to get ready.

BOX 1.1 **THE OPPORTUNITY COSTS OF STUDYING ECONOMICS** **CASE STUDIES & APPLICATIONS**

What are you sacrificing?

You may not have realised it, but you probably consider opportunity costs many times a day. The reason is that we are constantly making choices: what to buy, what to eat, what to wear, whether to go out, how much to study and so on. Each time we make such a choice, we are in effect rejecting some alternative. This alternative forgone is the opportunity cost of the action we chose.

Sometimes the opportunity costs of our actions are the direct monetary costs we incur. Sometimes it is more complicated.

Take the opportunity costs of your choices as a student of economics.

Buying a textbook costing £34.99

This does involve a direct money payment. What you have to consider is the alternatives you could have bought with the £34.99. You then have to weigh up the benefit from the best alternative against the benefit of the textbook.

 1. *What might prevent you from making the best decision?*

Coming to classes

You may or may not be paying your own course fees. Even if you are, there is no extra (marginal) monetary cost in coming to classes once the fees have been paid. You will not get a refund by skipping classes!

So are the opportunity costs zero? No: by coming to classes you are *not* working in the library; you are *not* having an extra hour in bed; you are *not* sitting drinking coffee with friends, and so on. If you are making a rational decision to come to classes, then you will consider such possible alternatives.

 2. *If there are several other things you could have done, is the opportunity cost the sum of all of them?*

Choosing to study at university or college

What are the opportunity costs of being a student in higher education? At first it might seem that the costs would include the following:

- Tuition fees.
- Books, stationery, etc.
- Accommodation expenses.
- Transport.
- Food, entertainment and other living expenses.

But adding these up does *not* give the *opportunity* cost. The opportunity cost is the *sacrifice* entailed by going to university or college *rather* than doing something else. Let us assume that the alternative is to take a job that has been offered. The correct list of opportunity costs of higher education would include:

- Tuition fees paid by you (as opposed to your parents or anyone else).
- Books, stationery, etc.
- *Additional* accommodation and transport expenses over what would have been incurred by taking the job.
- Wages that would have been earned in the job *less* any student allowance or grant received.

 3. *Why is the cost of food not included?*
4. *Make a list of the benefits of higher education.*
5. *Is the opportunity cost to the individual of attending higher education different from the opportunity costs to society as a whole?*

So how do you make a rational decision about when the alarm should go off? What you have to do is to weigh up the costs and benefits of *additional* sleep. Each extra minute in bed gives you more sleep (the marginal benefit) but gives you more of a rush when you get up (the marginal cost). The decision is therefore based on the costs and benefits of *extra* sleep, not on the *total* costs and benefits of a whole night's sleep.

This same principle applies to rational decisions made by consumers, workers and firms. For example, the car firm we were considering just now will weigh up the marginal costs and benefits of producing cars: in other words, it will compare the costs and revenue of producing *additional* cars. If additional cars add more to the firm's revenue than to its costs, it will be profitable to produce them.

Rational decision making involves weighing up the marginal benefit and marginal cost of any activity. If the marginal benefit exceeds the marginal cost, it is rational to do the activity (or to do more of it). If the marginal cost exceeds the marginal benefit, it is rational not to do it (or to do less of it).

Decision making based on marginal costs and benefits is the second of our **Threshold Concepts**, explored on the book's website.

The social implications of choice

Microeconomics does not just study how choices are made. It also looks at their consequences. Under certain conditions the consequences may be an efficient use of the nation's resources.

However, a whole series of possible problems can arise from the choices that people make, whether they are made by individuals, by firms or by the government. These problems include such things as inefficiency, waste, inequality and pollution.

Take the case of pollution. It might be profitable for a firm to tip toxic waste into a river. But what is profitable for the firm will not necessarily be 'profitable' for society. There may be serious environmental consequences of the firm's actions.

Throughout the book we will be considering how well the economy meets various economic and social objectives: whether micro or macro. We will examine why problems occur and what can be done about them.

> **Pause for thought**
>
> *Imagine that, as a student, you are short of money and that you are offered employment working in the student union shop. You can choose the number of hours each week that you work. How would you make a 'rational' decision about the number of hours to work in any given week?*

Recap

1. The subject of economics is usually divided into two main branches, macroeconomics and microeconomics.
2. Macroeconomics deals with aggregates such as the overall levels of unemployment, output, growth and prices in the economy.
3. Microeconomics deals with the activities of individual units within the economy: firms, industries, consumers, workers, etc. Because resources are scarce, people have to make choices. Society has to choose by some means or other what goods and services to produce, how to produce them and for whom to produce them. Microeconomics studies these choices.
4. Rational choices involve weighing up the marginal benefits of each activity against its marginal opportunity costs. If the marginal benefit exceeds the marginal cost, it is rational to choose to do more of that activity.

1.3 MODELLING ECONOMIC RELATIONSHIPS

How can diagrams be used to illustrate economic issues?

Economics books and articles frequently contain diagrams. The reason is that diagrams are very useful for illustrating economic relationships. Ideas and arguments that might take a long time to explain in words can often be expressed clearly and simply in a diagram.

Such diagrams are an example of an **economic model**. Models are a simplification of reality in order to show clearly how things are related. For example, a model could show how the demand for a product is related to price. It would show how demand changed as price changed. We would expect that as the price of a product rose, so the quantity demanded would fall. If you glance forward to Figure 2.1 on page 31, you will see a diagram relating the demand for potatoes to the price of potatoes.

To examine such relationships, we have to assume that other things that might affect the outcome do not change. For example, if we were modelling how the demand for Cheddar cheese was affected by changes in its price, we would have to assume that the price of other products, including other types of cheese, were held constant. This is known as the '*ceteris paribus*' assumption. *Ceteris paribus* is Latin for 'other things being equal' If the price of other products *did* change, we would then have to re-specify our model.

Modelling in economics is the third of our **Threshold Concepts**.

 Modelling in economics involves specifying how one variable (the 'dependent variable') depends on one or more other variables ('independent variables'). It involves 'holding constant' all other variables that might influence the outcome (the *ceteris paribus* assumption). A model can be expressed in words, as a graph, or mathematically in terms of one or more equations. In this book we use mainly verbal descriptions and graphs.

Two of the most common types of diagram used in economics are graphs and flow diagrams. In the next two sections we will look at one example of each. These examples are chosen to illustrate the distinction between microeconomic and macroeconomic issues.

The production possibility curve

We start by having a look at a **production possibility curve**. This diagram is a graph. Like many diagrams in economics it shows a simplified picture of reality – a picture stripped of all details that are unnecessary to illustrate the points being made. Of course, there are dangers in this. In the attempt to make a diagram simple enough to understand, we run the risk of oversimplifying. If this is the case, the diagram may be misleading.

A production possibility curve is shown in Figure 1.1. The graph is based on the data shown in Table 1.1.

Assume that some imaginary nation devotes all its resources – land, labour and capital – to producing just two goods, food and clothing. Various possible combinations that could be produced over a given period of time (e.g. a year) are shown in the table. Thus the country, by devoting all its resources to producing food, could produce 8 million units of food but no clothing. Alternatively, by producing, say, 7 million units of food it could release enough resources – land, labour and capital – to produce 2.2 million units of clothing. At the other extreme, it could produce 7 million units of clothing, with no resources at all being used to produce food.

The information in the table can be transferred to a graph (Figure 1.1). We measure units of food on one axis (in this case the vertical axis) and units of clothing on the other. The curve shows all the combinations of the two goods that can be produced with all the nation's resources fully and efficiently employed. For

Figure 1.1   A production possibility curve

Table 1.1   Maximum possible combinations of food and clothing that can be produced in a given time period

Units of food (millions)	Units of clothing (millions)
8.0	0.0
7.0	2.2
6.0	4.0
5.0	5.0
4.0	5.6
3.0	6.0
2.0	6.4
1.0	6.7
0.0	7.0

example, production could take place at point *x*, with 6 million units of food and 4 million units of clothing being produced. Production cannot take place beyond the curve. For example, production is not possible at point *w*: the nation does not have enough resources to do this.

Note that there are two simplifying assumptions in this diagram. First, it is assumed that there are just two types of good that can be produced. It is necessary to make this assumption since we only have two axes on our graph. The other assumption is that there is only one type of food and one type of clothing. This is implied by measuring their output in particular units (e.g. tonnes). If food differed in type, there would be the possibility of producing a greater tonnage of food for a given amount of clothing simply by switching production from one foodstuff to another.

These two assumptions are obviously enormous simplifications when we consider the complex modern economies of the real world. But despite this, the diagram still allows important principles to be illustrated, and illustrated simply.

Microeconomics and the production possibility curve

A production possibility curve illustrates the microeconomic issues of *choice* and *opportunity cost*.

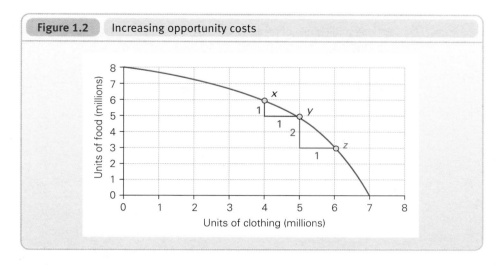

Figure 1.2   Increasing opportunity costs

If the country chose to produce more clothing, it would have to sacrifice the production of some food. This sacrifice of food is the opportunity cost of the extra clothing.

The fact that to produce more of one good involves producing less of the other is illustrated by the downward-sloping nature of the curve. For example, the country could move from point *x* to point *y* in Figure 1.2. In doing so it would be producing an extra 1 million units of clothing, but 1 million fewer units of food. Thus the opportunity cost of the 1 million extra units of clothing would be the 1 million units of food forgone.

It also illustrates the phenomenon of **increasing opportunity costs**. By this we mean that as a country produces more of one good it has to sacrifice ever-*increasing* amounts of the other. The reason for this is that different factors of production have different properties. People have different skills. Land differs in different parts of the country. Raw materials differ one from another; and so on. Thus as the nation concentrates more and more on the production of one good, it has to start using resources that are less and less suitable – resources that would have been better suited to producing other goods. In our example, then, the production of more and more clothing will involve a growing *marginal cost*: ever-increasing amounts of food have to be sacrificed for each additional unit of clothing produced.

It is because opportunity costs increase that the production possibility curve is bowed outward rather than being a straight line. Thus in Figure 1.2 as production moves from point *x* to *y* to *z*, so the amount of food sacrificed rises for each additional unit of clothing produced. The opportunity cost of the fifth million units of clothing is 1 million units of food. The opportunity cost of the sixth million units of clothing is 2 million units of food.

Macroeconomics and the production possibility curve

There is no guarantee that resources will be fully employed, or that they will be used in the most efficient way possible. The nation may thus be producing at a point inside the curve: for example, point *v* in Figure 1.3.

What we are saying here is that the economy is producing less of both goods than it could possibly produce, either because some resources are not being used (for example, workers may be unemployed), or because it is not using the most efficient methods of production possible, or a combination of the two. By using its

TC 1
p 7

KI 1
p 5

Definition

Increasing opportunity costs

When additional production of one good involves ever-increasing sacrifices of another.

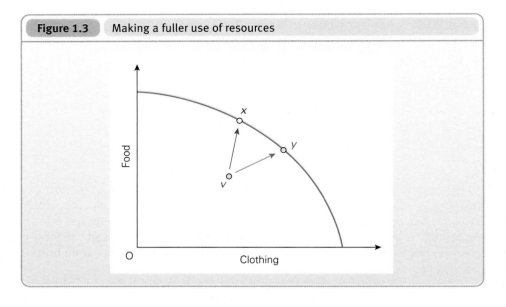

Figure 1.3   Making a fuller use of resources

KI 1
p 5

TC 3
p 11

resources to the full, however, the nation could move out on to the curve: to point *x* or *y*, for example. It could thus produce more clothing *and* more food.

Here we are not concerned with the combination of goods produced (a microeconomic issue), but with whether the total amount produced is as much as it could be (a macroeconomic issue).

Over time, the production possibilities of a nation are likely to increase. **Investment** in new plant and machinery will increase the stock of capital; new raw materials may be discovered; technological advances are likely to take place; through education and training, labour is likely to become more productive. This growth in potential output is illustrated by an outward shift in the production possibility curve. This will then allow actual output to increase: for example, from point *x* to point *x'* in Figure 1.4.

Definition

Investment
The production of items that are not for immediate consumption.

Pause for thought

Will economic growth necessarily involve a parallel outward shift in the production possibility curve? Explain.

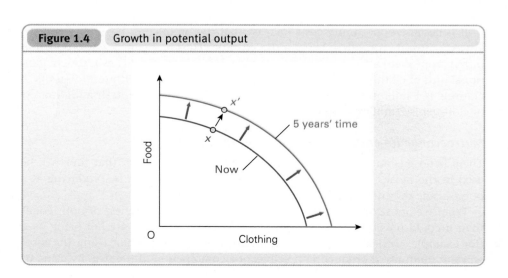

Figure 1.4   Growth in potential output

The circular flow of goods and incomes

The process of satisfying human wants involves producers and consumers. The relationship between them is two-sided and can be represented in a flow diagram (see Figure 1.5).

The consumers of goods and services are labelled 'households'. Some members of households, of course, are also workers, and in some cases are the owners of other factors of production too, such as land. The producers of goods and services are labelled 'firms'.

Firms and households are in a twin 'demand and supply' relationship with each other.

First, in the top half of the diagram, households demand goods and services, and firms supply goods and services. In the process, exchange takes place. In a money economy (as opposed to a **barter economy**), firms exchange goods and services for money. In other words, money flows from households to firms in the form of consumer expenditure, while goods and services flow the other way – from firms to households.

This coming together of buyers and sellers is known as a **market** – whether it be a street market, a shop, the Internet, an auction, a mail-order system or whatever. Thus we talk about the market for apples, the market for oil, for cars, for houses, for televisions and so on.

Second, firms and households come together in the market for factors of production. This is illustrated in the bottom half of the diagram. This time the demand and supply roles are reversed. Firms demand the use of factors of production owned by households – labour, land and capital. Households supply them. Thus the services of labour and other factors flow from households to firms, and in exchange firms pay households money – namely, wages, rent, dividends and interest. Just as

> **Definitions**
>
> **Barter economy**
> An economy where people exchange goods and services directly with one another without any payment of money. Workers would be paid with bundles of goods.
>
> **Market**
> The interaction between buyers and sellers.

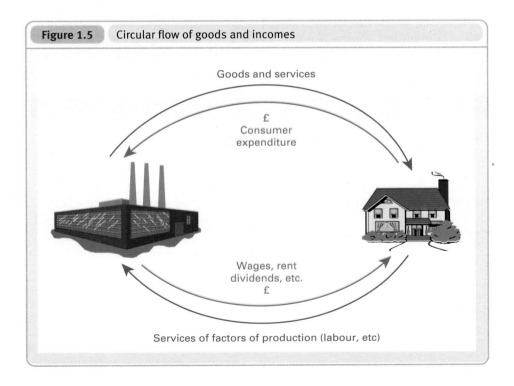

Figure 1.5 Circular flow of goods and incomes

Goods and services

£
Consumer
expenditure

Wages, rent
dividends, etc.
£

Services of factors of production (labour, etc)

we referred to particular goods markets, so we can also refer to particular factor markets – the market for bricklayers, for secretaries, for hairdressers, for land, and so on.

There is thus a circular flow of incomes. Households earn incomes from firms, and firms earn incomes from households. The money circulates. There is also a circular flow of goods and services, but in the opposite direction. Households supply factor services to firms, which then use them to supply goods and services to households.

The flow diagram in Figure 1.5, like the production possibility curve, can help us to distinguish between micro- and macroeconomics.

Microeconomics is concerned with the composition of the circular flow: *what* combinations of goods makes up the goods flow; *how* the various factors of production are combined to produce these goods; *for whom* the wages, dividends, rent and interest are paid out.

Macroeconomics is concerned with the total size of the flow and what causes it to expand and contract.

Techniques of analysis

If you glance through the book, you will see that there are many diagrams and tables and some equations. But this does not mean that there are many mathematical techniques that you will have to master in order to study this book. In fact, there are relatively few techniques – and simple ones at that! But they are ones which we use many times in many different contexts. You will find that if you are new to the subject, you will very quickly become familiar with these techniques. To help you check your understanding of them, you should visit Appendix A on the book's website (**www.pearsoned.co.uk/sloman**).

This book does not use calculus. If, however, your course does, you will find some optional 'Maths Cases' on the book's website that use differentiation to explore some of the theories we cover. The rules of differentiation and their use to find maximum and minimum points are given in Web appendix B in MyEconLab.

Recap

1. The production possibility curve shows the possible combinations of two goods that a country can produce in a given period of time. Assuming that the country is already producing on the curve, the production of more of one good will involve producing less of the other. This opportunity cost is illustrated by the slope of the curve.

2. If the economy is producing within the production possibility curve as a result of idle resources or inefficiency, it can produce more of both goods by taking up this slack. In the longer term it can only produce more of both by shifting the curve outwards through investment, technological progress, etc.

3. The circular flow of goods and incomes shows the interrelationships between firms and households in a money economy. Firms and households come together in markets. In goods markets, firms supply goods and households demand goods. In the process, money flows from households to firms in return for the goods and services that the firms supply. In factor markets, firms demand factors of production and households supply them. In the process, money flows from firms to households in return for the services of the factors that households supply.

ECONOMIC SYSTEMS

How do countries differ in the way their economies are organised?

All societies are faced with the problem of scarcity. They differ considerably, however, in the way they tackle the problem. One important difference between societies is in the degree of government control of the economy.

At the one extreme lies the completely planned or **command economy**, where all the economic decisions are taken by the government.

At the other extreme lies the completely **free-market economy**. In this type of economy there is no government intervention at all. All decisions are taken by individuals and firms. Households decide how much labour and other factors to supply, and what goods to consume. Firms decide what goods to produce and what factors to employ. The pattern of production and consumption that results depends on the interactions of all these individual demand and supply decisions.

In practice, all economies are a mixture of the two. It is therefore the *degree* of government intervention that distinguishes different economic systems. Thus in the former communist countries of eastern Europe, the government played a large role, whereas in the United States, the government plays a much smaller role.

It is nevertheless useful to analyse the extremes in order to put the different **mixed economies** of the real world into perspective.

We start by having a brief look at the command economy. Then for the rest of this chapter we will see how a free-market economy operates. In subsequent chapters we will examine the various ways in which governments intervene in market economies: i.e. we will look at the various forms of **mixed market economy**.

The command economy

The command economy is usually associated with a socialist or communist economic system, where land and capital are collectively owned. The state plans the allocation of resources at three important levels:

- It plans the allocation of resources between current consumption and investment for the future. By sacrificing some present consumption and diverting resources into investment, it could increase the economy's growth rate. The amount of resources it chooses to devote to investment will depend on its broad macroeconomic strategy: the importance it attaches to growth as opposed to current consumption.
- At a microeconomic level it plans the output of each industry and firm, the techniques that will be used and the labour and other resources required by each industry and firm.

  In order to ensure that the required inputs are available, the state would probably conduct some form of **input–output analysis**. All industries are seen as users of *inputs* from other industries and as producers of *output* for consumers or other industries. For example, the steel industry uses inputs from the coal and iron-ore industries and produces output for the vehicle and construction industries. Input–output analysis shows, for each industry, the sources of all its inputs and the destination of all its output. By its use the state attempts to match up the inputs and outputs of each industry so that the planned demand for each industry's product is equal to its planned supply.

Definitions

Centrally planned or command economy
An economy where all economic decisions are taken by the central authorities.

Free-market economy
An economy where all economic decisions are taken by individual households and firms, with no government intervention.

Mixed economy
An economy where economic decisions are made partly by the government and partly through the market.

Mixed market economy
A market economy where there is some government intervention.

Input–output analysis
This involves dividing the economy into sectors where each sector is a user of inputs from and a supplier of outputs to other sectors. The technique examines how these inputs and outputs can be matched to the total resources available in the economy.

■ It plans the distribution of output between consumers. This will depend on the government's aims. It may distribute goods according to its judgement of people's *needs*; or it may give more to those who produce more, thereby providing an *incentive* for people to work harder.

It may distribute goods and services directly (for example, by a system of rationing); or it may decide the distribution of money incomes and allow individuals to decide how to spend them. If it does the latter, it may still seek to influence the pattern of expenditure by setting appropriate prices: low prices to encourage consumption, and high prices to discourage consumption.

Assessment of the command economy

With central planning, the government could take an overall view of the economy. It could direct the nation's resources in accordance with specific national goals.

High growth rates could be achieved if the government directed large amounts of resources into investment. Unemployment could be largely avoided if the

---

BOX 1.2   THE RISE AND FALL OF PLANNING IN THE FORMER SOVIET UNION

When everything didn't go according to plan

Early years

The Bolsheviks under the leadership of Lenin came to power in Russia with the October revolution of 1917. The Bolsheviks, however, were opposed by the White Russians and civil war ensued.

During this period of *War Communism*, the market economy was abolished. Industry and shops were nationalised; workers were told what jobs to do; there were forced requisitions of food from peasants to feed the towns; the money economy collapsed as rampant inflation made money worthless; workers were allocated goods from distribution depots.

With the ending of the civil war in 1921, the economy was in bad shape. Lenin embarked on a *New Economic Policy*. This involved a return to the use of markets. Smaller businesses were returned to private hands, and peasants were able to sell their food rather than having it requisitioned. The economy began to recover.

Lenin died in 1924 and Stalin came to power.

The Stalinist system

The Soviet economy underwent a radical transformation from 1928 onwards. The key features of the Stalinist approach were collectivisation, industrialisation and central planning.

Collectivisation of agriculture

Peasant farms were abolished and replaced by large-scale collective farms where land was collectively owned and worked. Collectivisation initially caused massive disruption and famine, with peasants slaughtering their animals rather than giving them up to the collective. People died in their thousands. Despite an initial fall in output, more food was provided for the towns, and

many workers left the land to work in the new industries.

In addition to the collective farms, state farms were established. These were owned by the state and were run by managers appointed by the state. Workers were paid a wage rather than having a share in farm income.

Both collective and state farms were given quotas of output that they were supposed to deliver for which the state would pay a fixed price.

Industry and central planning

A massive drive to industrialisation took place. To achieve this a vast planning apparatus was developed. At the top was *Gosplan*, the central planning agency. This prepared five-year plans and annual plans.

The five-year plans specified the general direction in which the economy was to move. The annual plans gave the details of just what was to be produced and with what resources for some 200 or so key products. Other products were planned at a lower level – by various industrial ministries or regional authorities.

The effect was that all factories were given targets that had to be achieved. It was the task of the planning authorities to ensure that the targets were realistic: that there were sufficient resources to meet the targets. The system operated without the aid of the price mechanism and the profit motive. The main incentive was the bonus: bonuses were paid to managers and workers if targets were achieved.

In the early years, very high growth rates were achieved; but this was at a cost of low efficiency. The poor flow of information from firms to the planners led to many inconsistencies in the plans. The targets were often totally unrealistic, and as a result there were frequent government carefully planned the allocation of labour in accordance with production requirements and labour skills. National income could be distributed more equally or in accordance with needs. The social repercussions of production and consumption (e.g. the effects on the environment) could be taken into account, provided the government was able to predict these effects and chose to take them into account.

In practice, a command economy could achieve these goals only at considerable social and economic cost. The reasons are as follows:

■ The larger and more complex the economy, the greater the task of collecting and analysing the information essential to planning, and the more complex the plan. Complicated plans are likely to be costly to administer and involve cumbersome bureaucracy.

■ If there is no system of prices, or if prices are set arbitrarily by the state, planning is likely to involve the inefficient use of resources. It is difficult to assess the relative efficiency of two alternative techniques that use different inputs, if there is

---

CASE STUDIES & APPLICATIONS

shortages and sometimes surpluses. With incentives purely geared to meeting targets, there was little product innovation and goods were frequently of poor quality and finish.

The limits of planning

Although most resources were allocated through planning, there were nevertheless some goods that were sold in markets. Any surpluses above their quota that were produced by collective farms could be sold in collective farm markets (street markets) in the towns. In addition, the workers on collective farms were allowed to own their own small private plots of land, and they too could sell their produce in the collective farm markets.

A large 'underground economy' flourished in which goods were sold on the black market and in which people did second 'unofficial' jobs (e.g. as plumbers, electricians or garment makers).

Gorbachev's reforms

Stalin died in 1953. The planning system, however, remained largely unchanged until the late 1980s.

During the 1970s growth had slowed down and by the time Mikhail Gorbachev came to power in 1985 many people were pressing for fundamental economic reforms. Gorbachev responded with his policy of *perestroika* (economic reconstruction), which among other things included the following:

■ Making managers more involved in preparing their own plans rather than merely being given instructions.

■ Insisting that firms cover their costs of production. If they could not, the state might refuse to bale them out

and they could be declared bankrupt. The aim of this was to encourage firms to be more efficient.

■ Improving the incentive system by making bonuses more related to genuine productivity. Workers had come to expect bonuses no matter how much or how little was produced.

■ Organising workers into small teams or 'brigades' (typically of around 10–15 workers). Bonuses were then awarded to the whole brigade according to its productivity. The idea was to encourage people to work more effectively together.

■ Stringent checks on quality by state officials and the rejection of substandard goods.

■ Allowing one-person businesses and co-operatives (owned by the workers) to be set up.

■ A greater willingness by the state to raise prices if there were substantial shortages.

These reforms, however, did not halt the economic decline. What is more, there was now an unhappy mix of planning and the market, with people unclear as to what to expect from the state. Many managers resented the extra responsibilities they were now expected to shoulder and many officials saw their jobs threatened. Queues lengthened in the shops and people became increasingly disillusioned with *perestroika*.

Following a failed coup in 1991, in which hard-line communists had attempted to reimpose greater state control, and with the consequent strengthening of the position of Boris Yeltsin, the Russian president and the main advocate of more radical reforms, both the Soviet Union and the system of central planning came to an end.

Russia embarked upon a radical programme of market reforms in which competition and enterprise were intended to replace state central planning (see Case Study 1.7 in MyEconLab).

no way in which the value of those inputs can be ascertained. For example, how can a rational decision be made between an oil-fired and a coal-fired furnace if the prices of oil and coal do not reflect their relative scarcity?

■ It is difficult to devise appropriate incentives to encourage workers and managers to be more productive without a reduction in quality. For example, if bonuses are given according to the quantity of output produced, a factory might produce shoddy goods, since it can probably produce a larger quantity of goods by cutting quality. To avoid this problem, a large number of officials may have to be employed to check quality.

■ Complete state control over resource allocation would involve a considerable loss of individual liberty. Workers would have no choice where to work; consumers would have no choice what to buy.

■ The government might enforce its plans even if they were unpopular.

■ If production is planned, but consumers are free to spend money incomes as they wish, then there will be a problem if the consumer wishes change. Shortages will occur if consumers decide to buy more, and surpluses will occur if they decide to buy less.

Most of these problems were experienced in the former USSR and the other Eastern Bloc countries, and were part of the reason for the overthrow of their communist regimes (see Box 1.2).

> **Pause for thought**
>
> *Queues were a common feature of the former Soviet Union. Why do you think they were so commonplace? Is a system of queuing a fair way of allocating scarce goods and resources?*

The free-market economy

Free decision making by individuals

The free-market economy is usually associated with a pure capitalist system, where land and capital are privately owned. All economic decisions are made by households and firms, which are assumed to act in their own self-interest. The following assumptions are usually made:

■ Firms seek to maximise profits.
■ Consumers seek to get the best value for money from their purchases.
■ Workers seek to maximise their wages relative to the human cost of working in a particular job.

It is also assumed that individuals are free to make their own economic choices; consumers are free to decide what to buy with their incomes; workers are free to choose where and how much to work; firms are free to choose what to sell and what production methods to use.

The resulting supply and demand decisions of firms and households are transmitted to each other through their effect on *prices*.

The price mechanism

> **Definition**
>
> **The price mechanism**
> The system in a market economy whereby price changes that occur in response to changes in demand and supply have the effect of making demand equal to supply.

The **price mechanism** works as follows. Prices respond to *shortages* and *surpluses*. Shortages cause prices to rise. Surpluses cause prices to fall.

If consumers decide they want more of a good (or if producers decide to cut back supply), demand will exceed supply. The resulting *shortage* will encourage sellers to *raise* the price of the good. This will act as an incentive to producers to supply more, since production will now be more profitable. At the same time, it will discourage consumers from buying so much. *The price will continue rising until the shortage has thereby been eliminated.*

If, on the other hand, consumers decide they want less of a good (or if producers decide to produce more), supply will exceed demand. The resulting *surplus* will encourage sellers to *reduce* the price of the good. This will act as a disincentive to producers, who will supply less, since production will now be less profitable. It will encourage consumers to buy more. *The price will continue falling until the surplus has thereby been eliminated.*

 This price, where demand equals supply, is called the **equilibrium price**. By **equilibrium** we mean a point of balance or a point of rest: in other words, a point towards which there is a tendency to move.

The same analysis can be applied to factor markets. If the demand for a particular type of labour exceeds its supply, the resulting shortage will drive up the wage rate (i.e. the price of labour) as employers compete with each other for labour. The rise in the wage rate will have the effect of curbing firms' demand for that type of labour and encouraging more workers to take up that type of job. Wages will continue rising until demand equals supply: until the shortage is eliminated.

Likewise if there is a surplus of a particular type of labour, the wage will fall until demand equals supply. As with price, the wage rate where the demand for labour equals the supply is known as the *equilibrium* wage rate.

The response of demand and supply to changes in price illustrates a very important feature of how economies work:

 People respond to incentives. It is important, therefore, that incentives are appropriate and have the desired effect. This is another of our Threshold Concepts. For details, see MyEconLab.

The effect of changes in demand and supply

How will the price mechanism respond to changes in consumer demand or producer supply? After all, the pattern of consumer demand changes. For example, people may decide they want more mountain bikes and fewer racers. Likewise the pattern of supply also changes. For example, changes in technology may allow the mass production of microchips at lower cost, while the production of hand-built furniture becomes relatively expensive.

In all cases of changes in demand and supply, the resulting changes in *price* act as both *signals* and *incentives*.

 A change in demand. A rise in demand is signalled by a rise in price. This then acts as an incentive for firms to produce more of the good: the quantity supplied rises. Firms divert resources from goods with lower prices relative to costs (and hence lower profits) to those goods that are more profitable.

A fall in demand is signalled by a fall in price. This then acts as an incentive for firms to produce less: such goods are now less profitable to produce. Thus the quantity supplied falls.

A change in supply. A rise in supply is signalled by a fall in price. This then acts as an incentive for consumers to buy more: the quantity demanded rises. A fall in supply is signalled by a rise in price. This then acts as an incentive for consumers to buy less: the quantity demanded falls.

 Changes in demand or supply cause markets to adjust. Whenever such changes occur, the resulting 'disequilibrium' will bring an automatic change in prices, thereby restoring equilibrium (i.e. a balance of demand and supply).

The interdependence of markets

The interdependence of goods and factor markets. A rise in demand for a good will raise its price and profitability. Firms will respond by supplying more. But to do this they will need more inputs. Thus the demand for the inputs will rise, which in turn will raise the price of the inputs. The suppliers of inputs will respond to this incentive by supplying more. This can be summarised as follows:

1. Goods market
    - Demand for the good rises.
    - This creates a shortage.
    - This causes the price of the good to rise.
    - This eliminates the shortage by choking off some of the demand and encouraging firms to produce more.
2. Factor market
    - The increased supply of the good causes an increase in the demand for factors of production (i.e. inputs) used in making it.
    - This causes a shortage of those inputs.
    - This causes their prices to rise.
    - This eliminates their shortage by choking off some of the demand and encouraging the suppliers of inputs to supply more.

Goods markets thus affect factor markets.

It is common in economics to summarise an argument like this by using symbols. It is a form of shorthand. Figure 1.6 summarises this particular sequence of events.

Interdependence exists in the other direction too: factor markets affect goods markets. For example, the discovery of raw materials will lower their price. This will lower the production costs of firms using these raw materials and increase the supply of the finished goods. The resulting surplus will lower the price of the good, which will encourage consumers to buy more.

Pause for thought

Summarise this last paragraph using symbols like those in Figure 1.6.

The interdependence of different goods markets. A rise in the price of one good will encourage consumers to buy alternatives. This will drive up the price of alternatives. This in turn will encourage producers to supply more of the alternatives.

Interdependence and the public interest. Even though all individuals are merely looking to their own self-interest in the free-market economy, they are in fact being encouraged to respond to the wishes of others through the incentive of the price mechanism. For example, if consumers want more of a product, firms will supply more – not out of the goodness of their hearts, but because it is profitable to do so.

Figure 1.6   The price mechanism: the effect of a rise in demand

It is often claimed that this is a major advantage of a free-market economy. We will be examining this claim in subsequent chapters.

Competitive markets

In the next chapter we will examine the working of the price mechanism in more detail. We will look first at demand, then at supply, and then we will put the two together to look at the determination of price.

The markets we will be examining are highly competitive markets, with many firms competing against each other. In economics we call this **perfect competition**. This is where consumers and producers are too numerous to have any control over prices: they are **price takers**.

In the case of consumers, this means that they have to accept the prices as given for the things that they buy. On most occasions this is true. For example, when you get to the supermarket checkout you cannot start haggling with the checkout operator over the price of a can of beans or a tub of margarine.

In the case of firms, perfect competition means that producers are too small and face too much competition from other firms to be able to raise prices. Take the case of farmers selling wheat. They have to sell it at the current market price. If individually they try to sell at a higher price, no one will buy, since purchasers of wheat (for example, flour millers) can get all the wheat they want at the market price.

Of course, many firms *do* have the power to choose their prices. This does not mean that they can simply charge whatever they like. They will still have to take account of overall consumer demand and their competitors' prices. Ford, when setting the price of its Focus cars, will have to ensure that they remain competitive with Astras, Golfs, 307s, etc. Nevertheless, most firms have some flexibility in setting their prices: they have a degree of 'market power'.

If this is the case, then why do we study *perfect* markets, where firms are price takers? One reason is that they provide a useful approximation to the real world and give us many insights into how a market economy works. Many markets do function very similarly to the markets we shall be describing.

Another is that perfect markets provide an ideal against which to compare the real world. It is often argued that perfect markets benefit the consumer, whereas markets dominated by big business may operate against the consumer's interests. For example, the consumer may end up paying higher prices in a market dominated by just a few firms than in one operating under perfect competition.

Definitions

Perfect competition (preliminary definition)
A situation where the consumers and producers of a product are price takers. (There are other features of a perfectly competitive market; these are examined in Chapter 4.)

Price taker
A person or firm with no power to be able to influence the market price.

Recap

1. The economic systems of different countries vary according to the extent to which they rely on the market or the government to allocate resources.

2. At the one extreme, in a command economy, the state makes all the economic decisions. It plans how many resources to allocate for present consumption and how many for investment for future output. It plans the output of each industry, the methods of production it will use and the amount of resources it will be allocated. It plans the distribution of output between consumers.

3. A command economy has the advantage of being able to address directly various national economic goals, such as rapid growth and the avoidance of unemployment and inequality. A command economy, however, is likely to be inefficient: a large bureaucracy will be needed to collect and process information; prices and the choice of production methods are likely to be arbitrary; incentives may be inappropriate; shortages and surpluses may result.

4. At the other extreme is the free-market economy. In this economy, decisions are made by the interaction of demand and supply. Price changes act as the mechanism whereby demand and supply are balanced. If there is a shortage of a product, its price will rise until the shortage is eliminated. If there is a surplus, its price will fall until that is eliminated.

5. In the next chapter we will be studying perfect markets. These are markets where both producers and consumers are price takers.

QUESTIONS

1. Imagine that you won millions of pounds on the National Lottery. Would your 'economic problem' be solved?

2. Would redistributing incomes from the rich to the poor reduce the overall problem of scarcity?

3. In what way does specialisation reduce the problem of scarcity?

4. Which of the following are macroeconomic issues, which are microeconomic ones and which could be either depending on the context?

   (a) Inflation.
   (b) Low wages in certain service industries.
   (c) The rate of exchange between the pound and the euro.
   (d) Why the price of cabbages fluctuates more than that of cars.
   (e) The rate of economic growth this year compared with last year.
   (f) The decline of traditional manufacturing industries.

5. Assume that in a household one parent currently works full time and the other stays at home to look after the family. How would you set about identifying and calculating the opportunity costs of the second parent now taking a full-time job? How would such calculations be relevant in deciding whether it is worth taking that job?

6. When you made the decision to study economics, was it a 'rational' decision (albeit based on the limited information you had available at the time)? What additional information would you like to have had in order to ensure that your decision was the right one?

7. Assume you are looking for a job and are offered two. One is more unpleasant to do, but pays more. How would you make a rational choice of which of the two jobs to accept?

8. Imagine that a country can produce just two things: goods and services. Assume that over a given time period it could produce any of the following combinations:

Units of goods	0	10	20	30	40	50	60	70	80	90	100
Units of services	80	79	77	74	70	65	58	48	35	19	0

   (a) Draw the country's production possibility curve.
   (b) Assuming that the country is currently producing 40 units of goods and 70 units of services, what is the opportunity cost of producing another 10 units of goods?
   (c) Explain how the figures illustrate the principle of increasing opportunity cost.
   (d) Now assume that technical progress leads to a 10 per cent increase in the output of goods for any given amount of resources. Draw the new production possibility curve. How has the opportunity cost of producing extra units of services altered?

9. Under what circumstances would the production possibility curve be (a) a straight line, (b) bowed in towards the origin? Are these circumstances ever likely?

10. Using a chart similar to that in Figure 1.6, trace through the following effects: (a) a fall in demand for a good; (b) an increased supply of a factor of production. (In the case of (b) you will need to consider the factor market first, and then the goods market.)

Additional case studies in the Essentials of Economics MyEconLab (www.pearsoned.co.uk/sloman)

1.1   **Scarcity and abundance.** If scarcity is the central economic problem, is anything truly abundant?

1.2   **Global economics.** This examines how macroeconomics and microeconomics apply at the global level and identifies some key issues.

1.3   **Buddhist economics.** A different perspective on economic problems and economic activity.

1.4   **Green economics.** This examines some of the environmental costs that society faces today. It also looks at the role of economics in analysing these costs and how the problems can be tackled.

1.5   **Positive and normative statements.** A crucial distinction when considering matters of economic policy.

1.6   **Adam Smith (1723–90).** Smith, the founder of modern economics, argued that markets act like an invisible hand guiding production and consumption.

1.7   **Free-market medicine in Russia.** This examines the operation of the fledgling market economy in Russia and the successes and difficulties in moving from a planned to a market economy.

Websites relevant to this chapter

Numbers and sections refer to websites listed in the Web appendix and hotlinked from this book's website at **www.pearsoned.co.uk/sloman**.

■ For news articles relevant to this chapter, see the *Economics News Articles* link from the book's website.

■ For a tutorial on finding the best economics websites see site C8 (*The Internet Economist*).

■ For general economics news sources, see websites in section A of the Web Appendix at the end of the book, and particularly A1–9, 24, 38, 39. See also A38 and 39 for links to newspapers worldwide; and A42 and A44 for links to economics news articles from newspapers worldwide.

■ For sources of economic data, see sites in section B and particularly B1–4, 33, 34.

■ For general sites for students of economics, see sites in section C and particularly C1–7.

■ For sites giving links to relevant economics websites, organised by topic, see sites I4, 7, 8, 11, 12, 17, 18.

■ For news on the Russian economy (Box 1.2), see sites A14, 15. See also the *Economic Systems and Theories > Transition Economies* section of site I7.

Web appendices

1.1   **Some techniques of economic analysis.** This appendix explains how economists use graphs, tables and simple equations to represent economic data.

1.2   **Elementary differentiation.** This gives the rules for simple differentiation. Although this book does not use calculus (of which differentiation is part), the techniques are widely used by economists and you will need to use calculus if you progress to more advanced economic courses.

B Part

Microeconomics

CHAPTER MAP

Markets, demand and supply

In this section of the book we focus on microeconomics. Despite being 'small economics' – in other words, the economics of the individual parts of the economy, rather than the economy as a whole – it is still concerned with many of the big issues of today.

We will study why the pattern of production and consumption changes over time; why some people are rich and others poor; why our lives seem to be dominated by market forces beyond our control. We will look at the world of big business at one extreme and highly competitive markets at the other. We will look at many of the seemingly intractable problems we face: from the growing problem of pollution, to our limited power as consumers, to the widening inequality of incomes in society.

We will look at how markets work. We will examine what determines how much of any product gets produced and sold, and why some goods rise in price, whereas others fall. In the process we will be looking at one of the most important theories in the whole of economics: the theory of supply and demand.

After studying this chapter, you should be able to answer the following questions:

- How do markets operate?
- What determines the amount that consumers buy of a product?
- What determines how much producers supply of a product?
- How are market prices determined and when are they likely to rise or fall?
- How do markets respond to changes in demand or supply?
- What are the major strengths and weaknesses of a free-market economy?

2.1   DEMAND

How much will people buy of any item?

The relationship between demand and price

The headlines announce, 'Major crop failures in Brazil and East Africa: coffee prices soar'. Shortly afterwards you find that coffee prices have doubled in the shops. What do you do? Presumably you will cut back on the amount of coffee you drink. Perhaps you will reduce it from, say, six cups per day to two. Perhaps you will give up drinking coffee altogether.

This is simply an illustration of the general relationship between price and consumption: *when the price of a good rises, the quantity demanded will fall*. This relationship is known as the **law of demand**. There are two reasons for this law:

■ People will feel poorer. They will not be able to afford to buy so much of the good with their money. The purchasing power of their income (their *real income*)[1] has fallen. This is called the **income effect** of a price rise.

■ The good will now be dearer relative to other goods. People will thus switch to alternative or 'substitute' goods. This is called the **substitution effect** of a price rise.

Similarly, when the price of a good falls, the quantity demanded will rise. People can afford to buy more (the income effect), and they will switch away from consuming alternative goods (the substitution effect).

Therefore, returning to our example of the increase in the price of coffee, we will not be able to afford to buy as much as before, and we will probably drink more tea, cocoa, fruit juices or even water instead.

A word of warning: be careful about the meaning of the words **quantity demanded**. They refer to the amount consumers are willing and able to purchase at a given price over a given period (e.g. a week, or a month, or a year). They do *not* refer to what people would simply *like* to consume. You might like to own a luxury yacht, but your demand for luxury yachts will almost certainly be zero at the current price.

The demand curve

Consider the hypothetical data in Table 2.1. The table shows how many kilos of potatoes per month would be purchased at various prices.

Columns (2) and (3) show the **demand schedules** for two individuals, Tracey and Darren. Column (4), by contrast, shows the total **market demand schedule**. This is the total demand by all consumers. To obtain the market demand schedule for potatoes, we simply add up the quantities demanded at each price by *all* consumers: i.e. Tracey, Darren and everyone else who demands potatoes. Notice that we are talking about demand *over a period of time* (not at a *point* in time). Thus we would talk about daily demand, or weekly demand, or annual demand or whatever.

---

[1] 'Real income' is income measured in terms of its purchasing power: i.e. after taking price changes into account. Thus if prices doubled and your money income stayed the same, your real income would have halved. In other words, you would only be able to buy half as much as before with your income.

Table 2.1	The demand for potatoes (monthly)			
	Price (pence per kilo) (1)	Tracey's demand (kilos) (2)	Darren's demand (kilos) (3)	Total market demand (tonnes: 000s) (4)
A	20	28	16	700
B	40	15	11	500
C	60	5	9	350
D	80	1	7	200
E	100	0	6	100

Figure 2.1   Market demand curve for potatoes (monthly)

The demand schedule can be represented graphically as a **demand curve**. Figure 2.1 shows the market demand curve for potatoes corresponding to the schedule in Table 2.1. The price of potatoes is plotted on the vertical axis. The quantity demanded is plotted on the horizontal axis.

Point *E* shows that at a price of 100p per kilo, 100 000 tonnes of potatoes are demanded each month. When the price falls to 80p we move down the curve to point *D*. This shows that the quantity demanded has now risen to 200 000 tonnes per month. Similarly, if the price falls to 60p we move down the curve again to point *C*: 350 000 tonnes are now demanded. The five points on the graph (*A–E*) correspond to the figures in columns (1) and (4) of Table 2.1. The graph also enables us to read off the likely quantities demanded at prices other than those in the table.

A demand curve could also be drawn for an individual consumer. Like market demand curves, individuals' demand curves generally slope downwards from left to right: the lower the price of a product, the more is a person likely to buy.

Two points should be noted at this stage:

■ In textbooks, demand curves (and other curves too) are only occasionally used to plot specific data. More frequently they are used to illustrate general theoretical arguments. In such cases, the axes will simply be price and quantity, with the units unspecified.

■ The term demand 'curve' is used even when the graph is a straight line! In fact, when using demand curves to illustrate arguments we frequently draw them as straight lines – it's easier.

Other determinants of demand

Price is not the only factor that determines how much of a good people will buy. Demand is also affected by the following:

Tastes. The more desirable people find the good, the more they will demand. Tastes are affected by advertising, by fashion, by observing other consumers, by considerations of health and by the experiences from consuming the good on previous occasions.

The number and price of substitute goods (i.e. competitive goods). The higher the price of **substitute goods**, the higher will be the demand for this good as people switch from the substitutes. For example, the demand for coffee will depend on the price of tea. If tea goes up in price, the demand for coffee will rise.

The number and price of complementary goods. **Complementary goods** are those that are consumed together: cars and petrol, shoes and polish, fish and chips. The higher the price of complementary goods, the fewer of them will be bought and hence the less will be the demand for this good. For example, the demand for electricity will depend on the price of electrical goods. If the price of electrical goods goes up, so that fewer are bought, the demand for electricity will fall.

Income. As people's incomes rise, their demand for most goods will rise. Such goods are called **normal goods**. There are exceptions to this general rule, however. As people get richer, they spend less on **inferior goods** such as cheap margarine, and switch to better-quality goods.

Distribution of income. If national income were redistributed from the poor to the rich, the demand for luxury goods would rise. At the same time, as the poor got poorer they might have to turn to buying inferior goods, whose demand would thus rise too.

Expectations of future price changes. If people think that prices are going to rise in the future, they are likely to buy more now before the price does go up.

To illustrate these six determinants, let us look at the demand for butter:

■ Tastes: if it is heavily advertised, demand is likely to rise. If, on the other hand, there is a cholesterol scare, people may demand less for health reasons.

■ Substitutes: if the price of margarine goes up, the demand for butter is likely to rise as people switch from one to the other.

■ Complements: if the price of bread goes up, people will buy less bread and hence less butter to spread on it.

■ Income: if people's incomes rise, they may well turn to consuming butter rather than margarine, or feel that they can afford to spread butter more thickly on their bread.

■ Income distribution: if income is redistributed away from the poor, they may have to give up consuming butter and buy cheaper margarine instead, or simply buy less butter and use it more sparingly.

Definitions

Substitute goods
A pair of goods which are considered by consumers to be alternatives to each other. As the price of one goes up, the demand for the other rises.

Complementary goods
A pair of goods consumed together. As the price of one goes up, the demand for both goods will fall.

Normal good
A good whose demand rises as people's incomes rise.

Inferior good
A good whose demand falls as people's incomes rise.

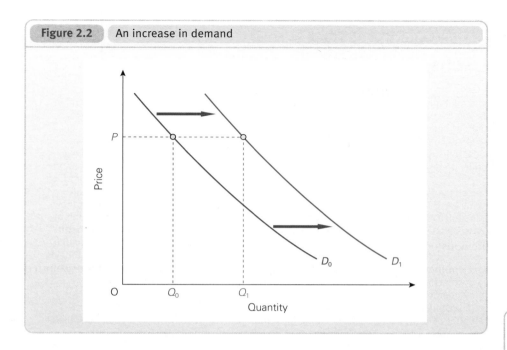

Figure 2.2   An increase in demand

- Expectations: if it is announced in the news that butter prices are expected to rise in the near future, people are likely to buy more now and stock up their freezers while current prices last.

Movements along and shifts in the demand curve

A demand curve is constructed on the assumption that 'other things remain equal' (sometimes known by the Latin term *ceteris paribus*). In other words, it is assumed that none of the determinants of demand, other than price, changes.[2] The effect of a change in price is then simply illustrated by a movement along the demand curve: for example, from point *B* to point *D* in Figure 2.1 when the price of potatoes rises from 40p to 80p per kilo.

What happens, then, when one of these other determinants does change? The answer is that we have to construct a whole new demand curve: the curve shifts. If a change in one of the other determinants causes demand to rise – say, income rises – the whole curve will shift to the right. This shows that at each price, more will be demanded than before. Thus in Figure 2.2 at a price of P, a quantity of Q_0 was originally demanded. But now, after the increase in demand, Q_1 is demanded. (Note that D_1 is not necessarily parallel to D_0.)

If a change in a determinant other than price causes demand to fall, the whole curve will shift to the left.

To distinguish between shifts in and movements along demand curves, it is usual to distinguish between a change in *demand* and a change in the *quantity demanded*. A shift in demand is referred to as a **change in demand**, whereas a movement along the demand curve as a result of a change in price is referred to as a **change in the quantity demanded**.

Definitions

Ceteris paribus
Latin for 'other things being equal'. This assumption has to be made when making deductions from theories.

Change in demand
The term used for a shift in the demand curve. It occurs when a determinant of demand *other* than price changes.

Change in the quantity demanded
The term used for a movement along the demand curve to a new point. It occurs when there is a change in price.

Pause for thought

The price of cinema tickets rises and yet it is observed that cinema attendance increases. Does this means that the demand curve for cinema tickets is upward sloping?

---

[2] We make this assumption to keep the analysis simple at the outset. We can then drop the assumption by changing things one at a time and seeing what happens.

BOX 2.1   GETTING SATISFACTION

Characteristics, utility and the demand curve

When you buy something, it's normally because you want it. You want it because you expect to get pleasure, satisfaction or some other sort of benefit from it. This applies to everything from cups of coffee, to train journeys, to music downloads, to jeans, to insurance. Economists use the term 'utility' to refer to the benefit we get from consumption.

Kelvin Lancaster[a] popularised the idea that individuals derive their utility from the characteristics or attributes of goods and services. So, for instance, the utility we derive from that morning cup of tea or coffee may come from outputs such as 'the quenching of thirst' and 'flavour'. It may be that each morning we decide to consume our drink in our favourite coffee shop. Then, in fact, the utility is influenced not only by the characteristics of the tea or coffee itself but from the characteristics of the environment in which we are consuming our drink.

Clearly, the nature and amount of utility that people get varies from one product to another, and from one person to another. But there is a simple rule that applies to virtually all people and all products. *As you consume more of a product, and thus become more satisfied, so your desire for additional units of it will decline.*

Economists call this rule the **principle of diminishing marginal utility**.

KEY IDEA 7

The principle of diminishing marginal utility. The more of a product a person consumes over a given period of time, the less will be the additional utility gained from one more unit.

For example, the second cup of tea in the morning gives you less additional satisfaction than the first cup. The third cup gives less still. We call the additional utility you get from consuming an extra unit of a product the marginal utility (*MU*). So the rule says that the marginal utility will fall as we consume more of a product over a given period of time.

There is a problem, however, with the concept of marginal utility. How can it be measured? After all, we cannot get inside each other's heads to find out just how much pleasure we are getting from consuming a product! One way round the problem is to measure marginal utility in money terms: in other words, the amount that a person would be prepared to pay for one more unit of a product. Thus if you were prepared to pay 50p for an extra packet of crisps per week, then we would say that your marginal utility from consuming it is 50p. As long as you are prepared to pay more or the same as the actual price, you will buy an extra packet. If you are not prepared to pay that price, you will not.

We can now see how this relates to a downward-sloping demand curve. As the price of a good falls, it will be worth buying extra units. You will buy more because the price will now be below the amount you are prepared to pay: i.e. price is less than your marginal utility. But as you buy more, your marginal utility from consuming each extra unit will get less and less. How many extra units do you buy? You will stop when the marginal utility has fallen to the new lower price of the good: when $MU = P$.

Marginal utility analysis is explored further in Web Appendix 2.1. An alternative approach to analysing demand, known as 'indifference analysis', is explored in Web Appendix 2.2.

TC 2
p 10

1. As well as economists, who might be interested in the influences on the utility derived by individuals when consuming goods and services?
2. How will your marginal utility from the consumption of electricity be affected by the number of electrical appliances you own?
3. How will your marginal utility from the consumption of butter depend on the amount of margarine you consume?

---

[a] Lancaster, K. (1966). A new approach to consumer theory. *The Journal of Political Economy*, 74. pp. 132–157.

Definitions

Principle of diminishing marginal utility
As more units of a good are consumed, additional units will provide less additional satisfaction than previous units.

Marginal utility (*MU*)
The extra satisfaction gained from consuming one extra unit of a good within a given time period.

Recap

1. When the price of a good rises, the quantity demanded per period of time will fall. This is known as the 'law of demand'. It applies both to individuals' demand and to the whole market demand.

2. The law of demand is explained by the income and substitution effects of a price change.

3. The relationship between price and quantity demanded per period of time can be shown in a table (or 'schedule') or as a graph. On the graph, price is plotted on the vertical axis and quantity demanded per period of time on the horizontal axis. The resulting demand curve is downward sloping (negatively sloped).

4. Other determinants of demand include tastes, the number and price of substitute goods, the number and price of complementary goods, income, the distribution of income and expectations of future price changes.

5. If price changes, the effect is shown by a movement along the demand curve. We call this effect 'a change in the quantity demanded'.

6. If any other determinant of demand changes, the whole curve will shift. We call this effect 'a change in demand'. A rightward shift represents an increase in demand; a leftward shift represents a decrease in demand.

SUPPLY
2.2

How much of any item will firms want to produce?

Supply and price

Imagine you are a farmer deciding what to do with your land. Part of your land is in a fertile valley. Part is on a hillside where the soil is poor. Perhaps, then, you will consider growing vegetables in the valley and keeping sheep on the hillside.

Your decision will largely depend on the price that various vegetables will fetch in the market and likewise the price you can expect to get from sheep and wool. As far as the valley is concerned, you will plant the vegetables that give the best return. If, for example, the price of potatoes is high, you will probably use a lot of the valley for growing potatoes. If the price gets higher, you may well use the whole of the valley, perhaps being prepared to run the risk of potato disease. If the price is very high indeed, you may even consider growing potatoes on the hillside, even though the yield per hectare is much lower there. In other words, the higher the price of a particular crop, the more you are likely to grow in preference to other crops.

This illustrates the general relationship between supply and price: *when the price of a good rises, the quantity supplied will also rise.* There are three reasons for this:

■ As firms supply more, they are likely to find that beyond a certain level of output costs rise more and more rapidly. Only if price rises will it be worth producing more and incurring these higher costs.

In the case of the farm we have just considered, once potatoes have to be grown on the hillside, the costs of producing them will increase. Also, if the land has to be used more intensively, say by the use of more and more fertilisers, again the costs of producing extra potatoes are likely to rise quite rapidly. It is the same for manufacturers. Beyond a certain level of output, costs are likely to rise rapidly as workers have to be paid overtime and as machines approach capacity working. If higher output involves higher costs of production, producers will need to get a higher price if they are to be persuaded to produce extra output.

Definitions

Supply schedule
A table showing the different quantities of a good that producers are willing and able to supply at various prices over a given time period. A supply schedule can be for an individual producer or group of producers, or for all producers (the market supply schedule).

Supply curve
A graph showing the relationship between the price of a good and the quantity of the good supplied over a specified period of time.

Table 2.2   The supply of potatoes (monthly)

	Price of potatoes (pence per kilo)	Farmer X's supply (tonnes)	Total market supply (tonnes: 000s)
a	20	50	100
b	40	70	200
c	60	100	350
d	80	120	530
e	100	130	700

■ The higher the price of the good, the more profitable it becomes to produce. Firms will thus be encouraged to produce more of it by switching from the production of less profitable goods.

■ Given time, if the price of a good remains high, new producers will be encouraged to set up in production. Total market supply thus rises.

The first two determinants affect supply in the short run. The third affects supply in the long run. We distinguish between short-run and long-run supply in Chapter 3 (pages 69–70).

The supply curve

The amount that producers would like to supply at various prices can be shown in a **supply schedule**. Table 2.2 shows a monthly supply schedule for potatoes, both for an individual farmer (farmer X) and for all farmers together (the whole market).

The supply schedule can be represented graphically as a **supply curve**. A supply curve may be an individual firm's supply curve or a market curve (i.e. that of the whole industry).

Figure 2.3 shows the *market* supply curve of potatoes. As with demand curves, price is plotted on the vertical axis and quantity on the horizontal axis. Each of the points a–e corresponds to a figure in Table 2.2. For example, a price rise from 60p per kilo to 80p per kilo will cause a movement along the supply curve from point c to point d: total market supply will rise from 350 000 tonnes per month to 530 000 tonnes per month.

Not all supply curves will be upward-sloping (positively sloped). Sometimes they will be vertical, or horizontal, or even downward-sloping. This will depend largely on the time period over which firms' response to price changes is considered. This question is examined in Chapter 3 in the section on the elasticity of supply (Section 3.3) and in more detail in Chapters 4 and 5.

Other determinants of supply

Like demand, supply is not simply determined by price. The other determinants of supply are as follows:

The costs of production. The higher the costs of production, the less profit will be made at any price. As costs rise, firms will cut back on production, probably switching to alternative products whose costs have not risen so much.

The main reasons for a change in costs are:

■ Change in input prices: costs of production will rise if wages, raw material prices, rents, interest rates or any other input prices rise.

Figure 2.3   Market supply curve of potatoes (monthly)

- Change in technology: technological advances can fundamentally alter the costs of production. Consider, for example, how the microchip revolution has changed production methods and information handling in virtually every industry in the world.
- Organisational changes: various cost savings can be made in many firms by reorganising production.
- Government policy: costs will be lowered by government subsidies and raised by various taxes.

The profitability of alternative products (substitutes in supply). If some alternative product (a **substitute in supply**) becomes more profitable to supply than before, producers are likely to switch from the first good to this alternative. Supply of the first good falls. Other goods are likely to become more profitable if their prices rise or their costs of production fall. For example, if the price of carrots goes up, or the cost of producing carrots comes down, farmers may decide to produce more carrots. The supply of potatoes is therefore likely to fall.

The profitability of goods in joint supply. Sometimes when one good is produced, another good is also produced at the same time. These are said to be **goods in joint supply**. An example is the refining of crude oil to produce petrol. Other grade fuels will be produced as well, such as diesel and paraffin. If more petrol is produced, due to a rise in demand, then the supply of these other fuels will rise too.

Nature, 'random shocks' and other unpredictable events. In this category we would include the weather and diseases affecting farm output, wars affecting the supply of imported raw materials, the breakdown of machinery, industrial disputes, earthquakes, floods and fire, and so on.

The aims of producers. A profit-maximising firm will supply a different quantity from a firm that has a different aim, such as maximising sales. For most of the time we shall assume that firms are profit maximisers.

Definitions

Substitutes in supply
These are two goods where an increased production of one means diverting resources away from producing the other.

Goods in joint supply
These are two goods where the production of more of one leads to the production of more of the other.

Expectations of future price changes. If price is expected to rise, producers may temporarily reduce the amount they sell. Instead they are likely to build up their stocks and release them on to the market only when the price does rise. At the same time they may plan to produce more, by installing new machines, or taking on more labour, so that they can be ready to supply more when the price has risen.

The number of suppliers. If new firms enter the market, supply is likely to rise.

Movements along and shifts in the supply curve

The principle here is the same as with demand curves. The effect of a change in price is illustrated by a movement along the supply curve: for example, from point *d* to point *e* in Figure 2.3 when price rises from 80p to 100p. Quantity supplied rises from 530 000 to 700 000 tonnes per month.

If any other determinant of supply changes, the whole supply curve will shift. A rightward shift illustrates an increase in supply. A leftward shift illustrates a decrease in supply. Thus in Figure 2.4, if the original curve is S_0, the curve S_1 represents an increase in supply (more is supplied at each price), whereas the curve S_2 represents a decrease in supply (less is supplied at each price).

A movement along a supply curve is often referred to as a **change in the quantity supplied**, whereas a shift in the supply curve is simply referred to as a **change in supply**.

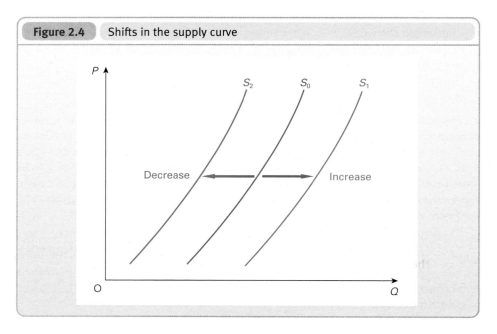

Figure 2.4   Shifts in the supply curve

Definitions

Change in the quantity supplied
The term used for a movement along the supply curve to a new point. It occurs when there is a change in price.

Change in supply
The term used for a shift in the supply curve. It occurs when a determinant *other* than price changes.

Recap

1. When the price of a good rises, the quantity supplied per period of time will usually also rise. This applies both to individual producers' supply and to the whole market supply.

2. There are two reasons in the short run why a higher price encourages producers to supply more: (a) they are now willing to incur higher costs per unit associated with producing more; (b) they will switch to producing this product instead of now less profitable ones. In the long run there is a third reason: new producers will be attracted into the market.

3. The relationship between price and quantity supplied per period of time can be shown in a table (or schedule) or as a graph. As with a demand curve, price is plotted on the vertical axis and quantity per period of time on the horizontal axis. The resulting supply curve is upward-sloping (positively sloped).

4. Other determinants of supply include the costs of production, the profitability of alternative products, the profitability of goods in joint supply, random shocks and expectations of future price changes.

5. If price changes, the effect is shown by a movement along the supply curve. We call this effect 'a change in the quantity supplied'.

6. If any determinant *other* than price changes, the effect is shown by a shift in the whole supply curve. We call this effect 'a change in supply'. A rightward shift represents an increase in supply; a leftward shift represents a decrease in supply.

THE DETERMINATION OF PRICE   2.3

How much of any item will actually be bought and sold and at what price?

Equilibrium price and output

We can now combine our analysis of demand and supply. This will show how the actual price of a product and the actual quantity bought and sold are determined in a free and competitive market.

Let us return to the example of the market demand and market supply of potatoes, and use the data from Tables 2.1 and 2.2. These figures are given again in Table 2.3.

What will be the price and output that actually prevail? If the price started at 20p per kilo, demand would exceed supply by 600 000 tonnes (A – a). Consumers would be unable to obtain all they wanted and would thus be willing to pay a higher price. Producers, unable or unwilling to supply enough to meet the demand, will be only too happy to accept a higher price. The effect of the shortage, then, will be to drive up the price. The same would happen at a price of 40p per kilo. There would still be a shortage; price would still rise. But as the price rises, the quantity demanded falls and the quantity supplied rises. The shortage is progressively eliminated.

Table 2.3	The market demand and supply of potatoes (monthly)	
Price of potatoes (pence per kilo)	**Total market demand (tonnes: 000s)**	**Total market supply (tonnes: 000s)**
20	700 (A)	100 (a)
40	500 (B)	200 (b)
60	350 (C)	350 (c)
80	200 (D)	530 (d)
100	100 (E)	700 (e)

What would happen if the price started at a much higher level: say at 100p per kilogram? In this case supply would exceed demand by 600 000 tonnes ($e - E$). The effect of this surplus would be to drive the price down as farmers competed against each other to sell their excess supplies. The same would happen at a price of 80p per kilo. There would still be a surplus; price would still fall.

In fact, only one price is sustainable. This is the price where demand equals supply: namely 60p per kilogram, where both demand and supply are 350 000 tonnes. When supply matches demand the market is said to **clear**. There is no shortage and no surplus.

As we saw on page 21, the price, where demand equals supply, is called the *equilibrium price*. In Table 2.3, if the price starts at other than 60p per kilo, there will be a tendency for it to move towards 60p. The equilibrium price is the only price at which producers' and consumers' wishes are mutually reconciled: where the producers' plans to supply exactly match the consumers' plans to buy.

Definition

Market clearing

A market clears when supply matches demand, leaving no shortage or surplus.

> **KEY IDEA 8**
> **TC 5**
>
> *Equilibrium is the point where conflicting interests are balanced.* Only at this point is the amount that demanders are willing to purchase the same as the amount that suppliers are willing to supply. It is a point which will be automatically reached in a free market through the operation of the price mechanism. This is another of our *threshold concepts*. For details, visit MyEconLab.

Demand and supply curves

The determination of equilibrium price and output can be shown using demand and supply curves. Equilibrium is where the two curves intersect.

Figure 2.5 shows the demand and supply curves of potatoes corresponding to the data in Table 2.3. Equilibrium price is P_e (60p) and equilibrium quantity is Q_e (350 000 tonnes).

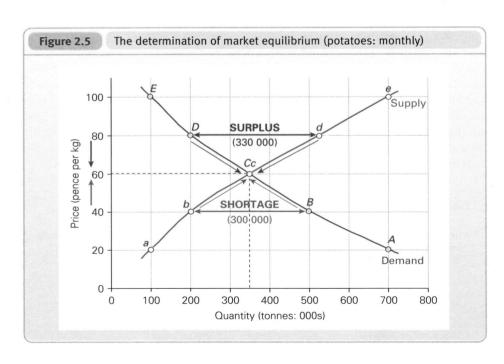

Figure 2.5   The determination of market equilibrium (potatoes: monthly)

At any price above 60p, there would be a surplus. Thus at 80p there is a surplus of 330 000 tonnes ($d - D$). More is supplied than consumers are willing and able to purchase at that price. Thus a price of 80p fails to clear the market. Price will fall to the equilibrium price of 60p. As it does so, there will be a movement along the demand curve from point D to point C, and a movement along the supply curve from point d to point c.

At any price below 60p, there would be a shortage. Thus at 40p there is a shortage of 300 000 tonnes ($B - b$). Price will rise to 60p. This will cause a movement along the supply curve from point b to point c and along the demand curve from point B to point C.

Point Cc is the equilibrium: where demand equals supply.

Movement to a new equilibrium

The equilibrium price will remain unchanged only so long as the demand and supply curves remain unchanged. If either of the curves shifts, a new equilibrium will be formed.

A change in demand

If one of the determinants of demand changes (other than price), the whole demand curve will shift. This will lead to a movement along the supply curve to the new intersection point.

For example, in Figure 2.6, if a rise in consumer incomes led to the demand curve shifting to D_2, there would be a shortage of $h - g$ at the original price P_{e_1}. This would cause price to rise to the new equilibrium P_{e_2}. As it did so, there would be a movement along the supply curve from point g to point i, and along the new demand curve (D_2) from point h to point i. Equilibrium quantity would rise from Q_{e_1} to Q_{e_2}.

The effect of the shift in demand, therefore, has been a movement along the supply curve from the old equilibrium to the new: from point g to point i.

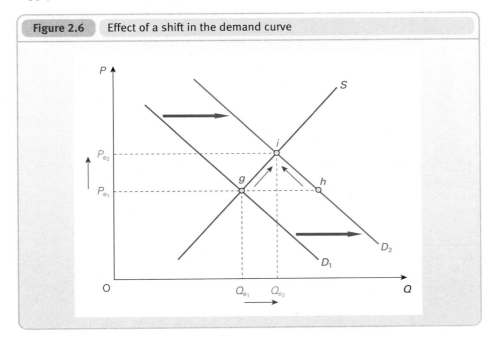

Figure 2.6   Effect of a shift in the demand curve

BOX 2.2   **UK HOUSE PRICES**

From raising the roof to falling through the floor

Headlines about UK house prices are commonplace. If we draw up a list of British obsessions we could perhaps add house prices to a list, including the weather, football and the lives of the rich and famous! Sometimes these headlines speak of rapidly increasing house prices and the problems facing households looking to get their feet on the first rung of the housing ladder. At other times, the headlines refer to falling house prices and the possibility that some households will be faced with 'negative housing equity' whereby the outstanding value of a mortgage is greater than the value of the property against which it is secured.

These changing headlines reflect two important characteristics of UK house prices: (i) their volatility; and (ii) their tendency to rise over the long term. These characteristics can be observed in the chart. House prices in 2008 were some 44 times higher than back in 1970, equivalent to an annual increase of around about 10.5 per cent. During the same period, consumer prices increased by the much smaller factor of 10.4 and this equates to an annual increase of 6.4 per cent. The fact that actual or nominal UK house prices have increased more quickly than consumer prices leads economists to talk about an increase in the *real* price of housing. In other words, the price of housing has increased relative to the average price of a basket of consumer goods and services.

House prices have not only grown more quickly than the average price of consumer goods and services, they have also increased more quickly than incomes. Household incomes increased by some 9 per cent a year between 1970 and 2008, some $1\frac{1}{2}$ percentage points less than house prices. While the difference might not seem a lot in a single year, it is quite significant over time and helps explain why UK house prices increased from around $2\frac{1}{2}$ times annual income in 1970 to over 4 times annual income in 2008.

The chart nicely captures the *volatility* in house prices. This is done by observing the annual rate of change in house prices, better known as the annual rate of house price inflation. There were marked increases in house prices in the early 1970s and early 1980s, with annual house price inflation rates approaching or exceeding 30 per cent. On each occasion house price inflation rates soon moderated, but house prices continued to increase.

We see further very strong growth in house prices in the late 1980s, but this time it is followed by house price falls. Indeed, house prices fell in each of the first four years of the 1990s. By the end of the 1990s house price inflation picked up again and the UK experienced a protracted period of robust growth.

UK house price inflation (all houses, all buyers)

Source: Based on data from Department of Communities and Local Government

But by 2008 the UK was again experiencing falling house prices. It is fair to say that UK house prices have truly been on a roller-coaster ride!

The determinants of house prices

KI 6
p 21

House prices are determined by demand and supply. If demand rises (i.e. shifts to the right) or if supply falls (i.e. shifts to the left), the equilibrium price of houses will rise. Similarly, if demand falls or supply rises, the equilibrium price will fall.

But why have UK house prices increased over the long term and more quickly than incomes and consumer prices? The answer is that demand has grown faster than supply. And why have we seen such volatility in house prices? The answer here lies in *fluctuations* in demand combined with a stock of housing that changes only slowly.

Let us examine the various factors that affected the demand for houses.

Incomes (actual and anticipated). The second half of the 1980s and from 1997 to 2007 were periods of rapidly rising incomes. The economy was experiencing an economic 'boom'. Many people wanted to spend their extra incomes on housing: either buying a house for the first time, or moving to a better one. What is more, many people thought that their incomes would continue to grow, and were thus prepared to stretch themselves financially in the short term by buying an expensive house, confident that their mortgage payments would become more and more affordable over time.

The early 1990s and 2008/9, by contrast, were periods of recession, with rising unemployment and either falling or much more slowly growing incomes. People had much less confidence about their ability to afford large mortgages.

The desire for home ownership. Many British households aspire to owner-occupation. This has often been reflected in government policies. Two examples include tax relief on mortgage interest payments and the 'right to buy scheme' which, initiated under Prime Minister Thatcher's government in the 1980s, gives council tenants the right to buy their property from councils or housing associations. In the 1980s, both these policies were believed to have fuelled the growth in housing demand. Tax relief on home loans was subsequently reduced and then removed in April 2000.

The cost of mortgages. Interest rates affect the cost of servicing a given mortgage. Debt servicing relates to the repayment of capital and to interest payments. When interest rates fall, the costs of servicing debt fall. This helps to fuel the demand for housing. During the period from 1997 interest rates were historically low which

enabled people to afford larger mortgages and thus afford to buy more expensive houses. In contrast, at the end of the 1980s and into the early 1990s, and again from 2004 to 2008, interest rates were rising. Mortgages were becoming increasingly unaffordable for many people.

The availability of mortgages. In the two housing boom periods of the late 1980s and from 1997 to 2007, mortgages were readily available. With house prices rising, banks and building societies were prepared to accept smaller deposits on houses, and to lend a larger multiple of people's income. After all, if borrowers were to default, lenders would still have a very good chance of getting all their money back.

In the early 1990s, however, and again from 2008, banks and building societies were more cautious about granting mortgages. They were aware that, with falling house prices, rising unemployment and the growing problem of negative equity, there was an increased danger that borrowers would default on payments.

Speculation. A belief that house prices will continue to move in a particular direction can exacerbate house price movements. For instance, both in the late 1980s and during much of the 2000s there was a belief that house prices would continue to rise. This encouraged people to buy as soon as possible, and to take out the biggest mortgage possible, before prices went up any further. There was also an effect on supply. Those with houses to sell held back until the last possible moment in the hope of getting a higher price. The net effect was for a rightward shift in the demand curve for houses and a leftward shift in the supply curve. The effect of this speculation, therefore, was to help bring about the very effect that people were predicting (see Section 3.5).

In the early 1990s, and again from 2008, the opposite occurred. With house prices falling, those thinking of buying houses held back, hoping to buy at a lower price. People with houses to sell tried to sell as quickly as possible before prices fell any further. Again the effect of this speculation was to aggravate the change in prices – this time a fall in prices.

Thus speculation tends to increase house price volatility.

1. *Draw supply and demand diagrams to illustrate what happened to UK house prices (a) during the early and middle parts of the 2000s; (b) during the late 2000s.*
2. *What similarities exist between the causes of the house price boom and bust of the late 1980s/early 1990s and that of the 2000s?*
3. *If actual house prices are rising can real house prices fall? Explain you answer.*

BOX 2.3   STOCK MARKET PRICES

Demand and supply in action

Firms that are quoted on the stock market (see Case Study 4.1 in MyEconLab) can raise money by issuing shares. These are sold on the 'primary stock market'. People who own the shares receive a 'dividend' on them, normally paid six-monthly. The amount varies with the profitability of the company.

People or institutions that buy these shares, however, may not wish to hold on to them forever. This is where the 'secondary stock market' comes in. It is where existing shares are bought and sold. There are stock markets, primary and secondary, in all the major countries of the world.

There are more than 3200 shares and other securities listed on the London Stock Exchange and trading in them takes place each Monday to Friday (excluding Bank Holidays). The prices of shares depend on demand and supply. For example, if the demand for Tesco shares at any one time exceeds the supply on offer, the price will rise until demand and supply are equal. Share prices fluctuate throughout the trading day and sometimes price changes can be substantial.

To give an overall impression of share price movements, stock exchanges publish share price indices. The best-known one in the UK is the FTSE ('footsie') 100, which stands for the 'Financial Times Stock Exchange' index of the 100 largest companies' shares. The index represents an average price of these 100 shares. The index was first calculated on 3 January 1984 with a base level of 1000 points. The chart shows the opening monthly value of the FTSE 100 since January 1995.

From its start in 1984 to the end of 2008, the FTSE 100 increased by an average of 7.7 per cent each year. However, this figure masks some significant variations in the prices of shares. For instance, the first three years of the new millennium saw the FTSE 100 fall by some 43 per cent and in 2008 the index fell by almost one-third!

In contrast, share prices rose by 132 per cent from 1995 to 2000. The long-run upward trend in share prices combined with their volatility is something we also see in UK house prices (see Box 2.2).

But what causes share prices to change? Why were they so high in 1999, but only just over half that value just three years later? The answer lies in the determinants of the demand and supply of shares.

Demand

There are five main factors that affect the demand for shares.

The dividend yield. This is the dividend on a share as a percentage of its price. The higher the dividend yields on shares the more attractive they are as a form of saving. One of the main explanations of rising stock market prices from 2003 to 2007 was high profits and resulting high dividends. Similarly, the slowdown in the world economy after 2007 led to falling profits and falling dividends.

The price of and/or return on substitutes. The main substitutes for shares in specific companies are other shares. Thus if, in comparison with other shares, Tesco shares are expected to pay high dividends relative to the

Financial Times Stock Exchange Index (FTSE) (3/1/84 = 1000)

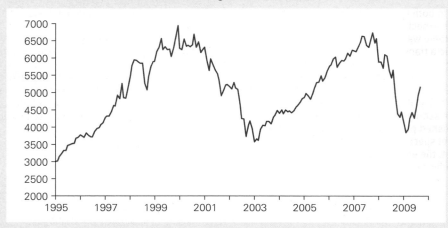

share price, people will buy Tesco shares. As far as shares in general are concerned, the main substitutes are other forms of saving. Thus if the interest rate on savings accounts in banks and building societies fell, people with such accounts would be tempted to take their money out and buy shares instead.

Another major substitute is property. If house prices rise rapidly, as they did at the start of the 2000s (see Box 2.2), this will reduce the demand for shares as many people switch to buying property in anticipation of even higher prices. If house price growth is weak or even negative, as it was during the first half of the 1990s, this makes shares relatively more attractive as an investment and can boost the demand for them. Of course, other factors may affect *both* house prices *and* shares in the same way. Thus the 'credit crunch' of the late 2000s, when finance became both harder and more expensive to obtain, resulted in both falling house prices *and* falling share prices as the economy slowed down and profits fell.

Incomes. If the economy is growing rapidly and people's incomes are thus rising rapidly, they are likely to buy more shares. For instance, in the second half of the 1990s, when household sector disposable income grew by an average of 3 per cent per year, share prices rose rapidly (see chart).

Wealth. 'Wealth' or 'net worth' is the accumulated value of people's financial and physical assets, less any financial liabilities (see Chapter 8)). The households sector's wealth increased in the second half of the 1990s and people used their increased wealth to buy shares. It was a similar picture in the mid-2000s. Much of the wealth worldwide was in relatively 'liquid' form – i.e. in a form that can easily be turned into cash (and hence used to buy shares).

Expectations. In both the mid- to late 1980s and the 1990s, people expected share prices to go on rising. In the 1980s there was a sense that the UK economy had undergone a transformation enabling permanently higher rates of economic growth. In the case of the late 1990s, reforms to policy-making, including central bank independence (see Chapter 12), again suggested better economic times lay ahead and an end to 'boom and bust'. These positive sentiments encouraged people to buy shares and pushed prices up even more. Of course, this can further fuel speculation and further share buying.

By contrast, the early and late 2000s saw confidence shaken. Negative sentiment helps to push prices down as people hold back from buying. If this negative sentiment persists it can cause significant falls. In the early part of the decade many countries experienced a temporary slowing of economic growth. This combined with other negative factors, such as the 11 September 2001 attack on the World Trade Center and various corporate scandals, such as the accounting fraud concerning the giant US company Enron.

In the late 2000s, there was a global financial crisis followed by a severe economic slowdown. Stock markets plummeted. Between October 2007 and 2008 the FTSE 100 fell by almost a half (see chart). Furthermore the FTSE and other stock markets around the world moved wildly as investors tried to gauge of the severity of the crisis. Share prices moved sharply in response to releases of economic data, firms' trading figures and policy initiatives designed to stabilise the financial system and to get banks lending again.

Supply

The factors affecting supply are largely the same as those affecting demand, but in the opposite direction.

If the return on alternative forms of saving falls, people with shares are likely to hold on to them, as they represent a better form of saving. The supply of shares to the market will fall. If incomes or wealth rises, people again are likely to want to hold on to their shares.

As far as expectations are concerned, if people believe that share prices will rise, they will hold on to the shares they have. Supply to the market will fall, thereby pushing up prices. If, however, they believe that prices will fall, as they did in 2008, they will sell their shares now before prices do fall. Supply will increase, driving down the price.

Share prices and business

Companies are crucially affected by their share price. If a company's share price falls, this is taken as a sign that 'the market' is losing confidence in the company. This will make it more difficult to raise finance, not only by issuing additional shares in the primary market, but also from banks.

It will also make the company more vulnerable to a takeover bid. This is where one company seeks to buy out another by offering to buy all its shares. A takeover will succeed if the owners of more than half of the company's shares vote to accept the offered price. Shareholders are more likely to agree to the takeover if the company's shares have not being doing very well recently.

1. *If the rate of economic growth in the economy is 3 per cent in a particular year, can we expect share prices to rise by 3 per cent that year? Explain your answer.*
2. *Of what importance do you think the publication of economic and financial data by firms and governments is in affecting share prices?*

A change in supply

Likewise, if one of the determinants of supply changes (other than price), the whole supply curve will shift. This will lead to a movement *along* the *demand* curve to the new intersection point.

For example, in Figure 2.7, if costs of production rose, the supply curve would shift to the left: to S_2. There would be a shortage of $g - j$ at the old price of P_{e_1}. Price would rise from P_{e_1} to P_{e_3}. Quantity would fall from Q_{e_1} to Q_{e_3}. In other words, there would be a movement along the demand curve from point g to point k, and along the new supply curve (S_2) from point j to point k.

To summarise: a shift in one curve leads to a movement along the other curve to the new intersection point. Sometimes a number of determinants might change. This may lead to a shift in *both* curves. When this happens, equilibrium simply moves from the point where the old curves intersected to the point where the new ones intersect.

KI 6
p 21

> **Pause for thought**
>
> *Is the following statement true? 'An increase in demand will cause an increase in price. This increase in price will cause a reduction in demand, until demand is reduced back to its original level.' Explain your answer and try using a demand and supply diagram to illustrate what is going on.*

Figure 2.7	Effect of a shift in the supply curve

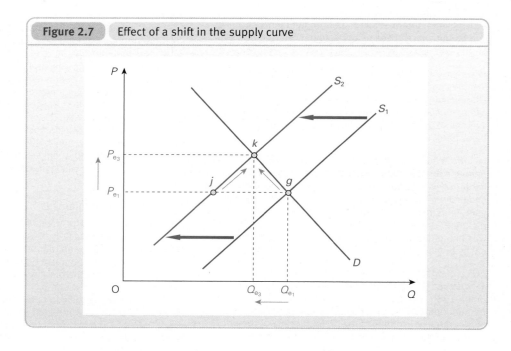

Recap

1. If the demand for a good exceeds the supply, there will be a shortage. This will lead to a rise in the price of the good.

2. If the supply of a good exceeds the demand, there will be a surplus. This will lead to a fall in the price.

3. Price will settle at the equilibrium. The equilibrium price is the one that clears the market: the price where demand equals supply.

4. If the demand or supply curve shifts, this will lead either to a shortage or to a surplus. Price will therefore either rise or fall until a new equilibrium is reached at the position where the supply and demand curves now intersect.

THE FREE-MARKET ECONOMY   2.4

How well does it serve us?

Advantages of a free-market economy

The fact that a free-market economy functions automatically is one of its major advantages. There is no need for costly and complex bureaucracies to co-ordinate economic decisions. The economy can respond quickly to changing demand and supply conditions.

When markets are highly competitive, no one has great power. Competition between firms keeps prices down and acts as an incentive to firms to become more efficient. The more firms there are competing, the more responsive they will be to consumer wishes.

The more efficiently firms can combine their factors of production, the more profit they will make. The more efficiently workers work, the more secure will be their jobs and the higher their wages. The more carefully consumers decide what to buy, the greater the value for money they will receive.

Thus people pursuing their own self-interest through buying and selling in competitive markets helps to minimise the central economic problem of scarcity, by encouraging the efficient use of the nation's resources in line with consumer wishes. From this type of argument, the following conclusion is often drawn by defenders of the free market: 'The pursuit of private gain results in the social good.' This is obviously a highly significant claim and has profound moral implications (see Threshold Concepts 5 and 6).

KEY IDEA 9 TC 4 p 21 ***People gain from voluntary interaction.*** **When people buy from or sell to other people, or when they are employed by or employ other people, both parties will gain from the interaction. This is the sixth of our threshold concepts.**

Problems with a free-market economy

In practice, however, markets do not achieve maximum efficiency in the allocation of scarce resources, and governments feel it necessary to intervene to rectify this and other problems of the free market. The problems of a free market are as follows:

- Competition between firms is often limited. A few giant firms may dominate an industry. In these cases they may charge high prices and make large profits. Rather than merely responding to consumer wishes, they may attempt to persuade consumers by advertising. Consumers are particularly susceptible to advertisements for products that are unfamiliar to them.
- Lack of competition and high profits may remove the incentive for firms to be efficient.
- Power and property may be unequally distributed. Those who have power and/or property (e.g. big business, unions, landlords) will gain at the expense of those without power and property.
- The practices of some firms may be socially undesirable or have adverse environmental consequences. For example, a chemical works may pollute the environment.

BOX 2.4 | **THE COFFEE CRISIS OF 2000 TO 2004**

An unfair bean count?

The cultivating, processing and retailing of coffee is a big industry. Yet, the late 1990s and early 2000s marked something of a crisis for coffee producers. During this period the world supply of coffee rose relative to demand, causing a slump in the price. The graph shows the trend in the average price of coffee

(there are many varieties and prices) between 1996 and 2009. Having reached $1.80 per lb in May 1997 (an imperial pound (lb) is equivalent to 454 grams). It then fell more or less continuously over the next five years, reaching around $44 in 2002: a fall of some 75 per cent.

Coffee prices (average of all coffees) and output

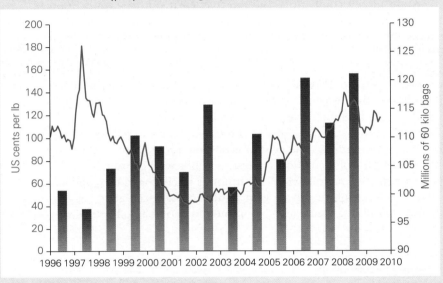

Source: International Coffee Organization (ICO)

- Some socially desirable goods would simply not be produced by private enterprise. What firm would build and operate a lighthouse, unless it were paid for by the government?
- A free-market economy may lead to macroeconomic instability. There may be periods of recession with high unemployment and falling output, and other periods of rising prices.

- Finally, there is the ethical objection that a free-market economy, by rewarding self-interested behaviour, may encourage selfishness, greed, materialism and the acquisition or pursuit of power.

We shall be examining these various problems in more detail in later chapters.

The mixed economy

Because of the problems of both free-market and command economies, all real-world economies are a mixture of the two systems. The economies of the former communist bloc all used the market mechanism to some extent. All market economies involve some degree of government intervention.

During this period, the supply of coffee increased by around 3.6 per cent a year, outstripping the 1.5 per cent annual increase in demand. The growth in supply was largely caused by new plantings in Vietnam and Brazil. In 2002 world demand was estimated to be around 106 million bags; but production was over 120 million bags with a further 40 million bags held in stock.

The effect of the low price on many coffee growers, who are mainly to be found in some of the world's poorest countries, was catastrophic. Many farmers were driven into debt; others left the land and migrated to cities, worsening the often appalling conditions there. Others switched to growing narcotic drugs, such as coca in Vietnam.

As we can see from the chart, the price of coffee recovered after 2004, peaking in July 2008 at $133 per lb, its highest level since July 1997. In part, this was due to farmers diversifying into other crops; in part, it was due to buoyant global demand, with the emergence of new coffee markets, such as China and Russia, and strong demand in coffee-producing countries themselves.

In 2008, however, a combination of good harvests and a recovery in the coffee prices caused supply to increase substantially. Although demand was still growing in developing countries, the onset of recession in developed countries was halting the growth in demand and, as a result, the world growth in supply outstripped the world growth in demand. By the end of 2008 the price had fallen back to $103 per lb.

You might be wondering why the price of a latte or an espresso in your favourite coffee shop did not follow the price received by coffee growers in the early and late 2000s. Well, of the price you pay for a cup of coffee only a very small part is accounted for by the coffee beans. The rest pays for the wages of staff, overheads, advertising and profits.

Fine, but why has the price of instant coffee in supermarkets not more closely followed the price of coffee? In particular, why did it not fall more noticeably during the 'crisis years' of the early 2000s? The answer here lies in the actions of coffee roasters. About a half of the world production of coffee is bought by just four huge companies – Kraft, Nestlé, Procter & Gamble and Sara Lee. These companies did not, in general, pass on the reduction in the price of coffee to producers but substantially increased their profits. (We will be looking at the behaviour of large firms in Chapter 5, in the section on oligopoly.)

1. *What do you think caused the large increase in the price of coffee in 1997?*
2. *Use supply and demand diagrams to explain (a) the fall in coffee prices in the late 1990s and early 2000s; (b) the increase in coffee prices from 2004 to 2008*

The material in this box has largely been drawn from the ICO website (www.ico.org).

KEY IDEA 10 / **TC 7**

Government intervention may be able to rectify various failings of the market. Government intervention in the market can be used to achieve various economic objectives that may not be best achieved by the market. Governments are not perfect, however, and their actions may bring adverse as well as beneficial consequences.

The fact that government intervention can, at least in principle, correct market failures is the seventh of our 15 threshold concepts.

In mixed market economies, the government may control the following:

■ **Relative prices** of goods and inputs, by taxing or subsidising them or by direct price controls.

■ Relative incomes, by the use of income taxes, welfare payments or direct controls over wages, profits, rents, etc.

■ The pattern of production and consumption, by the use of legislation (e.g. making it illegal to produce unsafe goods), by direct provision of goods and services (e.g. education and defence), by taxes and subsidies or by nationalisation.

Definition

Relative price
The price of one good compared with another (e.g. good X is twice the price of good Y).

■ The macroeconomic problems of unemployment, inflation, lack of growth, balance of trade deficits and exchange rate fluctuations, by the use of taxes and government expenditure, the control of bank lending and interest rates, the direct control of prices, and the control of the foreign exchange rate.

Just how the government intervenes, and what the effects of the various forms of intervention are, will be examined in detail in later chapters.

The relative merits of alternative mixtures of government and the market depend on the weight attached to various political and economic goals: goals such as liberty, equality, efficiency in production, the fulfilling of consumer wishes, economic growth and full employment. No one type of mixed market economy is likely to be superior in all respects.

> **Pause for thought**
>
> *Why do governments on the political right tend to intervene less in markets than governments on the political left? Does this mean that whether something is an economic 'problem' depends on your perspective?*

Recap

1. A free-market economy functions automatically, and if there is plenty of competition between producers, this can help to protect consumers' interests.

2. In practice, however, competition may be limited; there may be great inequality; there may be adverse social and environmental consequences; there may be macroeconomic instability.

3. All real-world economies are some mixture of the market and government intervention. Governments intervene in market economies in various ways in order to correct the failings of the free market. The degree and form of government intervention depend on the aims of governments and the nature of the problems they are attempting to tackle.

QUESTIONS

1. Why do the prices of fresh vegetables fall when they are in season? Could an individual farmer prevent the price falling?

2. If you were the owner of a clothes shop, how would you set about deciding what prices to charge for each garment at the end-of-season sale?

3. The number of owners of mobile phones has grown rapidly and hence the demand for mobile phones has also grown rapidly. Yet the prices of mobile phones have fallen. Why?

4. Assume that oil begins to run out and that extraction becomes more expensive. Trace through the effects of this on the market for oil and the market for other fuels.

5. This question is concerned with the supply of oil for central heating. In each case consider whether there is a movement along the supply curve (and in which direction) or a shift in it (and whether left or right).

   (a) New oil fields start up in production.
   (b) The demand for central heating rises.
   (c) The price of gas falls.
   (d) Oil companies anticipate an upsurge in demand for central heating oil.
   (e) The demand for petrol rises.
   (f) New technology decreases the costs of oil refining.
   (g) All oil products become more expensive.

6. The weekly demand and supply schedules for t-shirts (in millions) in a free market are as follows:

Price (£)	8	7	6	5	4	3	2	1
Quantity demanded	6	8	10	12	14	16	18	20
Quantity supplied	18	16	14	12	10	8	6	4

   (a) What is the equilibrium price and quantity?
   (b) Assume that changes in fashion cause the demand for t-shirts to rise by 4 million at each price. What will be the new equilibrium price and quantity? Has equilibrium quantity risen as much as the rise in demand? Explain why or why not.
   (c) Now plot the data in the table on a graph and mark the equilibrium. Also plot the new data corresponding to (b) and mark the new equilibrium.

7. On separate demand and supply diagrams for bread, sketch the effects of the following: (a) a rise in the price of wheat; (b) a rise in the price of butter and margarine; (c) a rise in the price of rice, pasta and potatoes. In each case, state your assumptions.

8. For what reasons might the price of foreign holidays rise? In each case identify whether these are reasons affecting demand or supply (or both).

9. If both demand and supply change, and if we know in which direction they have shifted but not how much, why is it that we will be able to predict the direction in which *either* price *or* quantity will change, but not both? (Clue: consider the four possible combinations and sketch them if necessary: (a) *D* left, *S* left; (b) *D* right, *S* right; (c) *D* left, *S* right; (d) *D* right, *S* left.)

10. What will happen to the equilibrium price and quantity of butter in each of the following cases? You should state whether demand or supply (or both) have shifted and in which direction. (In each case assume *ceteris paribus*.)

   (a) A rise in the price of margarine.
   (b) A rise in the demand for yoghurt.
   (c) A rise in the price of bread.
   (d) A rise in the demand for bread.
   (e) An expected rise in the price of butter in the near future.
   (f) A tax on butter production.
   (g) The invention of a new, but expensive, process for removing all cholesterol from butter, plus the passing of a law which states that all butter producers must use this process.

Log on to MyEconlab and complete the studyplan exercises for this chapter to see how much you have learnt and where you need to revise most. Make sure you access all the supporting textbook resources including the online workbook, newsblog, audio animations, guided solutions and ebook.

Additional case studies in the *Essentials of Economics* MyEconLab (www.pearsoned.co.uk/sloman)

2.1 **The interdependence of markets.** A case study in the operation of markets, examining the effects on a local economy of the discovery of a large coal deposit.

2.2 **Bentham and the philosophy of utilitarianism.** This looks at the historical and philosophical underpinning of the ideas of utility maximisation.

2.3 **Stocks and flows.** This examines one of the most important distinctions in economics and one that we shall come across on several occasions.

2.4 **Adjusting to oil price shocks.** A case study showing how demand and supply analysis can be used to examine the price changes in the oil market since 1973.

2.5 **Rationing.** A case study in the use of rationing as an alternative to the price mechanism. In particular, it looks at the use of rationing in the UK during the Second World War.

Websites relevant to this chapter

Numbers and sections refer to websites listed in the Web appendix and hotlinked from this book's website at **www.pearsoned.co.uk/sloman**.

■ For news articles relevant to this chapter, see the Economics News Articles link from the book's website.

■ For general news on markets, see websites in section A, and particularly A2, 3, 4, 5, 8, 9, 18, 24, 25, 26, 36. See also sites A42 and A44 for links to economics news articles from newspapers worldwide.

■ For links to sites on markets, see the relevant sections of I4, 7, 11, 17.

■ For data on the housing market (Box 2.2), see sites B7, 8, 11 and E2.

■ For student resources relevant to this chapter, see sites C1–7, 9, 10, 19; D3.

■ For sites favouring the free market, see C17 and E34.

Web appendices

2.1 **Marginal utility theory.** This develops the analysis of Box 2.1 and shows how the marginal utility the consumer receives from a product affects demand.

2.2 **Indifference analysis.** This examines the choices consumers make between products and shows how these choices are affected by the prices of the products.

CHAPTER MAP

Markets in action

In this chapter we explore the working of markets in more detail. We start by examining one of the most important concepts in the whole of economics – that of elasticity (Sections 3.1–3.4).

A bumper harvest may seem like good news for farmers: after all, they will be able to sell more. But is it good news? Although they will sell more, the effect of the increased supply will be to drive down the price – and that's bad news for farmers! So will the increased sales (the good news) be enough to compensate for the reduction in price (the bad news)? Will farmers end up earning more or less from their bumper harvest? It all depends on just how much the price falls, and this depends on the *price elasticity of demand* for their produce. This is a measure of how *responsive* demand is to a change in price.

It is not just the responsiveness of *demand* that is important in determining the functioning of markets. It is also the responsiveness of *supply*. Why, do you think, do some firms respond to a rise in price by producing a lot more, whereas others only produce a little more? Is it simply because of different technologies? We will discover just what influences the price elasticity of supply in Section 3.3.

The chapter closes by looking at what happens if governments set about *controlling* prices. Why will shortages occur if the government sets the price too low, or surpluses if it sets it too high? When might governments feel that it is a good idea to fix prices?

After studying this chapter, you should be able to answer the following questions:

- How responsive is consumer demand to changes in prices and changes in incomes?
- How responsive is firms' output to a change in price?
- How does this responsiveness (or 'elasticity') of demand and supply affect the working of markets?
- Why are markets likely to be more responsive in the long run than the short run to changes in demand or supply?
- How will people respond if they anticipate a change in price?
- What will happen if the government sets a price either above or below the market equilibrium?

3.1   PRICE ELASTICITY OF DEMAND

How responsive is demand to a change in price?

When the price of a good rises, the quantity demanded will fall. That much is fairly obvious. But in most cases we will want to know more than this. We will want to know just *how much* the quantity demanded will fall. In other words, we will want to know how *responsive* demand is to a rise in price.

Take the case of two products: oil and cauliflowers. In the case of oil, a rise in price is likely to result in only a slight fall in the quantity demanded. If people want to continue driving, they have to pay the higher prices for fuel. A few may turn to riding bicycles, and some people may try to make fewer journeys, but for most people, a rise in the price of petrol and diesel will make little difference to how much they use their cars.

In the case of cauliflowers, however, a rise in price may lead to a substantial fall in the quantity demanded. The reason is that there are alternative vegetables that people can buy. Many people, when buying vegetables, are very conscious of their prices and will buy whatever is reasonably priced.

We call the responsiveness of demand to a change in price the **price elasticity of demand**. If we know the price elasticity of demand for a product, we can predict the effect on price and quantity of a shift in the *supply* curve for that product. For example, we can predict the effect of the bumper harvest that we considered at the beginning of the chapter.

Figure 3.1 shows the effect of a shift in supply with two quite different demand curves (*D* and *D'*). Curve *D'* is more elastic than curve *D* over any given price range. In other words, for any given change in price, there will be a larger change in quantity demanded along curve *D'* than along curve *D*.

Assume that initially the supply curve is S_1, and that it intersects with both demand curves at point *a*, at a price of P_1 and a quantity of Q_1. Now supply shifts to S_2. What will happen to price and quantity? In the case of the less elastic demand

Definition

Price elasticity of demand

The responsiveness of quantity demanded to a change in price.

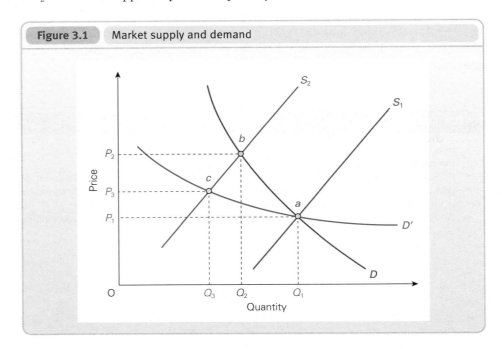

> **Figure 3.1   Market supply and demand**

curve D, there is a relatively large rise in price (to P_2) and a relatively small fall in quantity (to Q_2): equilibrium is at point b. In the case of the more elastic demand curve D', however, there is only a relatively small rise in price (to P_3) but a relatively large fall in quantity (to Q_3): equilibrium is at point c.

Measuring the price elasticity of demand

What we want to compare is the size of the change in quantity demanded with the size of the change in price. But since price and quantity are measured in different units, the only sensible way we can do this is to use percentage or proportionate changes. This gives us the following **formula for the price elasticity of demand** ($P\varepsilon_D$) for a product: percentage (or proportionate) change in quantity demanded divided by the percentage (or proportionate) change in price. Putting this in symbols gives:

$$P\varepsilon_D = \frac{\%\Delta Q_D}{\%\Delta P}$$

where ε (the Greek epsilon) is the symbol we use for elasticity, and Δ (the capital Greek delta) is the symbol we use for a 'change in'.

Thus if a 40 per cent rise in the price of oil caused the quantity demanded to fall by a mere 10 per cent, the price elasticity of oil over this range would be:

$-10\%/40\% = -0.25$

On the other hand, if a 5 per cent fall in the price of cauliflowers caused a 15 per cent rise in the quantity demanded, the price elasticity of demand for cauliflowers over this range would be:

$15\%/-5\% = -3$

Cauliflowers have a more elastic demand than oil, and this is shown by the figures. But just what do these two figures show? What is the significance of minus 0.25 and minus 3?

Interpreting the figure for elasticity

The use of proportionate or percentage measures

Elasticity is measured in proportionate or percentage terms for the following reasons:

■ It allows comparison of changes in two qualitatively different things, and thus which are measured in two different types of unit: i.e. it allows comparison of *quantity* changes with *monetary* changes.

■ It is the only sensible way of deciding *how big* a change in price or quantity is. Take a simple example. An item goes up in price by £1. Is this a big increase or a small increase? We can answer this only if we know what the original price was. If a can of beans goes up in price by £1, that is a huge price increase. If, however, the price of a house goes up by £1, that is a tiny price increase. In other words, it is the percentage or proportionate increase in price that we look at in deciding how big a price rise it is.

The sign (positive or negative)

Demand curves are generally downward-sloping. This means that price and quantity change in opposite directions. A *rise* in price (a positive figure) will cause a *fall* in the quantity demanded (a negative figure). Similarly a *fall* in price will cause a *rise* in the quantity demanded. Thus when working out price elasticity of demand we

Definition

Formula for price elasticity of demand ($P\varepsilon_D$)

The percentage (or proportionate) change in quantity demanded divided by the percentage (or proportionate) change in price: $\%\Delta Q_D \div \%\Delta P$.

either divide a negative figure by a positive figure, or a positive figure by a negative. Either way, we end up with a negative figure.

The value (greater or less than 1)

If we now ignore the negative sign and just concentrate on the value of the figure, this tells us whether demand is elastic or inelastic.

■ **Elastic demand** ($\varepsilon > 1$). This is where a change in price causes a proportionately larger change in the quantity demanded. In this case the value of elasticity will be greater than 1, since we are dividing a larger figure by a smaller figure.

■ **Inelastic demand** ($\varepsilon < 1$). This is where a change in price causes a proportionately smaller change in the quantity demanded. In this case elasticity will be less than 1, since we are dividing a smaller figure by a larger figure.

■ **Unit elastic demand** ($\varepsilon = 1$). This is where price and quantity demanded change by the same proportion. This will give an elasticity equal to 1, since we are dividing a figure by itself.

Determinants of price elasticity of demand

The price elasticity of demand varies enormously from one product to another. Table 3.1 gives some examples. But why do some products have a highly elastic demand, whereas others have a highly *in*elastic demand? What determines price elasticity of demand?

The number and closeness of substitute goods. This is the most important determinant. The more substitutes there are for a good, and the closer they are, the more will people switch to these alternatives when the price of the good rises: the greater, therefore, will be the price elasticity of demand.

Returning to our examples of oil and cauliflowers, there is no close substitute for oil and thus demand is relatively inelastic. There are plenty of alternatives to cauliflowers, however, and thus demand is relatively elastic.

The proportion of income spent on the good. The higher the proportion of our income we spend on a good, the more we will be forced to cut consumption when its price rises: the bigger will be the income effect and the more elastic will be the demand.

Table 3.1	Estimates of price elasticity of demand for the USA
Product	**Price elasticity of demand**
Food	−0.21
Medical services	−0.22
Housing	
Rental	−0.18
Owner-occupied	−1.20
Electricity	−1.14
Cars	−1.20
Beer	−0.26
Wine	−0.88
Cigarettes	−0.35
Transatlantic air travel	−1.30
Imports	−0.58

Source: W. Nicholson, *Intermediate Microeconomics*, 9th edition (South-Western, 2004)

Thus salt has a very low price elasticity of demand. We spend such a tiny fraction of our income on salt, that we would find little difficulty in paying a relatively large percentage increase in its price: the income effect of a price rise would be very small. By contrast, there will be a much bigger income effect when a major item of expenditure rises in price. For example, if mortgage interest rates rise (the 'price' of loans for house purchase), people may have to cut down substantially on their demand for housing, being forced to buy somewhere smaller and cheaper, or to live in rented accommodation.

The time period. When price rises, people may take time to adjust their consumption patterns and find alternatives. The longer the time period after a price change, then, the more elastic is the demand likely to be.

To illustrate this, let us return to our example of oil. Between December 1973 and June 1974 the price of crude oil quadrupled, which led to similar increases in the prices of petrol and other oil products (such as central heating oil). Over the next few months, there was only a very small fall in the consumption of oil products. Demand was highly inelastic. The reason was that people still wanted to drive their cars and heat their houses.

Over time, however, as the higher oil prices persisted, new fuel-efficient cars were developed and many people switched to smaller cars or moved closer to their work. Similarly, people switched to gas or solid-fuel central heating, and spent more money insulating their houses to save on fuel bills. Demand was thus much more elastic in the long run.

Recap

1. Price elasticity of demand is a measure of the responsiveness of demand to a change in price.

2. It is defined as the proportionate (or percentage) change in quantity demanded divided by the proportionate (or percentage) change in price. Given that demand curves are downward-sloping, price elasticity of demand will have a negative value.

3. If quantity changes proportionately more than price, the figure for elasticity will be greater than 1 (ignoring the sign): demand is elastic. If the quantity changes proportionately less than price, the figure for elasticity will be less than 1 (again, ignoring the sign): demand is inelastic. If quantity and price change by the same proportion, the elasticity has a value of (minus) 1: demand is unit elastic.

4. Demand will be more elastic the greater the number and closeness of substitute goods, the higher the proportion of income spent on the good and the longer the time period that elapses after the change in price.

PRICE ELASTICITY OF DEMAND AND CONSUMER EXPENDITURE   3.2

How much do we spend on a good at a given price?

One of the most important applications of price elasticity of demand concerns its relationship with the total amount of money that consumers spend on a product. **Total consumer expenditure (*TE*)** is simply price times quantity purchased.

$$TE = P \times Q$$

For example, if consumers buy 3 million units (*Q*) at a price of £2 per unit (*P*), they will spend a total of £6 million (*TE*). Note that total consumer expenditure

Figure 3.2   Price elasticity of demand and total expenditure

(a) Elastic demand between two points

(b) Inelastic demand between two points

will be the same as the **total revenue (TR)** received by firms from the sale of the product (before any taxes or other deductions).

What will happen to consumer expenditure (and hence firms' revenue) if there is a change in price? The answer depends on the price elasticity of demand.

Elastic demand

As price rises so quantity demanded falls, and vice versa. When demand is elastic, quantity demanded changes proportionately more than price. Thus the change in quantity has a bigger effect on total consumer expenditure than does the change in price. For example, when the price rises, there will be such a large fall in consumer demand that less will be spent than before. This can be summarised as follows:

- P rises; Q falls proportionately more; therefore TE falls.
- P falls: Q rises proportionately more; therefore TE rises.

In other words, total expenditure changes in the same direction as *quantity*.

This is illustrated in Figure 3.2(a). The areas of the rectangles in the diagram represent total expenditure. But why? The area of a rectangle is its height multiplied by its length. In this case, this is price multiplied by quantity purchased, which, as we have seen, gives total expenditure.

Demand is elastic between points *a* and *b*. A rise in price from £4 to £5 causes a proportionately larger fall in quantity demanded: from 20 million to 10 million. Total expenditure *falls* from £80 million (the blue shaded area) to £50 million (the striped area).

When demand is elastic, then, a rise in price will cause a fall in total consumer expenditure and thus a fall in the total revenue that firms selling the product receive. A reduction in price, however, will result in consumers spending more, and hence firms earning more.

Inelastic demand

When demand is inelastic, it is the other way around. Price changes proportionately more than quantity. Thus the change in price has a bigger effect on total consumer expenditure than does the change in quantity. To summarise the effects:

Pause for thought

If a firm faces an elastic demand curve, why will it not necessarily be in the firm's interests to produce more? (Clue: you will need to distinguish between revenue and profit. We will explore this relationship in the next chapter.)

- *P* rises; *Q* falls proportionately less; therefore *TE* rises.
- *P* falls; *Q* rises proportionately less; therefore *TE* falls.

In other words, total consumer expenditure changes in the same direction as *price*.

This is illustrated in Figure 3.2(b). Demand is inelastic between points *a* and *c*. A rise in price from £4 to £8 causes a proportionately smaller fall in quantity demanded: from 20 million to 15 million. Total expenditure *rises* from £80 million (the blue shaded area) to £120 million (the striped area).

In this case, firms' revenue will increase if there is a rise in price, and fall if there is a fall in price.

Special cases

Figure 3.3 shows three special cases: (a) a totally inelastic demand ($P\varepsilon_D = 0$); (b) an infinitely elastic demand ($P\varepsilon_D = -\infty$); and (c) a unit elastic demand ($P\varepsilon_D = -1$).

Totally inelastic demand. This is shown by a vertical straight line. No matter what happens to price, quantity demanded remains the same. It is obvious that the more the price rises, the bigger will be the level of consumer expenditure. Thus in Figure 3.3(a) consumer expenditure will be higher at P_2 than at P_1.

Infinitely elastic demand. This is shown by a horizontal straight line. At any price above P_1 in Figure 3.3(b) demand is zero. But at P_1 (or any price below) demand is 'infinitely' large.

This seemingly unlikely demand curve is in fact relatively common for an *individual producer*. In a perfect market, as we have seen, firms are small relative to the whole market (like the small-scale grain farmer). They have to accept the price as given by supply and demand in the *whole market*, but at that price they can sell as much as they produce. (Demand is not *literally* infinite, but as far as the firm is concerned it is.) In this case, the more the individual farmer produces, the more revenue will be earned. In Figure 3.3(b), more revenue is earned at Q_2 than at Q_1.

Unit elastic demand. This is where price and quantity change in exactly the same proportion. Any rise in price will be exactly offset by a fall in quantity, leaving total revenue unchanged. In Figure 3.3(c) the striped area is exactly equal to the blue shaded area: in both cases total expenditure is £800.

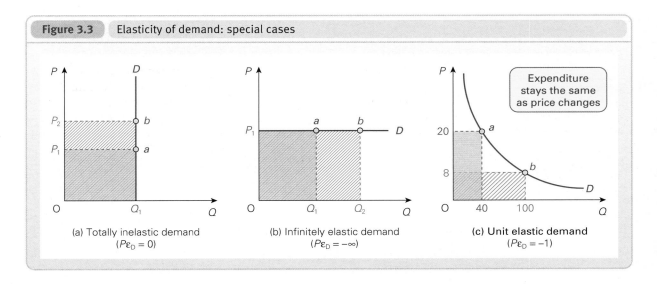

| Figure 3.3 | Elasticity of demand: special cases |

(a) Totally inelastic demand
($P\varepsilon_D = 0$)

(b) Infinitely elastic demand
($P\varepsilon_D = -\infty$)

(c) Unit elastic demand
($P\varepsilon_D = -1$)

Expenditure stays the same as price changes

BOX 3.1	THE MEASUREMENT OF ELASTICITY	EXPLORING ECONOMICS

We have defined price elasticity as the percentage or proportionate change in quantity demanded divided by the percentage or proportionate change in price. But how, in practice, do we measure these changes for a specific demand curve?

A common mistake that students make is to think that you can talk about the elasticity of a whole *curve*. The mistake here is that in most cases the elasticity will vary along the length of the curve.

Take the case of the demand curve illustrated in Figure (a). Between points *a* and *b*, total expenditure rises ($P_2Q_2 > P_1Q_1$): demand is thus elastic between these two points. Between points *b* and *c*, however, total revenue falls ($P_3Q_3 < P_2Q_2$). Demand here is inelastic.

Normally, then, we can refer to the elasticity only of a *portion* of the demand curve, not of the *whole* curve.

There is, however, an exception to this rule. This is when the elasticity just so happens to be the same all the way along a curve, as in the three special cases illustrated in Figure 3.3.

(a) Different elasticities along different portions of a demand curve

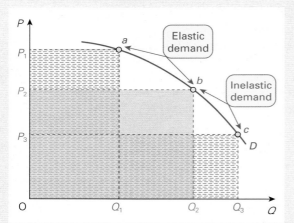

Although we cannot normally talk about the elasticity of a whole curve, we can nevertheless talk about the elasticity between any two points on it. Remember the formula we used was:

$$\frac{\% \text{ or proportionate } \Delta Q}{\% \text{ or proportionate } \Delta P} \quad \text{(where } \Delta \text{ means 'change in')}$$

The way we measure a *proportionate* change in quantity is to divide that change by the level of Q: i.e. $\Delta Q/Q$. Similarly, we measure a proportionate change in price by dividing that change by the level of P: i.e. $\Delta P/P$. Price elasticity of demand can thus now be rewritten as:

$$\frac{\Delta Q}{Q} \div \frac{\Delta P}{P}$$

But just what value do we give to P and Q? Consider the demand curve in Figure (b). What is the elasticity of demand between points *m* and *n*? Price has fallen by £2 (from £8 to £6), but what is the proportionate change? Is it 2/8 or 2/6? The convention is to express the change as a proportion of the average of the two prices, £8 and £6: in other words to take the mid-point price, £7. Thus the proportionate change is 2/7.

Similarly the proportionate change in quantity between points *m* and *n* is 10/15, since 15 is mid-way between 10 and 20.

Thus using the **average (or 'mid-point') formula**, elasticity between *m* and *n* is given by:

$$\frac{\Delta Q}{\text{average } Q} \div \frac{\Delta P}{\text{average } P} = \frac{10}{15} \div \frac{-2}{7} = -2.33$$

Since 2.33 is greater than 1, demand is elastic between *m* and *n*.

(b) Measuring elasticity using the arc method

 Referring again to Figure (b), what is the price elasticity of demand between a price of (a) £6 and £4; (b) £4 and £2? What do you conclude about the elasticity of a straight-line demand curve as you move down it?

In this box we have looked at the measurement of elasticity over a segment of the demand curve. This gives what is known as 'arc elasticity'. An alternative is to measure elasticity at a single point on the demand curve. This gives, not surprisingly, what is known as 'point elasticity'. This method is examined in Web Appendix 3.1.

Definition

Average (or 'mid point') formula for price elasticity of demand
$\Delta Q_D/\text{average } Q_D \div \Delta P/\text{average } P$

You might have thought that a demand curve with unit elasticity would be a straight line at 45° to the axes. Instead it is a curve. The reason for its particular shape is that the proportionate *rise* in quantity must equal the proportionate *fall* in price (and vice versa). As we move down the demand curve, in order for the *proportionate* change in both price and quantity to remain constant there must be a bigger and bigger *absolute* rise in quantity and a smaller and smaller absolute fall in price.

> **Pause for thought**
>
> *Two customers go to the fish counter at a supermarket to buy some cod. Neither looks at the price. Customer A orders 1 kilo of cod. Customer B orders £3 worth of cod. What is the price elasticity of demand of each of the two customers?*

| BOX 3.2 | ADVERTISING AND ITS EFFECT ON DEMAND CURVES | CASE STUDIES & APPLICATIONS |

How to increase sales and price

When we are told that brand X will make us more beautiful, enrich our lives, wash our clothes whiter, help us attract more friends, give us a new taste sensation or allow us to save the planet, just what are the advertisers up to? 'Trying to sell the product', you may reply. In fact there is a bit more to it than this. Advertisers are trying to do two things:

■ Shift the product's demand curve to the right.
■ Make it less price elastic.

This is illustrated in the diagram.

Effect of advertising on the demand curve

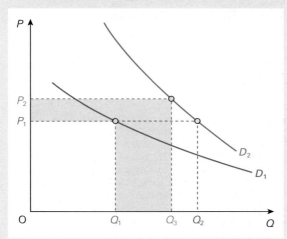

D_1 shows the original demand curve with price at P_1 and sales at Q_1. D_2 shows the curve after an advertising campaign. The rightward shift allows an increased quantity (Q_2) to be sold at the original price. If the demand is also made highly inelastic, the firm can also raise its price and still have a substantial increase in sales. Thus in the diagram, price can be raised to P_2 and sales will be Q_3 still substantially above Q_1. The total gain in revenue is shown by the shaded area.

How can advertising bring about this new demand curve?

Shifting the demand curve to the right

This can occur in two ways. First, if the advertising brings the product to more people's attention, then the market for the good grows and the demand curve shifts to the right. Second, if the advertising increases people's desire for the characteristics or attributes of a product, they will be prepared to pay a higher price for each unit purchased.

Making the demand curve less elastic

This will occur if the advertising creates a greater attachment to a product, a range of products or indeed to an organisation (brand loyalty). In other words, advertising can be used to affect perceptions of the characteristics of products and even those of firms.

If advertising is successful in generating a sense of uniqueness amongst consumers for a product it allows a firm to raise the price of the product without a significant fall in sales. If it is successful in differentiating its brand then the firm can raise prices across its range of products, again without hitting sales. Successful advertising therefore reduces the size of the substitution effect since consumers have been led to believe that there are few, if any, close substitutes.

1. *Think of some recent advertising campaigns and identify what 'characteristics' the advertising was attempting to highlight.*
2. *Imagine that 'Sunshine' sunflower margarine, a well-known brand, is advertised with the slogan, 'It helps you live longer'. What do you think would happen to the demand curve for a supermarket's own brand of sunflower margarine? Consider both the direction of shift and the effect on elasticity. Will the elasticity differ markedly at different prices? How will this affect the pricing policy and sales of the supermarket's own brand? What do you think might be the response of government to the slogan?*

BOX 3.3	WHAT WE PAY TO WATCH SPORT	CASE STUDIES & APPLICATIONS

How do we get satisfaction from attending matches?

One of the decisions that football, rugby, cricket and other sporting clubs need to make is the price of season tickets. Many organisations, including professional sports clubs, are not price takers but *choose* what price to set.

Often the price charged to watch sporting events seems especially high. Using the example of the price of football season tickets we consider why this might be the case.

For sports fans, especially those of team sports, there can be incredibly strong emotional ties. For some supporters of a particular club utility is largely derived from an attachment or loyalty to the club. These supporters would find it difficult, if not impossible, to support another club. The stronger the sense of loyalty commanded by a club the fewer the number of substitutes there are to attending that club's matches.

Attachment to a football club works in the same way as attachment does to any product by reducing the number of substitutes. The fewer the number of substitutes to which customers (fans) can turn, the lower the price elasticity of demand and the higher is likely to be the price that is charged. So, loyalty really can come at a cost!

We now consider two further characteristics of team sports, such as football, which if they change *may* affect both the position and slope of the demand curve for season tickets. (Box 3.2 considered how advertising can affect the position and slope of demand curves.)

The demand for success

Supporters are attracted to success. If a club is generally expected to perform well it can effectively 'sell' this expected success. An increase in the likelihood of success can move the demand curve for season tickets to the right and even make the product less price elastic (see the diagram in Box 3.2).

'Success' can work in the same way as 'loyalty' by reducing the number of substitutes and allowing a high price to be charged. But, more than this, an increase in the expectation of success, can allow a firm to raise its price and yet still sell more season tickets. It is for this reason that clubs often make announcements about player signings or a change in its manager as soon as they can at the end of a season and sometimes even before the end of a season!

The probability of success is, in part, dependent on the league in which a club competes. It is even possible to argue that revenues from season tickets can increase as a result of relegation. Why? Well, relegation might be expected to increase the proportion of matches a club might win. For instance, Leeds, Leicester and Norwich are examples of English football clubs which, having played relatively recently in the English Premier League, found themselves competing in the third tier of English football ('League 1'). Each of these clubs will have taken into account, when setting the price of season tickets, an expectation amongst supporters that their club would win a higher proportion of matches in a lower league. Indeed, Leicester City was promoted straight back to the second tier (the Championship) having lost only four matches in the 2008/9 League 1 season.

The demand for superstars

Sports fans are attracted by the 'quality' of the sporting event they are attending or by the opportunity to watch 'superstars'. For some supporters it might matter less that 'their' club is regularly winning, but more that they can watch household names grace their club's ground. Therefore, promotion to the top league might be expected to move the demand curve for season tickets to the right, but it may also make matches 'must see' events making the demand curve less price elastic.

By purchasing season tickets, the supporters of the so-called 'big clubs' are usually able to see 'big names' and experience a 'high win percentage'. This combination of characteristics makes for a highly demanded 'product' with few substitutes. The final result: a high price!

1. *What common factor might explain the high price paid for drinks on trains or at pop concerts and the high price paid by supporters for season tickets to watch top football clubs?*
2. *A football club is newly promoted to the top league in its country. How might this impact on the position and slope of its demand curve for season tickets? How might this demand curve change for the following season if it was to survive relegation by finishing one place above relegation?*

For example, a rise in quantity from 200 to 400 is the same proportionate change as a rise from 100 to 200, but its absolute size is double. A fall in price from £5 to £2.50 is the same percentage as a fall from £10 to £5, but its absolute size is only half.

Recap

1. The total expenditure on a product is found by multiplying the quantity sold by the price of the product.

2. When demand is price elastic, a rise in price will lead to a reduction in total expenditure on the good and hence a reduction in the total revenue of producers.

3. When demand is price inelastic, a rise in price will lead to an increase in total expenditure on the good and hence an increase in the total revenue of producers.

PRICE ELASTICITY OF SUPPLY ($P\varepsilon_s$)

3.3

How responsive is supply to a change in price?

When price changes, there will be not only a change in the quantity demanded, but also a change in the quantity *supplied*. Frequently we will want to know just how responsive quantity supplied is to a change in price. The measure we use is the **price elasticity of supply**.

Figure 3.4 shows two supply curves. Curve S_2 is more elastic between any two prices than curve S_1. Thus, when price rises from P_1 to P_2 there is a larger increase in quantity supplied with S_2 (namely, Q_1 to Q_3) than there is with S_1 (namely, Q_1 to Q_2). For any shift in the demand curve there will be a larger change in quantity supplied and a smaller change in price with curve S_2 than with curve S_1. Thus the effect on price and quantity of a shift in the demand curve will depend on the price elasticity of supply.

The **formula for the price elasticity of supply** ($P\varepsilon_s$) is: the percentage (or proportionate) change in quantity supplied divided by the percentage (or proportionate) change in price.

> **Definitions**
>
> **Price elasticity of supply**
> The responsiveness of quantity supplied to a change in price.
>
> **Formula for price elasticity of supply (arc method)**
> ΔQ_s/average $Q_s \div \Delta P$/average P.

Figure 3.4   Two supply curves of different elasticity

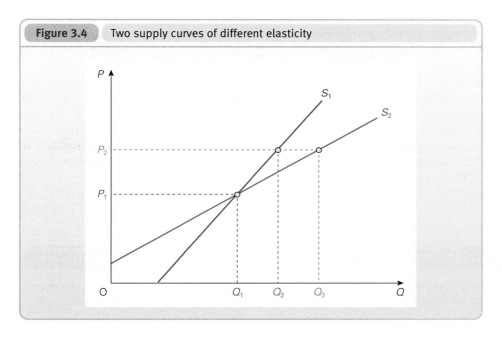

Putting this in symbols gives:

$$P\varepsilon_S = \frac{\%\Delta Q_S}{\%\Delta P}$$

In other words, the formula is identical to that for the price elasticity of demand, except that quantity in this case is quantity *supplied*. Thus if a 10 per cent rise in price caused a 25 per cent rise in the quantity supplied, the price elasticity of supply would be:

25%/10% = 2.5

and if a 10 per cent rise in price caused only a 5 per cent rise in the quantity, the price elasticity of supply would be:

5%/10% = 0.5

In the first case, supply is elastic ($P\varepsilon_S > 1$); in the second it is inelastic ($P\varepsilon_S < 1$). Notice that, unlike the price elasticity of demand, the figure is positive (assuming that the supply curve is upward-sloping). This is because price and quantity supplied change in the *same* direction.

The determinants of price elasticity of supply

The amount that costs rise as output rises.   The less the additional costs of producing additional output, the more will firms be encouraged to produce for a given price rise: the more elastic will supply be.

Supply is thus likely to be elastic if firms have plenty of spare capacity, if they can readily get extra supplies of raw materials, if they can easily switch away from producing alternative products and if they can avoid having to introduce overtime working (at higher rates of pay). If all these conditions hold, costs will be little affected by a rise in output and supply will be relatively elastic. The less these conditions apply, the less elastic will supply be.

Time period

■ Immediate time period. Firms are unlikely to be able to increase supply by much immediately. Supply is virtually fixed, or can vary only according to available stocks. Supply is highly inelastic.
■ Short run. If a slightly longer time period is allowed to elapse, some inputs can be increased (e.g. raw materials) while others will remain fixed (e.g. heavy machinery). Supply can increase somewhat.
■ Long run. In the long run, there will be sufficient time for all inputs to be increased and for new firms to enter the industry. Supply, therefore, is likely to be highly elastic. In some circumstances the long-run supply curve may even slope downwards (see Section 4.2).

Recap

1. Price elasticity of supply measures the responsiveness of supply to a change in price. It has a positive value.

2. Supply will be more elastic the less costs per unit rise as output rises and the longer the time period.

OTHER ELASTICITIES   3.4

How does demand respond to changes in income and to changes in the price of other goods?

Income elasticity of demand

So far we have looked at the responsiveness of demand and supply to a change in price. But price is just one of the determinants of demand and supply. In theory, we could look at the responsiveness of demand or supply to a change in *any* one of their determinants. We could have a whole range of different types of elasticity of demand and supply.

 KEY IDEA 11 / TC 8 — **Elasticity.** The responsiveness of one variable (e.g. demand) to a change in another (e.g. price). This concept is fundamental to understanding how markets work and is thus one of our Threshold Concepts (no. 8). The more elastic variables are, the more responsive is the market to changing circumstances.

In practice there are just two other elasticities that are particularly useful to us, and both are demand elasticities.

The first is the **income elasticity of demand** ($Y\varepsilon_D$). This measures the responsiveness of demand to a change in consumer incomes (Y).[1] It enables us to predict how much the demand curve will shift for a given change in income. The **formula for income elasticity of demand** is: the percentage (or proportionate) change in demand divided by the percentage (or proportionate) change in income. Putting this in symbols gives:

$$Y\varepsilon_D = \frac{\%\Delta Q_D}{\%\Delta Y}$$

In other words, the formula is identical to that for the price elasticity of demand, except that we are dividing the change in demand by the change in *income* that caused it rather than by a change in price. Thus if a 2 per cent rise in income caused an 8 per cent rise in a product's demand, then its income elasticity of demand would be:

8%/2% = 4

The major determinant of income elasticity of demand is the degree of 'necessity' of the good. In a developed country, the demand for luxury goods expands rapidly as people's incomes rise, whereas the demand for basic goods, such as bread, rises only a little. Thus items such as cars and holidays abroad have a high income elasticity of demand, whereas items such as potatoes and bus journeys have a low income elasticity of demand (see Table 3.2).

Definitions

Income elasticity of demand ($Y\varepsilon_D$)
The responsiveness of demand to a change in consumer incomes.

Formula for income elasticity of demand
The percentage (or proportionate) change in demand divided by the percentage (or proportionate) change in income: $\%\Delta Q_D \div \%\Delta Y$.

Pause for thought

Assume that you decide to spend a quarter of your income on clothes. What is (a) your income elasticity of demand; (b) your price elasticity of demand?

---

[1] Note that we use the letter Y rather than the letter I to stand for 'income'. This is normal practice in economics. The reason is that the letter I is used for 'investment'.

Table 3.2	Estimates of income elasticity of demand for the USA

Product	Income elasticity of demand
Food	+0.28
Medical services	+0.22
Housing	
Rental	+1.00
Owner-occupied	+1.20
Electricity	+0.61
Cars	+3.00
Beer	+0.38
Wine	+0.97
Cigarettes	−0.50
Transatlantic air travel	+1.40
Imports	+2.73

Source: W. Nicholson, *Intermediate Microeconomics*, 9th edition (South-Western, 2004)

Definitions

Normal goods

Goods whose demand increases as consumer incomes increase. They have a positive income elasticity of demand. Luxury goods will have a higher income elasticity of demand than more basic goods.

Inferior goods

Goods whose demand *decreases* as consumer incomes increase. Such goods have a negative income elasticity of demand.

Cross-price elasticity of demand

The responsiveness of demand for one good to a change in the price of another.

Formula for cross-price elasticity of demand ($C\varepsilon_{D_{ab}}$)

The percentage (or proportionate) change in demand for good a divided by the percentage (or proportionate) change in price of good b: $\%\Delta Q_{D_a} \div \%\Delta P_b$.

The demand for some goods actually decreases as income rises. These are *inferior goods* such as cheap margarine. As people earn more, so they switch to butter or better-quality margarine. Unlike **normal goods**, which have a positive income elasticity of demand, **inferior goods** have a negative income elasticity of demand.

Income elasticity of demand is an important concept to firms considering the future size of the market for their product. If the product has a high income elasticity of demand, sales are likely to expand rapidly as national income rises, but may also fall significantly if the economy moves into recession. (See Case Study 3.3, *Income elasticity of demand and the balance of payments*, in MyEconLab. This shows how the concept of income elasticity of demand can help us understand why so many developing countries suffer from chronic balance of trade problems.)

TC 8
p 67

Cross-price elasticity of demand ($C\varepsilon_{D_{ab}}$)

This is often known by its less cumbersome title of **cross elasticity of demand**. It is a measure of the responsiveness of demand for one product to a change in the price of another (either a substitute or a complement). It enables us to predict how much the demand curve for the first product will shift when the price of the second product changes. For example, knowledge of the cross elasticity of demand for Coca-Cola to the price of Pepsi would allow Coca-Cola to predict the effect on its own sales if the price of Pepsi were to change.

The **formula for the cross-price elasticity of demand** ($C\varepsilon_{D_{ab}}$) is: the percentage (or proportionate) change in demand for good a divided by the percentage (or proportionate) change in price of good b. Putting this in symbols gives:

$$C\varepsilon_{D_{ab}} = \frac{\%\Delta Q_{D_a}}{\%\Delta P_b}$$

If good b is a *substitute* for good a, a's demand will *rise* as b's price rises. In this case, cross elasticity will be a positive figure. For example, if the demand for butter rose by 2 per cent when the price of margarine (a substitute) rose by 8 per cent, then the cross elasticity of demand for butter with respect to margarine would be:

$2\%/8\% = 0.25$

If good b is *complementary* to good a, however, a's demand will *fall* as b's price rises and thus as the quantity of b demanded falls. In this case, cross elasticity of demand will be a negative figure. For example, if a 4 per cent rise in the price of bread led to a 3 per cent fall in demand for butter, the cross elasticity of demand for butter with respect to bread would be:

$$-3\%/4\% = -0.75$$

The major determinant of cross elasticity of demand is the closeness of the substitute or complement. The closer it is, the bigger will be the effect on the first good of a change in the price of the substitute or complement, and hence the greater the cross elasticity, either positive or negative.

Firms will wish to know the cross elasticity of demand for their product when considering the effect on the demand for their product of a change in the price of a rival's product or of a complementary product. These are vital pieces of information for firms when making their production plans.

Another example of the usefulness of the concept of cross elasticity of demand is in the field of international trade and the balance of payments. A government will wish to know how a change in domestic prices will affect the demand for imports. If there is a high cross elasticity of demand for imports (because they are close substitutes for home-produced goods), and if prices at home rise due to inflation, the demand for imports will rise substantially, thus worsening the balance of trade.

Recap

1. Income elasticity of demand measures the responsiveness of demand to a change in income. For normal goods it has a positive value; for inferior goods it has a negative value.

2. Demand will be more income elastic the more luxurious the good and the less rapidly demand is satisfied as consumption increases.

3. Cross-price elasticity of demand measures the responsiveness of demand for one good to a change in the price of another. For substitute goods the value will be positive; for complements it will be negative.

4. The cross-price elasticity will be more elastic the closer the two goods are as substitutes or complements.

MARKETS AND ADJUSTMENT OVER TIME   3.5

How do markets respond over the longer term to a change in demand or supply?

The full adjustment of price, demand and supply to a situation of disequilibrium will not be instantaneous. It is necessary, therefore, to analyse the time path which supply takes in responding to changes in demand, and which demand takes in responding to changes in supply.

Short-run and long-run adjustment

As we have already seen, the price elasticities of demand and supply vary with the time period under consideration. The reason is that producers and consumers take

Figure 3.5 Response of supply to an increase in demand

A bigger response in market supply in the long run than in the short run

Figure 3.6 Response of demand to an increase in supply

A bigger response in market demand in the long run than in the short run

time to respond to a change in price. The longer the time period, the bigger the response, and thus the greater the elasticity of demand and supply.

This is illustrated in Figures 3.5 and 3.6. In both cases, as equilibrium moves from points *a* to *b* to *c*, there is a large short-run price change (P_1 to P_2) and a small short-run quantity change (Q_1 to Q_2), but a small long-run price change (P_1 to P_3) and a large long-run quantity change (Q_1 to Q_3).

Price expectations and speculation

In a world of shifting demand and supply curves, prices do not stay the same. Sometimes they go up; sometimes they come down. If prices are likely to change in the foreseeable future, this will affect the behaviour of buyers and sellers *now*. If, for example, it is now December and you are thinking of buying a new winter coat, you might decide to wait until the January sales, and in the meantime make do with your old coat. If, on the other hand, when January comes you see a new summer jacket in the sales, you might well buy it now and not wait until the summer for fear that the price will have gone up by then. Thus a belief that prices will go up will cause people to buy now; a belief that prices will come down will cause them to wait.

The reverse applies to sellers. If you are thinking of selling your house and prices are falling, you will want to sell it as quickly as possible. If, on the other hand, prices are rising sharply, you will wait as long as possible so as to get the highest price. Thus a belief that prices will come down will cause people to sell now; a belief that prices will go up will cause them to wait.

> **KEY IDEA 12 TC 9**
>
> ***People's actions are influenced by their expectations.*** People respond not just to what is happening now (such as a change in price), but to what they anticipate will happen in the future. Understanding the crucial role that expectations play in determining economic behaviour makes this a Threshold Concept, the ninth of our 15.

This behaviour of looking into the future and making buying and selling decisions based on your predictions is called **speculation**. Speculation is often based on current trends in price behaviour. If prices are currently rising, people may then try to decide whether they are about to peak and go back down again, or whether they are likely to go on rising. Having made their prediction, they will then act on it. This speculation will thus affect demand and supply, which in turn will affect price. Speculation is commonplace in many markets: the stock exchange, the foreign exchange market and the housing market are three examples.

Speculation tends to be **self-fulfilling**. In other words, the actions of speculators tend to bring about the very effect on prices that speculators had anticipated. For example, if speculators believe that the price of British Airways shares is about to rise, they will buy more BA shares. But by doing this they will ensure that the price *will* rise. The prophecy has become self-fulfilling.

Speculation can either help to reduce price fluctuations or aggravate them: it can be stabilising or destabilising.

Stabilising speculation

Speculation will tend to have a **stabilising** effect on price fluctuations when suppliers and/or demanders believe that a change in price is only *temporary*.

Assume, for example, that there has recently been a rise in price, caused, say, by an increase in demand. In Figure 3.7(a) demand has shifted from D_1 to D_2. Equilibrium has moved from point a to point b, and price has risen from P_1 to P_2. How do people react to this rise in price.

Given that they believe this rise in price to be only temporary, suppliers bring their goods to market now, before price falls again. Supply shifts from S_1 to S_2. Demanders, however, hold back until price does fall. Demand shifts from D_2 to D_3. The equilibrium moves to point c, with price falling back towards P_1.

A good example of stabilising speculation occurs in agricultural commodity markets. Take the case of wheat. When it is harvested in the autumn there will be

Definitions

Speculation
Where people make buying or selling decisions based on their anticipations of future prices.

Self-fulfilling speculation
The actions of speculators tend to cause the very effect that they had anticipated.

Stabilising speculation
Where the actions of speculators tend to reduce price fluctuations.

Figure 3.7   Speculation (initial price rise)

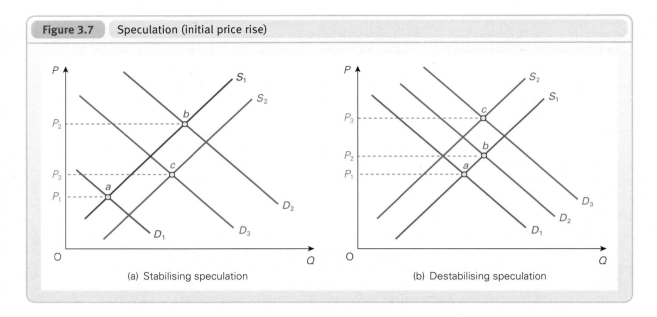

(a) Stabilising speculation   (b) Destabilising speculation

a plentiful supply. If all this wheat were to be put on the market, the price would fall to a very low level. Later in the year, when most of the wheat would have been sold, the price would then rise to a very high level. This is all easily predictable.

So what do farmers do? The answer is that they speculate. When the wheat is harvested they know the price will tend to fall, and so instead of bringing it all to market they put a lot of it into store. The more the price falls, the more they will put into store *anticipating that the price will later rise*. But this holding back of supplies prevents prices from falling. In other words, it stabilises prices.

Later in the year, when the price begins to rise, they will gradually release grain on to the market from the stores. The more the price rises, the more they will release on to the market *anticipating that the price will fall again by the time of the next harvest*. But this releasing of supplies will again stabilise prices by preventing them rising so much.

Rather than the farmers doing the speculation, it could be done by grain merchants. When there is a glut of wheat in the autumn, and prices are relatively low, they buy wheat on the grain market and put it into store. When there is a shortage in the spring and summer they sell wheat from their stores. In this way they stabilise prices just as the farmers did when they were the ones that operated the stores.

Destabilising speculation

Definition

Destabilising speculation
Where the actions of speculators tend to make price movements larger.

Speculation will tend to have a **destabilising** effect on price fluctuations when suppliers and/or buyers believe that a change in price heralds similar changes to come.

Assume again that there has recently been a rise in price, caused by an increase in demand. In Figure 3.7(b), demand has shifted from D_1 to D_2 and price has risen from P_1 to P_2. This time, believing that the rise in price heralds further rises to come, suppliers wait until the price rises further. Supply shifts from S_1 to S_2. Demanders buy now before any further rise in price. Demand shifts from D_2 to D_3. As a result, the price continues to rise: to P_3.

Box 2.2 examined the housing market. In this market, speculation is frequently destabilising. Assume that people see house prices beginning to move upwards.

This might be the result of increased demand brought about by a cut in mortgage interest rates or by growth in the economy. People may well believe that the rise in house prices signals a boom in the housing market: that prices will go on rising. Potential buyers will thus try to buy as soon as possible before prices rise any further. This increased demand (as in Figure 3.7(b)) will thus lead to even bigger price rises. This mirrors what happened to UK house prices from the late 1990s through to 2007.

However, during 2008 house prices started to fall. This time potential buyers believed that prices would fall further and thus held off entering the market. The result was even bigger price falls!

Pause for thought

Draw two diagrams like Figures 3.7(a) and (b), only this time assume an initial fall in demand and hence price. The first diagram should show the effects of stabilising speculation and the second the effect of destabilising speculation.

Short selling

A form of speculation that can be very damaging to markets is the practice of **short selling**. This is where people take advantage of anticipated falls in prices, such as those of currencies (exchange rates) and shares, by selling the commodity even though they do not possess it! For instance, if investors want to take advantage of an expected fall in the price of particular shares, they can borrow them from dealers who do own some and agree to return them on a specified date. They pay a fee for doing this. In the meantime they sell the shares on the market at the current price and wait, hoping the share price falls. They are now 'short' of the shares (i.e. they don't possess them but still owe them). They will then need to make a judgement about the right time to buy the shares so as to try and make the most profit, but they must do this prior to the agreed time for returning the shares.

Although anyone can short sell, it is largely traders from various financial institutions that engage in this practice. Huge bonuses can be earned from their employers if the short selling is profitable. This encourages an atmosphere of risk taking and looking to short-term gains rather than providing long-term capital to firms.

The practice of short selling has increased in recent years and added to the instability of markets like those for foreign currency and shares. During 2008, for instance, worries about bad debts and losses in the banking sector led many traders to short sell the shares of banks and other financial institutions felt to be most at risk.

Definition

Short selling (or shorting)
Where investors borrow an asset, such as shares or foreign currency; sell the asset, hoping the price will soon fall; then buy it back later and return it to the lender. Assuming the price has fallen, the short seller will make a profit of the difference (minus any fees).

Conclusion

In some circumstances, then, the action of speculators can help keep price fluctuations to a minimum (stabilising speculation). This is most likely when markets are relatively stable in the first place, with only moderate underlying shifts in demand and supply.

In other circumstances, however, speculation can make price fluctuations much worse. This is most likely in times of uncertainty, when there are significant changes in the determinants of demand and supply. Given this uncertainty, people may see price changes as signifying some trend. They then 'jump on the bandwagon' and do what the rest are doing, further fuelling the rise or fall in price.

Dealing with uncertainty and risk

When price changes are likely to occur, buyers and sellers will try to anticipate them. Unfortunately on many occasions no one can be certain just what these price changes will be. Take the case of stocks and shares. If you anticipate that the price of, say, HSBC shares is likely to go up substantially in the near future, you may well decide to buy some now and then sell them later after the price has risen. But you cannot be certain that they will go up in price: they may fall instead. If you buy the shares, therefore, you will be taking a gamble.

Now gambles can be of two types. The first is where you know the odds. Let us take the simplest case of a gamble on the toss of a coin. Heads you win; tails you lose. You know that the odds of winning are precisely 50 per cent. If you bet on the toss of a coin, you are said to be operating under conditions of **risk**. *Risk is when the probability of an outcome is known.* Risk itself is a measure of the *variability* of an outcome. For example, if you bet £1 on the toss of a coin, such that heads you win £1 and tails you lose £1, then the variability is –£1 to +£1.

The second form of gamble is the more usual. This is where the odds are not known or are known only roughly. Gambling on the stock exchange is like this. You may have a good idea that a share will go up in price, but is it a 90 per cent chance, an 80 per cent chance or what? You are not certain. Gambling under these sort of conditions is known as operating under **uncertainty**. *This is when the probability of an outcome is not known.*

Risk and uncertainty pervade the whole of economic life and decisions are constantly having to be made whose outcome cannot be known for certain.

KEY IDEA 13

People's actions are influenced by their attitudes towards risk. Many decisions are taken under conditions of risk or uncertainty. Generally, the lower the probability of (or the more uncertain) the desired outcome of an action, the less likely will people be to undertake the action.

Reducing the problem of uncertainty

Stockholding. Suppliers can reduce the problem of uncertainty by holding stocks. For instance, wheat farmers uncertain as to what the price of wheat will be when they take it to market can make use of storage facilities and wait until the price is 'right'. They can put the wheat into store if the price is low and then wait until it goes up. Alternatively, if the price of wheat is high at harvest time, they can sell it straight away.

Futures or forward markets. A futures market involves buyers and sellers agreeing prices today for the future delivery of commodities or financial instruments. For example, our wheat farmer could be quoted a price today for the delivery of a quantity of wheat in six months' time. This price is known as a **future price**. No matter what happens to the **spot price** (i.e. the current market price) in the meantime, the selling price has been agreed. Of course, the farmer will lose out if the spot price turns out to be greater than the agreed future price.

Prices in futures market are determined in the same way as in other markets: by demand and supply. Such markets will naturally attract speculators, largely financial institutions, who never actually handle the commodities themselves.

Web appendix 3.2 gives fuller analysis of risk and uncertainty. It also examines the role of insurance as a way of reducing or eliminating risk.

Definitions

Risk
When an outcome may or may not occur, but its probability of occurring is known. It is a measure of the variability of that outcome.

Uncertainty
When an outcome may or may not occur and its probability of occurring is not known.

Future price
A price agreed today at which an item (e.g. a commodity) will be exchanged at some set date in the future.

Spot price
The current market price.

Pause for thought

The demand for pears is more price elastic than the demand for bread and yet the price of pears fluctuates more than that of bread. Why should this be so? If pears could be stored as long and as cheaply as flour, would this affect the relative price fluctuations? If so, how?

Recap

1. A complete understanding of markets must take into account the time dimension.

2. Given that producers and consumers take time to respond fully to price changes, we can identify different equilibria after the lapse of different lengths of time. Generally, short-run supply and demand tend to be less price elastic than long-run supply and demand. As a result, any shifts in *demand* or *supply* curves will tend to have a relatively bigger effect on price in the short run and a relatively bigger effect on quantity in the long run.

3. People often anticipate price changes and this will affect the amount they demand or supply. This speculation will tend to stabilise price fluctuations if people believe that the price changes are only temporary. However, speculation will tend to destabilise these fluctuations (i.e. make them more severe) if people believe that prices are likely to continue to move in the same direction as at present (at least for some time).

4. Many economic decisions are taken under conditions of risk or uncertainty. Uncertainty over future prices can be tackled by holding stocks or through transactions in futures markets.

MARKETS WHERE PRICES ARE CONTROLLED   **3.6**

What happens if the government fixes prices?

At the equilibrium price, there will be no shortage or surplus. The equilibrium price, however, may not be the most *desirable* price. The government, therefore, may prefer to keep prices above or below the equilibrium price.

Setting a minimum (high) price

If the government sets a **minimum price** above the equilibrium (a price floor), there will be a surplus: $Q_s - Q_d$ in Figure 3.8. Price will not be allowed to fall to eliminate this surplus. The government may do this for various reasons:

> **Definition**
>
> **Minimum price**
> A price floor set by the government or some other agency. The price is not allowed to fall below this level (although it is allowed to rise above it).

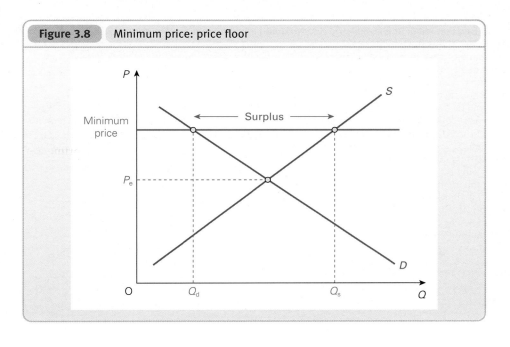

Figure 3.8   Minimum price: price floor

■ To protect producers' incomes. If the industry is subject to supply fluctuations (e.g. crops, due to fluctuations in weather) and if industry demand is price inelastic, prices are likely to fluctuate severely. Minimum prices will prevent the fall in producers' incomes that would accompany periods of low prices.

■ To create a surplus (e.g. of grains), particularly in periods of plenty, which can be stored in preparation for possible future shortages.

■ In the case of wages (the price of labour), minimum wages legislation can be used to prevent workers' wage rates from falling below a certain level (see Box 6.4).

There are various methods the government can use to deal with the surpluses associated with minimum prices.

■ The government could buy the surplus and store it, destroy it or sell it abroad in other markets.

■ Supply could be artificially lowered by restricting producers to particular quotas. In Figure 3.8, supply could therefore be reduced to Q_d.

| BOX 3.4 | AGRICULTURE AND MINIMUM PRICES |

A problem of surpluses

Governments in many countries intervene in agricultural markets. The problems of fluctuating prices, dependency on foreign food imports, and the maintenance of farmers' and farm workers' incomes are but a few of the reasons for such intervention. The form that government intervention takes varies, from a series of subsidies or tax reliefs for farmers, to the more formal fixing of high minimum prices or direct payments.

Until recently, the fixing of high minimum prices was the main policy used by the European Union in its Common Agricultural Policy (CAP). Here 'Intervention Boards' of the EU buy up any surpluses that result at a given 'intervention' price, usually set above the equilibrium.

The effects of this system are illustrated in the diagram, which shows the demand and supply of a particular agricultural product. Assume that the EU demand is D_{EU} and that EU supply is S_{EU}. Assume also that the world price is P_w. This will be the equilibrium price, since any shortage at P_w (i.e. $b - a$) will be imported at that price. Thus before intervention, EU demand is Q_{d_1} and EU supply is Q_{s_1} and imports are $Q_{d_1} - Q_{s_1}$.

Now assume that the EU sets an intervention price of P_i. At this high price, there will be a surplus of $d - e$ (i.e. $Q_{s_2} - Q_{d_2}$). Assume for the moment that none of this surplus is exported. It will all, therefore, be bought by the appropriate Intervention Board. The cost to the EU of buying this surplus is shown by the total shaded area ($edQ_{s_2}Q_{d_2}$: i.e. the surplus multiplied by the intervention price). Unless the food is thrown away or otherwise disposed of, there will obviously then be the additional costs of storing this food: costs that have been very high in some years as wine 'lakes' and grain and dairy 'mountains' have built up.

An alternative to storing the food is for the Board to sell the surpluses on the world market at the world price (P_w). In this case, the net cost to the Intervention Board would only be the shaded area $edcf$: in other words, the amount purchased by the Board ($d - e$) multiplied by the difference in price paid by the Board and the price it receives on the world market ($P_i - P_w$).

Alternatively, export subsidies could be paid to farmers who sell on world markets to bring the amount they receive up to the intervention price: i.e. a subsidy of $P_i - P_w$. Here the Board would only need to purchase what had not been managed to be sold.

The system of high minimum prices in agricultural products

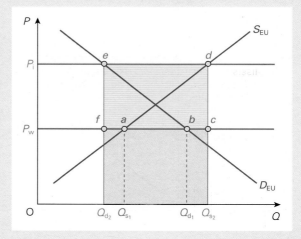

■ Demand could be raised by advertising, by finding alternative uses for the good, or by reducing consumption of substitute goods (e.g. by imposing taxes or quotas on substitutes, such as imports).

One of the problems with minimum prices is that firms with surplus on their hands may try to evade the price control and cut their prices.

Another problem is that high prices may cushion inefficiency. Firms may feel less need to find more efficient methods of production and cut their costs if their profits are being protected by the high price. Also the high price may discourage firms from producing alternative goods which they could produce more efficiently or which are in higher demand, but which nevertheless have a lower (free-market) price.

One of the best-known examples of governments fixing high minimum prices is the Common Agricultural Policy (CAP) of the European Union. This is examined in Box 3.4.

TC 4
p 21

Pause for thought

Draw a supply and demand diagram with the price of labour (the wage rate) on the vertical axis and the quantity of labour (the number of workers) on the horizontal axis. What will happen to employment if the government raises wages from the equilibrium to some minimum wage above the equilibrium?

CASE STUDIES & APPLICATIONS

Over time the high prices will encourage farmers to produce more. Indeed they know the Intervention Boards will buy as much as they offer for sale. This results in a rightward shift in the supply curve and hence an even greater surplus.

Assessing the system of high minimum prices

The justifications for such a policy are that it stabilises domestic prices for farmers, reduces dependency on food imports by boosting domestic production and it boosts farmers' incomes. This also encourages them to invest in agriculture, which results in a growth in agricultural productivity.

Price support has, however, been criticised on a number of counts:

■ Food surpluses have been a costly waste of scarce resources.
■ The system had harmful effects on the environment. Farmers boosted output by using more chemical fertilisers and pesticides; and they gained land by removing hedgerows, trees and ponds. This caused pollution and affected wildlife and its habitats.
■ The system increased inequalities within agriculture. Only larger farmers were able to boost output and gain more income. These tended to be located near each other, so only some EU regions gained.
■ Prices for some agricultural commodities were kept higher than others, so producers of some commodities gained much more than others.
■ Higher food prices penalise poor consumers, who spend a larger proportion of their income on food than do the rich.

■ Subsidised EU exports have had a doubly damaging effect on agriculture in developing countries: (a) exporters of foodstuffs find it very difficult to compete with subsidised EU exports; (b) farmers in developing countries who are producing for their domestic market find that they cannot compete with cheap imports of food from the EU. Agriculture in the developing world thus declines. Farmers' incomes are too low to invest in the land. Many migrate to the overcrowded cities, with little or no paid employment.
■ Trade disputes arose because export subsidies gave EU exports an unfair advantage and took export markets from other exporting countries.

As a result of these problems, various reforms to the CAP have been implemented. In particular, high prices have been cut and land taken out of production ('set aside'). Price cuts have boosted EU demand, while price cuts and set-aside have reduced EU supply. This has reduced considerably subsidised EU exports.

Farmers' incomes are now boosted by direct payments unrelated to current output. These are designed to 'decouple', or break the direct link, between support to farmers and the level of production. In order to try to help the environment directly and support the rural community more generally, 'Rural Development' policy makes grants and other incentives available for farmers to farm less intensively or to diversify into alternative rural industries (such as tourism and forestry).

 What is the effect on output of replacing high minimum prices with grants to farmers unrelated to current production?

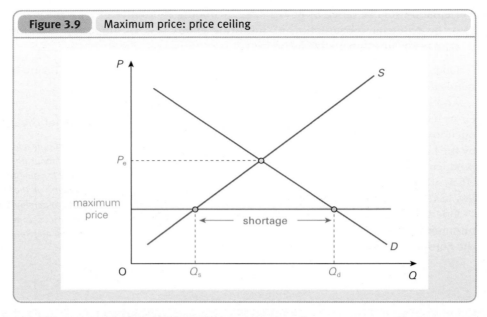

Figure 3.9   Maximum price: price ceiling

Definitions

Maximum price

A price ceiling set by the government or some other agency. The price is not allowed to rise above this level (although it is allowed to fall below it).

Rationing

Where the government restricts the amount of a good that people are allowed to buy.

Underground markets

Where people ignore the government's price and/or quantity controls and sell illegally at whatever price equates illegal demand and supply.

Setting a maximum (low) price

If the government sets a **maximum price** below the equilibrium (a price ceiling), there will be a shortage: $Q_d - Q_s$ in Figure 3.9. Price will not be allowed to rise to eliminate this shortage. The government may set maximum prices to prevent them rising above a certain level. This will normally be done for reasons of fairness. In wartime, or times of famine, the government may set maximum prices for basic goods so that poor people can afford to buy them.

TC 7 p 49

The resulting shortages, however, create further problems. If the government merely sets prices and does not intervene further, the shortages will lead to the following:

■ Allocation on a 'first come, first served' basis. This is likely to lead to queues developing, or firms adopting waiting lists. Queues were a common feature of life in the former communist eastern European countries where governments kept prices below the level necessary to equate demand and supply. In recent years, as part of their economic reforms, they have allowed prices to rise. This has had the obvious benefit of reducing or eliminating queues, but at the same time it has made life very hard for those on low incomes.

■ Firms deciding which customers should be allowed to buy: for example, giving preference to regular customers.

Neither of the above may be considered to be fair. Certain needy people may be forced to go without. Therefore, the government may adopt a system of **rationing**. People could be issued with a set number of coupons for each item rationed.

A major problem with maximum prices is likely to be the emergence of **underground markets**, where customers, unable to buy enough in legal markets, may well be prepared to pay very high prices: prices above P_e in Figure 3.9.

Another problem is that the maximum prices reduce the quantity produced of an already scarce commodity. For example, artificially low prices in a famine are likely to reduce food supplies: if not immediately, then at the next harvest, because of less being sown. In many developing countries, governments control the price of basic foodstuffs in order to help the urban poor. The effect, however, is to reduce incomes for farmers, who are then encouraged to leave the land and flock into the ever-growing towns and cities.

TC 7
p 49

To minimise these types of problem the government may attempt to reduce the shortage by encouraging supply: by drawing on stores, by direct government production, or by giving subsidies or tax relief to firms. Alternatively, it may attempt to reduce demand: by the production of more alternative goods (e.g. home-grown vegetables in times of war) or by controlling people's incomes.

One example of a maximum price is considered in Box 3.5. The 'price' in this case is the rent paid by tenants for private rented accommodation. Should the government set a rent ceiling in order to guarantee affordable accommodation? Would there be any problems with such a policy?

BOX 3.5 **RENT CONTROL**

CASE STUDIES & APPLICATIONS

Cheap housing for all?

TC 7
p 49

The purpose of rent control is to protect tenants from paying high rent, as well as to provide cheap housing for the very poor. However, many economists argue that in practice such rent controls only succeed in making a larger part of the population worse off. How is this so?

Referring to the diagram, assume that the rent for a particular type of accommodation is initially at the equilibrium level, R_0, where $D = S$. Now assume that legislation is passed that sets a rent ceiling of R_1. Despite this reduction in rent, the supply of rental accommodation will fall only slightly in the short run, as landlords cannot quickly transfer their accommodation to other uses. In the diagram this is shown by a movement from point a to point b on the relatively inelastic supply curve S.

With the rent set below equilibrium, there will be a shortage of rented property. In the short run, however, this will be relatively small (i.e. $Q_2 - Q_1$), and hence only a relatively small number of people will be unable to find accommodation. The remainder will benefit from the lower rents.

In the long run, however, many landlords will respond to the lower rent by putting their accommodation to other uses. The supply curve will become more elastic

(curve S') and the supply of rented property will fall to Q_3 (point c). Shortages now increase (to $Q_2 - Q_3$) as less rental housing is available. More people become homeless – more, perhaps, than in an unregulated market.

Rent controls may have further adverse effects. First, on equity grounds it is somewhat arbitrary as to who gets and who does not get housing at the lower rent. Second, in the long run, those landlords who still keep their property available for rent may cut maintenance costs and let their property fall into disrepair.

Those in favour of rent controls counter these arguments by claiming that the demand and supply curves of rented accommodation are very inelastic. Take the case of the demand curve. People have got to live somewhere. If rent control is abolished, many people will just have to pay the higher rent, or become homeless.

So is this a fair argument? The price elasticity of demand for rented accommodation depends on substitutes. The obvious substitute for renting is to purchase. If mortgages for house *purchase* are easily obtainable, at low interest rates and with only a small deposit required, then this may be a viable alternative for many people and will thus make demand for rented accommodation more elastic. If, however, house purchase is not affordable for many potential first-time buyers, then the demand for rented accommodation will indeed be relatively inelastic.

Effect of rent control

1. *How could housing supplied by the public sector be made to rectify some of the problems we have identified above? (What would it do to the supply curve?)*
2. *If the government gives poor people rent allowances (i.e. grants), how will this affect the level of rents in an uncontrolled market? What determines the size of the effect?*
3. *The case for and against rent controls depends to a large extent on the long-run elasticity of supply. Do you think it will be relatively elastic or inelastic? Give reasons.*

| BOX 3.6 | THE EFFECT OF IMPOSING TAXES ON GOODS | EXPLORING ECONOMICS |

Who ends up paying?

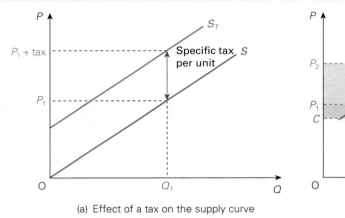

(a) Effect of a tax on the supply curve

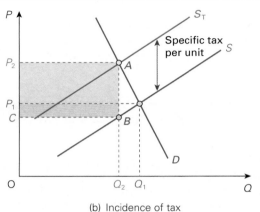

(b) Incidence of tax

Another example of government intervention in markets is the imposition of taxes on goods. These indirect taxes, as they are called, include taxes such as value added tax (VAT) and excise duties on cigarettes, petrol and alcoholic drinks.

These taxes can be a fixed amount per unit sold – a specific tax. An example is the tax on petrol, which is set at so much per litre. Alternatively, they can be a percentage of the price, or value added, at each stage of production – an ad valorem tax. An example is VAT.

When a tax is levied on a good or service, this has the effect of shifting the supply curve upwards by the amount of the tax (see diagram (a)). In the case of a specific tax, it will be a parallel shift, since the amount of the tax is the same at all prices.

But why does the supply curve shift upwards by the amount of the tax? In diagram (a), the supply curve (S) shows that, to supply Q_1, producers need to receive a price of P_1. Now a tax is levied of an amount shown by the arrows. For producers to continue receiving P_1 and hence producing Q_1, the price charged to consumers has to be $P_1 +$ tax. Thus the new supply curve is shown by the red line S_T.

The Incidence of the tax

What will be the effect of the tax on the price and the quantity sold? This is illustrated in diagram (b). Before the tax is imposed, Q_1 units are sold at a price of P_1. The effect of the tax is to shift the supply curve to S_T. Price rises to P_2 and quantity falls to Q_2.

Notice, however, that price does not rise by the full amount of the tax, because the demand curve is downward sloping. The amount of the tax is $P_2 - C$, whereas the price increase is only $P_2 - P_1$. Thus the burden or incidence of such taxes is distributed between consumers and producers. Consumers pay to the extent that price rises. Producers pay to the extent that this rise in price is not sufficient to cover the tax.

We can also show in diagram (b) the revenue the government receives from the tax. The tax per unit is $P_2 - C$ and the quantity sold is Q_2 (shown by the distance CB). Thus the revenue raised is the total area of the shaded rectangle, P_2ABC.

The rise in price from P_1 to P_2 multiplied by the number of goods sold (Q_2) (the green area) is the amount of the tax passed on to consumers and thus represents the consumers' share of the tax. The remainder (the lilac area) is the producers' share. This is the amount by which the producers' net price is below the original price (i.e. $P_1 - C$) multiplied by Q_2.

Elasticity and the incidence of taxation

It is easy to see that the less elastic is demand:

■ the less quantity sold falls and hence the greater the revenue the government raises from the tax.
■ the more price rises and hence the greater the proportion of the tax paid by consumers.

Thus in most countries, cigarettes, petrol and alcohol have been major targets for indirect taxes. In many cases the tax accounts for well over half of the market price! Demand for each of them is high and relatively inelastic. Thus the tax raises a lot of revenue and does not curb demand greatly.

 Demand tends to be more elastic in the long run than in the short run. Assume that a tax is imposed on a good that was previously untaxed. How will the incidence of this tax change as time passes?

TC 8
p 67

Recap

1. The government may fix minimum or maximum prices. If a minimum price is set above the equilibrium price, a surplus will result. If a maximum price is set below the equilibrium price, a shortage will result.

2. Minimum prices are set as a means of protecting the incomes of suppliers or creating a surplus for storage in case of future reductions in supply. If the government is not deliberately trying to create a surplus, it must decide what to do with it.

3. Maximum prices are set as a means of keeping prices down for the consumer. The resulting shortage will cause queues, waiting lists or the restriction of sales by firms to favoured customers. Alternatively, the government could introduce a system of rationing. If it does, then underground markets are likely to arise. This is where goods are sold illegally above the maximum price.

QUESTIONS

1. Draw a diagram with two supply curves, one steeply sloping and one gently sloping. Ensure that the two curves cross. Draw a demand curve through the point where they cross and mark the equilibrium price and quantity. Now assume that the demand curve shifts to the right. Show how the shape of the supply curve will determine just what happens to price and quantity.

2. Which of the following will have positive signs and which will have negative ones? (a) price elasticity of demand; (b) income elasticity of demand (normal good); (c) income elasticity of demand (inferior good); (d) cross elasticity of demand (with respect to changes in price of a substitute good); (e) cross elasticity of demand (with respect to changes in price of a complementary good); (f) price elasticity of supply.

3. Demand for oil might be relatively elastic over the longer term, and yet it could still be observed that over time people consume more oil (or only very slightly less) despite rising oil prices. How can this apparent contradiction be explained?

4. Is the demand curve for any football club's season tickets much the same as that facing any other football club? Explain.

5. Assume that a football club has the following demand curve for season tickets

   $Q_d = 50\,000 - 50P$

   (a) What quantity of season tickets is demanded when season tickets are free ($P = 0$)?
   (b) At what price do season tickets cease to be bought ($Q = 0$)?
   (c) Using the information from (a) and (b) sketch the demand curve for the club.

   (d) What amount of season tickets is demanded at £600 and £700? What revenue is generated from season ticket sales at each price?
   (e) Using the average (mid-point) formula in Box 3.1 estimate the price elasticity between £600 and £700.
   (f) What can we say about the price elasticity of demand between the points on the demand curve corresponding to season ticket prices of £600 and £700?
   (g) In what price range does raising season ticket prices increase revenues from season ticket sales?

6. How might a firm set about making the demand for its brand less elastic?

7. Assuming that a firm faces an inelastic demand and wants to increase its total revenue, in what direction should it change its price? Is there any limit to how far it should go in changing its price in this direction?

8. Why are both the price elasticity of demand and the price elasticity of supply likely to be greater in the long run?

9. Which are likely to have the highest cross elasticity of demand: two brands of coffee, or coffee and tea? Explain.

10. Redraw both diagrams in Figure 3.7, only this time assume that it was an initial shift in supply that caused price to change in the first place.

11. What are the advantages and disadvantages of speculation from the point of view of (a) the consumer; (b) firms?

12. Give some examples of decisions you have taken recently that were made under conditions of

uncertainty. With hindsight do you think you made the right decisions?

13. Assume that the (weekly) market demand and supply of tomatoes are given by the figures shown below:

Price (£ per kilo)	4.00	3.50	3.00	2.50	2.00	1.50	1.00
Q_d (000 kilos)	30	35	40	45	50	55	60
Q_s (000 kilos)	80	68	62	55	50	45	38

(a) What are the equilibrium price and quantity?
(b) What will be the effect of the government fixing a minimum price of (i) £3.00 per kilo; (ii) £1.50 per kilo?
(c) Suppose that the government paid tomato producers a subsidy of £1.00 per kilo. (i) Give the new supply schedule. (ii) What will be the new equilibrium price? (iii) How much will this cost the government?

(d) Alternatively, suppose that the government guaranteed tomato producers a price of £2.50 per kilo. (i) How many tomatoes would it have to buy in order to ensure that all the tomatoes produced were sold? (ii) How much would this cost the government?
(e) Alternatively, suppose it bought all the tomatoes produced at £2.50. (i) At what single price would it have to sell them in order to dispose of the lot? (ii) What would be the net cost of this course of action?

14. Think of two things that are provided free. In each case, identify when and in what form a shortage might occur. In what ways are/could these shortages be dealt with? Are they the best solution to the shortages?

15. Think of some examples where the price of a good or service is kept below the equilibrium. In each case consider the advantages and disadvantages of the policy.

Log on to MyEconlab and complete the studyplan exercises for this chapter to see how much you have learnt and where you need to revise most. Make sure you access all the supporting textbook resources including the online workbook, newsblog, audio animations, guided solutions and ebook.

Additional case studies in the *Essentials of Economics* MyEconLab (www.pearsoned.co.uk/sloman)

3.1   Shall we put up our price? This uses the concept of price elasticity of demand to explain why prices are higher where firms face little or no competition.

3.2   Any more fares? Pricing on the buses: an illustration of the relationship between price and total revenue.

3.3   Income elasticity of demand and the balance of payments. This examines how a low income elasticity of demand for the exports of many developing countries can help to explain their chronic balance of payments problems.

3.4   Elasticities of demand for various foodstuffs. An examination of the evidence about price and income elasticities of demand for food in the UK.

3.5   The role of the speculator. This assesses whether the activities of speculators are beneficial or harmful to the rest of society.

3.6   Underground markets. How underground markets can develop when prices are fixed below the equilibrium.

3.7   **The fallacy of composition.** An illustration of how something that applies to an individual may not apply to a larger group. The example is taken from agriculture.

3.8   **The cobweb model.** An outline of the theory that explains price fluctuations in terms of time lags in supply.

3.9   **Speculation and short selling.** How speculative activity can be very damaging to stock markets.

3.10   **Dealing in futures markets.** How buying and selling in futures markets can reduce uncertainty.

Websites relevant to this chapter

Numbers and sections refer to websites listed in the Web appendix and hotlinked from this book's website at **www.pearsoned.co.uk/sloman**.

■ For news articles relevant to this chapter, see the *Economics News Articles* link from the book's website.

■ For general news on markets and market intervention, see websites in section A, and particularly A1–5, 7–9, 18, 24, 25, 26, 33, 36. See also A38 and 39 for links to newspapers worldwide; and A42 and A44 for links to economics news articles from newspapers worldwide.

■ For information on advertising (Box 3.2), see site E37.

■ For information on agriculture and the Common Agricultural Policy (Box 3.4), see sites E14 and G9.

■ For student resources relevant to this chapter, see sites C17, 9, 10, 19; D3.

■ For sites favouring the free market, see C17 and E34.

Web appendices

3.1   **Point elasticity.** An alternative way of measuring elasticity.

3.2   **Risk and uncertainty.** An analysis of consumer decision-making when knowledge is imperfect. The appendix also looks at the role of insurance in reducing or eliminating uncertainty.

CHAPTER MAP

Chapter

The supply decision

So far we have assumed that supply curves are generally upward sloping: that a higher price will encourage firms to supply more. But just how much will firms choose to supply at each price? It depends largely on the amount of profit they will make. If a firm can increase its profits by producing more, it will normally do so.

Profit is made by firms earning more from the sale of goods than they cost to produce. A firm's total profit is thus the difference between its total sales revenue (*TR*) and its total costs of production (*TC*). In order then to discover how a firm can maximise its profit or even get a sufficient level of profit, we must first consider what determines costs and revenue.

In Sections 4.1 and 4.2 we examine short-run and long-run costs respectively. Over the short run a firm will be limited in what inputs it can expand. For example, a manufacturing company might be able to use more raw materials, or possibly more labour, but it will not have time to open up another factory. Over the long run, however, a firm will have much more flexibility. It can, if it chooses, expand the whole scale of its operations.

In Section 4.3 we turn to the revenue side and see how a firm's revenue varies with output. Finally, Section 4.4 puts revenue and cost together to see how profit is determined. In particular, we shall see how profit varies with output and how the point of maximum profit is found.

After studying this chapter, you should be able to answer the following questions:

- What is the relationship between inputs and outputs in both the short and long run?
- How do costs vary with output and just what do we mean by 'costs'?
- What is meant by 'economies of scale' and what are the reasons for such economies?
- How does a firm's sales revenue vary with output?
- How do we measure profits?
- At what output will a firm maximise its profits? How much profit will it make at this output?

4.1 PRODUCTION AND COSTS: SHORT RUN

How do a firm's costs vary with output over the short term?

The cost of producing any level of output will depend on the amount of inputs used and the price the firm must pay for them. Let us first focus on the quantity of inputs used.

 KEY IDEA 14 *Output depends on the amount of resources and how they are used.* Different amounts and combinations of inputs will lead to different amounts of output. If output is to be produced efficiently, inputs should be combined in the optimum proportions.

Short-run and long-run changes in production

If a firm wants to increase production, it will take time to acquire a greater quantity of certain inputs. For example, a manufacturer can use more electricity by turning on switches, but it might take a long time to obtain and install more machines, and longer still to build a second or third factory.

If, then, the firm wants to increase output in a hurry, it will only be able to increase the quantity of certain inputs. It can use more raw materials, more fuel, more tools and possibly more labour (by hiring extra workers or offering overtime to its existing workforce). But it will have to make do with its existing buildings and most of its machinery.

The distinction we are making here is between **fixed factors** and **variable factors**. A *fixed* factor is an input that cannot be increased within a given time period (e.g. buildings). A *variable* factor is one that can.

The distinction between fixed and variable factors allows us to distinguish between the short run and the long run.

The short run. The **short run** is a time period during which at least one factor of production is fixed. In the short run, then, output can be increased only by using more variable factors. For example, if a shipping line wanted to carry more passengers in response to a rise in demand, it could possibly accommodate more passengers on existing sailings if there were space. It could possibly increase the number of sailings with its existing fleet, by hiring more crew and using more fuel. But in the short run it could not buy more ships: there would not be time for them to be built.

The long run. The **long run** is a time period long enough for all inputs to be varied. Given long enough, a firm can build a second factory and install new machines.

The actual length of the short run will differ from firm to firm. It is not a fixed period of time. Thus if it takes a farmer a year to obtain new land, buildings and equipment, the short run is any time period up to a year and the long run is any time period longer than a year. On the other hand, if it takes a shipping company three years to obtain an extra ship, the short run is any period up to three years and the long run is any period longer than three years.

For the remainder of this section we will concentrate on *short-run* production and costs. We will look at the long run in Section 4.2.

Definitions

Fixed factor
An input that cannot be increased in supply within a given time period.

Variable factor
An input that *can* be increased in supply within a given time period.

Short run
The period of time over which at least one factor is fixed.

Long run
The period of time long enough for *all* factors to be varied.

Production in the short run: the law of diminishing returns

Production in the short run is subject to *diminishing returns*. You may well have heard of 'the law of diminishing returns': it is one of the most famous of all 'laws' of economics. To illustrate how this law underlies short-run production let us take the simplest possible case where there are just two factors: one fixed and one variable.

Take the case of a farm. Assume that the fixed factor is land and the variable factor is labour. Since the land is fixed in supply, output per period of time can be increased only by increasing the number of workers employed. But imagine what would happen as more and more workers crowded on to a fixed area of land. The land cannot go on yielding more and more output indefinitely. After a point the additions to output from each extra worker will begin to diminish.

We can now state the **law of diminishing (marginal) returns**.

> **Definition**
>
> **Law of diminishing (marginal) returns**
> When one or more factors are held fixed, there will come a point beyond which the extra output from additional units of the variable factor will diminish.

> **KEY IDEA 15**
>
> *The law of diminishing marginal returns.* When increasing amounts of a variable factor are used with a given amount of a fixed factor, there will come a point when each extra unit of the variable factor will produce less extra output than the previous unit.

Box 4.1 is a case study illustrating the law of diminishing returns. Another good example is given in Web Case 4.3, which looks at diminishing returns to the application of nitrogen fertiliser on farmland. Box 4.2 shows that the law has potentially dire implications for us and the future inhabitants of our planet.

The relationship between inputs and output is explained in more detail in Web Appendix 4.1, which looks at the short-run 'production function'.

Measuring costs of production

We are now ready to look at short-run costs. First of all, we will need to define just what we mean by costs. The term is used differently by economists and accountants.

| **BOX 4.1** | **DIMINISHING RETURNS IN THE BREAD SHOP** | CASE STUDIES & APPLICATIONS |

Is the baker using his loaf?

KI 5
p 87

Just up the road from where John lives is a bread shop. Like many others, he buys his bread there on a Saturday morning. Not surprisingly, Saturday morning is the busiest time of the week for the shop and as a result it takes on extra assistants.

During the week only one assistant serves the customers, but on a Saturday morning there used to be five serving. But could they serve five times as many customers? No, they could not. There were diminishing returns to labour.

The trouble is that certain factors of production in the shop are fixed:

■ The shop is a fixed size. It gets very crowded on Saturday morning. Assistants sometimes have to wait while customers squeeze past each other to get to the counter, and with five serving, the assistants themselves used to get in each other's way.

■ There is only one cash till. Assistants frequently had to wait while other assistants used it.
■ There is only one pile of tissue paper for wrapping the bread. Again the assistants often had to wait.

The fifth and maybe even the fourth assistant ended up serving very few extra customers.

John is still going to the same bread shop and they still have only one till and one pile of tissue paper. But now only three assistants are employed on a Saturday! The shop, however, is just as busy.

 How would you advise the baker as to whether he should (a) employ four assistants on a Saturday; (b) extend his shop, thereby allowing more customers to be served on a Saturday morning?

BOX 4.2   MALTHUS AND THE DISMAL SCIENCE OF ECONOMICS

Population growth + diminishing returns = starvation

KI 15
p 87

The law of diminishing returns has potentially cataclysmic implications for the future populations of the world.

If the population of the world grows rapidly, then food output may not keep pace with it. There will be diminishing returns to labour as more and more people crowd on to the limited amount of land available.

This is already a problem in some of the poorest countries of the world, especially in sub-Saharan Africa. The land is barely able to support current population levels. Only one or two bad harvests are needed to cause mass starvation – witness the appalling famines in recent years in Ethiopia and Sudan.

The relationship between population and food output was analysed as long ago as 1798 by the Reverend Thomas Robert Malthus (1766–1834) in his *Essay on the Principle of Population*. This book was a bestseller and made Robert Malthus perhaps the best known of all social scientists of his day.

Malthus argued as follows:

> I say that the power of population is indefinitely greater than the power in the earth to produce subsistence for man.
>
> Population when unchecked, increases in a geometrical ratio. Subsistence increases only in an arithmetical ratio. A slight acquaintance with numbers will show the immensity of the first power in comparison with the second.[a]

What Malthus was saying is that world population tends to double about every 25 years or so if unchecked. It grows geometrically, like the series: 1, 2, 4, 8, 16, 32, 64, etc. But food output, because of diminishing returns, cannot keep pace with this. It is likely to grow at only an arithmetical rate, like the series: 1, 2, 3, 4, 5, 6, 7, etc. It is clear that population, if unchecked, will soon outstrip food supply.

So what is the check on population growth? According to Malthus, it is starvation. As population grows, so food output per head will fall until, with more and more people starving, the death rate will rise. Only then will population growth stabilise at the rate of growth of food output.

---

[a] T. R. Malthus, *First Essay on Population* (Macmillan, 1926), pp. 13–14.

Have Malthus's gloomy predictions been borne out by events? Two factors have mitigated the forces that Malthus described:

- The rate of population growth tends to slow down as countries become more developed. Although improved health prolongs life, this tends to be more than offset by a decline in the birth rate as people choose to have smaller families.
- Technological improvements in farming have greatly increased food output per hectare.

The growth in food output has thus exceeded the rate of population growth in developed countries. Also certain developing countries have seen significant advances in agriculture. These include the 'green revolution' of the 1960s, whereby new high-yielding crop varieties were developed (especially in the cases of wheat and rice), and the development of genetically modified crops in recent years. In some countries food output growth has outstripped population growth. India, for example, now exports grain.

Nevertheless, the Malthusian spectre is very real for some of the poorest developing countries, which are simply unable to feed their populations satisfactorily. It is these poorest countries of the world which have some of the highest rates of population growth – around 3 per cent per annum in many African countries.

A further cause for concern arises from the move in Asia towards a westernised diet, with meat and dairy products playing a larger part. This further increases pressure on the land, since cattle require considerably more grain to produce meat than would be needed to feed humans a vegetarian diet.

A third factor is cited by some commentators, who remain unconvinced of the strength of Malthus's gloomy prognostication for the world. They believe that he seriously underestimated mankind's capacity to innovate; perhaps human ingenuity is one resource that doesn't suffer from diminishing returns.

 Why might it be possible for there to be a zero marginal productivity of labour on many family farms in poor countries and yet just enough food for all the members of the family to survive?

When measuring costs, economists always use the concept of **opportunity cost**. Remember from Chapter 1 how we defined opportunity cost. It is the cost of any activity measured in terms of the *sacrifice* made in doing it: in other words, the cost measured in terms of the opportunities forgone.

 TC 1
p 7

How do we apply this principle of opportunity cost to a firm? First we must discover what factors of production it is using. Then we must measure the sacrifice involved. To do this it is necessary to put factors into two categories.

Factors not owned by the firm: explicit costs

The opportunity cost of those factors not already owned by the firm is simply the price that the firm has to pay for them. Thus if the firm uses £100 worth of electricity, the opportunity cost is £100. The firm has sacrificed £100 that could have been spent on something else.

These costs are called **explicit costs** because they involve direct payment of money by firms.

Factors already owned by the firm: implicit costs

When the firm already owns factors (e.g. machinery), it does not as a rule have to pay out money to use them. Their opportunity costs are thus **implicit costs**. They are equal to what the factors could earn for the firm in some alternative use, either within the firm or hired out to some other firm.

Here are some examples of implicit costs:

■ A firm owns some buildings. The opportunity cost of using them is the rent it could have received by letting them out to another firm.
■ A firm draws £100 000 from the bank out of its savings in order to invest in new plant and equipment. The opportunity cost of this investment is not just the £100 000 (an explicit cost), but also the interest it thereby forgoes (an implicit cost).
■ The owner of the firm could have earned £15 000 per annum by working for someone else. This £15 000, then, is the opportunity cost of the owner's time.

If there is no alternative use for a factor of production, as in the case of a machine designed to make a specific product, and if it has no scrap value, the opportunity cost of using it is *zero*. In such a case, if the output from the machine is worth more than the cost of all the *other* inputs involved, the firm might as well use the machine rather than let it stand idle.

What the firm paid for the machine – its **historic cost** – is irrelevant. Not using the machine will not bring that money back. It has been spent. These costs are sometimes referred to as 'sunk costs'.

Costs and output

A firm's costs of production depend on its output. The reason is simple. The more it produces, the greater the quantity of factors of production it must use. The more factors it uses, the greater its costs will be. More precisely, this relationship depends on two elements:

■ The productivity of the factors. The greater their productivity, the smaller will be the quantity of them that is needed to produce a given level of output, and hence the lower will be the cost of that output.
■ The price of the factors. The higher their price, the higher will be the costs of production.

KI 14
p 86

Definitions

Opportunity cost
Cost measured in terms of the best alternative forgone.

Explicit costs
The payments to outside suppliers of inputs.

Implicit costs
Costs that do not involve a direct payment of money to a third party, but which nevertheless involve a sacrifice of some alternative.

Pause for thought

Assume that a farmer decides to grow wheat on land that could be used for growing barley. Barley sells for £100 per tonne. Wheat sells for £150 per tonne. Seed, fertiliser, labour and other costs of growing crops are £80 per tonne for both wheat and barley. What are the farmer's costs and profit per tonne of growing wheat?

Definition

Historic costs
The original amount the firm paid for factors it now owns.

In the short run, some factors used by the firm are fixed in supply. Their total costs, therefore, are fixed, in the sense that they do not vary with output. Rent on land is a **fixed cost**. It is the same whether the firm produces a lot or a little.

The total cost of variable factors, however, does vary with output. The cost of raw materials is a **variable cost**. The more that is produced, the more raw materials are used and therefore the higher is their total cost.

Total cost (*TC*) is thus total fixed cost (*TFC*) plus total variable cost (*TVC*)

Average and marginal cost

In addition to total costs (fixed and variable), there are two other categories of costs that are particularly important for our analysis of profits. These are average cost and marginal cost.

Average cost (*AC*) is cost per unit of production.

$$AC = TC/Q$$

Thus if it costs a firm £2000 to produce 100 units of a product, the average cost would be £20 for each unit (£2000/100).

Like total cost, average cost can be divided into the two components, fixed and variable. In other words, average cost equals **average fixed cost** ($AFC = TFC/Q$) plus **average variable cost** ($AVC = TVC/Q$).

$$AC = AFC + AVC$$

Marginal cost (*MC*) is the *extra* cost of producing *one more unit*: that is, the rise in total cost per one unit rise in output.

$$MC = \frac{\Delta TC}{\Delta Q}$$

where Δ means 'a rise in'.

For example, assume that a firm is currently producing 1 000 000 boxes of matches a month. It now increases output by 1000 boxes (another batch): $\Delta Q = 1000$. Assume that, as a result, total costs rise by £40: $\Delta TC = £40$. What is the cost of producing one more box of matches? It is:

$$MC = \frac{\Delta TC}{\Delta Q} = \frac{£40}{1000} = 4\text{p}$$

(Note that all marginal costs are variable, since, by definition, there can be no extra fixed costs as output rises.) Table 4.1 shows costs for an imaginary firm, firm X, over a given period of time (e.g. a week). The table shows how average and marginal costs can be derived from total costs. It is assumed that total fixed costs are £12 000 (column 2) and that total variable costs are as shown in column 3.

The figures for *TVC* have been chosen to illustrate the law of diminishing returns. Initially, *before* diminishing returns set in, *TVC* rises less and less rapidly as more variable factors are added. For example, in the case of a factory with a fixed supply of machinery, initially as more workers are taken on the workers can do increasingly specialist tasks and make a fuller use of the capital equipment. Above a certain output (3 units in Table 4.1), diminishing returns set in. Given that extra workers (the extra variable factors) are producing less and less extra output, the extra units of output they do produce will be costing more and more in terms of

Table 4.1 Costs for firm X

Output (Q) (1)	TFC (£000) (2)	TVC (£000) (3)	TC(TFC + TVC) (£000) (4)	AFC(TFC/Q) (£000) (5)	AVC(TVC/Q) (£000) (6)	AC(TC/Q) (£000) (7)	MC(ΔTC/ΔQ) (£000) (8)
0	12	0	12	–	–	–	
							10
1	12	10	22	12	10	22	
							6
2	12	16	28	6	8	14	
							5
3	12	21	33	4	7	11	
							7
4	12	28	40	3	7	10	
							12
5	12	40	52	2.4	8	10.4	
							20
6	12	60	72	2	10	12	
							31
7	12	91	103	1.7	13	14.7	

wage costs. Thus *TVC* rises more and more rapidly. You can see this by examining column 3.

The figures in the remaining columns in Table 4.1 are derived from columns 1 to 3. Look at the figures in each of the columns and check how the figures are derived. Note the figures for marginal cost are plotted between the lines to illustrate that marginal cost represents the increase in costs as output increases from one unit to the next. We can use the figures in Table 4.1 to draw *MC*, *AFC*, *AVC* and *AC* curves.

KI 15
p 87

Marginal cost (MC). The shape of the *MC* curve follows directly from the law of diminishing returns. Initially, in Figure 4.1, as more of the variable factor is used, extra units of output cost less than previous units. *MC* falls.

Figure 4.1   Average and marginal costs

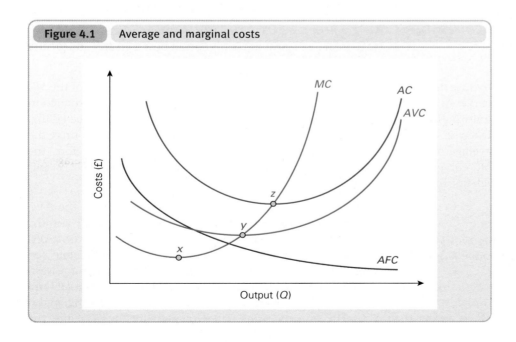

BOX 4.3   THE RELATIONSHIP BETWEEN AVERAGES AND MARGINALS

In this chapter we have just examined the concepts of *average* and *marginal* cost. We shall be coming across several other average and marginal concepts later on. It is useful at this stage to examine the general relationship between averages and marginals. In all cases there are three simple rules that relate them.

To illustrate these rules, consider the following example.

Imagine over the first four matches of the football season Sloman FC has conceded a total of 8 goals, and so an average of 2 goals per match.

Now assume in their next match against White FC they concede a further 2 goals (the marginal goals conceded). This will not affect Sloman FC's average goals conceded per match. It will remain at 2. Their sixth match is against the much-feared Garratt FC who put 8 goals past the hapless keeper. This worsens the team's defensive record, with the average number of goals conceded per match rising; not to 8, of course, but to 3. This is found by dividing the total number of goals conceded (18) by the number of matches (6).

If then in the next match Sloman FC manage to 'keep a clean sheet' with no goals conceded, this will pull the average goals conceded per match back down.

From this example we can derive the three universal rules about averages and marginals:

■ If the marginal equals the average, the average will not change.
■ If the marginal is above the average, the average will rise.
■ If the marginal is below the average, the average will fall.

An opening batsman for a university cricket club scores the following number of runs in five successive innings:

Innings:	1	2	3	4	5
Runs:	20	20	50	10	0

These can be seen as the marginal number of runs from each innings. Calculate the total and average number of runs after each innings. Show how the average and marginal scores illustrate the three rules above.

Pause for thought

Before you read on, can you explain why the marginal cost curve will always cut the average cost curve at its lowest point.

Beyond a certain level of output, diminishing returns set in. This is shown as point *x*. Thereafter *MC* rises. Additional units of output cost more and more to produce, since they require ever-increasing amounts of the variable factor.

Average fixed cost (AFC). This falls continuously as output rises, since total fixed costs are being spread over a greater and greater output.

Average (total) cost (AC). The shape of the *AC* curve depends on the shape of the *MC* curve. As long as new units of output cost less than the average, their production must pull the average cost down. That is, if *MC* is less than *AC*, *AC* must be falling. Likewise, if new units cost more than the average, their production must drive the average up. That is, if *MC* is greater than *AC*, *AC* must be rising. Therefore, the *MC* curve crosses the *AC* curve at its minimum point (point *z* in Figure 4.1). This relationship between averages and marginals is explored in Box 4.3.

Pause for thought

Why is the minimum point of the AVC curve at a lower level of output than the minimum point of the AC curve?

Average variable cost (AVC). Since *AVC* = *AC* − *AFC*, the *AVC* curve is simply the vertical difference between the *AC* and the *AFC* curves. Note that as *AFC* gets less, the gap between *AVC* and *AC* narrows. Since all marginal costs are variable (by definition, there are no marginal fixed costs), the same relationship holds between *MC* and *AVC* as it did between *MC* and *AC*. That is, if *MC* is less than *AVC*, *AVC* must be falling, and if *MC* is greater than *AVC*, *AVC* must be rising. Therefore, as with the *AC* curve, the *MC* curve crosses the *AVC* curve at its minimum point (point *y* in Figure 4.1).

Recap

1. Production in the short run is subject to diminishing returns. As greater quantities of the variable factor(s) are used, so each additional unit of the variable factor will add less to output than previous units: i.e. output will rise less and less rapidly.

2. When measuring costs of production, we should be careful to use the concept of opportunity cost. In the case of inputs not owned by the firm, the opportunity cost is simply the explicit cost of purchasing or hiring them. It is the price paid for them. In the case of inputs already owned by the firm, it is the implicit cost of what the factor could have earned for the firm in its best alternative use.

3. As some factors are fixed in supply in the short run, their total costs are fixed with respect to output. In the case of variable factors, their total cost increases as more output is produced and hence as more of them are used. Total cost can be divided into total fixed and total variable cost.

4. Marginal cost is the cost of producing one more unit of output. It will probably fall at first but will start to rise as soon as diminishing returns set in.

5. Average cost, like total cost, can be divided into fixed and variable costs. Average fixed cost will decline as more output is produced. The reason is that the total fixed cost is being spread over a greater and greater number of units of output. Average variable cost will tend to decline at first, but once the marginal cost has risen above it, it must then rise. The same applies to average cost.

PRODUCTION AND COSTS: LONG RUN   4.2

How do a firm's costs vary with output over the longer term?

In the long run, *all* factors of production are variable. There is time for the firm to build a new factory (maybe in a different part of the country), to install new machines, to use different techniques of production, and in general to combine its inputs in whatever proportion and in whatever quantities it chooses.

In the long run, then, a firm will have to make a number of decisions: about the scale of its operations and the techniques of production it will use. These decisions will affect the costs of production. It is important, therefore, to get them right.

The scale of production

If a firm were to double all of its inputs – something it could do in the long run – would it double its output? Or would output more than double or less than double? We can distinguish three possible situations:

Constant returns to scale. This is where a given percentage increase in inputs will lead to the same percentage increase in output.

Increasing returns to scale. This is where a given percentage increase in inputs will lead to a larger percentage increase in output.

Decreasing returns to scale. This is where a given percentage increase in inputs will lead to a smaller percentage increase in output.

Notice the terminology here. The words 'to scale' mean that *all* inputs increase by the same proportion. Decreasing returns *to scale* are therefore quite different from diminishing *marginal* returns (where only the *variable* factor increases). The differences between marginal returns to a variable factor and returns to scale are illustrated in Table 4.2.

Table 4.2	Short-run and long-run increases in output				
Short run			**Long run**		
Input 1	**Input 2**	**Output**	**Input 1**	**Input 2**	**Output**
3	1	25	1	1	15
3	2	45	2	2	35
3	3	60	3	3	60
3	4	70	4	4	90
3	5	75	5	5	125

In the short run, input 1 is assumed to be fixed in supply (at 3 units). Output can be increased only by using more of the variable factor (input 2). In the long run, however, both input 1 and input 2 are variable.

In the short-run situation, diminishing returns can be seen from the fact that output increases at a decreasing rate (25 to 45 to 60 to 70 to 75) as input 2 is increased. In the long-run situation, the table illustrates increasing returns to scale. Output increases at an *increasing* rate (15 to 35 to 60 to 90 to 125) as both inputs are increased.

Economies of scale

The concept of increasing returns to scale is closely linked to that of **economies of scale**. A firm experiences economies of scale if costs per unit of output fall as the scale of production increases. Clearly, if a firm is getting increasing returns to scale from its factors of production, then as it produces more it will be using smaller and smaller amounts of factors per unit of output. Other things being equal, this means that it will be producing at a lower average cost.

There are a number of reasons why firms are likely to experience economies of scale. Some are due to increasing returns to scale; some are not.

Specialisation and division of labour. In large-scale plants, workers can do more simple, repetitive jobs. With this **specialisation and division of labour** less training is needed; workers can become highly efficient in their particular job, especially with long production runs; there is less time lost by workers switching from one operation to another; and supervision is easier. Workers and managers can be employed who have specific skills in specific areas.

Indivisibilities. Some inputs are of a minimum size: they are indivisible. The most obvious example is machinery. Take the case of a combine harvester. A small-scale farmer could not make full use of one. They only become economical to use, therefore, on farms above a certain size. The problem of **indivisibilities** is made worse when different machines, each of which is part of the production process, are of a different size. For example, if there are two types of machine, one producing 6 units a day, the other packaging 4 units a day, a minimum of 12 units per day will have to be produced, involving two production machines and three packaging machines, if all machines are to be fully utilised.

The 'container principle'. Any capital equipment that contains things (e.g. blast furnaces, oil tankers, pipes, vats) tends to cost less per unit of output the larger its size. The reason has to do with the relationship between a container's volume and its

KI 14
p 86

surface area. A container's cost depends largely on the materials used to build it and hence roughly on its surface area. Its output depends largely on its volume. Large containers have a bigger volume relative to surface area than do small containers. For example, a container with a bottom, top and four sides, with each side measuring 1 metre, has a volume of 1 cubic metre and a surface area of 6 square metres (6 surfaces of 1 square metre each). If each side was doubled in length to 2 metres, the volume would be 8 cubic metres and the surface area 24 square metres (6 surfaces of 4 square metres each). Thus an eightfold increase in capacity has been gained at only a fourfold increase in the container's surface area, and hence an approximate fourfold increase in cost.

Greater efficiency of large machines. Large machines may be more efficient in the sense that more output can be gained for a given amount of inputs. For example, only one worker may be required to operate a machine, whether it be large or small. Also, a large machine may make more efficient use of raw materials.

By-products. With production on a large scale, there may be sufficient waste products to make some by-product.

Multi-stage production. A large factory may be able to take a product through several stages in its manufacture. This saves time and cost moving the semi-finished product from one firm or factory to another. For example, a large cardboard-manufacturing firm may be able to convert trees or waste paper into cardboard and then into cardboard boxes in a continuous sequence.

All the above are examples of **plant economies of scale**. They are due to an individual factory or workplace or machine being large. There are other economies of scale that are associated with the *firm* being large – perhaps with many factories.

Organisational economies. With a large firm, individual plants can specialise in particular functions. There can also be centralised administration of the firms. Often, after a merger between two firms, savings can be made by **rationalising** their activities in this way.

Spreading overheads. There are some expenditures that are only economic when the *firm* is large, such as research and development: only a large firm can afford to set up a research laboratory. This is another example of indivisibilities, only this time at the level of the firm rather than the plant. The greater the firm's output, the more these **overhead costs** are spread.

Financial economies. Large firms may be able to obtain finance at lower interest rates than small firms. They may be able to obtain certain inputs cheaper by buying in bulk. (These are examples of economies of scale which are not the result of increasing returns to scale.)

Definitions

Plant economies of scale
Economies of scale that arise because of the large size of the factory.

Rationalisation
The reorganising of production (often after a merger) so as to cut out waste and duplication and generally to reduce costs.

Overheads
Costs arising from the general running of an organisation, and only indirectly related to the level of output.

Economies of scope. Often a firm is large because it produces a range of products. This can result in each individual product being produced more cheaply than if it were produced by a single-product firm. The reason for these **economies of scope** is that various overhead costs and financial and organisational economies can be shared among the products. For example, a firm that produces a whole range of CD players, DVD players and recorders, amplifiers, games consoles, TVs and so on can benefit from shared marketing and distribution costs and the bulk purchase of electronic components.

Diseconomies of scale

When firms get beyond a certain size, costs per unit of output may start to increase. There are several reasons for such **diseconomies of scale**:

■ Management problems of co-ordination may increase as the firm becomes larger and more complex, and as lines of communication get longer. There may be a lack of personal involvement by management.
■ Workers may feel 'alienated' if their jobs are boring and repetitive, and if they feel an insignificantly small part of a large organisation. Poor motivation may lead to shoddy work.
■ Industrial relations may deteriorate as a result of these factors and also as a result of the more complex interrelationships between different categories of worker.
■ Production-line processes and the complex interdependencies of mass production can lead to great disruption if there are hold-ups in any one part of the firm.

Whether firms experience economies or diseconomies of scale depends on the conditions applying in each individual firm.

The size of the whole industry

As an *industry* grows in size, this can lead to **external economies of scale** for its member firms. This is where a firm, whatever its own individual size, benefits from the *whole industry* being large. For example, the firm may benefit from having access to specialist raw material or component suppliers, labour with specific skills, firms that specialise in marketing the finished product, and banks and other financial institutions with experience of the industry's requirements. What we are referring to here is the **industry's infrastructure**: the facilities, support services, skills and experience that can be shared by its members.

The member firms of a particular industry might, however, experience external **diseconomies of scale**. For example, as an industry grows larger, this may create a growing shortage of specific raw materials or skilled labour. This will push up their prices, and hence the firms' costs.

The relationship between inputs and outputs in the long run is examined in Web Appendices 4.2 and 4.3. These look at ways of combining inputs so as to minimise costs for a given output or maximise output for a given cost.

Long-run average cost

We turn now to *long-run* cost curves. Since there are no fixed factors in the long run, there are no long-run fixed costs. For example, the firm may rent more land in order to expand its operations. Its rent bill therefore goes up as it expands its output. All costs, then, in the long run are variable costs.

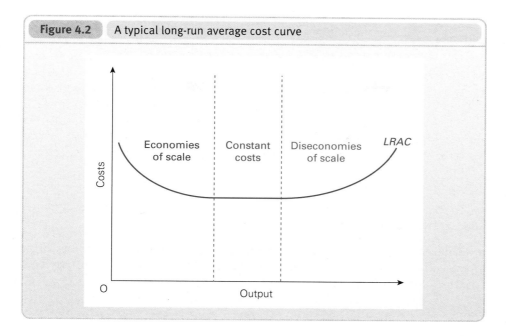

Figure 4.2   A typical long-run average cost curve

Although it is possible to draw long-run total, marginal and average cost curves, we will concentrate on **long-run average cost (*LRAC*) curves**. These can take various shapes, but a typical one is shown in Figure 4.2.

It is often assumed that as a firm expands, it will initially experience economies of scale and thus face a downward-sloping *LRAC* curve. After a point, however, all such economies will have been achieved and thus the curve will flatten out. Then, possibly after a period of constant *LRAC*, the firm will get so large that it will start experiencing diseconomies of scale and thus a rising *LRAC*. At this stage, production and financial economies begin to be offset by the managerial problems of running a giant organisation.

The effect of this is to give a saucer-shaped curve, as in Figure 4.2.

Assumptions behind the long-run average cost curve

There are three key assumptions that we make when constructing long-run average cost curves:

Factor prices are given. At each level of output it is assumed that a firm will be faced with a given set of factor prices. If factor prices *change*, therefore, both short- and long-run cost curves will shift. Thus an increase in nationally negotiated wage rates would shift the curves upwards.

However, factor prices might be different at *different* levels of output. For example, one of the economies of scale that many firms enjoy is the ability to obtain bulk discount on raw materials and other supplies. In such cases the curve does *not* shift. The different factor prices are merely experienced at different points along the curve, and are reflected in the shape of the curve. Factor prices are still given for any particular level of output.

The state of technology and factor quality are given. These are assumed to change only in the *very* long run (see below). If a firm gains economies of scale, it is because it is being able to exploit *existing* technologies and make better use of the existing availability of factors of production.

> **Definition**
>
> **Long-run average cost curve**
>
> A curve that shows how average cost varies with output on the assumption that *all* factors are variable. (It is assumed that the least-cost method of production will be chosen for each output.)

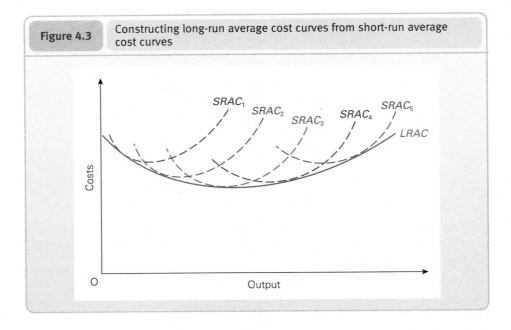

Figure 4.3 Constructing long-run average cost curves from short-run average cost curves

Firms choose the least-cost combination of factors for each output. The assumption here is that firms operate efficiently: that they choose the cheapest possible way of producing any level of output. If the firm did not operate efficiently, it would be producing at a point above the *LRAC* curve.

The relationship between long-run and short-run average cost curves

Take the case of a firm that has just one factory and faces a short-run average cost curve illustrated by $SRAC_1$ in Figure 4.3.

In the long run, it can build more factories. If it thereby experiences economies of scale (due, say, to savings on administration), each successive factory will allow it to produce with a new lower *SRAC* curve. Thus with two factories it will face curve $SRAC_2$, with three factories curve $SRAC_3$, and so on. Each *SRAC* curve corresponds to a particular amount of the factor that is fixed in the short run: in this case, the factory. (Many more *SRAC* curves could be drawn between the ones shown, since factories of different sizes could be built or existing ones could be expanded.)

From this succession of short-run average cost curves we can construct a long-run average cost curve. This is shown in Figure 4.3. This is known as the **envelope curve**, since it envelops the short-run curves.

Long-run cost curves in practice

Firms do experience economies of scale. Some experience continuously falling *LRAC* curves. Others experience economies of scale up to a certain output and thereafter constant returns to scale.

Evidence is inconclusive on the question of diseconomies of scale. There is little evidence to suggest the existence of *technical* diseconomies, but the possibility of diseconomies due to managerial and industrial relations problems cannot be ruled out.

Some evidence on economies of scale in the UK is considered in Box 4.4.

Definition

Envelope curve
A long-run average cost curve drawn as the tangency points of a series of short-run average cost curves.

Postscript: Decision making in different time periods

We have distinguished between the short run and the long run. Let us introduce two more time periods to complete the picture. The complete list then reads as follows.

Very short run (immediate run). *All* factors are fixed. Output is fixed. The supply curve is vertical. On a day-to-day basis a firm may not be able to vary output at all. For example, a flower seller, once the day's flowers have been purchased from the wholesaler, cannot alter the amount of flowers available for sale on that day. In the very short run, all that may remain for a producer to do is to sell an already produced good.

Short run. At least one factor is fixed in supply. More can be produced, but the firm will come up against the law of diminishing returns as it tries to do so.

Long run. All factors are variable. The firm may experience constant, increasing or decreasing returns to scale. But although all factors can be increased or decreased, they are of a fixed *quality*.

Very long run. All factors are variable, *and* their quality and hence productivity can change. Labour productivity can increase as a result of education, training, experience and social factors. The productivity of capital can increase as a result of new inventions (new discoveries) and innovation (putting inventions into practice).

Improvements in factor quality will reduce costs and thus shift the short- and long-run cost curves downwards.

Just how long the 'very long run' is will vary from firm to firm. It will depend on how long it takes to develop new techniques, new skills or new work practices.

It is important to realise that decisions *for* all four time periods can be made *at* the same time. Firms do not make short-run decisions *in* the short run and long-run decisions *in* the long run. They can make both short-run and long-run decisions today. For example, assume that a firm experiences an increase in consumer demand and anticipates that it will continue into the foreseeable future. It thus wants to increase output. Consequently, it makes the following four decisions *today*.

■ (*Very short run*) It accepts that for a few days it will not be able to increase output. It informs its customers that they will have to wait. It may temporarily raise prices to choke off some of the demand.

■ (*Short run*) It negotiates with labour to introduce overtime working as soon as possible, to tide it over the next few weeks. It orders extra raw materials from its suppliers. It launches a recruitment drive for new labour so as to avoid paying overtime longer than is necessary.

■ (*Long run*) It starts proceedings to build a new factory. The first step may be to discuss requirements with a firm of consultants.

■ (*Very long run*) It institutes a programme of research and development and/or training in an attempt to increase productivity.

Although we distinguish these four time periods, it is the middle two we are primarily concerned with. The reason for this is that there is very little the firm can do in the *very* short run. And in the *very* long run, although the firm will obviously want to increase the productivity of its inputs, it will not be in the position to make precise calculations of how to do it. It will not know precisely what inventions will be made, or just what will be the results of its own research and development.

> **Pause for thought**
>
> *Why are Christmas trees and fresh foods often sold cheaply on Christmas Eve? Why do shops find it most profitable to lower the price of these items to the point where the price elasticity of demand equals −1?*

| BOX 4.4 | MINIMUM EFFICIENT SCALE |

The extent of economies of scale in practice

Two of the most important studies of economies of scale have been those made by C. F. Pratten[a] in the late 1980s and by a group advising the European Commission[b] in 1997. Both studies found strong evidence that many firms, especially in manufacturing, experienced substantial economies of scale.

In a few cases long-run average costs fell continuously as output increased. For most firms, however, they fell up to a certain level of output and then remained constant.

The extent of economies of scale can be measured by looking at a firm's *minimum efficient scale (MES)*. The *MES* is the size beyond which no significant additional economies of scale can be achieved: in other words, the point where the *LRAC* curve flattens off. In Pratten's studies he defined this level as the minimum scale above which any possible doubling in scale would reduce average costs by less than 5 per cent (i.e. virtually the bottom of the *LRAC* curve). In the diagram *MES* is shown at point *a*.

The *MES* can be expressed in terms either of an individual factory or of the whole firm. Where it refers to the minimum efficient scale of an individual factory, the *MES* is known as the *minimum efficient plant size (MEPS)*.

The *MES* can then be expressed as a percentage of the total size of the market or of total domestic production. Table (a), based on the Pratten study, shows *MES* for plants and firms in various industries. The first column shows *MES* as a percentage of total UK production. The second column shows *MES* as a percentage of total EU production. Table (b), based on the 1997 study, shows *MES* for various plants as a percentage of total EU production.

Expressing *MES* as a percentage of total output gives an indication of how competitive the industry could be. In some industries (such as footwear and tufted carpets), economies of scale were exhausted (i.e. *MES* was reached) with plants or firms that were still small relative to total UK production and even smaller relative to total EU production. In such industries there would be room for many firms and thus scope for considerable competition.

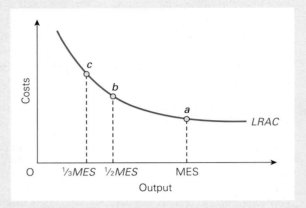

In other industries, however, even if a single plant or firm were large enough to produce the whole output of the industry in the UK, it would still not be large enough to experience the full potential economies of scale: the *MES* is greater than 100 per cent. Examples from Table (a) include factories producing cellulose fibres, and car manufacturers. In such industries there is no possibility of competition. In fact, as long as the *MES* exceeds 50 per cent there will not be room for more than one firm large enough to gain full economies of scale. In this case the industry is said to be a *natural monopoly*. As we shall see in Chapters 5 and 7, when competition is lacking, consumers may suffer by firms charging prices considerably above costs.

A second way of measuring the extent of economies of scale is to see how much costs would increase if production were reduced to a certain fraction of *MES*. The normal fractions used are $1/2$ or $1/3$*MES*. This is illustrated in the diagram. Point *b* corresponds to $1/2$*MES*; point *c* to $1/3$*MES*. The greater the percentage by which *LRAC* at point *b* or *c* is higher than at point *a*, the greater will be the economies of scale to be gained by producing at *MES* rather than at $1/2$*MES* or $1/3$*MES*. For example, the table shows that greater economies of scale can be gained by moving from $1/2$*MES* to *MES* in the production of electric motors than of cigarettes.

[a] C. F. Pratten, 'A survey of the economies of scale', in *Research on the 'Costs of Non-Europe'*, vol. 2 (Office for Official Publications of the European Communities, 1988)

[b] European Commission/Economists Advisory Group Ltd, 'Economies of Scale', *The Single Market Review, Sub-series V, Volume 4*. Office for official publications of the European Communities, Luxembourg, 1997

Table (a)

Product	MES as % of production		% additional cost at $\frac{1}{2}$MES
	UK	EU	
Individual plants			
Cellulose fibres	125	16	3
Rolled aluminium semi-manufactures	114	15	15
Refrigerators	85	11	4
Steel	72	10	6
Electric motors	60	6	15
TV sets	40	9	9
Cigarettes	24	6	1.4
Ball-bearings	20	2	6
Beer	12	3	7
Nylon	4	1	12
Bricks	1	0.2	25
Tufted carpets	0.3	0.04	10
Shoes	0.3	0.03	1
Firms			
Cars	200	20	9
Lorries	104	21	7.5
Mainframe computers	>100	n.a.	5
Aircraft	100	n.a.	5
Tractors	98	19	6

Source: See footnote a

The main purpose of the studies was to determine whether the single EU market is big enough to allow both economies of scale and competition. The tables suggest that in all cases, other things being equal, the EU market is indeed large enough for this to occur. The second study also found that 47 of the 53 manufacturing sectors analysed had scope for further exploitation of economies of scale.

In 2007 and 2008 the European Commission agreed to fund a number of research projects to conduct further investigations of *MES* across different industries and to consider the impact of the expansion of the EU.

Table(b)

Plants	MES as % of total EU production
Aerospace	12.19
Tractors and agricultural machinery	6.57
Electric lighting	3.76
Steel tubes	2.42
Shipbuilding	1.63
Rubber	1.06
Radio and TV	0.69
Footwear	0.08
Carpets	0.03

Source: See footnote b

1. *Why might a firm operating with one plant achieve MEPS and yet not be large enough to achieve MES? (Clue: are all economies of scale achieved at plant level?)*
2. *Why might a firm producing bricks have an MES that is only 0.2 per cent of total EU production and yet face little effective competition from other EU countries?*

Recap

1. In the long run, a firm is able to vary the quantity it uses of all factors of production. There are no fixed factors and hence no long-run fixed costs.

2. If it increases all factors by the same proportion, it may experience constant, increasing or decreasing returns to scale.

3. Economies of scale occur when costs per unit of output fall as the scale of production increases. This can be the result of a number of factors, some of which are directly due to increasing (physical) returns to scale. These include the benefits of specialisation and division of labour, the use of larger and more efficient machines, and the ability to have a more integrated system of production. Other economies of scale arise from the financial and administrative benefits of large-scale organisations.

4. When constructing long-run cost curves it is assumed that factor prices are given, that the state of technology is given and that firms will choose the least-cost method of production for each given output.

5. The *LRAC* curve can be downward sloping, upward sloping or horizontal, depending in turn on whether there are economies of scale, diseconomies of scale or neither. Typically *LRAC* curves are drawn as saucer-shaped. As output expands, initially there are economies of scale. When these are exhausted the curve will become flat. When the firm becomes very large it may begin to experience diseconomies of scale. If this happens, the *LRAC* curve will begin to slope upwards again.

6. An envelope curve can be drawn which shows the relationship between short-run and long-run average cost curves. The *LRAC* curve envelops the short-run *AC* curves: it is 'tangential' to them (i.e. just touches them).

7. Four distinct time periods can be distinguished. In addition to the short- and long-run periods, we can also distinguish the very-short- and very-long-run periods. The very short run is when all factors are fixed. The very long run is where not only the quantity of factors but also their quality is variable (as a result of changing technology, etc.).

4.3 REVENUE

How does a firm's revenue vary with its level of sales?

Remember that we defined a firm's total profit as its total revenue minus its total costs of production. In the last two sections we looked at costs. We now turn to revenue.

As with costs, we distinguish between three revenue concepts: total revenue (*TR*), average revenue (*AR*) and marginal revenue (*MR*).

Total, average and marginal revenue

Total revenue (TR)

Total revenue is the firm's total earnings per period of time from the sale of a particular amount of output (*Q*).

For example, if a firm sells 1000 units (*Q*) per month at a price of £5 each (*P*), then its monthly total revenue will be £5000: in other words, £5 × 1000 ($P \times Q$). Thus:

$$TR = P \times Q$$

Average revenue (AR)

Average revenue is the amount that the firm earns per unit sold. Thus:

$$AR = TR/Q$$

So if the firm earns £5000 (*TR*) from selling 1000 units (*Q*), it will earn £5 per unit. But this is simply the price! Thus:

$$AR = P$$

(The only exception to this is when the firm is selling its products at different prices to different consumers. In this case *AR* is simply the (weighted) average price.)

Marginal revenue (MR)

Marginal revenue is the extra total revenue gained by selling one more unit (per time period). So if a firm sells an extra 20 units this month compared with what it expected to sell, and in the process earns an extra £100, then it is getting an extra £5 for each extra unit sold: *MR* = £5. Thus:

$$MR = \Delta TR / \Delta Q$$

We now need to see how each of these three revenue concepts (*TR*, *AR* and *MR*) varies with output. We can show this relationship graphically in the same way as we did with costs.

The relationship will depend on the market conditions under which a firm operates. A firm that is too small to be able to affect market price will have different-looking revenue curves from a firm that is able to choose the price it charges. Let us examine each of these two situations in turn.

> **Definitions**
>
> **Marginal revenue**
> The extra revenue gained by selling one more unit per period of time:
> $MR = \Delta TR / \Delta Q$
>
> **Price taker**
> A firm that is too small to be able to influence the market price.

Revenue curves when price is not affected by the firm's output

Average revenue

If a firm is very small relative to the whole market, it is likely to be a **price taker**. That is, it has to accept the price given by the intersection of demand and supply in the whole market. But, being so small, it can sell as much as it is capable of producing at that price. This is illustrated in Figure 4.4. Diagram (a) shows market demand and supply. Equilibrium price is £5. Diagram (b) looks at the demand for an individual firm that is tiny relative to the whole market. (Look at the difference in the scale of the horizontal axes in the two diagrams.)

Figure 4.4   Deriving a firm's *AR* and *MR*: price-taking firm

Being so small, any change in its output will be too insignificant to affect the market price. It thus faces a horizontal demand 'curve' at this price. It can sell 200 units, 600 units, 1200 units or whatever without affecting this £5 price.

Average revenue is thus constant at £5. The firm's average revenue curve must therefore lie along exactly the same line as its demand curve.

Marginal revenue

In the case of a horizontal demand curve, the marginal revenue curve will be the same as the average revenue curve, since selling one more unit at a constant price (*AR*) merely adds that amount to total revenue. If an extra unit is sold at a constant price of £5, an extra £5 is earned.

Revenue curves when price varies with output

The curves *AR* and *MR* will look quite different when price does vary with the firm's output.

If a firm has a relatively large share of the market, it will face a downward-sloping demand curve. This means that if it is to sell more, it must lower the price. But it could also choose to raise its price. If it does so, however, it will have to accept a fall in sales.

Average revenue

Remember that average revenue equals price. If, therefore, the price has to be reduced to sell more output, average revenue will fall as output increases.

Table 4.3 gives an example of a firm facing a downward-sloping demand curve. The demand curve (which shows how much is sold at each price) is given by the first two columns.

Note that, as in the case of a price-taking firm, the demand curve and the *AR* curve lie along exactly the same line (see Figure 4.5). The reason for this is simple: *AR* = *P*, and thus the curve relating price to quantity (the demand curve) must be the same as that relating average revenue to quantity (the *AR* curve).

Marginal revenue

When a firm faces a downward-sloping demand curve, marginal revenue will be less than average revenue, and may even be negative. But why?

If a firm is to sell more per time period, it must lower its price (assuming it does not advertise). This will mean lowering the price not just for the extra units it hopes to sell, but also for those units it would have sold had it not lowered the price.

Table 4.3	Revenues for a firm facing a downward-sloping demand curve		
Q (units)	P = AR (£)	TR (£)	MR (£)
1	8	8	
			6
2	7	14	
			4
3	6	18	
			2
4	5	20	
			0
5	4	20	
			−2
6	3	18	
			−4
7	2	14	

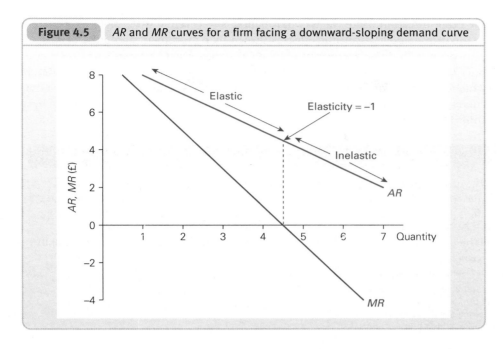

Figure 4.5   *AR* and *MR* curves for a firm facing a downward-sloping demand curve

Thus the marginal revenue is the price at which it sells the last unit, *minus* the loss in revenue it has incurred by reducing the price on those units it could otherwise have sold at the higher price. This can be illustrated with Table 4.3.

Assume that price is currently £7. Two units are thus sold. The firm now wishes to sell an extra unit. It lowers the price to £6. It thus gains £6 from the sale of the third unit, but loses £2 by having to reduce the price by £1 on the two units it could otherwise have sold at £7. Its net gain is therefore £6 − £2 = £4. This is the marginal revenue: it is the extra revenue gained by the firm from selling one more unit. Try using this method to check out the remaining figures for *MR* in Table 4.3. (Note that in the table the figures for *MR* are entered in the spaces between the figures for the other three columns.)

There is a simple relationship between marginal revenue and *price elasticity of demand*. Remember from Chapter 3 (page 60) that if demand is price elastic, a *decrease* in price will lead to a proportionately larger increase in the quantity demanded and hence to an *increase* in revenue. Marginal revenue will thus be positive. If, however, demand is inelastic, a decrease in price will lead to a proportionately smaller increase in sales. In this case the price reduction will more than offset the increase in sales and as a result revenue will fall. Marginal revenue will be negative.

If, then, marginal revenue is a positive figure (i.e. if sales per time period are 4 units or less in Figure 4.5), the demand curve will be elastic at that quantity, since a rise in quantity sold (as a result of a reduction in price) would lead to a rise in total revenue. If, on the other hand, marginal revenue is negative (i.e. at a level of sales of 5 or more units in Figure 4.5), the demand curve will be inelastic at that quantity, since a rise in quantity sold would lead to a *fall* in total revenue.

Thus the demand (*AR*) curve of Figure 4.5 is elastic to the left of point *r* and inelastic to the right.

Shifts in revenue curves

We saw in Chapter 2 that a change in *price* will cause a movement along a demand curve. It is similar with revenue curves, except that here the causal connection is in the other direction. Here we ask what happens to revenue when there is a change in the firm's *output*. Again the effect is shown by a movement along the curves.

A change in any *other* determinant of demand, such as tastes, income or the price of other goods, will shift the demand curve. As this change affects the price at which each level of output can be sold, there will be a shift in all three revenue curves. An increase in revenue is shown by a vertical shift upwards; a decrease by a shift downwards.

Recap

1. Total revenue (*TR*) is the total amount a firm earns from its sales in a given time period. It is simply price times quantity: $TR = P \times Q$.

2. Average revenue (*AR*) is total revenue per unit: $AR = TR/Q$. In other words, $AR = P$.

3. Marginal revenue is the extra revenue earned from the sale of one more unit per time period: $MR = \Delta TR/\Delta Q$.

4. The *AR* curve will be the same as the demand curve for the firm's product. In the case of a price taker, the demand curve and hence the *AR* curve will be a horizontal straight line and will also be the same as the *MR* curve.

5. A firm that faces a downward-sloping demand curve must obviously also face the same downward-sloping *AR* curve. The *MR* curve will also slope downwards, but will be below the *AR* curve and steeper than it.

6. When demand is price elastic, marginal revenue will be positive. When demand is price inelastic, marginal revenue will be negative.

7. A change in output is represented by a movement along the revenue curves. A change in any other determinant of revenue will shift the curves up or down.

4.4 PROFIT MAXIMISATION

How much output should a firm produce if it wants to maximise its profit?

We are now in a position to put costs and revenue together to find the output at which profit is maximised, and also to find out how much that profit will be. We take the case of a firm facing a downward-sloping demand curve, whose revenue, costs and profit are shown in Table 4.4. Note, we use the capital Greek letter pi (*Π*) to stand for 'profit'.

Finding the maximum profit that the firm can make is a two-stage process. The first stage is to find the profit-maximising output. To do this we use the *MC* and *MR* curves. The second stage is to find out just how much profit is at this output. To do this we use the *AR* and *AC* curves.

Stage 1: Using marginal curves to arrive at the profit-maximising output

There is a very simple **profit-maximising rule**: if profits are to be maximised, *MR* *must equal MC*. From Table 4.4 it can be seen that $MR = MC$ at an output of 3. This is shown as point *e* in Figure 4.6.

But why are profits maximised when $MR = MC$? The simplest way of answering this is to see what the position would be if *MR* did not equal *MC*.

Referring to Figure 4.6, at a level of output below 3, *MR* exceeds *MC*. This means that by producing more units there will be a bigger addition to revenue (*MR*) than to cost (*MC*). Total profit will *increase*. As long as MR exceeds MC, profit can be increased by increasing production.

At a level of output above 3, *MC* exceeds *MR*. All levels of output above 3 thus add more to cost than to revenue and hence *reduce* profit. As long as MC exceeds MR, profit can be increased by cutting back on production.

Definition

Profit-maximising rule
Profit is maximised where marginal revenue equals marginal cost.

Table 4.4   Revenue, cost and profit

Q (units)	P = AR (£)	TR (£)	MR (£)	TC (£)	AC (£)	MC (£)	TΠ (£)	AΠ (£)
0	9	0		6	–		–6	–
1	8	8	8	10	10	4	–2	–2
2	7	14	6	12	6	2	2	1
3	6	18	4	14	$4^2/3$	2	4	$-1^1/3$
4	5	20	2	18	$4^1/2$	4	2	$^1/2$
5	4	20	0	25	5	7	–5	–1
6	3	18	–2	36	6	11	–18	–3
7	2	14	–4	56	8	20	–42	–6

Figure 4.6   Finding the profit-maximising output using marginal curves

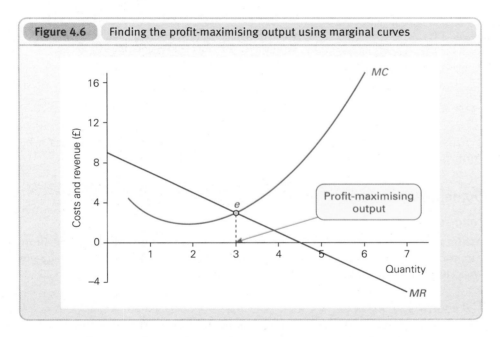

Profits are thus maximised where $MC = MR$: at an output of 3. This can be confirmed by reference to the $TΠ$ column in Table 4.4.

Students worry sometimes about the argument that profits are maximised when $MR = MC$. Surely, they say, if the last unit is making no profit, how can profit be at a *maximum*? The answer is very simple. If you cannot add anything more to a total, the total must be at the maximum. Take the simple analogy of going up a hill. When you cannot go any higher, you must be at the top.

Stage 2: Using average curves to measure the size of the profit

Once the profit-maximising output has been discovered, we now use the average curves to measure the *amount* of profit at the maximum. Both marginal and average curves corresponding to the data in Table 4.4 are plotted in Figure 4.7.

First, average profit ($AΠ$) is found. This is simply $AR - AC$. At the profit-maximising output of 3, this gives a figure for $AΠ$ of £6 – £$4^2/3$ = £$1^1/3$. Then total profit is obtained by multiplying average profit by output:

$$TΠ = AΠ × Q$$

Pause for thought

What will be the effect on a firm's profit-maximising output of a rise in fixed costs?

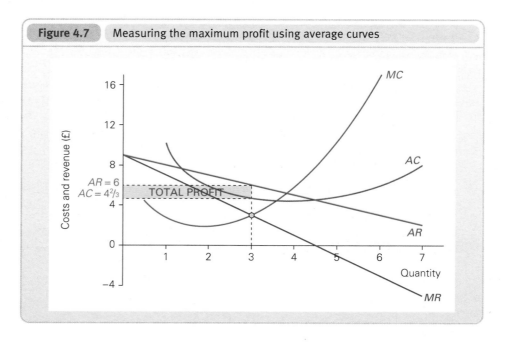

Figure 4.7 Measuring the maximum profit using average curves

This is shown as the shaded area. It equals £1⅓ × 3 = £4. This can again be confirmed by reference to the *TΠ* column in Table 4.4.

Some qualifications

Long-run profit maximisation

Assuming that the *AR* and *MR* curves are the same in the long run as in the short run, long-run profits will be maximised at the output where *MR* equals the *long-run MC*. The reasoning is the same as with the short-run case.

The meaning of 'profit'

One element of cost is the opportunity cost to the owners of the firm incurred by being in business. This is the minimum return that the owners must make on their capital in order to prevent them from eventually deciding to close down and perhaps move into some alternative business. It is a *cost* since, just as with wages, rent, etc., it has to be covered if the firm is to continue producing. This opportunity cost to the owners is sometimes known as **normal profit**, and is *included in the cost curves*.

What determines this normal rate of profit? It has two components. First, someone setting up in business invests capital in it. There is thus an opportunity cost. This is the interest that could have been earned by lending it in some riskless form (e.g. by putting it in a savings account in a bank). Nobody would set up a business unless they expected to earn at least this rate of profit. Running a business is far from riskless, however, and hence a second element is a return to compensate for risk. Thus:

Normal profit (%) = Rate of interest on a riskless loan + A risk premium

The risk premium varies according to the line of business. In those businesses with fairly predictable patterns, such as food retailing, it is relatively low. Where outcomes are very uncertain, as in mineral exploration or the manufacture of fashion garments, it is relatively high.

Definition

Normal profit
The opportunity cost of being in business. It consists of the interest that could be earned on a riskless asset, plus a return for risk taking. It is counted as a cost of production.

Thus if owners of a business earn normal profit, they will (just) be content to remain in that industry. If they earn more than normal profit, they will also (obviously) prefer to stay in this business. If they earn less than normal profit, then after a time they will consider leaving and using their capital for some other purpose.

Given that normal profits are included in costs, any profit that is shown diagrammatically (e.g. the shaded area in Figure 4.7) must therefore be over and above normal profit. It is known by several alternative names: **supernormal profit**, pure profit, economic profit, abnormal profit, producer's surplus (or sometimes simply profit). They all mean the same thing: the excess of total profit over normal profit.

Loss minimising

Sometimes there is no output at which the firm can make a profit. Such a situation is illustrated in Figure 4.8: the *AC* curve is above the *AR* curve at all levels of output.

In this case, the output where *MR* = *MC* will be the loss-minimising output. The amount of loss at the point where *MR* = *MC* is shown by the shaded area in Figure 4.8.

Whether or not to produce at all

The short run. Fixed costs have to be paid even if the firm is producing nothing at all. Rent has to be paid, business rates have to be paid, and so forth. Providing, therefore, that the firm is more than covering its *variable* costs, it can go some way to paying off these fixed costs and therefore will continue to produce.

It will shut down if it cannot cover its variable costs: that is, if the *AVC* curve is above, or the *AR* curve is below, that illustrated in Figure 4.9. This situation is known as the **short-run shut-down point**.

The long run. All costs are variable in the long run. If, therefore, the firm cannot cover its long-run average costs (which include normal profit), it will close down. The **long-run shut-down point** will be where the *AR* curve is tangential to (i.e. just touches) the *LRAC* curve.

Figure 4.8   Loss-minimising output

Figure 4.9 The short-run shut-down point

Driving up profits

One key to a company's success is the logistics of its operations. 'Logistics' refers to the management of the inflow of resources to a company and the outflow of finished goods from it; in other words it refers to 'supply-chain management'. This includes the purchasing of raw materials, transporting them, production sequencing, stock control, delivery to wholesalers or retailers, and so on.

Logistics depend on the provision of high quality and timely information. As IT systems have become increasingly sophisticated, they have enabled modern developments in logistics to transform the operation of many industries.

Driving down costs

With the widespread use of containerisation and development of giant distribution companies, such as UPS and DHL, transporting materials and goods around the world has become much faster and much cheaper. Instead of having to make parts in-house, companies can now use the logistics industry to obtain them at lower cost elsewhere, often from the other side of the world.

With improved systems for ordering materials, and deliveries becoming more and more reliable, firms no longer need keep large stocks of parts; they simply buy them as they need them. The same opportunity to save costs lies with the finished product: a company can keep lower levels of stocks when its own delivery mechanisms are more efficient.

The globalisation of logistics, with increasing use of the Internet, has resulted in a hugely complex logistics industry. Firms that were once solely concerned with delivery are now employed to manage companies' supply chains and achieve substantial cost savings for them.

Driving up revenues

Efficient logistics has not just resulted in lower costs. The flexibility it has given firms has allowed many to increase their sales.

Carrying lower levels of stocks and switching from supplier to supplier, with the process often being managed by a logistics company, can allow companies to change the products they offer more rapidly. They can be more responsive to consumer demand and thereby increase their sales.

A well-known example of a company benefiting from this approach is Primark. This low-cost fashion retailer focuses much more on buying, logistics and supply-chain management, than on branding or advertising.

1. *What dangers are there in keeping stocks to a minimum and relying on complex supply chains?*
2. *Which industries do you think would benefit most from reduced transport times for their finished products? Think of an industry, other than low-cost fashion, which would benefit from the ability to switch rapidly the products offered.*

Recap

1. Total profit equals total revenue minus total cost.

2. Graphically, profits are maximised at the output where marginal revenue equals marginal cost. Having found this output, the level of maximum profit can be found by finding the average profit ($AR - AC$) and then multiplying it by the level of output.

3. Normal profit is the minimum profit that must be made to persuade a firm to stay in business in the long run. It is counted as part of the firm's costs.

Supernormal profit is any profit over and above normal profit.

4. For a firm that cannot make a profit at any level of output, the point where $MR = MC$ represents the loss-minimising output.

5. In the short run, a firm will close down if it cannot cover its variable costs. In the long run, it will close down if it cannot make normal profits.

QUESTIONS

1. Up to roughly how long is the short run in the following cases?

   (a) A mobile disco firm.
   (b) Electricity power generation.
   (c) A small grocery retailing business.
   (d) 'Superstore Hypermarkets plc'.

   In each case specify your assumptions.

2. Given that there is a fixed supply of land in the world, what implications can you draw from the law of diminishing returns about the effects of an increase in world population on food output per head?

3. The following are some costs incurred by a shoe manufacturer. Decide whether each one is a fixed cost or a variable cost or has some element of both.

   (a) The cost of leather.
   (b) The fee paid to an advertising agency.
   (c) Wear and tear on machinery.
   (d) Business rates on the factory.
   (e) Electricity for heating and lighting.
   (f) Electricity for running the machines.
   (g) Basic minimum wages agreed with the union.
   (h) Overtime pay.
   (i) Depreciation of machines as a result purely of their age (irrespective of their condition).

4. What economies of scale is a large department store likely to experience?

5. Why are many firms likely to experience economies of scale up to a certain size and then diseconomies of scale after some point beyond that?

6. Name some industries where external economies of scale are gained. What are the specific external economies in each case?

7. Examine Figure 4.2 (on page 97). What would (i) the firm's long-run total cost curve, and (ii) its long-run marginal cost curve look like?

8. Under what circumstances is a firm likely to experience a flat-bottomed *LRAC* curve?

9. Draw a downward-sloping demand curve. Now choose scales for both axes. Read off various points on the demand curve and use them to construct a table showing price and quantity. Use this table to work out the figures for a marginal revenue column. Now use these figures to draw an *MR* curve.

10. Copy Figure 4.5 (which is based on Table 4.3). Now assume that incomes have risen and that, as a result, two more units per time period can be sold at each price. Construct a new table and plot the resulting new *AR* and *MR* curves on your diagram. Are the new curves parallel to the old ones?

11. Using the data in Table 4.3, construct a *total revenue* curve and mark the parts of the curve where the price elasticity of demand is (a) elastic; (b) unit elastic; (c) inelastic.

12. From the information given in the following table, construct a table like Table 4.4.

Q	0	1	2	3	4	5	6	7
P	12	11	10	9	8	7	6	5
TC	2	6	9	12	16	21	28	38

13. Use your table to draw a diagram like Figures 4.7. Use this diagram to show the profit-maximising output and the level of maximum profit. Confirm your findings by reference to the table you have constructed.

14. Normal profits are regarded as a cost (and are included in the cost curves). Explain why.

15. What determines the size of normal profit? Will it vary with the general state of the economy?

16. A firm will continue producing in the short run even if it is making a loss, providing it can cover its variable costs. Explain why. Just how long will it be willing to continue making such a loss?

17. The price of pocket calculators and digital watches fell significantly in the years after they were first introduced, and at the same time demand for them increased substantially. Use cost and revenue diagrams to illustrate these events. Explain the reasoning behind the diagram(s) you have drawn.

18. The table below shows the average cost and average revenue (price) for a firm at each level of output.

    (a) Construct a table to show *TC*, *MC*, *TR* and *MR* at each level of output (put the figures for

MC and *MR* midway between the output figures).
(b) Using *MC* and *MR* figures, find the profit-maximising output.
(c) Using *TC* and *TR* figures, check your answer to (b).
(d) Plot the *AC*, *MC*, *AR* and *MR* figures on a graph.
(e) Mark the profit-maximising output and the *AR* and *AC* at this output.
(f) Shade in an area to represent the level of profits at this output.

19. In February 2000, Unilever, the giant consumer products company, announced that it was to cut 25 000 jobs, close 100 plants and rely more on the Internet to purchase its supplies. It would use part of the money saved to increase promotion of its leading brands, such as Dove skin-care products, Lipton tea, Omo detergents and Calvin Klein cosmetics. The hope was to boost sales and increase profits. What was the likely effect of meeting these targets on its total costs, total revenue, average costs and average revenue? Give reasons for your answer.

Output	1	2	3	4	5	6	7	8	9	10
AC (£)	7.00	5.00	4.00	3.30	3.00	3.10	3.50	4.20	5.00	6.00
AR (£)	10.00	9.50	9.00	8.50	8.00	7.50	7.00	6.50	6.00	5.50

Log on to MyEconlab and complete the studyplan exercises for this chapter to see how much you have learnt and where you need to revise most. Make sure you access all the supporting textbook resources including the online workbook, newsblog, audio animations, guided solutions and ebook.

Additional case studies in the *Essentials of Economics* MyEconLab (www.pearsoned.co.uk/sloman)

4.1   The legal and organisational structure of firms. This case looks at the distinction between sole proprietorships, partnerships, private limited companies and public limited companies. It also distinguishes between U-form, M-form and H-form organisations.

4.2   Division of labour in a pin factory. This is the famous example of division of labour given by Adam Smith in his *Wealth of Nations* (1776).

4.3   Diminishing returns to nitrogen fertiliser. This case study provides a good illustration of diminishing returns in practice by showing the effects on grass yields of the application of increasing amounts of nitrogen fertiliser.

4.4   **The fallacy of using historic costs.** This looks at the example of the pricing of Christmas trees.

4.5   **Followers of fashion.** This case study examines the effects of costs on prices of fashion-sensitive goods.

4.6   **Cost curves in practice.** What do cost curves look like when fixed factors are divisible?

4.7   **Putting on a duplicate.** This examines the effects on marginal costs of additional passengers on a coach journey.

Websites relevant to this chapter

Numbers and sections refer to websites listed in the Web appendix and hotlinked from this book's website at **www.pearsoned.co.uk/sloman**.

- For news articles relevant to this chapter, see the *Economics News Articles* link from the book's website.

- For student resources relevant to this chapter, see sites C1–7, 9, 10, 14, 19, 20.

- For a case study examining costs, see site D2.

- For sites that look at companies, their scale of operation and market share, see B2 (third link); E4, 10; G7, 8.

- For links to sites on various aspects of production and costs, see section *Microeconomics > Production* in site I7.

Web appendices

4.1   **The short-run production function.** An analysis of how output varies with increases in the quantity of the variable factor used. The appendix looks at the concepts of total, average and marginal product.

4.2   **The optimum combination of factors.** This appendix examines how factors can be combined so as to minimise costs for any given output. It uses the concept of marginal product and develops the 'equi-marginal principle' developed in Web Appendix 2.1.

4.3   **Isoquant analysis.** This develops a model to show the optimum combination of factors to minimise costs for any given output or maximise output for any given cost. The analysis is similar to indifference analysis, developed in Web Appendix 2.2.

CHAPTER MAP

Market structures

As we saw in Chapter 4, a firm's profits are maximised where its marginal cost equals its marginal revenue: *MC* = *MR*. But we will want to know more than this.

What determines the *amount* of profit that a firm will make? Will its profits be large, or just enough for it to survive, or so low that it will be forced out of business? Will the price charged to the consumer be high or low? And, more generally, will the consumer benefit from the decisions a firm makes?

The answers to these questions depend on the amount of competition that a firm faces. A firm in a highly competitive environment will behave quite differently from a firm facing little or no competition. In particular, a firm facing competition from many other firms will be forced to keep its prices down and be as efficient as possible, simply to survive.

Even if a firm faces only one or two rivals, competition might be quite intense. Firms might put a lot of effort into producing more efficiently or into developing new or better products in order to gain a larger share of the market. They may, however, collude with each other to keep prices up.

When firms face little or no competition (like the local water company or a major pharmaceutical company), they may have considerable power over prices and we may end up paying a lot more.

In this chapter we look at different types of market and how well they serve the consumer.

After studying this chapter, you should be able to answer the following questions:

- What determines the degree of market power of a firm?
- Why does operating under conditions of perfect competition make being in business a constant battle for survival?
- How do firms get to become monopolies and remain so?
- At what price and output will a monopolist maximise profits and how much profit will it make?
- How well or badly do monopolies serve the consumer compared with competitive firms?
- How are firms likely to behave when there are just a few of them competing ('oligopolies')? Will they engage in all-out competition or will they collude with each other?
- What strategic games are oligopolists likely to play in their attempt to out-do their rivals? What determines the output of these 'games'?
- Why may firms charge different consumers different prices for an identical product?

5.1 THE DEGREE OF COMPETITION

How much competition does a firm face?

It is traditional to divide industries into categories according to the degree of competition that exists between the firms within the industry. There are four such categories.

At one extreme is **perfect competition** where there are very many firms competing. Each firm is so small relative to the whole industry that it has no power to influence price. It is a price taker. At the other extreme is **monopoly**, where there is just one firm in the industry, and hence no competition from *within* the industry. In the middle come **monopolistic competition**, which involves quite a lot of firms competing and where there is freedom for new firms to enter the industry, and **oligopoly**, where there are only a few firms and where entry of new firms is restricted.

To distinguish more precisely between these four categories, the following must be considered:

■ How freely can firms enter the industry: is entry free or restricted? If it is restricted, just how great are the barriers to the entry of new firms?
■ The nature of the product. Do all firms produce an identical product, or do firms produce their own particular brand or model or variety?
■ The degree of control the firm has over price. Is the firm a price taker or can it choose its price, and if so, how will changing its price affect its profits? What we are talking about here is the nature of the demand curve it faces. How elastic is it? If the firm puts up its price, will it lose (a) all its sales (a horizontal demand curve), or (b) a large proportion of its sales (a relatively elastic demand curve), or (c) just a small proportion of its sales (a relatively inelastic demand curve)?

TC 8
p 67

Market power benefits the powerful at the expense of others. When firms have market power over prices, they can use this to raise prices and profits above the perfectly competitive level. Other things being equal, the firm will gain at the expense of the consumer. Similarly, if consumers or workers have market power they can use this to their own benefit.

Table 5.1 shows the differences between the four categories.

The market structure under which a firm operates will determine its behaviour. Firms under perfect competition behave quite differently from firms that are monopolists, which behave differently again from firms under oligopoly or monopolistic competition.

This behaviour (or 'conduct') in turn affects the firm's performance: its prices, profits, efficiency, etc. In many cases it also affects other firms' performance: *their* prices, profits, efficiency, etc. The collective conduct of all the firms in the industry affects the whole industry's performance.

Economists thus see a causal chain running from market structure to the performance of that industry.

Structure → Conduct → Performance

Table 5.1	Features of the four market structures				
Type of market	**Number of firms**	**Freedom of entry**	**Nature of product**	**Examples**	**Implication for demand curve for firm**
Perfect competition	Very many	Unrestricted	Homogeneous (undifferentiated)	Cabbages, carrots (these approximate to perfect competition)	Horizontal. The firm is a price taker
Monopolistic competition	Many/several	Unrestricted	Differentiated	Builders, restaurants	Downward sloping, but relatively elastic. The firm has some control over price
Oligopoly	Few	Restricted	1. Undifferentiated or 2. Differentiated	1. Cement 2. Cars, electrical appliances	Downward sloping, relatively inelastic but depends on reactions of rivals to a price change
Monopoly	One	Restricted or completely blocked	Unique	Many prescription drugs, local water company	Downward sloping, more inelastic than oligopoly. The firm has considerable control over price

First we look at the two extreme market structures: perfect competition and monopoly (Sections 5.2 and 5.3). Then we turn to look at the two intermediate cases of monopolistic competition and oligopoly (Sections 5.4 and 5.5).

These two intermediate cases are sometimes referred to collectively as **imperfect competition**. The vast majority of firms in the real world operate under imperfect competition. It is still worth studying the two extreme cases, however, because they provide a framework within which to understand the real world. Some industries tend more to the competitive extreme, and thus their performance corresponds to some extent to perfect competition. Other industries tend more to the other extreme: for example, when there is one dominant firm and a few much smaller firms. In such cases their performance corresponds more to monopoly.

> **Definition**
>
> **Imperfect competition**
> The collective name for monopolistic competition and oligopoly.

> **Pause for thought**
>
> *Give one more example in each of the four market categories in Table 5.1.*

Recap

1. There are four alternative market structures under which firms operate. In ascending order of firms' market power, they are: perfect competition, monopolistic competition, oligopoly and monopoly.

2. The market structure under which a firm operates affects its conduct, which in turn affects its performance.

PERFECT COMPETITION   5.2

What happens when there are very many firms all competing against each other? Is this good for us as consumers?

The theory of perfect competition illustrates an extreme form of capitalism. In it, firms are entirely subject to market forces. They have no power whatsoever to affect the price of the product. The price they face is determined by the interaction of demand and supply in the whole *market*.

Assumptions

The model of perfect competition is built on four assumptions:

- Firms are *price takers*. There are so many firms in the industry that each one produces an insignificantly small proportion of total industry supply, and therefore has *no power whatsoever* to affect the price of the product. It faces a horizontal demand 'curve' at the market price: the price determined by the interaction of demand and supply in the whole market.
- There is complete *freedom of entry* into the industry for new firms. Existing firms are unable to stop new firms setting up in business. Setting up a business takes time, however. Freedom of entry, therefore, applies in the long run.
- All firms produce an *identical product*. (The product is 'homogeneous'.) There is therefore no branding or advertising.
- Producers and consumers have *perfect knowledge* of the market. That is, producers are fully aware of prices, costs and market opportunities. Consumers are fully aware of price, quality and availability of the product.

These assumptions are very strict. Few, if any, industries in the real world meet these conditions. Certain agricultural markets are perhaps closest to perfect competition. The market for certain fresh vegetables, such as potatoes, is an example. A potato grower is likely to face competition from so many others that he or she cannot affect the market price of any given variety of potatoes; there is freedom for farmers to set up in business growing potatoes; for any variety and grade of potatoes, each farmer produces a virtually identical product (potatoes are not branded by grower); knowledge of the market by both producers and consumers is very good.

> **Pause for thought**
>
> *It is sometimes claimed that the market for various stocks and shares is perfectly competitive, or nearly so. Take the case of the market for shares in a large company, such as BP. Go through each of the four assumptions above and see if they apply in this case. (Don't be misled by the first assumption. The 'firm' in this case is not BP itself, but rather the owners of the shares.)*

The short-run equilibrium of the firm

> **Definition**
>
> **Short run under perfect competition**
> The period during which there is too little time for new firms to enter the industry.

In the **short run** we assume that the number of firms in the industry cannot be increased; there is simply not time for new firms to enter the market.

Figure 5.1 shows a short-run equilibrium for both industry and a firm under perfect competition. Both parts of the diagram have the same scale for the vertical axis. The horizontal axes have totally different scales, however. For example, if the horizontal axis for the firm were measured in, say, thousands of units, the horizontal axis for the whole industry might be measured in millions or tens of millions of units, depending on the number of firms in the industry.

Let us examine the determination of price, output and profit in turn.

Price

The price is determined in the industry by the intersection of demand and supply. Being a price taker, the firm faces a horizontal demand (or average revenue) 'curve' at this price. It can sell all it can produce at the market price (P_e), but nothing at a price above P_e.

Output

The firm will maximise profit where marginal cost equals marginal revenue ($MR = MC$), at an output of Q_e. Note that, since the price is not affected by the firm's output, marginal revenue will equal price (see pages 103–4 and Figure 4.4).

Figure 5.1   Short-run equilibrium of industry and firm under perfect competition

(a) Industry

(b) Firm

Thus the firm's *MR* 'curve' and *AR* 'curve' (= demand 'curve') are the same horizontal straight line.

Profit

If the average cost (*AC*) curve (which includes normal profit) dips below the average revenue (*AR*) 'curve', the firm will earn supernormal profit. Supernormal profit per unit at Q_e is the vertical difference between *AR* and *AC* at Q_e. Total supernormal profit is the shaded rectangle in Figure 5.1 (i.e. profit per unit times quantity sold).

The short-run supply curve

The *firm's* short-run supply curve will be its (short-run) marginal cost curve. But why? A supply curve shows how much will be supplied at each price: it relates quantity to price. The marginal cost curve relates quantity to marginal cost. But, under perfect competition, given that $P = MR$, and $MR = MC$, P must equal MC. Thus the supply curve and the *MC* curve will follow the same line.

For example, in Figure 5.2(b), if price were P_1, profits would be maximised at Q_1 where $P_1 = MC$. Thus point *a* is one point on the supply curve. At a price of P_2,

Figure 5.2   Deriving the short-run supply curve

(a) Industry

(b) Firm

Q_2 would be produced. Thus point *b* is another point on the supply curve, and so on.

So, under perfect competition, the firm's supply curve depends entirely on production costs. This demonstrates why the firm's supply curve is upward sloping. Since marginal costs rise as output rises (due to diminishing marginal returns), a higher price will be necessary to induce the firm to increase its output.

Note that the firm will not produce at a price below *AVC* (see pages 109–10). Thus the supply curve is only that portion of the *MC* curve above point *e*.

What will be the short-run supply curve of the whole *industry*? This is simply the sum of the short-run supply curves (and hence *MC* curves) of all the firms in the industry. Graphically this will be a *horizontal* sum, since it is *quantities* that are being added.

Pause for thought

Will the industry supply be zero below a price of P_s in Figure 5.2?

The long-run equilibrium of the firm

Definition

The long run under perfect competition

The period of time which is long enough for new firms to enter the industry.

In the **long run**, if typical firms are making supernormal profits, new firms will be attracted into the industry. Likewise, if existing firms can make supernormal profits by increasing the scale of their operations, they will do so, since all factors of production are variable in the long run.

The effect of the entry of new firms and/or the expansion of existing firms is to increase industry supply. This is illustrated in Figure 5.3. At a price of P_1 supernormal profits are earned. The industry supply curve will thus shift to the right as new firms enter. This in turn leads to a fall in price.

Supply will go on increasing, and price falling, until firms are making only normal profits. This will be when price has fallen to the point where the demand 'curve' for the firm just touches the bottom of its long-run average cost curve. Q_L is thus the long-run equilibrium output of the firm, with P_L the long-run equilibrium price.

Since the *LRAC* curve is tangential to (i.e. just touching) all possible short-run *AC* curves (see Section 5.2), the full long-run equilibrium will be as shown in Figure 5.4 where:

$$LRAC = AC = MC = MR = AR$$

Figure 5.3   Long-run equilibrium under perfect competition

Figure 5.4   Long-run equilibrium of the firm under perfect competition

$LRAC = (SR)AC = (SR)MC = MR = AR$

The incompatibility of perfect competition and substantial economies of scale

Why is perfect competition so rare in the real world – if it even exists at all? One important reason for this has to do with economies of scale.

In many industries, firms may have to be quite large if they are to experience the full potential economies of scale. But perfect competition requires there to be *many* firms. Firms must therefore be small under perfect competition: too small in most cases for economies of scale.

Once a firm expands sufficiently to achieve economies of scale, it will usually gain market power. It will be able to undercut the prices of smaller firms, which will thus be driven out of business. Perfect competition is destroyed.

Perfect competition could exist in any industry, therefore, only if there were no (or virtually no) economies of scale.

Is perfect competition good for consumers?

Generally it is argued that perfect competition is a 'good thing', and that the more perfect an industry becomes the better. We explore the arguments in Section 5.3 (pages 126–8) after we have looked at monopoly, but at this stage the main points in favour of perfect competition can be identified.

■ Price equals marginal cost. Why is this desirable? To answer this, consider what would happen if they were not equal. If price were greater than marginal cost, this would mean that consumers were putting a higher value (P) on the production of extra units than they cost to produce (MC). Therefore more ought to be produced. If price were less than marginal cost, consumers would be putting a lower value on extra units than they cost to produce. Therefore less ought to be produced. When they are equal, therefore, production levels are just right. But, as we shall see later, it is only under perfect competition that $MC = P$.

BOX 5.1   E-COMMERCE

A return of power to the people?

The relentless drive towards big business in recent decades has seen many markets become more concentrated and increasingly dominated by large producers. And yet forces are at work that are undermining this dominance and bringing more competition to markets. One of these forces is *e-commerce*.

In this case study, we will consider just how far e-commerce is returning 'power to the people'.

Moving markets back towards perfect competition?

To see the extent to which e-commerce is making markets more competitive, let's look at the assumptions of perfect competition.

Large number of firms. The growth of e-commerce has led to many new firms starting up in business. It's not just large firms like Amazon.com that are providing increased competition for established firms, but the thousands of small online companies that are being established every day. Many of these firms are selling directly to us as consumers. This is known as 'B2C' e-commerce (business-to-consumers). But many more are selling to other firms ('B2B'). More and more companies, from the biggest to the smallest, are transferring their purchasing to the Web and are keen to get value for money.

The reach of the Web is global. This means that firms, whether conventional or Web-based, have to keep an eye on the prices and products of competitors in the rest of the world, not just in the local neighbourhood. Firms' demand curves are thus becoming very price elastic. This is especially so for goods that are cheap to transport, or for services such as insurance and banking where no transport is required.

Perfect knowledge. There are various ways in which e-commerce is adding to the consumer's knowledge. There is greater price transparency, with consumers able to compare prices online. Online shopping agents, such as Kelkoo and DealTime, can quickly locate a list of alternative suppliers. There is greater information on product availability and quality and this information is available at very little cost to the consumer. Virtual shopping malls, full of e-retailers, place the high-street retailer under intense competitive pressure.

The pressure is even greater in the market for intermediate products. Many firms are constantly searching for cheaper sources of supply, and the Internet provides a cheap and easy means of conducting such searches.

Freedom of entry. Internet companies often have lower start-up costs than their conventional rivals. Their premises are generally much smaller, with no 'shop-front' costs and lower levels of stockholding; in fact many of these businesses are initially operated from their owners' homes. Marketing costs can also be relatively low, especially given the ease with which companies can be located with search engines. Internet companies are often smaller and more specialist, relying on Internet 'outsourcing' (buying parts, equipment and other supplies through the Internet), rather than making everything themselves. They are also more likely to use delivery firms rather than having their own transport fleet. All this makes it relatively cheap for new firms to set up and begin trading over the Internet.

One consequence of the rise of e-commerce is that the distinction between firms and consumers is becoming increasingly blurred. With the rise of eBay, more and more

■ The combination of (long-run) production being at minimum average cost and the firm making only normal profit keeps prices at a minimum.

■ Perfect competition is a case of 'survival of the fittest'. Inefficient firms will be driven out of business, since they will not be able to make even normal profits. This encourages firms to be as efficient as possible and, where possible, to invest in new improved technology.

In general, it can be argued that perfectly competitive markets result in economic efficiency.

 KEY IDEA 17   *Economic efficiency* is achieved when each good is produced at the minimum cost and where consumers get maximum benefit from their income.

people are finding going into business incredibly easy. Some people are finding a market for all the junk they've collected over the years, while others are selling products they produce at home and yet others specialise in selling-on products using the marketing power of eBay. As a consequence there are some 90 million active eBay users worldwide, and hundreds of thousands of people make a full-time living from buying and selling on eBay. Annual sales on eBay are worth over £40 billion.

Not only do these factors make markets more price competitive, they also bring other benefits. Costs are driven down, as firms economise on stockholding, rely more on outsourcing and develop more efficient relationships with suppliers. 'Procurement hubs', online exchanges and trading communities are now well established in many industries. The competition also encourages innovation, which improves quality and the range of products.

What are the limits to e-commerce?

In 20 years, will we be doing all our shopping on the Internet? Will the only shopping malls be virtual ones? Although e-commerce is revolutionising some markets, it is unlikely that things will go anything like that far.

The benefits of 'shop shopping' are that you get to see the good, touch it and use it. You can have instant possession of it: you don't have to wait. Many people like wandering round the shops, meeting friends, seeing what takes their fancy, trying on clothes, browsing through DVDs and so on. 'Retail therapy' for many is a leisure activity.

Online shopping is limited by current technology; Internet access may be slow and frustrating; 'surfing' may instead become 'wading'; you have to wait for goods to be delivered; and what if deliveries are late or fail completely? Online shopping requires access to a credit or debit card, which might not be available to everyone, particularly younger consumers and those on low incomes.

Also costs might not be as low as expected. How efficient is it to have many small deliveries of goods? How significant are the lost cost savings from economies of scale that larger producers or retailers are likely to generate?

Nevertheless, e-commerce has made many markets, both retail and B2B, more competitive. This is especially so for services and for goods whose quality is easy to identify online. Many firms are being forced to face up to having their prices determined by the market.

1. *Why may the Internet work better for replacement buys than for new purchases?*
2. *Give three examples of products that are particularly suitable for selling over the Internet and three that are not. Explain your answer.*
3. *In 2008 eBay sellers called for a boycott of the site, following changes in the fees being charged and the removal of their ability to leave feedback on buyers. Explain how eBay can both increase competition across the economy and simultaneously acquire very substantial monopoly power.*

Recap

1. The assumptions of perfect competition are: a very large number of firms, complete freedom of entry, a homogeneous product and perfect knowledge of the good and its market by both producers and consumers.

2. In the short run, there is not time for new firms to enter the market, and thus supernormal profits can persist. In the long run, however, any supernormal profits will be competed away by the entry of new firms.

3. The short-run equilibrium for the firm will be where the price, as determined by demand and supply in the market, is equal to marginal cost. At this output the firm will be maximising profit.

4. The long-run equilibrium will be where the market price is just equal to firms' long-run average cost.

5. There can be no substantial economies of scale to be gained in a perfectly competitive industry. If there were, the industry would cease to be perfectly competitive as the large, low-cost firms drove the small, high-cost ones out of business.

5.3   MONOPOLY

What happens when there is only one firm in the market? Do we as consumers suffer?

What is a monopoly?

This may seem a strange question because the answer appears obvious. A monopoly exists when there is only one firm in the industry.

But whether an industry can be classed as a monopoly is not always clear. It depends how narrowly the industry is defined. For example, a textile company may have a monopoly on certain types of fabric, but it does not have a monopoly on fabrics in general. The consumer can buy fabrics other than those supplied by the company. A rail company may have a monopoly over rail services between two cities, but it does not have a monopoly over public transport between these two cities. People can travel by coach or air. They could also use private transport.

To some extent, the boundaries of an industry are arbitrary. What is more important for a firm is the amount of monopoly *power* it has, and that depends on the closeness of substitutes produced by rival industries. The Post Office, before 2006, had a monopoly over the delivery of letters, but it faced competition in communications from telephone, faxes and e-mail.

Barriers to entry

For a firm to maintain its monopoly position, there must be barriers to the entry of new firms. As we shall see, barriers also exist under oligopoly, but in the case of monopoly they must be high enough to block the entry of new firms. Barriers can take various forms.

Economies of scale. If the monopolist's costs go on falling significantly up to the output that satisfies the whole market, the industry may not be able to support more than one producer. This case is known as **natural monopoly**. It is particularly likely if the market is small. For example, two bus companies might find it unprofitable to serve the same routes, each running with perhaps only half-full buses, whereas one company with a monopoly of the routes could make a profit. Electricity transmission via a national grid is another example of a natural monopoly.

Even if a market could support more than one firm, a new entrant is unlikely to be able to start up on a very large scale. Thus the monopolist that is already experiencing economies of scale can charge a price below the cost of the new entrant and drive it out of business. If, however, the new entrant is a firm already established in another industry, it may be able to survive this competition.

Network economies. When a product or service is used by everyone in the market, there are benefits to all users from having access to other users. Thus eBay, by providing such large **network economies** makes it very difficult for other online auction houses to compete. Similar network economies apply to Microsoft's Windows (see Case Study 5.4 in MyEconLab), Adobe's *Acrobat* (for pdf files) and airlines operating interconnecting routes (see Case Study 5.5 in MyEconLab).

Economies of scope. A firm that produces a range of products is also likely to experience a lower average cost of production. For example, a large pharmaceutical

Definitions

Natural monopoly
A situation where long-run average costs would be lower if an industry were under monopoly than if it were shared between two or more competitors.

Network economies
The benefits to consumers of having a network of other people using the same product or service.

company producing a range of drugs and toiletries can use shared research, marketing, storage and transport facilities across its range of products. These lower costs make it difficult for a new single-product entrant to the market, since the large firm will be able to undercut its price and drive it out of the market.

Product differentiation and brand loyalty. If a firm produces a clearly differentiated product, where the consumer associates the product with the brand, it will be very difficult for a new firm to break into that market. Rank Xerox invented, and patented, the plain paper photocopier. After this legal monopoly (see below) ran out, people still associated photocopiers with Rank Xerox. It is still not unusual to hear someone say that they are going to 'Xerox the article' or, for that matter, 'Hoover their carpet'. Other examples of strong brand image include Guinness, Kellogg's Cornflakes, Coca-Cola, Nescafé and Sellotape.

Lower costs for an established firm. An established monopoly is likely to have developed specialised production and marketing skills. It is more likely to be aware of the most efficient techniques and the most reliable and/or cheapest suppliers. It is likely to have access to cheaper finance. It is thus operating on a lower cost curve. New firms would therefore find it hard to compete and would be likely to lose any price war.

Ownership of, or control over, key inputs or outlets. If a firm governs the supply of vital inputs (say, by owning the sole supplier of some component part), it can deny access to these inputs to potential rivals. On a world scale, the de Beers company has a monopoly in fine diamonds because all diamond producers market their diamonds through de Beers.

Similarly, if a firm controls the outlets through which the product must be sold, it can prevent potential rivals from gaining access to consumers. For example, Birds Eye Wall's used to supply freezers free to shops on the condition that they stocked only Wall's ice-cream in them.

Legal protection. The firm's monopoly position may be protected by patents on essential processes, by copyright, by various forms of licensing (allowing, say, only one firm to operate in a particular area) and by tariffs (i.e. customs duties) and other trade restrictions to keep out foreign competitors. Examples of monopolies protected by patents include most new medicines developed by pharmaceutical companies (e.g. anti-AIDS drugs), Microsoft's Windows operating systems, and agro-chemical companies, such as Monsanto, with various genetically modified plant varieties and pesticides.

Mergers and takeovers. The monopolist can put in a takeover bid for any new entrant. The sheer threat of takeovers may discourage new entrants.

Aggressive tactics. An established monopolist can probably sustain losses for longer than a new entrant. Thus it could start a price war, mount massive advertising campaigns, offer attractive after-sales service, introduce new brands to compete with new entrants, and so on.

Equilibrium price and output

Since there is, by definition, only one firm in the industry, the firm's demand curve is also the industry demand curve.

Compared with other market structures, demand under monopoly tends to be less elastic at each price. The monopolist can raise its price and consumers have no

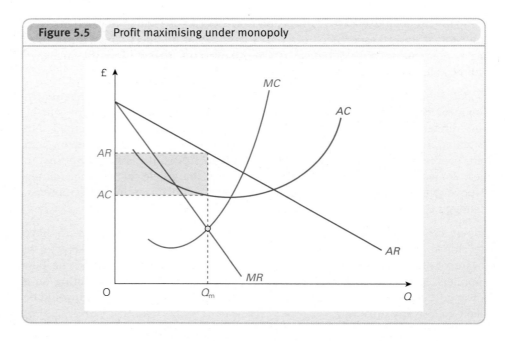

Figure 5.5   Profit maximising under monopoly

alternative firm to turn to within the industry. They either pay the higher price, or go without the good altogether.

Unlike the firm under perfect competition, the monopoly firm is thus a 'price maker'. It can choose what price to charge. Nevertheless, it is still constrained by its demand curve. A rise in price will reduce the quantity demanded.

As with firms in other market structures, a monopolist will maximise profit where *MR* = *MC*. In Figure 5.5 profit is maximised at Q_m. The supernormal profit obtained is shown by the shaded area.

These profits will tend to be larger the less elastic is the demand curve (and hence the steeper is the *MR* curve), and thus the bigger is the gap between *MR* and price (*AR*). The actual elasticity will depend on whether reasonably close substitutes are available in *other* industries. The demand for a rail service will be much less elastic (and the potential for profit greater) if there is no bus service to the same destination.

Since there are barriers to the entry of new firms, a monopolist's supernormal profits will not be competed away in the long run. The only difference, therefore, between short-run and long-run equilibrium is that in the long run the firm will produce where *MR = long-run MC*.

Monopoly versus perfect competition: which best serves the public interest?

Because it faces a different type of market environment, the monopolist will produce a quite different output and at a quite different price from a perfectly competitive industry.

Let us compare the two.

Short-run price and output. Figure 5.6 compares the profit-maximising position for an industry under monopoly with that under perfect competition. Note that we are comparing the monopoly with the whole *industry* under perfect competition. That

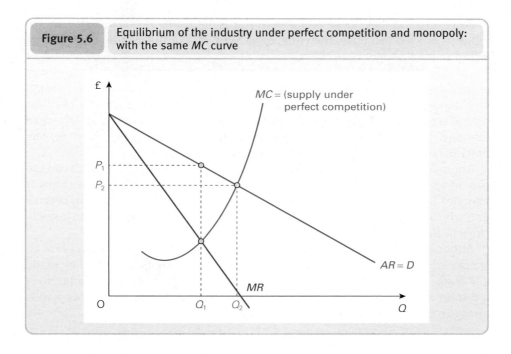

Figure 5.6 | Equilibrium of the industry under perfect competition and monopoly: with the same *MC* curve

way we can assume, for sake of comparison, that they both face the same demand curve. We also assume for the moment that they both face the same cost curves.

The monopolist will produce Q_1 at a price of P_1. This is where $MC = MR$. If the same industry were under perfect competition, however, it would produce at Q_2 and P_2 – a higher output and a lower price. But why? The reason is that for each of the firms in the industry – and it is at this level that the decisions are made – marginal revenue is the same as price. Remember that the *firm* under perfect competition faces a perfectly elastic demand (*AR*) curve, which also equals *MR* (see Figure 5.1). Thus producing where $MC = MR$ also means producing where $MC = P$. When *all* firms under perfect competition do this, price and quantity in the *industry* will be given by P_2 and Q_2 in Figure 5.6.

In the short run, therefore, it would seem (other things being equal) that perfect competition better serves the consumer's interest than does monopoly.

Long-run price and output. Under perfect competition, freedom of entry eliminates supernormal profit and forces firms to produce at the bottom of their *LRAC* curve. The effect, therefore, is to keep long-run prices down. Under monopoly, however, barriers to entry allow profits to remain supernormal in the long run. The monopolist is not forced to operate at the bottom of the *AC* curve. Thus, other things being equal, long-run prices will tend to be higher, and hence output lower, under monopoly.

Thus, again, it would *seem* that perfect competition better serves the consumer's interests. But this assumes that the cost curves are the *same* under both perfect competition and monopoly. Let us, therefore, turn to costs.

Costs under monopoly. The sheer survival of a firm in the long run under perfect competition requires that it uses the most efficient known technique, and develops new techniques wherever possible. The monopolist, however, sheltered by barriers

> **Pause for thought**
>
> *If the shares in a monopoly (such as a water company) were very widely distributed among the population, would the shareholders necessarily want the firm to use its monopoly power to make larger profits?*

to entry, can still make large profits even if it is not using the most efficient technique. It has less incentive, therefore, to be efficient. For this reason, costs may be *higher* under monopoly (another criticism of monopoly).

On the other hand, the monopoly may be able to achieve substantial economies of scale due to larger plant, centralised administration and the avoidance of unnecessary duplication (e.g. a monopoly water company would eliminate the need for several sets of rival water mains under each street). If this results in an *MC* curve substantially below that of the same industry under perfect competition, the monopoly may even produce a *higher* output at a *lower* price.

Another reason why a monopolist may operate with lower costs is that it can use part of its supernormal profits for research and development and investment. It may not have the same *incentive* to become efficient as the perfectly competitive firm which is fighting for survival, but it may have a much greater *ability* to become efficient than has the small firm with limited funds.

Although a monopoly faces no competition in the goods market, it may face an alternative form of competition in financial markets. A monopoly, with potentially low costs, which is currently run inefficiently, is likely to be subject to a takeover bid from another company. This **competition for corporate control** may thus force the monopoly to be efficient in order to prevent being taken over.

Innovation and new products. The promise of supernormal profits, protected perhaps by patents, may encourage the development of new (monopoly) industries producing new products. It is this chance of making monopoly profits that encourages many people to take the risks of going into business.

Potential competition or potential monopoly? The theory of contestable markets

Potential competition

The theory of contestable markets argues that what is crucial in determining price and output is not whether an industry is *actually* a monopoly or competitive, but whether there is the real *threat* of competition.

If a monopoly is protected by high barriers to entry – say, it owns all the raw materials – then it will be able to make supernormal profits with no fear of competition.

If, however, another firm *could* take over from it with little difficulty, it will behave much more like a competitive firm. The threat of competition has a similar effect to actual competition.

As an example, consider a catering company that is given permission by a factory to run its canteen. The catering company has a monopoly over the supply of food to the workers in that factory. If, however, it starts charging high prices or providing a poor service, the factory could offer the running of the canteen to an alternative catering company. This threat may force the original catering company to charge 'reasonable' prices and offer a good service.

Perfectly contestable markets

A market is **perfectly contestable** when the costs of entry and exit by potential rivals are zero, and when such entry can be made very rapidly. In such cases, the moment the possibility of earning supernormal profits occurs, new firms will enter, thus driving profits down to a normal level. The sheer threat of this happening, so the theory goes, will ensure that the firm already in the market will (a) keep its

---

Definitions

Competition for corporate control
The competition for the control of companies through takeovers.

Perfectly contestable market
A market where there is free and costless entry and exit.

| BOX 5.2 | BREAKING SKY'S MONOPOLY ON LIVE PREMIER LEAGUE FOOTBALL | CASE STUDIES & APPLICATIONS |

The impact of opening up the market

The early days of Sky

The structure of English football was changed with the formation of the FA Premier League for the 1992/3 football season. One justification for this was the promise of higher payments by TV companies. Live league football had been shown on free-to-air television throughout the 1980s and the clubs were very aware that this was potentially a very lucrative source of revenue.

The first contract to acquire the live and exclusive FA Premier League football broadcasting rights for the United Kingdom and the Republic of Ireland was worth £191 million over five seasons. A consequence of Sky being awarded the contract was that live top-flight English league football was no longer available on terrestrial and free-to-air television. Those who wanted to watch live football matches on television had to sign up with Sky, buying both a basic package and the additional Sky sports channels; Sky thus had a monopoly.

Attempts to reduce monopoly power

Both the Premier League and Sky's coverage proved to be hugely successful with viewers and advertisers and this was reflected in the price paid for subsequent packages. That starting in 1997 cost Sky £670 million for four seasons, while in 2003 BSkyB, as the company was now formally known, paid over £1 billion for exclusive rights for three seasons.

However, over this period the European Commission was expressing increasing concern about the extent of Sky's monopoly. The Commission started legal proceedings in 2002, filing a statement of objections, but was thwarted when the League agreed a new contract with Sky before ironing out an EC-approved deal.

At this time Sky did agree to sub-license up to eight 'top quality Premier League matches' each season to another broadcaster in order to win European approval. The Commission trumpeted this pledge as meaning 'that for the first time in the history of the Premier League free-to-air television will have a realistic opportunity to show live Premier League matches'. These hopes were dashed, however, when no rival broadcaster met the asking price set by Sky.

In 2005 the European Commission announced that Sky's monopoly would be broken. From 2007, the next set of rights, for a three-season period, would be sold in six 'balanced' packages of 23 games per season, with no broadcaster allowed more than five packages. The Commission claimed the deal would give fans 'greater choice and better value'.

However, concern was expressed about the impact on incomes of the Premiership clubs. While some commentators expected a more competitive process to result in roughly the same total income as was paid by Sky in 2003, just over £1 billion, others suggested that Sky paid a premium for the guarantee that it would be the sole broadcaster. Thus one effect of the new process might be reduced revenues for the clubs.

The outcome of the European Commission ruling

Revenues did not fall! Rather, the amount paid for the rights for matches played over the three seasons beginning 2007/8 was up by nearly 30 per cent from that for the three seasons from 2004/5. Sky won four of the six available packages, paying £1.31 billion. Setanta, an Irish-based satellite broadcaster, won the remaining two packages and paid £392 million.

The rights for the three seasons from 2010/11 were put out to auction early in 2009. The result was a further 5 per cent increase in revenues. This time Sky successfully bid for five packages, paying £1.62 billion, and Setanta a single package for which they paid £159 million.

In June 2009 Setanta failed to meet a payment to the Premier League as part settlement of its rights to the package for the 2009/10 season. This led the Premier League to auction both the TV rights for the 2009/10 season and the three seasons from 2010/11. The result was that Disney-owned US broadcaster ESPN bought up all the rights previously owned by Setanta with no net loss in revenues for the Premier League.

Chasing the Premier Leage dream was not only costly for Setanta but coincided with a widening of the financial gap between the Premier League and the rest of the football pyramid. It also increased concerns about the amounts of debt amassed by established football clubs in the Premier League and those in the lower leagues.

Nonetheless, armchair fans can now access 92 live English Premier League fixtures, though they need to subcribe to the packages of two broadcasters. Attendances at matches remain buoyant and the success of English teams in the UEFA Champions league illustrates the influence of the Premier League in world football.

The monopoly power that accrued initially to Sky, and that is currently shared with ESPN, has been incredibly important in making the Premier League what it is today.

1. What other examples of monopoly power exist in football? Could this power be reduced?
2. Assess the impact of the pay broadcasters' emergence on (a) football fans, (b) other viewers.

prices down, so that it just makes normal profits, and (b) produce as efficiently as possible, taking advantage of any economies of scale and any new technology. If the existing firm did not do this, entry would take place, and potential competition would become actual competition.

Contestable markets and natural monopolies

So why in such cases are the markets not *actually* perfectly competitive? Why do they remain monopolies?

The most likely reason has to do with economies of scale and the size of the market. To operate on a minimum efficient scale, the firm may have to be so large relative to the market that there is only room for one such firm in the industry. If a new firm does come into the market, then one or other of the two firms will not survive the competition. The market is simply not big enough for both of them.

If, however, there are no entry or exit costs, new firms will be perfectly willing to enter even though there is only room for one firm, provided they believe that they are more efficient than the existing firm. The existing firm, knowing this, will be forced to produce as efficiently as possible and with only normal profit.

The importance of costless exit

Setting up in a new business usually involves large expenditures on plant and machinery. Once this money has been committed, it becomes fixed costs. If these fixed costs are no higher than those of the existing firm, then the new firm could win the battle. But, of course, there is always the risk that it might lose.

But does losing the battle really matter? Can the firm not simply move to another market?

It does matter if there are substantial costs of exit. This will be the case if the capital equipment cannot be transferred to other uses – for example, a new blast furnace constructed by a new rival steel company. In this case, these fixed costs are known as **sunk costs**. The losing firm is left with capital equipment it cannot use. The firm may therefore be put off entering in the first place. The market is not perfectly contestable, and the established firm can make supernormal profit.

If, however, the capital equipment can be transferred, the exit costs will be zero (or at least very low), and new firms will be more willing to take the risks of entry. For example, a rival coach company may open up a service on a route previously operated by only one company, and where there is still only room for one operator. If the new firm loses the resulting battle, it can still use the coaches it has purchased. It simply uses them for a different route. The cost of the coaches is not a sunk cost.

Costless exit, therefore, encourages firms to enter an industry, knowing that, if unsuccessful, they can always transfer their capital elsewhere.

The lower the exit costs, the more contestable the market. This implies that firms already established in other similar markets may provide more effective competition against monopolists, since they can simply transfer capital from one market to another. For example, studies of airlines in the USA show that entry to a particular route may be much easier for an established airline, which can simply transfer planes from one route to another.

Contestability and the consumer's interests

The more contestable the market, the more will a monopoly be forced to act like a firm under perfect competition. If, therefore, a monopoly operates in a perfectly

> **Definition**
>
> **Sunk costs**
> Costs that cannot be recouped (e.g. by transferring assets to other uses).

contestable market, it might bring the 'best of both worlds' for the consumer. Not only will it be able to achieve low costs through economies of scale, but also the potential competition will keep profits and hence prices down.

KI 17
p 122

> **Pause for thought**
>
> *Think of two examples of highly contestable monopolies (or oligopolies). How well is the consumer's interest served?*

Recap

1. A monopoly is where there is only one firm in an industry. In practice, it is difficult to determine where a monopoly exists because it depends on how narrowly an industry is defined.

2. Barriers to the entry of new firms will normally be necessary to protect a monopoly from competition. Such barriers include economies of scale (making the firm a natural monopoly or at least giving it a cost advantage over new (small) competitors), control over supplies of inputs or over outlets, patents or copyright, and tactics to eliminate competition (such as takeovers or aggressive advertising).

3. Profits for the monopolist will be maximised (as for other firms) where $MC = MR$.

4. If demand and cost curves are the same in a monopoly and a perfectly competitive industry, the monopoly will produce a lower output and at a higher price than the perfectly competitive industry.

5. On the other hand, any economies of scale will, in part, be passed on to consumers in lower prices, and the monopolist's high profits may be used for research and development and investment, which in turn may lead to better products at possibly lower prices.

6. Potential competition may be as important as actual competition in determining a firm's price and output strategy.

7. The threat of this competition is greater the lower are the entry and exit costs to and from the industry. If the entry and exit costs are zero, the market is said to be perfectly contestable. Under such circumstances an existing monopolist will be forced to keep its profits down to the normal level if it is to resist entry of new firms. Exit costs will be lower, the lower are the sunk costs of the firm.

MONOPOLISTIC COMPETITION   5.4

What happens if there are quite a lot of firms competing, but each firm tries to attract us to its particular product or service?

Very few markets in practice can be classified as perfectly competitive or as a pure monopoly. The vast majority of firms do compete with other firms, often quite aggressively, and yet they are not price takers: they do have some degree of market power. Most markets, therefore, lie between the two extremes of monopoly and perfect competition, in the realm of 'imperfect competition'. As we saw in Section 5.1, there are two types of imperfect competition: namely, monopolistic competition and oligopoly.

Monopolistic competition is nearer to the competitive end of the spectrum. It can best be understood as a situation where there are a lot of firms competing but where each firm does nevertheless have some degree of market power (hence the term 'monopolistic' competition): each firm has some discretion as to what price to charge for its products.

Assumptions

■ There are *quite a large number of firms*. As a result each firm has only a small share of the market, and therefore its actions are unlikely to affect its rivals to any great

TC 3
p 11

extent. What this means is that each firm in making its decisions does not have to worry how its rivals will react. It assumes that what its rivals choose to do will *not* be influenced by what it does.

This is known as the assumption of **independence**. (As we shall see later, this is not the case under oligopoly. There we assume that firms believe that their decisions *do* affect their rivals, and that their rivals' decisions will affect them. Under oligopoly we assume that firms are *inter*dependent.)

■ There is *freedom of entry* of new firms into the industry. If any firm wants to set up in business in this market, it is free to do so.

In these two respects, therefore, monopolistic competition is like perfect competition.

■ Unlike perfect competition, however, each firm produces a product or provides a service in some way different from its rivals. As a result it can raise its price without losing all its customers. Thus its demand curve is downward sloping, albeit relatively elastic given the large number of competitors to which customers can turn. This is known as the assumption of **product differentiation**.

Petrol stations, restaurants, hairdressers and builders are all examples of monopolistic competition.

A typical feature of monopolistic competition is that, although there are many firms in the industry, there is only one firm in a particular location. This applies particularly in retailing. There may be several newsagents in a town, but only one in a particular street. In a sense, therefore, it has a local monopoly. People may be prepared to pay higher prices there to avoid having to go elsewhere.

Equilibrium of the firm

Short run

As with other market structures, profits are maximised at the output where $MC = MR$. The diagram is the same as for the monopolist, except that the AR and MR curves are more elastic. This is illustrated in Figure 5.7(a). As with perfect competition, it is possible for the monopolistically competitive firm to make supernormal profit in the short run. This is shown as the shaded area.

Just how much profit the firm will make in the short run depends on the strength of demand: the position and elasticity of the demand curve. The further to the right the demand curve is relative to the average cost curve, and the less elastic the demand curve is, the greater will be the firm's short-run profit. Thus a firm whose product is considerably differentiated from its rivals may be able to earn considerable short-run profits.

Long run

If typical firms are earning supernormal profit, new firms will enter the industry in the long run. As new firms enter, they will take some of the customers away from the established firms. The demand for the established firms' product will therefore fall. Their demand (AR) curve will shift to the left, and will continue doing so as long as supernormal profits remain and thus new firms continue entering.

Long-run equilibrium will be reached when only normal profits remain: when there is no further incentive for new firms to enter. This is illustrated in Figure 5.7(b).

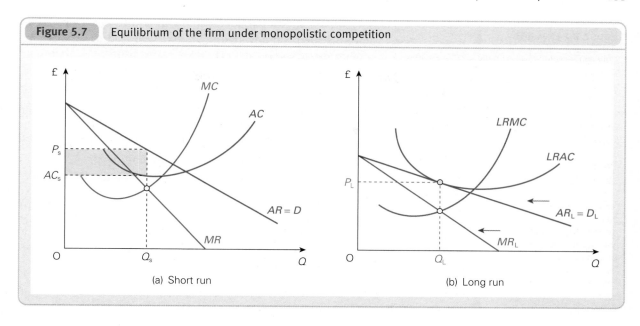

> **Figure 5.7**   Equilibrium of the firm under monopolistic competition

(a) Short run

(b) Long run

The firm's demand curve settles at D_L, where it just touches the firm's *LRAC* curve. Output will be Q_L: where $AR_L = LRAC$. (At any other output, *LRAC* is greater than *AR* and thus less than normal profit would be made.)

Non-price competition

One of the biggest problems with the simple model in Figure 5.7 is that it concentrates on price and output decisions. In practice, the profit-maximising firm under monopolistic competition will also need to decide the exact variety of product to produce and how much to spend on advertising it. This will lead the firm to take part in **non-price competition**.

Non-price competition involves two major elements: product development and advertising.

The major aims of *product development* are to produce a product that will sell well (i.e. one in high or potentially high demand) and one that is different from rivals' products (i.e. has a relatively inelastic demand due to lack of close substitutes). For shops or other firms providing a service, 'product development' takes the form of attempting to provide a service which is better than, or at least different from, that of rivals: personal service, late opening, certain lines stocked, and so on.

The major aim of *advertising* is to sell the product. This can be achieved not only by informing people of the product's existence and availability, but also by trying to persuade them to purchase it. Like product development, successful advertising will both increase demand and also make the firm's demand curve less elastic, since it stresses the specific characteristics of this firm's product over its rivals' (see Box 3.2 on page 63).

Product development and advertising not only increase a firm's demand and hence revenue, they also involve increased costs. So how much should a firm advertise, say to maximise profits?

For any given price and product, the optimal amount of advertising is where the revenue from *additional* advertising (MR_A) is equal to its cost (MC_A). As long as

Definition

Non-price competition
Competition in terms of product promotion (advertising, packaging, etc.) or product development.

TC 8
p 67

TC 2
p 10

Pause for thought

Why will additional advertising lead to smaller and smaller increases in sales?

$MR_A > MC_A$, additional advertising will add to profit. But extra amounts spent on advertising are likely to lead to smaller and smaller increases in sales. Thus MR_A falls, until $MR_A = MC_A$. At that point no further profit can be made. It is at a maximum.

Several problems arise with this analysis. These include:

- The effect of product development and advertising on demand will be difficult for a firm to forecast.
- Product development can affect a firm's future costs. For example, it may impact on production costs or 'aftercare' costs, such as servicing and repair.
- Product development and advertising are likely to have different effects at different prices. Profit maximisation, therefore, will involve the more complex choice of the optimum combination of price, type of product, and level and variety of advertising.

Monopolistic competition and the public interest

Comparison with perfect competition

It is often argued that monopolistic competition leads to a less efficient allocation of resources than perfect competition.

Figure 5.8 compares the long-run equilibrium positions for two firms. One firm is under perfect competition and thus faces a horizontal demand curve. It will produce an output of Q_1 at a price of P_1. The other is under monopolistic competition and thus faces a downward-sloping demand curve. It will produce the lower output of Q_2 at the higher price of P_2. A crucial assumption here is that a firm would have the *same* long-run average cost (*LRAC*) curve in both cases. Given this assumption, monopolistic competition has the following disadvantages:

- Less will be sold and at a higher price.
- Firms will not be producing at the least-cost point.

KI 17
p 122

| Figure 5.8 | Long-run equilibrium of the firm under perfect and monopolistic competition |

By producing more, firms would move to a lower point on their *LRAC* curve. Thus firms under monopolistic competition are said to have **excess capacity**. In Figure 5.8 this excess capacity is shown as $Q_1 - Q_2$. In other words, monopolistic competition is typified by quite a large number of firms (e.g. petrol stations), all operating at less than optimum output, and thus being forced to charge a price above that which they could charge if they had a bigger turnover. How often have you been to a petrol station and had to queue for the pumps?

So how does this affect the consumer? Although the firm under monopolistic competition may charge a higher price than under perfect competition, the difference may be very small. Although the firm's demand curve is downward sloping, it is still likely to be highly elastic due to the large number of substitutes. Furthermore, the consumer may benefit from monopolistic competition by having a greater variety of products to choose from. Each firm may satisfy some particular requirement of particular consumers.

> **Definition**
>
> **Excess capacity (under monopolistic competition)**
> In the long run firms under monopolistic competition will produce at an output below their minimum-cost point.

Comparison with monopoly

The arguments are very similar here to those when comparing perfect competition and monopoly.

On the one hand, freedom of entry for new firms and hence the lack of long-run supernormal profits under monopolistic competition are likely to help keep prices down for the consumer and encourage cost saving. On the other hand, monopolies are likely to achieve greater economies of scale and have more funds for investment and research and development.

Recap

1. Monopolistic competition occurs where there is free entry to the industry and quite a large number of firms operating independently of each other, but where each firm has some market power as a result of producing differentiated products or services.

2. In the short run, firms can make supernormal profits. In the long run, however, freedom of entry will drive profits down to the normal level. The long-run equilibrium of the firm is where the (downward-sloping) demand curve just touches the long-run average cost curve.

3. The long-run equilibrium is one of excess capacity. Given that the demand curve is downward sloping, the point where it just touches the *LRAC* curve will not be at the bottom of the *LRAC* curve. Increased production would thus be possible at *lower* average cost.

4. Firms under monopolistic competition may engage in non-price competition, in the forms of product development and advertising, in order to maintain an advantage over their rivals.

5. Monopolistically competitive firms, because of excess capacity, may have higher costs, and thus higher prices, than perfectly competitive firms, but consumers may gain from a greater diversity of products.

6. Monopolistically competitive firms may have fewer economies of scale than monopolies and conduct less research and development, but the competition may keep prices lower than under monopoly. Whether there will be more or less choice for the consumer is debatable.

OLIGOPOLY   5.5

What happens if there are just a few firms that dominate the market? Will they compete or get together?

Oligopoly occurs when just a few firms between them share a large proportion of the industry.

There are, however, significant differences in the structure of industries under oligopoly and similarly significant differences in the behaviour of firms. The firms may produce a virtually identical product (e.g. metals, chemicals, sugar, petrol). Most oligopolists, however, produce differentiated products (e.g. cars, soap powder, soft drinks, electrical appliances). Much of the competition between such oligopolists is in terms of the marketing of their particular brand.

The two key features of oligopoly

Despite the differences between oligopolies, there are two crucial features that distinguish oligopoly from other market structures.

Barriers to entry

Unlike firms under monopolistic competition, there are various barriers to the entry of new firms. These are similar to those under monopoly (see pages 124–5). The size of the barriers, however, will vary from industry to industry. In some cases entry is relatively easy, whereas in others it is virtually impossible.

Interdependence of the firms

> **Definition**
>
> **Interdependence (under oligopoly)**
> One of the two key features of oligopoly. Each firm will be affected by its rivals' decisions. Likewise its decisions will affect its rivals. Firms recognise this interdependence. This recognition will affect their decisions.

Because there are only a few firms under oligopoly, each firm has to take account of the others. This means that they are mutually dependent: they are **interdependent**. Each firm is affected by its rivals' actions. If a firm changes the price or specification of its product, for example, or the amount of its advertising, the sales of its rivals will be affected. The rivals may then respond by changing their price, specification or advertising. No firm can therefore afford to ignore the actions and reactions of other firms in the industry.

 KEY IDEA 18 *People often think and behave strategically.* How you think others will respond to your actions is likely to influence your own behaviour. Firms, for example, when considering a price or product change will often take into account the likely reactions of their rivals.

It is impossible, therefore, to predict the effect on a firm's sales of, say, a change in the price of its product without first making some assumption about the reactions of other firms. Different assumptions will yield different predictions. For this reason there is no single generally accepted theory of oligopoly. Firms may react differently and unpredictably.

Competition and collusion

Oligopolists are pulled in two different directions:

■ The interdependence of firms may make them wish to *collude* with each other. If they can club together and act as if they were a monopoly, they could jointly maximise industry profits.
■ On the other hand, they will be tempted to *compete* with their rivals to gain a bigger share of industry profits for themselves.

These two policies are incompatible. The more fiercely firms compete to gain a bigger share of industry profits, the smaller these industry profits will become! For example, price competition drives down the average industry price, while competition through advertising raises industry costs. Either way, industry profits fall.

Sometimes firms will collude. Sometimes they will not. The following sections examine first **collusive oligopoly** (both open and tacit), and then **non-collusive oligopoly**.

Collusive oligopoly

KI 16
p 116

When firms under oligopoly engage in collusion, they may agree on prices, market share, advertising expenditure, etc. Such collusion reduces the uncertainty they face. It reduces the fear of engaging in competitive price cutting or retaliatory advertising, both of which could reduce total industry profits.

A cartel

A formal collusive agreement is called a **cartel**. The cartel will maximise profits if it acts like a monopoly: if the members behave as if they were a single firm. This is illustrated in Figure 5.9.

The total market demand curve is shown with the corresponding market *MR* curve. The cartel's *MC* curve is the *horizontal* sum of the *MC* curves of its members (since TC 2
p 10 we are adding the *output* of each of the cartel members at each level of marginal cost). Profits are maximised at Q_1 where $MC = MR$. The cartel must therefore set a price of P_1 (at which Q_1 will be demanded).

Having agreed on the cartel price, the members may then compete against each other using *non-price competition*, to gain as big a share of resulting sales (Q_1) as they can.

Alternatively, the cartel members may somehow agree to divide the market between them. Each member would be given a **quota**. The sum of all the quotas must add up to Q_1. If the quotas exceeded Q_1, either there would be output unsold if price remained fixed at P_1, or the price would fall.

But if quotas are to be set by the cartel, how will it decide the level of each individual member's quota? The most likely method is for the cartel to divide the

Definitions

Collusive oligopoly
Where oligopolists agree (formally or informally) to limit competition between themselves. They may set output quotas, fix prices, limit product promotion or development, or agree not to 'poach' each other's markets.

Non-collusive oligopoly
Where oligopolists have no agreement between themselves, formal, informal or tacit.

Cartel
A formal collusive agreement.

Quota (set by a cartel)
The output that a given member of a cartel is allowed to produce (production quota) or sell (sales quota).

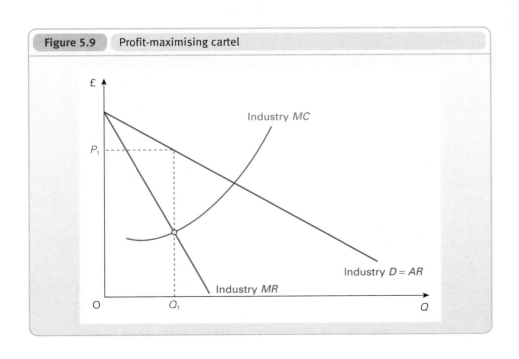

Figure 5.9   Profit-maximising cartel

BOX 5.3	OPEC – THE RISE AND FALL AND RISE AGAIN OF A CARTEL

The history of the world's most famous cartel

OPEC is probably the best known of all cartels. It was set up in 1960 by the five major oil-exporting countries: Saudi Arabia, Iran, Iraq, Kuwait and Venezuela. As of 2009, there were 12 members. OPEC's stated objectives are:

■ Stabilisation of oil markets to secure an efficient, economic and regular supply of petroleum
■ Steady income for producers and a fair return to capital to those investing in the petroleum industry

The years leading up to 1960 had seen the oil-producing countries increasingly in conflict with the international oil companies, which extracted oil under 'concessionary agreement'. Under this scheme, oil companies were given the right to extract oil in return for royalties. This meant that the oil-producing countries had little say over output and price levels.

The early years

Despite the formation of OPEC in 1960, it was not until 1973 that control of oil production was effectively transferred from the oil companies to the oil countries, with OPEC making the decisions on how much oil to produce and thereby determining its oil revenue. By this time OPEC consisted of 13 members.

OPEC's pricing policy over the 1970s consisted of setting a market price for Saudi Arabian crude (the market leader), and leaving other OPEC members to set their prices in line with this: a form of dominant 'firm' price leadership.

As long as demand remained buoyant, and was price inelastic, this policy allowed large price increases with consequent large revenue increases. In 1973/4, after the Arab–Israeli war, OPEC raised the price of oil from around $3 per barrel to over $12. The price was kept at roughly this level until 1979. And yet the sales of oil did not fall significantly.

 Illustrate what was happening here on a demand and supply diagram. Remember that demand was highly inelastic and was increasing over time.

After 1979, however, following a further increase in the price of oil from around $15 to $40 per barrel, demand did fall. This was largely due to the recession of the early 1980s (although, as we shall see later on when we look at macroeconomics, this recession was in turn largely caused by governments' responses to the oil price increases).

The use of quotas

Faced by declining demand, OPEC after 1982 agreed to limit output and allocate production quotas in an attempt to keep the price up. A production ceiling of 16 million barrels per day was agreed in 1984.

The cartel was beginning to break down, however, due to the following:

Oil prices

- The world recession and the resulting fall in the demand for oil.
- Growing output from non-OPEC members.
- 'Cheating' by some OPEC members who exceeded their quota limits.

With a glut of oil, OPEC could no longer maintain the price. The 'spot' price of oil (the day-to-day trading price of oil on the open market) was falling, as the graph shows.

The trend of lower oil prices was reversed in the late 1980s. With the world economy booming, the demand for oil rose and along with it the price. Then in 1990 Iraq invaded Kuwait and the Gulf War ensued. With the cutting-off of supplies from Kuwait and Iraq, the supply of oil fell and there was a sharp rise in its price.

But with the ending of the war and the recession of the early 1990s, the price rapidly fell again and only recovered slowly as the world economy started expanding once more.

On the demand side, the development of energy-saving technology plus increases in fuel taxes led to a relatively slow growth in consumption. On the supply side, the growing proportion of output supplied by non-OPEC members, plus the adoption in 1994 of a relatively high OPEC production ceiling of $24^1/_2$ million barrels per day, meant that supply more than kept pace with demand.

The situation for OPEC deteriorated further in the late 1990s, following the recession in the Far East. Oil demand fell by some 2 million barrels per day. By early 1999, the price had fallen to around $10 per barrel – a mere $2.70 in 1973 prices! In response, OPEC members agreed to cut production by 4.3 million barrels per day. The objective was to push the price back up to around $18–20 per barrel.

But, with the Asian economy recovering and the world generally experiencing more rapid economic growth, the price rose rapidly and soon overshot the $20 mark. By early 2000 it had reached $30: a tripling in price in just 12 months. With the world economy then slowing down, however, the price rapidly fell back, reaching $18 in November 2001.

However, in late 2001 the relationship between OPEC and non-OPEC oil producers changed. The 10 members of the OPEC cartel decided to cut production by 1.5 million barrels a day. This followed an agreement with five of the major oil producers outside of the cartel to reduce their output too, the aim being to push oil prices upwards and then stabilise them at around $25 per barrel.

The alliance between OPEC and non-OPEC oil producers is the first such instance of its kind in the oil industry. As a result, it seemed that OPEC might now once again be able to control the market for oil.

The price surge of 2003–8 . . .

But how successfully could this alliance cope with crisis? With worries over an impending war with Iraq and a strike in Venezuela, the oil price rose again in late 2002, passing the $30 mark in early 2003. OPEC claimed that it could maintain supply and keep prices from surging even with an Iraq war, but with prices rising rapidly above $30, many doubted that it could.

In 2004 the situation worsened with supply concerns related to the situation in Iraq, Saudi Arabia, Russia and Nigeria, and the oil price rose to over $50 in October 2004. OPEC tried to relax the quotas, but found it difficult to adjust supply sufficiently quickly to make any real difference to the price.

From 2006, oil prices increased more sharply than they ever had before and, for the first time in years, the real price of oil exceeded that seen in the 1970s. The major cause of the increases was very substantial increases in demand, particularly from India and China, coupled with continuing concerns about supply. The implications of the sharp price increases were substantial: inflationary pressures built up across the world, while the income of OPEC nations doubled in the first half of 2008.

By July 2008 the price had reached $147. Some analysts were predicting a price of over $200 per barrel by the end of the year.

. . . and then the fall

But then, with the growing banking turmoil and fears of a recession, the price began to fall – and rapidly so. When the price dropped below $100 in September 2008 the majority of the world breathed a sigh of relief. But as the economic outlook became gloomier and the demand for oil fell, so the price plummeted, reaching $34 by the end of the year – less than a quarter of the price just five months previously – and hovering around the $40 mark in the first quarter of 2009. Whilst this was good news for the consumer, it was potentially damaging for investment in oil exploration and development and also for investment in alternative energy supplies.

OPEC responded to the falling price by announcing cuts in production, totalling some 14 per cent between August 2008 and January 2009, which represented a global cut of about 5 per cent. Yet 2009 was to see something of a recovery in the global economy and this helped to fuel the demand for oil. As a result, the price of oil began to rebound during 2009. This again helps to demonstrate the volatility of the price of oil.

The recent history of OPEC illustrates the difficulty of using supply quotas to achieve a particular price. With demand being price inelastic but income elastic (responsive to changes in world income, such as rising demand from China), and with considerable speculative movements in demand, the equilibrium price for a given supply quota can fluctuate wildly.

What conditions facilitate the formation of a cartel? Which of these conditions were to be found in the oil market in (a) the early 1970s; (b) the mid-1980s; (c) the early 2000s?

market between the members according to their current market share. That is the solution most likely to be accepted as 'fair'.

In many countries, including the UK, cartels are illegal. They are seen by the government as a means of driving up prices and profits, and thereby as being against the public interest. Where open collusion is illegal, firms may simply break the law, or get round it. For example, in November 2001, the EU imposed record fines totalling €855.2 million on eight pharmaceutical companies for meeting secretly to fix the prices of vitamins (see Case Study 5.14 in MyEconLab). Alternatively, firms may stay within the law, but still *tacitly* collude by watching each other's prices and keeping theirs similar. Firms may tacitly 'agree' to avoid price wars or aggressive advertising campaigns.

Tacit collusion

One form of **tacit collusion** is where firms keep to the price that is set by an established leader. The leader may be the largest firm: the firm that dominates the industry. This is known as **dominant firm price leadership**. Alternatively, the price leader may simply be the one that has proved to be the most reliable to follow: the one that is the best barometer of market conditions. This is known as **barometric firm price leadership**.

Dominant firm price leadership. How does the leader set the price? This depends on the assumptions it makes about its rivals' reactions to its price changes. If it assumes that rivals will simply follow it by making exactly the same percentage price changes up or down, then a simple model can be constructed. This is illustrated in Figure 5.10. The leader assumes that it will maintain a constant market share (say, 50 per cent).

The leader will maximise profits where its marginal revenue is equal to its marginal cost. It knows its current position on its demand curve (say, point *a*). It

Figure 5.10 A price leader aiming to maximise profits for a given market share

then estimates how responsive its demand will be to industry-wide price changes and thus constructs its demand and *MR* curves on that basis. It then chooses to produce Q_L at a price of P_L: at point *l* on its demand curve (where $MC = MR$). Other firms then follow that price. Total market demand will be Q_T, with followers supplying that portion of the market not supplied by the leader: namely, $Q_T - Q_L$.

There is one problem with this model. That is the assumption that the followers will want to maintain a constant market share. It is possible that if the leader raises its price, the followers may want to supply more at this new price. On the other hand, the followers may decide merely to maintain their market share for fear of invoking retaliation from the leader, in the form of price cuts or an aggressive advertising campaign.

Barometric firm price leadership. A similar exercise can be conducted by a barometric firm. Although the firm is not dominating the industry, its price will be followed by the others. It merely tries to estimate its demand and *MR* curves – assuming, again, a constant market share – and then produces where $MR = MC$ and sets price accordingly.

In practice, which firm is taken as the barometer may frequently change. Whether we are talking about oil companies, car producers or banks, any firm may take the initiative in raising prices. If the other firms are merely waiting for someone to take the lead – say, because costs have risen – they will all quickly follow suit. For example, if one of the bigger building societies or banks raises its mortgage rates by 1 per cent, this is likely to stimulate the others to follow suit.

Other forms of tacit collusion. An alternative to having an established leader is for there to be an established set of simple 'rules of thumb' that everyone follows. One such example is **average cost pricing**. Here producers, instead of equating *MC* and *MR*, simply add a certain percentage for profit on top of average costs. Thus, if average costs rise by 10 per cent, prices will automatically be raised by 10 per cent. This is a particularly useful rule of thumb in times of inflation, when all firms will be experiencing similar cost increases.

Another rule of thumb is to have certain **price benchmarks**. Thus clothes may sell for £9.95, £14.95, £19.95, etc. (but not £12.31, £16.42 or £20.04). If costs rise, then firms simply raise their price to the next benchmark, knowing that other firms will do the same.

Rules of thumb can also be applied to advertising (e.g. you do not criticise other firms' products, only praise your own); or to the design of the product (e.g. lighting manufacturers tacitly agreeing not to bring out an everlasting light bulb).

Factors favouring collusion

Collusion between firms, whether formal or tacit, is more likely when firms can clearly identify with each other or some leader and when they trust each other not to break agreements. It is easier for firms to collude if the following conditions apply:

- There are only very few firms, all well known to each other.
- They are open with each other about costs and production methods.
- They have similar production methods and average costs, and are thus likely to want to change prices at the same time and by the same percentage.
- They produce similar products and can thus more easily reach agreements on price.

Pause for thought

If a firm has a typically shaped average cost curve and sets prices 10 per cent above average cost, what will its supply curve look like?

- There is a dominant firm.
- There are significant barriers to entry and thus there is little fear of disruption by new firms.
- The market is stable. If industry demand or production costs fluctuate wildly, it will be difficult to make agreements, partly due to difficulties in predicting and partly because agreements may frequently have to be amended. There is a particular problem in a declining market where firms may be tempted to undercut each other's price in order to maintain their sales.
- There are no government measures to curb collusion.

Non-collusive oligopoly: the breakdown of collusion

In some oligopolies, there may be only a few (if any) factors favouring collusion. In such cases, the likelihood of price competition is greater.

Even if there is collusion, there will always be the temptation for individual oligopolists to 'cheat', by cutting prices or by selling more than their allotted quota. The danger, of course, is that this would invite retaliation from the other members of the cartel, with a resulting price war. Price would then fall and the cartel could well break up in disarray.

When considering whether to break a collusive agreement, even if only a tacit one, a firm will ask: (1) 'How much can we get away with without inviting retaliation?' and (2) 'If a price war does result, will we be the winners? Will we succeed in driving some or all of our rivals out of business and yet survive ourselves, and thereby gain greater market power?'

The position of rival firms, therefore, is rather like that of generals of opposing armies or the players in a game. It is a question of choosing the appropriate *strategy*: the strategy that will best succeed in outwitting your opponents. The strategy a firm adopts will, of course, be concerned not just with price but also with advertising and product development.

Non-collusive oligopoly: assumptions about rivals' behaviour

Even though oligopolists might not collude, they will still need to take account of rivals' likely behaviour when deciding their own strategy. In doing so they will probably look at rivals' past behaviour and make assumptions based on it. There are three well-known models, each based on a different set of assumptions.

Assumption that rivals produce a given quantity: the Cournot model

One assumption is that rivals will produce a particular *quantity*. This is most likely when the market is stable and the rivals have been producing a relatively constant quantity for some time. The task, then, for the individual oligopolist is to decide its own price and quantity given the presumed output of its competitors.

The earliest model based on this assumption was developed by the French economist Augustin Cournot[1] in 1838. The **Cournot model** (which is developed in Web Appendix 5.2) takes the simple case of just two firms (a **duopoly** producing an identical product: for example, two electricity-generating companies supplying the whole country.

TC 9
p 71

KI 18
p 136

TC 3
p 11

> **Definitions**
>
> **Cournot model**
> A model of duopoly where each firm makes its price and output decisions on the assumption that its rival will produce a particular quantity.
>
> **Duopoly**
> An oligopoly where there are just two firms in the market.

---

[1] See http://cepa.newschool.edu/het/profiles/cournot.htm for a profile of Cournot and his work.

Figure 5.11   The Cournot model of duopoly: Firm A's profit-maximising position

Firm A believes that Firm B will produce Q_{B1}

Firm A's profit-maximising output and price are Q_{A1} and P_A

This is illustrated in Figure 5.11 which shows the profit-maximising price and output for Firm A. The total market demand curve is shown as D_M. Assume that Firm A believes that its rival, Firm B, will produce Q_{B1} units. Thus Firm A perceives its own demand curve (D_{A1}) to be Q_{B1} units less than total market demand. In other words, the horizontal gap between D_M and D_{A1} is Q_{B1} units. Given its perceived demand curve of D_{A1}, its marginal revenue curve will be MR_{A1} and the profit-maximising output will be Q_{A1}, where $MR_{A1} = MC_A$. The profit-maximising price will be P_{A1}.

If Firm A believed that Firm B would produce *more* than Q_{B1}, its perceived demand and *MR* curves would be further to the left and the profit-maximising quantity and price would both be lower.

Profits in the Cournot model. Industry profits will be *less* than under a monopoly or a cartel. The reason is that price will be lower than the monopoly price. This can be seen from Figure 5.11 If this were a monopoly, then to find the profit-maximising output, we would need to construct an *MR* curve corresponding to the market demand curve (D_M). This would intersect with the *MC* curve at a higher output than Q_{A1} and a *higher* price (given by D_M).

Nevertheless, profits in the Cournot model will be higher than under perfect competition, since price is still above marginal cost.

Assumption that rivals set a particular price: the Bertrand model

An alternative assumption is that rival firms set a particular price and stick to it. This scenario is more realistic when firms do not want to upset customers by frequent price changes or want to produce catalogues which specify prices. The task, then, for a given oligopolist is to choose its own price and quantity in the light of the prices set by rivals.

The most famous model based on this assumption was developed by another French economist, Joseph Bertrand, in 1883. Bertrand again took the simple case of a duopoly, but his conclusions apply equally to oligopolies with three or more firms.

TC 9
p 71

TC 3
p 11

Definitions

Nash equilibrium

The position resulting from everyone making their optimal decision based on their assumptions about their rivals' decisions. Without collusion, there is no incentive for any firm to move from this position.

Takeover bid

Where one firm attempts to purchase another by offering to buy the shares of that company from its shareholders.

Kinked demand theory

The theory that oligopolists face a demand curve that is kinked at the current price, demand being significantly more elastic above the current price than below. The effect of this is to create a situation of price stability.

The outcome is one of price cutting until all supernormal profits are competed away. The reason is simple. If Firm A assumes that its rival, Firm B, will hold price constant, then Firm A should undercut this price by a small amount and as a result gain a large share of the market. At this point, Firm B will be forced to respond by cutting its price. What we end up with is a price war until price is forced down to the level of average cost, with only normal profits remaining.

Nash equilibrium. The equilibrium outcome in either the Cournot or Bertrand model is not in the *joint* interests of the firms. In each case, total profits are less than under a monopoly or cartel. But, in the absence of collusion, the outcome is the result of each firm doing the best it can, given its assumptions about what its rivals are doing. The resulting equilibrium is known as a **Nash equilibrium** after John Nash, a US mathematician (and subject of the film *A Beautiful Mind*) who introduced the concept in 1951.

In practice, when competition is intense, as in the Bertrand model, the firms may seek to collude long before profits have been reduced to a normal level. Alternatively firms may put in a **takeover bid** for their rival(s).

The kinked demand-curve assumption

In 1939 a theory of non-collusive oligopoly was developed simultaneously on both sides of the Atlantic: in the USA by Paul Sweezy and in Britain by R. L. Hall and C. J. Hitch. This **kinked demand theory** has since become perhaps the most famous of all theories of oligopoly. The model seeks to explain how it is that, even when there is no collusion at all between oligopolists, prices can nevertheless remain stable.

The theory is based on two asymmetrical assumptions:

■ If an oligopolist cuts its price, its rivals will feel forced to follow suit and cut theirs, to prevent losing customers to the first firm.

■ If an oligopolist raises its price, however, its rivals will *not* follow suit since, by keeping their prices the same, they will thereby gain customers from the first firm.

On these assumptions, each oligopolist will face a demand curve that is *kinked* at the current price and output (see Figure 5.12). A rise in price will lead to a large fall in sales as customers switch to the now relatively lower-priced rivals. The firm will thus be reluctant to raise its price. Demand is relatively elastic above the kink. On the other hand, a fall in price will bring only a modest increase in sales, since rivals lower their prices too and therefore customers do not switch. The firm will thus also be reluctant to lower its price. Demand is relatively inelastic below the kink. Thus oligopolists will be reluctant to change prices at all.

This price stability can be shown formally by drawing in the firm's marginal revenue curve, as in Figure 5.13.

To see how this is done, imagine dividing the diagram into two parts either side of Q_1. At quantities less than Q_1 (the left-hand part of the diagram), the *MR* curve will correspond to the shallow part of the *AR* curve. At quantities greater than Q_1 (the right-hand part), the *MR* curve will correspond to the steep part of the *AR* curve. To see how this part of the *MR* curve is constructed, imagine extending the steep part of the *AR* curve back to the vertical axis. This and the corresponding *MR* curve are shown by the dashed lines in Figure 5.13.

As you can see, there will be a gap between points *a* and *b*. In other words, there is a vertical section of the *MR* curve between these two points. Profits are maximised

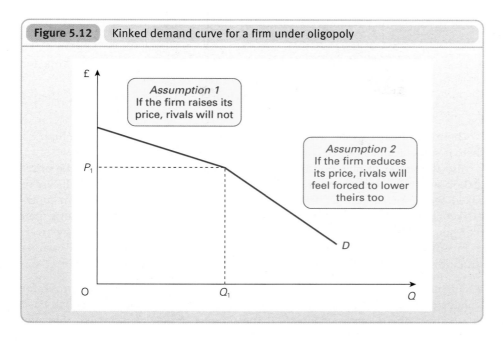

Figure 5.12   Kinked demand curve for a firm under oligopoly

Figure 5.13   Stable price under conditions of a kinked demand curve

where $MC = MR$. Thus, if the MC curve lies anywhere between MC_1 and MC_2 (i.e. between points a and b), the profit-maximising price and output will be P_1 and Q_1. Thus prices will remain stable *even with a considerable change in costs*.

Oligopoly and the consumer

If oligopolists act collusively and jointly maximise industry profits, they will in effect be acting together as a monopoly. In such cases, prices may be very high. This is clearly not in the best interests of consumers.

Furthermore, in two respects, oligopoly may be more disadvantageous than monopoly:

■ Depending on the size of the individual oligopolists, there may be less scope for economies of scale to mitigate the effects of market power.

■ Oligopolists are likely to engage in much more extensive advertising than a monopolist.

These problems will be less severe, however, if oligopolists do not collude, if there is some degree of price competition and if barriers to entry are weak.

Also the power of oligopolists in certain markets may to some extent be offset if they sell their product to other powerful firms. Thus oligopolistic producers of baked beans or soap powder sell a large proportion of their output to giant supermarket chains, which can use their market power to keep down the price at which they purchase these products. This phenomenon is known as **countervailing power**.

In some respects, oligopoly has *advantages* to society over other market structures:

■ Oligopolists, like monopolists, can use part of their supernormal profit for research and development. Unlike monopolists, however, oligopolists will have a considerable *incentive* to do so. If the product design is improved, this may allow the firm to capture a larger share of the market, and it may be some time before rivals can respond with a similarly improved product. If, in addition, costs are reduced by technological improvement, the resulting higher profits will improve the firm's capacity to withstand a price war.

■ Non-price competition through product differentiation may result in greater choice for the consumer. Take the case of stereo equipment. Non-price competition has led to a huge range of different products of many different specifications, each meeting the specific requirements of different consumers.

It is difficult to draw any general conclusions, since oligopolies differ so much in their performance.

> **Definition**
>
> **Countervailing power**
> Where the power of a monopolistic/oligopolistic seller is offset by powerful buyers which can prevent the price from being pushed up.

> **Pause for thought**
>
> *Assume that two brewers announce that they are about to merge. What information would you need to help you decide whether the merger would be in the consumer's interest?*

Recap

1. An oligopoly is where there are just a few firms in the industry with barriers to the entry of new firms. Firms recognise their mutual dependence.

2. Oligopolists want to maximise their joint profits. This tends to make them collude to keep prices high. On the other hand, they want the biggest share of industry profits for themselves. This tends to make them compete.

3. They are more likely to collude if there are few of them; if they are open with each other; if they have similar products and cost structures; if there is a dominant firm; if there are significant entry barriers; if the market is stable; and if there is no government legislation to prevent collusion.

4. Collusion can be open or tacit.

5. A formal collusive agreement is called a 'cartel'. A cartel aims to act as a monopoly. It can set price and leave the members to compete for market share, or it can assign quotas. There is always a temptation for cartel members to 'cheat' by undercutting the cartel price if they think they can get away with it and not trigger a price war.

6. Tacit collusion can take the form of price leadership. This is where firms follow the price set by either a dominant firm in the industry or one seen as a reliable 'barometer' of market conditions. Alternatively, tacit collusion can simply involve following various rules of thumb such as average cost pricing and benchmark pricing.

7. Even when firms do not collude they will still have to take into account their rivals' behaviour.

8. In the Cournot model firms assume that their rivals output is given and then choose the profit-maximising price and output in the light of this assumption. The resulting price and profit are lower than under monopoly, but still higher than under perfect competition.

9. In the Bertrand model firms assume that their rivals' price is given. This will result in prices being competed down until only normal profits remain.

10. In the kinked-demand curve model, firms are likely to keep their prices stable unless there is a large shift in costs or demand.

11. Whether consumers benefit from oligopoly depends on the particular oligopoly and how competitive it is; whether there is any countervailing power; whether the firms engage in extensive advertising and of what type; whether product differentiation results in a wide range of choice for the consumer; and how much of the profits are ploughed back into research and development.

GAME THEORY   5.6

Thinking strategically about rivals' behaviour

KI 18
p 136

Economists use **game theory** to model the strategic interactions between 'players', such as firms, where those choices affect the interests of others. As we have seen, the behaviour of a firm under non-collusive oligopoly depends on how it thinks its rivals will react to its decisions. By using game theory we can try and understand the decisions that these firms make in relation to variables like price, advertising and product development.

> **Definition**
>
> **Game theory (or games theory or the theory of games)**
> The study of alternative strategies that oligopolists may choose to adopt, depending on their assumptions about their rivals' behaviour.

Single-move games

The simplest type of 'game' is a single-move or single-period game. This involves just one 'move' by each firm involved. For example, two or more firms are bidding for a contract which will be awarded to the lowest bidder. When the bids are all made the contract will be awarded to the lowest bidder; the 'game' is over.

> **Pause for thought**
>
> *Can you think of other examples within economics where game theory could help to analyse the choices made by individuals, groups or organisations?*

Simple dominant strategy games

Consider the case where there are just two firms with identical costs, products and demand. They are both considering which of two alternative prices to charge. Table 5.2 shows typical profits they could each make.

Let us assume that at present both firms (X and Y) are charging a price of £2 and that they are each making a profit of £10 million, giving a total industry profit of £20 million. This is shown in the top left-hand cell (A).

Now assume they are both (independently) considering reducing their price to £1.80. In making this decision they will need to take into account what their rival might do, and how this will affect them. Let us consider X's position. In our simple example there are just two things that its rival, firm Y, might do. Either Y could cut its price to £1.80, or it could leave its price at £2. What should X do?

TC 9
p 71

One alternative is to go for the *cautious* approach and think of the worst thing that its rival could do. If X kept its price at £2, the worst thing for X would be if its rival Y cut its price. This is shown by cell C: X's profit falls to £5 million.

Table 5.2	Profits for firms X and Y at different prices

		X's price	
		£2.00	£1.80
Y's price	£2.00	A £10m each	B £5m for Y £12m for X
	£1.80	C £12m for Y £5m for X	D £8m each

If, however, X cut its price to £1.80, the worst outcome would again be for Y to cut its price, but this time X's profit only falls to £8 million. In this case, then, if X is cautious, it will *cut its price to £1.80*. Note that Y will argue along similar lines, and if it is cautious, it too will cut its price to £1.80. This policy of adopting the safer strategy is known as **maximin**. Following a maximin strategy, the firm will opt for the alternative that will maximise its minimum possible profit.

An alternative strategy is to go for the *optimistic* approach and assume that your rivals react in the way most favourable to you. Here the firm goes for the strategy that yields the highest possible profit. In X's case this again means cutting price, only this time on the optimistic assumption that firm Y will leave its price unchanged. If firm X is correct in its assumption, it will move to cell B and achieve the maximum possible profit of £12 million. This strategy of going for the maximum possible profit is known as **maximax**. Note that again the same argument applies to Y. Its maximax strategy will be to cut price and hopefully end up in cell C.

Given that in this 'game' *both* approaches, maximin and maximax, lead to the *same* strategy (namely, cutting price), this is known as a **dominant strategy game**.

The result is that the firms will end up in cell D, earning a lower profit (£8 million each) than if they had charged the higher price (£10 million each in cell A).

As we saw in the Cournot and Bertrand models above, the equilibrium outcome where there is no collusion between the firms (cell D in this game) is known as a **Nash equilibrium**. The Nash equilibrium in this game is cell D.

In our example, collusion rather than a price war would have benefited both firms. Yet, even if they did collude, both would be tempted to cheat and cut prices. This is known as the **prisoner's dilemma**. An example is given in Box 5.4.

More complex games with no dominant strategy

More complex 'games' can be devised with more than two firms, many alternative prices, differentiated products and various forms of non-price competition (e.g. advertising). In such cases, the cautious (maximin) strategy may suggest a different policy (e.g. do nothing) from the high-risk (maximax) strategy (e.g. cut prices substantially).

In complex and changing situations, firms may alter their tactics in the light of new circumstances. Thus in some cases firms may compete hard for a time (in price or non-price terms) and then realise that maybe no one is winning. Firms may then jointly raise prices and reduce advertising. Later, after a period of tacit collusion, competition may break out again. This may be sparked off by the entry of a new

Definitions

Maximin
The strategy of choosing the policy whose worst possible outcome is the least bad.

Maximax
The strategy of choosing the policy that has the best possible outcome.

Dominant strategy game
Where the *same* policy is suggested by different strategies.

Nash equilibrium
The position resulting from everyone making their optimal decision based on their assumptions about their rivals' decisions. Without collusion, there is no incentive for any firm to move from this position.

Prisoner's dilemma
Where two or more firms (or people), by attempting independently to choose the best strategy for whatever the other(s) are likely to do, end up in a worse position than if they had co-operated in the first place.

BOX 5.4   THE PRISONER'S DILEMMA

Game theory is relevant not just to economics. A famous non-economic example is the prisoner's dilemma.

Nigel and Amanda have been arrested for a joint crime of serious fraud. Each is interviewed separately and given the following alternatives:

■ First, if they say nothing, the court has enough evidence to sentence both to a year's imprisonment.
■ Second, if either Nigel or Amanda *alone* confesses, he or she is likely to get only a three-month sentence but the partner could get up to 10 years.
■ Third, if both confess, they are likely to get three years each.

What should Nigel and Amanda do?

Alternatives for Nigel and Amanda

	Amanda's alternatives	
	Not confess	Confess
Not confess	**A** Each gets 1 year	**C** Nigel gets 10 years / Amanda gets 3 months
Confess	**B** Nigel gets 3 months / Amanda gets 10 years	**D** Each gets 3 years

(Nigel's alternatives)

Let us consider Nigel's dilemma. Should he confess in order to get the short sentence (the maximax strategy)? This is better than the year he would get for not confessing. There is, however, an even better reason for confessing. Suppose Nigel doesn't confess but, unknown to him, Amanda does confess. Then Nigel ends up with the long sentence. Better than this is to confess and to get no more than three years: this is the safest (maximin) strategy.

Amanda is in the same dilemma. The result is simple. When both prisoners act selfishly by confessing, they both end up in position D with relatively long prison terms. Only when they collude will they end up in position A with relatively short prison terms, the best combined solution.

Of course the police know this and will do their best to prevent any collusion. They will keep Nigel and Amanda in separate cells and try to persuade each of them that the other is bound to confess.

Thus the choice of strategy depends on:

■ Nigel's and Amanda's risk attitudes: i.e. are they 'risk lovers' or 'risk-averse'?
■ Nigel's and Amanda's estimates of how likely the other is to own up.

1. Why is this a dominant strategy 'game'?
2. How would Nigel's choice of strategy be affected if he had instead been involved in a joint crime with Jeremy, Pauline, Diana and Dave, and they had all been caught?

Let us now look at two real-world examples of the prisoner's dilemma.

Standing behind the goal!

Dean is following his beloved Leicester at yet another away match. He is sitting behind the goal his team are attacking. They break forward at rapid pace. With the prospect of a goal he stands to get a better view. Others follow his lead: after all, if they stayed sitting, they would not see at all.

In this Nash equilibrium, most people are worse off, since, except for tall people, their view is likely to be worse and they lose the comfort of sitting down. If only Dean and others like him could just sit down!

Too much advertising

Why do firms spend so much on advertising? If they are aggressive, they do so to get ahead of their rivals (the maximax approach). If they are cautious, they do so in case their rivals increase their advertising (the maximin approach).

Although in both cases it may be in the individual firm's best interests to increase advertising, the resulting Nash equilibrium is likely to be one of excessive advertising: the total spent on advertising (by all firms) is not recouped in additional sales.

Give one or two other examples (economic or non-economic) of the prisoner's dilemma.

firm, by the development of a new product design, by a change in market demand, or simply by one or more firms no longer being able to resist the temptation to 'cheat'. In short, the behaviour of particular oligopolists may change quite radically over time.

Repeated games

In many situations firms will *react* to what their rivals do; their rivals, in turn, will react to what they do. In other words, the game moves back and forth from one 'player' to the other like a game of chess or cards. Firms will still have to think strategically (as you do in chess), considering the likely responses of their rivals to their own actions. These multiple-move games are known as *repeated games* or *extensive-form games*.

One of the simplest repeated games is the *tit-for-tat*. This is where a firm will cut prices, or make some other aggressive move, *only* if the rival does so first. To illustrate this repeated game let us look again at the example we considered in Table 5.2, but this time we will extend it beyond one time period.

Assume that firm X is adopting the tit-for-tat strategy. If firm Y cuts its price from £2.00 to £1.80, then firm X will respond in round 2 by also cutting its price. The two firms will end up in cell D – worse off than if neither had cut their price. If, however, firm Y had left its price at £2.00 then firm X would respond by leaving its price unchanged too. Both firms would remain in cell A with a higher profit than cell D.

As long as firm Y knows that firm X will respond in this way, it has an incentive not to cut its price. Thus it is in X's interests to make sure that Y clearly 'understands' how X will react to any price cut. In other words, X will make a threat.

The importance of threats and promises

In many situations, an oligopolist will make a threat or promise that it will act in a certain way. As long as the threat or promise is **credible** (i.e. its competitors believe it), the firm can gain and it will influence its rivals' behaviour.

Take the simple situation where a large oil company, such as Esso, states that it will match the price charged by any competitor within a given radius. Assume that competitors believe this 'price promise' but also that Esso will not try to *undercut* their price. In the simple situation where there is only one other filling station in the area, what price should it charge? Clearly it should charge the price that would maximise its profits, assuming that Esso will charge the *same* price. In the absence of other filling stations in the area, this is likely to be a relatively high price.

Now assume that there are several filling stations in the area. What should the company do now? Its best bet is probably to charge the same price as Esso and hope that no other company charges a lower price and forces Esso to cut its price. Assuming that Esso's threat is credible, other companies are likely to reason in a similar way.

The importance of timing

Most decisions by oligopolists are made by one firm at a time rather than simultaneously by all firms. Sometimes a firm will take the initiative. At other times it will respond to decisions taken by other firms.

Take the case of a new generation of large passenger aircraft that can fly further without refuelling. Assume that there is a market for a 500-seater version of this type of aircraft and a 400-seater version, but that the market for each size of aircraft is not big enough for the two manufacturers, Boeing and Airbus, to share it profitably. Let us also assume that the 400-seater market would give an annual

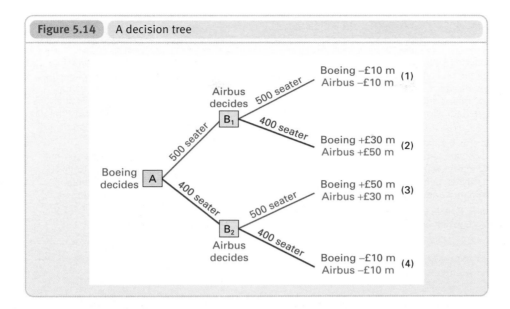

Figure 5.14   A decision tree

profit of £50 million to a single manufacturer and that the 500-seater would give an annual profit of £30 million, but that if both manufacturers produced the same version, they would each make an annual loss of £10 million.

Assume that Boeing announces that it is building the 400-seater plane. What should Airbus do? The choice is illustrated in Figure 5.14. This diagram is called a **decision tree** and shows the sequence of events. The small square at the left of the diagram is Boeing's decision point (point A). If it had decided to build the 500-seater plane, we would move up the top branch. Airbus would now have to make a decision (point B_1). If it too built the 500-seater plane, we would move to outcome 1: a loss of £10 m for both manufacturers. Clearly, with Boeing building a 500-seater plane, Airbus would choose the 400-seater plane: we would move to outcome 2, with Boeing making a profit of £30 million and Airbus a profit of £50 million. Airbus would be very pleased!

Boeing's best strategy at point A, however, would be to build the 400-seater plane. We would then move to Airbus's decision point B_2. In this case, it is in Airbus's interests to build the 500-seater plane. Its profit would be only £30 million (outcome 3), but this is better than the £10 m loss if it too built the 400-seater plane (outcome 4). With Boeing deciding first, the Nash equilibrium will thus be outcome 3.

There is clearly a **first-mover advantage** here. Once Boeing has decided to build the more profitable version of the plane, Airbus is forced to build the less profitable one. Naturally, Airbus would like to build the more profitable one and be the first mover. Which company succeeds in going first depends on how advanced they are in their research and development and in their production capacity.

More complex decision trees. The aircraft example is the simplest version of a decision tree, with just two companies and each one making only one key decision. In many business situations, much more complex trees could be constructed. The 'game' would be more like chess, with many moves and several options on each move. If there were more than two companies, the decision tree would be more complex still.

KI 18
p 136

Definitions

Decision tree (or game tree)
A diagram showing the sequence of possible decisions by competitor firms and the outcome of each combination of decisions.

First-mover advantage
When a firm gains from being the first to take action.

Pause for thought

Give an example of decisions that two firms could make in sequence, each one affecting the other's next decision.

Recap

1. Game theory is a way of modelling behaviour in strategic situations where the outcome for an individual or firm depends on the choices made by others. It enables us to examine various strategies that firms can adopt when the outcome of each is not certain.

2. The simplest type of 'game' is a single-move or single-period game. Many single-period games have predictable outcomes, no matter what assumptions each firm makes about its rivals' behaviour. Such games are known as dominant strategy games.

3. Non-collusive oligopolists will have to work out a price strategy. They can adopt a low-risk 'maximin' strategy

of choosing the policy that has the least-bad worst outcome, or a high-risk 'maximax' strategy of choosing the policy with the best possible outcome, or some compromise. Either way, a 'Nash' equilibrium is likely to be reached which is not in the best interests of the firms collectively. It will entail a lower level of profit than if they had colluded.

4. In repeated games, firms will respond not only to what rival firms do, but what they say they will do. To this end, a firm's threats of promises must be credible, if they are to influence rivals' decisions. A decision tree can be constructed to show the possible sequence of moves in a repeated game.

5.7 PRICE DISCRIMINATION

In what situations will firms be able to charge different prices to different consumers? How will we as consumers benefit or lose from the process?

Up to now we have assumed that a firm will sell its output at a single price. Sometimes, however, firms may practise **price discrimination**. This is where consumers are grouped into two or more independent markets and a separate price is charged in each market, even though there is no difference in costs of production or supply. Examples include different-priced seats on buses for adults and children, different prices for the same seats on aircraft (depending on when they are booked), and different prices charged for the same product in different countries or different parts of the same country. (There are other forms of price discrimination, but this – known as 'third-degree price discrimination' – is the most common.)

Conditions necessary for price discrimination to operate

As we shall see, a firm will be able to increase its profits if it can engages in price discrimination. But under what circumstances will it be able to charge discriminatory prices? There are three conditions that must be met:

■ The firm must be able to set its price. Thus price discrimination will be impossible under perfect competition, where firms are price takers.
■ The markets must be separate. Consumers in the low-priced market must not be able to resell the product in the high-priced market. For example, children must not be able to resell a half-priced child's cinema ticket for use by an adult.
■ Demand elasticity must differ in each market. The firm will charge the higher price in the market where demand is less elastic, and thus less sensitive to a price rise.

Advantages to the firm

Price discrimination allows the firm to earn a higher revenue from any given level of sales. Figure 5.15 represents a firm's demand curve. If it is to sell 200 units without

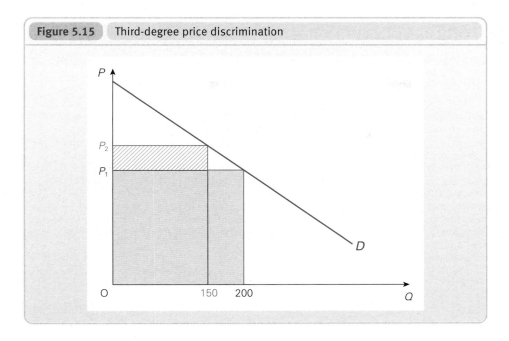

Figure 5.15 Third-degree price discrimination

price discrimination, it must charge a price of P_1. The total revenue it earns is shown by the blue area. If, however, it can practise price discrimination by selling 150 of those 200 units at the higher price of P_2, it will gain the pink-striped area in addition to the blue area.

Another advantage the firm gains by price discrimination is that it may be able to use it to drive competitors out of business. If a firm has a monopoly in one market (e.g. the home market), it may be able to charge a high price due to its relatively inelastic demand, and thus make high profits. If it is under oligopoly in another market (e.g. the export market), it may use the high profits in the first market to subsidise a very low price in the oligopolistic market, thus forcing its competitors out of business.

 Large bus companies in the UK have been accused of doing this. They use the profits made from the high fares on routes where they face no competition to subsidise fares on routes where they do face competition, often from a small rival attempting to break into the market. The aim is to drive the small company out of business. Sometimes on these routes, the large company charges fares that are below cost (thereby making a temporary loss on these routes). This practice is known as **predatory pricing**.

Price discrimination and the consumer

No clear-cut decision can be made over the desirability of price discrimination from the point of view of the consumer. Some people will benefit from it; others will lose. Those paying the higher price will probably feel that price discrimination is unfair to them. On the other hand, those charged the lower price may thereby be able to obtain a good or service they could otherwise not afford: e.g. concessionary bus fares for senior citizens.

Competition. As explained above, a firm may use price discrimination to drive competitors out of business. On the other hand, it might use its profits from its

Definition

Predatory pricing
Selling at a price below average variable cost in order to drive competitors from the market.

BOX 5.5   PROFIT-MAXIMISING PRICES AND OUTPUT FOR A PRICE-DISCRIMINATING FIRM

EXPLORING ECONOMICS

Identifying different prices in different markets

Assuming that a firm wishes to maximise profits, what discriminatory prices should it charge and how much should it produce?

Assume that the firm sells an identical product in two separate markets X and Y with demand and *MR* curves as shown in the diagrams.

Diagram (c) shows the *MC* and *MR* curves for the firm as a whole. This *MR* curve is found by adding the amounts sold in the two markets at each level of *MR* (in other words, the horizontal addition of the two *MR* curves). Thus, for example, with output of 1000 units in market X and 2000 in market Y, making 3000 in total, revenue would increase by £5 if one extra unit were sold, whether in market X or Y.

Total profit is maximised where $MC = MR$: i.e. at an output of 3000 units in total. This output must then be divided between the two markets so that *MC* is equal to *MR* in each market: i.e. $MC = MR = £5$ in each market. *MR* must be the same in both markets, otherwise revenue could be increased by switching output to the market with the higher *MR*.

The profit-maximising price in each market will be given by the relevant demand curve. Thus, in market X, 1000 units will be sold at £9 each; in market Y, 2000 units will be sold at £7 each.

 Why is the higher price charged in the market with the less elastic demand curve?

Profit-maximising output under third-degree price discrimination

(a) Market X   (b) Market Y   (c) Total (markets X + Y)

high-priced market to break into another market and withstand a possible price war. Competition is thereby increased.

Profits. Price discrimination raises a firm's profits. This could be seen to be against the interests of the consumer, especially if the average price of the product is raised. On the other hand, the higher profits may be reinvested and lead to lower costs in the future.

Recap

1. Price discrimination is where a firm sells the same product at different prices in different markets.

2. Price discrimination allows the firm to earn a higher revenue from a given level of sales.

3. Some people will gain from price discrimination; others will lose. It is likely to be particularly harmful when it is used as a means of driving competitors from the market (predatory pricing).

QUESTIONS

1. A perfectly competitive firm faces a price of £14 per unit. It has the following short-run cost schedule.

Output	0	1	2	3	4	5	6	7	8
TC (£)	10	18	24	30	38	50	66	91	120

   (a) Copy the table and put in additional rows for average cost and marginal cost at each level of output. (Enter the figures for marginal cost in the space between each column.)
   (b) Plot AC, MC and MR on a diagram.
   (c) Mark the profit-maximising output.
   (d) How much (supernormal) profit is made at this output?
   (e) What would happen to the price in the long run if this firm were typical of others in the industry? Why would we need to know information about long-run average cost in order to give a precise answer to this question?

2. If the industry under perfect competition faces a downward-sloping demand curve, why does an individual firm face a horizontal demand curve?

3. On a diagram similar to Figure 5.3, show the long-run equilibrium for both firm and industry under perfect competition. Now assume that the demand for the product falls. Show the short-run and long-run effects.

4. If supernormal profits are competed away under perfect competition, why will firms have an incentive to become more efficient?

5. Is it a valid criticism of perfect competition to argue that it is incompatible with economies of scale?

6. As an illustration of the difficulty in identifying monopolies, try and decide which of the following are monopolies: British Telecom; a local evening newspaper; a water company; the village post office; the Royal Mail; Interflora; the London Underground; ice-creams in the cinema; Guinness; food sold in a train buffet car; Tipp-Ex; the board game 'Monopoly'.

7. Try this brain teaser. A monopoly would be expected to face an inelastic demand. After all, there are no direct substitutes. And yet, if it produces where $MR = MC$, MR must be positive, and demand must therefore be elastic. Therefore the monopolist must face an elastic demand! Can you solve this conundrum?

8. For what reasons would you expect a monopoly to charge (a) a higher price, and (b) a lower price than if the industry were operating under perfect competition?

9. In which of the following industries are exit costs likely to be low: (a) steel production; (b) market gardening; (c) nuclear power generation; (d) specialist financial advisory services; (e) production of fashion dolls; (f) production of a new drug; (g) contract catering; (h) mobile discos; (i) car ferry operators? Are these exit costs dependent on how narrowly the industry is defined?

10. Think of three examples of monopolies (local or national) and consider how contestable their markets are.

11. Think of ten different products or services and estimate roughly how many firms there are in the market. You will need to decide whether 'the market' is a local one, a national one or an international one. In what ways do the firms compete in each of the cases you have identified?

12. Assume that a monopolistically competitive industry is in long-run equilibrium. On a diagram like Figure 5.7, show the effect of a fall in demand on a firm's price and profit in (a) the short run and (b) the long run.

13. Imagine there are two types of potential customer for jam sold by a small food shop. The one is the person who has just run out and wants some now. The other is the person who looks in the cupboard, sees that the pot of jam is less than half full and thinks, 'I will soon need some more'. How will the price elasticity of demand differ between these two customers?

14. Why may a food shop charge higher prices than supermarkets for 'essential items' and yet very similar prices for delicatessen items?

15. Firms under monopolistic competition generally have spare capacity. Does this imply that if, say, half of the petrol stations were closed down, the consumer would benefit? Explain.

16. Will competition between oligopolists always reduce total industry profits?

17. In which of the following industries is collusion likely to occur: bricks, beer, margarine, cement, crisps, washing powder, carpets?

18. Devise a box diagram like that in Table 5.2 (on page 148), only this time assume that there are three firms each considering the two strategies of keeping price the same or reducing it by a set amount. Is the game still a 'dominant strategy game'?

19. What do you understand by a 'repeated game'? Give examples of how the outcomes from a repeated game may differ from those in single-move games?

20. Which of the following are examples of effective countervailing power?

(a) Power stations buying coal from a large mining company.
(b) A large office hiring a photocopier from Rank Xerox.
(c) Marks and Spencer buying clothes from a garment manufacturer.

(d) A small village store (but the only one for miles around) buying food from a wholesaler.

21. Is it the size of the purchasing firm that is important in determining its power to keep down the prices charged by its suppliers?

22. If a cinema could sell all its seats to adults in the evenings at the end of the week, but only a few on Mondays and Tuesdays, what price discrimination policy would you recommend to the cinema in order for it to maximise its weekly revenue?

23. Think of two examples of price discrimination. In what ways do the consumers gain or lose? What information would you need to be certain in your answer?

Log on to MyEconlab and complete the studyplan exercises for this chapter to see how much you have learnt and where you need to revise most. Make sure you access all the supporting textbook resources including the online workbook, newsblog, audio animations, guided solutions and ebook.

Additional case studies in the *Essentials of Economics* MyEconLab (www.pearsoned.co.uk/sloman)

5.1 **Is perfect best?** An examination of the meaning of the word 'perfect' in perfect competition.

5.2 **B2B electronic marketplaces.** This case study examines the growth of firms trading with each other over the Internet (business to business or 'B2B') and considers the effects on competition.

5.3 **Concentration ratios.** One way of measuring the degree of market power in an industry.

5.4 **Windows cleaning.** The examination of Microsoft's market dominance by the US Department of Justice.

5.5 **Airline deregulation in the USA and Europe.** Whether the deregulation of various routes has led to more competition and lower prices.

5.6 **Competition in the pipeline?** Monopoly in the supply of gas.

5.7 **X-inefficiency.** A type of inefficiency suffered by many large firms, resulting in a wasteful use of resources.

5.8 **Edward Chamberlin (1899–1967).** The birth of the monopolistic competition model.

5.9 **The motor vehicle repair and servicing industry.** A case study of monopolistic competition.

5.10 **Curry wars.** Monopolistic competition in the take-away food market.

5.11 **Bakeries: oligopoly or monopolistic competition?** A case study on the bread industry, showing that small-scale local bakeries can exist alongside giant national bakeries.

5.12 **Oligopoly in the brewing industry.** A case study showing how the UK brewing industry is becoming more concentrated.

5.13 **Supermarket wars?** Is there genuine competition or tacit collusion in the UK supermarket sector?

5.14 **The global vitamin cartel.** A case study showing oligopolistic collusion in the production and sale of vitamins.

5.15 **Cartels set in concrete, steel and cardboard.** This examines some of the best-known Europe-wide cartels of recent years.

5.16 **Merger activity.** This examines mergers in Europe: their causes and consequences.

5.17 **A product's life cycle.** How market conditions vary at different stages in a product's life.

5.18 **Peak load pricing.** An example of price discrimination.

5.19 **How do UK companies set prices?** A summary of the findings of a Bank of England survey on how firms set prices in practice.

Websites relevant to this chapter

Numbers and sections refer to websites listed in the Web appendix and hotlinked from this book's website at **www.pearsoned.co.uk/sloman**.

■ For news articles relevant to this chapter, see the *Economics News Articles* link from the book's website.

■ For general news on companies and markets, see websites in section A, and particularly A2, 3, 4, 5, 8, 9, 18, 24, 25, 26, 36. See also A38 and 39 for links to newspapers worldwide; and A42 and A44 for links to economics news articles from newspapers worldwide.

■ For sites that looks at competition and market power, see B2 (third link); E4, 10, 18; G7, 8. See also links in I7, 11, 14 and 17.

■ For sites on game theory, see D4; C20; I17 and 4 (in the EconDirectory section).

Web appendices

5.1 **Measuring monopoly power.** An examination of how the degree of monopoly power possessed by a firm can be measured.

5.2 **The Cournot model.** An extension of the analysis given in the text.

CHAPTER MAP

Wages and the distribution of income

Why do pop stars, footballers and stockbrokers earn such large incomes? Why, on the other hand, do cleaners, hospital porters and workers in clothing factories earn very low incomes?

The explanation for differences in wages lies in the working of labour markets. In the first part of the chapter we will consider how labour markets operate. In particular, we will focus on the determination of wage rates in different types of market: ones where employers are wage takers, ones where they can choose the wage rate, and ones where wage rates are determined by a process of collective bargaining.

In Section 6.4 we ask the more general question of why some people are rich and others poor, and consider the degree of inequality in our society: a society that includes the super-rich, with their luxury yachts and their villas abroad, and people living in slum conditions, with not enough to feed and clothe themselves or their children properly; a society where people begging in the streets are an all too familiar sight.

The chapter closes with a consideration of what can be done to reduce inequality. Is the solution to tax the rich very heavily so that the money can be redistributed to the poor? Or might this discourage people from working so hard? Would it be better, then, to focus on benefits and increase the support for the poor?

After studying this chapter, you should be able to answer the following questions:

- How has the UK labour market changed over the years?
- How are wage rates determined in a perfect labour market?
- What are the determinants of the demand and supply of labour and their respective elasticities?
- What forms of market power exist in the labour market and what determines the power of employers and labour?
- What effects do powerful employers and trade unions have on wages and employment?
- What are the causes of inequality and how do we measure inequality?
- What can the government do to reduce inequality?

6.1 LABOUR MARKET TRENDS

How has the pattern of employment changed in recent years?

The labour market has undergone great change in recent years. Advances in technology, changes in the pattern of output, a need to be competitive in international markets and various social changes have all contributed to changes in work practices and in the structure and composition of the workforce.

Major changes include the following:

■ A shift from agricultural and manufacturing to service-sector employment. Figure 6.1 reveals that employment in agriculture has been falling over a long historical period. The fall in manufacturing employment, however, has been more recent, starting in the 1960s and gathering pace since. By contrast, employment in the service industries has grown steadily since 1946. In fact since 1979, it has expanded by over 7 million jobs.

■ A rise in part-time employment. In 1971 approximately one in six workers in the UK was part-time; by 2009 this had risen to one worker in four. In the EU as a whole, the figure is one in six. The growth in part-time work reflects the growth in the service sector, where many jobs are part-time.

■ A rise in female participation rates. Women now constitute approximately half of the paid labour force. The rise in participation rates is strongly associated with the growth in the service sector and the creation of part-time positions. In the early 1970s in the UK, around 36 per cent of jobs were filled by women; by the end of the 2000s this was 46 per cent.

■ A rise in the proportion of workers employed on fixed-term contracts, or on a temporary or casual basis. Many firms nowadays prefer to employ only their core workers/managers on a permanent ('continuing') basis. They feel that it gives them more flexibility in responding to changing market conditions to have the

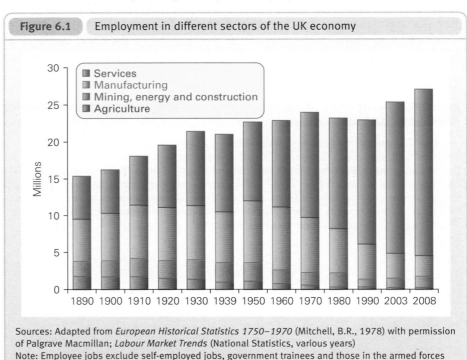

| Figure 6.1 | Employment in different sectors of the UK economy |

Sources: Adapted from *European Historical Statistics 1750–1970* (Mitchell, B.R., 1978) with permission of Palgrave Macmillan; *Labour Market Trends* (National Statistics, various years)
Note: Employee jobs exclude self-employed jobs, government trainees and those in the armed forces

remainder of their workers employed on a short-term basis, and, perhaps, to make use of agency staff or to contract out work.

Box 6.1 considers in more detail some of the notable patterns in recent UK employment data.

| BOX 6.1 | PATTERNS IN UK EMPLOYMENT | CASE STUDIES & APPLICATIONS |

The story of the disappearing full-time male?

We consider here some of the changes that have occurred in both the level and type of employment in the UK.

An increase in total employment. Total employment in the UK increased from 24.6 million in February 1971 (74.9% of working age) to 29.2 million in February 2009 (73.6% of working age). This increase is almost entirely due to rising female employment, which increased by almost one-half to 13.5 million. As a result, the male:female share of employment changed from 63:37 to 54:46.

Growth in part-time employment. The UK has also seen a marked growth in the number of part-time workers (see table). One-quarter of all jobs are now part-time and, of these, three-quarters are filled by women. However, there has also been a growth in part-time work amongst men, doubling between 1992 and 2009 to over 1.8 million. While men still overwhelmingly work full-time, nearly 12 per cent in 2009 had part-time jobs.

Growth in workers with second jobs. The UK has also seen considerable growth in the number of workers with more than one job. Some 1.17 million employees (493 000 men and 676 000 women) had second jobs in 2009, compared to 700 000 in 1984.

No systematic trend in total hours worked. An alternative way of measuring the labour input is the number of labour hours worked in a given week. When looking at labour's effect on the volume of goods produced in an economy, this measure allows us to control for changes in the intensity to which labour is used, such as the increase in the number of part-time workers or changes in the amount of overtime by workers.

The chart shows the number of labour hours (millions) supplied *per week* since 1971Q1. While labour hours increased between 1994 and 2008, there is no clear systematic trend over the longer term.

Upward trend in the total number of hours supplied by women. There are, however, contrasting gender trends.

Hours worked per week in the UK

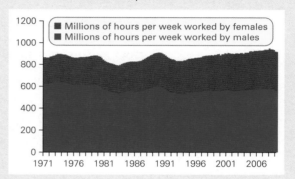

Source: Based on *Time Series Data* from *Economic and Labour Market Review* (National Statistics)

The total number of male hours worked declined with the recession of the early 1980s and levels have never moved above the 600 million per week that were regularly seen in the 1970s. Female hours have, by contrast, shown an upward trend since the 1970s. Interestingly, the number of female hours supplied was not affected by the recessions of the early 1980s and 1990s and remained constant during 2008 as the global financial crisis caused economic activity to contract sharply.

The male–female split of hours supplied has moved from 73:27 in 1971 to 62:38 in 2009. This is less marked than the move in the male–female split of employment from 63:37 to 54:46, reflecting the higher proportion of women in part-time employment.

 What might explain why the total number of labour hours supplied by female workers has been less sensitive to economic downturns than that of male workers?

Gender and part-time mix of employment

| | Employment | | Part-time | | | | |
	Millions	% female	Millions	% of employed	% female	As % of females in employment	As % of males in employment
1984	24.28	41.7	4.99	20.5	87.3	43.0	4.5
1994	25.50	45.3	6.10	24.5	82.6	44.6	7.8
2004	28.49	45.9	7.35	25.8	77.9	43.8	10.6
2009	29.20	46.2	7.54	25.8	75.7	42.2	11.7

Source: *Labour Force Survey* (National Statistics)

6.2 WAGE DETERMINATION IN A PERFECT MARKET

Why are some people paid higher wage rates than others?

Perfect labour markets

When looking at the market for labour, it is useful to make a similar distinction to that made in goods markets: the distinction between perfect and imperfect markets. That way we can gain a clearer understanding of the effects of power, or lack of it, in the labour market. Although in practice few labour markets are totally perfect, many do at least approximate to it.

The key assumption of a perfect labour market is that everyone is a **wage taker**. In other words, neither employers nor employees have any economic power to affect wage rates. This situation is not uncommon. Small employers are likely to have to pay the 'going wage rate' to their employees, especially where the employee is of a clear category, such as an electrician, a bar worker, a secretary or a porter. As far as employees are concerned, being a wage taker means not being a member of a union and therefore not being able to use collective bargaining to push up the wage rate.

Wage rates and employment under perfect competition are determined by the interaction of the market demand and supply of labour. This is illustrated in Figure 6.2. The curves show the total number of hours workers would supply and the number of hours of labour firms would demand for each wage rate in a particular labour market. The equilibrium market wage rate is W_e, where demand equals supply. Equilibrium employment in terms of the total number of hours people are employed in the market is Q_e.

Generally it would be expected that the supply and demand curves slope the same way as in goods markets. The higher the wage rate paid for a certain type of job, the more workers will want to do that job. This gives an upward-sloping supply curve of labour. On the other hand, the higher the wage rate that employers have to pay, the less labour they will want to employ. Either they will simply produce less output, or they will substitute other factors of production, like machinery, for labour. Thus the demand curve for labour slopes downwards.

We now turn to look at the supply and demand for labour in more detail.

TC 5
p 40

The supply of labour

As we have seen, the supply of labour in each market will typically be upward sloping. The *position* of the market supply curve of labour will depend on the number of people willing and able to do the job at each given wage rate. This depends on three things:

Definition

Wage taker
An employer (or employee) who is unable to influence the wage rate.

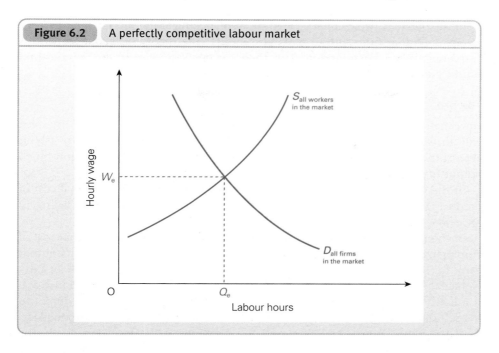

Figure 6.2   A perfectly competitive labour market

- The number of qualified people.
- The non-wage benefits or costs of the job, such as the pleasantness or otherwise of the working environment, job satisfaction or dissatisfaction, status, power, the degree of job security, holidays, perks and other fringe benefits.
- The wages and non-wage benefits in alternative jobs.

A change in the wage rate will cause a movement along the supply curve. A change in any of these other three determinants will shift the whole curve.

> **Pause for thought**
>
> *Which way will the supply curve shift if the wage rates in alternative jobs rise?*

The elasticity of supply of labour

How *responsive* will the supply of labour be to a change in the wage rate? If the market wage rate goes up, will a lot more labour become available or only a little? This responsiveness (elasticity) depends on (a) the difficulties and costs of changing jobs and (b) the time period.

Another way of looking at the elasticity of supply of labour is in terms of the **mobility of labour**: the willingness and ability of labour to move to another job, whether in a different location (geographical mobility) or in a different industry (occupational mobility). The mobility of labour (and hence the elasticity of supply of labour) will be higher when there are alternative jobs in the same location, when alternative jobs require similar skills and when people have good information about these jobs.

> **Definition**
>
> **Mobility of labour**
> The willingness and ability of labour to move to another job.

It is also much higher in the long run, when people have the time to acquire new skills and when the education system has had time to adapt to the changing demands of industry.

The demand for labour: the marginal productivity theory

The market demand curve for labour will typically be downward sloping. To see why, let us examine how many workers an individual firm will want to employ.

In the previous two chapters, when we were looking at the production of goods, we assumed that firms aim to maximise profits. The theory of labour demand is based on the same assumption. This theory is generally known as the **marginal productivity theory**.

The profit-maximising approach

How many workers should a firm employ in order to maximise profits? The firm will answer this question by weighing up the costs of employing extra labour against the benefits. It will use exactly the same principles as in deciding how much output to produce.

In the goods market, the firm will maximise profits where the marginal cost of producing an extra unit of a *good* equals the marginal revenue from selling it: $MC = MR$.

In the labour market, the firm will maximise profits where the marginal cost of employing an extra *worker* equals the marginal revenue that the worker's output earns for the firm: MC of labour = MR of labour. The reasoning is simple. If an extra worker adds more to a firm's revenue than to its costs, the firm's profits will increase. It will be worth employing that worker. But as more workers are employed, diminishing returns to labour will set in (see page 87). Each extra worker will produce less than the previous one, and thus earn less revenue for the firm. Eventually the marginal revenue from extra workers will fall to the level of their marginal cost. At that point, the firm will stop employing extra workers. There are no additional profits to be gained. Profits are at a maximum.

Measuring the marginal cost and revenue of labour

Marginal cost of labour (MC_L)
This is the extra cost of employing one more worker. Under perfect competition the firm is too small to affect the market wage. It faces a horizontal supply curve. In other words, it can employ as many workers as it chooses at the market wage rate. Thus the additional cost of employing one more person will simply be the wage rate: $MC_L = W$.

Marginal revenue of labour (MRP_L)
The marginal revenue that the firm gains from employing one more worker is called the **marginal revenue product of labour** (MRP_L). The MRP_L is found by multiplying two elements – the *marginal physical product* of labour (MPP_L) and the marginal revenue gained by selling one more unit of output (MR).

$$MRP_L = MPP_L \times MR$$

The MPP_L is the extra output produced by the last worker. Thus if the last worker produces 100 tonnes of output per week (MPP_L), and if the firm earns an extra £2 for each additional tonne sold (MR), then the worker's MRP is £200. This extra worker is adding £200 to the firm's revenue.

The profit-maximising level of employment for a firm

The MRP_L curve is illustrated in Figure 6.3. As more workers are employed, there will come a point when diminishing returns set in (point x). Thereafter the MRP_L curve slopes downwards. The figure also shows the MC_L 'curve' at the current market wage W_e.

Profits are maximised at an employment level of Q_e, where MC_L (i.e. the wage rate, W) = MRP_L. Why? At levels of employment less than Q_e, MRP_L exceeds MC_L.

TC 2
p 10

KI 15
p 87

KI 15
p 87

TC 2
p 10

Definitions

Marginal productivity theory
The theory that the demand for a factor depends on its marginal revenue product.

Marginal revenue product (of a factor)
The extra revenue a firm earns from employing one more unit of a variable factor: $MRP_{factor} = MPP_{factor} \times MR_{good}$

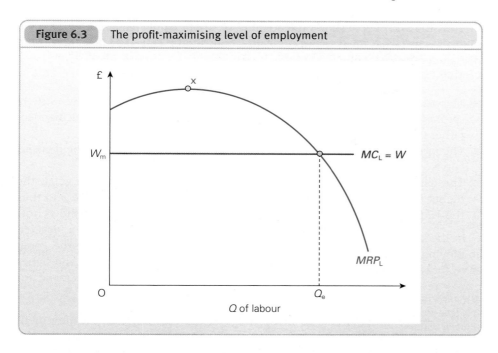

Figure 6.3   The profit-maximising level of employment

The firm will increase profits by employing more labour. At levels of employment greater than Q_e, MC_L exceeds MRP_L. In this case the firm will increase profits by reducing employment.

Derivation of the firm's demand curve for labour

No matter what the wage rate, the quantity of labour demanded will be found from the intersection of W and MRP_L (see Figure 6.4). At a wage rate of W_1, Q_1 labour is demanded (point *a*); at W_2, Q_2 is demanded (point *b*); at W_3, Q_3 is demanded (point *c*).

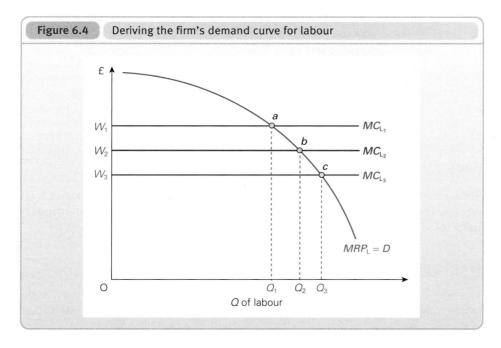

Figure 6.4   Deriving the firm's demand curve for labour

Thus the MRP_L curve shows the quantity of labour employed at each wage rate. But this is just what the demand curve for labour shows. Thus the MRP_L curve is the demand curve for labour.

There are three determinants of the demand for labour by a firm:

- The wage rate. This determines the position *on* the demand curve. (Strictly speaking we would refer here to the wage determining the 'quantity demanded' rather than the 'demand'.)
- The productivity of labour (MPP_L). This determines the position *of* the demand curve.
- The demand for the good. The higher the market demand for the good, the higher will be its market price, and hence the higher will be the MR, and thus the MRP_L. This too determines the position of the demand curve. It shows how the demand for labour (and other factors) is a **derived demand**: i.e. one derived from the demand for the good. For example, the higher the demand for houses, and hence the higher their price, the higher will be the demand for bricklayers.

A change in the wage rate is represented by a movement along the demand curve for labour. A change in the productivity of labour or in the demand for the good *shifts* the curve.

Definition

Derived demand
The demand for a factor of production depends on the demand for the good which uses it.

Pause for thought

If the productivity of a group of workers rises by 10 per cent, will the wage rate they are paid also rise by 10 per cent? Explain why or why not.

Market demand and its elasticity

For the same reason that the firm's demand for labour is downward sloping, so the whole market demand for labour will be downward sloping. At higher wage rates, firms in total will employ less labour.

The *elasticity* of this market demand for labour (with respect to changes in the wage rate) depends on various factors. Elasticity will be greater:

KI 11
p 67

The greater the price elasticity of demand for the good. A rise in the wage rate, being a cost of production, will drive up the price of the good. If the market demand for the good is elastic, this rise in price will lead to a lot less being sold and hence a lot fewer people being employed.

The easier it is to substitute labour for other factors and vice versa. If labour can be readily replaced by other inputs (e.g. machinery), then a rise in the wage rate will lead to a large reduction in labour as workers are replaced by these other inputs.

The greater the wage cost as a proportion of total costs. If wages are a large proportion of total costs and the wage rate rises, total costs will rise significantly; therefore production will fall significantly, and so too will the demand for labour.

The longer the time period. Given sufficient time, firms can respond to a rise in wage rates by reorganising their production processes. For example they could introduce robot production lines.

Wages and profits under perfect competition

The wage rate (W) is determined by the interaction of demand and supply in the labour market. This will be equal to the value of the output that the last person produces (MRP_L).

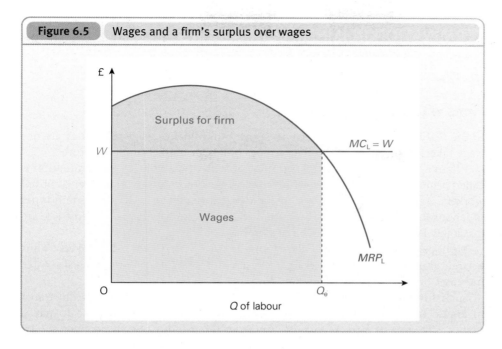

Figure 6.5   Wages and a firm's surplus over wages

Profits to the individual firm arise from the fact that the MRP_L curve slopes downward (diminishing returns), with the last worker adding less to the revenue of firms than previous workers already employed.

If *all* workers in the firm receive a wage equal to the *MRP* of the last worker, everyone but the last worker will receive a wage *less* than their *MRP*. This excess of MRP_L over W of previous workers provides a surplus to the firm over its wages bill (see Figure 6.5). Part of this will be required for paying non-wage costs; part will be profits for the firm.

Perfect competition between firms will ensure that profits are kept down to *normal* profits. If the surplus over wages is such that *supernormal* profits are made, new firms will enter the industry. The price of the good (and hence MRP_L) will fall, and the wage rate will be bid up, until only normal profits remain.

TC 4
p 21

KI 17
p 122

Recap

1. Wage rates in a competitive labour market are determined by the interaction of demand and supply.

2. The market supply of labour curve will normally be upward sloping. Its elasticity will depend on the occupational and geographical mobility of labour. The more readily labour can transfer between jobs and regions, the more elastic will be the supply of labour.

3. The demand for labour depends on labour's productivity. A profit-maximising employer will continue taking on extra workers until MRP_L has fallen (due to diminishing returns) to equal MC_L (= W under perfect competition).

4. The firm's demand curve for labour is its MRP_L curve.

5. The elasticity of demand for labour depends on the elasticity of demand for the good, the ease of substituting labour for other factors and vice versa, wages as a proportion of total costs, and the time period involved.

6. If supernormal profits are made, new firms will enter the industry. The price of the good will fall, and the wage rate will be bid up, until only normal profits remain.

6.3   WAGE DETERMINATION IN IMPERFECT MARKETS

How are wage rates affected by big business and by unions?

Firms with power

Definitions

Monopsony
A market with a single buyer or employer.

Oligopsony
A market with just a few buyers or employers.

In the real world, many firms have the power to influence wage rates: they are not wage takers. This is one of the major types of labour market 'imperfection'.

When a firm is the only employer of a particular type of labour, this situation is called a **monopsony**. The Post Office used to be a monopsony employer of postal workers. Another example is when a factory is the only employer of certain types of labour in that district. It therefore has local monopsony power. When there are just a few employers, this is called **oligopsony**.

Monopsonists (and oligopsonists too) are 'wage setters' not 'wage takers'. Thus a large employer in a small town may have considerable power to resist wage increases or even to force wage rates down.

KI 16
p 116

Such firms face an upward-sloping supply curve of labour. This is illustrated in Figure 6.6. If the firm wants to take on more labour, it will have to pay a higher wage rate to attract workers away from other industries. But conversely, by employing less labour it can get away with paying a lower wage rate. The supply curve shows the wage rate that must be paid to attract a given quantity of labour. The wage rate it pays is the *average cost* to the firm of employing labour (AC_L): i.e. the cost per worker. The supply curve is also therefore the AC_L curve.

The *marginal* cost of employing one more worker (MC_L) will be above the wage (AC_L): see Figure 6.6. The reason is that the wage rate has to be raised to attract extra workers. The MC_L will thus be the new higher wage paid to the new employee *plus* the small rise in the total wages bill for existing employees: after all, they will be paid the higher wage too.

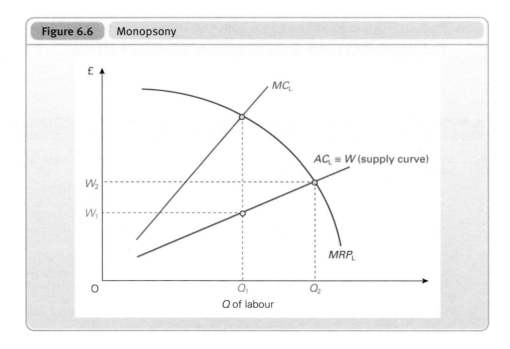

Figure 6.6   Monopsony

The profit-maximising employment of labour would be at Q_1, where $MC_L = MRP_L$. The wage (found from the AC_L curve) would thus be W_1.

If this had been a perfectly competitive labour market, employment would have been at the higher level Q_2, with the wage rate at the higher level W_2, where $W = MRP_L$. What in effect the monopsonist is doing, therefore, is forcing the wage rate down by restricting the number of workers employed.

The role of trade unions

How can unions influence the determination of wages, and what might be the consequences of their actions?

The extent to which unions will succeed in pushing up wage rates depends on their power and militancy. It also depends on the power of firms to resist and on their ability to pay higher wages. In particular, the scope for unions to gain a better deal for their members depends on the sort of market in which the employers are producing.

Unions facing competitive employers

If the employers are producing under perfect or monopolistic competition, unions can raise wage rates only at the expense of employment. Firms are only earning normal profit. Thus if unions force up the wage rate, the marginal firms will go bankrupt and leave the industry. Fewer workers will be employed. The fall in output will lead to higher prices. This will enable the remaining firms to pay a higher wage rate.

Figure 6.7 illustrates these effects. If unions force the wage rate up from W_1 to W_2, employment will fall from Q_1 to Q_2. There will be a surplus of people ($Q_3 - Q_2$) wishing to work in this industry for whom no jobs are available.

The union is in a doubly weak position. Not only will jobs be lost as a result of forcing up the wage rate, but also there is a danger that these unemployed people

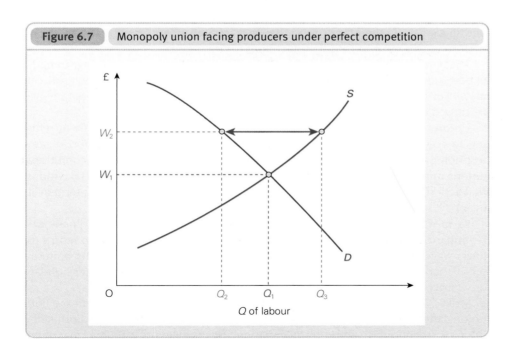

Figure 6.7   Monopoly union facing producers under perfect competition

will undercut the union wage, unless the union can prevent firms from employing non-unionised labour.

Wage rates can be increased without a reduction in the level of employment only if, as part of the bargain, the productivity of labour is increased. This is called a **productivity deal**. The *MRP* curve, and hence the *D* curve in Figure 6.7, shifts to the right.

Bilateral monopoly

What happens when a union monopoly faces a monopsony employer? What will the wage rate be? What will the level of employment be? Unfortunately, economic theory cannot give a precise answer to these questions. There is no 'equilibrium' level as such (see Box 6.2). Ultimately the wage rate and level of employment will depend on the relative bargaining strengths and skills of unions and management.

Strange as it may seem, unions may be in a stronger position to make substantial gains for their members when they are facing a powerful employer. There is often considerable scope for them to increase wage rates *without* this leading to a reduction in employment, or even for them to increase both the wage rate *and* employment. The reason is that if firms have power in the *goods* market too, and are making supernormal profit, then there is scope for a powerful union to redistribute some of these profits to wages.

The actual wage rate under bilateral monopoly is usually determined through a process of negotiation or 'collective bargaining'. The outcome of this bargaining will depend on a wide range of factors, which vary substantially from one industry or firm to another.

Collective bargaining

Sometimes when unions and management negotiate, *both* sides can gain from the resulting agreement. For example, the introduction of new technology may allow higher wages, improved working conditions and higher profits. Usually, however, one side's gain is the other's loss. Higher wages means lower profits. Either way, both sides will want to gain the maximum for themselves.

The outcome of the negotiations will depend on the relative bargaining strengths of both sides. In bargaining there are various threats or promises that either side can make. For these to be effective, of course, the other side must believe that they will be carried out.

Union *threats* might include strike action, **picketing**, **working to rule** or refusing to co-operate with management – for example, in the introduction of new technology. Alternatively, in return for higher wages or better working conditions, unions might *offer* no-strike agreements (or an informal promise not to take industrial action), increased productivity, reductions in the workforce, or long-term deals over pay.

In turn, employers might threaten employees with plant closure, **lock-outs**, redundancies or the employment of non-union labour. Alternatively, in return for lower wage increases, they might offer various 'perks' such as productivity bonuses, profit-sharing schemes, better working conditions, more overtime, better holidays or security of employment.

Strikes, lock-outs and other forms of industrial action impose costs on both unions and firms. Unions lose pay. Firms lose revenue. It is usually in both sides' interests, therefore, to settle by negotiation. Nevertheless to gain the maximum

| BOX 6.2 | WAGES UNDER BILATERAL MONOPOLY | EXPLORING ECONOMICS |

All to play for?

There is no single equilibrium wage rate under bilateral monopoly. This box shows why.

Assume first that there is no union. The diagram shows that a monopsonist employer will maximise profits by employing Q_1 workers at a wage rate of W_1. (Q_1 is where $MRP_L = MC_L$).

What happens when a union is introduced into this situation? Wages will now be set by negotiation between unions and management. Once the wage rate has been agreed, the employer can no longer drive the wage rate down by employing fewer workers. If it tried to pay less than the agreed wage, it could well be faced by a strike, and thus have a zero supply of labour!

Similarly, if the employer decided to take on *more* workers, it would not have to *increase* the wage rate as long as the negotiated wage were above the free-market

wage: as long as the wage rate were above that given by the supply curve S_1.

The effect of this is to give a new supply curve that is horizontal up to the point where it meets the original supply curve. For example, let us assume that the union succeeds in negotiating a wage rate of W_2. The supply curve will be horizontal at this level to the left of point x. To the right of this point it will follow the original supply curve S_1, since to acquire more than Q_3 workers it would have to raise the wage rate above W_2.

If the supply curve is horizontal to the left of point x at a level of W_2, so too will be the MC_L curve. The reason is simply that the extra cost to the employer of taking on an extra worker (up to Q_3) is merely the negotiated wage rate: no rise has to be given to existing employees. If MC_L is equal to the wage, the profit-maximising employment ($MC_L = MRP_L$) will now be where $W = MRP_L$. At a negotiated wage rate of W_2, the firm will therefore choose to employ Q_1 workers.

What this means, therefore, is that the union can push the wage right up from W_1 to W_2 and the firm will still *want* to employ Q_1. In other words, a wage rise can be obtained *without* a reduction in employment.

The union could go further still. By threatening industrial action, it may be able to push the wage rate above W_2 and still insist that Q_1 workers are employed (i.e. no redundancies). The firm may be prepared to see profits drop right down to normal level rather than face a strike and risk losses. The absolute upper limit to the wage rate will be that at which the firm is forced to close down.

Bilateral monopoly

KI 13
p 74

1. *If the negotiated wage rate were somewhere between W_1 and W_2, how would the resulting level of employment compare with that at W_1?*
2. *What in practice will determine just how much the agreed wage rate is above W_1?*

advantage, each side must persuade the other that it will carry out its threats if pushed.

The approach described so far has essentially been one of confrontation. The alternative is for both sides to concentrate on increasing the total net income of the firm by co-operating on ways to increase efficiency or the quality of the product. This approach is more likely when unions and management have built up an atmosphere of trust over time.

The past 30 years has seen a considerable decline in union membership in the UK, falling from 55 per cent of employees in 1979 to 27.5 per cent in 2008. Union density rates vary considerably across countries from around 70 per cent in Sweden, Denmark and Finland to under 12 per cent in the USA and 8 per cent in France. Case Study 6.6 in MyEconLab charts the rise and decline of the labour movement in the UK and offers various explanations.

Definitions

Efficiency wage hypothesis
The hypothesis that the productivity of workers is affected by the wage rate that they receive.

Efficiency wage rate
The profit-maximising wage rate for the firm after taking into account the effects of wage rates on worker motivation, turnover and recruitment.

The efficiency wage hypothesis

We have seen that a union may be able to force an employer to pay a wage above the market-clearing rate. But it may well be in employers' interests to do so, even in non-unionised sectors.

One explanation for this phenomenon is the **efficiency wage hypothesis**. This states that the productivity of workers rises as the wage rate rises. As a result, employers are frequently prepared to offer wage rates above the market-clearing level, attempting to balance increased wage costs against gains in productivity. But why may higher wage rates lead to higher productivity? There are three main explanations.

Less 'shirking'. In many jobs it is difficult to monitor the effort that individuals put into their work. Workers may thus get away with shirking or careless behaviour. The business could attempt to reduce shirking by imposing a series of sanctions, the most serious of which would be dismissal. The greater the wage rate currently received, the greater will be the cost to the individual of dismissal, and the less likely it is, therefore, that workers will shirk. The business will benefit not only from the additional output, but also from a reduction in the costs of having to monitor workers' performance. As a consequence, the **efficiency wage rate** for the business will lie above the market-determined wage rate.

Reduced labour turnover. If workers receive on-the-job training or retraining, then to lose a worker once the training has been completed is a significant cost to the business. Labour turnover, and hence its associated costs, can be reduced by paying a wage above the market-clearing rate. By paying such a wage rate, the business is seeking a degree of loyalty from its employees.

Improved morale. A simple reason for offering wage rates above the market-clearing level is to motivate the workforce – to create the feeling that the firm is a 'good' employer that cares about its employees. As a consequence, workers might be more industrious and more willing to accept the introduction of new technology (with the reorganisation that it involves).

The paying of efficiency wages above the market-clearing wage will depend upon the type of work involved. Workers who occupy skilled positions, especially where the business has invested time in their training (thus making them costly to replace) are likely to receive efficiency wages considerably above the market wage. By contrast, workers in unskilled positions, where shirking can be easily monitored, where little training takes place and where workers can be easily replaced, are unlikely to command an 'efficiency wage premium'. In such situations, rather than keeping wage rates high, the business will probably try to pay as little as possible.

KI 17
p 122

TC 4
p 21

Recap

1. Where a firm has monopoly power in employing labour, it is known as a 'monopsonist'. Such a firm will employ workers to the point where $MRP_L = MC_L$. Since the wage is below MC_L, the monopsonist, other things being equal, will employ fewer workers at a lower wage than would be employed in a perfectly competitive labour market.

2. If a union has monopoly power, its power to raise wages will be limited if the employer operates under perfect or monopolistic competition in the goods market. A rise in wage rates will force the employer to cut back on employment, unless there is a corresponding rise in productivity.

3. In a situation of bilateral monopoly (where a monopoly union faces a monopsony employer) the union may have considerable scope to raise wage rates above the monopsony level. There is no unique equilibrium wage. The wage rate will depend on the outcome of a process of collective bargaining between union and management.

4. Collective bargaining is the process by which employers and unions negotiate wage levels and the terms and conditions of employment. Both sides can use threats and promises to determine the outcome of the negotiating process. The success of such threats and promises depends upon factors such as the power of the union or the employer; attitudes and the determination to win; scope for compromise; negotiating skills; information; and the role of government.

5. The efficiency wage hypothesis states that a firm might pay above the market-clearing wage rate so as to: reduce shirking; reduce labour turnover; improve the quality of labour recruited; and stimulate worker morale. The level of efficiency wage rates will largely be determined by the types of job workers do, and the level and scarcity of the skills they possess.

CAUSES OF INEQUALITY   6.4

Why are some people rich and others poor?

Inequality in the UK

Table 6.1 shows the distribution of household incomes in the UK. The population is placed into five equal-sized groups (or 'quintiles') of households, from the poorest 20 per cent of households up to the richest 20 per cent. Income is measured before government intervention (original income) and then after the receipt of cash benefits from government and the payment of all types of tax (post-tax income). The following points can be drawn from these statistics:

■ In 2007/8, the richest 20 per cent of households earned 51 per cent of original income, and even after the deduction of taxes their share of post-tax income was still 44 per cent.

■ The poorest 20 per cent, by contrast, earned a mere 3 of original income, and even after the receipt of benefits their share of post-tax income was only 6 per cent.

Inequality grew dramatically in the 1980s and 1990s in the UK and many other countries. Between 1977 and 2007/8, the share of post-tax income of the poorest 40 per cent of households fell from 21 per cent to 18 per cent; while the share of the top 20 per cent grew from 36 per cent to 44 per cent.

Distribution of income by source

Households' original income is made up of employment income, income from financial products and income from occupational pensions. If we add to original income the cash benefits paid by government we derive a measure of household income known as gross income. Figure 6.8 shows the sources of gross household incomes in 1975 and 2007/8. Wages and salaries constitute by far the largest element. However, their share fell from 77 per cent to 66 per cent of national income between 1975 and 2007/8. Conversely, the share coming from social security benefits and pensions rose from 12 per cent to 21 per cent, reflecting the growing proportion of the population past retirement age.

Table 6.1	Distribution of UK income by quintile group of households							
	1977		**1987**		**1997/8**		**2007/8**	
	Original income	Post-tax income	Original income	Post-tax income	Original income	Post-tax income	Original income	Post-tax income
Lowest 20%	4	8	2	8	2	7	3	6
Next 20%	11	13	7	12	7	11	8	12
Middle 20%	20	19	16	16	15	16	14	16
Next 20%	26	24	25	22	25	22	24	22
Highest 20%	39	36	50	43	51	44	51	44
All	100	100	100	100	100	100	100	100

Source: *Economic and Labour Market Review* (National Statistics)

Figure 6.8	Sources of UK household income as a percentage of gross household income

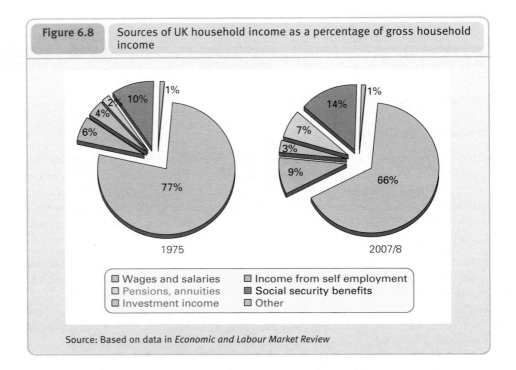

1975   2007/8

- ☐ Wages and salaries
- ☐ Pensions, annuities
- ☐ Investment income
- ☐ Income from self employment
- ☐ Social security benefits
- ☐ Other

Source: Based on data in *Economic and Labour Market Review*

In contrast to wages and salaries, investment income (dividends, interest and rent) accounts for a relatively small percentage of household income – a mere 3 per cent in 2007/8.

With the growth of small businesses and the increased number of people being 'employed' on a freelance basis, the proportion of incomes coming from self-employment has grown. It rose from 6 per cent in 1975 to 9 per cent in 2007/8.

Distribution of wages and salaries by occupation

The major cause of differences in incomes between individuals in employment is the differences in wages and salaries between different occupations. Differences in full-time wages and salaries are illustrated in Figure 6.9. This shows the average gross weekly earnings of full-time adult workers in selected occupations in 2008. As you can see, there are considerable differences in pay between different occupations.

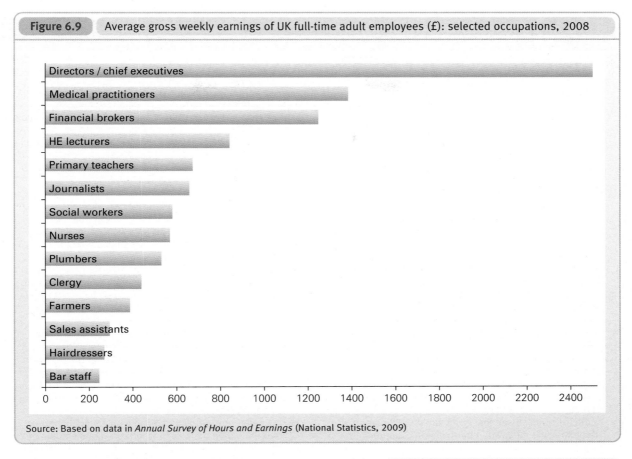

Figure 6.9   Average gross weekly earnings of UK full-time adult employees (£): selected occupations, 2008

Source: Based on data in *Annual Survey of Hours and Earnings* (National Statistics, 2009)

Differences in weekly earnings are mainly the result of differences in hourly rates of pay (see Box 6.3), but are also partly explained by differences in the number of hours worked (including the amount of overtime).

Since the late 1970s, wage differentials have widened. Part of the explanation lies in a shift in the demand for labour. Many firms have adopted new techniques that require a more highly educated workforce. Wage rates in some of these skilled occupations have increased substantially.

At the same time there has been a decline in the number of unskilled jobs in industry, and along with it, a decline in the power of unions to represent such people. Where low-skilled jobs remain, there is intense pressure on employers to reduce wage costs if they are competing with companies based in developing countries, where wage rates are much lower.

As prospects for the unskilled decline in industry, so people with few qualifications increasingly compete for low-paid service-sector jobs (e.g. in supermarkets, fast-food outlets and call centres). The growth in people seeking part-time work has also kept wage rates down in this sector.

Pause for thought

If fringe benefits (such as long holidays, company cars, free clothing/uniforms, travel allowances and health insurance) were included, do you think the level of inequality would increase or decrease? Explain why.

Causes of inequality

We turn now to identify the major causes of inequality. The problem has many dimensions and there are many factors that determine the pattern and depth of

BOX 6.3   EQUAL PAY FOR EQUAL WORK?

Wage inequalities between men and women

Table (a) Average hourly pay (excluding overtime) for full-time UK employees, *aged 18 and over, 1970–2008* (£)

	1970	1974	1978	1982	1986	1990	1994	1998	2002	2004	2006	2008
Men	0.67	1.05	2.00	3.55	4.82	6.89	8.65	10.65	12.92	13.73	14.29	15.54
Women	0.42	0.71	1.48	2.62	3.58	5.28	6.88	8.39	10.32	11.21	11.24	12.88
Women's pay as a % of men's	63.1	67.4	73.9	73.9	74.3	76.6	79.5	78.8	79.9	81.6	78.7	82.9

Source: *Annual Survey of Hours and Earnings* (National Statistics, 2009)

Women earn less than men. How much less depends on how earnings are measured, but on the most widely used definition (see Table (a)), women in the UK earn some 17 per cent less than men. The gender wage gap has narrowed over the years, however; in 1970, women earned 37 per cent less than men.

A similar picture can be seen throughout the EU. In 2005, women's average hourly pay was 85 per cent of men's. The figure varies from one country to another. In Germany it was 78 per cent, whereas in Belgium it was 93 per cent.

The inequality between male and female earnings can in part be explained by the fact that men and women are occupationally segregated. Seeing that women predominate in poorly paid occupations, the difference in earnings is somewhat to be expected. But if you consider Table (b), you can see that quite substantial earnings differentials persist within particular occupations.

1. *If we were to look at weekly rather than hourly pay and included the effects of overtime, what do you think would happen to the pay differentials in Table (a)?*
2. *In Table (b), which of the occupations have a largely female workforce?*

So why has this inequality persisted? There are a number of possible reasons:

■ The marginal productivity of labour in typically female occupations may be lower than in typically male occupations. This may in part be due to simple questions of physical strength. Very often, however, it is due to the fact that women tend to work in more labour-intensive occupations. If there is less capital equipment per female worker than there is per male worker, then it would be expected that the marginal

product of a woman would be less than that of a man. Evidence from the EU as a whole suggests that occupational segregation is a significant factor in explaining pay differences.

■ Many women take career breaks to have children. For this reason, employers are sometimes more willing to invest money in training men (thereby increasing their marginal productivity), and more willing to promote men.

■ Women tend to be less geographically mobile than men. If social norms are such that the man's job is seen as somehow more 'important' than the woman's, then a couple will often move if necessary for the man to get promotion. The woman, however, will have to settle for whatever job she can get in the same locality as her partner.

■ A smaller proportion of women workers are members of unions than men. Even when they are members of unions, these are often in jobs where unions are weak (e.g. clothing industry workers and shop assistants).

■ Part-time workers (mainly women) have less bargaining power, less influence and less chance of obtaining promotion.

■ Custom and practice. Despite equal pay legislation, many jobs done wholly or mainly by women continue to be low-paid, irrespective of productivity.

■ Prejudice. In many jobs women are discriminated against when it comes to promotion, especially to senior positions. Women are seriously underrepresented in boardrooms. This phenomenon is known as 'the glass ceiling'. It is very difficult to legislate against when the employer can simply claim that the 'better' person was promoted.

Which of the above reasons could be counted as economically 'irrational' (i.e. paying different wage rates to women and men for other than purely economic reasons)? Certainly the last two would classify. Paying different wage

inequality. It is thus wrong to try to look for a single cause, or even the major one. What follows then is a list of the possible determinants of inequality:

■ Differences in ability. People differ in intelligence, strength, dexterity, etc. Some of these differences are innate and some are acquired through the process of 'socialisation' – education, home environment, peer group, etc.

Table (b) Average hourly pay, excluding overtime, for selected occupations, full-time UK employees on adult rates, 2008

Occupation	Men	Women	Women's pay as
	£ per hour		a % of men's
Social workers	15.73	15.79	100.4
Nurses	15.05	14.83	98.5
Hairdressers, barbers	7.37	7.05	95.7
Telephonists	10.06	9.60	95.4
Bar staff	6.43	5.89	91.6
Chefs, cooks	8.25	7.54	91.4
Librarians	15.12	13.48	89.2
Secondary school teachers	22.87	20.21	88.4
Sales and retail assistants	8.07	7.13	88.4
Police officers (sergeant and below)	17.41	15.33	88.1
Laboratory technicians	12.66	10.91	86.2
Solicitors, lawyers and judges	31.73	25.90	81.6
Assemblers and routine operatives	9.94	7.93	79.8
Management consultants & economists	25.96	20.17	77.7
Medical practitioners	36.60	28.25	77.2
Personnel managers	30.19	22.18	73.5
Directors / chief executives of major organisations	69.83	46.87	67.1
All occupations	15.54	12.88	82.9
Average *gross weekly* pay (incl. overtime)	631.10	485.50	76.9
Average weekly hours worked (incl. overtime)	40.8	37.6	
Average weekly overtime	1.9	0.7	

Source: *Annual Survey of Hours and Earnings* (National Statistics, 2009)

rates on these grounds would not be in the profit interests of the employer.

Some of the others, however, are more difficult to classify. The causes of the inequality in wage rates may be traced back beyond the workplace: perhaps to the educational system, or to a culture that discourages women from being so aggressive in seeking promotion or 'self-advertisement'.

It is interesting to consider the role that maternity pay and leave may play in the continuation of unequal incomes between women and men. In July 2008 Nicola Brewer, chief executive of the Equality and Human Right Commission, gave a speech in which she called for a rethinking of family policy. In particular she suggested that over-generous treatment of mothers, compared with fathers, was a contributory factor in continuing inequality. By 2010 mothers in the UK will have become entitled to 52 weeks' paid maternity leave while fathers receive two weeks' paternity pay. Ms Brewer argued that this policy perpetuated the view that childcare was a woman's issue rather than a parental one.

The right to request flexible working until the point where a child reaches the age of 16 (a right that is much more likely to be invoked by women than men) is likely to strengthen the view of many employers that women are less valuable employees.

3. *If employers were forced to give genuinely equal pay for equal work, how would this affect the employment of women and men? What would determine the magnitude of these effects?*

4. *How could family policy ensure that parents are able to work, while reducing pay differentials?*

5. *What measures could a government introduce to increase the number of women getting higher-paid jobs?*

■ Differences in attitude. Some people are adventurous, willing to take risks, willing to move for better jobs, keen to push themselves forward. Others are much more cautious.

■ Differences in qualifications. These are reflections of a number of things: ability, attitudes towards study, access to educational establishments, the quality of tuition, attitudes and income of parents, etc.

BOX 6.4	MINIMUM WAGE LEGISLATION

A way of helping the poor?

The Labour government introduced a statutory UK minimum wage in April 1999. The rate was £3.60 per hour for those aged 22 and over and £3.00 for those between 18 and 21. In 2004 an additional rate was introduced for 16- and 17-year-olds. The rates have been increased every year and in 2009/10 were £5.80, £4.83 and £3.57.

The call for a minimum wage grew stronger during the 1990s as the number of low-paid workers within the UK increased. There were many people working as cleaners, kitchen hands, garment workers, security guards and shop assistants, who were receiving pittance rates of pay, sometimes less than £2 per hour. There were several factors explaining the growth in the size of the low-pay sector.

■ *Unemployment*. Very high rates of unemployment since the early 1980s had shifted the balance of power from workers to employers. Employers were able to force many wage rates downwards, especially of unskilled and semi-skilled workers.

■ *Growth in part-time employment*. Changes in the structure of the UK economy, in particular the growth in the service sector and the growing proportion of women seeking work, had led to an increase in part-time employment, with many part-time workers not receiving the same rights, privileges and hourly pay as their full-time equivalents.

■ *Changes in labour laws*. The abolition of wages councils in 1993, which had set legally enforceable minimum hourly rates in various low-paid industries, and the introduction of various new laws to reduce the power of labour had taken away what little protection there was for low-paid workers.

Assessing the arguments

The principal argument against imposing a national minimum wage concerns its impact on employment. Many fear that unemployment will rise as employers respond to higher wage costs by shedding labour. If you raise wage rates above the equilibrium level, there will be surplus labour: i.e. unemployment (see Figure 6.7 on page 169). However, the impact of a national minimum wage on employment is not so simple.

In the case of a firm operating in *competitive* labour and goods markets, the demand for low-skilled workers is relatively wage-sensitive. Any rise in wages paid by this employer would lead to a large fall in its sales and hence in employment. But given that *all* firms face the minimum wage, individual employers are more able to pass on higher wages in higher prices, knowing that their competitors are doing the same.

When employers have a degree of *monopsony* power, however, it is not even certain that they would *want* to reduce employment. Remember what we argued in the diagram in Box 6.2 (on page 171) when we were examining the effects of unions driving up wages. The argument is the same with a minimum wage. The minimum wage can be as high as W_2 and the firm will still want to employ as many workers as at W_2. The point is that the firm can no longer drive down the wage rate by employing fewer workers, so the incentive to cut its workforce has been removed. Indeed, if the minimum wage rate were above W_1 but below W_2, the firm would now want to employ *more* workers (where the minimum wage rate (= MC_L) is equal to the MRP_L). What is effectively happening is that the minimum wage is redistributing the firm's income from profits to wages.

The above three sets of factors will cause differences in people's marginal productivity and hence differences in wage rates. Wages will also reflect the following:

■ Differences in hours worked. Some people do a full-time job plus overtime, or a second job; others work only part-time.

■ Differences in the pleasantness/unpleasantness of jobs. Other things being equal, unpleasant, arduous or dangerous jobs will need to pay higher wage rates.

■ Differences in power. Monopoly power in the supply of labour or goods, and monopsony power in the demand for labour, are unequally distributed in the economy.

■ Differences in the demand for goods. Workers employed in expanding industries will tend to have a higher marginal revenue product because their output has a higher market value.

■ Discrimination, whether by race, sex, age, social background, etc.

Inequality is not just the result of differences in wages. It is also caused by the following:

In the long run, the effect on unemployment will depend on the extent to which the higher wages are compensated by higher labour productivity.

Evidence from the USA and other countries suggests that modest increases in the minimum wage have had a neutral effect upon employment. Similarly in the UK, there is little evidence to suggest that employers have responded by employing fewer workers. In fact, unemployment rates have fallen. This, however, can be explained by a buoyant economy and increasing labour market flexibility (see Case Study 6.2 in MyEconLab).

Whether there would continue to be little effect if the minimum wage were to rise substantially is another matter! The issue, then, seems to be how *high* can the minimum wage be set before unemployment begins to rise.

The impact of the minimum wage in the UK

Some 1.3 million workers benefit from the minimum wage. The main beneficiaries have been women – the majority of whom work part-time and many of whom are lone parents – and people from ethnic minorities. Even the Conservative Party, previously staunch opponents of a minimum wage, has dropped its opposition.

The biggest weakness of minimum wages as a means of relieving poverty is that they only affect the employed. One of the main causes of poverty is unemployment. Clearly the unemployed do not benefit from the minimum wage.

Another cause of poverty is a large number of dependants in a family. If there is only one income earner, he or she may be paid above the minimum wage and yet the family could be very poor. By contrast, many of those who have been helped by the minimum wages are second income earners in a family.

These are not arguments against minimum wages. They merely suggest that minimum wages cannot be the sole answer to poverty.

In the UK, the TUC estimated that there are around 150 000 workers who receive less than the minimum wage and whose employers are breaking the law. It is likely that these workers do not report this as they feel intimidated and fear that they will lose their jobs.

As the economy moved towards recession in 2008/9, employers called for only moderate increases in the minimum wage in order to reduce the likelihood of increased unemployment. The rate awarded from October 2009 was a mere 1.2 per cent (7p).

1. *If an increase in wage rates for the low-paid led to their being more motivated, how would this affect the marginal revenue product and the demand for such workers? What implications does your answer have for the effect on employment in such cases? (See page 172 on the efficiency wage hypothesis.)*
2. *If a rise in the minimum wage encourages employers to substitute machines for workers, will this necessarily lead to higher long-term unemployment in (a) that industry and (b) the economy in general?*

■ Differences in household composition. Other things being equal, the more dependants there are in a household, the lower the income will be *per member* of that household. Figure 6.10 gives an extreme example of this. It shows the average household income in the UK in 2007 of four different categories of household.

The average income of households with two adults and four or more children was considerably less than that of households with only one man and one woman. This means that they had a very much lower income *per member* of the household. There is a twin problem for many large households. Not only may there be relatively more children and old-age dependants, but also the total household income will be reduced if one of the adults stays at home to look after the family, or works only part-time.

■ Inequality of wealth. People with wealth are able to obtain an income other than from their own labour (e.g. from rent or dividends on shares). The greater the inequality of wealth, the greater is the inequality of income likely to be.

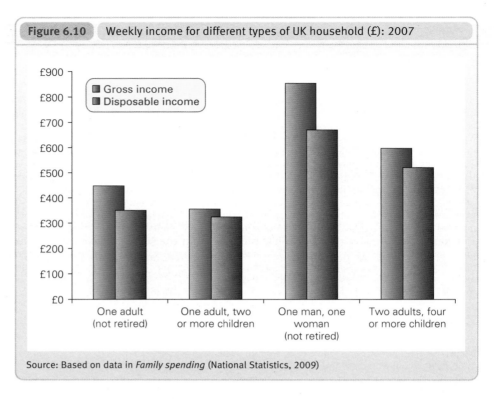

Figure 6.10   Weekly income for different types of UK household (£): 2007

Source: Based on data in *Family spending* (National Statistics, 2009)

Pause for thought

Which of these causes of inequality are reflected in differences in the marginal revenue product of labour?

■ Degree of government support. The greater the support for the poor, the less will be the level of inequality in the economy.

■ Unemployment. This has been one of the major causes of poverty and hence inequality in recent years.

Recap

1. Wages and salaries constitute by far the largest source of income, and thus inequality can be explained mainly in terms of differences in wages and salaries. These differences reflect differences in the productivity of workers, consumer demand, power and discrimination.

2. Apart from differences in wages and salaries between occupations, other determinants of income inequality include differences in household composition, inequality of wealth, unemployment and the level of government benefits.

6.5 THE REDISTRIBUTION OF INCOME

How can income be redistributed from rich to poor? What will be the effects of doing so?

In this section we will look at policies to redistribute incomes more equally, and in particular we will focus on the use of government social security benefits and taxation. In doing so, we will be focusing on the economic and social goal of 'equity'.

Equity is where income is distributed in a way that is considered to be fair or just. Note that an equitable distribution is not the same as a totally equal distribution and that different people have different views on what is equitable.

Taxation

If taxes are to be used as a means of achieving greater equality, the rich must be taxed proportionately more than the poor. The degree of redistribution will depend on the degree of 'progressiveness' of the tax. In this context, taxes may be classified as follows:

- **Progressive tax**. As people's income (Y) rises, the percentage of their income paid in the tax (T) rises. In other words, the average rate of tax (T/Y) rises. Income taxes are progressive (but much less progressive in the UK than they used to be).
- **Regressive tax**. As people's income rises, the percentage of their income paid in the tax falls: T/Y falls. An extreme form of regressive tax is a lump-sum tax. This is levied at a fixed *amount* (not rate) irrespective of income. The 'poll tax', introduced in Scotland in 1989 and in England and Wales in 1990 as the new form of local taxation, was an example of such a tax. But it proved massively unpopular with the electorate, and was replaced by the 'council tax' (based on property values) in 1993.
- **Proportional tax**. As people's income rises, the percentage of their income paid in the tax stays the same: T/Y is constant.

The more progressive a tax, the more it will redistribute incomes away from the rich. Regressive taxes will have the opposite effect, since they tax the rich proportionately less than the poor.

Details of tax rates in the UK are given in Case Study 6.13 in MyEconLab. This case study also examines how progressive or regressive the various types of tax are.

Definitions

Progressive tax
A tax whose average rate with respect to income rises as income rises.

Regressive tax
A tax whose average rate with respect to income falls as income rises.

Proportional tax
A tax whose average rate with respect to income stays the same as income rises.

Problems with using taxes to redistribute incomes

Assuming that it is desirable to redistribute incomes from rich to poor, how successfully can taxes accomplish this, and at what economic cost?

Taxation takes away income. It can thus reduce the incomes of the rich. But no taxes, however progressive, can *increase* the incomes of the poor. This will require subsidies (i.e. benefits).

But what about tax cuts? Can bigger tax cuts not be given to the poor? This is possible only if the poor are already paying taxes in the first place. Take the two cases of income tax and taxes on goods and services.

- Income tax. If the government cuts income tax, then anyone currently paying it will benefit. A cut in tax *rates* will give proportionately more to the rich, since they have a larger proportion of taxable income relative to total income. An increase in personal *allowances*, on the other hand, will give the same *absolute* amount to everyone above the new tax threshold. This will therefore represent a smaller proportionate gain to the rich. In either case, however, there will be no gain at all to those people below the tax threshold. They paid no income tax in the first place. These poorest of all people therefore gain nothing at all from income tax cuts.
- Taxes on goods and services. Since taxes such as VAT and excise duties on alcoholic drinks, tobacco, petrol and gambling are generally regressive, any cut

in their rate will benefit the poor proportionately more than the rich. A more dramatic effect would be obtained by cutting the rate most on those goods consumed relatively more by the poor (e.g. on domestic fuel).

The government may not wish to cut the overall level of taxation, given its expenditure commitments. In this case, it can switch the burden of taxes from regressive to progressive taxes: it could cut taxes on certain goods and services and raise income taxes and taxes on company profits. That way, at least some benefit is gained by the very poor.

Taxation and incentives

One of the major justifications given by the Conservative governments after 1979 for *cutting* both the basic and higher rates of income tax was that it increased the incentive to work.

This whole question of incentives is highly charged politically. If the Conservatives are correct, then there is a trade-off between output and equity. High and progressive income taxes can lead to a more equal distribution of income, but a smaller national output. Alternatively, by cutting taxes there will be a bigger national output, but less equally divided. If many on the political left are correct, however, by raising income taxes we can have both a more equal society and a *bigger* national output: there is no trade-off.

The key to analysing these arguments is to distinguish between the *income effect* and the *substitution effect* of raising taxes. Raising income tax does two things.

- It reduces disposable incomes. People therefore are encouraged to work *more* in an attempt to maintain their consumption of goods and services. This is called the **income effect**. 'I have to work more to make up for the higher taxes', a person might say.
- It reduces the opportunity cost of leisure. Since higher income taxes reduce take-home pay, an extra hour taken in leisure now involves a smaller sacrifice in consumption. Thus people may substitute leisure for consumption, and work less. This is called the **substitution effect**. 'What is the point of doing overtime', another person might say, 'if so much of the overtime pay is going in taxes?'

The relative size of the income and substitution effects is likely to differ for different types of people. For example, the *income* effect is likely to dominate for those people with a substantial proportion of long-term commitments, such as those with families, with mortgages and other debts. They may feel forced to work *more* to maintain their disposable income. Clearly for such people, higher taxes are *not* a disincentive to work. The income effect is also likely to be relatively large for people on higher incomes, for whom an increase in tax rates represents a substantial cut in income.

The *substitution* effect is likely to dominate for those with few commitments: those whose families have left home, the single, and second income earners in families where that second income is not relied on for 'essential' consumption. A rise in tax rates for these people is likely to encourage them to work less.

Although high income earners may work more when there is a tax *rise*, they may still be discouraged by a steeply progressive tax *structure*. If they have to pay very high marginal rates of tax, it may simply not be worth their while seeking promotion or working harder (see Case Study 6.15 in MyEconLab).

One final point should be stressed. For many people there is no choice in the amount they work. The job they do dictates the number of hours worked, irrespective of changes in taxation.

TC 4
p 21

TC 1
p 7

Definitions

Income effect of a tax rise

Tax increases reduce people's incomes and thus encourage people to work more.

Substitution effect of a tax rise

Tax increases reduce the opportunity cost of leisure and thus encourage people to work less.

Benefits

Benefits can be either benefits in kind or cash benefits.

Benefits in kind

Some individuals receive forms of benefit from the state, not as direct monetary payments, but in the form of the provision of free or subsidised goods or services. These are known as **benefits in kind**. The two largest items in most countries are health care and education. They are very differently distributed, however. This difference can largely be explained on age grounds. Old people use a large proportion of health services, but virtually no education services.

Benefits in kind tend to be consumed roughly equally by the different income groups. Nevertheless they do have some equalising effect, since they represent a much larger proportion of poor people's income than rich people's. They have a far smaller redistributive effect, however, than cash benefits.

Cash benefits

Means-tested benefits. **Means-tested benefits** are available only to those whose income (and savings in some instances) fall below a certain level. To obtain such benefits, therefore, people must apply for them and declare their personal circumstances to the authorities.

The benefits could be given as grants or merely as loans. They could be provided as general income support or for the meeting of specific needs, such as rents, fuel bills and household items.

Universal benefits. **Universal benefits** are those that everyone is entitled to, irrespective of their income, if they fall into a certain category. Examples include state pensions, and unemployment, sickness and incapacity benefits.

Figure 6.11 shows the expenditure on social cash benefits in selected European countries since 1998. These include unemployment, sickness, invalidity, maternity, family, survivors' (widows' and orphans') and housing benefits and state pensions.

> **Pause for thought**
>
> *How will tax cuts affect the willingness of women with employed partners to return to paid work after having brought up a family? (Clue: think about the size of the income and substitution effects.)*

> **Definitions**
>
> **Benefits in kind**
> Goods or services which the state provides directly to the recipient at no charge or at a subsidised price. Alternatively, the state can subsidise the private sector to provide them.
>
> **Means-tested benefits**
> Benefits whose amount depends on the recipient's income or assets.
>
> **Universal benefits**
> Benefits paid to everyone in a certain category irrespective of their income or assets.

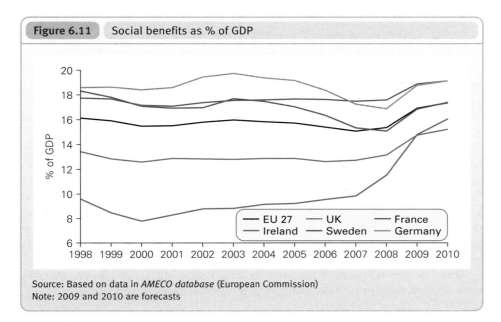

Figure 6.11   Social benefits as % of GDP

Legend: EU 27 — UK — France — Ireland — Sweden — Germany

Source: Based on data in *AMECO database* (European Commission)
Note: 2009 and 2010 are forecasts

As you can see, benefits as a percentage of GDP (national income) vary from one country to another. For instance, the Irish and UK percentages were significantly below the average for the EU-27 (the 27 EU member countries as of 2007) for most of this period.

Differences between countries reflect a multitude of factors: some economic, but others not. Amongst the reasons are: differences in the coverage and levels of particular benefits, rates of unemployment, incomes, rates of economic growth and demographic factors such as the age structure of the population. But, cultural and historic traditions can matter too, such as views concerning the role of governments – a theme we will pick up in Chapter 7.

The system of benefits in the UK and their redistributive effects are examined in Case Study 6.16 in MyEconLab.

Benefits and the redistribution of income

It might seem that means-tested benefits are a much more efficient system of redistributing income from the rich to the poor: the money is directed to those most in need. With universal benefits, by contrast, many people may receive them who have little need for them. Do families with very high incomes need child benefit? Would it not be better for the government to redirect the money to those who are genuinely in need?

There are, however, serious problems in attempting to redistribute incomes by the use of means-tested benefits:

■ Not everyone entitled to means-tested benefits applies for them, whether from ignorance of what is available, from the complexities of claiming or from reluctance to reveal personal circumstances. Thus some of the poorest families may receive no support.

■ The levels of income above which people become ineligible for benefits may be set too low. Even if they were raised, there will always be some people just above these levels who will still find difficulties.

■ Means tests based purely on *income* (or even universal benefits based on broad categories) ignore the very special needs of many poor people. A person earning £80 a week living in a small, well-appointed flat with a low rent will have less need of assistance than another person who also earns £80 per week but lives in a cold, draughty and damp house with large bills to meet. If means tests are to be fair, then *all* of a person's circumstances need to be taken into account.

The tax/benefit system and the problem of disincentives: the 'poverty trap'

When means-tested benefits are combined with a progressive income tax system, there can be a serious problem of disincentives. As poor people earn more money, so not only do they start paying income taxes and national insurance, but also they begin losing means-tested benefits. Theoretically, it is possible to have a marginal tax-plus-lost-benefit rate in excess of 100 per cent. In other words, for every extra £1 earned, taxes and lost benefits add up to more than £1. High marginal tax-plus-lost-benefit rates obviously act as a serious disincentive. What is the point of getting a job or trying to earn more money, if you end up earning little more or actually losing money?

This situation is known as the **poverty trap**. People are trapped on low incomes with no realistic means of bettering their position.

Definition

Poverty trap
Where poor people are discouraged from working or getting a better job because any extra income they earn will be largely taken away in taxes and lost benefits.

The problem of the poverty trap would be overcome by switching to a system of universal benefits unrelated to income. For example, *everyone* could receive a flat payment from the state fixed at a sufficiently high level to cover their basic needs. There would still be *some* disincentive, but this would be confined to an income effect: people would not have the same need to work if the state provided a basic income. But there would no longer be the disincentive to work caused by a resulting *loss* of benefits (a substitution effect).

The big drawback with universal benefits, however, is their cost. If they were given to everyone and were large enough to help the poor, their cost would be enormous. Thus although the benefits themselves would not create much disincentive effect, the necessary taxation to fund them almost certainly would.

There is no ideal solution to this conundrum. On the one hand, the more narrowly benefits are targeted on the poor, the greater the problem of the poverty trap. On the other hand, the more widely they are spread, the greater the cost of providing any given level of support to individuals.

A compromise proposal is that of a **negative income tax**. This is examined in Case Study 6.17 in MyEconLab. Box 6.5 examines the use of tax credits – a form of negative income tax – in the UK.

> **Pause for thought**
>
> *Does the targeting of benefits to those in greatest need necessarily increase the poverty trap?*

> **Definition**
>
> **Negative income tax**
> A combined system of taxes and benefits. Below a certain level of income people pay a negative tax: in other words they receive benefits. As people earn more, they gradually lose their benefits until beyond a certain level they begin paying taxes – the tax becomes positive.

Recap

1. Taxes can be categorised as progressive, regressive or proportional. Progressive taxes have the effect of reducing inequality. The more steeply progressive they are, the bigger the reduction in inequality.

2. Taxes on their own cannot increase the incomes of the poor. Cutting taxes, however, *can* help the poor if the cuts are carefully targeted.

3. Using taxes to redistribute incomes can cause disincentives. Raising taxes has two effects on the amount people wish to work. On the one hand, people will be encouraged to work more in order to maintain their incomes. This is the income effect. On the other hand, they will be encouraged to substitute leisure for income (i.e. to work less), since an hour's leisure now costs less in forgone income. This is the substitution effect. The relative size of the income and substitution effects will depend on the nature of the tax change. The substitution effect is more likely to outweigh the income effect for those with few commitments, for people just above the tax threshold of the newly

raised tax and in cases where the highest rates of tax are increased.

4. Benefits can be cash benefits or benefits in kind. They can be universal or means-tested. Universal benefits include child benefit, state pensions, unemployment benefits, and sickness and invalidity benefits. Benefits in kind include health care, education and free school meals.

5. Means-tested benefits can be specifically targeted to those in need and are thus more 'cost-effective'. However, there can be serious problems with such benefits, including: limited take-up, time-consuming procedures for claimants, some relatively needy people falling just outside the qualifying limit and inadequate account taken of *all* relevant circumstances affecting a person's needs.

6. The poverty trap occurs when the combination of increased taxes and reduced benefits removes the incentive for poor people to earn more. The more steeply progressive this combined system is at low incomes, the bigger the disincentive effect.

BOX 6.5   UK TAX CREDITS

An escape from the poverty trap?

Tax credits (which share characteristics with negative income taxes) were introduced in the UK in 1999 in the form of working families tax credit, which was replaced in 2003 by working tax credit (WTC) and child tax credit (CTC). These credits are paid either as tax relief or as a cash benefit.

Working tax credit is designed for working people on low incomes. To be eligible for the basic amount (see the table), people without children must be aged 25 or over and work at least 30 hours per week. People with children, the over-50s returning to work and the disabled must work at least 16 hours per week. Couples and lone parents receive an additional amount. There is a further addition for anyone with children who works at least 30 hours per week, or for couples who jointly work at least 30 hours per week. This is designed as an incentive for people to move from part-time to full-time work. Recipients of WTC also get paid 80 per cent of eligible childcare costs up to £175 per week for one child and £300 for two or more children. For each pound earned above a threshold amount, relief is reduced by 39p.

Child tax credit provides support to families with children, whether or not anyone in the family works. It is paid in addition to WTC and child benefit. There is a basic rate and an additional amount per child. Relief tapers off for incomes over a threshold amount although the full adult element is awarded to households with an income of up to £50 000 (2009/10). (See table for rates of WTC and CTC.)

WTC and CTC rates (£ annual): 2009/10

Working tax credit (WTC)

Basic element	1 890
Addition for couples and lone parents	1 860
Addition for those working 30 hours or more	775
Income threshold (above which WTC is reduced)	6 420

Child tax credit (CTC)

Family element	545
Baby addition	545
Additional amount per child	2 235
Income threshold (above which CTC is reduced)	16 040

Source: HM Revenue and Customs

Apart from targeting support at poorer families, these tax credits are intended to improve incentives to work, by reducing the poverty trap. In other words, the aim is to reduce the financial penalties for parents working by tapering off more slowly the rate at which benefits are lost. With a lost-benefit rate of 39 per cent, the combined marginal tax-plus-lost-benefit rate (the 'marginal deduction rate') is typically around 70 per cent, depending on a person's marginal rate of tax and other means-tested benefits received.

Although the introduction of these tax credits has reduced the typical marginal deduction rate for poor families, the rate is still very high. For many poor parents, therefore, the incentive to work is still relatively low.

There is another effect from reducing the rate at which benefit tapers off. Some benefit will now be available to slightly less poor families. Although this is good in terms of providing support for them, there is now more of a disincentive for parents in such families to work extra hours, or to take a better job, since the marginal deduction rate is now higher. In other words, although they are better off, they will take home less for each extra hour worked.

WTC and CTC illustrate the general problem of providing support to poor people which is affordable for taxpayers without creating disincentives to work. The more gently the support tapers off (and hence the less the disincentive to earn extra money), the more costly it is to finance and hence the higher tax rates are needed elsewhere. The problems with using negative income taxes are explored in Case Study 6.17 in MyEconLab.

WTC and CTC are major elements of the UK Labour government's policy on poverty, which is focused on families. The policy concentrates on eliminating worklessness in households where children are living, lifting them out of poverty and breaking the 'cycle of deprivation'.

A major criticism of tax credits lies in the complexity of the system. This has two consequences: first it is estimated that of the seven million households eligible for the benefits, around two million fail to claim them; second the system is administratively costly and prone to errors. Despite this, tax credits have contributed to reductions in the number of children living in poverty in the UK since 2000.

Economists sometimes refer to an 'unemployment trap'. People are discouraged from taking work in the first place. Explain how such a 'trap' arises. Do working tax credits and child tax credits create an unemployment trap? What are the best ways of eliminating, or at least reducing, the unemployment trap?

QUESTIONS

1. If a firm faces a shortage of workers with very specific skills, it may decide to undertake the necessary training itself. If, on the other hand, it faces a shortage of unskilled workers, it may well offer a small wage increase in order to obtain the extra labour. In the first case it is responding to an increase in demand for labour by attempting to shift the supply curve. In the second case it is merely allowing a movement along the supply curve. Use a demand and supply diagram to illustrate each case. Given that elasticity of supply is different in each case, do you think that these are the best policies for the firm to follow?

2. For what types of reason does the marginal revenue product differ between workers in different jobs?

3. Why, do you think, are some of the lowest-paid jobs the most unpleasant?

4. The wage rate a firm has to pay and the output it can produce vary with the number of workers as shown in the table below (all figures are hourly). Assume that output sells at £2 per unit.

Number of workers	1	2	3	4	5	6	7	8
Wage rate (AC_L) (£)	3	4	5	6	7	8	9	10
Total output (TPP_L)	10	22	32	40	46	50	52	52

(a) Copy the table and add additional rows for TC_L, MC_L, TRP_L and MRP_L. Put the figures for MC_L and MRP_L in the spaces between the columns.

(b) How many workers will the firm employ in order to maximise profits?

(c) What will be its hourly wage bill at this level of employment?

(d) How much hourly revenue will it earn at this level of employment?

(e) Assuming that the firm faces other (fixed) costs of £30 per hour, how much hourly profit will it make?

(f) Assume that the workers now form a union and that the firm agrees to pay the negotiated wage rate to all employees. What is the maximum to which the hourly wage rate could rise without causing the firm to try to reduce employment below that in (b) above? (See the diagram in Box 6.2.)

(g) What would be the firm's hourly profit now?

5. The figures shown in the table below are for a monopsonist employer. Fill in the missing figures for columns (3) and (4). How many workers should the firm employ if it wishes to maximise profits?

6. To what extent can trade unions be seen to be (a) an advantage, (b) a disadvantage to (i) workers in unions, (ii) employers bargaining with unions, (iii) non-union members in firms where there is collective bargaining, (iv) workers in non-unionised jobs?

7. Identify four groups of workers, two with very high wages and two with very low wages. Explain why they get the wages they do.

8. Do any of the following contradict marginal productivity theory: (a) wage scales related to length of service (incremental scales); (b) nationally negotiated wage rates; (c) discrimination; (d) firms taking the lead from other firms in determining this year's pay increase?

9. For what reasons is the average gross weekly pay of women only around 77 per cent of that of men in the UK?

10. Does the existence of overtime tend to increase or decrease inequality?

11. Distinguish between proportional, progressive and regressive taxation. Could a progressive tax have a constant marginal rate?

Number of workers (1)	Wage rate (£) (2)	Total cost of labour (£) (3)	Marginal cost of labour (£) (4)	Marginal revenue product (£) (5)
1	100	100		
2	105	210	110	230
3	110	330	120	240
4	115			240
5	120			230
6	125			210
7	130			190
8	135			170
9	140			150
10	145			130

12. If a person earning £5000 per year pays £500 in a given tax and a person earning £10 000 per year pays £800, is the tax progressive or regressive? Explain.

13. A proportional tax will leave the distribution of income unaffected. Why should this be so, given that a rich person will pay a larger absolute amount than a poor person?

14. Under what circumstances would a rise in income tax act as (a) a disincentive and (b) an incentive to effort?

15. Who is likely to work harder as a result of a cut in income tax rates – a person on a high income or a person on a low income? Why? Would your answer be different if personal allowances were zero?

16. What tax changes (whether up or down) will both have a positive incentive effect and also redistribute incomes more equally?

17. What is meant by 'the poverty trap'? Would a system of universal benefits be the best solution to the problem of the poverty trap?

18. How would you go about deciding whether person A or person B gets more personal benefit from each of the following: (a) an electric fire; (b) a clothing allowance of £x; (c) draught-proofing materials; (c) child benefit? Do your answers help you in deciding how best to allocate benefits?

Log on to MyEconlab and complete the studyplan exercises for this chapter to see how much you have learnt and where you need to revise most. Make sure you access all the supporting textbook resources including the online workbook, newsblog, audio animations, guided solutions and ebook.

Additional case studies in the *Essentials of Economics* MyEconLab (www.pearsoned.co.uk/sloman)

6.1   **Labour as a factor of production.** An examination of some of the ethical consequences of treating labour as an 'input' into production.

6.2   **Flexible labour markets.** This looks at the changes in the ways that firms organise their workforces.

6.3   **Telecommuters.** This case study looks at the growth in the number of people working from home.

6.4   **Life at the mill.** Monopsony in Victorian times as reported by Friedrich Engels.

6.5   **Poverty in the past.** Extreme poverty in Victorian England.

6.6   **The rise and decline of the labour movement.** A brief history of trade unions in the UK.

6.7   **How useful is marginal productivity theory?** How accurately does the theory describe employment decisions by firms?

6.8   **Profit sharing.** An examination of the case for and against profit sharing as a means of rewarding workers.

6.9   **Ethnic minorities in the UK labour market.** This case study looks at differences in income and employment between different ethnic groups in the UK.

6.10 **How can we define poverty?** This examines different definitions of poverty and, in particular, distinguishes between absolute and relative measures of poverty.

6.11 **How to reverse the UK's increased inequality.** Recommendations of the Rowntree Foundation.

6.12 **Adam Smith's maxims of taxation.** This looks at the principles of a good tax system as identified by Adam Smith.

6.13 **Taxation in the UK.** This case study looks at the various types of tax in the UK. It gives the current tax rates and considers how progressive the system is.

6.14 **The poll tax.** This case charts the introduction of the infamous poll tax (or 'community charge') in the UK and its subsequent demise.

6.15 **The Laffer curve.** This curve suggests that raising tax rates beyond a certain level will *reduce* tax revenue. But will cutting tax rates increase revenue?

6.16 **The system of benefits in the UK.** A description of the various benefits used in the UK and their redistributive effects.

6.17 **Negative income tax and redistribution.** This case looks at the possible effects of introducing negative income taxes (tax credits).

Websites relevant to this chapter

Numbers and sections refer to websites listed in the Web appendix and hotlinked from this book's website at **www.pearsoned.co.uk/sloman**.

- For news articles relevant to this chapter, see the *Economics News Articles* link from the book's website.

- For general news on labour markets, see websites in section A, and particularly A1, 2, 4, 5 and 7. See also A38, A39 and A44 for links to economics news articles from newspapers worldwide.

- For data on labour markets, see links in B1 or 2, especially to *Labour Market Trends* on the National Statistics site. See also B9 and links in B19; and the *resources > statistics* links in H3.

- For information on international labour standards and employment rights, see site H3.

- Sites I7 and 11 contain links to Labour economics, Labour force and markets and Labour unions in the Microeconomics section and to Distribution of income and wealth in the Macroeconomics section. Site I4 has links in the Directory section to Labour and Labour Economics. Site I17 in the Labour Economics section has links to various topics, such as Labour Unions, Minimum Wage, Poverty and Work.

- Links to the TUC and Confederation of British Industry sites can be found at E32 and 33.

- For information on poverty and inequality, see sites B18; E9, 13.

- For information on taxes, benefits and the redistribution of income, see E9, 30, 36; G5, 13. See also *The Virtual Economy* at D1.

- For student resources relevant to this chapter, see sites C1–7, 9, 10, 19; D3.

Web appendices

6.1 **Deriving the individual's supply curve of labour.** This uses indifference analysis (see Web Appendix 2.2) to explain the shape of an individual worker's supply curve of labour and explains why at high wage rates the curve may become backward bending.

6.2 **Economic rent and transfer earnings.** This appendix examines a way of classifying the earnings of a factor of production and shows how these earnings depend on the price elasticity of supply of the factor.

6.3 **Lorenz curves and Gini coefficients.** Two methods of measuring inequality.

CHAPTER MAP

Market failures and government policy

To what extent should we rely on markets to allocate resources? In recent years, governments throughout the world have tended to put more reliance on markets as the means of allocating resources. Policies of privatisation, deregulation, and cutting government expenditure and taxes have been widely adopted by governments of all political persuasions.

Despite this increased reliance on markets, markets often fail. At a general level, while we observe the tendency for a country's national income to increase over time, it is inherently unstable and its distribution unequal. But, more than this, we witness and contribute to activities that adversely affect the lives of others, no more so than our impact on the environment. At the same time, many aspects of our lives seem to be dominated by the interests of big business and the quality of many of the goods we buy is very poor.

While both the extent and nature of government involvement in economies varies from one country to another, all governments are still expected to play a major role. This involvement ranges from supporting and regulating businesses, to the passing of laws to protect the individual, to providing or enabling access to key services such as education, health care and law and order, to social protection in the form of pensions and social security, to the provision of infrastructure, such as a country's rail track or road network.

In this chapter we identify the various ways in which the market fails to look after society's interests (Sections 7.1–7.4). Then we look at how the government can set about putting right these failings (Sections 7.5–7.7). Then we look at some of the shortcomings of governments, and ask: should we have more or less intervention? In the final section we turn to problems of the environment as a case study in market failure and government intervention.

After studying this chapter, you should be able to answer the following questions:

- What is the meaning of a 'socially efficient' allocation of resources and to what extent will a perfectly competitive market achieve social efficiency?
- For what reasons do real-world markets fail to achieve social efficiency?
- How can governments put right the failings of the market?
- How successful are they likely to be?
- How can economists explain environmental degradation?
- What policies can be pursued to achieve environmental sustainability?

7.1   SOCIAL EFFICIENCY

Is this something that the free market will achieve?

In order to decide the optimum amount of government intervention, it is first necessary to identify the various social goals that intervention is designed to meet. Two of the major objectives of government intervention identified by economists are **social efficiency** and **equity**.

Equity

KI 19
p 181

Most people would argue that the free market fails to lead to a *fair* distribution of resources, if it results in some people living in great affluence whilst others live in dire poverty. Clearly what constitutes 'fairness' is a highly contentious issue: those on the political right generally have a quite different view from those on the political left. Nevertheless, most people would argue that the government does have some duty to redistribute incomes from the rich to the poor through the tax and benefit system, and perhaps to provide various forms of legal protection for the poor (such as a minimum wage rate). We looked at the causes of inequality and policies of redistribution in Chapter 6. In this chapter, therefore, we focus on the second issue: that of social efficiency.

Social efficiency

KI 17
p 122

If the marginal benefits to society – or 'marginal social benefits' (*MSB*) – of producing (or consuming) any given good or service exceed the marginal costs to society – or 'marginal social costs' (*MSC*) – then it is said to be socially efficient to produce (or consume) more. For example, if people's gains from having additional motorways exceed *all* the additional costs to society (both financial and non-financial), then it is socially efficient to construct more motorways.

If, however, the marginal social costs of producing (or consuming) any good or service exceed the marginal social benefits, then it is socially efficient to produce (or consume) less.

It follows that if the marginal social benefits of any activity are equal to the marginal social costs, then the current level is the optimum. To summarise: to achieve social efficiency in the production of any good or service, the following should occur:

TC 2
p 10

$MSB > MSC \rightarrow$ produce more

$MSC > MSB \rightarrow$ produce less

$MSB = MSC \rightarrow$ keep production at its current level

Similar rules apply to consumption. For example, if the marginal social benefits of consuming more of any good or service exceed the marginal social cost, then society would benefit from more of the good being consumed.

Social efficiency is an example of 'allocative efficiency': in other words, the best allocation of resources between alternative uses.

Allocative efficiency in any activity is achieved where any reallocation would lead to a decline in net benefit. It is achieved where marginal benefit equals marginal cost. Private efficiency is achieved where marginal private benefit equals marginal private cost (*MB = MC*). Social efficiency is achieved where marginal social benefit equals marginal social cost (*MSB = MSC*).

Definitions

Social efficiency
Production and consumption at the point where *MSB = MSC*.

Equity
A fair distribution of resources.

The concept of allocative efficiency is another of our Threshold Concepts (no. 10). It is a threshold concept, because to understand it is to understand how to make the most of scarce resources: and scarcity is the core problem of economics for all of us.

In the real world, however, the market rarely leads to social efficiency: the marginal social benefits of most goods and services do not equal the marginal social costs. Part of the problem is that many of our actions have spillover effects on other people (these are known as 'externalities'), part is a lack of competition, part is a lack of knowledge by both producers and consumers, and part is the fact that markets may take a long time to adjust to any disequilibrium, given the often considerable short-run immobility of factors of production.

> **KEY IDEA 21**
>
> *Markets generally fail to achieve social efficiency.* There are various types of market failure. Market failures provide one of the major justifications for government intervention in the economy.

In this chapter we examine these various 'failings' of the free market and what the government can do to rectify the situation. We also examine why the government itself may fail to achieve social efficiency.

General equilibrium

Markets are in a constant state of flux. Demand changes as consumer tastes change and as income changes; supply changes as technology, the availability of natural resources and costs change. These changes in demand and supply cause markets to adjust to a new equilibrium.

At any one time, it is useful to look at the overall equilibrium towards which markets are heading: the **general equilibrium** of all markets.

> **KEY IDEA 22**
> **TC 11**
>
> *General equilibrium.* The situation where all individual markets in the economy are in equilibrium: in other words, where demand equals supply in all markets. If demand or supply changes in any market, there are likely to be ripple effects into other markets (i.e. for substitute or complementary goods, in both demand and supply), until a new general equilibrium is reached. This is Threshold Concept 11.

> **Definition**
>
> **General equilibrium**
> Where all the millions of markets throughout the economy are in a simultaneous state of equilibrium.

The concept of general equilibrium is a threshold concept because it gives us an insight into how market forces apply to a whole economy, and not just to its individual parts. It is about seeing how the whole jigsaw fits together and how changes ripple throughout the economy.

We can then ask, whether this general equilibrium is socially efficient, or whether a reallocation of resources in the economy would lead to greater social efficiency.

An economy where all markets are perfectly competitive and where there are no externalities *will* be socially efficient when there is a state of general equilibrium. Why will this be so? Take the case of goods markets. In any given goods markets, the consumer will achieve private efficiency where marginal utility (i.e. marginal benefit) equals price (see Box 2.1 on page 34); and the producer where marginal cost equals price (see Section 5.2, page 118). Given that all producers and consumers face the same market price, in equilibrium marginal utility will equal marginal cost.

But will this be socially efficient? In the absence of externalities, benefits from consumption are confined to the consumers themselves. In other words, as members of society, their benefit is the whole social benefit. Thus $P = MU = MSB$. Likewise, the costs of production are confined to the producers: there are no costs imposed on *other* members of society. Thus $P = MC = MSC$.

To summarise:

$$MU = MSB = P = MC = MSC$$

and hence:

$$MSB = MSC$$

Thus equilibrium in any market under perfect competition with no externalities is socially efficient. When this applies to all markets, then general equilibrium is socially efficient.

Web Appendix 7.1 looks at social efficiency in more detail.

7.2 MARKET FAILURES: EXTERNALITIES AND PUBLIC GOODS

What will happen if certain markets are 'missing'?

Externalities

The market will not lead to social efficiency if the actions of producers or consumers affect people *other than themselves*. As we saw above, these effects on other people are known as **externalities**: they are the side-effects, or 'third-party' effects, of production or consumption. Externalities can be either desirable or undesirable. Whenever other people are affected beneficially, there are said to be **external benefits**. Whenever other people are affected adversely, there are said to be **external costs**.

 KEY IDEA 23 *Externalities are spillover costs or benefits.* Where these exist, even an otherwise perfect market will fail to achieve social efficiency.

Thus the full cost to society (the **social cost**) of the production of any good or service is the private cost faced by firms plus any externalities of production (positive or negative). Likewise the full benefit to society (the **social benefit**) from the consumption of any good is the private benefit enjoyed by consumers plus any externalities of consumption (positive or negative).

There are four major types of externality.

External costs of production (MSC > MC)

When a chemical firm dumps waste into a river or pollutes the air, the community bears costs additional to those borne by the firm. The marginal *social* cost (*MSC*) of chemical production exceeds the marginal private cost (*MC*). Diagrammatically, the *MSC* curve is above the *MC* curve. This is shown in Figure 7.1(a), which assumes that the firm in other respects is operating in a perfect market, and is therefore a price taker (i.e. faces a horizontal demand curve).

The firm maximises profits at Q_1: the output where marginal cost equals price (see Section 5.2). The price is what people buying the good are prepared to pay for

Definitions

Externalities
Costs or benefits of production or consumption experienced by society but not by the producers or consumers themselves. Sometimes referred to as 'spillover' or 'third-party' costs or benefits.

External benefits
Benefits from production (or consumption) experienced by people *other* than the producer (or consumer).

External costs
Costs of production (or consumption) borne by people *other* than the producer (or consumer).

Social cost
Private cost plus externalities in production.

Social benefit
Private benefit plus externalities in consumption.

Figure 7.1   Externalities in production

(a) External costs   (b) External benefits

one more unit (if it wasn't, they wouldn't buy it) and therefore reflects their marginal benefit. We assume no externalities from consumption, and therefore the marginal benefit to consumers is the same as the marginal *social* benefit (*MSB*). The *socially* optimum output would be Q_2, where P (i.e. *MSB*) = *MSC*. The firm, however, produces Q_1 which is more than the optimum. Thus external costs lead to over-production from society's point of view.

The problem of external costs arises in a free-market economy because no one has legal ownership of the air or rivers and no one, therefore, can prevent or charge for their use as a dump for waste. Such a 'market' is missing. Control must, therefore, be left to the government or local authorities.

Other examples include extensive farming that destroys hedgerows and wildlife, and global warming caused by CO_2 emissions from power stations.

External benefits of production (MSC < MC)

If a forestry company plants new woodlands, there is a benefit not only to the company itself, but also to the world through a reduction of CO_2 in the atmosphere (forests are a carbon sink). The marginal *social* cost of providing timber, therefore, is less than the marginal *private* cost to the company.

In Figure 7.1(b), the *MSC* curve is *below* the *MC* curve. The level of output provided by the forestry company is Q_1 where $P = MC$, a *lower* level than the social optimum, Q_2, where $P = MSC$.

Another example of external benefits in production is that of research and development. If other firms have access to the results of the research, then clearly the benefits extend beyond the firm that finances it. Since the firm only receives the private benefits, it will conduct a less than optimal amount of research.

External costs of consumption (MSB < MB)

Figure 7.2(a) shows the marginal benefit and price to a motorist (i.e. the consumer) of using a car. It is assumed that the marginal benefit declines as the motorist travels

Figure 7.2	Externalities in consumption

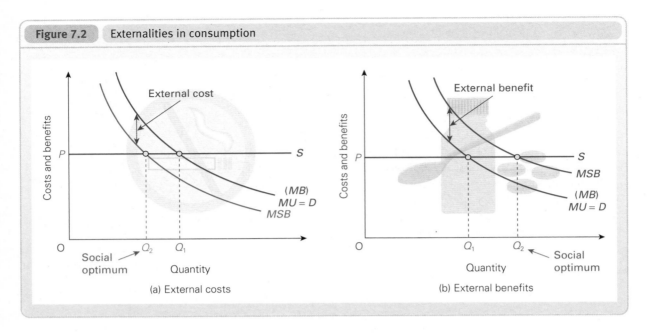

(a) External costs

(b) External benefits

further.[1] The optimal distance travelled for this motorist will be Q_1 miles: i.e. where marginal benefit (MB) = price (P) (where price is the cost of petrol, oil, wear and tear, etc. per mile). The reasoning is as follows: if the marginal benefit from the consumption of any good or service, measured in terms of what you are prepared to pay for it, exceeds its price (i.e. the marginal cost to the consumer), the consumer will gain by consuming more of it. If, however, the marginal benefit is less than the price, the consumer will gain by consuming less. The optimum level of consumption from the motorist's point of view, therefore, will be where $MB = P$: i.e. Q_1 miles.

When people use their cars, however, other people suffer from their exhaust fumes, the added congestion, the noise, etc. These 'negative externalities' make the marginal social benefit of using cars less than the marginal private benefit of the motorist. Thus the MSB curve is below the MB curve. Assuming that there are no externalities in *production*, and therefore that marginal social cost is given by the price, the *social* optimum will be where $MSB = P$: i.e. at Q_2. But this is less than the actual level of consumption, Q_1. Thus, when there are negative externalities in consumption, the actual level of consumption will be too great from society's point of view.

Other examples of negative externalities of consumption include the effects on other people of noisy radios in public places, the smoke from cigarettes, and litter.

External benefits of consumption (MSB > MB)

When people travel by train rather than by car, other people benefit by there being less congestion and exhaust and fewer accidents on the roads. Thus the marginal

[1] To understand this, consider your own position (assuming you had a car). If you had only a little money available for motoring, or if the price of petrol were very high, then you would only use your car for essential journeys: journeys with a high marginal private benefit (or 'marginal utility' as it is often referred to by economists). If your income increased, or if the price of petrol came down, you would use your car more (i.e. travel additional miles), but these additional journeys would be yielding you less additional benefit per mile than previous journeys, since they would be less essential to you. The more miles you travel, the less essential each *additional* mile: i.e. the marginal benefit diminishes. This is an example of the **principle of diminishing marginal utility**, which we saw in Box 1.2.

KI 17
p 34

social benefit of rail travel is *greater* than the marginal private benefit to the rail passenger. There are external benefits from rail travel. In Figure 7.2(b), the *MSB* curve is *above* the private *MB* curve. The actual level of consumption (Q_1) is thus below the socially optimal level of consumption (Q_2).

Other examples include the beneficial effects for other people of deodorants, vaccinations and attractive clothing.

To summarise: whenever there are external benefits, there will be too little produced or consumed. Whenever there are external costs, there will be too much produced or consumed. The market will not equate *MSB* and *MSC*.

The above arguments have been developed in the context of perfect competition, with prices given to the producer or consumer by the market. Externalities also occur in all other types of market.

Public goods

There is a category of goods where the positive externalities are so great that the free market, whether perfect or imperfect, may not produce at all. They are called **public goods**. Examples include lighthouses, pavements, flood-control dams, public drainage, public services such as the police and even government itself.

Public goods have two important characteristics: *non-rivalry* and *non-excludability*.

- If I consume a bar of chocolate, it cannot then be consumed by someone else. If, however, I enjoy the benefits of street lighting, it does not prevent you or anyone else doing the same. There is thus what we call **non-rivalry** in the consumption of such goods. These goods tend to have large external benefits relative to private benefits. This makes them socially desirable, but privately unprofitable. No single individual would pay to have a pavement built along his or her street. The private benefit would be too small relative to the cost. And yet the social benefit to all the other people using the pavement may far outweigh the cost.

- If I spend money erecting a flood-control dam to protect my house, my neighbours will also be protected by the dam. I cannot prevent them enjoying the benefits of my expenditure. This feature of **non-excludability** means that they would get the benefits free, and would therefore have no incentive to pay themselves. This is known as the **free-rider problem**.

KEY IDEA 24

The free-rider problem. People are often unwilling to pay for things if they can make use of things other people have bought. This problem can lead to people not purchasing things that would be to the benefit of themselves and other members of society.

When goods have these two features, the free market will simply not provide them. Thus these public goods can only be provided by the government or by the government subsidising private firms. (Note that not all goods and services produced by the public sector come into the category of 'public goods and services': thus education and health are publicly provided, but they *can* be, and indeed are, privately provided as well.)

Pause for thought

Is it likely that the MSB curve will be parallel to the MB curve in each of the diagrams of Figure 7.2?

Definitions

Public good
A good or service that has the features of non-rivalry and non-excludability and as a result would not be provided by the free market.

Non-rivalry
Where the consumption of a good or service by one person will not prevent others from enjoying it.

Non-excludability
Where it is not possible to provide a good or service to one person without it thereby being available to others to enjoy.

Pause for thought

Which of the following have the property of non-rivalry: (a) a can of drink; (b) public transport; (c) a commercial radio broadcast; (d) the sight of flowers in a public park?

Definition

Free-rider problem
Where it is not possible to exclude other people from consuming a good that someone has bought.

Recap

1. Social efficiency will be achieved where $MSC = MSB$ for each good and service. In practice, however, markets fail to achieve social efficiency. One reason for this is the existence of externalities.

2. Externalities are spillover costs or benefits. Whenever there are external costs, the market will (other things being equal) lead to a level of production and consumption *above* the socially efficient level. Whenever there are external benefits, the market

will (other things being equal) lead to a level of production and consumption *below* the socially efficient level.

3. Public goods will not be provided by a free market. The problem is that they have large external benefits relative to private benefits and without government intervention it would not be possible to prevent people having a 'free ride' and thereby escaping contributing to their cost of production.

7.3 MARKET FAILURES: MONOPOLY POWER

What problems arise from big business?

Whenever markets are imperfect, whether as pure monopoly or monopsony, or whether as some form of imperfect competition, the market will fail to equate MSB and MSC, even if there are no externalities.

Take the case of monopoly. A monopoly will produce less than the socially efficient output. This is illustrated in Figure 7.3. A monopoly faces a downward-sloping demand curve, and therefore marginal revenue is below average revenue $(= P = MSB)$. Profits are maximised at an output of Q_1, where marginal revenue equals marginal cost (see Figure 5.5 on page 126). If there are no externalities, the socially efficient output will be at the higher level of Q_2, where $MSB = MSC$.

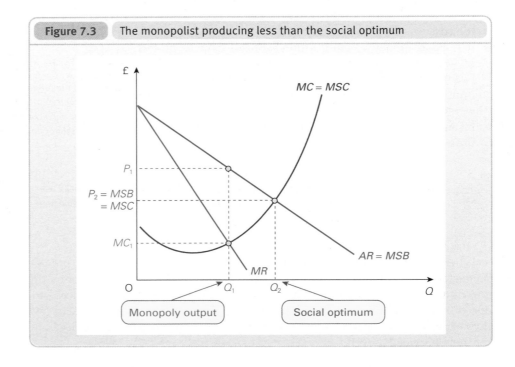

| Figure 7.3 | The monopolist producing less than the social optimum |

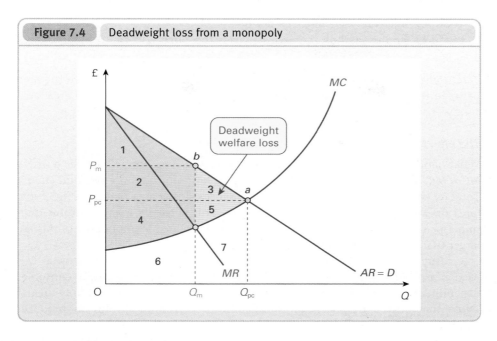

Figure 7.4   Deadweight loss from a monopoly

Deadweight loss under monopoly

Consumer and producer surplus

One way of analysing the welfare loss that occurs under monopoly is to use the concepts of *consumer* and *producer surplus*. Consumer surplus is the excess of consumers' total benefit (or 'utility') from consuming a good over their total expenditure on it. Producer surplus is just another name for profit. The two concepts are illustrated in Figure 7.4. The diagram shows an industry that is initially under perfect competition and then becomes a monopoly (but faces the same revenue and cost curves).

Let us start by examining consumer and producer surplus under *perfect competition*.

Consumer surplus. Under perfect competition the industry will produce an output of Q_{pc} at a price of P_{pc}, where $MC = P (= AR)$: i.e. at point *a* (see pages 126–7).

Consumers' total benefit is given by the area under the demand curve (the sum of all the areas 1–7). The reason for this is that each point on the demand curve shows how much the last consumer is prepared to pay (i.e. the benefit to the marginal consumer). The area under the demand curve thus shows the total of all these marginal benefits from zero consumption to the current level: i.e. it gives total benefit.

Consumers' total expenditure is $P_{pc} \times Q_{pc}$ (area 4 + 5 + 6 + 7).

Consumer surplus is the difference between total benefit and total expenditure: in other words, the area between the price and the demand curve (area 1 + 2 + 3).

Producer surplus. **Producer surplus** (profit) is the difference between total revenue and total cost.

Total cost is the area under the *MC* curve (area 6 + 7). The reason for this is that each point on the marginal cost curve shows what the last unit costs to produce. The area under the *MC* curve thus gives all the marginal costs starting from an output of zero to the current output: i.e. it gives total costs.[2]

Definitions

Consumer surplus
The excess of what a person would have been prepared to pay for a good (i.e. the utility) over what that person actually pays.

Producer surplus
The excess of total revenue over total cost: i.e. profit.

---

[2] Strictly speaking, the sum of all marginal costs gives total *variable* costs. Producers' surplus is therefore total revenue minus total variable costs: i.e. total profit plus total fixed costs.

Total revenue is $P_{pc} \times Q_{pc}$ (area 4 + 5 + 6 + 7).

Producer surplus is thus the area between the price and the MC curve (area 4 + 5).

Total (private) surplus. Total consumer plus producer surplus is therefore the area between the demand and MC curves. This is shown by the total shaded area (area 1 + 2 + 3 + 4 + 5).

The effect of monopoly on total surplus

What happens when the industry is under *monopoly*? The firm will produce where $MC = MR$, at an output of Q_m and a price of P_m (at point b on the demand curve). Total revenue is $P_m \times Q_m$ (area 2 + 4 + 6). Total cost is the area under the MC curve (area 6). Thus producer surplus is area 2 + 4. This is clearly a *larger* surplus than under perfect competition (since area 2 is larger than area 5): monopoly profits are larger than profits under perfect competition.

KI 16
p 116

Consumer surplus, however, will be much smaller. With consumption at Q_m, total benefit to consumers is given by area 1 + 2 + 4 + 6, whereas consumer expenditure is given by area 2 + 4 + 6. Consumer surplus, then, is simply area 1. (Note that area 2 has been transformed from consumer surplus to producer surplus.)

Total surplus under monopoly is therefore area 1 + 2 + 4: a smaller surplus than under perfect competition. 'Monopolisation' of the industry has resulted in a loss of total surplus of area 3 + 5. The producer's gain is less than consumers' loss. This net loss of total surplus is known as the **deadweight welfare loss** of monopoly.

KI 21
p 193

Conclusions

As was shown in Section 5.3, there are possible social *advantages* from powerful firms; advantages such as economies of scale and more research and development. These advantages may outweigh deadweight loss from monopoly power. It can be argued that an ideal situation would be where firms are large enough to gain economies of scale and yet were somehow persuaded or compelled to produce where $P = MC$ (assuming no externalities).

Pause for thought

Assume that a monopoly existed in an industry where there were negative externalities. Could the socially efficient output be Q_m in Figure 7.4? If so, would this make monopoly socially efficient?

OTHER MARKET FAILURES   7.4

In what other ways may a market fail to make the best use of scarce resources?

Ignorance and uncertainty

Perfect competition assumes that consumers, firms and factor suppliers have perfect knowledge of costs and benefits. In the real world there is often a great deal of ignorance and uncertainty. Thus people are unable to equate marginal benefit with marginal cost.

Consumers purchase many goods only once or a few times in a lifetime. Cars, washing machines, televisions and other consumer durables fall into this category. Consumers may not be aware of the quality of such goods until they have purchased them, by which time it is too late. Advertising may contribute to people's ignorance by misleading them as to the benefits of a good.

Firms are often ignorant of market opportunities, prices, costs, the productivity of labour (especially white-collar workers), the activity of rivals, etc.

Many economic decisions are based on expected future conditions. Since the future can never be known for certain, many decisions may turn out to be wrong.

In some cases it may be possible to obtain the information through the market. There may be an agency that will sell you the information, or a newspaper, magazine or website that contains the information. In such cases you will have to decide whether the cost to you of obtaining the information is worth the benefit it will provide you. A problem here is that you may not have sufficient information to judge how reliable the information is that you are obtaining!

Protecting people's interests

Dependants

People do not always make their own economic decisions. They are often dependent on decisions made by others. Parents make decisions on behalf of their children; partners on each other's behalf; younger adults on behalf of old people; managers on behalf of shareholders, etc.

A free market will respond to these decisions, however good or bad they may be; whether they be in the interest of the dependant or not. Thus the government may feel it necessary to protect dependants.

Poor economic decision making by individuals on their own behalf

The government may feel that people need protecting from poor economic decisions that they make on their *own* behalf. It may feel that in a free market people will consume too many harmful things. Thus if the government wants to discourage smoking and drinking, it can put taxes on tobacco and alcohol. In more extreme cases it could make various activities illegal: activities such as prostitution, certain types of gambling, and the sale and consumption of drugs.

On the other hand, the government may feel that people consume too little of things that are good for them: things such as education, health care and sports facilities. Such goods are known as **merit goods**. The government could either provide them free or subsidise their production.

> **Definition**
>
> **Merit goods**
> Goods which the government feels that people should consume but tend to underconsume and which therefore ought to be subsidised or provided free.

> **Pause for thought**
>
> *How do merit goods differ from public goods?*

The principal–agent problem

The problem of dependants is an example of a wider issue, known as the **principal –agent problem**. One of the features of a complex modern economy is that people (principals) have to employ others (agents) to carry out their wishes. If you want to go on holiday, it is easier to go to a travel agent to sort out the arrangements than to do it all yourself. Likewise, if you want to buy a house, it is more convenient to go to an estate agent. The point is that these agents have specialist knowledge and can save you, the principal, a great deal of time and effort. This is merely an example of the benefits of specialisation and the division of labour.

It is the same with firms. They employ people with specialist knowledge and skills to carry out specific tasks. Companies frequently employ consultants to give them advice, or engage the services of specialist firms such as an advertising agency. It is the same with the employees of the company. They can be seen as 'agents' of their employer. In the case of workers, they can be seen as the agents of management. Junior managers are the agents of senior management. Senior managers are the agents of the directors, who are themselves agents of the shareholders. Thus in large firms there is often a complex chain of principal–agent relationships. Indeed, it is often claimed that in large companies there tends to be a 'divorce' between the owners of the firm (the shareholders), who are the principals, and the controllers of the firm (the managers), who are the shareholders' agents.

These relationships have an inherent danger for the principal: there is **asymmetric information** between the two sides. The agent knows more about the situation than the principal – in fact, this is part of the reason why the principal employs the agent in the first place. The danger is that the agent may well not act in the principal's best interests, and may be able to get away with it because of the principal's imperfect knowledge. The estate agent trying to sell you a house may not tell you about the noisy neighbours or that the vendor is prepared to accept a much lower price. A second-hand car dealer may 'neglect' to tell you about the rust on the underside of the car or that it has a history of unreliability.

> **KEY IDEA 25** *The principal–agent problem.* Where people (principals), as a result of a lack of knowledge, cannot ensure that their best interests are served by their agents. Agents may take advantage of this situation to the disadvantage of the principals.

So how can principals tackle the problem? There are two elements in the solution:

■ The principals must have some way of *monitoring* the performance of their agents. Thus a company might employ efficiency experts to examine the operation of its management.

■ There must be *incentives* for agents to behave in the principals' interests. Thus managers' salaries could be more closely linked to the firm's profitability.

In a competitive market, managers' and shareholders' interests are more likely to coincide. Managers have to ensure that the company remains efficient or it may not survive the competition and they might lose their jobs. In monopolies and oligopolies, however, where supernormal profits can often be relatively easily earned, the interests of shareholders and managers are likely to diverge. Here it will be in shareholders' interests to institute incentive mechanisms that ensure that their agents, the managers, are motivated to strive for profitability.

TC 4 p 21

Definitions

Principal–agent problem Where people (principals), as a result of lack of knowledge, cannot ensure that their best interests are served by their agents.

Asymmetric information Where one party in an economic relationship (e.g. an agent) has more information than another (e.g. the principal).

Immobility of factors and time lags in response

Even under conditions of perfect competition, factors may be very slow to respond to changes in demand or supply. Labour, for example, may be highly immobile both occupationally and geographically. This can lead to large price changes and hence to large supernormal profits and high wages for those in the sectors of rising demand or falling costs. The long run may be a very long time coming!

In the meantime, there will be further changes in the conditions of demand and supply. Thus the economy is in a constant state of disequilibrium and the long run never comes. As firms and consumers respond to market signals and move towards equilibrium, so the equilibrium position moves and the social optimum is never achieved.

 KEY IDEA 26 *The problem of time lags.* Many economic actions can take a long time to take effect. This can cause problems of instability and an inability of the economy to achieve social efficiency.

Whenever monopoly/monopsony power exists, the problem is made worse as firms or unions put up barriers to the entry of new firms or factors of production.

Macroeconomic goals

As we shall see later in the book, the key macroeconomic objectives relate in one way or another to the total level of spending or the total level of output in an economy. These objectives include strong and stable rates of economic growth, full employment, stable prices and a balance of international payments. Unfortunately the free market is unlikely to achieve these objectives simultaneously.

In the late 2000s an increasingly important macroeconomic goal for many governments was to ensure the stability of the financial system. This is an example of where a market failure in a particular sector is highly significant in other sectors too. In this case, intense competition amongst financial institutions and weaknesses in systems of regulation led to unsustainable lending practices and to the collapse or near-collapse of financial institutions around the world (see Chapter 10 for more on the financial system).

Sections C and D of this book examine the various macroeconomic problems and the methods of government intervention in more detail.

How far can economists go in advising governments?

Certain goals, such as growth in national income, changes in the distribution of income and greater efficiency, are relatively easy to quantify. Others, such as enlightenment or the sense of community well-being, are virtually impossible to quantify. For this reason, economics tends to concentrate on the means of achieving a relatively narrow range of goals. The danger is that by economists concentrating on a limited number of goals, they may well influence the policy makers – the government, local authorities, various pressure groups, etc. – into doing the same, and thus into neglecting other perhaps important social goals.

Different objectives are likely to conflict. For example, economic growth may conflict with greater equality. In the case of such 'trade-offs', all the economist can do is to demonstrate the effects of a given policy, and leave the policy makers to decide whether the benefits in terms of one goal outweigh the costs in terms of another goal.

 TC 1 p 7

| BOX 7.1 | SHOULD HEALTH-CARE PROVISION BE LEFT TO THE MARKET? |

A case of multiple market failures

In the UK, the National Health Service provides free hospital treatment, a free general practitioner service and free prescriptions for certain categories of people (such as pensioners and children). Their marginal cost to the patient is thus zero. Of course, these services use resources and they thus have to be paid for out of taxes.

But why are these services not sold directly to the patient, thereby saving the taxpayer money? There are, in fact, a number of reasons why the market would fail to provide the optimum amount of health care.

People may not be able to afford treatment

This is a problem connected with the distribution of income. Because income is unequally distributed, some people will be able to afford better treatment than others, and the poorest people may not be able to afford treatment at all. On grounds of equity, therefore, it is argued that health care should be provided free – at least for poor people.

The concept of equity that is usually applied to health care is that of treatment according to medical need rather than according to the ability to pay.

1. *Does this argument also apply to food and other basic goods?*

Difficulty for people in predicting their future medical needs

If you were suddenly taken ill and required a major operation, it could be very expensive indeed for you if you had to pay. On the other hand, you may go through life requiring very little, if any, medical treatment. In other words, there is great uncertainty about your future medical needs. As a result it would be very difficult to plan your finances and budget for possible future medical expenses if you had to pay for treatment. Medical insurance is a possible solution to this problem, but there is still a problem of equity. Would the chronically sick or very old be able to obtain cover, and if so, would they be able to afford the premiums?

Externalities

Health care generates a number of benefits *external* to the patient. If you are cured of an infectious disease, for example, it is not just you who benefits but also others, since you will not infect them. In addition if you have a job you will be able to get back to work, thus reducing the disruption there. These external benefits of health care could be quite large.

If the sick had to pay the cost of their treatment, they may decide not to be treated – especially if they are poor. They may not take into account the effect that their illness has on other people. The market, by equating *private* benefits and costs, would produce too little health care.

KEY IDEA 27

Societies face trade-offs between economic objectives. For example, the goal of faster growth may conflict with that of greater equality; the goal of lower unemployment may conflict with that of lower inflation (at least in the short run). This is an example of opportunity cost: the cost of achieving more of one objective may be achieving less of another. The existence of trade-offs means that policy makers must make choices.

Recap

1. Ignorance and uncertainty may prevent people from consuming or producing the levels they would otherwise choose. Information may sometimes be provided (at a price) by the market, but it may be imperfect and in some cases not available at all.

2. Markets may respond sluggishly to changes in demand and supply. The time lags in adjustment can lead to a permanent state of disequilibrium and to problems of instability.

3. In a free market there may be inadequate provision for dependants and an inadequate output of merit goods. Also, because of asymmetric information, agents may not always act in the best interests of their principals.

4. Although economists cannot make ultimate pronouncements on the rights and wrongs of the market – that involves making moral judgements (and economists here are no different from any other people) – they can point out the consequences of the market and of various government policies, and also the trade-offs that exist between different objectives.

Patient ignorance

Markets only function well to serve consumer wishes if the consumer has the information to make informed decisions. For many products that we buy, we have a pretty good idea how much we will like them. In the case of health care, however, 'consumers' (i.e. patients) may have very poor knowledge. If you have a pain in your chest, it may be simple muscular strain, or it may be a symptom of heart disease. You rely on the doctor (the *supplier* of the treatment) to give you the information: to diagnose your condition. Two problems could arise here with a market system of allocating health care.

The first is that unscrupulous doctors might advise more expensive treatment than is necessary; they might even have an agreement with certain drugs companies that they will try to persuade you to buy an expensive branded product rather than an identical cheaper version. This is an example of the principal–agent problem and the problem of asymmetric information (see page 202).

The second is that patients suffering from the early stages of a serious disease might not consult their doctor until the symptoms become acute, by which time it might be too late to treat the disease, or very expensive to do so. With a free health service, however, a person is likely to receive an earlier diagnosis of serious conditions.

Oligopoly

If doctors and hospitals operated in the free market as profit maximisers, it is unlikely that competition would drive down their prices. Instead they might collude to fix standard prices for treatment, so as to protect their incomes. Even if doctors did compete openly, it is unlikely that consumers would have enough information to enable them to 'shop around' for the best value.

We have to be careful though; to argue that the market system will fail to provide an optimal allocation of health-care resources does not in itself prove that *free provision* is the best alternative. For example, with no charge for GP appointments it is likely that some patients will consult their doctors over trivial complaints.

In the USA there is much more reliance on *private medical insurance* with only the very poor getting free treatment. Alternatively, the government may simply *subsidise* health care, so as to make it cheaper rather than free. This is the case with prescriptions and dental treatment in the UK, where many people have to pay part of the cost of treatment. Also the government can *regulate* the behaviour of the providers of health care, to prevent exploitation of the patient. Thus only people with certain qualifications are allowed to operate as doctors, nurses, pharmacists, etc.

2. If health care is provided free, the demand is likely to be high. How is this high demand dealt with? Is this a good way of dealing with it?
3. Go through each of the market failings identified in this box. In each case, consider what alternative policies are open to a government to tackle them. What are the advantages and disadvantages of these alternatives?

GOVERNMENT INTERVENTION: TAXES AND SUBSIDIES   7.5

Will taxing the bad and subsidising the good solve the problem of externalities?

Faced with all the problems of the free market, what is a government to do?

There are several policy instruments that the government can use. At one extreme it can totally replace the market by providing goods and services itself. At the other extreme it can merely seek to persuade producers, consumers or workers to act differently. Between the two extremes the government has a number of instruments it can use to change the way markets operate. These include taxes, subsidies, laws and regulatory bodies. In this and the next two sections we examine these different forms of government intervention.

The use of taxes and subsidies

A policy instrument particularly favoured by many economists is that of taxes and subsidies. They can be used for two main purposes: (a) to promote greater social efficiency by altering the composition of production and consumption, and (b) to redistribute incomes. We examined their use for the second purpose in the last chapter. Here we examine their use to achieve greater social efficiency.

When there are imperfections in the market, social efficiency will not be achieved. Marginal social benefit (*MSB*) will not equal marginal social cost (*MSC*). A different level of output would be more desirable. Taxes and subsidies can be used to correct these imperfections. Essentially the approach is to tax those goods or activities where the market produces too much, and subsidise those where the market produces too little.

Taxes and subsidies to correct externalities

The rule here is simple: the government should impose a tax equal to the marginal external cost (or grant a subsidy equal to the marginal external benefit).

Assume, for example, that a chemical works emits smoke from a chimney and thus pollutes the atmosphere. This creates external costs for the people who breathe in the smoke. The marginal social cost of producing the chemicals thus exceeds the marginal private cost to the firm: $MSC > MC$.

This is illustrated in Figure 7.5. The marginal pollution cost (the externality) is shown by the vertical distance between the MC and MSC curves. For simplicity, it is assumed that the firm is a price taker. It produces Q_1 where $P = MC$ (its profit-maximising output), but in doing so takes no account of the external pollution costs it imposes on society.

If the government now imposes a tax on production equal to the marginal pollution cost, it will effectively 'internalise' the externality. The firm will have to pay an amount in tax equal to the external cost it creates. It will therefore now

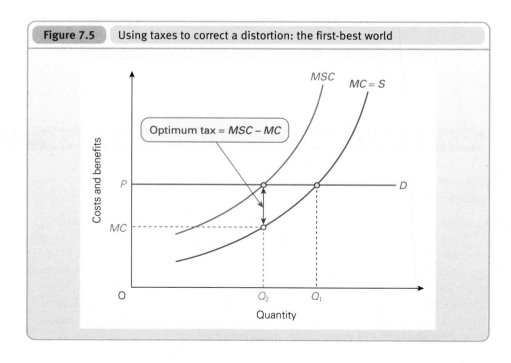

Figure 7.5 Using taxes to correct a distortion: the first-best world

maximise profits at Q_2, where $P = MC + $ tax. But this is the socially optimum output where $MSB = MSC$.

Taxes and subsidies to correct for monopoly

If the problem of monopoly that the government wishes to tackle is that of *excessive profits*, it can impose a lump-sum tax on the monopolist: that is, a tax of a fixed absolute amount irrespective of how much the monopolist produces, or the price it charges. Since a lump-sum tax is an additional *fixed* cost to the firm, and hence will not affect the firm's marginal cost, it will not reduce the amount that the monopolist produces (which *would* be the case with a per-unit tax). Two examples of such taxes are the 'windfall tax' imposed in 1997 by the UK Labour government on the profits of various privatised utilities, and in 2005 on the profits of oil companies operating in the North Sea following large increases in world oil prices.

If the government is concerned that the monopolist produces less than the socially efficient output, it could give the monopolist a *per-unit subsidy* (which would encourage the monopolist to produce more). But would this not *increase* the monopolist's profit? The answer to this is to impose a harsh lump-sum tax in addition to the subsidy. The tax would not undo the subsidy's benefit of encouraging the monopolist to produce more, but it could be used to reduce the monopolist's profits below the original (i.e. pre-subsidy) level.

Advantages of taxes and subsidies

Many economists favour the tax/subsidy solution to market imperfections (especially the problem of externalities) because it still allows the market to operate. It forces firms to take on board the full social costs and benefits of their actions. It is also adjustable according to the magnitude of the problem.

Moreover, if firms are taxed for polluting, they are encouraged to find cleaner ways of producing. The tax acts as an incentive over the longer run to reduce pollution. Likewise, by subsidising *good* practices, firms are given the incentive to adopt more good practices.

Disadvantages of taxes and subsidies

Infeasible to use different tax and subsidy rates. Each firm produces different levels and types of externalities and operates under different degrees of imperfect competition. It would be administratively very difficult and expensive, if not impossible, to charge every offending firm its own particular tax rate (or grant every relevant firm its own particular rate of subsidy). Even in the case of pollution where it is possible to measure a firm's emissions, there would still have to be a different tax rate for each pollutant and even for each environment, depending on its ability to absorb the pollutant and the number of people affected.

Using combinations of lump-sum taxes and per-unit subsidies to correct monopoly distortions to price, output and profit would also probably be impractical. Given that cost and revenue curves differ substantially from one firm to another, separate tax and subsidy rates would be needed for each firm. An army of tax inspectors would be necessary to administer the system!

Lack of knowledge. Even if a government did decide to charge a tax equal to each offending firm's marginal external costs, it would still have the problem of measuring those costs and apportioning blame. The damage to lakes and forests from acid

Pause for thought

Why is it easier to use taxes and subsidies to tackle the problem of car exhaust pollution than to tackle the problem of peak-time traffic congestion in cities?

rain has been a major concern since the beginning of the 1980s. But just how serious is that damage? What is its current monetary cost? How long-lasting is the damage? Just what and who is to blame? These are questions that cannot be answered precisely. It is thus impossible to fix the 'correct' pollution tax on, say, a particular coal-fired power station.

Despite these problems, it is nevertheless possible to charge firms by the amount of a particular emission. For example, firms could be charged for chimney smoke by so many parts per million of a given pollutant. Although it is difficult to 'fine-tune' such a system so that the charge reflects the precise number of people affected by the pollutant and by how much, it does go some way to internalising the externality. As Box 7.4 on pages 222–3 shows, many countries in recent years have introduced 'green' taxes, seeing them as an effective means of protecting the environment.

Recap

1. Taxes and subsidies are one means of correcting market distortions.

2. Externalities can be corrected by imposing tax rates equal to the size of marginal external costs, and granting rates of subsidy equal to marginal external benefits.

3. Taxes and subsidies can also be used to affect monopoly price, output and profit. Subsidies can be used to persuade a monopolist to increase output (and reduce price) to the competitive level.

Lump-sum taxes can then be used to reduce monopoly profits without affecting the new price or output.

4. Taxes and subsidies have the advantages of 'internalising' externalities and of providing incentives to reduce external costs. On the other hand, they may be impractical to use when different rates are required for each case, or when it is impossible to know the full effects of the activities that the taxes or subsidies are being used to correct.

7.6 GOVERNMENT INTERVENTION: LAWS AND REGULATION

Should the government try to stop 'bad behaviour' by big business?

Laws prohibiting or regulating undesirable structures or behaviour

Laws are frequently used to correct market imperfections. Laws can be of three main types: those that prohibit or regulate behaviour that imposes external costs, those that prevent firms providing false or misleading information, and those that prevent or regulate monopolies and oligopolies. For example, in the UK, under the 2002 Enterprise Act, it is a criminal offence for two or more firms to engage in cartel agreements, such as price fixing, market sharing or supply restriction (see pages 137 and 140). Convicted offenders may receive a prison sentence of up to five years and/or an unlimited fine.

Advantages of legal restrictions

- They are usually simple and clear to understand and are often relatively easy to administer. For example, various polluting activities could be banned or restricted.

- When the danger is very great, or when the extent of the danger is not as yet known, it might be much safer to ban various practices altogether (e.g. the use of various toxic chemicals) rather than to rely on taxes.
- When a decision needs to be taken quickly, it might be possible to invoke emergency action. For example, in Athens it was found to be simpler to ban or restrict the use of private cars during a chemical smog emergency than to tax their use.
- Because consumers suffer from imperfect information, consumer protection laws can make it illegal for firms to sell shoddy or unsafe goods, or to make false or misleading claims about their products.

Disadvantages of legal restrictions

The main problem is that legal restrictions tend to be a rather blunt weapon. If, for example, a firm were required to reduce the effluent of a toxic chemical to 20 tonnes per week, there would be no incentive for the firm to reduce it further. With a tax on the effluent, however, the more the firm reduced the effluent, the less tax it would pay. Thus with a system of taxes there is a *continuing* incentive to cut pollution, to improve safety, or whatever.

Regulatory bodies

Rather than using the blunt weapon of general legislation to ban or restrict various activities, a more 'subtle' approach can be adopted. This involves the use of various regulatory bodies. Having identified possible cases where action might be required (e.g. potential cases of pollution or misleading information), the regulatory body would probably conduct an investigation and then prepare a report containing its findings and recommendations. It might also have the power to enforce its decisions.

In most industrial countries, governments have in place a 'competition policy' which attempts to control the worst abuses of market power. In the EU, the European Commission can order an investigation of firms operating in two or more EU countries if it is suspected that they are engaging in anti-competitive practices. These include such things as price fixing by oligopolists (see Case Studies 5.14 and 5.15 in MyEconLab), the refusal by a manufacturer to supply retailers that discount its products, or a firm conducting 'predatory pricing' – deliberately selling at a loss in part of the market in order to undercut the price of a new entrant. Practices that are found after investigation to be detrimental to competition are prohibited and heavy fines can be imposed, even for a first offence.

In the UK, the Office of Fair Trading (OFT) is the official body that investigates and reports on suspected cases of anti-competitive practices. The OFT can order such firms to cease or modify these practices. If they do not, the OFT can impose fines of up to 10 per cent of the firm's worldwide annual revenue. Alternatively the OFT can refer such firms to the Competition Commission. The Commission then conducts an investigation, and makes a ruling.

In the UK there are also regulatory bodies for each of the major privatised utilities (see Box 7.2).

The advantage of such bodies is that a case-by-case approach can be adopted and, as a result, the most appropriate solution adopted. However, investigations may be expensive and time-consuming, only a few cases may be examined and offending firms may make various promises of good behaviour which, owing to a lack of follow-up by the regulatory body, may not in fact be carried out.

> **Pause for thought**
>
> *What other forms of intervention are likely to be necessary to back up the work of regulatory bodies?*

BOX 7.2   REGULATING PRIVATISED INDUSTRIES

Is it the best way of dealing with their monopoly power?

From the early 1980s, the Thatcher and Major governments engaged in extensive programmes of 'privatisation', returning most of the nationalised industries to the private sector. Nationalised industries, they claimed, were bureaucratic, inefficient, unresponsive to consumer wishes and often a burden on the taxpayer.

Other countries have followed similar programmes of privatisation in what has become a worldwide phenomenon. Privatisation has been seen by many governments as a means of revitalising ailing industries and raising revenues to ease budgetary problems.

However, privatisation has brought its own problems. Consumers have complained of poor service and high prices. The result is that governments have been increasingly concerned to *regulate* the behaviour of these industries, many of which have considerable market power.

The system of regulation in the UK

In each of the major privatised industries – gas and electricity, telecommunications, water and railways – there is a separate regulatory office. Their legal authority is contained in the Act of privatisation, but their real power lies in the terms of their licences and price-setting formulae.

The price-setting formulae are essentially of the 'RPI minus X' variety. What this means is that the industries can raise their prices by the rate of increase in the retail price index (*RPI*) (i.e. by the rate of inflation) *minus* a certain percentage (X) to take account of expected increases in efficiency. The idea is that this will force the industry to pass such cost savings on to the consumer. The licence also permits the regulator to monitor other aspects of the behaviour of the industry and to require it to take various measures. For example, the Office of Rail Regulation sets minimum standards for the punctuality and frequency of trains. Generally, however, the approach has been one of negotiation with the industry.

Assessing the system of regulation in the UK

The system that has evolved in the UK has various advantages.

■ It is a *discretionary* system, with the regulator able to judge individual examples of the behaviour of the industry on their own merits. The regulator has a detailed knowledge of the industry, which would not be available to government ministers or other bodies such as the Office of Fair Trading. The regulator could thus be argued to be the best person to decide on whether the industry is acting in the public interest.
■ The system is *flexible*, since it allows for the licence and price formula to be changed as circumstances change.
■ The 'RPI minus X' formula provides an *incentive* for the privatised firms to be as efficient as possible. If they can lower their costs by more than X, they will, in theory, be able to make larger profits and keep them. If, on the other hand, they do not succeed in reducing costs sufficiently, they will make a loss. There is thus a continuing pressure on them to cut costs.

There are, however, some inherent problems with the way in which regulation operates in the UK.

■ The 'RPI minus X' formula was designed to provide an incentive for the firms to cut costs. But if X is too low, the firm might make excessive profits. Frequently regulators have underestimated the scope for cost reductions resulting from new technology and reorganisation, and have thus initially set X too low. As a result, instead of X remaining constant for a number of years, as intended, new higher values for X have been set after only one or two years. Alternatively, one-off price cuts have been ordered, as happened when the water companies were required by OFWAT to cut prices by an average of 10 per cent in 2000. In either case the incentive for the industry to cut costs is reduced. What is the point of being more efficient if the regulator is merely going to take away the extra profits?

Recap

1. Laws can be used to regulate activities that impose external costs, to regulate monopolies and oligopolies, and to provide consumer protection. Legal controls are often simpler and easier to operate than taxes, and are safer when the danger is potentially great. Nevertheless, legal controls tend to be rather a blunt weapon, although discretion can sometimes be allowed in the administration of the law.

2. Regulatory bodies can be set up to monitor and control activities that might be against the public interest (e.g. anti-competitive behaviour of oligopolists). They can conduct investigations of specific cases and can be very thorough. The investigations, however, may be expensive and time-consuming, and may not be acted on by the authorities.

TC 7
p 10

TC 4
p 21

Interestingly, in March 2008 OFGEM, the regulator of gas and electricity markets in the UK announced that it was going to embark on a review of *RPI – X* pricing and, in particular, whether this was consistent with tackling climate change. The results of this review were expected in 2010.

■ Regulation is becoming increasingly complex. This makes it difficult for the industries to plan and may lead to a growth of 'short-termism'. One of the claimed advantages of privatisation was to give greater independence to the industries from short-term government interference, and allow them to plan for the longer term. In practice, one type of interference may have been replaced by another.

■ There may also be the danger of **regulatory capture**. As regulators become more and more involved in their industry and get to know the senior managers at a personal level, so they are increasingly likely to see the managers' point of view and become less and less tough. Commentators do not believe that this has happened yet: the regulators are generally independently minded. But it is a danger for the future.

■ Alternatively, regulators could be captured by government. Instead of being totally independent, there to serve the interests of the consumer, they might bend to pressures from the government to do things which might help the government win the next election.

Increasing competition in the privatised industries

Where natural monopoly exists (see page 124), competition is impossible in a free market. Of course, the industry *could* be broken up by the government, with firms prohibited from owning more than a certain percentage of the industry. But this would lead to higher costs of production. Firms would be operating further back up a downward-sloping long-run average cost curve.

But many parts of the privatised industries are not natural monopolies. Generally it is only the *grid* that is a natural monopoly. In the case of gas and water, it is the pipelines. It would be wasteful to duplicate these. In the case of electricity it is the power lines: the national grid

and the local power lines. In the case of the railways it is the track. *Other* parts of these industries, however, have generally been opened up to competition (with the exception of water). Thus there are now many producers and sellers of electricity and gas. This is possible because they are given access, by law, to the national and local electricity grids and gas pipelines.

Even for the parts where there is a natural monopoly, they could be made contestable monopolies. One way of doing this is by granting operators a licence for a specific period of time. This is known as **franchising**, and has been the approach used for the railways. Once a company has been granted a franchise, it has the monopoly of passenger rail services over specific routes. But the awarding of the franchise can be highly competitive, with rival companies putting in competitive bids, in terms of both price (or, in the case of railways, the level of government subsidy required) and the quality of service.

Despite attempts to introduce competition into the privatised industries, they are still dominated by giant companies. Even if they are no longer strictly monopolies, they still have considerable market power. Competition is far from being perfect! The scope for price leadership or other forms of oligopolistic collusion is great. Thus although regulation through the price formula has been progressively abandoned as elements of competition have been introduced, the regulators have retained a role similar to that of the Office of Fair Trading: they can intervene to prevent cases of collusion and the abuse of monopoly power. The companies, however, do have the right of appeal to the Competition Commission.

1. *Should regulators of utilities that have been privatised into several separate companies allow (a) mergers between these companies or similar companies from abroad; (b) mergers with firms in other industries?*
2. *If an industry regulator adopts an RPI – X formula for price regulation, is it desirable that the value of X should be adjusted as soon as cost conditions change?*

Definitions

Regulatory capture
Where the regulator is persuaded to operate in the industry's interests rather than those of the consumer.

Franchising
Where a firm is granted the licence to operate a given part of an industry for a specified length of time.

7.7 OTHER FORMS OF GOVERNMENT INTERVENTION

What other means does the government have to correct market failures?

Changes in property rights

One cause of market failure is the limited nature of property rights. If someone dumps a load of rubble in your garden, you can insist that it is removed. If, however, someone dumps a load of rubble in his or her *own* garden, but which is next door to yours, what can you do? You can still see it from your window. It is still an eyesore. But you have no property rights over the next-door garden.

Property rights define who owns property, to what uses it can be put, the rights other people have over it and how it may be transferred. By *extending* these rights, individuals may be able to prevent other people imposing costs on them, or charge them for doing so.

The socially efficient level of charge would be one that was equal to the marginal external cost (and would have the same effect as the government charging a tax on the firm of that amount: see Figure 7.5). The **Coase theorem**[3] states that in an otherwise perfectly competitive market, the socially efficient charge *will* be levied. But why?

Let us take the case of river pollution by a chemical works that imposes a cost on people fishing in the river. If property rights to the river were now given to the fishing community they could impose a charge on the chemical works per unit of output. If they charged *less* than the marginal external cost, they would suffer more from the last unit (in terms of lost fish) than they were being compensated. If they charged *more*, and thereby caused the firm to cut back its output below the socially efficient level, they would be sacrificing receiving charges that would be greater than the marginal suffering. It will be in the sufferers' best interests, therefore, to charge an amount *equal* to the marginal externality.

In most instances, however, this type of solution is totally impractical. It is impractical when *many* people are *slightly* inconvenienced, especially if there are many culprits imposing the costs. For example, if I were disturbed by noisy lorries outside my home, it would not be practical to negotiate with every haulage company involved. What if I wanted to ban the lorries from the street but my next-door neighbour wanted to charge them 10p per journey? Who gets their way?

Where the extension of private property rights becomes a more practical solution is when the culprits are few in number, are easily identifiable and impose clearly defined costs. Thus a noise abatement Act could be passed which allowed me to prevent my neighbours playing noisy radios, having noisy parties or otherwise disturbing the peace in my home. The onus would be on me to report them. Or I could agree not to report them if they paid me adequate compensation.

But even in cases where only a few people are involved, there may still be the problem of litigation. Justice may not be free, and there is thus a conflict with equity. The rich can afford 'better' justice. They can employ top lawyers. Thus even

Definition

The Coase theorem
By sufferers from externalities doing deals with perpetrators (by levying charges or offering payments), the externality will be 'internalised' and the socially efficient level of output will be achieved.

Pause for thought

If the sufferers had no property rights, show how it would still be in their interests to 'bribe' the firm to produce the socially efficient level of output.

---

[3] Named after Ronald Coase, who developed the theory. See his 'The problem of social cost', *Journal of Law and Economics* (1960).

if I have a right to sue a large company for dumping toxic waste near me, I may not have the legal muscle to win.

Finally there is the broader question of *equity*. The extension of private property rights may favour the rich (who tend to have more property) at the expense of the poor. Ramblers may get great pleasure from strolling across a great country estate, along public rights of way. This may annoy the owner. If the owner's property rights are now extended to exclude the ramblers, is this a social gain?

Of course, equity considerations can also be dealt with by altering property rights, but in a different way. *Public* property like parks, open spaces, libraries and historic buildings could be extended. Also the property of the rich could be redistributed to the poor. Here it is less a question of the rights that ownership confers, and more a question of altering the ownership itself.

> **Pause for thought**
>
> *Would it be a good idea to extend countries' territorial waters in order to bring key open-seas fishing grounds within countries' territory? Could this help to solve the problem of over-fishing?*

Provision of information

When ignorance is a reason for market failure, the direct provision of information by the government or one of its agencies may help to correct that failure. An example is the information on jobs provided by job centres to those looking for work. They thus help the labour market to work better and increase the elasticity of supply of labour. Another example is the provision of consumer information – for example, on the effects of smoking, or of eating certain foodstuffs. Another is the provision of government statistics on prices, costs, employment, sales trends, etc. This enables firms to plan with greater certainty.

The direct provision of goods and services

In the case of public goods and services, such as streets, pavements, seaside illumination and national defence, the market may completely fail to provide. In this case the government must take over the role of provision. Central government, local government or some other public agency could provide these goods and services directly. Alternatively, they could pay private firms to do so. The public would pay through central and local taxation.

But just what quantity of the public good should be provided? How can the level of public demand or public 'need' be identified? Should any charge at all be made to consumers for each unit consumed?

With a pure public good, once it is provided the marginal cost of supplying one more consumer is zero. Take the case of a lighthouse. Once it is constructed and in operation, there is no extra cost of providing the service to additional passing ships. Even if it were *possible* to charge ships each time they make use of it, it would not be socially desirable. Assuming no external costs, MSC is zero. Thus $MSB = MSC$ at a price of zero. Zero is thus the socially efficient price.

But what about the construction of a new public good, like a new road or a new lighthouse? How can a rational decision be made by the government as to whether it should go ahead? This time the marginal cost is not zero: extra roads and lighthouses cost money to build. The solution is to identify all the costs and benefits to society from the project (private and external) and to weigh them up. This is known as **cost–benefit analysis** (see Web Appendix 7.2 for details of how cost–benefit analysis is conducted). If the social benefits of the project exceed the social costs, then it would be socially efficient to go ahead with it. Many proposed public projects are subjected to cost–benefit analysis in order to assess their desirability.

> **Definition**
>
> **Cost–benefit analysis**
> The identification, measurement and weighing-up of the costs and benefits of a project in order to decide whether or not it should go ahead.

The government could also provide goods and services directly which are *not* public goods. Examples include health and education. There are four reasons why such things are provided free or at well below cost.

Social justice. Society may feel that these things should not be provided according to ability to pay. Rather they should be provided as of right: an equal right based on need.

Large positive externalities. People other than the consumer may benefit substantially. If a person decides to get treatment for an infectious disease, other people benefit by not being infected. A free health service thus helps to combat the spread of disease.

Dependants. If education were not free, and if the quality of education depended on the amount spent, and if parents could choose how much or little to buy, then the quality of children's education would depend not just on their parents' income, but also on how much they cared. A government may choose to provide such things free in order to protect children from 'bad' parents. A similar argument is used for providing free prescriptions and dental treatment for all children.

Ignorance. Consumers may not realise how much they will benefit. If they had to pay, they may choose (unwisely) to go without. Providing health care free may persuade people to consult their doctors before a complaint becomes serious.

Recap

1. An extension of property rights may allow individuals to prevent others imposing costs on them, or to charge them for so doing. This is not practical, however, when many people are affected to a small degree, or where several people are affected but differ in their attitudes towards what they want doing about the 'problem'.

2. The government may provide information in cases where the private sector fails to provide an adequate level.

3. The government may also provide goods and services directly. These could be in the category of public goods or other goods where the government feels that provision by the market is inadequate.

7.8 MORE OR LESS INTERVENTION?

Can the government always put things right?

Government intervention in the market can itself lead to problems.

Drawbacks of government intervention

Shortages and surpluses. If the government intervenes by fixing prices at levels other than the equilibrium, this will create either shortages or surpluses (see Section 3.6).

If the price is fixed *below* the equilibrium, there will be a shortage. For example, if the rent of council houses is fixed below the equilibrium in order to provide cheap housing for poor people, demand will exceed supply. In the case of such shortages the government will have to adopt a system of waiting lists, or rationing, or giving certain people preferential treatment. Alternatively it will have to allow allocation to be on a first-come, first-served basis or allow queues to develop. Black markets are likely to occur.

If the price is fixed *above* the equilibrium price, there will be a surplus. Such surpluses are obviously wasteful. (The problem of food surpluses in the European Union was examined in Box 3.4.)

Poor information. The government may not know the full costs and benefits of its policies. It may genuinely wish to pursue the interests of consumers or any other group and yet may be unaware of people's wishes or misinterpret their behaviour.

Bureaucracy and inefficiency. Government intervention involves administrative costs. The more wide-reaching and detailed the intervention, the greater the number of people and material resources that will be involved. These resources may be used wastefully.

Lack of market incentives. If government intervention removes market forces or cushions their effect (by the use of subsidies, welfare provisions, guaranteed prices or wages, etc.), it may remove certain useful incentives. Subsidies may allow inefficient firms to survive. Welfare payments may discourage effort. The market may be imperfect, but it does tend to encourage efficiency by allowing the efficient to receive greater rewards.

Shifts in government policy. The economic efficiency of industry may suffer if government intervention changes too frequently. It makes it difficult for firms to plan if they cannot predict tax rates, subsidies, price and wage controls, etc.

Lack of freedom for the individual. Government intervention involves a loss of freedom for individuals to make economic choices. The argument is not just that the pursuit of individual gain is seen to lead to the social good, but that it is desirable in itself that individuals should be as free as possible to pursue their own interests with the minimum of government interference: that minimum being largely confined to the maintenance of laws consistent with the protection of life, liberty and property.

The case for non-intervention (*laissez-faire*), or very limited intervention, is not that the market is the *perfect* means of achieving given social goals, but that the above problems created by intervention are greater than the problems it overcomes.

Advantages of the free market

Although markets in the real world are not perfect, even imperfect markets can be argued to have positive advantages over government provision or even government regulation. These might include the following:

Automatic adjustments. Government intervention requires administration. A free-market economy, on the other hand, leads to automatic, albeit imperfect, adjustment to demand and supply changes.

Dynamic advantages of capitalism. The chances of making high monopoly/oligopoly profits will encourage business people to invest in new products and new techniques. Prices may be high initially, but consumers will gain from the extra choice of products. Furthermore, if profits are high, new firms will sooner or later break into the market and competition will ensue.

> **Pause for thought**
>
> *Are there any features of free-market capitalism that would discourage innovation?*

A high degree of competition even under monopoly/oligopoly. Even though an industry at first sight may seem to be highly monopolistic, competitive forces may still work as a result of the following:

■ A fear that excessively high profits might encourage firms to attempt to break into the industry (assuming that the market is contestable).
■ Competition from closely related industries (e.g. coach services for rail services, or electricity for gas).
■ The threat of foreign competition.
■ Countervailing powers (see page 146). Large powerful producers often sell to large powerful buyers. For example, the power of detergent manufacturers to drive up the price of washing powder is countered by the power of supermarket chains to drive down the price at which they purchase it. Thus power is to some extent neutralised.
■ The competition for corporate control (see page 128).

Should there be more or less intervention in the market?

No firm conclusions can be drawn in the debate between those who favour more and those who favour less government intervention, for the following reasons:

■ Many moral, social and political issues are involved which cannot be settled by economic analysis. For example, it could be argued that freedom to set up in business and freedom from government regulation are desirable for their own sake. As a fundamental ethical point of view this can be disputed, but not disproved.
■ In principle, the issue of whether a government ought to intervene in any situation could be settled by weighing up the costs and benefits of that intervention. However, such costs and benefits, even if they could be identified, are extremely difficult if not impossible to measure, especially when the costs are borne by different people from those who receive the benefits and when externalities are involved.
■ Often the effect of more or less intervention simply cannot be predicted: there are too many uncertainties.

Nevertheless, economists can make a considerable contribution to analysing problems of the market and the effects of government intervention.

Recap

1. Government intervention in the market may lead to shortages or surpluses; it may be based on poor information; it may be costly in terms of administration; it may stifle incentives; it may be disruptive if government policies change too frequently; it may remove certain liberties.

2. By contrast, a free market leads to automatic adjustments to changes in economic conditions; the prospect of monopoly/oligopoly profits may stimulate risk taking and hence research and development and innovation; there may still be a high degree of actual or potential competition under monopoly and oligopoly.

3. It is impossible to draw firm conclusions about the 'optimum' level of government intervention. This is partly due to the moral/political nature of the question, partly due to the difficulties of measuring costs and benefits of intervention/non-intervention, and partly due to the difficulties of predicting the effects of government policies, especially over the longer term.

THE ENVIRONMENT: A CASE STUDY IN MARKET FAILURE   **7.9**

How can economists contribute to the environmental debate?

The environmental problem

Global warming, pollution of the land, rivers and seas, the depletion of fish stocks, the chopping down of rainforests, the reduction in biodiversity, the dirty and rubbish-strewn nature of many cities and the despoiling of the countryside have become major concerns around the world in recent years. And yet, in many cases the degradation of the environment is getting worse.

There are some grounds for optimism, however. Many newer industrial processes are cleaner and make a more efficient use of resources. This leads to less waste and a slowdown in the rate of extraction of various minerals and fossil fuels.

In addition, as resources become scarcer, so their prices rise. This encourages people to use less of them, either by using more efficient technology or by switching to renewable alternatives. Thus as fossil fuels gradually run out, so a rise in their price will encourage the switch to solar, wave and wind power.

Finally, public opinion can put important pressure on governments and firms. Many firms have found it to be in their commercial interests to have a 'green image'. Likewise, governments see electoral advantage in policies to create a cleaner, greener environment.

Despite these developments, however, many aspects of environmental degradation continue to worsen. Many natural species continue to be destroyed; fish stocks in many parts of the world are dangerously low; tropical forests are being cut down at an alarming rate; toxic chemicals are widespread in the environment; fossil fuel usage grows apace as large developing countries, such as China and India, continue on a path of rapid industrialisation, and as road and air travel throughout the world seem inexorably to grow; global warming is set to accelerate, with consequent rises in sea levels and dramatically changing rainfall patterns.

Part of the problem is the growing pressure on the environment of a rapidly expanding world population (see Box 4.2 on page 88). But a major cause of the problem is the failure of the market system.

Market failures

The market system will fail to provide an adequate protection for the environment for a number of reasons.

The environment as a common resource. The air, the seas and many other parts of the environment are not privately owned. They are a global 'commons', and thus have the characteristic of 'non-excludability' (see page 197). Many of the 'services' provided by the environment do not have a price, so there is no economic incentive to economise on their use.

Yet most environmental resources are *scarce*: there is 'rivalry' in their use. This is where common resources differ from public goods. One person's use of a common resource diminishes the amount or quality available for others. At a zero price, these resources will be overused. This is why fish stocks in many parts of the world are severely depleted, why virgin forests are disappearing (cut down for timber or firewood), why many roads are so congested and why the atmosphere is becoming so polluted (being used as a common 'dump' for emissions). In each case, a resource that is freely available is overused. This is known as the 'tragedy of the commons'. Web Appendix 7.3 examines the economics of common resources.

Externalities. One of the major problems of the environment being a common resource is that of externalities. When people pollute the environment, the costs are borne mainly by others. The greater these external costs, the lower will be the socially efficient level of output (Q_2 in Figure 7.1(a) on page 195). Because no one owns the environment, there is no one to enforce property rights over it. If a company pollutes the air that I breathe, I cannot stop it because the air does not belong to me.

Ignorance. There have been many cases of people causing environmental damage without realising it, especially when the effects build up over a long time. Take the case of aerosols. It was not until the 1980s that scientists connected their use to ozone depletion. Even when the problems are known to scientists, consumers may not appreciate the full environmental costs of their actions. So even if people would like to be more 'environmentally friendly' in their activities, they might not have the knowledge to be so.

Pause for thought

Look through the categories of possible market failings in Sections 7.1 to 7.3. Are there any others, in addition to the four we have just identified, that will result in a socially inefficient use of the environment?

Inter-generational problems. The environmentally harmful effects of many activities are long-term, whereas the benefits are immediate. Thus consumers and firms are frequently prepared to continue with various practices and leave future generations to worry about their environmental consequences. The problem, then, is a reflection of the importance that people attach to the present relative to the future.

Policy alternatives

Charging for use of the environment (as a resource or a dump)

Definition

Environmental charges
Charges for using natural resources (e.g. water or national parks), or for using the environment as a dump for waste (e.g. factory emissions or sewage).

One way of 'pricing the environment' is for the government to impose **environmental charges** on consumers or firms. Thus *emissions charges* could be levied on firms discharging waste. Another example is the use of *user charges* to households for sewage disposal or rubbish collection. The socially efficient level of environmental use would be where the marginal social benefits and costs of that use were equal. This is illustrated in Figure 7.6, which shows the emission of toxic waste into a river by a chemical plant.

It is assumed that all the benefits from emitting the waste into the river accrue to the firm (i.e. there is no external benefit). Marginal private and marginal social benefits are thus the same ($MB = MSB$). The curve slopes downwards because, with a downward-sloping demand curve for the *good*, higher output will have a lower marginal benefit, and so too will the waste associated with it.

But what about the marginal costs? Without charges, the marginal private cost of using the river for emitting the waste is zero. The pollution of the river, however, imposes an external cost on those living by the river or using it for fishing or water supply. The marginal external cost rises as the river becomes less and less able to cope with increased levels of emission. As there is no private cost, the marginal social cost is the same as the marginal external cost.

Without a charge, the firm will emit L_1, since this is where its private marginal cost (= 0) equals its private marginal benefit. The socially efficient level of emission is L_2 and the socially efficient level of emission charge, therefore, is P_2.

Figure 7.6   An emissions charge

Environmental ('green') taxes and subsidies

Rather than charging for environmental use, a tax could be imposed on the output (or consumption) of a *good*, wherever external environmental costs are generated. These are known as **green taxes**. In this case, the good already has a price: the tax has the effect of increasing the price. To achieve a socially efficient output, the rate of tax should be equal to the marginal external cost (see Figure 7.5 on page 206). The alternative is to subsidise activities that reduce pollution (such as the installation of loft insulation). Here the rate of subsidy should be equal to the marginal external benefit.

Although green taxes and subsidies are theoretically a means of achieving social efficiency, they do have serious limitations (see Box 7.4).

Laws and regulations

The traditional way of tackling pollution has been to set maximum permitted levels of emission or resource use, or minimum acceptable levels of environmental quality, and then to fine firms contravening these limits. Clearly, there have to be inspectors to monitor the amount of pollution, and the fines have to be large enough to deter firms from exceeding the limit.

Virtually all countries have environmental regulations of one sort or another. For example, the EU has over 200 items of legislation covering areas such as air and water pollution, noise, the marketing and use of dangerous chemicals, waste management, the environmental impacts of new projects (such as power stations, roads and quarries), recycling, depletion of the ozone layer and global warming.

Given the uncertainty over the environmental impacts of pollutants, especially in the longer term, it is often better to play safe and set tough emissions or ambient standards. These could always be relaxed at a later stage if the effects turn out not to be so damaging, but it might be too late to reverse damage if the effects turn out to be more serious. Taxes may be a more sophisticated means of reaching a socially

TC 4
p 21

Definition

Green tax
A tax on output designed to charge for the adverse effects of production on the environment. The socially efficient level of a green tax is equal to the marginal environmental cost of production.

BOX 7.3　A DEEPER SHADE OF GREEN

How should we treat the environment?

How green are you? Do you see the environment as there for you to use as you choose, or do we all have responsibilities for looking after the environment – responsibilities towards each other, or to future generations, or to the animals and plants that share the planet with us, or even to the planet itself? In this box we examine some of the different approaches to looking after the environment, and ask what implications they have for sustainability.

The free-market approach. At one extreme, we could regard the world as there purely for ourselves: a resource that belongs to individual property owners to do with as they choose; or a 'common asset', such as the air and seas, for individuals to use for their own benefit. In this view of the world, we are entitled simply to weigh up the marginal costs and benefits to ourselves of any activity. Sustainability is only achieved in this free-market world to the extent that resource prices rise as they become scarce and to the extent that environmentally friendly technologies are in firms' (or consumers') private interests.

In terms of Figure 7.1(a) on page 195, assuming that there were external environmental costs (shown by the vertical difference between the *MSC* and *MC* curves), no account would be taken of these, and production would remain at the free-market level of Q_1.

The social-efficiency approach. A somewhat less extreme version of this view is one that takes the social costs and benefits of using the environment into account: i.e. not just the costs and benefits to the direct producer or consumer, but to people in general. Here we would apply the standard rules for social efficiency: that if marginal social benefit exceeds marginal social cost we should do more of the activity, and if marginal social cost exceeds marginal social benefit we should do less. In Figure 7.1(a), the social-efficiency approach would give an optimum output of Q_2.

Even though this approach does take into account environmental externalities (such as pollution) these environmental costs are only costs to the extent that they adversely affect *human beings*.

Within this general approach, however, more explicit account can be taken of sustainability, by including in the external costs the costs of our use of the environment today to *future* generations. For example, we could take into account the effects of global warming not just on ourselves, but on our children and their descendants.

The conservationist approach. Many environmentalists argue that our responsibilities should not be limited to each other, or even to future generations, but should include the environment for its own sake. Such a view would involve downplaying the relative importance of material consumption and economic growth and putting greater emphasis on the maintenance of ecosystems. Growth in consumption would be ethically acceptable only if it led to no (or only very minor) environmental degradation. Maintenance of the environment is thus seen as an ethical constraint on human activity. In Figure 7.1(a) the optimum production would be below Q_2 as long as the *MSC* curve only included costs to *society* and not the broader costs to the environment for its own sake.

The Gaia approach. The strongest approach to sustainability involves a fundamentally different ethical standpoint. Here the Earth itself, and its various natural species of animals and plants have moral rights. According to this 'Gaia philosophy', people are seen as mere custodians of the planet: the planet does not belong to us, any more than a dog belongs to the fleas on its back! This view of the environment is similar to that held by indigenous peoples living in marginal areas, such as the Aborigines in Australia and the Bushmen of the Kalahari, and to various other 'hunter–gatherer' peoples in developing countries. Their ethic is that the land they leave their descendants should be as good, if not better, than the land they inherited from their ancestors. Conservation is the 'prime directive'. This approach to the environment has been dubbed the 'deep green' approach.

In this approach, Figure 7.1(a) is irrelevant. The question is not whether environmental degradation is a price worth paying for the benefits of consumption. Production should be avoided that involves *any* environmental degradation.

1. If, according to the deep green approach, we should not do anything that involves environmental degradation, does this imply that the cost of environmental damage is infinite?
2. If the adverse effects on the environment of a person's actions were confined to that person's own property (e.g. a farmer cutting down hedgerows on his or her own land), would this matter if we took a social efficiency approach towards sustainability? Would there be any external *costs*?

efficient output, but regulations are usually more straightforward to devise, easier to understand by firms and easier to implement.

Education

People's attitudes are very important in determining the environmental consequences of their actions. Fortunately for the environment, people are not always out simply to maximise their own self-interest. If they were, then why would people often buy more expensive 'green' products, such as environmentally friendly detergents? The answer is that many people like to do their own little bit, however small, towards protecting the environment.

This is where education can come in. If children, and adults for that matter, were made more aware of environmental issues and the consequences of their actions, then people's consumption habits could change and more pressure would be put on firms to improve their 'green credentials'.

Tradable permits

A policy measure that has grown in popularity in recent years is that of **tradable permits**. This is a combination of regulations and market-based systems. A maximum permitted level of emission is set for a given pollutant for a given factory, and the firm is given a permit to emit up to this amount. If it emits less than this amount, it is given a credit for the difference, which it can then use in another of its factories, or sell to other firms. These other firms are then allowed to emit that amount *over* their permitted level. Thus the overall level of emissions is given by regulations, whereas their distribution is determined by the market.

Take the example of firms A and B, which are currently producing 12 units of a pollutant each. Now assume that a standard is set permitting them to produce only 10 units each. If firm A managed to reduce the pollutant to 8 units, it would be given a credit for 2 units. It could then sell this to firm B, enabling B to continue emitting 12 units. The effect would still be a total reduction of 4 units between the two firms. However, the trade in pollution permits allows pollution reduction to be concentrated where it can be achieved at lowest cost. In our example, if it cost firm B more to reduce its pollution than firm A, the permits could be sold from A to B at a price that was profitable to both (i.e. at a price above the cost of emission reduction to A, but below the cost of emission reduction to B). Given the resulting reduced cost of pollution control, it might be politically easier to impose tougher standards (i.e. impose lower permitted levels of emission).

The principle of tradable permits can be used as the basis of international agreements on pollution reduction. Each country could be required to achieve a certain percentage reduction in a pollutant (e.g. carbon dioxide – CO_2 – or sulphur dioxide – SO_2), but any country exceeding its reduction could sell its right to these emissions to other (presumably richer) countries.

A similar principle can be adopted for using natural resources. Thus fish quotas could be assigned to fishing boats or fleets or countries. Any parts of these quotas not used could then be sold.

The EU carbon trading system. In the EU, a carbon Emissions Trading Scheme (ETS) has been in place since January 2005 as part of the EU's approach to meeting its targets under the Kyoto Treaty (see Case Study 7.7 in MyEconLab). Each EU member state adopts a total CO_2 emissions quota in line with its Kyoto target. It then allocates emissions allowances, or credits, to all industrial plants producing significant amounts of CO_2 (some 12 000 across the EU). Companies that exceed their limits

Definition
Tradable permits Each firm is given a permit to produce a given level of pollution. If less than the permitted amount is produced, the firm is given a credit. This can then be sold to another firm, allowing it to exceed its original limit.

have to purchase credits to cover the difference, while those that reduce their emissions can sell their surplus credits for a profit. Companies can trade directly with each other or through brokers operating throughout Europe. More details can be found in Case Study 7.8 in MyEconLab.

Their growing popularity in the industrialised world

Increasingly countries are introducing 'green' taxes in order to discourage pollution as goods are produced, consumed or disposed of. The table shows the range of green taxes used around the world and the chart shows green tax revenues as a percentage of GDP in various countries.

As can be seen from the chart, they are higher than average in Scandinavian countries, reflecting the strength of their environmental concerns. They are lowest in the USA. By far the largest green tax revenues come from fuel taxes. Fuel taxes are relatively high in the UK and so, therefore, are green tax revenues.

There are various problems, however, with using the tax weapon in the fight against pollution.

Identifying the socially efficient tax rate. It will be difficult to identify the appropriate amount of tax for each firm, given that each one is likely to produce different amounts of pollutants for any given level of output. Even if two firms produce identical amounts of pollutants, the environmental damage might be quite different, because the ability of the environment to cope with it will differ between the two locations. Also, the number of people suffering will differ (a factor that is very important when considering the *human* impact of pollution). What is more,

Green tax revenues as a percentage of GDP

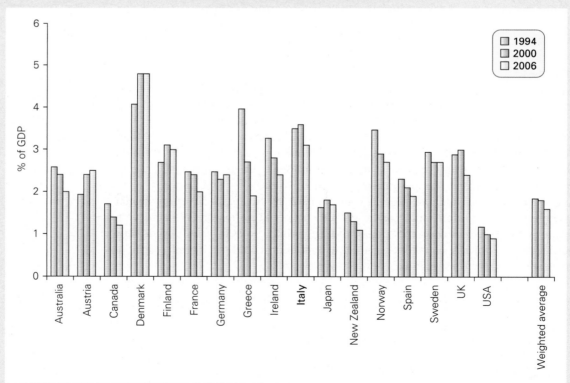

Source: Environmentally Related Taxes Database (OECD, 2009)

Assessing the system of tradable permits. The main advantage of tradable permits is that they combine the simplicity of regulations with the benefits of achieving pollution reduction in the most efficient way. There is also the advantage that firms have a financial incentive to cut pollution. This might then make it easier for governments to impose tougher standards (i.e. impose lower permitted levels of emission).

TC 4
p 21

CASE STUDIES & APPLICATIONS

Types of environmental taxes and charges

Motor fuels	**Other goods**	**Air transport**
Leaded/unleaded	Batteries	Noise charges
Diesel (quality differential)	Plastic carrier bags	Aviation fuels
Carbon/energy taxation	Glass containers	**Water**
Sulphur tax	Drink cans	Water charges
Other energy products	Tyres	Sewage charges
Carbon/energy tax	CFCs/halons	Water effluent charges
Sulphur tax or charge	Disposable razors/cameras	Manure charges
NO_2 charge	Lubricant oil charge	**Direct tax provisions**
Methane charge	Oil pollutant charge	Tax relief on green investment
Agricultural inputs	Solvents	Taxation on free company cars
Fertilisers	**Waste disposal**	Employer-paid commuting expenses taxable
Pesticides	Municipal waste charges	Employer-paid parking expenses taxable
Manure	Waste-disposal charges	Commuter use of public transport tax-deductible
Vehicle-related taxation	Hazardous waste charges	
Sales tax depends on car size	Landfill tax or charges	
Road tax depends on car size	Duties on waste water	

the harmful effects are likely to build up over time, and predicting these effects is fraught with difficulty.

Problems of demand inelasticity. The less elastic the demand for the product, the less effective will a tax be in cutting production and hence in cutting pollution. Thus taxes on petrol would have to be very high indeed to make significant reductions in the consumption of petrol and hence significant reductions in the exhaust gases that contribute towards global warming and acid rain.

Problems with international trade. If a country imposes pollution taxes on its industries, its products will become less competitive in world trade. To compensate for this, it may be necessary to give the industries tax rebates for exports. Also taxes would have to be imposed on imports of competitors' products from countries where there is no equivalent green tax.

Effects on employment. Reduced output in the industries affected by green taxes will lead to a reduction in employment. If, however, the effect was to encourage investment in new cleaner technology, employment might not fall. Furthermore, employment opportunities could be generated elsewhere, if the extra revenues from the green taxes were spent on alternative products (e.g. buses and trains rather than cars).

Redistributive effects. Many green taxes are regressive. The poor spend a higher proportion of their income on domestic fuel than the rich. A 'carbon tax' on such fuel therefore has the effect of redistributing incomes away from the poor. The poor also spend a larger proportion of their income on food than do the rich. Taxes on agriculture, designed to reduce the intensive use of fertilisers and pesticides, also tend to hit the poor proportionately more than the rich.

Not all green taxes, however, are regressive. The rich spend a higher proportion of their income on motoring than the poor. Thus petrol and other motoring taxes could have a progressive effect.

Despite these problems, such taxes can still move output closer to the socially efficient level. What is more, they do have the major advantage of providing a continuing incentive to firms to find cleaner methods of production and thereby save more on their tax bills.

Is it a good idea to use the revenues from green taxes to subsidise green alternatives (e.g. using petrol taxes for subsidising rail transport)? Consider the implications for wider tax policy in your answer.

| BOX 7.5 | THE PROBLEM OF URBAN TRAFFIC CONGESTION |

Does Singapore have the answer?

It takes only one hour to drive from one end of Singapore to the other. Yet the average Singaporean driver travels an estimated 20 800 km per year, more than the average US driver, and over 50 per cent more than the average Japanese driver. In Singapore in 2007 there were a little over 517 000 cars (excluding taxis), giving a vehicle density of 157 motor vehicles per km of road. This compares with a vehicle density in the USA of only 27 motor vehicles per km. It is hardly surprising that traffic congestion has become a major focus of public debate, particularly as the demand for cars is set to increase as consumer affluence grows.

The problem of traffic congestion

Traffic congestion is a classic example of the problem of externalities. When people use their cars, not only do they incur private costs (petrol, wear and tear on the vehicle, tolls, the time taken to travel, etc.), but also they impose costs on other people. These external costs include the following:

Congestion costs: time. When a person uses a car on a congested road, it will add to the congestion. This will therefore slow down the traffic even more and increase the journey time of other car users.

Congestion costs: monetary. Congestion increases fuel consumption, and the stopping and starting increases the costs of wear and tear. When a motorist adds to congestion, therefore, there will be additional monetary costs imposed on other motorists.

Environmental costs. When motorists use a road they reduce the quality of the environment for others. Cars emit fumes and create noise. This is bad enough for pedestrians and other car users, but can be particularly distressing for people living along the road. Driving can cause accidents – a problem that increases as drivers become more impatient as a result of delays.

Exhaust gases cause long-term environmental damage and are one of the main causes of the greenhouse effect and of the increased acidity of lakes and rivers and the poisoning of forests. They can also cause long-term health problems (e.g. for asthma sufferers).

The socially efficient level of road usage

These externalities mean that road usage will be above the social optimum. This is illustrated in the diagram. Costs and benefits are shown on the vertical axis and are measured in money terms. Thus any non-monetary costs or benefits (such as time costs) must be given a monetary value. The horizontal axis measures road usage in terms of cars per minute passing a specified point on the road.

For simplicity it is assumed that there are no external benefits from car use and that therefore marginal private and marginal social benefits are the same. The *MSB* curve is shown as downward sloping. The reason for this is that different road users put a different value on any given journey. If the marginal (private) cost of making the journey were high, only those for whom the journey had a high marginal benefit would travel along the road. If the

Actual and optimum road usage

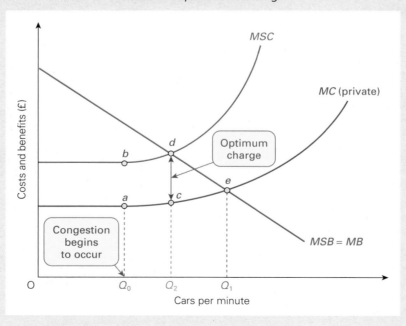

Cars per minute

marginal cost of making the journey fell, more people would make the journey: people choosing to make the journey as long as the marginal cost of the journey was less than the marginal benefit. Thus the greater the number of cars, the lower the marginal benefit.

The marginal (private) cost curve (MC) is likely to be constant up to the level of traffic flow at which congestion begins to occur. This is shown as point a in the diagram. Beyond this point, marginal cost is likely to rise as time costs increase (i.e. journey times lengthen) and as fuel consumption rises.

The marginal *social* cost curve (MSC) is drawn above the marginal private cost curve. The vertical difference between the two represents the external costs. Up to point b, external costs are simply the environmental costs. Beyond point b, there are also external congestion costs, since additional road users slow down the journey of *other* road users. These external costs get progressively greater as traffic grinds to a halt.

The actual level of traffic flow will be at Q_1, where marginal private costs and benefits are equal (point e). The socially efficient level of traffic flow, however, will be at the lower level of Q_2 where marginal social costs and benefits are equal (point d). In other words, there will be an excessive level of road usage.

So what can governments do to 'internalise' these externalities?

The Singapore solution

In contrast to its neighbours, many of which are suffering more acute urban traffic congestion problems, Singapore has an integrated transport policy. This includes the following:

■ Restricting the number of new car licences, and allowing their price to rise to the corresponding equilibrium. This makes car licences in Singapore among the most expensive in the world.
■ A 111-kilometre-long mass rail transit (MRT) system with subsidised fares. Trains are comfortable, clean and frequent. Stations are air-conditioned.
■ A programme of building new estates near MRT stations.
■ Cheap, frequent buses, serving all parts of the island.

But it is in respect to road usage that the Singaporean authorities have been most innovative.

The first innovation came in 1975. The city centre was made a restricted zone. Motorists who wished to enter this zone had to buy a ticket (an 'area licence') at any one of 33 entry points. Police were stationed at these entry points to check that cars had paid and displayed.

Then in 1990 a quota system for new cars was established. The government decides the total number of cars that the country should have, and issues just enough licences each month to maintain that total. These licences (or 'Certificates of Entitlement') are for 10 years and are

offered at auction. Their market price varies from around £10 000 to £30 000.

A problem with the licences is that they are a once-and-for-all payment, which does not vary with the amount that people use their car. In other words, their marginal cost (for additional miles driven) is zero. Many people feel that, having paid such a high price for their licence, they ought to use their car as much as possible in order to get value for money!

With traffic congestion steadily worsening, it was recognised that something more had to be done. Either the Area Licensing Scheme had to be widened, or some other form of charging had to be adopted. The decision was taken to introduce electronic road pricing (ERP). This alternative would not only save on police labour costs, but enable charge rates to be varied according to levels of congestion, times of the day, and locality.

What, then, would be the optimum charge? If the objective is to reduce traffic from Q_1 to Q_2 in the diagram, then a charge of $d - c$ should be levied.

Since 1998 all vehicles in Singapore have been fitted with an in-vehicle unit (IU). Every journey made requires the driver to insert a smart card containing pre-paid units into the IU. On specified roads, overhead gantries read the IU and deduct the appropriate charge from the card. If a car does not have sufficient funds on its smart card, the car's details are relayed to a control centre and a fine is imposed. The system has the benefit of operating on three-lane highways and does not require traffic to slow down.

The ERP system operates on roads subject to congestion and charges can vary every 5 or 20 minutes according to predicted traffic flows. Rates are published in advance but are reviewed every three months. The system is thus very flexible to allow traffic to be kept at the desired level.

The system was expensive to set up, however. Cheaper schemes have been adopted elsewhere, such as Norway and parts of the USA. These operate by funnelling traffic into a single lane in order to register the car, but they have the disadvantage of slowing the traffic down.

One message is clear from the Singapore solution. Road pricing alone is not enough. Unless there are fast, comfortable and affordable public transport alternatives, the demand for cars will be highly price inelastic. People have to get to work!

1. *Referring to a town or city with which you are familiar, consider what would be the most appropriate mix of policies to deal with its traffic congestion problems.*
2. *Explain how, by varying the charge debited from the smart card according to the time of day or level of congestion, a socially optimal level of road use can be achieved.*

There are, however, various problems with tradable permits. One is how to distribute the permissions in a way that all firms regard as fair. Another is the possibility that trade will lead to pollution being concentrated in certain geographical areas. Another is that it may reduce the pressure on dirtier factories (or countries) to cut their emissions.

Finally, the system will only lead to significant cuts in pollution if the permitted levels are low. Once the system is in place, the government might then feel the pressure is off to *reduce* the permitted levels. This was a major criticism of the first trading period of the EU's ETS in 2005–7. Emissions allowances were relatively generous. As a result many firms found it easy to produce surplus credits, which pushed their price to a low level, reaching a minuscule €0.02 per tonne by the end of 2007. This, in turn, made it cheap for 'dirty' firms to buy credits and thus reduced the pressure on them to cut pollution. In answer to this, the allowances were somewhat tighter in the second trading period (2008–12). By mid-2008, carbon was trading at around €28 per tonne. With the recession of 2008/9, however, the price fell as firms cut back production. By early 2009, the price was around €8 per tonne, although it rose again to about €14 by mid-2009.

> **Pause for thought**
>
> *To what extent does the introduction of tradable permits lead to a lower level of total pollution (as opposed to its redistribution)?*

How much can we rely on governments?

If governments are to be relied upon to set the optimum green taxes or regulations, several conditions must be met.

First, they must have the will to protect the environment. But governments are accountable to their electorates and must often appease various pressure groups, such as representatives of big business. In the USA, for example, there has been great resistance to cuts in greenhouse gases from the automobile, power and various other industries, many of which have powerful representation in Congress. One of the problems is that many of the environmental effects of our actions today will be on future generations, but governments represent today's generation, and today's generation may not be prepared to make the necessary sacrifices. This brings us back to the importance of education.

Second, it must be possible to identify just what the optimum is. This requires a knowledge of just what the environmental effects are of various activities, such as the emission of CO_2 into the atmosphere, and that is something on which scientists disagree.

Finally, there is the problem that many environmental issues are global and not just local or national. Many require concerted action by governments around the world. The history of international agreements on environmental issues, however, is plagued with difficulties between countries, which seem concerned mainly with their own national interests.

Recap

1. The effects of population pressures and market failures have led to growing environmental degradation.

2. The market fails to achieve a socially efficient use of the environment because large parts of the environment are a common resource, because production or consumption often generates environmental externalities, because of ignorance of the environmental effects of our actions, and because of a lack of concern for future generations.

3. One approach to protecting the environment is to impose charges for using the environment or taxes per unit of output. The problem with these methods is in identifying the appropriate charges or tax rates, since these will vary according to the environmental impact.

4. Another approach is to use laws and regulations, such as making certain practices illegal or putting limits on discharges. This is a less sophisticated alternative to taxes or charges, but it is safer when the environmental costs of certain actions are unknown.

5. Education can help to change attitudes towards the environment and the behaviour of consumers and firms.

6. Tradable permits are a mix of regulations and market-based systems. Firms are given permits to emit a certain level of pollution and these can then be traded. A firm that can reduce its pollution relatively cheaply below its permitted level can sell this credit to another firm that finds it more costly to do so. The system is an efficient and administratively cheap way of limiting pollution to a designated level. It can, however, lead to pollution being concentrated in certain areas and can reduce the pressure on firms to find cleaner methods of production.

7. Although governments can make a major contribution to reducing pollution, government action is unlikely to lead to the optimum outcome (however defined). Governments may be more concerned with short-run political considerations and will not have perfect information.

QUESTIONS

1. The table at the bottom of the page gives the costs and benefits of an imaginary firm operating under perfect competition whose activities create a certain amount of pollution. (It is assumed that the costs of this pollution to society can be accurately measured.)
   (a) What is the profit-maximising level of output for this firm?
   (b) What is the socially efficient level of output?
   (c) Why might the marginal pollution costs increase in the way illustrated in this example?

2. In Figure 7.1 (page 195) the MSC curve is drawn parallel to the MC curve. Under what circumstances would it have a steeper slope than the MC curve?

3. Give additional examples of each of the four types of externality to those given on pages 194–7.

4. Give some examples of public goods (other than those given on page 197). Does the provider of these goods or services (the government or local authority) charge for their use? If so, is the method of charging based on the amount of the good people use? Is it a good method of charging? Could you suggest a better method?

5. Distinguish between publicly provided goods, public goods and merit goods.

6. Name some goods or services provided by the government or local authorities that are not public goods.

7. Some roads could be regarded as a public good, but some could be provided by the market. Which types of road could be provided by the market? Why? Would it be a good idea?

Output (units)	Price per unit (MSB) (£)	Marginal (private) costs to the firm (MC) (£)	Marginal external (pollution) costs (MEC) (£)	Marginal social costs (MSC = MC + MEC) (£)
1	100	30	20	50
2	100	30	22	52
3	100	35	25	60
4	100	45	30	75
5	100	60	40	100
6	100	78	55	133
7	100	100	77	177
8	100	130	110	240

8. Assume that you have decided to buy an LCD television. How do you set about ensuring that you make the right choice between the available makes?

9. Assume that you wanted the information given in (a)–(h) below. In which cases could you (i) buy perfect information; (ii) buy imperfect information; (iii) obtain information without paying for it; (iv) not obtain information?

   (a) Which washing machine is the most reliable?
   (b) Which of two jobs that are vacant is the more satisfying?
   (c) Which builder will repair my roof most cheaply?
   (d) Which builder will make the best job of repairing my roof?
   (e) Which builder is best value for money?
   (f) How big a mortgage would it be wise for me to take out?
   (g) What course of higher education should I follow?
   (h) What brand of washing powder washes whiter?

   In which cases are there non-monetary costs to you of finding out the information? How can you know whether the information you acquire is accurate or not?

10. Make a list of pieces of information a firm might want to know and consider whether it could buy the information and how reliable that information might be.

11. Assume that a country had no state education at all. For what reasons might the private education system not provide the optimal allocation of resources to and within education?

12. Assume that a firm discharges waste into a river. As a result, the marginal social costs (*MSC*) are greater than the firm's marginal (private) costs (*MC*). The following table shows how *MC*, *MSC*, *AR*, *TR* and *MR* vary with output.

Output	1	2	3	4	5	6	7	8
MC	23	21	23	25	27	30	35	42
MSC	35	34	38	42	46	52	60	72
TR	60	102	138	168	195	219	238	252
AR	60	51	46	42	39	36.5	34	31.5
MR	60	42	36	30	27	24	19	14

   Assume that the marginal private benefit (*MB*) is given by the price (*AR*). Assume also that there are no externalities on the consumption side, and that therefore *MSB* = *MB*.

   (a) How much will the firm produce if it seeks to maximise profits?

   (b) What is the socially efficient level of output (assuming no externalities on the demand side)?
   (c) How much is the marginal external cost at this level of output?
   (d) What size of tax would be necessary for the firm to reduce its output to the socially efficient level?
   (e) Why is the tax less than the marginal externality?
   (f) Why might it be equitable to impose a lump-sum tax on this firm?
   (g) Why will a lump-sum tax not affect the firm's output (assuming that in the long run the firm can still make at least normal profit)?

13. On a diagram similar to Figure 7.5 (on page 206), demonstrate how a subsidy can correct for an external benefit.

14. Why might it be better to ban certain activities that cause environmental damage rather than to tax them?

15. To what extent could property rights (either public or private) be successfully extended and invoked to curb the problem of industrial pollution (a) of the atmosphere, (b) of rivers, (c) by the dumping of toxic waste, (d) by the erection of ugly buildings and (e) by the creation of high levels of noise?

16. What protection do private property rights in the real world give to sufferers of noise (a) from neighbours, (b) from traffic, (c) from transistor radios at the seaside?

17. How suitable are legal restrictions in the following cases?

   (a) Ensuring adequate vehicle safety (e.g. that tyres have sufficient tread or that the vehicle is roadworthy).
   (b) Reducing traffic congestion.
   (c) Preventing the abuse of monopoly power.
   (d) Ensuring that mergers are in the public interest.
   (e) Ensuring that firms charge a price equal to marginal cost.

18. How would you evaluate the following?

   (a) The external effects of building a reservoir in an area of outstanding natural beauty.
   (b) The external effects of acid rain pollution from a power station.

19. Many economists have argued that a form of 'congestion tax' ought to be imposed on motorists who use their cars on busy roads, to

take account of the external costs they impose on other road users and pedestrians. Compare the relative advantages and disadvantages of the following measures:

(a) Increasing the rate of duty on petrol.
(b) Increasing the annual road fund licence.
(c) Using a system such as that in Singapore (see Box 7.5), where charges are deducted from a pre-paid smart card inserted into a device in the car. Charges vary according to the time of day and/or the level of congestion.
(d) Installing cameras that record number plates of cars in a designated zone, and then fining their owners if a daily fixed fee for driving in the zone has not been paid (this system is used in London).

(e) Setting up toll booths to charge motorists for using certain stretches of road.
(f) The use of bus and cycle lanes at peak times.
(g) Subsidising public transport.

20. Give examples of how the government intervenes to protect the interests of dependants from bad economic decisions taken on their behalf.

21. What are the possible arguments in favour of fixing prices (a) below and (b) above the equilibrium? Are there any means of achieving the same social goals without fixing prices?

22. Make out a case for (a) increasing and (b) decreasing the role of the government in the allocation of resources.

Log on to MyEconlab and complete the studyplan exercises for this chapter to see how much you have learnt and where you need to revise most. Make sure you access all the supporting textbook resources including the online workbook, newsblog, audio animations, guided solutions and ebook.

Additional case studies in the *Essentials of Economics* MyEconLab (www.pearsoned.co.uk/sloman)

7.1 **Corporate social responsibility.** An examination of social responsibility as a goal of firms and its effect on business performance.

7.2 **The police as a public service.** The extent to which policing can be classified as a public good.

7.3 **Deadweight loss from taxes on goods and services.** This shows the welfare loss from the imposition of a tax, which must be weighed against the redistributive and other gains from the tax.

7.4 **Libertarianism.** The views of the 'neo-Austrian' right that market capitalism has dynamic advantages in creating incentives to innovate and take risks.

7.5 **Public choice theory.** This examines how economists have attempted to extend their analysis of markets to the field of political decision making.

7.6 **Perverse subsidies.** An examination of the use of subsidies around the world that are harmful to the environment.

7.7 **Selling the environment.** This looks at the proposals made at international climate conferences to use market-based solutions to global warming.

7.8 **The EU carbon trading system.** This examines the EU carbon Emissions Trading Scheme which began in 2005.

7.9 **Restricting car access to Athens.** A case study that examines how the Greeks have attempted to reduce local atmospheric pollution from road traffic.

7.10 The right track for reform? How successful has rail privatisation been in the UK?

7.11 Can the market provide adequate protection for the environment? This explains why markets generally fail to take into account environmental externalities.

7.12 Environmental auditing. Are businesses becoming greener? A growing number of firms are subjecting themselves to an 'environmental audit' to judge just how 'green' they are.

Websites relevant to this chapter

Numbers and sections refer to websites listed in the Web appendix and hotlinked from this book's website at **www.pearsoned.co.uk/sloman**.

■ For news articles relevant to this chapter, see the *Economics News Articles* link from the book's website.

■ For general news on market failures and government intervention, see websites in section A, and particularly A1–5, 18, 19, 24, 31. See also links to newspapers in A38 and 39; and see A42 and A44 for links to economics news articles from newspapers worldwide.

■ Sites I7 and 11 contain links to Competition and monopoly, Policy and regulation and Transport in the Microeconomics section; they also have an Industry and commerce section. Site I4 has links to Environmental and Environmental Economics in the EconDirectory section. Site I17 has several sections of links in the Issues in Society section.

■ UK and EU departments relevant to competition policy can be found at sites E10; G7, 8.

■ UK regulatory bodies can be found at sites E4, 11, 16, 18, 19, 21, 22, 25, 29.

■ For information on taxes and subsidies, see E30, 36; G13. For use of green taxes (Box 7.4), see H5; G11; E2, 14, 30.

■ For information on health and the economics of health care (Box 7.1), see E8; H9. See also links in I8 and 17.

■ For sites favouring the free market, see C17; E34. See also C18 for the development of ideas on the market and government intervention.

■ For the economics of the environment, see links in I4, 7, 11, 17. For policy on the environment and transport, see E2, 7, 11, 14, 29; G10, 11. See also H11.

■ For student resources relevant to this chapter, see sites C1–7, 9, 10, 19.

Web appendices

7.1 Private and social efficiency. This appendix uses general equilibrium analysis to show how a perfect market economy in the absence of externalities will lead to a socially optimal allocation of resources.

7.2 Cost–benefit analysis. A technique to help decide whether or not a project should go ahead.

7.3 The economics of common resources. Why commonly owned resources tend to be overused.

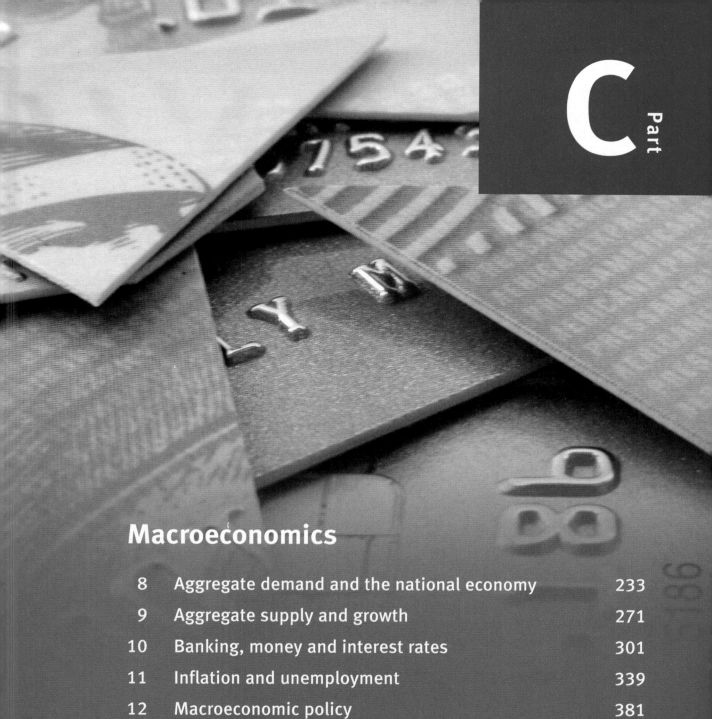

C Part

Macroeconomics

CHAPTER MAP

Aggregate demand and the national economy

We turn now to *macroeconomics*. This will be the subject for this third part of the book and most of the final part. As we have already seen, microeconomics focuses on *individual* markets. In macroeconomics we take a much loftier view. We examine the economy as a whole. We still examine demand and supply, but now it is the *total* level of spending in the economy and the total level of production. In other words, we examine *aggregate demand* and *aggregate supply*.

In particular, we will be examining four key topics. The first is national output. What determines the size of national output? What causes it to grow? Why do growth rates fluctuate? Why do economies sometimes surge ahead and at other times languish in recession?

The second is employment and unemployment. What causes unemployment? If people who are unemployed want jobs, and if consumers want more goods and services, then why does our economy fail to provide a job for everyone who wants one?

Then there is the issue of inflation. Why is it that the general level of prices always seems to rise, and only rarely fall? Why is inflation a problem, and would it be a good thing or a bad thing if prices did fall? Why do countries' central banks, such as the Bank of England, set targets for the rate of inflation?

The final topic, which is the subject of the final part of the book, concerns a country's economic relationships with other countries. We look at international trade and investment and at the flows of foreign currencies around the world.

In this chapter, after a preliminary look at the range of macroeconomic issues, we then focus on national output. In doing this we identify the key purchasers of goods and services in the economy and the ways in which these purchasers are connected. We see what determines the level of spending.

We go on to develop a simple model of the economy, in which prices are held constant, to consider how national output in any one year is determined.

After studying this chapter, you should be able to answer the following questions:

- What are the key macroeconomic issues faced by all countries?
- Who are the key groups of purchasers whose demands determine the total level of spending on a country's goods and services?
- What are the various flows of incomes around the economy? What causes these flows to expand or contract?
- How do we measure national output?
- What factors influence the level of spending by firms, households and government?
- What determines the level of national output at any one time?
- What is the effect on national income of an increase in spending?

8.1 INTRODUCTION TO MACROECONOMICS

What issues does macroeconomics tackle?

The first half of the book was concerned with microeconomics. By focusing on individual markets, microeconomics enables us to focus on individual decisions. For instance, we can analyse the decision-making process of firms as they decide on what goods and services to produce and how to produce them. Similarly, we can analyse individuals as they decide how to allocate their budget between different consumption options or what jobs to take.

As we saw on the previous page, the issues addressed by macroeconomists relate in one way or another to the total level of spending in the economy (aggregate demand) or the total level of output (aggregate supply). But macroeconomics is still concerned with understanding human behaviour. However, a macroeconomist will typically take a broader perspective than a microeconomist. This may involve analysing groups or sectors within the economy, such as the household or corporate sectors, or the government.

It is also worth keeping in mind that macroeconomics is often characterised by quite lively debates. These concern the precise causes of various macroeconomic problems and what policies are best to tackle them.

Key macroeconomic issues

We now outline four broad issues that are generally of concern to policy-makers. However, the attention given to them will inevitably be affected by the economic circumstances of the time – for example, whether the economy is booming or in recession.

Economic growth

Governments try to achieve high **rates of economic growth** over the long term: in other words, growth that is sustained over the years and is not just a temporary phenomenon. Governments also try to achieve *stable* growth, avoiding both recessions and excessive short-term growth that cannot be sustained. In practice, however, this can often prove difficult to achieve.

> **Definition**
>
> **Rate of economic growth**
> The percentage increase in output between two moments of time, typically over a 12-month period.

> **KEY IDEA 28** **TC 12** *Economies suffer from inherent instability.* As a result, economic growth and other macroeconomic indicators tend to fluctuate. This is Threshold Concept 12. It is a threshold concept because it is vital to recognise the fundamental instability in market economies. Analysing the ups and downs of the 'business cycle' occupies many macroeconomists.

Figure 8.1 shows how growth rates have fluctuated over the years for four economies.[1] As you can see, in all four cases there has been considerable volatility in their growth rates.

---

[1] Note that EU-12 stands for the 12 original members of the eurozone: Austria, Belgium, Germany, Greece, Finland, France, Ireland, Italy, Luxembourg, Netherlands, Portugal and Spain.

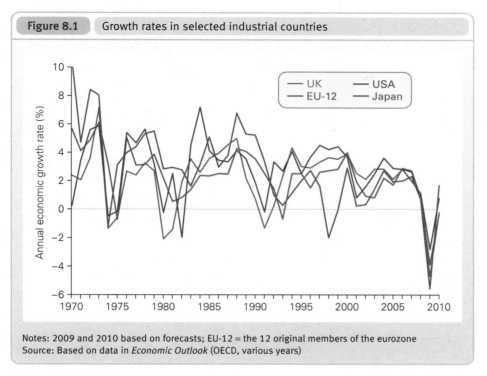

| Figure 8.1 | Growth rates in selected industrial countries |

Notes: 2009 and 2010 based on forecasts; EU-12 = the 12 original members of the eurozone
Source: Based on data in *Economic Outlook* (OECD, various years)

Unemployment

Reducing unemployment is another major macroeconomic aim of governments, not only for the sake of the unemployed themselves, but also because it represents a waste of human resources and because unemployment benefits are a drain on government revenues.

Unemployment in the 1980s and early 1990s was significantly higher than in the 1950s, 1960s and 1970s. Then, in the late 1990s and early 2000s, it fell in some countries, such as the UK and the USA. In others, such as Germany and France, it remained stubbornly high. This is illustrated in Figure 8.2, which shows unemployment rates (as a percentage of the labour force) for the same four economies.

You can also see that unemployment has fluctuated over the years with the ups and downs of the respective economies. For example, UK unemployment rose in the recessions of the early 1980s, early 1990s and late 2000s, but fell in the boom of the late 1980s and mid-to-late 1990s.

Inflation

By inflation we mean a general rise in prices throughout the economy. Government policy here is to keep inflation both low and stable. One of the most important reasons for this is that it will aid the process of economic decision-making. For example, businesses will be able to set prices and wage rates, and make investment decisions with far more confidence.

We have become used to low **inflation rates** and in some countries, like Japan, periods of deflation, with a general fall in prices. But, it was not long ago that inflation rates in most developed countries were in double figures. In 1975, UK inflation reached 24 per cent. Figure 8.3 illustrates annual rates of inflation (annual percentage change in the consumer prices) in the same four economies.

In most developed countries, governments have a particular target for the rate of inflation. In the UK the target for the growth of consumer prices is 2 per cent. The

> **Definition**
>
> **Inflation rate (annual)**
> The percentage increase in prices over a 12-month period.

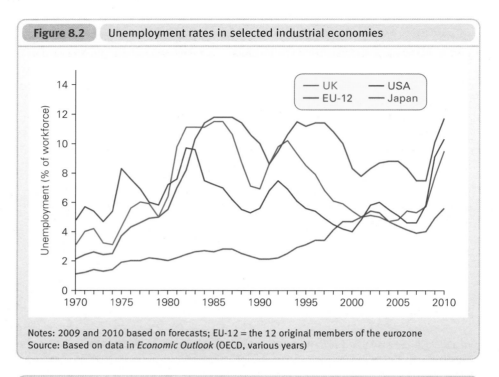

Figure 8.2   Unemployment rates in selected industrial economies

Notes: 2009 and 2010 based on forecasts; EU-12 = the 12 original members of the eurozone
Source: Based on data in *Economic Outlook* (OECD, various years)

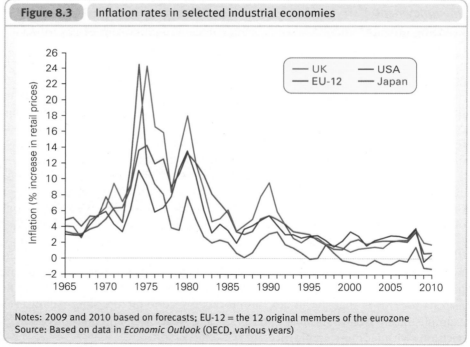

Figure 8.3   Inflation rates in selected industrial economies

Notes: 2009 and 2010 based on forecasts; EU-12 = the 12 original members of the eurozone
Source: Based on data in *Economic Outlook* (OECD, various years)

Definition

Balance of payments account

A record of the country's transactions with the rest of the world. It shows the country's payments to or deposits in other countries (debits) and its receipts or deposits from other countries (credits). It also shows the balance between these debits and credits under various headings.

Bank of England then adjusts interest rates to try to keep inflation on target (we see how this works in Chapter 12).

The balance of payments

A country's **balance of payments** account records all transactions between the residents of that country and the rest of the world. These transactions enter as either debit items or credit items. The debit items include all payments *to* other countries: these include the country's purchases of imports, the spending on investment it makes abroad and the interest and dividends paid to people abroad who have invested in the country. The credit items include all receipts *from* other countries: from the sales of exports, from inward investment expenditure and from interest and dividends earned from abroad.

The sale of exports and any other receipts earn foreign currency. The purchase of imports or any other payments abroad use up foreign currency. If we start to spend more foreign currency than we earn, one of two things must happen. Both are likely to be a problem.

The balance of payments will go into deficit. In other words, there will be a shortfall of foreign currencies. The government will therefore have to borrow money from abroad, or draw on its foreign currency reserves to make up the shortfall. This is a problem because, if it goes on too long, overseas debts will mount, along with the interest that must be paid; and/or reserves will begin to run low.

The exchange rate will fall. The **exchange rate** is the rate at which one currency exchanges for another. For example, the exchange rate of the pound into the dollar might be £1 = $1.60.

If the government does nothing to correct the balance of payments deficit, then the exchange rate must fall: for example, to $1.55 or $1.50, or lower. (We will show just why this is so in Chapter 12.) A falling exchange rate is a problem because it pushes up the price of imports and may fuel inflation. Also, if the exchange rate fluctuates, this can cause great uncertainty for traders and can damage international trade and economic growth.

In order to achieve the goals of high and sustainable economic growth, low unemployment, low inflation, a satisfactory balance of payments and stable exchange rates, the government (or **central bank**) may seek to control several 'intermediate' variables. These include taxes, government expenditure, interest rates and the supply of money. We will be looking at the relationship between all these in the coming chapters.

Definitions

Exchange rate
The rate at which one national currency exchanges for another. The rate is expressed as the amount of one currency that is necessary to purchase *one unit* of another currency (e.g. €1.55 = £1).

Central bank
a country's central bank is banker to the government and the banks as a whole (see Section 10.2). In most countries the central bank operates monetary policy by setting interest rates and influencing the supply of money. The central bank in the UK is the Bank of England; in the eurozone it is the European Central Bank (ECB) and in the USA it is the Federal Reserve Bank (the 'Fed').

Recap

1. Macroeconomics, like microeconomics, looks at issues such as output, employment and prices; but it looks at them in the context of the whole economy.

2. The four main macroeconomic goals that are generally of most concern to governments are economic growth, reducing unemployment, keeping inflation low and stable, and avoiding balance of payments and exchange rate problems.

THE CIRCULAR FLOW OF INCOME MODEL   8.2

How is spending related to income and who are the key groups of purchasers in the economy?

Unfortunately, the pursuit of any one of the four objectives that we have identified may make at least one of the others worse. For example, attempts to increase the rate of economic growth by giving tax cuts so as to boost consumer spending, and

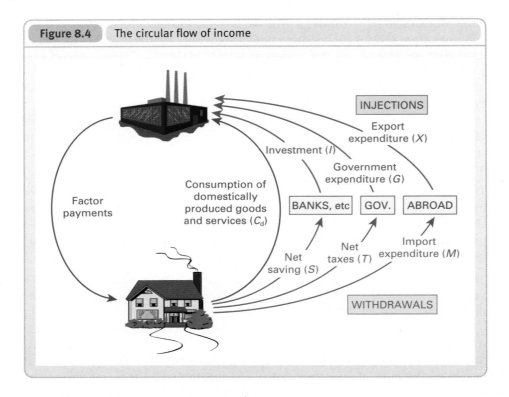

Figure 8.4   The circular flow of income

thereby encourage investment, may lead to higher inflation. It is thus important to understand the relationship between the four objectives.

One way in which the objectives are linked is through their relationship with **aggregate demand (AD)**. This is the total spending on goods and services made within the country by four groups of people: consumers on goods and services (*C*), firms on investment (*I*), the government on goods, services and investment (such as education, health and new roads) (*G*) and people abroad on this country's exports (*X*). From these four we have to subtract any imports (*M*) since aggregate demand refers only to spending on *domestic* firms. Thus:[2]

$$AD = C + I + G + X - M$$

To show how the four objectives are related to aggregate demand, we use a simple model of the economy. This is the *circular flow of income* model and is shown in Figure 8.4. It is an extension of the model we looked at back in the Chapter 1 (see Figure 1.5 on page 15).

If we look at the left-hand side of the diagram we can identify two major groups: *firms* and *households*. Each group has two roles. Firms are producers of goods and services; they are also the employers of labour and other factors of production. Households (which include all individuals) are the consumers of goods and services; they are also the suppliers of labour and various other factors of production. In the diagram there is an inner flow and various outer flows of incomes between these two groups.

---

[2] An alternative way of specifying this is to focus on just the component of each that goes to domestic firms. We use a subscript 'd' to refer to this component (i.e. with the imported component subtracted). Thus $AD = C_d + I_d + G_d + X$.

Definition

Aggregate demand (*AD*)
Total spending on goods and services made in the economy. It consists of four elements: consumer spending (*C*), investment (*I*), government spending (*G*) and the expenditure on exports (*X*), less any expenditure on foreign goods and services (*M*): $AD = C + I + G + X - M^2$.

TC 3
p 11

Before we look at the various parts of the diagram, a word of warning. Do not confuse *money* and *income*. Money is a stock concept. At any given time, there is a certain quantity of money in the economy (e.g. £100 billion). But that does not tell us the level of national *income*. Income is a flow concept (as is expenditure). It is measured as so much *per period of time*.

> **KEY IDEA 29** **Stocks and flows.** A stock is a quantity of something at a given point in time. A flow is an increase or decrease in something over a specified period of time. This is an important distinction and a common cause of confusion.

The relationship between money and income depends on how rapidly the money *circulates*: its 'velocity of circulation'. (We will examine this concept in detail later on.) If there is £100 billion of money in the economy and each £1 on average is paid out as income five times per year, then annual national income will be £500 billion.

The inner flow, withdrawals and injections

The inner flow

Firms pay money to households in the form of wages and salaries, dividends on shares, interest and rent. These payments are in return for the services of the factors of production – labour, capital and land – that are supplied by households. Thus on the left-hand side of the diagram, money flows directly from firms to households as 'factor payments'.

Households, in turn, pay money to domestic firms when they **consume domestically produced goods and services** (C_d). This is shown on the right-hand side of the inner flow. There is thus a circular flow of payments from firms to households to firms and so on.

If households spend *all* their incomes on buying domestic goods and services, and if firms pay out *all* this income they receive as factor payments to domestic households, and if the velocity of circulation does not change, the flow will continue at the same level indefinitely. The money just goes round and round at the same speed and incomes remain unchanged.

In the real world, of course, it is not as simple as this. Not all income gets passed on round the inner flow; some is *withdrawn*. At the same time, incomes are injected into the flow from outside.

To help understand this we need to recognise that there other groups of purchasers (i.e. demanders). So far we have identified households and firms as two key groups in the economy. If we introduce government into our model we have a third group. While this increases the complexity of our model it makes it more realistic and increases the ways in which the total spending on goods and services on the economy can be affected.

A fourth group in our economic model is overseas purchasers. This group comprises the foreign equivalents of our three domestic groupings. For instance, it includes French households and Japanese car manufacturers.

The final group in the model is financial institutions, such as banks and building societies and they play a key role. They are of course firms, though governments can take stakes in them or even own them outright. Financial institutions act as the link between those who wish to borrow and those who wish to save. In this way,

> **Definition**
>
> **The consumption of domestically produced goods and services (C_d)**
> The direct flow of payments from households to firms for goods and services produced within the country.

> **Pause for thought**
>
> *Would this argument still hold if prices rose?*

for instance, financial institutions can provide firms with the access to the credit they need to fund investment projects, such as the purchase of new machinery.

Let us now incorporate our additional purchasers and the financial system into our model. We begin by focusing on the withdrawals from and injections into the inner flow.

Withdrawals (W)

Only part of the incomes received by households will be spent on the goods and services of domestic firms. The remainder will be withdrawn from the inner flow. Likewise only part of the incomes generated by firms will be paid to UK households. The remainder of this will also be withdrawn. There are three forms of **withdrawals** (or 'leakages' as they are sometimes called).

Net saving (S). Saving is income that households choose not to spend but to put aside for the future. Savings are normally deposited in financial institutions such as banks and building societies. This is shown in the bottom right of Figure 8.4. Money flows from households to 'banks, etc'. What we are seeking to measure here, however, is the net flow from households to the banking sector. We therefore have to subtract from saving any borrowing or drawing on past savings by households to arrive at the *net* saving flow. Of course, if household borrowing exceeded saving, the net flow would be in the other direction: it would be negative.

Net taxes (T). When people pay taxes (to either central or local government), this represents a withdrawal of money from the inner flow in much the same way as saving: only in this case, people have no choice. Some taxes, such as income tax and employees' national insurance contributions, are paid out of household incomes. Others, such as VAT and excise duties, are paid out of consumer expenditure. Others, such as corporation tax, are paid out of firms' incomes before being received by households as dividends on shares. (For simplicity, however, taxes are shown in Figure 8.4 as leaving the circular flow at just one point. It does not affect the argument.)

When, however, people receive *benefits* from the government, such as unemployment benefits, child benefit and pensions, the money flows the other way. Benefits are thus equivalent to a 'negative tax'. These benefits are known as **transfer payments**. They transfer money from one group of people (taxpayers) to others (the recipients).

In the model, 'net taxes' (T) represents the *net* flow to the government from households and firms. It consists of total taxes minus benefits.

Import expenditure (M). Not all household consumption (C) is of totally home-produced goods (C_d). Households spend some of their incomes on imported goods and services, or on goods and services using imported components. Although the money that consumers spend on such goods initially flows to domestic retailers, it will eventually find its way abroad, either when the retailers or wholesalers themselves import them, or when domestic manufacturers purchase imported inputs to make their products. This expenditure on imports constitutes the third withdrawal from the inner flow. This money flows abroad.

As we shall see, households are not the only group to purchase imported goods and services or goods and services using imported components: firms and government do too. These expenditures also contribute towards the sum of import expenditures (M) and affect the level of aggregate demand.

Total withdrawals are simply the sum of net saving, net taxes and the expenditure on imports:

$$W = S + T + M$$

Injections (J)

Only part of the demand for firms' output arises from consumers' expenditure. The remainder comes from other sources outside the inner flow. These additional components of aggregate demand are known as **injections** (*J*). There are three types of injection.

Investment on domestically produced goods (I_d). This is firms' spending on domestically produced goods and services after obtaining the money from various financial institutions – either past savings or loans, or through a new issue of shares. They may invest in plant and equipment or may simply spend the money on building up stocks of inputs, semi-finished or finished goods. Not all of the investment expenditure (*I*) undertaken by domestic firms is on totally home-produced goods. Investment expenditure on goods and services produced overseas contributes towards import expenditure (*M*).

Government expenditure on domestically produced goods and services (G_d). When the government (both central and local) spends money on goods and services produced by domestic firms, this counts as an injection. (Note that government expenditure in this model does *not* include state benefits. These transfer payments, as we saw above, are the equivalent of negative taxes and have the effect of reducing the *T* component of withdrawals.) As well as providing goods and services by purchasing from firms, governments can actually own and run operations themselves. In these cases, the wages of public-sector staff will also be a component of the government's expenditure and are a flow of factor payments to households.

As with investment, not all government purchases (*G*) are on totally home-produced goods and services. Expenditures on items made overseas contribute towards import expenditure (*M*).

Export expenditure (X). Money flows into the circular flow from abroad when households, firms and governments abroad buy our exports of goods and services.

Total injections are simply the sum of investment and government expenditure (both only domestic products) and exports:

$$J = I_d + G_d + X$$

Aggregate demand, as we have seen, is the total spending on domestic firms. In other words it is the spending by the household sector on domestically produced goods and services (C_d), plus the three injections:

$$AD = C_d + J$$

The relationship between withdrawals and injections

There are indirect links between saving and investment via financial institutions, between taxation and government expenditure via the government (central and local), and between imports and exports via foreign countries. These links, however, do not guarantee that $S = I_d$ or $G_d = T$ or $M = X$.

Take investment and saving. The point here is that the decisions to save and invest are made by different people, and thus they plan to save and invest different amounts. Likewise the demand for imports may not equal the demand for exports. As far as the government is concerned, it may choose not to spend all its tax revenues: to run a 'budget surplus'; or it may choose to spend more than it receives in taxes: to run a 'budget deficit' – by borrowing to make up the difference.

Thus planned injections (J) may not equal planned withdrawals (W).

The circular flow of income and the four macroeconomic objectives

If planned injections are not equal to planned withdrawals, what will be the consequences? If injections exceed withdrawals, the level of expenditure will rise: there will be a rise in aggregate demand. This extra spending will increase firms' sales and thus encourage them to produce more. Total output in the economy will rise. Thus firms will pay out more in wages, salaries, profits, rent and interest. In other words, national income will rise.

The rise in aggregate demand will have the following effects upon the four macroeconomic objectives:

- There will be economic growth. The greater the initial excess of injections over withdrawals, the bigger will be the rise in national income.
- Unemployment will fall as firms take on more workers to meet the extra demand for output.
- Inflation will tend to rise. The greater the rise in aggregate demand relative to the capacity of firms to produce, the more will firms find it difficult to meet the extra demand, and the more likely they will be to raise prices.
- The exports and imports part of the balance of payments will tend to deteriorate. The higher demand sucks more imports into the country, and higher domestic inflation makes exports less competitive and imports relatively cheaper compared with home-produced goods. Thus imports will tend to rise and exports will tend to fall.

> **Pause for thought**
>
> *What will be the effect on each of the four objectives if planned injections are less than planned withdrawals?*

Disequilibrium and a chain reaction

When injections do not equal withdrawals, a state of *disequilibrium* will exist: aggregate demand will rise or fall. Disequilibrium results in a chain reaction so as to bring the economy back to a state of equilibrium where injections are equal to withdrawals.

To illustrate this chain reaction, let us consider the situation again where injections exceed withdrawals. Perhaps there has been a rise in business confidence so that investment has risen. Or perhaps there has been a tax cut so that withdrawals have fallen. As we have seen, the excess of injections over withdrawals will lead to a rise in national income. But as national income rises, so households will not only spend more on domestic goods (C_d), but also save more (S), pay more taxes (T) and buy more imports (M). In other words, withdrawals will rise. This will continue until they have risen to equal injections. At that point, national income will stop rising, and so will withdrawals. Equilibrium has been reached.

In Section 8.5 we return to the circular flow model to address in more detail how changes in aggregate demand can affect the level of national income. In other words, we will consider the chain reaction resulting from disequilibrium and its impact on an economy's size. But, now we consider in more detail the significance in money terms of our purchasers of goods and services that we identified in the model.

> ## Recap
>
> 1. The circular flow of income model depicts the flows of money round the economy. The inner flow shows the direct flows between firms and households. Money flows from firms to households in the form of factor payments, and back again as consumer expenditure on domestically produced goods and services.
>
> 2. Not all incomes get passed on directly round the inner flow. Some is withdrawn in the form of net saving, some is paid in net taxes, and some goes abroad as expenditure on imports.
>
> 3. Likewise not all expenditure on domestic firms is by domestic consumers. Some is injected from outside the inner flow in the form of investment expenditure, government expenditure and expenditure on the country's exports.
>
> 4. The circular flow will be in equilibrium when planned injections equals planned withdrawals. But, planned injections and withdrawals are unlikely to be the equal. This will result in a chain reaction that returns the economy to a position of equilibrium.

THE COMPONENTS OF AGGREGATE DEMAND   8.3

What are the main groups that spend money in the economy?

We have seen how the demand for the goods and services produced within a nation's borders originate from four broad groups of purchasers: its households, its firms, its government and the foreign equivalents of these across the world.

$$AD = C + I + G + X - M$$

The circular flow model demonstrates the interdependence of these groups as well as the significance of the financial system. Changes in the behaviour of these purchasers and of financial institutions can have significant effects on the economy. In this section we consider some of the possible influences on the expenditures by the purchasers of goods and services in order to develop an understanding of what drives *changes* in the level of aggregate demand. We then use our findings to inform and construct a demand-driven model of the economy in Section 8.5.

The magnitude of the components of aggregate demand

Before we look in detail at each of the components of aggregate demand, it is worth noting that their magnitude varies from country to country. Table 8.1 presents the average percentage composition of aggregate demand for a selection of developed countries over the period 2000 to 2007.

The first three columns show the expenditure shares of GDP for purchases made by a country's residents – households, firms and government.

Of these three components we can see that for each country the largest is the expenditure share on final goods by households (which include non-profit institutions, such as clubs and societies). Typically, household spending accounts for at least half of the total spending on a country's goods and services and in some cases, such as the UK and the US, considerably more. These figures help to explain why economic activity can be affected by changes in household spending and why it is important to consider what factors may affect household spending.

> **Pause for thought**
>
> 1. *What are the implications for economic growth rates of the figures for gross capital expenditure (public and private)?*
> 2. *Why are the figures for exports and imports so high for Singapore and relatively high for Ireland and so low for the USA and relatively low for Japan?*

Household consumption

As we can see in Table 8.1, the largest component of aggregate demand is household consumption. Therefore, in trying to understand the determination of a nation's

Table 8.1	Composition of GDP by type of expenditure, % (average 2000–7)					
	Household final consumption	**Gross capital expenditure (public and private)**	**Government final consumption**	**Imports**	**Exports**	**External balance (X − M)**
Australia	57.7	25.7	18.1	21.4	20.0	−1.4
France	56.3	20.1	23.4	26.7	26.9	0.1
Germany	58.8	18.3	18.8	34.6	38.8	4.2
Ireland	46.3	24.4	15.3	73.8	87.8	14.0
Japan	57.1	23.8	17.7	11.9	13.3	1.4
Singapore	42.9	22.9	11.2	192.3	215.3	23.1
Sweden	48.5	17.6	26.6	40.2	47.5	7.3
UK	64.5	17.7	20.7	29.6	26.6	−3.0
USA	70.2	18.9	15.6	15.3	10.6	−4.8

Source: United Nations

output and its changes from period to period a good starting point is to consider what might affect the volume of purchases by households.

Disposable income. Perhaps the first determinant you think of as capable of explaining consumption is **disposable income**. Disposable income is the income that the household sector has available for spending or saving after deductions, such as income tax and payments to social insurance schemes, and any additions, such as social benefits.

Evidence suggests that, over the long run, when people's disposable income rises, they will spend most of it. So if your disposable income rises from £20 000 at the age of 25 to £30 000 at the age of 35, you will spend most of this extra £10 000.

However, short-run changes in disposable income, such as those from one quarter of a year to the next, are relatively more variable than those in spending. For example, many people's income varies with the time of year. Examples include those working in the holiday industry or painting and decorating. However, such people are likely to spread their spending relatively evenly over the year.

Case Study 8.1 in MyEconLab looks at the evidence on how consumption varies with disposable income in both the short and long run.

TC 9
p 71

Expected future incomes. Many people take into account both current and expected future incomes when planning their current and future consumption. You might have a relatively low income when you graduate, but can expect (you hope!) to earn much more in the future.

You are thus willing to take on more debts now in order to support your consumption, not only as a student but shortly afterwards as well, anticipating that you will be able to pay back these loans later. It is similar with people taking out a mortgage to buy a house. They might struggle to pay the interest at first, but hope that this will become easier over time.

In fact, the financial system (such as banks and building societies) plays an important part in facilitating this **smoothing of consumption** by households. You can borrow when your income is low and pay back the loans later on when your income is higher.

The financial system and consumption. The financial sector can have a major impact on the household sector's spending. For example, if interest rates rise, loans become more expensive for households to 'service'. **Debt-servicing costs** are the costs

Definitions

Disposable income
Income after tax and other deductions and after the receipt of benefits.

Consumption smoothing
The act by households of smoothing their levels of consumption over time despite facing volatile incomes.

Debt-servicing costs
The costs incurred when repaying debt, including debt interest payments.

incurred in repaying the loans and the interest payments on the loan. Where the rate of interest rate on debt is variable any changes in interest rates affect the cost of servicing the debt.

Interest rate changes may also affect saving. For example, a rise in interest rates will increase the return on savings, giving households the incentive to substitute future consumption through saving in place of current consumption. Therefore, there is a substitution effect to increase saving and reduce consumption. But, in order for households to obtain a given amount of interest income they actually need to save less since interest rates are higher and so there is an income effect to save less and spend more.

Financial institutions can affect the strength of consumption if their ability and willingness to provide credit changes. The global financial crises of the second half of the 2000s saw credit criteria tighten dramatically. A tightening of credit practices, such as reducing overdraft facilities or reducing income multiples (the size of loans made available relative to household incomes), weakens consumption growth. In contrast, a relaxation of lending practices, as seen in many countries during the 1980s, can strengthen consumption growth.

> **Pause for thought**
>
> *In recent years there has been an increase in the use of individual voluntary arrangements (IVAs) whereby households who have got into financial trouble try to arrange a repayment schedule with their creditors. These arrangements often involve some of the debt being written off. What is the effect likely to be on borrowing?*

Household balance sheets

By borrowing and saving households accumulate financial liabilities (debts), financial assets (savings) and physical assets (property). Table 8.2 shows a summary balance sheet of the net worth of the UK household sector.

The net worth of the household sector is the sum of the sector's net financial wealth and its physical wealth.

- Net financial wealth is the balance of financial assets over financial liabilities. Financial assets include moneys in savings accounts, shares and pension funds. Financial liabilities include debts secured against property, largely residential mortgages, and unsecured debts, such as overdrafts and unpaid balances on credit cards.
- Physical wealth is predominantly the sector's residential housing wealth and is, therefore, affected by changes in house prices.

Policy-makers, including central bankers, will analyse the net worth of the household sector and the composition of its balance sheets. The sector's financial health or level of financial distress can have a significant impact on short-term prospects for household spending. For instance, a declining net worth to income ratio, could indicate greater financial distress. This could be induced by falling

---

Table 8.2   Summary of household balance sheets, 31 December 2008

	£ billion	Ratio to disposable income
Financial assets	3687	4.03
Financial liabilities	1572	1.72
Net financial wealth	**2115**	**2.31**
Physical wealth	4461	4.88
Net worth	**6575**	**7.19**

Source: *United Kingdom National Accounts: The Blue Book* (National Statistics, 2009)
Note: Figures include assets and liabilities of the NPISH (non-profit institutions serving households) sector

BOX 8.1   THE EXPLOSION OF DEBT

Did it affect household spending?

Many of us at some time or other will have experience of debt. As a student, you are probably experiencing it right now! We can categorise debt as either 'secured' or 'unsecured'; secured debt is debt where property acts as collateral which, if necessary, could be sold to pay off some or all of the debt.

As the table shows, households in the UK in 2008 had amassed a staggering £1.6 trillion of debt, of which 75 per cent was secured debt. Twenty years earlier the stock of debt was £311 billion, of which secured debt was 70 per cent.

One way of trying to put the size of household debt into context is to compare it with the sector's annual disposable income. This reveals that from being equivalent to just a little over a year's worth of disposable income in 1988, the total amount of debt had risen to 1.75 times annual income by 2008.

But, does this increase in debt have implications for household spending? For instance, does it affect the stability of household spending?

If households were making careful choices to take on more debt now, planning to be able to pay them off later when their incomes were higher, then perhaps we should not be too worried. But, how realistic is this?

By far the largest financial liability of the household sector is secured debt. Between 1970 and 2008 secured debt increased from £10.5 billion to £1.18 trillion – equivalent to an increase each year of some 13 per cent. Chart (a) shows the amount of secured debt as both percentages of annual GDP and household-sector disposable income in the UK since 1970. Both measures show an increase in the scale of debt during the 1980s and again from the mid-1990s through to the financial crisis of 2007–9, when the level of secured debt to both GDP and income reached historic highs.

Debt held by UK Household Sector: September 1988 and 2008

	September 1988			September 2008		
	£ billions	% of liabilities	% of annual disposable income	£ billions	% of liabilities	% of annual disposable income
Financial liabilities	311.2	100.0	109.5	1568.3	100.0	174.8
Secured debt	213.7	68.9	75.2	1182.7	75.4	131.8
Non-secured debt	97.5	31.1	34.4	385.6	24.6	43.0

Source: Based on data in *UK Economic Accounts* (National Statistics)
Note: Figures relate to both the household and NPISH (Non-Profit Institutions Serving Households) sectors. The NPISH sector comprises charities and voluntary organisations.

(a) Secured debt as a percentage of GDP and disposable income

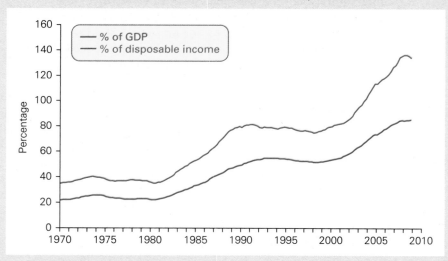

(b) Housing equity withdrawal and consumption as percentages of annual disposable income

So should we be concerned by the rise in the exposure to secured debt? Unlike unsecured debt, this debt is secured against property. Its increase reflects the growth in owner-occupation (the number of owner-occupiers in the UK increased from 9.6 to 18.6 million between 1971 and 2007) and the rise in the average price of housing by nearly 10 per cent per annum (see Box 2.2 on pages 42–3). Therefore, while the sector has been accumulating debt it has also been accumulating housing wealth. In other words, a large part of the increase in debt in the UK is explained by the purchase of residential housing.

But house prices are volatile. This, combined with the sheer scale of secured debt, creates the potential for significant short-term effects on household spending. When house prices are rising households may increase spending by borrowing additional sums from mortgage lenders. This is known as *housing equity withdrawal* (HEW).

When house prices fall, people may attempt to pay off more of their mortgage for fear of getting into 'negative equity' (owing more than the value of the house). To do this they have to cut back on consumption.

Chart (b) shows both the amounts of HEW and consumption as percentages of disposable income. Interestingly, they track each other very closely in the late 1980s, when rising HEW coincides with a rising propensity of households to consume out of income, and in the early 1990s when an injection of housing equity (negative HEW) coincides with a declining average propensity to consume.

The correlation is less clear during the bulk of the 2000s, however. It may be that for a large part of the decade households were extracting housing equity, on the back of strong house price growth, to repay unsecured debt. Later in the decade, as house prices fell, households were injecting housing equity. This coincided with a declining propensity to spend out of income during uncertain times.

The stock of debt amassed by households may also lead to changes in spending because of what are known as *cash flow effects*. For mortgage payers on variable interest rate mortgages, and most are, a rise in interest rates can mean substantial rises in monthly payments. This may force them to cut back on consumption. The impact across the household sector will be larger the higher the proportion of housing debt to national income.

1. Make a list of the ways in which the debt position of households could lead to changes in their spending.
2. In the late 2000s, the household sector faced declining levels of real disposable income. In what ways could their ability to use the financial system to smooth their spending have been affected in this period?

Note: An extended version of this box can be found in the web appendix to this chapter (Web Appendix 8.2).

house prices or falling share prices. In response to this we might see the sector engage in precautionary saving or repaying some of its outstanding debt. Therefore, the impact of worsening balance sheets is to weaken spending while improvements on the balance sheets enable consumption to strengthen.

Investment

There are five major determinants of investment.

Increased consumer demand. Investment is to provide extra capacity. This will only be necessary, therefore, if consumer demand increases. The bigger the increase in consumer demand, the more investment will be needed.

You might think that, since consumer demand depends on the level of national income, investment must too. But we are not saying that investment depends on the *level* of consumer demand; rather it depends on *how much it has risen*. If income and consumer demand are high but *constant*, there will be no point in firms expanding their capacity: no point in investing.

The relationship between investment and *increased* consumer demand is examined by the 'accelerator theory'. We will look at this theory in Section 9.4.

Expectations. Since investment is made in order to produce output for the future, investment must depend on firms' expectations about future market conditions. But,

TC 9
p 71

BOX 8.2   SURVEYS OF CONFIDENCE

What can policy-makers learn from their results?

How many times a time each day does somebody ask you how you are feeling? But, what would such a question mean in the context of a country? Well, once a month consumers and firms across the European Union are asked a series of questions, the answers to which are used to compile indicators of consumer and business confidence. For instance, consumers are asked about how they think their household finances will change over the next 12 months. They are offered various options such as 'get a lot better' or 'get a lot worse' and balances are then calculated on the basis of positive and negative replies.[a]

The European Union publishes its confidence indicators for each member country as well as averages for the whole EU. A summary indicator of confidence known as the *Economic Sentiment Index* attempts to measure the confidence of both consumers and firms.

But, why measure confidence? Does confidence perhaps affect the current, or maybe future, levels of aggregate demand? For instance, does low confidence amongst consumers affect their current or future spending plans or does low confidence amongst businesses affect their current for future investment plans? Or does confidence simply reflect the prevailing economic circumstances? In other words, perhaps confidence does not contribute to our understanding of demand changes, because it simply reflects other economic variables.

The chart plots the Economic Sentiment Index and the annual percentage change in real GDP across all EU countries for years from 1990.

The chart appears to show that sentiment is a *coincident indicator* of GDP growth; in other words we could use the path of the Economic Sentiment Index to track the path of GDP growth. Indeed, economic sentiment tracks output growth well throughout most of the period. Sentiment was high in the booms of the late 1990s and mid-2000s. Similarly, economic sentiment tracks the economic downturns of the early 1990s, early 2000s and late 2000s well too. However, there is no clear evidence that this measure of confidence *leads* actual output growth.

The evidence here points to measures of sentiment tracking rather than leading changes in output. This, however, does not mean that changes in sentiment do not *cause* changes in output. In fact, a likely scenario is that growth and sentiment interact. High growth leads to high confidence (high ESI), which in turn leads to more consumption and investment and hence higher growth, which in turn leads to higher confidence. The reverse is the case in a recession: low growth leads to lack of confidence (low ESI), which causes low or negative growth.

Measures of confidence are highly useful because they are published monthly. In contrast, measures of GDP are published annually or quarterly and with a considerable

[a] More information on the EU programme of business and consumer surveys can be found at **http://ec.europa.eu/ economy_finance/db_indicators/db_indicators8650_en.htm**.

future markets cannot be predicted with accuracy: they depend on consumer tastes, the actions of rivals and the whole state of the economy. Investment is thus *risky*.

Investment depends crucially on business confidence in the future (see Box 8.2). In the short run, therefore, we could expect periods of economic uncertainty, such as in the recessions of the early 1990s and late 2000s, to reduce capital expenditure by firms.

The cost and efficiency of capital equipment. If the cost of capital equipment goes down or machines become more efficient, the return on investment will increase. Firms will invest more. Technological progress is an important determinant here.

The rate of interest. One way of financing investment is by borrowing. A major part of this cost is the interest payments the firm must make. Thus the firm must weigh the annual income from the investment (minus operating costs) against the annual interest payments.

 The interest rate measures the opportunity cost of undertaking the project: the higher the rate of interest the higher its opportunity cost.

The availability of finance. Irrespective of interest rates, a firm cannot invest if it cannot raise the finance. The simplest way is to use the firm's own internal funds (i.e. ploughed-back profits). In the UK this has traditionally been the largest source of finance for firms. Given, however, that business profitability depends in large part on the general state of the economy, internal funds as a source of business finance are likely to show considerable cyclical variation.

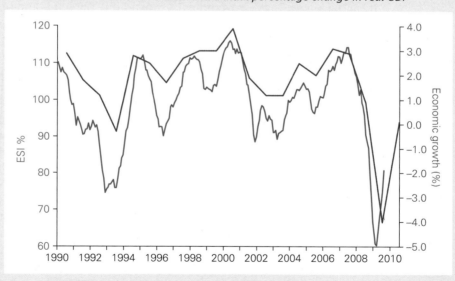

EU Economic Sentiment Index and annual percentage change in real GDP

Source: Based on data in *European Economy* (European Commission)

time delay. Therefore, measures of confidence are extremely timely for policy-makers and would appear to offer them some useful information about the likely path of output growth.

1. *What factors do you think might affect consumer and business confidence?*
2. *Is confidence something that an economist should be interested in?*

If it tries to borrow from banks but banks are cautious, perhaps feeling that the investment is too risky or the economic climate is too uncertain, the firm may be refused the loan. Bank lending has been the most volatile source of business finance, and has been particularly sensitive to the state of the economy.

Another way of raising finance is through the stock market. A public limited company (see Case Study 4.1 in MyEconLab) can make a new issue of shares and the money raised can be used to finance the investment. But the ease of raising money in this way depends on the state of the stock market.

In the boom of the mid-2000s, when profits were high, when share prices were rising (see Box 2.3 on pages 44–5) and banks were only too willing to lend, financing investment was relatively easy. After the credit crunch of 2007–9, however, both profits and share prices were falling. Also banks were becoming ultra-cautious, following their need to be baled out by governments around the world. Finance for investment thus became much harder to obtain.

Government expenditure

As we saw in Table 8.1, some government purchases can be categorised as capital expenditure. These are expenditures incurred in providing goods and services that will deliver longer-term consumption benefits, such as the education 'services' from school buildings.

The remaining expenditures involve the purchase of goods and services that are used or consumed in the short run. These other final consumption expenditures can involve day-to-day operational costs, such as paying teachers or purchasing items of stationery. Remember that government expenditures on benefits, grants and subsidies do not directly involve the purchase of a good or services, though they can affect aggregate demand through their impact on incomes. Therefore, these expenditures are treated as 'negative taxation'.

It can be argued that a government's expenditure on goods and services in any year is independent of the level of national income. The reason is as follows. In the months preceding the Budget each year, spending departments make submissions about their needs in the coming year. These are discussed with the Treasury and a sum is allocated to each department. That then (save for any unforeseen events) fixes government expenditure on goods and services for the following financial year.

Thus, again, for our purposes of modelling government expenditure we can take it as independent of the level of national income in the short term. Even if tax revenues turn out to be more or less than expected, this will not influence that year's government spending. The government can end up running either a budget surplus ($T > G$) or a budget deficit ($G > T$).

It may be that the level of government expenditure is affected by *changes* in national income, as we argued might be the case with private investment. In response to a recession, governments may look to support the economy by increasing its purchases of goods and services to support aggregate demand. For instance, governments may use their discretion to bring forward capital projects to boost aggregate demand and provide employment. This type of boost to aggregate demand was witnessed in many countries, including the UK and the USA, in response to the economic downturn of 2008/9.

Over the longer term, government expenditure *will* depend on national income. The higher the level of national income, the higher is the amount of tax revenue that the government receives, and hence the more it can afford to spend. The governments of richer nations clearly spend much more than those of developing countries.

Imports and exports

Imports

The sum of final expenditures by a country's households, firms and government is known as its **gross domestic final expenditure**. However, when estimating the country's GDP we must subtract imports as they are not part of this nation's production.

But what determines the level of import expenditure?

National income. In part, the factors that affect consumption, investment and government expenditure will affect import expenditure too. This is because some proportion of the demands by households, firms and government is satisfied by consuming foreign goods. Therefore, one influence on imports will be national income. We would expect more to be spent on imports as domestic incomes rise.

Exchange rates. Another factor affecting the consumption of foreign goods will be the rates of exchange between the domestic and foreign currencies. These are typically expressed as the number of foreign currency units per unit of domestic currency, for example the number of euros per US dollar.

If the number of foreign currency units which can be exchanged for 1 unit of domestic currency increases, then an **appreciation** of the domestic currency has occurred. This will lead to a decrease in the domestic-currency price of imported foreign goods and services relative to domestically produced goods and services (since one unit of domestic currency buys more foreign currency). Therefore, we would expect an appreciation to increase the sale of imports. Conversely a **depreciation** will lead to a fall in imports.

Exports

Exports are sold to people abroad, and thus depend largely on *their* incomes, not on incomes at home. Nevertheless, there are two indirect links between a country's national income and its exports:

- Via other countries' circular flows of income. If domestic incomes rise, more will be spent on imports. But this will cause a rise in other countries' incomes and lead them to buy more imports, part of which will be this country's exports.
- Via the exchange rate. A rise in domestic incomes will lead to a rise in imports. Other things being equal, this will lead to a depreciation in the exchange rate (we examine the reasons for this in Chapter 14). This will make it cheaper for people in other countries to buy this country's exports. Export sales will rise.

Definitions

Gross domestic final expenditure
Total expenditure by a country's residents on final goods and services. It thus includes expenditure on imports and excludes expenditure on exports.

Appreciation
A rise in the exchange rate of the domestic currency with foreign currencies.

Depreciation
A fall in the exchange rate of the domestic currency with foreign currencies.

Recap

1. Household spending (consumption) depends primarily on current and expected future disposable incomes and on the cost and availability of finance.

2. The financial system enables households to shift incomes across their lifetimes by borrowing or saving, but means that they accumulate stocks of assets and liabilities. Changes in the value of these assets and liabilities as well as in the costs of servicing debt can affect spending.

3. Private investment expenditure involves a highly heterogeneous set of purchases, but is likely to be affected by changes in interest rates, changes in consumer demand and in business confidence.

4. Government expenditure decisions are affected by economic and social considerations, but the political context is important too.

5. Import expenditure, like the total expenditure of households, firms and government, is affected by the level of national income. The exchange rate is also an important determinant.

6. Export expenditure is likely to depend on income levels overseas and on the rate of exchange.

8.4 THE EQUILIBRIUM LEVEL OF NATIONAL INCOME

How do changes in aggregate demand affect national income?

Having looked at the determinants of aggregate demand, we are now ready to see what happens if aggregate demand changes. The analysis we shall be using in this and the next section is based on the theory developed by John Maynard Keynes back in the 1930s, a theory that has had a profound influence on economics. Keynes argued that, without government intervention to steer the economy, countries could lurch from unsustainable growth to deep and prolonged recessions.

TC 3
p 11

The central argument is that the level of production in the economy depends on the level of aggregate demand. If people buy more, firms will produce more in response to this, providing they have spare capacity. If people buy less, firms will cut down their production and lay off workers. But just *how much* will national income rise or fall as aggregate demand changes?

The Keynesian analysis of output and employment can be explained most simply by returning to the circular flow of income diagram. Figure 8.5 shows a simplified version of the circular flow model that we looked at in Section 8.2.

We saw in Section 8.2 that aggregate demand will be constant when the total levels of injections (J) equals the total level of withdrawals (W). But, if injections (J) do not equal withdrawals (W), a state of disequilibrium exists. What will bring them back into equilibrium is a change in national income and employment.

Start with a state of equilibrium, where injections equal withdrawals. Now assume that there is a rise in injections. For example, firms increase their investment in response to a relaxation of banks' lending criteria. As a result aggregate demand ($C_d + J$) will be higher. Firms will respond to this increased demand by using more labour and other resources, and thus paying out more incomes (Y) to households. Household consumption will rise and so firms will sell more.

Firms will respond by producing more, and thus using more labour and other resources. Household incomes will rise again. Consumption and hence production

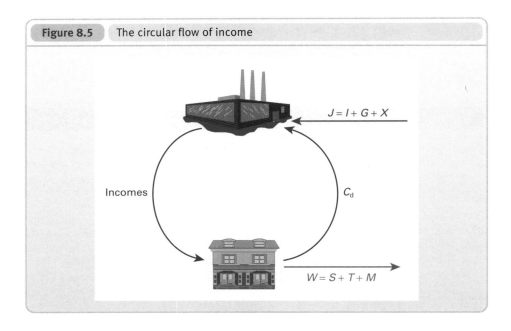

Figure 8.5 The circular flow of income

$J = I + G + X$

Incomes

C_d

$W = S + T + M$

will rise again, and so on. There will thus be a multiplied rise in incomes and employment. This is known as the **multiplier effect** and is an example of the 'principle of cumulative causation'.

 The principle of cumulative causation. An initial event can cause an ultimate effect that is much larger. This phenomenon of things building on themselves occurs throughout market economies. It is a fundamental principle in economics and is the thirteenth of our fifteen Threshold Concepts.

> **Definition**
>
> **Multiplier effect**
> An initial increase in aggregate demand of £xm leads to an eventual rise in national income that is greater than £xm.

The process, however, does not go on for ever. Each time household incomes rise, households save more, pay more taxes and buy more imports. In other words, withdrawals rise. When withdrawals have risen to match the increase in injections, equilibrium will be restored and national income and employment will stop rising. The process can be summarised as follows:

$$J > W \to Y\uparrow \to W\uparrow \text{ until } J = W$$

Similarly, an initial fall in injections (or rise in withdrawals) will lead to a multiplied fall in national income and employment:

$$J < W \to Y\downarrow \to W\downarrow \text{ until } J = W$$

Thus equilibrium in the circular flow of income can be at *any* level of output and employment.

Showing equilibrium with a Keynesian diagram

Equilibrium can be shown on a 'Keynesian' diagram. This plots various elements of the circular flow of income (such as consumption, withdrawals, injections and aggregate demand) against national income (i.e. GDP). There are two approaches to finding equilibrium: the withdrawals and injections approach and the income and expenditure approach. Let us examine each in turn.

The withdrawals and injections approach

In Figure 8.6, national income (Y) is plotted on the horizontal axis. Withdrawals (W) and injections (J) are plotted on the vertical axis.

As national income rises, so withdrawals (saving, taxes and imports) will rise. Thus the withdrawals curve slopes upwards. But, as we saw in Section 8.3, the impact of the current level of national income on the amount that businesses plan to invest, that the government plans to spend and that overseas residents plan to import from the UK (i.e. UK exports) may be slight and certainly debatable. Thus injections, for simplicity of our model, are assumed to be independent of national income. The injections line, therefore, is drawn as a horizontal straight line. (This does not mean that injections are constant over time, merely that they are constant with respect to national income. If injections rise, the whole line will shift upwards.)

Withdrawals equal injections at point x in the diagram. Equilibrium national income is thus Y_e. If national income were below this level, say at Y_1, injections would exceed withdrawals (by an amount $a - b$). This additional net expenditure injected into the economy would encourage firms to produce more. This in turn

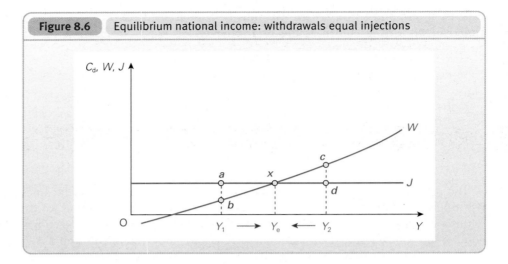

Figure 8.6   Equilibrium national income: withdrawals equal injections

would cause national income to rise. But as people's incomes rose, so they would save more, pay more taxes and buy more imports. In other words, withdrawals would rise. There would be a movement up along the W curve. This process would continue until $W = J$ at point x.

If, on the other hand, national income were initially at Y_2, withdrawals would exceed injections (by an amount $c - d$). This deficiency of demand would cause production and hence national income to fall. As it did so, there would be a movement down along the W curve until again point x was reached.

The income and expenditure approach

In Figure 8.7 the 45° line out from the origin plots $C_d + W$ against Y. It is a 45° line because, by definition, $Y = C_d + W$. To understand this, consider what can happen to national income: either it must be spent on domestically produced goods (C_d) or it must be withdrawn from the circular flow – there is nothing else that can happen to it. Thus if Y were £1000 billion, then $C_d + W$ must also be £1000 billion. If you draw a line such that whatever value is plotted on the horizontal axis (Y) is also plotted on the vertical axis ($C_d + W$), the line will be at 45 degrees (assuming that the axes are drawn to the same scale).

The green line plots aggregate demand. In this diagram it is known as the *aggregate expenditure line* (E). It consists of $C_d + J$: in other words, the total spending on the product of domestic firms (see Figure 8.5).

To show how this line is constructed, consider the brown line. This shows C_d. It is flatter than the 45° line. The reason is that for any given rise in national income, only *part* will be spent on domestic product, while the remainder will be withdrawn: i.e. C_d rises less quickly than Y. The proportion of the rise in national income which is spent on domestic goods and services is called the **marginal propensity to consume domestically produced goods (mpc_d)**. Therefore, if three quarters of the rise in national income is spent on home-produced items the mpc_d is $^3/_4$.

The E line consists of $C_d + J$. But we have assumed that J is constant with respect to changes in Y. Thus the E line is simply the C_d line shifted upwards by the amount of J.

TC 5
p 40

Definition

The marginal propensity to consume domestically produced goods (mpc_d)

The proportion of a rise in national income that is spent on goods and services produced within the country.

Figure 8.7	Equilibrium national income: real national income equals aggregate expenditure

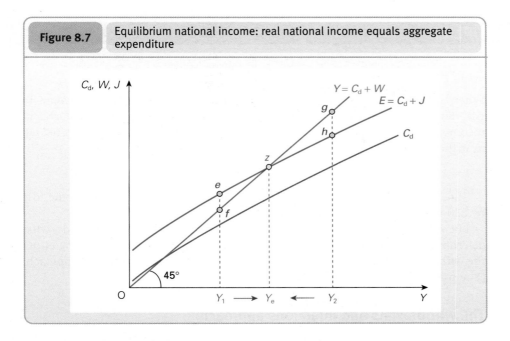

If aggregate expenditure exceeded national income, at say Y_1, there would be excess demand in the economy (of $e - f$). In other words, people would be buying more than was currently being produced. Firms would thus find their stocks dwindling and would therefore increase their level of production. In doing so, they would employ more factors of production. National income would thus rise. As it did so, C_d and hence E would rise. There would be a movement up along the E line. But because not all the extra income would be consumed (i.e. some would be withdrawn), expenditure would rise less quickly than income: the E line is flatter than the Y line. As income rises towards Y_e, the gap between Y and E gets smaller. Once point z is reached, $Y = E$. There is then no further tendency for income to rise.

If national income exceeded aggregate expenditure, at say Y_2, there would be insufficient demand for the goods and services currently being produced ($g - h$). Firms would find their stocks of unsold goods building up. They would thus respond by producing less and employing fewer factors of production. National income would thus fall and go on falling until Y_e was reached.

Note that if Y and E, and W and J were plotted on the same diagram, point z (in Figure 8.7) would be vertically above point x (in Figure 8.6).

Pause for thought

(a) Why does a − b in Figure 8.6 equal e − f in Figure 8.7?

(b) Why does c − d in Figure 8.6 equal g − h in Figure 8.7?

Recap

1. In the simple Keynesian model, equilibrium national income is where withdrawals equal injections, and where national income equals the total expenditure on domestic products: where $W = J$ and where $Y = E$.

2. The relationships between national income and the various components of the circular flow of income can be shown on a diagram, where national income is plotted on the horizontal axis and the various components of the circular flow are plotted on the vertical axis.

3. Equilibrium national income can be shown on this diagram either at the point where the W and J lines cross, or where the E line crosses the 45° line (Y).

8.5 THE MULTIPLIER

What will be the effect on output of a rise in spending?

When injections rise (or withdrawals fall), this will cause national income to TC 13 p 253 rise. But by how much? The answer is that there will be a *multiplied* rise in income: i.e. national income will rise by more than the rise in injections (or fall in withdrawals). The size of the **multiplier** is given by the letter k, where:

$$k = \Delta Y / \Delta J$$

Thus if injections rose by £10 million (ΔJ) and as a result national income rose by £30 million (ΔY), the multiplier would be 3.

But what determines the size of the rise in income (ΔY)? In other words, what determines the size of the multiplier? This can be shown graphically using either the withdrawals and injections approach or the income and expenditure approach. (You may omit one, if you choose.)

The withdrawals and injections approach

Assume that injections rise from J_1 to J_2 in Figure 8.8. Equilibrium will move from point a to point b. Income will thus rise from Y_{e_1} to Y_{e_2}. But this rise in income (ΔY) is bigger than the rise in injections (ΔJ) that caused it. This is the multiplier effect. It is given by $(c - a)/(b - c)$ (i.e. $\Delta Y/\Delta J$).

It can be seen that the size of the multiplier depends on the *slope of the W curve*. The flatter the curve, the bigger will be the multiplier: i.e. the bigger will be the rise in national income from any given rise in injections. The slope of the W curve is given by $\Delta W/\Delta Y$. This is the proportion of a rise in national income that is withdrawn, and is known as the **marginal propensity to withdraw** (*mpw*).

The point here is that the less is withdrawn each time money circulates, the more will be re-circulated and hence the bigger will be the rise in national income.

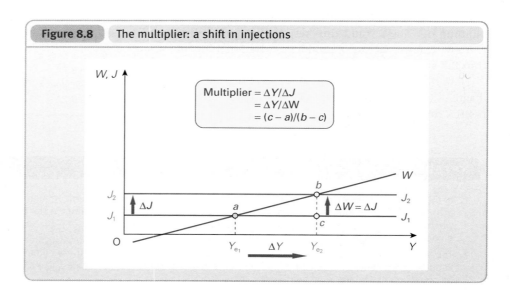

Figure 8.8   The multiplier: a shift in injections

The size of the multiplier thus varies inversely with the size of the *mpw*. The bigger the *mpw*, the smaller the multiplier; the smaller the *mpw*, the bigger the multiplier. In fact the **multiplier formula** is simply the inverse of the *mpw*:

$$k = 1/mpw$$

Thus if the *mpw* were $1/4$, the multiplier would be 4. So if *J* increased by £10 million, *Y* would increase by £40 million. To understand why, consider what must happen to withdrawals. Injections have risen by £10 million, thus withdrawals must rise by £10 million to restore equilibrium ($J = W$). But with an *mpw* of $1/4$, this £10 million rise in withdrawals must be one-quarter of the rise in national income that has resulted from the extra injections. Thus *Y* must rise by £40 million.

An alternative formula uses the concept of the marginal propensity to consume domestically produced goods (mpc_d) that we introduced earlier. This, as we saw, is the proportion of a rise in national income that is spent on domestically produced goods, and thus is not withdrawn. Thus if a quarter of a rise in national income is withdrawn, the remaining three-quarters will re-circulate as C_d. Thus:

$$mpw + mpc_d = 1$$

and

$$mpw = 1 - mpc_d$$

Thus the alternative formula for the multiplier is:

$$k = 1/(1 - mpc_d)$$

But why is the multiplier given by the formula $1/mpw$? This can be illustrated by referring to Figure 8.8. The *mpw* is the slope of the *W* line. In the diagram this is given by the amount $(b - c)/(c - a)$. The multiplier is defined as $\Delta Y/\Delta J$. In the diagram this is the amount $(c - a)/(b - c)$. But this is merely the inverse of the *mpw*. Thus the multiplier equals $1/mpw$.[3]

Definition

Multiplier formula
The formula for the multiplier is:

$k = 1/mpw$ or $1/(1 - mpc_d)$

The income and expenditure approach

Assume in Figure 8.9 that injections rise by £20 billion. The expenditure line thus shifts upward by £20 billion to E_2. The same effect would be achieved by withdrawals falling by £20 billion, and hence consumption of domestically produced goods rising by £20 billion. Equilibrium national income rises by £60 billion, from £100 billion to £160 billion (where the E_2 line crosses the *Y* line).

What is the size of the multiplier? It is $\Delta Y/\Delta J$; in other words, £60bn/£20bn = 3. This can be derived from the multiplier formula:

$$k = \frac{1}{1 - mpc_d}$$

Pause for thought

Think of two reasons why a country might have a steep E line, and hence a high value for the multiplier.

---

[3] In some elementary textbooks, the formula for the multiplier is given as $1/mps$ (where *mps* is the marginal propensity to save: the proportion of a rise in income saved). The reason for this is that it is assumed (for simplicity) that there is only one withdrawal, namely saving, and only one injection, namely investment. As soon as this assumption is dropped, $1/mps$ becomes the wrong formula.

Figure 8.9   The multiplier: a shift in the expenditure function

The mpc_d is given by $\Delta C_d/\Delta Y = \pounds 40bn/\pounds 60bn = {}^2/_3$ (i.e. the slope of the C_d line). Thus:

$$k = \frac{1}{1 - {}^2/_3} = \frac{1}{{}^1/_3} = 3$$

The multiplier: a numerical illustration

The multiplier effect does not work instantaneously. When there is an increase in injections, whether investment, government expenditure or exports, it takes time before this brings about the full multiplied rise in national income.

Consider the following example. Let us assume for simplicity that the mpw is $^1/_2$. This will give an mpc_d of $^1/_2$ also. Let us also assume that investment (an injection) rises by £160 million and stays at the new higher level. Table 8.3 shows what will happen.

As firms purchase more machines and construct more factories, the incomes of those who produce machines and those who work in the construction industry will

Table 8.3   The multiplier 'round'

Round	ΔJ (£m)	ΔY (£m)	ΔCd (£m)	ΔW (£m)
1	160	160	80	80
2	–	80	40	40
3	–	40	20	20
4	–	20	10	10
5	–	10	5	5
6	–	5	.	.
.		.	.	.
$1 \rightarrow °$		320	160	160

increase by £160 million. When this extra income is received by households, whether as wages or profits, half will be withdrawn ($mpw = \frac{1}{2}$) and half will be spent on the goods and services of domestic firms. This increase in consumption thus generates additional incomes for firms of £80 million over and above the initial £160 million (which is still being generated in each time period). When this additional £80 million of incomes is received by households (round 2), again half will be withdrawn and half will go on consumption of domestic product. This increases national income by a further £40 million (round 3). And so each time we go around the circular flow of income, national income increases, but by only half as much as the previous time ($mpc_d = \frac{1}{2}$).

If we add up the additional income generated in each round (assuming the process goes on indefinitely), the total will be £320 million: twice the rise in injections. The multiplier is 2.

The bigger the mpc_d (and hence the smaller the mpw), the more will expenditure rise each time national income rises, and hence the bigger will be the multiplier.

Recap

1. If injections rise (or withdrawals fall), there will be a multiplied rise in national income. The multiplier is defined as $\Delta Y/\Delta J$. Thus if a £10 million rise in injections led to a £50 million rise in national income, the multiplier would be 5.

2. The size of the multiplier depends on the marginal propensity to withdraw (mpw). The smaller the mpw, the less will be withdrawn each time incomes are generated round the circular flow, and thus the more will go round again as *additional* demand for domestic product. The multiplier formula is $1/mpw$ or $1/(1 - mpc_d)$.

APPENDIX: MEASURING NATIONAL INCOME AND OUTPUT

Three routes: one destination

To assess how fast the economy has grown we must have a means of *measuring* the value of the nation's output. The measure we use is *gross domestic product* (GDP).

GDP can be calculated in three different ways, which should all result in the same figure. These three methods are illustrated in the simplified circular flow of income shown in Figure 8.A1.

The product method

The first method of measuring GDP is to add up the value of all the goods and services produced in the country, industry by industry. In other words, we focus on firms and add up all their production. Thus method number one is known as the *product method*.

In the national accounts these figures are grouped together into broad categories such as manufacturing, construction and distribution. The figures for the UK economy for 2008 are shown in the top part of Figure 8.A2.

When we add up the output of various firms we must be careful to avoid *double counting*. For example, if a manufacturer sells a television to a retailer for £200 and the retailer sells it to the consumer for £300, how much has this television

Figure 8.A1 The circular flow of national income and expenditure

contributed to GDP? The answer is *not* £500. We do not add the £200 received by the manufacturer to the £300 received by the retailer: that would be double counting. Instead we either just count the final value (£300) or the value added at each stage (£200 by the manufacturer + £100 by the retailer).

The sum of all the values added by all the various industries in the economy is known as **gross value added at basic prices** (GVA).

How do we get from GVA to GDP? The answer has to do with taxes and subsidies on products. Taxes paid on goods and services (such as VAT and duties on petrol and alcohol) and any subsidies on products are *excluded* from gross value added (GVA), since they are not part of the value added in production. Nevertheless the way GDP is measured throughout the EU is at *market prices*: i.e. at the prices actually paid at each stage of production. Thus **GDP at market prices** (sometimes referred to simply as GDP) is GVA *plus* taxes on products *minus* subsidies on products. This is shown in the bottom panel of Figure 8.A2.

The income method

The second approach is to focus on the incomes generated from the production of goods and services. A moment's reflection will show that this must be the same as the sum of all values added at each stage of production. Value added is simply the difference between a firm's revenue from sales and the costs of its purchases from other firms. This difference is made up of wages and salaries, rent, interest and profit. In other words, it consists of the incomes earned by those involved in the production process.

Since GVA is the sum of all values added, it must also be the sum of all incomes generated: the sum of all wages and salaries, rent, interest and profit.

The middle panel of Figure 8.A2 shows how these incomes are grouped together in the official statistics. As you can see, the total is the same as that in the top panel of Figure 8.A2, even though the components are quite different.

Figure 8.A2 UK GDP: 2008

UK GVA (product-based measure): 2008

	Percentage of GVA
Agriculture, forestry and fishing £10 809 m	0.8
Mining, energy and water supply £67 895 m	5.2
Manufacturing £160 174 m	12.4
Construction £79 235 m	6.1
Wholesale and retail trade; repairs £140 923 m	10.9
Hotels and restaurants £35 410 m	2.7
Transport and communication £88 341 m	6.8
Banking, finance, insurance, etc. £119 836 m	9.2
Letting of property £297 781 m	23.0
Public administration and defence £63 605 m	4.9
Education, health and social work £168 388 m	13.0
Other services £63 936 m	4.9
Total GVA £1 296 332 m	100.0

UK GVA by category of income: 2008

	Percentage of GVA
Compensation of employees (wages and salaries) £769 662 m	59.4
Operating surplus (gross profit, rent and interest of firms government and other institutions) £429 003 m	33.1
Mixed incomes £83 369 m	6.4
Tax less subsidies on production (other than those on products) plus statistical discrepancy £14 298 m	1.1
Total GVA £1 296 332 m	100.0

From GVA to GDP: 2008

GVA (gross value added at basic prices)	£1 296 332 m
plus Taxes on products	£155 297 m
less Subsidies on products	£5 516 m
GDP (at market prices)	£1 446 113 m

Source: *United Kingdom National Accounts: The Blue Book* (National Statistics, 2009)

Note that we do not include transfer payments such as social security benefit and pensions. Since these are not payments for the production of goods and services, they are excluded from GVA. Conversely, part of people's gross income is paid in income taxes. Since it is this gross (pre-tax) income that arises from the production of goods and services, we count wages, profits, interest and rent *before* the deduction of income taxes.

As with the product approach, if we are working out GVA, we measure incomes before the payment of taxes on products or the receipt of subsidies on products, since it is these pre-tax-and-subsidy incomes that arise from the value added by production. When working out GDP, however, we add in these taxes and subtract these subsidies to arrive at a *market price* valuation.

The expenditure method

The final approach to calculating GDP is to add up all expenditure on final output (which will be at market prices). This will include the following:

- Consumer expenditure (*C*). This includes all expenditure on goods and services by households and by non-profit institutions serving households (NPISH) (e.g. clubs and societies).
- Government expenditure (*G*). This includes central and local government expenditure on final goods and services. Note that it includes non-marketed services (such as health and education), but excludes transfer payments, such as pensions and social security payments.
- Investment expenditure (*I*). This includes investment in capital, such as buildings and machinery. It also includes the value of any increase (+) or decrease (−) in inventories, whether of raw materials, semi-finished goods or finished goods.
- Exports of goods and services (*X*).
- Imports of goods and services (*M*). These have to be *subtracted* from the total in order to leave just the expenditure on *domestic* product. In other words, we subtract the part of consumer expenditure, government expenditure and investment that goes on imports. We also subtract the imported component (e.g. raw materials) from exports.

GDP (at market prices) = *C* + *G* + *I* + *X* − *M*

Table 8.A1 shows the calculation of UK GDP by the expenditure approach.

Table 8.A1	UK GDP at market prices by category of expenditure: 2008	
	£ million	**% of GDP**
Consumption expenditure of households and NPISH (C)	927 398	64.1
Gross capital formation (I)	246 435	17.0
Government final consumption (G)	313 019	21.6
Exports of goods and services (X)	421 501	29.1
less Imports of goods and services (M)	−459 899	−31.8
Statistical discrepancy	−2 341	−0.2
GDP at market prices	**1 446 113**	**100.0**

Source: *United Kingdom National Accounts: The Blue Book* (National Statistics, 2009)

Table 8.A2 UK GDP, GNY and NNY at market prices: 2008	
	£ million
Gross Domestic Product (GDP)	1 446 113
plus net income from abroad	25 142
Gross National Income (GNY)	1 471 255
less capital consumption (depreciation)	−162 272
Net national income (NNY)	1 308 983

Source: *United Kingdom National Accounts: The Blue Book* (National Statistics, 2009)

From GDP to national income

Gross national income

Some of the incomes earned in the country will go abroad. These include wages, interest, profit and rent earned in this country by foreign residents and remitted abroad, and taxes on production paid to foreign governments and institutions (e.g. the EU). On the other hand, some of the incomes earned by domestic residents will come from abroad. Again, these can be in the form of wages, interest, profit or rent, or in the form of subsidies received from governments or institutions abroad. Gross *domestic* product, however, is concerned with those incomes generated *within* the country, irrespective of ownership. If, then, we are to take 'net income from abroad' into account (i.e. these inflows minus outflows), we need a new measure. This is **gross national income (GNY)**.[4] It is defined as follows:

GNY at market prices = GDP at market prices + Net income from abroad

Thus GDP focuses on the value of domestic production, whereas GNY focuses on the value of incomes earned by domestic residents.

Net national income

The measures we have used so far ignore the fact that each year some of the country's capital equipment will wear out or become obsolete: in other words, they ignore **capital depreciation**. If we subtract an allowance for depreciation (or 'capital consumption') we get **net national income** (NNY).

NNY at market prices = GNY at market prices − Depreciation

Table 8.A2 shows GDP, GNY and NNY figures for the UK.

Households' disposable income

Finally, we come to a term called **households' disposable income**. It measures the income people have available for spending (or saving): i.e. after any deductions for income tax, national insurance, etc. have been made. It is the best measure to use if we want to see how changes in household income affect consumption.

How do we get from GNY at market prices to households' disposable income? We start with the incomes that firms receive[5] from production (plus income from

---

[4] In the official statistics, this is referred to as *GNI*. We use *Y* to stand for income, however, to avoid confusion with investment.

[5] We also include income from any public-sector production of goods or services (e.g. health and education) and production by non-profit institutions serving households.

abroad) and then deduct that part of their income that is *not* distributed to households. This means that we must deduct taxes that firms pay – taxes on goods and services (such as VAT), taxes on profits (such as corporation tax) and any other taxes – and add in any subsidies they receive. We must then subtract allowances for depreciation and any undistributed profits. This gives us the gross income that households receive from firms in the form of wages, salaries, rent, interest and distributed profits.

To get from this what is available for households to spend, we must subtract the money that households pay in income taxes and national insurance contributions, but add all benefits to households such as pensions and child benefit.

Households' disposable income = GNY at market prices – Taxes paid by firms
+ Subsidies received by firms – Depreciation
– Undistributed profits – Personal taxes
+ Benefits

Taking account of inflation

If we are to make a sensible comparison of one year's national income with another's, we must take inflation into account. For example, if this year national income is

---

BOX 8.3 **THE DISTINCTION BETWEEN REAL AND NOMINAL VALUES** EXPLORING ECONOMICS

Working out what is real

Which would you rather have: (a) a pay rise of 5 per cent when inflation is 2 per cent, or (b) a pay rise of 10 per cent when inflation is 9 per cent? Which debt would you rather have: (a) one where the interest rate is 10 per cent and inflation is 8 per cent, or (b) one where the interest rate is 5 per cent and the inflation rate is 1 per cent?

To answer these questions, you need to distinguish between real and nominal values. *Nominal values* are measured in current prices and take no account of inflation. Thus in the questions above, the nominal pay rises are (a) 5 per cent and (b) 10 per cent; the nominal interest rates are (a) 10 per cent and (b) 5 per cent. In each case it might seem that you are better off with alternative (b).

But if you opted for answers (b), you would be wrong. Once you take inflation into account, you would be better off in each case with alternative (a). What we need to do is to use *real values*. Real values take account of inflation. Thus in the first question, although the nominal pay rise in alternative (a) is 5 per cent, the real pay rise is only 3 per cent, since 2 of the 5 per cent is absorbed by higher prices. You are only 3 per cent better off in terms of what you can buy. In alternative (b) the real pay rise is only 1 per cent, since 9 of the 10 per cent is absorbed by higher prices. Thus in real terms, alternative (a) is better.

In the second question, although in alternative (a) you are paying 10 per cent in nominal terms, your debt is

being reduced in real terms by 8 per cent and thus you are paying a real rate of interest of only 2 per cent. In alternative (b), although the nominal rate of interest is only 5 per cent, your debt is being eroded by inflation by only 1 per cent. The real rate of interest is thus 4 per cent. Again, in real terms, you are better off with alternative (a).

The distinction between real and nominal values is a threshold concept, as understanding the distinction is fundamental to assessing statistics about the economy. Often politicians will switch between real and nominal values depending on which is more favourable to them. Thus a government wishing to show how strong economic growth has been will tend to use nominal growth figures. On the other hand, the opposition will tend to refer to real growth figures, as these will be lower (assuming a positive inflation rate).

It's easy to make the mistake of using nominal figures when we should really be using real ones. This is known as 'money illusion': the belief that a rise in money terms represents a real rise.

 When comparing two countries' GDP growth rates, does it matter if we use nominal figures, provided we use them for both countries?

10 per cent higher than last year, but at the same time prices are also 10 per cent higher, then the average person will be no better off at all. There has been no *real* increase in income.

An important distinction here is between **nominal GDP** and **real GDP**.

Definitions

Nominal GDP

GDP measured in current prices. These figures take no account of inflation.

Real GDP

GDP measured in constant prices that ruled in a chosen base year, such as 2000 or 2005. These figures *do* take account of inflation. When inflation is positive, real GDP figures will grow more slowly than nominal GDP figures.

BOX 8.4   **TRYING TO MAKE SENSE OF ECONOMIC DATA**   CASE STUDIES & APPLICATIONS

The apparently puzzling case of Japanese GDP

When a country is experiencing inflation, nominal GDP will rise faster than real GDP. The reason is that part of the rise in nominal GDP can be explained simply by the rise in prices.

The chart measures GDP in Japan and the UK. It is interesting to compare the two. In both cases the base year is 2000 and thus in both cases nominal and real GDP are the same in that year.

The UK experienced inflation every year from 1980 to 2008. Thus nominal GDP grew faster than real GDP. This can be seen from the graph where, before 2000, nominal GDP is below real GDP and after 2000, nominal GDP is above real GDP.

In Japan, however, things were different. From 1991 to 1999 nominal GDP was *greater* than real GDP. This is because the price level fell over the period; there was negative inflation (sometimes called 'deflation').

Now consider Japanese GDP after 2000. Here we find that real GDP is larger than the nominal GDP. This is explained by a decline in the average price level of domestically produced goods and services after 2000.

1. *If a country experiences a consistent rise in the average price level of domestically produced goods would we expect yearly real rates of economic growth to be higher or lower than nominal rates of growth? Explain your answer.*
2. *What effect would re-basing real GDP figures to a later year have on the figures if the country was experiencing (a) inflation; (b) deflation?*

Nominal and real GDP in Japan and the UK

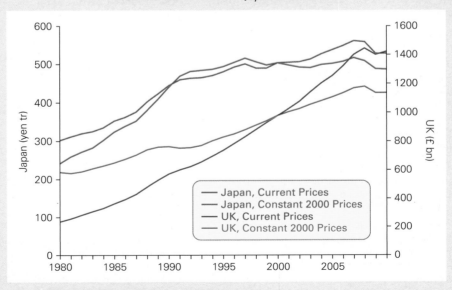

Source: *AMECO database* (© European Communities 2009)
Note: 2009 and 2010 based on forecasts

The distinction between nominal and real figures. Nominal figures are those using current prices, interest rates, etc. Real figures are figures corrected for inflation. This distinction is so important in assessing economic data that it is another of our Threshold Concepts.

Nominal GDP, sometimes called 'money GDP', measures GDP in the prices ruling at the time and thus takes no account of inflation. *Real* GDP, however, measures GDP in the prices that ruled in some particular year – the *base year*. Thus we could measure each year's GDP in, say, 2000 prices (known as 'GDP at constant 2000 prices'). This would enable us to see how much *real* GDP had changed from one year to another. In other words, it would eliminate increases in money GDP that were merely due to an increase in prices.

QUESTIONS

1. The table shows index numbers for real GDP (national output) for various countries (2003 = 100).

	2003	2004	2005	2006	2007	2008	2009
USA	100.0	103.6	106.7	109.6	111.9	113.1	110.2
Japan	100.0	102.7	104.7	106.9	109.4	108.7	102.7
Germany	100.0	100.7	101.7	104.9	107.6	108.7	103.3
France	100.0	102.2	104.2	106.6	108.9	109.7	107.4
UK	100.0	102.8	104.9	107.8	111.1	111.9	107.1

Sources: Various.

Using the formula $G = (Y_t - Y_{t-1})/Y_{t-1} \times 100$ (where G is the rate of growth, Y is the index number of output, t is any given year and $t - 1$ is the previous year):

(a) Work out the growth rate for each country for each year from 2004 to 2009.
(b) Plot the figures on a graph. Describe the pattern that emerges.

2. For simplicity, taxes are shown as being withdrawn from the inner flow of the circular flow of income (see Figure 8.4 on page 238) at just one point. In practice, different taxes are withdrawn at different points. At what point of the flow would the following be paid: (a) income taxes people pay on the dividends they receive on shares; (b) VAT; (c) business rates; (d) employees' national insurance contributions?

3. In terms of the UK circular flow of income, are the following net injections, net withdrawals or neither? If there is uncertainty, explain your assumptions.

(a) Firms are forced to take a cut in profits in order to give a pay rise.
(b) Firms spend money on research.
(c) The government increases personal tax allowances.

(d) The general public invests more money in building societies.
(e) UK investors earn higher dividends on overseas investments.
(f) The government purchases US military aircraft.
(g) People draw on their savings to finance holidays abroad.
(h) People draw on their savings to finance holidays in the UK.
(i) The government runs a budget deficit (spends more than it receives in tax revenues) and finances it by borrowing from the general public.
(j) The government runs a budget deficit and finances it by printing more money.

4. Identify the key purchasers of the goods and services produced within a country. Which of these groups of purchasers is the most significant in value terms?

5. What significance does the financial system have for household spending?

6. An economy is currently in equilibrium. The following figures refer to elements in its national income accounts.

	£bn
Consumption (total)	60
Investment	5
Government expenditure	8
Imports	10
Exports	7

(a) What is the current equilibrium level of national income?
(b) What is the level of injections?
(c) What is the level of withdrawals?

(d) Assuming that tax revenues are £7 billion, how much is the level of saving?

(e) If national income now rises to £80 billion and, as a result, the consumption of domestically produced goods rises to £58 billion, what is the mpc_d?

(f) What is the value of the multiplier?

(g) Given an initial level of national income of £80 billion, now assume that spending on exports rises by £4 billion, spending on investment rises by £1 billion and government expenditure falls by £2 billion. By how much will national income change?

7. What is the relationship between the mpc_d and the mpw?

8. Assume that the multiplier has a value of 3. Now assume that the government decides to increase aggregate demand in an attempt to reduce unemployment. It raises government expenditure by £100 million with no increase in taxes. Firms, anticipating a rise in their sales, increase investment by £200 million, of which £50 million consists of purchases of foreign machinery. How much will national income rise? (Assume no other changes in injections.)

9. On a Keynesian diagram, draw three W lines of different slopes, all crossing the J line at the same point. Now draw a second J line above the first. Mark the original equilibrium and all the new ones corresponding to each of the W lines. Using this diagram, show how the size of the multiplier varies with the mpw.

10. Why does the slope of the E line in a Keynesian diagram equal the mpc_d? (Clue: draw an mpc_d line.)

11. On a Keynesian diagram, draw two E lines of different slopes, both crossing the Y line at the same point. Now draw another two E lines, parallel with the first two and crossing each other vertically above the point where the first two crossed. Using this diagram, show how the size of the multiplier varies with the mpc_d.

12. What factors could explain why some countries have a higher multiplier than others?

Log on to MyEconlab and complete the studyplan exercises for this chapter to see how much you have learnt and where you need to revise most. Make sure you access all the supporting textbook resources including the online workbook, newsblog, audio animations, guided solutions and ebook.

Additional case studies in the *Essentials of Economics* MyEconLab (www.pearsoned.co.uk/sloman)

8.1 How does consumption behave? The case looks at evidence on the relationship between consumption and disposable income from the 1950s to the current day.

8.2 The paradox of thrift. How saving more can make the country worse off.

8.3 John Maynard Keynes (1883–1946). A profile of the great economist.

8.4 The Keynesian revolution. How Keynes's ideas revolutionised the approach to recession and mass unemployment and became economic orthodoxy in the 1950s and 60s.

8.5 Keynes's views on the consumption function. An analysis of how the assumptions made by Keynes affect the shape of the consumption function.

8.6 The relationship between income and consumption. Three alternative views of the consumption function.

8.7 **Durability and the future benefits of capital.** This case looks at ways in which an investment appraisal might take into account the timing of the benefits from the investment.

8.8 **Deriving the multiplier formula.** Using simple algebra to show how the multiplier formula is derived.

8.9 **The GDP deflator.** An examination of how GDP figures are corrected to take inflation into account.

8.10 **Simon Kuznets and the system of national income accounting**. This looks at the work of Simon Kuznets, who devised the system of national income accounting that is used around the world. It describes some of the patterns of economic growth that he identified.

8.11 **Comparing national income statistics.** The importance of taking the purchasing power of local currencies into account.

8.12 **Taking into account the redistributive effects of growth.** This case shows how figures for economic growth can be adjusted to allow for the fact that poor people's income growth would otherwise count for far less than rich people's.

8.13 **The use of ISEW.** An alternative measure to GDP for estimating economic welfare.

Websites relevant to this chapter

Numbers and sections refer to websites listed in the Web appendix and hotlinked from this book's website at **www.pearsoned.co.uk/sloman**.

■ For news articles relevant to this chapter, see the *Economics News Articles* link from the book's website.

■ For general news on macroeconomic issues, both national and international, see websites in section A, and particularly A1–5. See also links to newspapers worldwide in A38 and 39, and the news search feature in Google at A41. See also A42 for links to economics news articles from newspapers worldwide.

■ For macroeconomic data, including data on economic growth and the business cycle, see links in B1 or 2; also see B4 and 12. For UK data, see B3 and 34. For EU data, see G1 > Publications. For US data, see B25 and the *Data* section of B17. For international data, see B15, 21, 24, 31, 33. For links to data sets, see B28; I14.

■ For information on the development of ideas, see C12, 18; see also links under *Methodology and History of Economic Thought* in C14; and links to economists in I4 and I7. See also sites I7 and 11 > *Economic Systems and Theories* > *History of Economic Thought*.

■ For a model of the economy (based on the Treasury model), see *The Virtual Economy* (site D1). In addition to the model, where you can devise your own Budget, there are worksheets and outlines of theories and the work of famous economists.

■ For national income statistics for the UK (Appendix), see B1, *1. National Statistics* > the fourth link > *Economy* > *United Kingdom Economic Accounts* and *United Kingdom National Accounts – The Blue Book*.

■ For information on the United Nations' Human Development Index, a more broadly based measure of development than GDP, see site H17.

■ For student resources relevant to this chapter, see sites C1–7, 9, 10, 19.

Web appendices

8.1   **Using GDP statistics.** How well do GDP statistics measure a country's standard of living?

8.2   **The explosion of debt.** Does it affect household spending? (An extended version of Box 8.1.)

CHAPTER MAP

Aggregate supply and growth

In this chapter we focus on the factors that influence the aggregate supply of goods and services to an economy. We begin by constructing the aggregate demand and supply (AD–AS) model. This has an advantage over the circular flow and Keynesian models introduced in Chapter 8: it allows us to consider the impact of demand and supply changes not only on the level of output (real GDP), but also on the general level of prices in the economy.

We then turn to look at the causes of economic growth. Why does real GDP grow over time and what determines its rate?

We start by looking at short-run growth – growth rates over a few months or years. We see that growth rates fluctuate from year to year. In some years the economy booms, with real growth rates well in excess of their long run average. In other years, growth rates slow down or even become negative (i.e. a decline in output). We discuss the causes of these ups and downs in GDP, known as the *business cycle*.

Then we consider the drivers of long-term economic growth which help to raise the general standard of living in a country. At the heart of the debate about the drivers of long-run growth is a debate about technological progress. Therefore, we finish by considering what can be done to foster technological progress and whether or not this involves an active role for governments.

After studying this chapter, you should be able to answer the following questions:

- What is the effect on the economy of an increase in spending? Will output increase; will prices increase; or will there be some combination of the two?
- What is meant by the 'business cycle' and how does the actual output produced in the economy relate to what could potentially be produced?
- What are the causes of short-term fluctuations in economic growth? What is the role of changes in aggregate demand and changes in aggregate supply in determining the course of the business cycle?
- What determines the rate of economic growth over the long term?
- How do changes in (a) investment and (b) technological progress affect the long-term growth rate?
- What factors influence the rate of technological progress?

9.1 THE *AD–AS* MODEL

Moving on from the circular flow model of the economy

In the last chapter, we assumed that a rise in aggregate demand would be reflected purely in terms of an increase in national output (real GDP). We assumed that prices would not change. In practice, a rise in aggregate demand is likely to lead to a rise not only in GDP, but also in prices throughout the economy.

The problem with both the circular flow model and the Keynesian multiplier model is that they take no account of just how firms make supply decisions. These supply decisions, as well as being influenced by demand, are also influenced by prices. To be able to analyse the impact of changes in aggregate demand on national income *and* prices we make of the aggregate demand–supply (*AD/AS*) model. This is illustrated in Figure 9.1.

As with demand and supply curves for individual goods, we plot price on the vertical axis, except that now it is the *general* price level; and we plot quantity on the horizontal axis, except that now it is the *total quantity of national output* (GDP). Let us examine each curve in turn.

The aggregate demand curve

Remember what we said about aggregate demand in Chapter 8. It is the total level of spending on the country's products and consists of four elements: consumer spending on domestic products (C_d), private investment within the country (I_d), government expenditure on domestic goods and services (G_d) and expenditure on the country's exports (X). Thus:

$$AD = C_d + I_d + G_d + X$$

Figure 9.1   Aggregate demand and aggregate supply

The aggregate demand curve shows how much national output (GDP) will be demanded at each level of prices. The level of prices in the economy is shown by a price index (see Web appendix 9.1).

But why will the *AD* curve slope downwards: why will people demand fewer products as prices rise? There are three main reasons:

- *An international substitution effect.* If prices rise, people will be encouraged to buy fewer of the country's products and more imports instead (which are now relatively cheaper); the country will also sell fewer exports (which are now less competitive). Thus imports (a withdrawal) will rise and exports (an injection) will fall. Aggregate demand, therefore, will be lower.

- *An inter-temporal substitution effect.* As prices rise, people will need more money to pay for their purchases. With a given supply of money in the economy, this will have the effect of driving up interest rates (we will explore this in Chapter 10). The effect of higher interest rates will be to discourage borrowing and encourage saving, with individuals postponing current consumption in favour of future consumption. The effect will be a reduction in spending and hence in aggregate demand.

 - *Real balance effect.* If prices rise, the value of people's savings will be eroded. They may thus save more (and spend less) to compensate.

The aggregate supply curve

The aggregate supply curve shows the amount of goods and services that firms are willing to supply at any level of prices, other things remaining the same. The main variables that we hold constant when drawing the *short-run* aggregate supply curve are wage rates, the prices of other inputs, technology, and the labour force and the capital stock. Because these things obviously do change over time, we have to drop this assumption when drawing *long-run* aggregate supply curves. For now, we concentrate on the short-run *AS* curve.

Why do we assume that wage rates and other input prices are constant in the short run? Wage rates are frequently determined by a process of collective bargaining and, once agreed, will typically be set for a whole year, if not two. Even if they are not determined by collective bargaining, wage rates often change relatively infrequently. So too with the price of other inputs: except in perfect, or near perfect markets (such as the market for various raw materials), firms supplying capital equipment and other inputs tend to change their prices relatively infrequently. They do not immediately raise them when there is an increase in demand or lower them when demand falls. There is thus a 'stickiness' in both wage rates and the price of many inputs.

The short-run aggregate supply curve slopes upwards (as in Figure 9.1). In other words, the higher the level of prices, the more will be produced. The reason is simple: because we are holding wages and other input prices constant, as the prices of firms' products rise their profitability at each level of output will be higher than before. This will encourage them to produce more.

But what *limits* the increase in aggregate supply in response to an increase in prices? In other words, why is the aggregate supply curve not horizontal? There are two main reasons:

- Diminishing returns. With some factors of production fixed in supply, notably capital equipment, firms experience diminishing returns from their other factors, and hence have an upward-sloping marginal cost curve. In microeconomic

TC 14
p 266

TC 4
p 21

KI 15
p 87

analysis the upward-sloping cost curves of firms explain why the supply curves of individual goods and services slope upwards. Here in macroeconomics we are adding the supply curves of all goods and services and thus the aggregate supply curve also slopes upwards.

■ Growing shortages of certain variable factors. As firms collectively produce more, even inputs that can be varied may increasingly become in short supply. Skilled labour may be harder to find, for example.

Thus rising costs explain the upward-sloping aggregate supply curve. The more steeply costs rise as production increases, the less elastic will the aggregate supply curve be. It is likely that, as the level of GDP increases, and as full capacity is approached, so marginal costs will rise faster. The aggregate supply curve will thus tend to get steeper (as shown in Figure 9.1).

Equilibrium

The equilibrium price level will be where aggregate demand equals aggregate supply. To demonstrate this, consider what would happen if aggregate demand exceeded aggregate supply: for example, at P_2 in Figure 9.1. The resulting shortages throughout the economy would drive up prices. This would cause a movement up *along* both the *AD* and *AS* curves until $AD = AS$, at a price level of P_e and a level of national income of Y_e.

TC 5 p 40

Shifts in the AD or AS curves

If there is a change in the price level there will be a movement *along* the *AD* and *AS* curves. If any other determinant of *AD* or *AS* changes, the respective curve will shift. The analysis here is very similar to shifts and movements along demand and supply curves in individual markets (see pages 33 and 38).

The aggregate demand curve will shift if there is a change in any of its components – C_d, I_d, G_d or X. Thus if the government decides to spend more, or if customers spend more as a result of lower taxes, or if business confidence increases so that firms decide to invest more, the *AD* curve will shift to the right. A fall in any of these will cause the *AD* curve to shift to the left.

Similarly, the aggregate supply curve will shift if there is a change in any of the variables that are held constant when we plot the curve. Several of these variables, notably technology, the labour force and the stock of capital, change only slowly in the short run – normally shifting the curve gradually to the right. Wage rates (and other input prices) can change significantly in the short run, however, and are thus the major causes of shifts in the short-run supply curve.

What effect will an increase in the average wage rate have on the aggregate supply curve? Wages account for around 70 per cent of firms' costs. If, therefore, wages increase, costs increase and profitability falls, and this reduces the amount that firms wish to produce at any level of prices. Thus the aggregate supply curve shifts to the left. A similar effect will occur if other input prices increase. If, on the other hand, input prices fall the aggregate supply curve shifts to the right.

An important input is oil. Changes in the price of oil can shift the aggregate supply curve. A dramatic example of such shifts took place during the 2000s when oil prices initially rose in response to rising global demand, but fell sharply for a time at the end of the decade as the global economy weakened markedly (see Box 5.3).

Pause for thought

Give some examples of events that could shift (a) the AD curve to the left; (b) the AS curve to the right.

Effect of a shift in the aggregate demand curve

If there is an increase in aggregate demand, the *AD* curve will shift to the right. This will lead to a combination of higher prices and higher output, depending on the elasticity of the *AS* curve. The more elastic the *AS* curve, the more will output rise relative to prices. We will consider the shape of the *AS* curve in more detail in Chapter 11.

What we shall see is that the aggregate supply curve in the long run is generally much less elastic than the short-run curve and may well be vertical.

Recap

1. Equilibrium in the economy occurs where aggregate demand equals aggregate supply.

2. A diagram can be constructed to show aggregate demand and aggregate supply, with the price level on the vertical axis and national output (GDP) on the horizontal axis.

3. The *AD* curve is downward sloping, meaning that aggregate demand will be lower at a higher price level. The reason is that at higher prices: (a) there will be more imports and fewer exports; (b) interest rates will tend to be higher, resulting in reduced borrowing and increased saving; (c) people will be encouraged to save more to maintain the value of their savings.

4. The *AS* curve is upward sloping because the higher prices resulting from higher demand will encourage firms to produce more (assuming that factor prices and technology are fixed).

5. A change in the price level will cause a movement along the *AD* and *AS* curves. A change in any other determinant of either *AD* or *AS* will cause a shift in the respective curve.

6. The amount that prices and output rise as a result of an increase in aggregate demand will depend on the shape of the *AS* curve.

7. A rise in aggregate demand, to the extent that it results in higher prices, will not have a full multiplier effect on real national income.

INTRODUCING ECONOMIC GROWTH   9.2

What is the historical pattern of economic growth and can we expect it to continue?

Between 1993 and 2008 the UK enjoyed uninterrupted economic growth. During this period the UK saw its level of output increase over 63 consecutive quarters. In other words, the flow of output from production within each of these quarters was higher than in the previous quarter. The fact that growth should come to a halt as it did in the second quarter of 2008 and then become negative was, by historical standards, not a surprise; indeed it was the duration of sustained economic growth that appears unusual.

Despite this short-run volatility in the rate of growth, including periods of declining output, economies do experience increasing output over the long run. Short-run economic instability seems to go hand-in-hand with long-run growth.

These twin characteristics of growth are nicely captured in Figure 9.2, which plots for the UK both the *level* of real GDP (a measure of the economy's output) and quarter-to-quarter percentage *changes* in real GDP. It supports the idea that while the volume of output tends to grow over time, the rate of this growth is volatile; indeed we can identify periods of recession, which is defined as a period when output falls for two or more consecutive quarters.

| Figure 9.2 | Real GDP and quarterly economic growth in the UK |

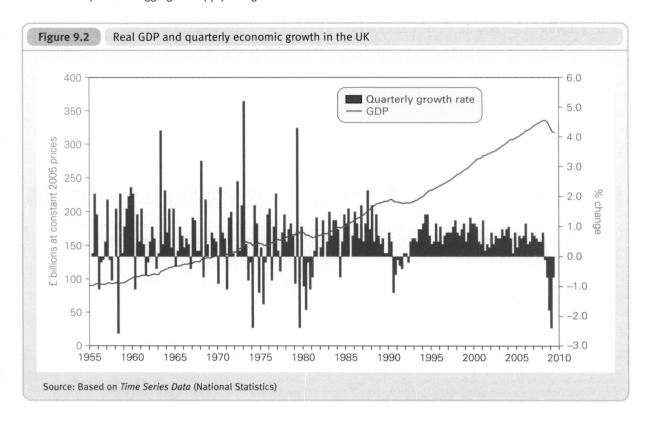

Source: Based on *Time Series Data* (National Statistics)

The distinction between actual and potential growth

Before examining the causes of economic growth, it is essential to distinguish between *actual* and *potential* economic growth. People frequently confuse the two.

Actual growth is the percentage increase in national output (real GDP) from one period to another. Normally this is expressed as an annual rate, but sometimes, as in Figure 9.2, as a quarterly one. When statistics on growth rates are published, it is actual growth they are referring to. Figure 9.3 shows annual growth rates for four economies (it is the same as Figure 8.1).

Potential growth is the speed at which the economy *could* grow. It is the percentage annual increase in the economy's *capacity* to produce: the rate of growth in *potential output*.

Two of the major factors contributing to potential economic growth are:

■ An increase in resources – natural resources, labour or capital.
■ An increase in the efficiency with which these resources are used, through advances in technology, improved labour skills or improved organisation.

Definitions

Actual growth
The percentage annual increase in national output actually produced.

Potential growth
The percentage annual increase in the capacity of the economy to produce.

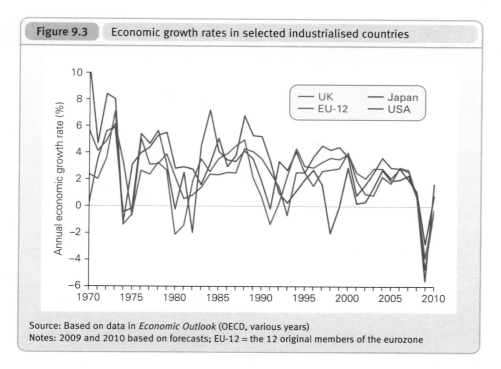

Figure 9.3   Economic growth rates in selected industrialised countries

Source: Based on data in *Economic Outlook* (OECD, various years)
Notes: 2009 and 2010 based on forecasts; EU-12 = the 12 original members of the eurozone

Potential output (i.e. potential GDP) is the level of output when the economy is operating at 'normal capacity utilisation'. This allows for firms having a planned degree of spare capacity to meet unexpected demand or for hold-ups in supply. It also allows for some unemployment as people move from job to job. Potential output is thus somewhat below full-capacity output, which is the absolute maximum that could be produced with firms working flat-out.

The difference between actual and potential output is known as the **output gap**. Thus if actual output exceeds potential output, the output gap is positive: the economy is operating above normal capacity utilisation. If actual output is below potential output, the output gap is negative: the economy is operating below normal capacity utilisation. Box 9.1 looks at the output gap for the UK and France since 1965.

If the actual growth rate is less than the potential growth rate, there will be an increase in spare capacity and probably an increase in unemployment: the output gap will become more negative (or less positive). To close a negative output gap, the actual growth rate would temporarily have to exceed the potential growth rate. In the long run, however, the actual growth rate will be limited to the potential growth rate.

There are thus two major policy issues concerned with economic growth: the short-run issue of ensuring that actual growth is such as to keep actual output as close as possible to potential output; and the long-run issue of what determines the rate of potential economic growth.

Definitions

Potential output
The sustainable level output that could be produced in the economy: i.e. one that involves a 'normal' level of capacity utilisation and does not result in rising inflation.

Output gap
The difference between actual and potential output. When actual output exceeds potential output, the gap is positive. When actual output is less than potential output, the gap is negative.

BOX 9.1   OUTPUT GAPS

An alternative measure of excess or deficient demand

If the economy grows, how fast and for how long can it grow before it runs into inflationary problems? On the other hand, what minimum rate must be achieved to avoid rising unemployment?

To answer these questions, economists have developed the concept of 'output gaps'.[a] As we have seen, the output gap is the difference between actual output and potential output.

If actual output is below potential output (the gap is negative), there will be a higher-than-normal level of unemployment as firms are operating below their normal level of capacity utilisation. There will, however, be a downward pressure on inflation, resulting from a lower-than-normal level of demand for labour and other resources. If actual output is above potential output (the gap is positive), there will be excess demand and a rise in inflation.

Generally, the gap will be negative in a recession and positive in a boom. In other words, output gaps follow the course of the business cycle.

Of course, to measure the output gap we first need to measure potential output. There are two main approaches to producing statistical estimates of potential output.

De-trending techniques. This approach is a purely mechanical exercise which involves smoothing the actual GDP figures. In doing this, it attempts to fit a trend growth path along the lines of the dashed line in Figure 9.4. The main disadvantage of this approach is that it is not grounded in economic theory and therefore does not take into consideration those factors that economists consider to be important in determining output levels over time.

Production function approach. Many institutions, such as the European Union, use an approach which borrows ideas from economic theory. Specifically, it uses the idea of a production function which relates output to a set of inputs. Estimates of potential output are generated by using statistics on the size of a country's capital stock (see Box 9.3), the potential available labour input and, finally, the productivity or effectiveness of these inputs in producing output.

The table shows the ratio of potential output in 2009 to that in 1965 for both France and the UK and what this equates to in terms of an annual rate of growth for potential output. We can see that the rate of growth in France's potential output is almost half a percentage point higher each year than that in the UK. Over the long term, the actual rate of economic growth in both countries is approximately the same as the potential rate. In other words, over the years, the average output gap tends towards zero.

---

[a]   See Giorno *et al.*, 'Potential output, output gaps and structural budget balances', *OECD Economic Studies*, no. 24, 1995: 1

Table 1 Potential and actual output in France and the UK

	Potential output in 2009/potential output in 1965	Equivalent annual rate of growth in potential output, %	Actual output in 2009/actual output in 1965	Equivalent annual rate of growth in actual output, %
France	3.34	2.78	3.33	2.77
UK	2.81	2.38	2.76	2.34

Source: Based on data in the annual macro-economic database [AMECO] of the European Commission's Directorate General for Economic and Financial Affairs.
Notes: 2009 figures based on forecasts

9.3   SHORT-TERM ECONOMIC GROWTH AND THE BUSINESS CYCLE

What is the pattern of economic growth from year to year?

Although growth in potential output varies to some extent over the years – depending on the rate of advance of technology, the level of investment and the discovery of new raw materials – it nevertheless tends to be much steadier than the growth in actual output.

Actual growth tends to fluctuate. In some years there is a high rate of economic growth: the country experiences a boom. In other years, economic growth is low or

TC 12
p 234

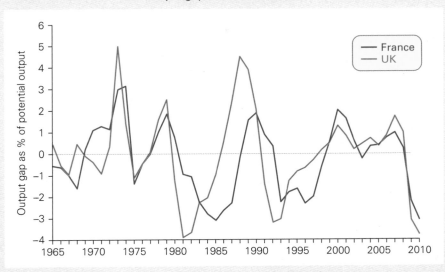

Output gaps in UK and France

Source: Based on data in *European Economy* (© European Communities 2009)

The chart shows that the output gaps have tended to fluctuate more in the UK than in France. This is particularly true during the 1980s and early 1990s. Interestingly, during this period the two economies appear to be out of synch. For instance, in 1988 when the UK was experiencing a positive output gap, with actual output estimated to be $4\frac{1}{2}$ per cent above the potential output, in France actual output was below its potential level.

We can use the information of output gaps to identify the length of a particular business cycle, its degree of economic volatility and the growth in potential output during the cycle. The trend growth rate in the UK was about $2\frac{1}{2}$ per cent per year over the full economic cycle to 2008 (i.e. from 1991: the equivalent point in the previous cycle).

Until the recession of the late 2000s growth rates in the UK had been relatively stable since 1992 compared with previous cycles. In fact, Gordon Brown was claiming in the early 2000s that 'boom and bust' were things of the past. During this period, therefore, output gaps, both positive and negative, were smaller than in the 1980s (or the 1970s for that matter).

Until the recession of 2008/9, it was argued that the greater stability in the UK economy created a climate that encouraged a long-term increase in investment and hence a long-term increase in potential growth. Whether that climate will be resumed in the future will have to be seen.

1. *Characterise the state of an economy during positive and negative output gaps.*
2. *Are all business cycles the same?*

even negative: the country experiences a slowdown or **recession**. This cycle of booms and recessions is known as the **business cycle** or **trade cycle**.

There are four 'phases' of the business cycle. They are illustrated in Figure 9.4.

1. *The upturn*. In this phase, a contracting or stagnant economy begins to recover, and growth in actual output resumes.
2. *The expansion*. During this phase, there is rapid economic growth: the economy is booming. A fuller use is made of resources, and the gap between actual and potential output narrows.
3. *The peaking out*. During this phase, growth slows down or even ceases.
4. *The slowdown, recession or slump*. During this phase, there is little or no growth or even a decline in output. Increasing slack develops in the economy.

Definitions

Recession
In official statistics, a recession is defined as when an economy experiences falling national output (negative growth) for two or more quarters.

Business cycle or **trade cycle**
The periodic fluctuations of national output round its long-term trend.

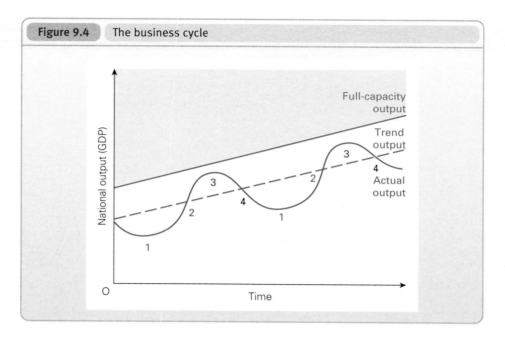

Figure 9.4   The business cycle

A word of caution: do not confuse a high *level* of output with a high rate of *growth* in output. The level of output is highest in phase 3. The rate of growth in output is highest in phase 2 (i.e. where the curve is steepest).

Long-term output trend. A line can be drawn showing the trend of national output over time (i.e. ignoring the cyclical fluctuations around the trend). This is shown as the dashed line in Figure 9.4. If, over time, firms on average operate with a 'normal' degree of capacity utilisation, the trend output line will be the same as the potential output line. Also, if the average level of capacity that is unutilised stays constant from one cycle to another, the trend line will have the same slope as the full-capacity output line. In other words, the trend (or potential) rate of growth will be the same as the rate of growth of capacity.

If, however, the level of unutilised capacity changes from one cycle to another, then the trend line will have a different slope from the full-capacity output line. For example, if unemployment and unused industrial capacity *rise* from one peak to another, or from one trough to another, the trend line will move further away from the full-capacity output line (i.e. it will be less steep).

Pause for thought

Figure 9.4 shows a decline in actual output in recession. Redraw the diagram, only this time show a mere slowing down of growth in phase 4.

The business cycle in practice

The business cycle illustrated in Figure 9.4 is a 'stylised' cycle. It is nice and smooth and regular. Drawing it this way allows us to make a clear distinction between each of the four phases. In practice, however, business cycles are highly irregular. They are irregular in two ways.

The length of the phases. Some booms are short-lived, lasting only a few months or so. Others are much longer, lasting perhaps three or four years. Likewise some recessions are short while others are long.

The magnitude of the phases. Sometimes in phase 2, there is a very high rate of economic growth, perhaps 4 per cent per annum or more. On other occasions in

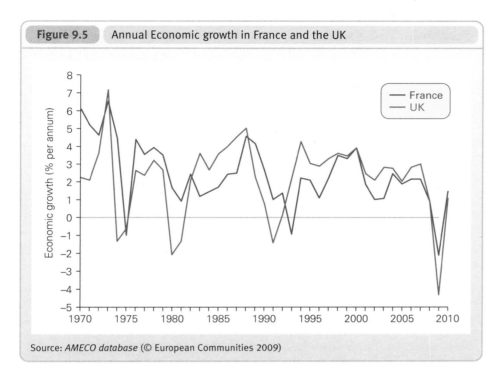

Figure 9.5 Annual Economic growth in France and the UK

Source: *AMECO database* (© European Communities 2009)

phase 2, growth is much gentler. Sometimes in phase 4 there is a recession, with an actual decline in output. On other occasions, phase 4 is merely a 'pause', with growth simply being low.

Nevertheless, despite the irregularity of the fluctuations and differences in magnitude, cycles are still clearly discernible. You can see this in Figure 9.5, which plots the annual rates of growth in France and the UK from 1970. While there is some similarity in the general patterns of growth in the two countries, the UK has experienced more marked downturns than France, with the contrasting experiences in the early 1980s being especially stark.

Recap

1. Actual growth must be distinguished from potential growth. The actual growth rate is the percentage annual increase in the output that is actually produced, whereas potential growth is the percentage annual increase in the capacity of the economy to produce (whether or not it is actually produced).

2. Actual growth will fluctuate with the course of the business cycle. The cycle can be broken down into four phases: the upturn, the expansion, the peaking out, and the slowdown or recession. In practice, the length and magnitude of these phases will vary: the cycle is thus irregular.

EXPLANATIONS OF THE BUSINESS CYCLE 9.4

Why isn't economic growth constant?

In this section we look at why growth in the short run tends to fluctuate. In other words, we examine the causes of the business cycle.

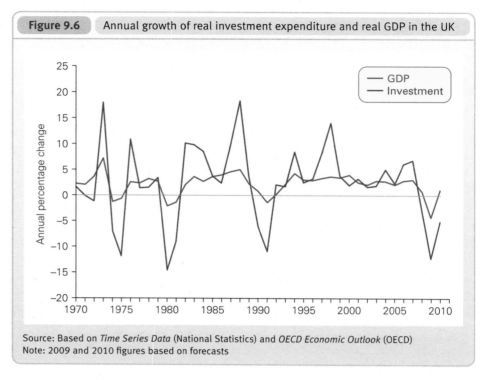

Figure 9.6   Annual growth of real investment expenditure and real GDP in the UK

Source: Based on *Time Series Data* (National Statistics) and *OECD Economic Outlook* (OECD)
Note: 2009 and 2010 figures based on forecasts

Fluctuations in aggregate demand

Keynesians blame fluctuations in output and employment on fluctuations in aggregate demand. They seek to explain why the growth in aggregate demand fluctuates, and then to devise appropriate stabilisation policies to iron out these fluctuations. A more stable economy, they argue, will provide a better climate for investment and the growth of both individual businesses and the economy as a whole.

Instability of investment: the accelerator

One of the major factors contributing to the ups and downs of the business cycle is the instability of investment. Figure 9.6 shows the annual percentage changes in real investment expenditures (gross capital formation) and annual growth in real GDP in the UK. You can see that investment is markedly more volatile than GDP.

In a recession, investment in new plant and equipment can all but disappear. After all, what is the point in investing in additional capacity if you cannot even sell what you are currently producing? When an economy begins to recover from a recession, however, and confidence returns, investment can rise very rapidly. In percentage terms, the rise in investment may be *several times that of the rise in income*. When the growth of the economy slows down, however, investment can fall dramatically.

The point is that investment depends not so much on the *level* of national income and consumer demand, as on their *rate of change*. The reason is that investment (except for replacement investment) is to provide *additional* capacity, and thus depends on how much demand has risen, not on its level. But growth rates change by much more than the level of output. For example, if economic growth is 1 per cent in 2010 and 2 per cent in 2012, then in 2012 output has gone up by 2 per cent, but growth has gone up by 100 per cent (i.e. it has doubled). Thus changes in investment tend to be much more dramatic than changes in national income. This is known as the **accelerator theory**. Box 9.2 gives an example of the accelerator effect.

TC 9
p 234

TC 9
p 71

TC 13
p 253

Definition

Accelerator theory
The *level* of investment depends on the *rate of change* of national income, and as a result tends to be subject to substantial fluctuations.

BOX 9.2	THE ACCELERATOR: AN EXAMPLE	EXPLORING ECONOMICS

Demonstrating the instability of investment

The following example illustrates some important features of the accelerator. It looks at the investment decisions made by a firm in response to change in the demand for its product. The firm is taken as representative of firms throughout the economy. The example is based on various strict assumptions. These help to keep the analysis simple.

- The firm's machines last exactly 10 years and then need replacing.
- At the start of the example, the firm has 10 machines in place, one 10 years old, one 9 years old, one 8 years old, one 7, one 6 and so on. Thus one machine needs replacing each year.
- Machines produce exactly 100 units of output per year. This figure cannot be varied.
- The firm always adjusts its output and its stock of machinery to match consumer demand.

The example shows what happens to the firm's investment over a six-year period when there is first a substantial rise in consumer demand, then a levelling off and then a slight fall. It illustrates the following features of the accelerator (see the table).

Investment will rise when the growth of national income (and hence consumer demand) is rising $(\Delta Y_{t+1} > \Delta Y_t)$. Years 1 to 2 illustrate this. The rise in consumer demand is zero in year 1 and 1000 units in year 2. Investment rises from 1 to 11 machines. The growth in investment may be considerably greater than the growth in consumer demand, giving a large accelerator effect. Between years 1 and 2, consumer demand doubles but investment goes up by a massive *11 times!*

Investment will be constant even when national income is growing, if the increase in income this year is the same as last year $(\Delta Y_{t+1} = \Delta Y_t)$. Years 2 to 3 illustrate this. Consumer demand continues to rise by 1000 units, but investment is constant at 11 machines.

Investment will fall even if national income is still growing, if the rate of growth is slowing down $(\Delta Y_{t+1} < \Delta Y_t)$. Years 3 to 4 illustrate this. Consumer demand rises now by 500 units (rather than the 1000 units last year). Investment falls from 11 to 6 machines.

If national income is constant, investment will be confined to replacement investment only. Years 4 to 5 illustrate this. Investment falls to the one machine requiring replacement.

If national income falls, even if only slightly, investment can be wiped out altogether. Years 5 to 6 illustrate this. Even though demand has fallen by only $^1/_{35}$, investment will fall to zero. Not even the machine that is wearing out will be replaced.

In practice, the accelerator will not be as dramatic and clear-cut as this. The effect will be extremely difficult to predict for the following reasons:

- Many firms may have spare capacity and/or carry stocks. This will enable them to meet extra demand without having to invest.
- The willingness of firms to invest will depend on their confidence of *future* demand. Just because demand has currently risen, firms are not going to rush out and spend large amounts of money on machines that will last many years if it is quite likely that next year demand will fall back again.
- Firms may make their investment plans a long time in advance and may be unable to change them quickly.
- Even if firms do decide to invest more, the producer goods industries may not have the capacity to meet a sudden surge in demand for machines.
- Machines do not as a rule suddenly wear out. A firm could thus delay replacing machines and keep the old ones for a bit longer if it was uncertain about its future level of demand.

All these points tend to reduce the magnitude of the accelerator and to make it very difficult to predict. Nevertheless the effect still exists. Firms still take note of changes in consumer demand when deciding how much to invest. Evidence shows that fluctuations in investment are far more severe than fluctuations in national income.

 If there is an initial change in injections or withdrawals, then theoretically this will set off a chain reaction between the multiplier and accelerator. Assuming that there is an initial rise in injections, trace through the multiplier and accelerator effects. Why is it unlikely that national income will go on rising more and more rapidly?

TC 12
p 234

The accelerator effect

Year	0	1	2	3	4	5	6
Quantity demanded by consumers (sales)	1000	1000	2000	3000	3500	3500	3400
Number of machines required	10	10	20	30	35	35	34
Induced investment (I_i) (extra machines)		0	10	10	5	0	0
Replacement investment (I_r)		1	1	1	1	1	0
Total investment ($I_i + I_r$)		1	11	11	6	1	0

Pause for thought

Under what circumstances would you expect a rise in national income to cause a large accelerator effect?

These fluctuations in investment, being injections into the circular flow of income, then have a multiplied effect on national income and will thus magnify the upswings and downswings of the business cycle.

Fluctuations in stocks

Firms hold stocks of finished goods. These stocks tend to fluctuate with the course of the business cycle, and these fluctuations in stocks themselves contribute to fluctuations in output.

Imagine an economy that is recovering from a recession. At first, firms may be cautious about increasing production: doing so may involve taking on more labour or making additional investment. Firms may not want to make these commitments if the recovery could soon peter out. They may, therefore, run down their stocks rather than increase output. Initially the recovery from recession will be slow.

If the recovery does continue, however, firms will start to gain more confidence and will increase their production. Also they will find that their stocks have got rather low and will need building up. This gives a further boost to production, and for a time the growth in output will exceed the growth in demand. This extra growth in output will then, via the multiplier, lead to a further increase in demand.

Once stocks have been built up again, the growth in output will slow down to match the growth in demand. This slowing down in output will, via the accelerator and multiplier, contribute to the ending of the expansionary phase of the business cycle.

As the economy slows down, firms may for a time be prepared to carry on producing and build up stocks. The increase in stocks thus cushions the effect of falling demand on output and employment.

If the recession continues, firms will be unwilling to go on building up stocks. But as firms attempt to reduce their stocks back to the desired level, production will fall *below* the level of sales, despite the fact that sales themselves are lower. This could therefore lead to a dramatic fall in output and, via the multiplier, to an even bigger fall in sales.

Eventually, once stocks have been run down to the minimum, production will have to rise again to match the level of sales. This will contribute to a recovery and the whole cycle will start again.

Why do booms and recessions persist for a period of time?

Why do booms and recessions last for several months or even years? There are two main reasons.

Time lags. It takes time for changes in injections and withdrawals to be fully reflected in changes in national income, output and employment. The multiplier process takes time. Moreover, consumers, firms and government may not all respond immediately to new situations. Their responses are spread out over a period of time.

'Bandwagon' effects. Once the economy starts expanding, growth expectations become buoyant. People think ahead and adjust their spending behaviour: they consume and invest more now. Likewise in a recession a mood of pessimism may set in. The effect is cumulative.

The multiplier and accelerator interact: they feed on each other. A rise in income causes a rise in investment (the accelerator). This, being an injection into the circular flow, causes a multiplied rise in income. This then causes a further accelerator effect, and a further multiplier effect, and so on.

Why do booms and recessions come to an end? What determines the turning points?

If booms or recessions can last for some time, then why do they not go on for ever? Why do they dome to an end?

Ceilings and floors. Actual output can go on growing more rapidly than potential output only as long as there is slack in the economy. As full employment is approached and as more and more firms reach full capacity, so a ceiling to output is reached.

At the other extreme, there is a basic minimum level of consumption that people tend to maintain. During a recession, people may not buy much in the way of luxury and durable goods, but they will still continue to buy food and other basic goods. There is thus a floor to consumption.

Echo effects. Durable consumer goods and capital equipment may last several years, but eventually they will need replacing. The replacement of goods and capital purchased in a previous boom may help to bring a recession to an end.

The accelerator. For investment to continue rising, consumer demand must rise at a faster and faster rate. If this does not happen, investment will fall back and the boom will break.

Random shocks. National or international political, social or natural events can affect the mood and attitudes of firms, governments and consumers, and thus affect aggregate demand.

Changes in government policy. In a boom, a government may become most worried by inflation and balance of trade deficits and thus pursue contractionary policies. In a recession, it may become most worried by unemployment and lack of growth and thus pursue expansionary policies. These government policies, if successful, will bring about a turning point in the cycle. This was the hope for the expansionary policies pursued by many governments during the global recession of the late 2000s.

Keynesians argue that governments should attempt to reduce cyclical fluctuations by the use of active stabilisation policies. A more stable economy will provide a better climate for long-term investment, which will lead to faster growth in both potential and actual output. The policy traditionally favoured by Keynesians for stabilising the economy is *fiscal policy*. This is considered in Chapter 12.

> **Pause for thought**
>
> *Why is it difficult to predict precisely when a recession will come to an end and the economy will start growing rapidly?*

Real business cycles: fluctuations in aggregate supply

New classical economists, unlike Keynesians, argue that the explanation of the business cycle lies not in fluctuations in aggregate demand, but rather in shifts in aggregate *supply*. In a recession, aggregate supply curves will shift to the left (output falls), while in a boom aggregate supply curves shift to the right (output rises). Since the new classical theory of cyclical fluctuations focuses on supply, it is known as **real business cycle theory**.

But what makes aggregate supply shift in the first place, and why, after an initial shift, will the aggregate supply curve *go on* shifting, causing a recession or boom to continue?

> **Definition**
>
> **Real business cycle theory**
> The new classical theory which explains cyclical fluctuations in terms of shifts in aggregate supply, rather than aggregate demand.

The initial shift in aggregate supply could come from a structural change: say, a shift in demand from older manufacturing industries to new service industries. Because of the immobility of labour, not all those laid off in the older industries will find work in the new industries. Structural unemployment (part of equilibrium unemployment) rises and output falls.

Alternatively, the initial shift in aggregate supply could come from a change in technology. For example, a technological breakthrough in telecommunications could shift aggregate supply to the right. Or it could come from an oil price increase, shifting aggregate supply to the left.

The persistence of supply-side effects

But why, when a shift occurs, does the effect persist? Why is there not a single rise or fall in aggregate supply? There are two main reasons. The first is that several changes may take months to complete. For example, a decline in demand for certain older industries, perhaps caused by growing competition from abroad, does not take place overnight. Likewise, a technological breakthrough does not affect all industries simultaneously.

The second reason is that these changes affect the profitability of investment. If investment rises, this will increase firms' capacity and aggregate supply will shift to the right. If investment falls (as a result, say, of the election of a government less sympathetic to industry), aggregate supply will shift to the left. In other words, investment is causing changes in output not through its effect on aggregate *demand* (through the multiplier), but rather through its effect on aggregate *supply*.

Turning points

So far we have seen how the theory of real business cycles explains persistent rises or falls in aggregate supply. But how does it explain *turning points*? Why do recessions and booms come to an end? The most likely explanation is that, once a shock has worked its way through, aggregate supply will stop shifting. If there is then any shock in the other direction, aggregate supply will start moving back again. For example, after a period of recession, an eventual rise in business confidence will cause investment to rise and hence aggregate supply to shift back to the right. Since these 'reverse shocks' are likely to occur at irregular intervals, they can help to explain why real-world business cycles are themselves irregular.

Recap

1. Keynesians explain cyclical fluctuations in the economy by examining the causes of fluctuations in the level of aggregate *demand*.

2. A major part of the Keynesian explanation of the business cycle is the instability of investment. The accelerator theory helps to explain this instability. It relates the level of investment to *changes* in national income and consumer demand. An initial increase in consumer demand can result in a very large percentage increase in investment; but as soon as the rise in consumer demand begins to level off, investment will fall; and even a slight fall in consumer demand can reduce investment to virtually zero.

Investment in stocks is also unstable and tends to amplify the business cycle.

3. Booms and recessions can persist because of time lags, 'bandwagon' effects and the *interaction* of the multiplier and accelerator.

4. Turning points are explained by ceilings and floors to output, echo effects, the accelerator, swings in government policy and random shocks.

5. Real business cycle theory focuses on aggregate supply shocks, which then persist for a period of time. Eventually their effect will peter out, and supply shocks in the other direction can lead to turning points in the cycle.

LONG-TERM ECONOMIC GROWTH   9.5

How does income per head today compare with that in the past?

Growth over the decades

Quite naturally, governments and individuals are concerned with the ups and downs of the business cycle. How does this year's economic performance compare with last year's? Are the various macroeconomic indicators, such as growth, unemployment and inflation, getting better or worse?

When we step back, however, and look at the longer span of history, these short-term fluctuations take on less significance. What we see is that economies tend to experience long-term economic growth, not long-term economic decline. Measured in terms of income per head (after adjusting for inflation), all developed nations are richer today than they were 50 years ago.

Figure 9.7 shows real GDP in France and the UK from 1960 to 2010. Two things emerge from the chart. First, the fluctuations in output appear minor compared with the long-term growth in output. Secondly, the long-term rate of growth in the two countries is different, with the British rate being lower than the French rate.

Such growth cannot be explained by a closing of the gap between actual and potential output: by an expansion of aggregate demand leading to a fuller use of resources. Instead, the explanation lies on the supply side. Countries' economic *capacity* has increased.

Comparing the growth performance of different countries

Although all developed countries (and most developing ones too) have experienced long-term economic growth, the *rate* of growth has differed from country to

| Figure 9.7 | Real GDP in France and the UK |

Source: *AMECO database* (European Commission) and *OECD Economic Outlook* (OECD)
Note: 2009 and 2010 based on forecasts

Table 9.1	Average annual percentage growth rate in GDP per person employed					
	1961–70	**1971–80**	**1981–90**	**1991–2000**	**2001–9**[b]	**1961–2009**[b]
France	4.9	2.8	2.2	1.8	0.9	2.5
Germany[a]	4.2	2.6	1.3	2.5	1.4	2.4
Italy	6.2	2.8	2.2	1.6	0.9	2.7
Ireland	4.2	3.7	3.8	3.3	2.1	3.4
Japan	8.6	3.7	3.0	1.1	1.6	3.6
Netherlands	3.8	2.7	1.6	1.5	1.3	2.2
Spain	6.7	4.2	1.9	1.1	0.7	3.0
UK	2.5	1.7	1.9	2.2	1.7	2.0
USA	2.3	1.2	1.3	1.7	1.6	1.6

[a] Up to 1991, figures are for West Germany only.
[b] 2009 projected.
Source: Based on data in *European Economy* (Commission of the European Union)

country. Table 9.1 shows the average annual growth in output per employed person for several developed countries for the four decades from 1961 to 2000 and for the most recent period. The effect of an average annual growth in output of just 2 or 3 per cent builds up over the years to a substantial rise in output.

Generally in the developed world, the less rich countries have grown faster than the richer ones. As a result, the income gap between developed countries has tended to narrow.

Figure 9.8 shows how many times greater output per person employed in 2009 was compared with that in 1960 in a selection of countries. We observe a marked contrast in the relative size of output per person employed at these two points in time across countries. For instance, in Japan output per person employed was approaching six times higher in 2009, while in Canada and the USA it was around twice as high.

Figure 9.8   Relative size of output per person employed in 1960 and 2009

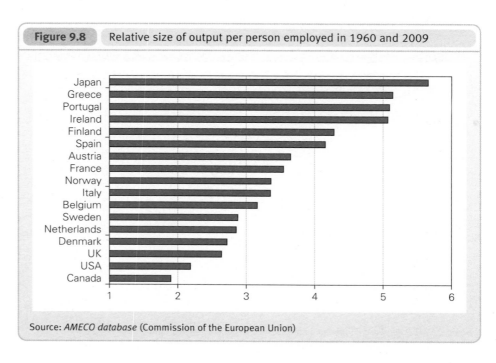

Source: *AMECO database* (Commission of the European Union)

But how is long-term growth per worker to be achieved? The answer is that there must be a growth in *potential output*. In other words the capacity of the economy must expand. Put another way, what is needed is an increase in aggregate supply (a 'supply-side' improvement) rather than simply an increase in aggregate demand. The next section explores the causes and effects of increasing potential output.

Before we go on, a word of caution. Long-term economic growth does not mean universal improvement. People are not necessarily happier; there are many stresses in modern living; the environment is in many respects more polluted; inequality has increased in most countries, especially over the past 20 years; for many people work is more demanding and the working day is longer than in the past; there is more crime and more insecurity. More is not always better.

Recap

1. The determinants of economic growth in the long run lie primarily on the supply side.

2. Most developed countries have experienced average annual rates of economic growth of 2 per cent or more over the past 50 years, but there have been considerable differences between countries.

3. The income gap between developed countries has tended to narrow as the less rich ones have grown faster than the richer ones.

EXPLANATIONS OF LONG-TERM GROWTH   9.6

Why is income per head today so much higher than a generation ago?

The causes of economic growth

The sources of growth in potential output can be grouped into two broad categories:

■ An increase in the *quantity* of factors. Here we would include an increase in the workforce or the average number of hours that people work, an increase in raw materials (e.g. discoveries of oil) and an increase in capital. Of these, for most countries it is an increase in the capital stock, brought about by investment, that is the most important source of growth.

■ An increase in the *productivity* of factors. Here we would include an increase in the skills of workers, a more efficient organisation of inputs by management and more productive capital equipment. Most significant here is technological progress. Developments of computer technology, of new techniques in engineering, of lighter, stronger and cheaper materials, of digital technology in communications and of more efficient motors have all contributed to a massive increase in the productivity of capital. Machines today can produce much more output than machines in the past that cost the same to manufacture.

 KEY IDEA 32 / **TC 15**   **Long-term growth in a country's output depends on a growth in the quantity and/or productivity of its resources.** Potential economic growth depends on the country's resources, technology and productivity. This is crucial to understanding what underlies the wealth of nations and why some countries have faster growth rates that others. It forms the 15th of our Threshold Concepts.

In this section, we will examine these two sources of growth, focusing first on capital accumulation (an increase in the *quantity* of capital) and then on technological progress (an increase in the *productivity* of factors).

Capital accumulation

An increase in capital per worker will generally increase output. In other words, the more equipment that is used by people at work, the more they are likely to produce. But to increase capital requires investment, and that investment requires resources – resources that could have been used for producing consumer goods. Thus more investment over the longer term requires more saving.

A simple model of economic growth

The rate of growth via capital accumulation depends on two things:

■ The marginal capital/output ratio (k). This is the amount of extra capital (ΔK) divided by the extra annual output that it produces (ΔY). Thus $k = \Delta K / \Delta Y$. The lower the value of k, the higher is the productivity of capital (i.e. the less extra capital you need to produce extra output).
■ The proportion of national income that is invested (i), which, assuming that all saving is invested, will equal the proportion of national income that is saved (s).

The formula for growth becomes:

$g = i/k$ (or $g = s/k$)

Thus if 20 per cent of national income went in new investment ($i = 20$ per cent), and if each £1 of new investment yielded 25p of extra income per year ($k = 4$), then the growth rate would be 5 per cent.

A simple example will demonstrate this. If national income is £100 billion, then £20 billion will be invested ($i = 20\%$). This will lead to extra annual output of £5 billion ($k = 4$). Thus national income grows to £105 billion: a growth of 5 per cent.

But what determines the rate of investment? There are a number of determinants. These include the confidence of business people about the future demand for their products, the profitability of business, the tax regime, the rate of growth in the economy and the rate of interest.

The neoclassical growth model

Although the above model is a useful starting point for examining economic growth arising from increased capital, two qualifications need to be made.

■ The first is that as capital per worker increases, so diminishing returns to capital are likely to set in. For example, if, in an office, you start equipping workers with PCs, at first output will increase very rapidly. But as more and more workers have their own PC rather than having to share, so the rate of increase in output slows down. When everyone has their own, output is likely to be at a maximum. Any additional PCs (of the same specification) will remain unused. Thus, for a given workforce, as the capital stock increases, so the marginal capital/output ratio (k) will rise and the growth rate will fall.
■ The second qualification is that, the larger the capital stock, the greater the proportion of investment that will be needed for replacement purposes, and the smaller the proportion that can be used for increasing the size of the capital stock.

Figure 9.9   Steady-state output

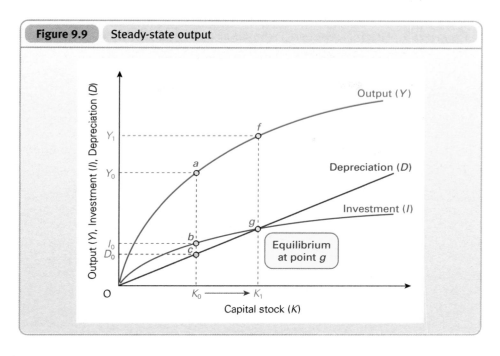

Let us now incorporate these two qualifications into a model of growth. This is known as the neoclassical or 'Solow' growth model, after the MIT economics professor and Nobel Prize winner, Robert Solow. This model is illustrated in Figure 9.9. The size of the capital stock (K) is measured on the horizontal axis; the level of national output (Y) is measured on the vertical axis. Assuming that the size of the workforce is constant, any increase in the capital stock means an increase in the average amount of capital per worker.

So how have we taken the two qualifications into account? First, consider the assumption of diminishing returns to capital. The Y curve shows that as the capital stock increases, so output increases. But, because of diminishing returns to capital the Y curve gets less and less steep. What will be the effect on investment? Increased output will mean increased saving and hence increased investment. This is shown by the investment curve (I). Note that the I curve has the same general shape as the Y curve because saving is assumed to be a given proportion of GDP. But, the higher the share of investment in GDP, the steeper will be this line.

Now consider our second qualification. There will be an increase in the amount of investment needed for replacement purposes as the capital stock increases. The depreciation (D) line shows the amount of depreciation of capital that takes place, and hence the amount of replacement investment required. The bigger the capital stock, the larger the amount of replacement investment required.

Assume initially that the size of the capital stock is K_0. This will generate an output of Y_0 (point a). This output, in turn, will generate saving and investment of I_0, but of this, D_0 will have to be used for replacement purposes. The difference $(b - c)$ will be available to increase the size of the capital stock. The capital stock will thus increase up to K_1 (point g). At this point, all investment will be required for replacement purposes. Output will therefore cease growing. Y_1 represents the steady-state level of national income.

Effect of an increase in the saving rate. If the saving rate increases, the investment curve will shift upwards. This is shown by a shift from I_1 to I_2 in Figure 9.10.

Definition

Steady-state national income
The long-run equilibrium level of national income. The level at which all investment is used to maintain the existing capital stock at its current level.

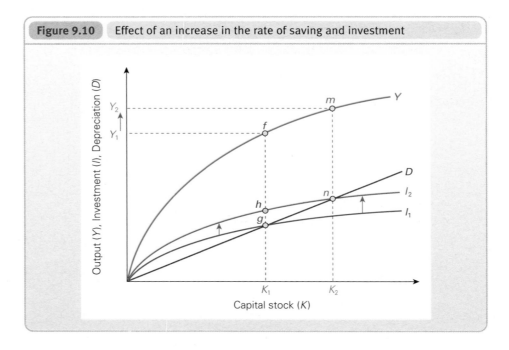

Figure 9.10   Effect of an increase in the rate of saving and investment

Investment is now above that which is necessary to maintain the capital stock at K_1. The capital stock will grow, therefore, and so will national income. But this growth is only temporary. Once the capital stock has risen to K_2, all the new higher level of investment will be absorbed in replacing capital ($I = D$ at point n). National income stops rising. Y_2 represents the new steady-state national income.

Does this mean, therefore, that there is no long-term gain from an increase in the saving rate? There *is* a gain, to the extent that income per worker is now higher (remember that we are assuming a constant labour force), and this higher income will be received not just once, but every year from now on as long as the saving rate remains at the new higher level. There is no increase in the long-term *growth rate*, however. To achieve that, we would have to look to the other determinants of growth.

What should be clear from the above analysis is that, without technological progress or some other means of increasing output from a given quantity of inputs, long-term growth cannot be sustained.

> **Pause for thought**
>
> *If there were a gradual increase in the saving rate over time, would this lead to sustained economic growth even without technological progress?*

Human capital and education. The analysis of Figures 9.9 and 9.10 need not be confined to the stock of physical capital: machines, buildings, tools, etc. It can also apply to human capital. Human capital refers to the skills and expertise of workers that have been acquired through education and training. If part of saving is used for investment in education and training, then the productivity of workers will rise, and so will output.

In Figures 9.9 and 9.10, therefore, the horizontal axis measures both physical and human capital. An increase in either has the effect of increasing the steady-state level of national income. In Box 9.3 we consider how capital is treated in countries' national accounts and look at rates of capital accumulation.

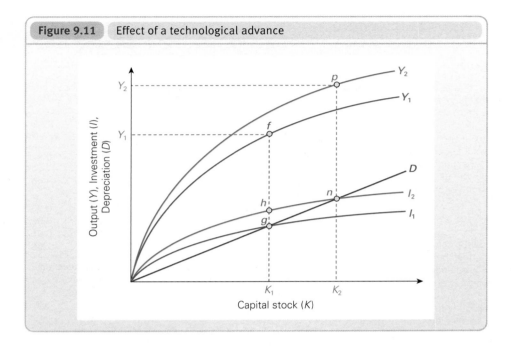

Figure 9.11   Effect of a technological advance

Technological progress

The effect of technological progress on output

Technological progress has the effect of increasing the output from a given amount of investment. This is shown in Figure 9.11. Initial investment and income curves are I_1 and Y_1; steady-state income is at a level of Y_1 (point f). A technological advance has the effect of shifting the Y line upwards, say to Y_2. The higher income curve leads to a higher investment curve (for a given rate of saving). This is shown by curve I_2. The new long-term equilibrium capital stock is thus K_2, and the new steady-state level of income is Y_2 (point p).

If there is a 'one-off' technological advance, the effect is the one we have just illustrated. National income rises to a higher level, but does not go on rising once the new steady-state level has been reached. But technological progress marches on over time. New inventions are made; new processes are discovered; old ones are improved. In terms of Figure 9.11, the Y curve *goes on* shifting upwards over time, as does the I curve too. The faster the rate of technological progress, the faster will the Y curve shift upwards and the higher will be the rate of economic growth.

Endogenous growth theory

It should be clear from what we have argued that an increase in technological progress is essential if a country wants to achieve faster rates of growth in the long term. But is this purely in the lap of the scientists and engineers? In the Solow growth model that we have been considering up to now, this is the type of assumption made. In other words, technological progress is simply a 'given': it is exogenously determined.

Whilst the neoclassical model identifies the importance of technological progress for enduring growth, it does not offer governments actual policy prescriptions. But cannot governments adopt policies that encourage scientific breakthroughs

BOX 9.3   GETTING INTENSIVE WITH CAPITAL

How quickly does it grow?

Do we really understand what is meant by capital accumulation? Do we really know what a country's capital stock includes?

In this box we take a look at two issues relating to capital. First, we consider what counts as capital in a country's national accounts. Secondly, we compare the growth of the capital stock in the UK and France and then see how this compares with the rates of economic growth in the two countries.

What is capital?

In a country's national accounts, capital consists of non-financial *fixed assets*. It does not include goods and services transformed or used up in the course of production; these are known as *intermediate goods and services*.

By focusing on the purchase of fixed assets, capital in the national accounts may be seen by some as being quite narrowly defined. For instance, some expenditures relating to staff development and to research and development are excluded. On the other hand, capital stock figures value parts of the country's infrastructure, such as its road, rail and telecommunications network. Further, it values the country's social capital, such as its school buildings, libraries and hospital building.

A country's stock of fixed assets can be valued at its replacement cost, regardless of its age: this is its *gross* value. It can also be valued at its written-down value known as its *net* value. The net value takes into account the *consumption of capital* which occurs through wear and tear (depreciation) or when capital becomes naturally obsolescent.

The table shows that the estimated *net* capital stock of the UK in 2008 was £3.01 trillion. To put this into context, this is roughly 2.1 times the value of GDP.

The table shows that there are five broad categories of fixed assets. The largest of these by value is *dwellings*, which includes houses, bungalows and flats. You might question why we include dwellings, but residential housing does yield rental incomes for landlords and,

UK net capital stock, 2008

	£ billions	% of fixed assets	Ratio to GDP
Dwellings	1216.9	40.4	0.84
Other buildings and works	1150.1	38.2	0.80
Plant, machinery and cultivated assets	508.9	16.9	0.35
Vehicles	83.0	2.8	0.06
Intangible assets	51.9	1.7	0.04
All fixed assets	**3010.8**	**100.0**	**2.08**

Source: Based on data from *Capital Stocks Tables for Publication* (National Statistics) and *UK Output, Income and Expenditure* (National Statistics)

more generally, it does provide all of us with important consumption services, most notably shelter.

The second largest component by value is *other buildings and works*. This includes buildings, other than dwellings, and most civil engineering and construction work. It will include structures such as factories, schools and hospitals and the country's railway track.

The third largest component is *plant, machinery and cultivated assets*. It includes electricity and telephone lines as well as tractors and fork lift trucks, while cultivated assets include livestock and forests. The next smaller component by value is *vehicles*. This includes lorries for haulage, buses and railway rolling stock for transportation and all civil aircraft. But, the smallest component of all is *intangible assets*. This includes computer software, original works of literature or art and mineral exploration.

How does capital grow? The UK and France compared

In models of economic growth an important measure of how much capital is being used is the amount of capital per person employed (per worker). This is also known as

Definition

Endogenous growth theory
A theory that the rate of economic growth depends on the rate of technological progress and diffusion, both of which depend on size of the capital stock and the capital goods industries, and also on institutions, incentives and the role of government.

and technological developments? What can be done to speed up the rate of innovation? This void is filled by endogenous growth theory. Endogenous growth models attempt to answer this by explicitly modelling technological advancement – a formal example will be demonstrated below.

But, what is at the heart of endogenous growth models? In short, endogenous growth models stress the importance of research and development, education and training and how nations can foster innovation. As you can imagine, there is considerable interest and debate surrounding endogenous growth models not just amongst academics but policy-makers too. Policy-makers are clearly interested in potential policies that could make their country a world leader in innovation and technological advancement, especially if this helps to sustain higher long-run rates of economic growth, and so higher standards of living.

EXPLORING
ECONOMICS

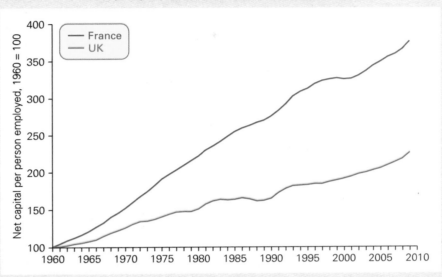

Net capital per person employed in France and the UK

Source: *AMECO database* (Commission of the European Union)

capital intensity. In the chart we plot the amounts of capital per worker in the UK and France since 1960. The series for each country is presented as an index (1960 = 100) so that we can compare across the two countries without worrying about local currencies. In both countries capital intensity has increased. Therefore, there is capital accumulation in both the UK and France.

The rate of capital accumulation in the two countries is, however, very different. If we compare the amount of capital per worker in 2009 with that in 1960, it is 3.75 times higher in France but only 2.25 times higher in the UK.

Generally, the higher the level of capital per worker, the greater will be the level of output (real GDP) per worker. If we compare the amount of output per worker in France

and the UK in 2009 with that in 1960 (see Figure 9.7), we find that its 3.6 times higher in France compared to 2.6 times higher in the UK.

A note of caution is necessary at this point. While there appears to be a statistical association between capital accumulation and economic growth, it is the role of economic theory to explore the relationship between the two. As you will see in this chapter there is considerable debate about this relationship!

1. *How does human capital (the skills and expertise of the workforce) fit into a national account's definition of capital?*
2. *Does the composition of a country's capital affect its long-run economic growth?*

In such models, a major determinant of technological progress is the size and composition of the capital stock. As economies accumulate capital, they are likely to devote more resources to the development and maintenance of capital goods industries. In other words, they are likely to have a larger sector devoted to producing and developing capital goods. This in turn may raise the rate of technological progress and enable further capital accumulation. A virtuous circle is created.

Investment in research and development is encouraged through the use of patents and copyrights. These provide some protection to firms (and individuals), enabling them to capture more of the benefits from their own ideas and thus providing them with an incentive to create and innovate. Furthermore, the striving for

Pause for thought

What is 'endogenous' about endogenous growth theory?

profit or the pursuit of competitive advantage over rivals are incentives that can drive this innovation and creativity.

But there are limits to the ability of firms to exclude other firms from prospering from their own ideas, such as the development of products, process and people. The virtuous circle is thus reinforced by externalities: the spillover of ideas from one firm to another. New ideas cannot be put back into the metaphorical bottle once its lid is off.

Policy implications

If there is a virtuous circle arising from firms investing and innovating, how are governments best placed to encourage it?

Equally important is the question of how to ensure the largest possible impact of such investments. For instance, to be able to take full advantage of technical innovations, workers and management need suitable flexibility and an appropriate array of skills. This may require new working practices and new forms of organisation.

Thus supply-side policy to encourage faster economic growth should focus not just on research and development, but also on investment, education and training, industrial organisation, work practices and the whole range of incentives that may be necessary to make optimum use of new techniques.

TC 15 p 289

A model of endogenous technological progress

We now present a simple, but more formal endogenous growth model. We have seen that endogenous growth theory argues that technological progress is *dependent* on various economic factors such as the rate of investment in research and development. This could be included as an element in the investment (I) term, i.e.

$$I = I_n + I_c$$

where I_n is investment in research and development of new technology (it could also include investment in training) and I_c is investment in capital that uses current technology. The greater the value of I_n/I_c, the faster will the Y curve (and I curve) shift upwards in Figure 9.9. Any policy, then, that increases the proportion of national income being devoted to R&D and training, will increase the long-run rate of economic growth.

The model also illustrates that the rate of economic growth is dependent not only on the resources devoted to new technologies, but on the responsiveness of national income to new technologies. In other words, growth depends not only on I_n/I_c but also the responsiveness of Y to I_n. The greater the value of $\Delta Y/I_n$, the greater will be the rate of economic growth.

The values of I_n and $\Delta Y/I_n$ are thought to depend on structural and institutional factors within the economy and on the role of government. These include

■ attitudes of business, such as their inclination to take risk
■ willingness of financial institutions to lend to support investment opportunities
■ tax incentives and government grants, for instance support for R&D
■ a research infrastructure (laboratories, the number and skills of researchers, etc.),
■ the degree of competition over the development of new products
■ the magnitude of external spillovers from the generation of new products, process and techniques.

Endogenous growth theory implies that the economy's production function (the Y line in Figures 9.9–9.11) will shift up over time. It may also become steeper. The reason is that the output from investment is not just confined to the firms doing the investing, but spills over to other firms which duplicate or build on the original firm's ideas.

Whatever the shape of the economy's production function, the more general point made by endogenous growth theorists is that investment, particularly in the development of new products, processes and techniques, drives technological progress. This technological progress makes further capital accumulation possible and so prevents the economy getting stuck at a 'steady state'.

Pause for thought

List a series of factors that you think could influence the significance of spillovers from investment.

Recap

1. The determinants of economic growth in the long run lie primarily on the supply side. They can be put into two broad categories: an increase in the quantity of factors and an increase in the productivity of factors.

2. An increased saving rate will lead to higher investment and hence to an increase in the capital stock. This, in turn, will lead to a higher level of national income. A larger capital stock, however, will require a higher level of replacement investment. Once this has risen to absorb all the extra investment, national income will stop rising: growth will cease. An increased saving rate will therefore lead only to a rise in output, not to a long-term rise in the rate of growth.

3. A higher long-term rate of growth will normally require a faster rate of technological progress. Endogenous growth theory argues that the rate of technological progress and its rate of diffusion depend on economic institutions and incentives. Supply-side policy could be used to alter these.

QUESTIONS

1. Why does the aggregate demand curve slope downwards? What factors would cause it to move to the left?

2. In what way will the nature of aggregate supply influence the effect of a change in aggregate demand on prices and real national income?

3. What shape do you think the aggregate supply curve would be at the current output if the economy was in a deep recession?

4. Referring to Figure 9.1, assume that the price level is currently above the equilibrium. Explain how the price level would return to its equilibrium level.

5. Why do cyclical swings seem much greater when we plot growth, rather than the level of output, on the vertical axis?

6. At what point of the business cycle is the country now? What do you predict will happen to growth over the next two years? On what basis do you make your prediction?

7. Why does investment in construction and producer goods industries tend to fluctuate more than investment in retailing and the service industries?

8. How can the interaction of the multiplier and accelerator explain cyclical fluctuations in national income? Why is it difficult to predict the size of the multiplier and accelerator?

9. Can governments induce cyclical fluctuations in national income? Can it ever be in the interests of governments to induce such volatility?

10. What are the determinants of long-run economic growth? Is long-run economic growth sustainable without technological progress?

11. What determines the rate of depreciation? What would happen if the rate of depreciation fell?

12. Explain the shapes of the I and Y curves in the Solow model of growth. What happens to these curves if the share of investment in national income rises?

13. What is the significance of the term 'endogenous' in endogenous growth theory? What, according to this theory, determines the long-run rate of economic growth?

14. What policy prescriptions do the neoclassical and endogenous growth theories offer policy-makers looking to raise their country's long-run growth rate?

15. For what possible reasons may one country experience a persistently faster rate of economic growth than another?

Log on to MyEconlab and complete the studyplan exercises for this chapter to see how much you have learnt and where you need to revise most. Make sure you access all the supporting textbook resources including the online workbook, newsblog, audio animations, guided solutions and ebook.

Additional case studies in the *Essentials of Economics* MyEconLab (www.pearsoned.co.uk/sloman)

9.1 **Introducing theories of economic growth.** An overview of classical and more modern theories of growth (a more detailed account of economic growth is given in Section 9.6).

9.2 **The multiplier–accelerator interaction.** A numerical example showing how the interaction of the multiplier and accelerator can cause cycles in economic activity.

9.3 **Has there been an accelerator effect since 1978?** An examination of the evidence for an accelerator effect in the UK.

9.4 **The phases of the business cycle.** A demand-side analysis of the factors contributing to each of the four phases.

9.5 **Productivity performance and the UK economy.** A detailed examination of how the UK's productivity compares with that in other countries.

9.6 **The USA: is it a 'new economy'?** An examination of whether US productivity increases are likely to be sustained.

9.7 **Technology and economic change.** How to get the benefits from technological advance.

9.8 **UK industrial performance.** This examines why the UK has had a poorer investment record than many other industrial countries and why it has suffered a process of 'deindustrialisation'.

9.9 **The R&D scoreboard.** An international comparison of spending by companies on research and development.

9.10 **The new economy.** Does globalisation bring economic success?

Websites relevant to this chapter

Numbers and sections refer to websites listed in the Web appendix and hotlinked from this book's website at **www.pearsoned.co.uk/sloman**.

- For news articles relevant to this chapter, see the *Economics News Articles* link from the book's website.

- For general news on macroeconomic issues, both national and international, see websites in section A, and particularly A1–5. See also links to newspapers worldwide in A38 and 39, and the news search feature in Google at A41. See also A42 and A44 for links to economics news articles from newspapers worldwide.

- For macroeconomic data, including data on economic growth and the business cycle, see links in B1 or 2; also see B4 and 12. For UK data, see B3 B34 and B36. For EU data, see B38 and G1 > *Publications*. For US data, see the *Data* section of B17 and B25. For international data, see B15, 21, 24, 31, 33.

- For information on the development of ideas, see C12, 18; see also links under *Methodology and History of Economic Thought* in C14; and links to economists in I4 and 17. See also sites I7 and 11 > *Economic Systems and Theories* > *History of Economic Thought*.

- For student resources relevant to this chapter, see sites C1–7, 9, 10, 19.

Web appendix

9.1   Deriving a price index for the economy. This explores how the process of chain linking is used to derive price indices for the components of aggregate demand and for the economy as a whole.

CHAPTER MAP

Banking, money and interest rates

In this chapter we are going to look at the important role that the banking system plays in the economy. Changes in the behaviour of financial institutions and in the amount of money can have a powerful effect on all the major macroeconomic indicators, such as inflation, unemployment, economic growth, exchange rates and the balance of payments.

But why do changes in the money supply affect the economy? Well, the supply of money and the demand for money between them determine the *rate of interest*, and this has a crucial impact on aggregate demand and the performance of the economy generally. But, more than this, many aspects of economic activity are dependent on the availability of money.

The very first question addressed in this chapter is to define what is actually meant by money (not as easy as it may seem), and to examine its functions. Then in Sections 10.2 and 10.3 we look at the operation of the financial sector of the economy and its role in determining the supply of money. This sector has come in for considerable scrutiny in recent times, following the banking turmoil associated with the 'credit crunch' of 2007–9.

We then turn to look at the demand for money. Here we are not asking how much money people would like. The answer to that would probably be 'as much as possible'! What we are asking is: how much of people's assets do they want to hold in the form of money?

Then, in Section 10.5, we put supply and demand together to show how interest rates are determined, or how money supply must be manipulated to achieve a chosen rate of interest. We will see how changes in money supply and/or interest rates affect aggregate demand and the level of activity in the economy.

After studying this chapter, you should be able to answer the following questions:

- What are the functions of money?
- What determines the amount of money in the economy? What causes it to grow and what is the role of banks in this process?
- Why do central banks, such as the Bank of England and the European Central Bank, play a crucial role in the functioning of economies?
- What is the relationship between money and interest rates? What is the role of various financial institutions in this relationship?
- How will a change in the money supply affect the level of aggregate demand? How will this, in turn, affect the level of real GDP?

10.1 THE MEANING AND FUNCTIONS OF MONEY

What is this thing called 'money'?

Before going any further we must define precisely what we mean by 'money' – not as easy a task as it sounds. Money is more than just notes and coin. In fact the main component of a country's money supply is not cash, but deposits in banks and other financial institutions. Only a very small proportion of these deposits are kept by the banks in their safes or tills in the form of cash. The bulk of the deposits appear merely as bookkeeping entries in the banks' accounts.

KI 29
p 239

This may sound very worrying. Will a bank have enough cash to meet its customers' demands? The answer in the vast majority of cases is yes. Only a small fraction of a bank's total deposits will be withdrawn at any one time, and banks always seek to ensure that they have the ability to meet their customers' demands. The chances of banks running out of cash are very low indeed. The only circumstance where this could become possible is if people lost confidence in a bank and started to withdraw money in what is known as a 'run on the bank'. This happened with the Northern Rock Bank in 2008. But in these circumstances the central bank or government would intervene to protect people's deposits by making more cash available to the bank or, in the last resort, by nationalising the bank (as happened with Northern Rock).

KI 13
p 74

What is more, the bulk of all but very small transactions are not conducted in cash at all. By the use of cheques, credit cards and debit cards, most money is simply transferred from the purchaser's to the seller's bank account without the need for first withdrawing it in cash.

What items should be included in the definition of money? To answer this we need to identify the *functions* of money.

The functions of money

The main purpose of money is for buying and selling goods, services and assets: i.e. as a medium of exchange. It also has two other important functions. Let us examine each in turn.

A medium of exchange

In a subsistence economy where individuals make their own clothes, grow their own food, provide their own entertainments, etc., people do not need money. If people want to exchange any goods, they will do so by barter. In other words, they will do swaps with other people.

The complexities of a modern developed economy, however, make barter totally impractical for most purposes (see Case Study 10.1 in MyEconLab). What is necessary is a medium of exchange that is generally acceptable as a means of payment for goods and services and as a means of payment for labour and other factor services. 'Money' is any such medium.

To be a suitable physical means of exchange, money must be light enough to carry around, must come in a number of denominations, large and small, and must not be easy to forge. Alternatively, money must be in a form that enables it to be transferred indirectly through some acceptable mechanism. For example, money in the form of bookkeeping entries in bank accounts can be transferred from one account to another by the use of mechanisms such as debit cards and direct debits.

Definition

Medium of exchange
Something that is acceptable in exchange for goods and services.

A means of evaluation

Money allows the value of goods, services and assets to be compared. The value of goods is expressed in terms of prices, and prices are expressed in money terms. Money also allows dissimilar things, such as a person's wealth or a company's assets, to be added up. Similarly, a country's GDP is expressed in money terms. Money thus serves as a 'unit of account'.

A means of storing wealth

People need a means whereby the fruits of *today's* labour can be used to purchase goods and services in the *future*. People need to be able to store their wealth: they want a means of saving. Money is one such medium in which to hold wealth. It can be saved.

What should count as money?

What items, then, should be included in the definition of money? Unfortunately, there is no sharp borderline between money and non-money.

Cash (notes and coin) obviously counts as money. It readily meets all the functions of money. Goods (fridges, cars and cabbages) do not count as money. But what about various financial assets such as savings accounts and stocks and shares? Do they count as money? The answer is: it depends on how narrowly money is defined.

Countries thus use several different measures of money supply. All include cash, but they vary according to what additional items are included. To understand their significance and the ways in which money supply can be controlled, it is first necessary to look at the various types of account in which money can be held and at the various financial institutions involved.

> **Pause for thought**
>
> *Why are debit cards not counted as money?*

> **Recap**
>
> 1. Money's main function is as a medium of exchange. In addition, it is a means of evaluation and a means of storing wealth.
>
> 2. What counts as money depends on how narrowly it is defined. All definitions include cash, but they vary according to what other financial assets are included.

THE FINANCIAL SYSTEM   10.2

Where do banks and other financial institutions fit in?

In order to understand the role of the financial sector in determining the supply of money, it is important to distinguish different types of financial institution. Each type has a distinct part to play in determining the size of the money supply.

The key role of banks in the monetary system

By far the largest element of money supply is bank deposits. It is not surprising, then, that banks play an absolutely crucial role in the monetary system.

BOX 10.1   FINANCIAL INTERMEDIATION

What is it that banks do?

Banks and other financial institutions are known as *financial intermediaries*. They all have the common function of providing a link between those who wish to lend and those who wish to borrow. In other words, they act as the mechanism whereby the supply of funds is matched to the demand for funds. In this process, they provide five important services.

Expert advice

Financial intermediaries can advise their customers on financial matters: on the best way of investing their funds and on alternative ways of obtaining finance. This should help to encourage the flow of savings and the efficient use of them.

Expertise in channelling funds

Financial intermediaries have the specialist knowledge to be able to channel funds to those areas that yield the highest return. They also have the expertise to assess risks and to refuse loans for projects considered too risky or to charge a risk premium to others. This all encourages the flow of saving as it gives savers the confidence that their savings will earn a good rate of interest. Financial intermediaries also help to ensure that projects that are potentially profitable will be able to obtain finance. They help to increase allocative efficiency.

Maturity transformation

Many people and firms want to borrow money for long periods of time, and yet many depositors want to be able to withdraw their deposits on demand or at short notice. If people had to rely on borrowing directly from other people, there would be a problem here: the lenders would not be prepared to lend for a long enough period. If you had £100 000 of savings, would you be prepared to lend it to a friend to buy a house if the friend was going to take 25 years to pay it back? Even if there was no risk whatsoever of your friend defaulting, most people would be totally unwilling to tie up their savings for so long.

This is where a bank or building society comes in. It borrows money from a vast number of small savers, who are able to withdraw their money on demand or at short notice. It then lends the money to house purchasers for a long period of time by granting mortgages (typically these are paid back over 20 to 30 years). This process whereby financial intermediaries lend for longer periods of time than they borrow is known as *maturity transformation*. They are able to do this because with a large number of depositors it is highly unlikely that they would all want to withdraw their deposits at the same time. On any one day, although some people will be withdrawing money, others will be making new deposits.

Risk transformation

You may be unwilling to lend money directly to another person in case they do not pay up. You are unwilling to take the risk. Financial intermediaries, however, by lending to large numbers of people, are willing to risk the odd case of default. They can absorb the loss because of the interest they earn on all the other loans. This spreading of risks is known as *risk transformation*. What is more, financial intermediaries may have the expertise to be able to assess just how risky a loan is.

Transmitting payments

In addition to channelling funds from depositors to borrowers, certain financial institutions have another important function. This is to provide a means of transmitting payments. Thus by the use of debit cards, credit cards, Internet and telephone banking, cheques, direct debits, etc., money can be transferred from one person or institution to another without having to rely on cash.

 Which of the above are examples of economies of scale?

Definition

Retail banking
Branch, telephone, postal and Internet banking for individuals and businesses at published rates of interest and charges. Retail banking involves the operation of extensive branch networks.

Banking can be divided into two main types: *retail banking* and *wholesale banking*. Most banks today conduct both types of business and are thus known as 'universal banks'.

Retail banking is the business conducted by the familiar high-street banks, such as Barclays, Lloyds, HSBC, Royal Bank of Scotland and NatWest (part of the RBS group). They operate bank accounts for individuals and businesses, attracting deposits and granting loans at published rates of interest.

The other major type of banking is **wholesale banking**. This involves receiving large deposits from and making large loans to companies or other banks and financial institutions; these are known as *wholesale deposits and loans*. As far as companies are concerned, these may be for short periods of time to account for the non-matching of a firm's payments and receipts from its business. They may be for longer periods of time, for various investment purposes. Because wholesale deposits and loans often involve very large sums of money, banks compete against each other for them and negotiate individual terms with the firm to suit the firm's particular requirements.

In the past, there were many independent wholesale banks, known as *investment banks*. These included famous names such as Morgan Stanley, Rothschild, S G Hambros and Goldman Sachs. With the worldwide financial crisis of 2008, however, most of the independent investment banks merged with universal banks. Today, most wholesale banking is conducted in a division of the major universal banks.

Banks are in the business of deposit taking and lending. To understand this, we must distinguish between banks' liabilities and assets. The total liabilities and assets for the UK banks are set out in a balance sheet in Table 10.1.

Liabilities

Customers' deposits in banks (and other deposit-taking institutions such as building societies) are **liabilities** to these institutions. This means simply that the customers have the claim on these deposits and thus the institutions are liable to meet the claims.

There are four major types of deposit: sight deposits, time deposits, certificates of deposit and 'repos'.

Sight deposits. **Sight deposits** are any deposits that can be withdrawn on demand by the depositor without penalty. In the past, sight accounts did not pay interest. Today, however, there are many sight accounts that do. In fact, there is quite aggressive competition nowadays between banks to offer apparently very attractive interest rates on such accounts, although these are often on balances up to a relatively small amount.

Table 10.1 Balance sheet of UK banks (end of March 2009)

Sterling liabilities	£bn	%	Sterling assets	£bn	%
Sight deposits		(27.2)	Notes and coin	5.9	(0.2)
UK banks, etc.	110.5		Balances with Bank of England		(1.9)
UK public sector	12.0		Reserve balances	57.9	
UK private sector	769.7		Cash ratio deposits	2.1	
Non-residents	126.6		Market loans		(15.2)
Time deposits		(36.7)	UK banks, etc.	195.5	
UK banks, etc.	90.5		CDs, etc.	43.1	
UK public sector	26.5		Non-residents	248.6	
UK private sector	697.9		Bills of exchange	39.2	(1.2)
Non-residents	388.4		Reverse repos	271.4	(8.5)
Certificates of deposit (CDs)	260.8	(8.0)	Investments	434.2	(13.5)
Repos	336.9	(10.3)	Advances	1794.1	(55.9)
Sterling capital & other funds	354.2	(10.8)	Miscellaneous	114.5	(3.6)
Other	102.5	(3.1)			
Total sterling liabilities	**3276.7**	(100.0)	**Total sterling assets**	**3206.8**	(100.0)
Liabilities in other currencies	4573.8		Assets in other currencies	4643.6	
Total liabilities	7850.4		Total assets	7850.4	

Source: Based on data in Table B1.2 of *Bankstats* (Bank of England)

The most familiar form of sight deposits are current accounts at banks. Depositors are issued with cheque books and/or debit cards (e.g. Visa/Delta or Switch/Maestro) that enable them to spend the money directly without first having to go to the bank and draw the money out in cash. In the case of debit cards, the person's account is electronically debited when the purchase is made and the card is 'swiped' across the machine and the pin entered. This process is known as EFTPOS (electronic funds transfer at point of sale).

An important feature of current accounts is that banks often allow customers to be overdrawn. That is, they can draw on their account and make payments to other people in excess of the amount of money they have deposited.

Time deposits. **Time deposits** require notice of withdrawal. However, they normally pay a higher rate of interest than sight accounts. With some types of account, a depositor can withdraw a certain amount of money on demand, but there will be a penalty of so many days' lost interest. They are not cheque-book or debit-card

---

Definition

Time deposits
Deposits that require notice of withdrawal or where a penalty is charged for withdrawals on demand.

BOX 10.2	BANKS' BALANCE SHEETS

Whose deposits are they?

At the start of 2009 UK resident banks (excluding the Bank of England) had total liabilities of £7.9 trillion. Of this, 40 per cent was made up of sterling liabilities and 60 per cent of other currency liabilities. Chart (a) shows both the growth in the total liabilities of UK resident banks and its composition between being denominated in sterling and other currencies. The share of liabilities denominated in sterling fell across much of the 2000s, from a 50 per cent share at the turn of the millennium, though the decline was especially marked in the second half of the decade.

We can see from Table 10.1 that time and sight deposits make up the bulk of banks' liabilities. But who makes these deposits? Perhaps your gut response is that it must be firms and individuals. Well, consider the case of UK sterling deposits. We can apportion these deposits to resident banks in the UK, to the public sector, to the non-bank private sector (firms and households) and to non-residents. Chart (b) shows the share of sterling deposits held by each of these sectors.

Private-sector deposits do indeed constitute the largest element of deposits in UK banks: about two-thirds of the total for much of the 2000s. The public sector's share, by contrast, has been much smaller, typically a little over 1 per cent of all deposits. However, this share, though still

(a) UK banks' liabilities (£ billions)

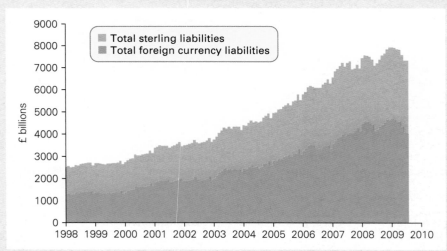

Source: *Monetary and Financial Statistics* (Bank of England)

accounts, although some allow customers to use cash cards. The most familiar form of time deposits are the deposit and savings accounts in banks and the various savings accounts in building societies. No overdraft facilities exist with time deposits.

A substantial proportion of time deposits are from the *banking sector*: i.e. other banks and other financial institutions. Inter-bank lending has grown over the years as money markets have become deregulated and as deposits are moved from one currency to another to take advantage of differences in rates of interest between different countries. A large proportion of overseas deposits are from foreign banks. Box 10.2 looks at the banking sector's balance sheets and the significance of deposits from the banking sector.

As we shall see below, however, inter-bank lending virtually dried up in 2008. Banks became increasingly fearful that if they lent money to other banks, the other banks might default on payment. The reason was that many banks held assets based on mortgages granted to people unable to pay. As these assets fell in value, so banks became less and less able to raise enough money to pay back inter-bank loans.

EXPLORING
ECONOMICS

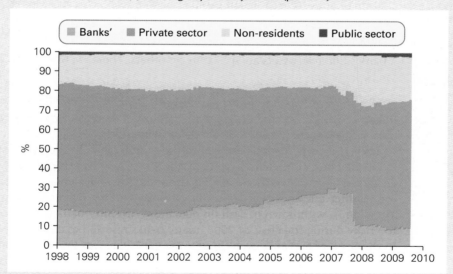

(b) Sterling deposits by sector (per cent)

Source: *Monetary and Financial Statistics* (Bank of England)

relatively small, started to rise sharply from the middle of 2008 as the government took steps to stabilise the financial system (see Box 10.4).

An interesting insight from Chart (b) is the significance of banks placing deposits with other banks. However, one result of the financial crisis in the late 2000s was that activity in the inter-bank market was severely restricted. At the end of 2006, almost 30 per cent of sterling deposits were from the UK banking sector! However, this share of

deposits shrank markedly afterwards, so that by 2009 less than 10 per cent of sterling deposits were from the UK banking sector.

Why do you think banks became reluctant to deposit money with other banks during the financial crisis of the late 2000s?

Certificates of deposit. **Certificates of deposit (CDs)** are certificates issued by banks to customers (usually firms) for large deposits of a fixed term (e.g. £100 000 for 18 months). They can be sold by one customer to another, and thus provide a means whereby the holders can get money quickly if they need it without the *banks* that have issued the CD having to supply the money. (This makes them relatively 'liquid' to the depositor but 'illiquid' to the bank: we examine this below.) The use of CDs has grown rapidly in recent years. Their use by firms has meant that, at a wholesale level, sight accounts have become *less* popular.

Sale and repurchase agreements (repos). If banks have a temporary shortage of funds, they can sell some of their financial assets to other banks or to the central bank – the Bank of England in the UK and the European Central Bank in the eurozone (see below) – and later repurchase them on some agreed date, typically a fortnight later. These **sale and repurchase agreements (repos)** are in effect a form of loan – the bank borrowing for a period of time using some of its financial assets as the security for the loan. One of the major assets to use in this way are government bonds, normally called 'gilt-edged securities' or simply 'gilts' (see below). Sale and repurchase agreements involving gilts are known as *gilt repos*.

Capital and other funds

This consists largely of the share capital in banks. Since shareholders cannot take their money out of banks, it provides a source of funding to meet sudden increases in withdrawals from depositors and to cover bad debts. As we shall see below, it is vital that banks have sufficient capital.

Assets

A bank's financial **assets** are its claims on others. There are three main categories of assets.

Cash and reserve balances in the central bank (Bank of England in the UK, ECB in the eurozone). Banks need to hold a certain amount of their assets as cash. This is largely used to meet the day-to-day demands of customers.

They also keep 'reserve balances' in the central bank. In the UK these earn interest at the Bank of England's repo rate (or 'Bank Rate' as it is called), if kept within an agreed target range. These are like the banks' own current accounts and are used for clearing purposes (i.e. for settling the day-to-day payments between banks). They can be withdrawn in cash on demand. With inter-bank lending being seen as too risky during the crisis of 2008, many banks resorted to depositing surplus cash in the Bank of England, even though the Bank Rate was lower than the inter-bank rate (known as 'LIBOR', which stands for 'London Inter-Bank Offered Rate').

In the UK, banks and building societies are also required to deposit a small fraction of their assets as 'cash ratio deposits' with the Bank of England. These cannot be drawn on demand and earn no interest.

As you can see from Table 10.1, cash and balances in the Bank of England account for a very small proportion of banks' assets. The vast majority of banks' assets are in the form of various types of loan – to individuals and firms, to other financial institutions and to the government. These are 'assets' because they represent claims that the banks have on other people. Loans can be grouped into two types: short- and long-term.

Short-term loans. These are in the form of *market loans, bills of exchange* or *reverse repos*. The market for these various types of loan is known as the **money market**.

Definitions

Certificates of deposit (CDs)
Certificates issued by banks for fixed-term interest-bearing deposits. They can be resold by the owner to another party.

Sale and repurchase agreements (repos)
An agreement between two financial institutions whereby one in effect borrows from another by selling its assets, agreeing to buy them back (repurchase them) at a fixed price and on a fixed date.

Assets
Possessions, or claims held on others.

Money market
The market for short-term loans and deposits.

■ **Market loans** are made primarily to other banks or financial institutions. This inter-bank lending consists of (a) money lent 'at call' (i.e. reclaimable on demand or at 24 hours' notice); (b) money lent for periods up to one year, but typically a few weeks; (c) CDs (i.e. certificates of deposits made in other banks or building societies). The rate at which banks lend to each other is known as the **LIBOR** (London inter-bank offered rate). The LIBOR has a major influence on the other rates that banks charge. As inter-bank lending can be anything from overnight to 12 months, the LIBOR will vary from length of loan to another.

■ **Bills of exchange** are loans either to companies (**commercial bills**) or to the government (**Treasury bills**). These are, in effect, an IOU, with the company issuing them (in the case of commercial bills), or the Bank of England on behalf of the government (in the case of Treasury bills), promising to pay the holder a specified sum on a particular date (the 'maturity date'), typically three months later. Since bills do not pay interest, they are sold below their face value (at a 'discount') but redeemed on maturity at the face value. This enables the purchaser, in this case the bank, to earn a return.

The price paid for bills will depend on demand and supply. For example, the more Treasury bills that the Bank of England offers for sale at its weekly tender of bills (i.e. the higher the supply), the lower will be their equilibrium price, and hence the higher will be their rate of return (i.e. their rate of interest, or 'rate of discount').

■ **Reverse repos**. When a sale and repurchase agreement is made, the financial institution *purchasing* the assets (e.g. gilts) is, in effect, giving a short-term loan. The other party agrees to buy back the assets (i.e. pay back the loan) on a set date. The assets temporarily held by the bank making the loan are known as 'reverse repos'. Reverse repos are typically for one week, but can be for as little as overnight or as long as one year.

Longer-term loans. These consist primarily of loans to customers, both personal customers and businesses. These loans, also known as *advances*, are of four main types: fixed-term (repayable in instalments over a set number of years – typically, six months to five years), overdrafts (often for an unspecified term), outstanding balances on credit-card accounts and mortgages (typically for 25 years).

Banks also make *investments*. These are partly in government bonds (gilts), which are effectively loans to the government. The government sells bonds, which then pay a fixed sum each year as interest. Once issued, they can then be bought and sold on the stock exchange. Banks are normally only prepared to buy bonds that have less than five years to maturity (the date when the government redeems the bonds). Banks also invest in various subsidiary financial institutions and in building societies.

Liquidity and profitability

As we have seen, banks keep a range of liabilities and assets. The balance of items in this range is influenced by three important considerations: profitability, liquidity and capital adequacy.

Profitability. Profits are made by lending money out at a higher rate of interest than that paid to depositors. The average interest rate received by banks on their assets is greater than that paid by them on their liabilities.

Liquidity. The **liquidity** of an asset is the ease with which it can be converted into cash without loss. Cash itself, by definition, is perfectly liquid.

Definitions

Market loans
Short-term loans (e.g. money at call and short notice).

LIBOR
The London inter-bank offered rate – the rate at which banks lend to each other. The LIBOR varies with the length of loan.

Bills of exchange
Certificates promising to repay a stated amount on a certain date, typically three months from the issue of the bill. Bills pay no interest as such, but are sold at a discount and redeemed at face value, thereby earning a rate of discount for the purchaser.

Commercial bills
Bills of exchange issued by firms.

Treasury bills
Bills of exchange issued by the Bank of England on behalf of the government. They are a means whereby the government raises short-term finance.

Reverse repos
Gilts or other assets that are purchased under a sale and repurchase agreement. They become an asset to the purchaser.

Liquidity
The ease with which an asset can be converted into cash without loss.

Some assets, such as money lent at call to other financial institutions, are highly liquid. Although not actually cash, these assets can be converted into cash virtually on demand with no financial penalty. Other short-term inter-bank lending is also very liquid. The only issue here is one of confidence that the money will actually be repaid. This was a worry in the financial crisis of autumn 2008, when many banks stopped lending to each other on the inter-bank market for fear that the borrowing bank might become insolvent.

Other assets, such as gilts, can be converted into cash straight away by selling them on the stock exchange, but with the possibility of some financial loss, given that their market price fluctuates. Such assets, therefore, are not as liquid as money at call.

Other assets are much less liquid. Personal loans to the general public or mortgages for house purchase can be redeemed by the bank only as each instalment is paid. Other advances for fixed periods are repaid only at the end of that period.

Banks must always be able to meet the demands of their customers for withdrawals of money. To do this, they must hold sufficient cash or other assets that can be readily turned into cash. In other words, banks must maintain sufficient liquidity.

Capital adequacy. Banks must have sufficient capital (i.e. funds) to allow them to meet all demands from depositors and to cover losses if borrowers default on payment. Capital adequacy is a measure of a bank's capital relative to its assets, where the assets are weighted according to the degree of risk. The more risky the assets, the greater the amount of capital that will be required.

A measure of capital adequacy is given by the **capital adequacy ratio (CAR)**. This is given by the following formula:

$$CAR = \frac{\text{Tier One capital} + \text{Tier Two capital}}{\text{Risk-weighted assets}}$$

Tier One capital includes bank reserves (from retained profits) and ordinary share capital, where dividends to shareholders vary with the amount of profit the bank makes. Such capital thus places no burden on banks in times of losses as no dividend need be paid. What is more, unlike depositors, shareholders cannot ask for their money back. Tier Two capital consists largely of preference shares. These pay a fixed rate of interest and thus do continue to place a burden on the bank even when losses are made (unless the bank goes out of business).

Risk-weighted assets are the value of assets, where each type of asset is multiplied by a risk factor. Under the internationally agreed Basel II Accord, cash and government bonds have a risk factor of zero and are thus not included. Inter-bank lending between the major banks has a risk factor of 0.2 and is thus included at only 20 per cent of its value; residential mortgages have a risk factor of 0.35; personal loans, credit-card debt and overdrafts have a risk factor of 1; loans to companies carry a risk factor of 0.2, 0.5, 1 or 1.5, depending on the credit rating of the company. Thus the greater the average risk factor of a bank's assets, the greater will be the value of its risk-weighted assets, and the lower will be its CAR.

The greater the CAR, the greater the capital adequacy of a bank. Under Basel II, banks are required to have a CAR of at least 8 per cent (i.e. 0.08). They are also required to hold a ratio of Tier One capital to risk-weighted assets of at least 4 per cent.

In times of lack of confidence of investors and/or of recession, more borrowers are likely to default on payment and thus a higher CAR may be necessary if the bank is to avoid becoming insolvent. Also, in such times, borrowing companies or other banks may have their credit rating downgraded, giving them a higher risk factor, thereby reducing the bank's CAR. This was the problem in 2008. Many

Definition

Capital adequacy ratio (CAR)

The ratio of a bank's capital (reserves and shares) to its risk-weighted assets. Under the Basel II Accord, a bank's CAR should be a minimum of 8 per cent.

banks needed an injection of capital (i.e. the sale of more shares) from either the private sector or the government, in order to maintain a high enough CAR to satisfy investors.

The balance between profitability and liquidity

Profitability is the major aim of banks and most other financial institutions. However, the aims of profitability and liquidity tend to conflict. In general, the more liquid an asset, the less profitable it is, and vice versa. Personal and business loans to customers are profitable to banks, but highly illiquid. Cash is totally liquid, but earns no profit. Thus financial institutions like to hold a range of assets with varying degrees of liquidity and profitability.

For reasons of *profitability*, the banks will want to 'borrow short' (at low rates of interest, such as on current accounts) and 'lend long' (at higher rates of interest, such as on personal loans). The difference in the average maturity of loans and deposits is known as the maturity gap. In general terms, the larger the maturity gap between loans and deposits, the greater the profitability. For reasons of *liquidity*, however, banks will want a relatively small gap: if there is a sudden withdrawal of deposits, banks will need to be able to call in enough loans.

The ratio of an institution's liquid assets to total assets is known as its liquidity ratio. For example, if a bank had £100 million of assets, of which £10 million were liquid and £90 million were illiquid, the bank would have a 10 per cent liquidity ratio. If a financial institution's liquidity ratio is too high, it will make too little profit. If the ratio is too low, there will be the risk that customers' demands may not be able to be met: this would cause a crisis of confidence and possible closure. Institutions thus have to make a judgement as to what liquidity ratio is best – one that is neither too high nor too low.

Balances in the central bank, short-term loans (i.e. those listed above) and government bonds with less than 12 months to maturity would normally be regarded as liquid assets.

Over the years, banks had reduced their liquidity ratios (i.e. the ratio of liquid assets to total assets). This was not a problem as long as banks could always finance lending to customers by borrowing on the inter-bank market. In 2008, however, banks became increasingly worried about bad debt. They thus felt the need to increase their liquidity ratios and hence cut back on lending and chose to keep a higher proportion of deposits in liquid form. In the UK, for example, banks substantially increased their level of reserves in the Bank of England.

> **Definitions**
>
> **Maturity gap**
> The difference in the average maturity of loans and deposits.
>
> **Liquidity ratio**
> The proportion of a bank's total assets held in liquid form.
>
> **Secondary marketing**
> Where assets are sold before maturity to another institution or individual.

> **Pause for thought**
>
> *Why are government bonds that still have 11 months to run regarded as liquid, whereas overdrafts granted for a few weeks are not?*

Secondary marketing and securitisation

As we have seen, one way of reconciling the two conflicting aims of liquidity and profitability is for financial institutions to hold a mixture of liquid and illiquid assets. Another way is through the secondary marketing of assets. This is where holders of assets sell them to someone else before the maturity date. This allows banks to close the maturity gap for *liquidity* purposes, but maintain the gap for *profitability* purposes.

Certificates of deposit (CDs) are a good example of secondary marketing. CDs are issued for fixed-period deposits in a bank (e.g. one year) at an agreed interest rate. The bank does not have to repay the deposit until the year is up. CDs are thus illiquid liabilities for the bank, and they allow it to increase the proportion of illiquid

Definitions

Securitisation

Where future cash flows (e.g. from interest rate or mortgage payments) are turned into marketable securities, such as bonds.

Special-purpose vehicle (SPV)

Legal entities created by financial institutions for conducting specific financial functions, such as bundling assets together into fixed-interest bonds and selling them.

Collateralised debt obligations (CDOs)

These are a type of security consisting of a bundle of fixed-income assets, such as corporate bonds, mortgage debt and credit-card debt.

Sub-prime debt

Debt where there is a high risk of default by the borrower (e.g. mortgage holders who are on low incomes facing higher interest rates and falling house prices).

assets without having a dangerously high maturity gap. But the holder of the CD in the meantime can sell it to someone else (through a broker). It is thus liquid to the holder. Because CDs are liquid to the holder, they can be issued at a relatively *low* rate of interest and thus allow the bank to increase its profitability.

Another example of secondary marketing is when a financial institution sells some of its assets to another financial institution. The advantage to the first institution is that it gains liquidity. The advantage to the second one is that it gains profitable assets. The most common method for the sale of assets has been through a process known as **securitisation**.

Securitisation occurs when a financial institution pools some of its assets, such as residential mortgages, and sells them to an intermediary known as a **special-purpose vehicle (SPV)**. SPVs are legal entities created by the financial institution. In turn, the SPV funds its purchase of the assets by issuing bonds to investors (note-holders). These bonds are known as **collateralised debt obligations (CDOs)**. The sellers (e.g. banks) get cash now rather than having to wait and can use it to fund loans to customers. The buyers make a profit if the income yielded by the CDOs are as expected. Such bonds can be very risky, however, as the future cash flows may be *less* than anticipated.

The securitisation chain is illustrated in Figure 10.1. The financial institution looking to sell its assets is referred to as the 'originator' or the 'originator-lender'. Working from left to right, we see the originator-lender sells its assets to another financial institution, the SPV, which then bundles assets together into CDOs and sells them to investors (e.g. banks or pension funds) as bonds. Now working from right to left, we see that by purchasing the bonds issued by the SPV, the investors provide the funds for the SPV's purchase of the lender's assets. The SPV is then able to use the proceeds from the bond sales (CDO proceeds) to provide the originator-lender with liquidity.

The effect of secondary marketing is to reduce the liquidity ratio that banks feel they need to keep. It has the effect of increasing their maturity gap.

Dangers of secondary marketing. There are dangers to the banking system, however, from secondary marketing. To the extent that banks individually feel that they can operate with a lower liquidity ratio, so this will lead to a lower national liquidity ratio. This may lead to an excessive expansion of credit (illiquid assets) in times of economic boom.

Also, there is an increased danger of banking collapse. If one bank fails, this will have a knock-on effect on those banks which have purchased its assets. In the specific case of securitisation, the strength of the chain is potentially weakened if individual financial institutions move into riskier market segments, such as **sub-prime** residential mortgage markets. Should the income streams of the originator's

Figure 10.1   Securitisation chain

assets dry up – for instance, if individuals default on their loans – then the impact is felt by the whole of the chain. In other words, institutions and investors are exposed to the risks of the originator's lending strategy.

The issue of securitisation and its impact on the liquidity of the financial system from 2006 is considered in Box 10.3.

The central bank

The Bank of England is the UK's central bank. The European Central Bank (ECB) is the central bank for the countries using the euro. The Federal Reserve Bank of America (the Fed) is the USA's central bank. All countries with their own currency have a central bank and these fulfil two vital roles in the economy.

The first is to oversee the whole monetary system and ensure that banks and other financial institutions operate as stably and as efficiently as possible.

The second is to act as the government's agent, both as its banker and in carrying out monetary policy. The Bank of England traditionally worked in very close liaison with the Treasury, and there used to be regular meetings between the Governor of the Bank of England and the Chancellor of the Exchequer. Although the Bank may have disagreed with Treasury policy, it always carried it out. With the election of the Labour government in 1997, however, the Bank of England was given independence to decide the course of monetary policy. In particular, this meant that the Bank of England and not the government would now decide interest rates.

Another example of an independent central bank is the European Central Bank, which operates the monetary policy for the eurozone countries. Similarly, the Fed is independent of both the President and Congress, and its chairman is generally regarded as having great power in determining the country's economic policy. Although the degree of independence of central banks from government varies considerably around the world, there has been a general move in recent years to make central banks more independent.

If the UK were to adopt the euro, there would be a much reduced role for the Bank of England. At present, however, within its two broad roles, it has a number of different functions. Although we will consider the case of the Bank of England, the same principles apply to other central banks.

It issues notes

The Bank of England is the sole issuer of banknotes in England and Wales (in Scotland and Northern Ireland, retail banks issue banknotes). The amount of banknotes issued by the Bank of England depends largely on the demand for notes from the general public. If people draw more cash from their bank accounts, the banks will have to draw more cash from their balances in the Bank of England.

It acts as a bank

To the government. It keeps the two major government accounts: the 'Exchequer' and the 'National Loans Fund'. Taxation and government spending pass through the Exchequer. Government borrowing and lending pass through the National Loans Fund. The government tends to keep its deposits in the Bank of England to a minimum. If the deposits begin to build up (from taxation), the government will probably spend them on paying back government debt. If, on the other hand, it runs short of money, it will simply borrow more.

BOX 10.3	RESIDENTIAL MORTGAGES AND SECURITISATION

Was this the cause of the credit crunch?

The conflict between profitability and liquidity may have sown the seeds for the credit crunch that affected economies across the globe in the second half of the 2000s.

To understand this, consider the size of the 'advances' item in the banking sector's balance sheet – 56 per cent of the value of sterling assets (see Table 10.1). The vast majority of these are to households. Advances secured against property have, in recent times, accounted for around 80 per cent by value of all household advances. *Residential mortgages* involve institutions lending long.

The number of residential mortgages rose as both the size of the housing stock and the proportion of households who are owner-occupiers grew. Figures from the Department of Communities and Local Government show that the owner-occupation rate rose from 50 per cent in 1971 to 70 per cent in 2006.

But, what further fuelled the growth in the *value* of residential mortgages was the long-term increase in house prices from 1996 to 2008. While UK house prices are volatile, the trend has been for them to grow more quickly than consumer prices and so for the real price of housing to rise.

Securitisation of mortgages

One way in which individual institutions can achieve the necessary liquidity to expand the size of their mortgage lending (illiquid assets) is through *securitisation*. Securitisation grew especially rapidly in the UK and the USA. In the UK this was particularly true amongst banks; building societies have historically made greater use of retail deposits to fund advances.

Figures from the Bank of England show that the value of the securitisation of secured lending to individuals (e.g. mortgage debt) plus loan transfers (a disposal of assets without the issue of bonds by an SPV) increased from just over £0.3 billion in 1998 to £102.5 billion in 2008 (see chart).

Securitisation is akin to financial re-engineering. It provides banks (originator-lenders) with liquidity and enables them to engage in further lending opportunities. The attraction of these fixed-income products for the investors (noteholders) is the potential for higher returns than on similarly rated products. However, the noteholders have no recourse should people with mortgages fall into arrears or, worse still, default on their mortgages.

Risks and the sub-prime market

The securitisation of assets is not without risks for all those in the securitisation chain and consequently for the financial system as a whole.

The pooling of advances in itself *reduces* the cash-flow risk facing investors. However, there is a moral hazard problem here. The pooling of the risks may encourage originator-lenders to lower their credit criteria by offering higher income multiples (advances relative to annual household incomes) or higher loan-to-value ratios (advances relative to the price of housing).

Towards the end of 2006 the USA witnessed an increase in the number of defaults by households on residential mortgages. This was a particular problem in the sub-prime market – higher-risk households with poor credit ratings. Similarly, the number falling behind with their payments rose. This was on the back of rising interest rates.

To banks. Banks' deposits in the Bank of England consist of reserve balances and cash ratio deposits (see Table 10.1). As we have seen, the reserve balances are used for clearing purposes between the banks and to provide them with a source of liquidity. Banks undertake to hold a target level of reserves over any given month. If the average balance over the month is within ±1 per cent of a bank's chosen target, the bank is paid at Bank Rate. In times of uncertainty, banks may choose to hold greater reserve balances.

In addition, under its Operational Standing Facilities system, the Bank of England is prepared to lend to banks, on demand, through reverse repos[1] at 0.25 percentage point above Bank Rate or to receive extra deposits at 0.25 percentage point below Bank Rate.

---

[1] Note that a repo to a bank (the borrower) is a reverse repo to the Bank of England (the lender).

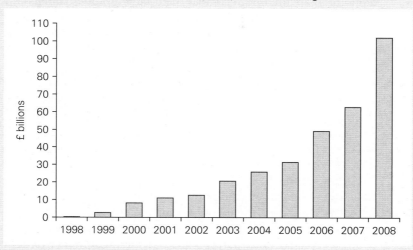

UK banks' securitisation/loan transfers of secured lending to individuals

Source: *Monetary and Financial Statistics*, Table A5.7 (Bank of England)

These problems in the US sub-prime market were the catalyst for the liquidity problem that beset financial systems in 2007 and 2008. Where these assets were securitised, investors, largely other financial institutions, suffered from the contagion arising from arrears and defaults.

Securitisation also internationalised the contagion. Investors are global so that advances, such as a US family's residential mortgage, can cross national borders.

This resulted in institutions writing-off debts, a deterioration of their balance sheets, the collapse in the demand for securitised assets and the drying-up of liquidity.

 Does securitisation necessarily involve a moral hazard problem?

To overseas central banks. The Bank of England holds deposits of sterling (and similarly the ECB holds deposits of euros) made by the authorities of other countries as part of their official reserves and/or for purposes of intervening in the foreign exchange market in order to influence the exchange rate of their currency. We will examine exchange rates in Chapter 14.

It manages the government's borrowing programme

Whenever the government runs a budget deficit (i.e. spends more than it receives in tax and other revenues), it will have to finance that deficit by borrowing. It can borrow by issuing bonds (gilts), National Savings certificates or Treasury bills. The Bank of England organises this borrowing.

Even when the government runs a budget surplus, the Bank of England will still have to manage the national debt (the accumulated borrowing from the past). The reason is that old bonds will be maturing and new issues of bonds will probably be necessary to replace them.

It provides liquidity, as necessary, to banks

It attempts to ensure that there is always an adequate supply of liquidity to meet the legitimate demands of depositors in banks. As we shall see below, it does this through the discount and repo markets. In the crisis of 2008/9, the Bank of England, along with other central banks around the world, supplied massive amounts of extra liquidity in an attempt to combat the decline in inter-bank lending (see Box 10.4).

The Bank of England also operates a Discount Window Facility, whereby it allows banks to borrow gilts for up to a year against a wide range of assets as collateral. These gilts could then be sold on the money markets to provide banks with extra liquidity.

It oversees the activities of banks and other financial institutions

It advises banks on good banking practice. It discusses government policy with them and reports back to the government. It requires all recognised banks to maintain adequate liquidity: this is called **prudential control**. Since May 1997, the Bank of England has ceased to be responsible for the detailed supervision of banks' activities. This responsibility passed to the Financial Services Authority (FSA). As we shall see below, however, in 2007/8 many banks experienced a large rise in bad debts (much of it securitised 'sub-prime' mortgage debt) and a considerable shortage of liquidity. This raised the question of whether the FSA, or the Bank of England for that matter, were sufficiently watchful of banks' liquidity and the risks of liquidity shortage. Some commentators argued that a much tighter form of prudential control should have been imposed.

This was one of the major issues discussed at the summit of leaders of 20 of the world's largest economies (the 'G20') in April 2009. It was agreed that much greater international co-ordination of bank regulation and surveillance was necessary to ensure that banks maintained sufficient liquidity and capital and were not over-exposed to risky assets, such as sub-prime mortgage debt.

It operates the government's monetary and exchange rate policy

Monetary policy. The Bank of England's Monetary Policy Committee (MPC) sets Bank Rate at its monthly meetings. This nine-member committee consists of four experts appointed by the Chancellor of the Exchequer and four senior members of the Bank of England, plus the Governor in the chair. By careful management of the issue and repurchasing of gilts and Treasury bills, the Bank of England then keeps interest rates in line with the level decided by the MPC. It also, in the process, influences the size of the money supply. Details of this are given in Section 12.2.

Exchange rate policy. The Bank of England manages the country's gold and foreign currency reserves on behalf of the Treasury. This is done through the **exchange equalisation account**. As we shall see in Chapter 14, by buying and selling foreign currencies on the foreign exchange market, the Bank of England can affect the exchange rate.

> **Definitions**
>
> **Prudential control**
> The insistence by the Bank of England that banks maintain adequate liquidity.
>
> **Exchange equalisation account**
> The gold and foreign exchange reserves account in the Bank of England.

> **Pause for thought**
>
> 1. *Would it be possible for an economy to function without a central bank?*
> 2. *What effect would a substantial increase in the sale of government bonds and Treasury bills have on interest rates?*

The role of the money market

It is through the money market that a central bank exercises control of the economy. The market deals in short-term lending and borrowing.

We take the case of the London money market, which is normally divided into the 'discount' and 'repo' markets and the 'parallel' or 'complementary' market.

The discount and repo markets

The markets for bills of exchange (the discount market) and for repos play a crucial role in ensuring that banks have sufficient liquidity to meet all their needs.

Assume that bank customers start drawing out more cash. As a result, banks find themselves short of liquid assets. What can they do? The answer is that they borrow from the Bank of England. There are two ways in which this can be done.

The first is to enter a repo agreement, whereby the Bank of England buys gilts from the banks (thereby supplying them with money) on the condition that the banks buy the gilts back at a fixed price and on a fixed date, typically two weeks later. The repurchase price will be above the sale price. The difference is the equivalent of the interest that the banks are being charged for having what amounts to a loan from the Bank of England. The repurchase price (and hence the 'repo rate') is set by the Bank of England to reflect the Bank Rate chosen by the MPC.

The second method is to sell Treasury bills back to the Bank of England before they have reached maturity (i.e. before the three months are up). This process is known as **rediscounting**. The Bank of England will pay a price below the face value, thus effectively charging interest to the banks. Again, the price is set so that the 'rediscount rate' reflects Bank Rate.

In being prepared to rediscount bills or provide money through gilt repos, the Bank of England is thus the ultimate guarantor of sufficient liquidity in the monetary system and is known as **lender of last resort**.

The need for banks to acquire liquidity in this way is not uncommon. This shortage of liquidity allows the Bank of England to control interest rates. If the banks are forced to obtain liquidity from the Bank of England, they will be borrowing at the Bank of England's *chosen rate* (i.e. the repo rate). The banks will then have to gear their other rates to it, and other institutions will gear their rates to those of the banks.

The Bank of England manages liquidity not only in order to achieve the rate of interest set by MPC each month but also to ensure the *stability* of the financial system. Box 10.4 details the timeline of responses by the Bank of England to the stresses in the money markets from Summer 2007.

The parallel money markets

The parallel money markets include the following:

■ The inter-bank market (wholesale loans from one bank to another from one day to up to several months). Inter-bank lending has traditionally been a major source of liquidity. Bank with surplus liquidity lend to other banks, which then use this as the basis for loans to individuals and companies. As we shall see below, during the financial crisis of 2008, inter-bank lending virtually ceased as banks became worried that the bank they were lending to might default.
■ The market for certificates of deposit.
■ The inter-companies deposit market (short-term loans from one company to another arranged through the market).
■ The foreign currencies market (dealings in foreign currencies deposited short term in London).
■ The building society market (wholesale borrowing by the building societies).
■ The commercial paper market (borrowing in sterling by companies, banks and other financial institutions by the issue of short-term (less than one year) 'promissory notes'. These, like bills of exchange, are sold at a discount and redeemed at their face value, but in the interim can be traded on the market at any time).

> **Definitions**
>
> **Rediscounting bills of exchange**
> Buying bills before they reach maturity.
>
> **Lender of last resort**
> The role of the Bank of England as the guarantor of sufficient liquidity in the monetary system.

BOX 10.4 | TACKLING THE CREDIT CRUNCH

Cleansing the banking system

A central bank manages liquidity to influence interest rates *and* to ensure stability of the financial system. From summer 2007, central banks, including the ECB, the Federal Reserve and the Bank of England, became increasingly pro-active in injecting liquidity into the financial system so as to underpin the lending activities of financial institutions.

But, why were financial institutions short of liquidity? As we saw in Box 10.3, they were forced to write off bad debts, particularly those emanating from the securitisation of sub-prime residential mortgages. The deterioration in the balance sheets of banks meant that there was less surplus capital to fund advances.

The LIBOR spread

The impact on the UK's inter-bank market is illustrated in chart (a). It depicts the Bank of England's Bank Rate, the one-month LIBOR, which is the rate at which institutions lend to each other for one month (see above, page 309), and the differential (or 'spread') between the LIBOR and Bank Rate. The spread of the LIBOR over the Bank Rate jumped to 0.75 percentage point in August 2007 and, though falling back a little, was still frequently pushing 0.5 percentage point through 2008.

Then with the crisis of October 2008, the spread widened considerably to over 1.1 percentage points. Despite a cut in Bank Rate from 5 to 4.5 per cent, the LIBOR actually *rose* (see chart (a)). This upward pressure on the spread is consistent with a shortage of surplus funds and fears by potential lenders that borrowing banks might go bust, leaving any unsecured debt unpaid. The spread then began to fall in response to initial measures

to 'normalise' the banking system, and though it rose again early in 2009, it fell back again in response to further measures.

Considerable media attention was focused on the impact of the credit crunch on households and firms. The attention on the housing and mortgage markets was particularly stark. Chart (b) shows the spread of the average mortgage rate over Bank Rate. Compared with the spread for the LIBOR, that for the mortgage rate is consistently positive. But, as with the LIBOR spread, the spread for mortgage rates rose considerably in October 2008. The mortgage spread continued to rise to over $3^1/_2$ percentage points in 2009. This reflected the very low Bank Rate and attempts by banks to strengthen their balance sheets.

Supplying liquidity through repos

The Bank of England provides liquidity to banks via 'open-market operations' (see Section 12.2). This involves the use of repos. The Bank of England offers funds for a fixed term against eligible collateral of a financial institution (such as government bonds – gilt repos).

In normal circumstances these repo operations are predominantly very short-term, such as overnight 'fine-tuning' repo operations. But, as we have seen, in the period from summer 2007 circumstances ceased to be 'normal'. In response to the liquidity shortage, the Bank of England increased the maturity of its repo operations and expanded the type of collateral it was willing to lend against. It also increased the number of institutions it was prepared to lend to. For instance, on 18 March 2008 the

(a) One-month LIBOR and Bank of England Bank Rate

Source: *Statistical Interactive Database* (Bank of England)

(b) *Spread of average mortgage rate over Bank of England Bank Rate*

Source: *Statistical Interactive Database* (Bank of England)

Bank offered £10 billion in 3-month repos (much longer than the typical 1 to 14 days) and another £15 billion on 15 April 2008.[a]

This, however, was still not enough and on 21 April 2008 it introduced a 'Special Liquidity Scheme'. This enabled banks to swap high-quality, but illiquid assets, such as mortgages and credit-card debt (but not sub-prime debt), for special one-year Treasury Bills that could then be exchanged for cash in the money markets. Banks could renew the swaps annually for up to three years. Responsibility for losses on their loans, however, stayed with the banks.[b] By September 2008, some £100 billion had been made available to banks under the scheme.

Bailing out banks under threat

As the credit crisis deepened through 2008, it became obvious that the measures of central banks around the world to supply extra liquidity were totally insufficient to tackle the problem. At the heart of the issue was a lack of trust between banks. With the securitisation of sub-prime debt, banks feared that many of the assets of other banks' were 'toxic'. In other words, these assets were becoming increasingly worthless as their market value plummeted. Why should bank A lend to bank B, if bank B might not be able to pay back the loan?

But this only made the problem worse. As inter-bank lending dried up, so banks with a high proportion of sub-prime assets, looked increasingly vulnerable. As fear of bankruptcy spread, so several banks had to be bailed out by their respective governments.

In addition, governments felt it increasingly necessary to buy up toxic debts from banks. In the USA, after much debate, Congress accepted the Paulson Plan. This committed a staggering $700 billion to buy up bad debt of banks in return for a government stake in the banks.

But even this was insufficient to restore confidence and governments turned to even more drastic measures. The UK led the way with a three-pronged bailout package in October 2008.

Britain's three-pronged rescue plan

A rescue plan for the banking system was announced on 8 October 2008. It involved making an additional £400 billion available to banks in the UK (the same size as the Paulson Plan for a country only $^1/_5$ of the size of the USA). There were three elements of the initial plan:

- *Extra capital*. A total of up to £50 billion of extra capital would be provided to the seven largest banks and the largest building society as the government and FSA felt necessary. This was to tackle their growing capital inadequacy as the riskiness of their assets increased. The new capital was to be in the form of new shares owned by the government – a form of partial nationalisation. The government ended up owning large stakes in the Royal Bank of Scotland (over 70 per cent) and the newly formed Lloyds Banking Group

---

[a] Further details of the Bank's open-market operations in managing the stability of the financial system during the liquidity crisis can be found in the Bank's Financial Stability Report. **www.bankofengland.co.uk/publications/fsr/index.htm**.
[b] See **www.bankofengland.co.uk/markets/sls/**.

(over 60 per cent) (formed from the merger of HBOS and Lloyds/TSB).

The net result was a significant increase in banks' capital ratios. For example, RBS's Tier One ratio rose by 4 percentage points. All banks would have a Tier One ratio of at least 9 per cent, giving them a considerable margin above the Basel II minimum capital adequacy ratio.

■ *Additional liquidity.* An additional £100 billion was made available under the Special Liquidity Scheme (see above). What is more, riskier assets would be acceptable for swapping for Treasury Bills than previously.

■ *Guaranteeing loans on the inter-bank market.* Under the Credit Guarantee Scheme, £250 billion was made available for loan guarantees for new inter-bank lending. In other words, if bank A lends to bank B and bank B then defaults, the government would pay bank A. The hope was that this would 'kick-start' inter-bank lending.

A few days later, European leaders announced a similar rescue package for eurozone banks, worth €1.5 trillion. National governments would provide extra capital by buying preference shares; they would also guarantee inter-bank lending until the end of 2009. In addition they announced that no major bank would be allowed to fail.

Subsequent measures

Over the next few months the scale of bank losses in many countries turned out to be even worse than first thought. Also, as the global recession deepened, banks were reluctant to restore lending for fear of incurring further bad debt (i.e. assets, such as loans and securitised bonds, which could not be redeemed in full – if at all). But increasing lending was vital to prevent further weakening aggregate demand. Thus governments had to take additional measures.

In February 2009 the UK government published details of its Asset Protection Scheme. Under the scheme, in return for a fee, financial institutions could insure themselves against losses from 1 January 2009 incurred on those assets placed in the scheme. These assets could include corporate loans, residential property loans and 'structured' credit assets, such as collateralised debt obligations (CDOs). In return for taking out the insurance, banks had to agree to lending commitments to both businesses and individuals.

Over in the USA, the Treasury announced in March 2009 details of a $1 trillion package – 'Public–Private Investment Program' – to deal with 'legacy assets' such as CDOs. Its intention, like the UK's Asset Protection Scheme, was to cleanse banks' balance sheets. The approach taken was rather different and was designed to attract private capital to purchase 'legacy assets'. So as to encourage private investors, such as insurance companies and private equity funds, to take part, low-interest loans were provided by the government and these loans were to be guaranteed against losses.

These and other measures of support for bank lending and for the cleansing of banks' balance sheets were mirrored in various aspects across the world. They were intended to ensure the long-term stability of the financial system while in the short run lessening the depth of the oncoming recession.

1. *Why may supplying extra liquidity to banks not necessarily be successful in averting a slowdown in borrowing and spending?*
2. *Why is there a potential 'moral hazard' in supporting failing banks? How could the terms of a bailout help to reduce this moral hazard?*

The parallel markets have grown in size and importance in recent years. The main reasons for this have been (a) the opening-up of markets to international dealing, given the abolition of exchange controls in 1979, (b) the deregulation of banking and money market dealing and (c) the volatility of interest rates and exchange rates, and thus the desire of banks to keep funds in a form that can be readily switched from one form of deposit to another, or from one currency to another. The main areas of growth have been in inter-bank deposits, certificates of deposit and the foreign currency markets.

Although the Bank of England has not traditionally dealt directly in the parallel markets and has not provided 'last resort' lending facilities, it nevertheless closely monitors the various money market rates of interest and if necessary seeks to influence them, through its dealings in the discount and repo markets.

In October 2008, at the height of the credit crisis, the Bank of England announced that it would guarantee loans on the

Pause for thought

Why should Bank of England determination of the rate of interest in the discount and repo markets also influence rates of interest in the parallel markets?

inter-bank market. With banks worried that other banks might default on loans, inter-bank lending had all but dried up. By removing the risk of default for lenders, the Bank of England was hoping to encourage banks to start lending to each other again (see Box 10.4).

Recap

1. Central to the financial system are the retail and wholesale arms of banks. Between them they provide the following important functions: giving expert advice, channelling capital to areas of highest return, maturity transformation, risk transformation and the transmission of payments. Some of these banks had to be rescued by the government in 2008 – they were too important to the health of the economy to allow them to fail.

2. Banks' liabilities include both sight and time deposits. They also include certificates of deposit and repos. Their assets include: notes and coin, balances with the central bank, market loans, bills of exchange (Treasury bills and commercial bills), reverse repos, advances to customers (the biggest item – including overdrafts, personal loans, credit card debt and mortgages) and investments (government bonds and inter-bank investments). In the years up to 2008 they had increasingly included securitised assets.

3. Banks aim to make profits, but they must also have a sufficient capital base and maintain sufficient liquidity. Liquid assets, however, tend to be relatively unprofitable and profitable assets tend to be relatively illiquid. Banks therefore need to keep a balance of profitability and liquidity in their range of assets.

4. The Bank of England is the UK's central bank. It issues notes; it acts as banker to the government, to banks and to various overseas central banks; it manages the government's borrowing programme; it ensures sufficient liquidity for the financial sector; it operates the country's monetary and exchange rate policy.

5. The money market is the market in short-term deposits and loans. It consists of the discount and repo markets and the parallel money markets.

6. The Bank of England operates in the repo and discount markets. By buying (rediscounting) bills and through gilt repos, it provides liquidity to the banks at the rate of interest chosen by the Monetary Policy Committee (Bank Rate). It is always prepared to lend in this way in order to ensure adequate liquidity in the economy. To supplement this process, the Bank of England introduced a Special Liquidity Scheme in 2008 as inter-bank lending declined during the credit crunch.

7. The parallel money markets consist of various markets in short-term finance between various financial institutions.

THE SUPPLY OF MONEY   10.3

How is it measured and what determines its size?

If money supply is to be monitored and possibly controlled, it is obviously necessary to measure it. But what should be included in the measure? Here we need to distinguish between the *monetary base* and *broad money*.

The **monetary base** (or 'high-powered money' or 'narrow money') consists of cash (notes and coin) in circulation outside the central bank.[2]

But the monetary base gives us a very poor indication of the effective money supply, since it excludes the most important source of liquidity for spending:

> **Definition**
>
> **Monetary base**
> Notes and coin outside the central bank.

---

[2] Before 2006, there used to be a measure of narrow money called 'M0'. This included cash in circulation outside the Bank of England and banks' non-interest-bearing 'operational balances' in the Bank of England, with these balances accounting for a tiny proportion of the whole. Since 2006, the Bank of England has allowed banks to hold interest-bearing reserve accounts, which are much larger than the former operational balances. The Bank of England thus decided to discontinue M0 as a measure and focus on cash in circulation as its measure of the monetary base.

namely, bank deposits. The problem is which deposits to include. We need to answer three questions:

- Should we include just sight deposits, or time deposits as well?
- Should we include just retail deposits, or wholesale deposits as well?
- Should we include just bank deposits, or building society (savings institution) deposits as well?

In the past there has been a whole range of measures, each including different combinations of these accounts. However, financial deregulation, the abolition of foreign exchange controls and the development of computer technology have led to huge changes in the financial sector throughout the world. This has led to a blurring of the distinctions between different types of account. It has also made it very easy to switch deposits from one type of account to another. For these reasons, the most usual measure that countries use for money supply is **broad money**, which in most cases includes both time and sight deposits, retail and wholesale deposits, and bank and building society (savings institution) deposits.

In the UK, this measure of broad money is known as M4. In most other European countries and the USA, it is known as M3. There are, however, minor differences between countries in what is included.

As we have seen, bank deposits of one form or another constitute by far the largest component of (broad) money supply. To understand how money supply expands and contracts, and how it can be controlled, it is thus necessary to understand what determines the size of bank deposits. Banks can themselves expand the amount of bank deposits, and hence the money supply, by a process known as 'credit creation'.

> **Definition**
>
> **Broad money**
> Cash in circulation plus retail and wholesale bank and building society deposits.

The creation of credit

To illustrate this process in its simplest form, assume that banks have just one type of liability – deposits – and two types of asset – balances with the central bank (to achieve liquidity) and advances to customers (to earn profit).

Banks want to achieve profitability while maintaining sufficient liquidity. Assume that they believe that sufficient liquidity will be achieved if 10 per cent of their assets are held as balances with the central bank. The remaining 90 per cent will then be in advances to customers. In other words, the banks operate a 10 per cent liquidity ratio.

Assume initially that the combined balance sheet of the banks is as shown in Table 10.2. Total deposits are £100 billion, of which £10 billion (10 per cent) are kept in balances with the central bank. The remaining £90 billion (90 per cent) are lent to customers.

Now assume that the government spends more money – £10 billion, say, on roads or education. It pays for this with cheques drawn on its account with the

Table 10.2 Banks' original balance sheet			
Liabilities	**£bn**	**Assets**	**£bn**
Deposits	100	Balances with the central bank	10
		Advances	90
Total	100	Total	100

Table 10.3	The initial effect of an additional deposit of £10 billion		
Liabilities	**£bn**	**Assets**	**£bn**
Deposits (old)	100	Balances with the central bank (old)	10
Deposits (new)	10	Balances with the central bank (new)	10
		Advances	90
Total	110	Total	110

central bank. The people receiving the cheques deposit them in their banks. Banks return these cheques to the central bank and their balances correspondingly increase by £10 billion. The combined banks' balance sheet now is shown in Table 10.3.

But this is not the end of the story. Banks now have surplus liquidity. With their balances in the central bank having increased to £20 billion, they now have a liquidity ratio of 20/110, or 18.2 per cent. If they are to return to a 10 per cent liquidity ratio, they need only retain £11 billion as balances at the central bank (£11 billion/£110 billion = 10 per cent). The remaining £9 billion they can lend to customers.

Assume now that customers spend this £9 billion in shops and the shopkeepers deposit the cheques in their bank accounts. When the cheques are cleared, the balances in the central bank of the customers' banks will duly be debited by £9 billion, but the balances in the central bank of the shopkeepers' banks will be credited by £9 billion: leaving *overall balances in the central bank unaltered*. There is still a surplus of £9 billion over what is required to maintain the 10 per cent liquidity ratio. The new deposits of £9 billion in the shopkeepers' banks, backed by balances in the central bank, can thus be used as the basis for *further* loans. Ten per cent (i.e. £0.9 billion) must be kept back in the central bank, but the remaining 90 per cent (i.e. £8.1 billion) can be lent out again.

When the money is spent and the cheques are cleared, this £8.1 billion will still remain as surplus balances in the central bank and can therefore be used as the basis for yet more loans. Again, 10 per cent must be retained and the remaining 90 per cent can be lent out. This process goes on and on until eventually the position is as shown in Table 10.4.

The initial increase in balances with the central bank of £10 billion has allowed banks to create new advances (and hence deposits) of £90 billion, making a total increase in money supply of £100 billion.

> **Pause for thought**
>
> *If banks choose to operate with a 5 per cent liquidity ratio and receive an extra £100 million of cash deposits: (a) What is the size of the bank deposits multiplier? (b) How much will total deposits have expanded after the multiplier has worked through? (c) How much will total credit have expanded?*

Table 10.4	The full effect of an additional deposit of £10 billion		
Liabilities	**£bn**	**Assets**	**£bn**
Deposits (old)	100	Balances with the central bank (old)	10
Deposits (new: inital)	10	Balances with the central bank (new)	10
(new: subsequent)	90	Advances (old)	90
		Advance (new)	90
Total	200	Total	200

TC 13
p 253

This effect is known as the **bank deposits multiplier**. In this simple example, with a liquidity ratio of $^1/_{10}$ (i.e. 10 per cent), the bank deposits multiplier is 10. An initial increase in deposits of £10 billion allowed total deposits to rise by £100 billion. In this simple world, therefore, the bank deposits multiplier is the inverse of the liquidity ratio (L).

Bank deposits multiplier = $^1/_L$

The creation of credit: the real world

In practice, the creation of credit is not as simple as this. There are three major complications.

Banks' liquidity ratio may vary

Banks may choose a different liquidity ratio. At certain times, banks may decide that it is prudent to hold a bigger proportion of liquid assets. If Christmas or the summer holidays are approaching and people are likely to make bigger cash withdrawals, banks may decide to hold more liquid assets.

On the other hand, there may be an upsurge in consumer demand for credit. Banks may be very keen to grant additional loans and thus make more profits, even though they have acquired no additional assets. They may simply go ahead and expand credit, and accept a lower liquidity ratio.

Customers may not want to take up the credit on offer. Banks may wish to make additional loans, but customers may not want to borrow. There may be insufficient demand. But will the banks not then lower their interest rates, thus encouraging people to borrow? Possibly; but if they lower the rate they charge to borrowers, they must also lower the rate they pay to depositors. But then depositors may switch to other institutions such as building societies.

Banks may not operate a simple liquidity ratio

The fact that banks hold a number of fairly liquid assets, such as money at call, bills of exchange and certificates of deposit, makes it difficult to identify a simple liquidity ratio. If the banks use extra cash to buy such liquid assets, can they then use *these* assets as the basis for creating credit? It is largely up to banks' judgements on their overall liquidity position. In practice, therefore, the size of the bank deposits multiplier will vary and is thus difficult to predict in advance.

Some of the extra cash may be withdrawn by the public

If extra cash comes into the banking system, and as a result extra deposits are created, part of them may be held by households and non-bank firms (known in this context as the **non-bank private sector**) as cash outside the banks. In other words, some of the extra cash leaks out of the banking system. This will result in an overall multiplier effect that is smaller than the full bank deposits multiplier. This overall multiplier is known as the **money multiplier**. It is defined as the change in total money supply expressed as a proportion of the change in the monetary base that caused it: $\Delta M_s/\Delta M_b$ (where M_s is total broad money supply and M_b is the monetary base).

TC 13
p 253

Definition

Banks deposits multiplier
The number of times greater the expansion of bank deposits is than the additional liquidity in banks that causes it: 1/*L* (the inverse of the liquidity ratio).

Pause for thought

How will an increased mobility of savings and other capital between institutions affect this argument?

Definitions

Non-bank private sector
Households and non-bank firms. In other words, everyone in the country other than banks and the government (central and local).

Money multiplier
The number of times greater the expansion of money supply is than the expansion of the monetary base that caused it: $\Delta M_s/\Delta M_b$.

Figure 10.2 Money multiplier: ratio of M4 to notes and coin

Source: *Monetary and Financial Statistics* (Bank of England)

The money multiplier in the UK

In the UK, the money multiplier is usually given by ΔM4/Δcash in circulation. The UK money multiplier grew rapidly after 2004. An indication of this is given by the ratio of the level of M4 to the level of cash in circulation. This is plotted in Figure 10.2. We can see that the ratio more than doubled through the 1980s to around 25. But from the beginning of the 1990s until the mid-2000s the value of this ratio was relatively steady. It then increased markedly. In other words, for a given monetary base (i.e. cash in circulation), much more credit was created. The effect of this was to give a bigger money multiplier: in other words, for a given *change* in cash in circulation, there would be a bigger *change* in M4 than previously.

But why did M4 increase in this way relative to the monetary base? The next section looks at factors determining the money supply.

> **Pause for thought**
>
> *Which would you expect to fluctuate more, the money multiplier (ΔM4/Δcash), or the simple ratio, M4/cash, illustrated in Figure 10.2?*

What causes money supply to rise?

There are four sets of circumstances in which the money supply can rise.

Banks choose to hold a lower liquidity ratio

If banks collectively choose to hold a lower liquidity ratio, they will have surplus liquidity. The banks have tended to choose a lower liquidity ratio over time because of the increasing use of direct debits and debit-card and credit-card transactions.

Surplus liquidity can be used to expand advances, which will lead to a multiplied rise in broad money supply (e.g. M4).

An important trend in recent years has been the growth in *inter-bank lending*. Table 10.1 showed that short-term loans to other banks (including overseas banks) and CDs are now the two largest elements in banks' liquid assets. These assets may be used by a bank as the basis for expanding loans and thereby starting a chain of credit creation. But although these assets are liquid to an *individual bank*, they do not add to the liquidity of the banking system *as a whole*. By using them for credit creation, the banking system is operating with a lower *overall* liquidity ratio.

This was a major element in the banking crisis of 2008. By operating with a collectively low liquidity ratio, banks were vulnerable to people defaulting on debt, such as mortgages. The problem was compounded by the holding of sub-prime debt in the form of securitised assets. Realising the vulnerability of other banks, banks became increasingly unwilling to lend to each other. The resulting decline in inter-bank lending reduced the amount of credit created.

> **Pause for thought**
>
> *What effects do debit cards and cash machines (ATMs) have on (a) banks' prudent liquidity ratios; (b) the size of the bank deposits multiplier?*

The non-bank private sector chooses to hold less cash

Households and firms may choose to hold less cash. Again, the reason may be a greater use of cards, direct debits, etc. This means that a greater proportion of the cash base will be held as deposits in banks rather than in people's wallets, purses or safes outside banks. The extra cash deposits allow banks to create more credit.

BOX 10.5 **CREDIT AND THE MONEY SUPPLY**

Who's driving the M4?

M4 is the UK's main broad aggregate measure of the money supply. But who holds this money?

One method of analysing holdings of M4 involves measuring the net lending of all monetary and financial institutions (MFIs) to three groups: the domestic private sector (households and firms), the public sector and non-residents. *Net* lending is total lending minus total deposits: known as M4 outstanding.

M4 lending outstanding is sterling denominated credit to the non-bank private sector. As we can see in Table (a) this is the most significant 'counterpart' to M4. The non-bank private sector had £2.4 trillion of debt outstanding with MFIs at the end of 2008. We can also see from the table that the public sector was a net saver with MFIs in 2008, a position that it has held since the middle of the 2000s and the onset of the global financial crisis.

We can also analyse changes in the level of net lending to each group and relate them to changes in M4. In other words, we can analyse the behaviour of different sectors and trace through their impact on the money supply.

The chart considers the impact of the non-bank sector on M4. It shows the changes in the amount of net borrowing over a 12-month period (i.e. annual changes) from MFIs to non-bank financial corporations (such as insurance companies), non-financial corporations and the household sector. As you can see, in the second half of the 2000s, non-bank financial corporations were borrowing larger sums to add to their existing stock of debt. On the other hand, non-financial corporations and households were borrowing increasingly smaller amounts. Indeed, in the case of the household sector, at the end of 2008 and into 2009 deposits made to MFIs exceeded the sums being borrowed. Later in 2009, the same applied to private (non-bank) companies (see chart).

There were two reasons for this for this massive reduction in bank lending.

On the demand side, people, worried by a deepening recession, were keen to reduce their debts. This was helped by lower interest rates and hence lower mortgage repayments and payments on other debt.

On the supply side, there was a reduced availability of credit as banks became more cautions about lending. It is not surprising that the government and the Bank of England were making concerted attempts to get banks lending again (see Box 10.4).

Table (a) MFIs balance sheet counterparts to M4 at end of 1998 and 2008

M4 lending outstanding to:	1998 £ billion	2008 £ billion
Non-bank private sector	894.2	2384.0
Other financial corporations	26.7	172.4
Public sector	25.3	−19.6
Non-residents	25.2	−68.4
Other MFI assets outstanding	−188.0	−518.6
Total M4	783.3	1949.8

Source: *Monetary and Financial Statistics* (Bank of England)

 What factors influence the net lending to households and non-financial corporations?

The above two reasons for an expansion of broad money supply (M4) are because more credit is being created for a given monetary base. As Figure 10.2 showed, the ratio of M4 to cash rose substantially after 2004. The other two reasons for an expansion of money supply are reasons why the monetary base itself might expand.

An inflow of funds from abroad

Sometimes the Bank of England will choose to build up the foreign currency reserves. To do this it will buy foreign currencies on the foreign exchange market using sterling. When the recipients of this extra sterling deposit it in UK banks, or spend it on UK exports and the exporters deposit in UK banks, credit will be created on the basis of it, leading to a *multiplied* increase in money supply.

A public-sector deficit

A public-sector deficit is the difference between public-sector expenditure and public-sector receipts. In the UK this is known as the public-sector net cash requirement (PSNCR). To meet this deficit, the government has to borrow money by selling

CASE STUDIES & APPLICATIONS

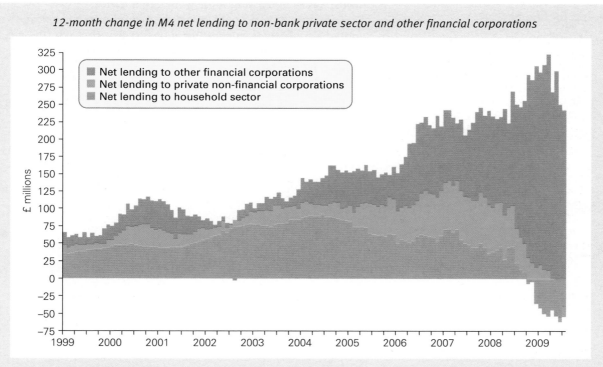

12-month change in M4 net lending to non-bank private sector and other financial corporations

Source: *Monetary and Financial Statistics* (Bank of England)

interest-bearing securities (Treasury bills and gilts). In general, the bigger the public sector's deficit, the greater will be the growth in the money supply. Just how the money supply will be affected, however, depends on who buys the securities.

Such securities could be sold to the Bank of England. In this case, the Bank of England credits the government's account to the value of the securities it has purchased. When the government spends the money, it pays with cheques drawn on its account with the Bank of England. When the recipients of these cheques pay them into their bank accounts, the banks will present the cheques to the Bank of England and their balances there will be duly credited. These additional balances will then become the basis for credit creation. There will be a multiplied expansion of the money supply.

Similarly, if the government borrows through additional Treasury bills, and if these are purchased by the banking sector, there will be a multiplied expansion of the money supply. The reason is that, although banks' balances at the central bank will go down when the banks purchase the bills, they will go up again when the government spends the money. In addition, the banks will now have additional liquid assets (bills), which can be used as the basis for credit creation.

If, however, the government securities are purchased by the 'non-bank private sector' (the name given to the general public and non-bank firms), the money supply will remain unchanged. When people buy the bonds or bills, they will draw money from their banks. When the government spends the money, it will be redeposited in banks. There is no increase in money supply. It is just a case of existing money changing hands.

The government could attempt to minimise the boost to money supply by financing the budget deficit through the sale of gilts, since, even if these were partly purchased by the banks, they could not be used as the basis for credit creation.

Definition

Exogenous money supply
Money supply that does not depend on the demand for money but is set by the authorities (i.e. the central bank or the government).

Pause for thought

Identify the various factors that could cause a fall in the money supply.

The relationship between money supply and the rate of interest

Simple monetary theory often assumes that the supply of money is totally independent of interest rates. The money supply is **exogenous**. This is illustrated in Figure 10.3(a). The supply of money is assumed to be determined by the government

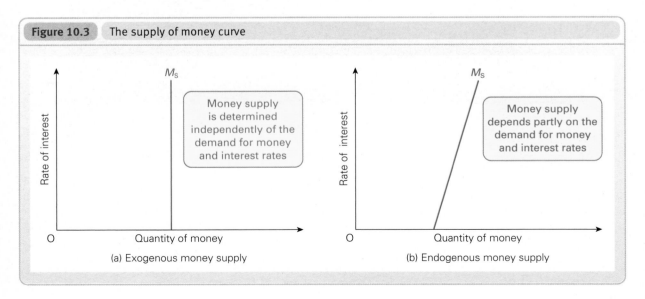

Figure 10.3 The supply of money curve

(a) Exogenous money supply

Rate of interest — Quantity of money — M_S

Money supply is determined independently of the demand for money and interest rates

(b) Endogenous money supply

Rate of interest — Quantity of money — M_S

Money supply depends partly on the demand for money and interest rates or central bank ('the authorities'): what the authorities choose it to be, or what they allow it to be by their choice of the level and method of financing the budget deficit.

In practice, money supply is **endogenous**, with higher interest rates leading to increases in the supply of money. This is illustrated in Figure 10.3(b). The argument is that the supply of money is responding to the demand for money. If people start borrowing more money, the resulting shortage of money in the banks will drive up interest rates. But if banks have surplus liquidity or are prepared to operate with a lower liquidity ratio, they will create extra credit in response to the increased demand and higher interest rates: money supply will expand. If banks find themselves short of liquidity, they can always borrow from the central bank through repos. Some economists go further still. They argue that money supply is not only endogenous, but the 'curve' is effectively horizontal; money supply expands passively to match the demand for money.

> **Definition**
>
> **Endogenous money supply**
> Money supply that is determined (at least in part) by the demand for money.

Recap

1. Money supply can be defined in a number of different ways, depending on what items are included. A useful distinction is between narrow money and broad money. Narrow money includes just cash and possibly banks' balances at the central bank. Broad money also includes deposits in banks and possibly various other short-term deposits in the money market. In the UK, M4 is the preferred measure of broad money. In the eurozone it is M3.

2. Bank deposits expand through a process of credit creation. If banks' liquid assets increase, they can be used as a base for increasing loans. When the loans are redeposited in banks, they form the base for yet more loans, and thus takes place a process of multiple credit expansion. The ratio of the increase of money to an expansion of the liquidity base is called the 'bank deposits multiplier'. It is the inverse of the liquidity ratio.

3. In practice, it is difficult to predict the precise amount by which money supply will expand if there is an increase in banks' liquidity. The reasons are that banks may choose to hold a different liquidity ratio; customers may not take up all the credit on offer; there may be no simple liquidity ratio, given the range of near-money assets; and some of the extra cash may leak away into extra cash holdings by the general public.

4. (Broad) money supply will rise if (a) banks choose to hold a lower liquidity ratio and thus create more credit for an existing amount of liquidity; (b) the non-bank private sector chooses to hold less cash; (c) the government runs a deficit and some of it is financed by borrowing from the banking sector; (d) there is an inflow of funds from abroad.

5. Simple monetary theory assumes that the supply of money is independent of interest rates. In practice, a rise in demand for money, and hence a rise in interest rates, will often lead to an increase in money supply.

THE DEMAND FOR MONEY   10.4

How much money do we want to hold at any one time?

The demand for money refers to the desire to *hold* money: to keep your wealth in the form of money, rather than spending it on goods and services or using it to purchase financial assets such as bonds or shares. It is usual to distinguish three reasons why people want to hold their assets in the form of money:

The transactions motive. Since money is a medium of exchange, it is required for conducting transactions. But since people only receive money at intervals (e.g. weekly or monthly) and not continuously, they require to hold balances of money in cash or in current accounts.

The precautionary motive. Unforeseen circumstances can arise, such as a car breakdown. Thus individuals often hold some additional money as a precaution. Firms too keep precautionary balances because of uncertainties about the timing of their receipts and payments. If a large customer is late in making payment, a firm may be unable to pay its suppliers unless it has spare liquidity.

The assets or speculative motive. Money is not just a medium of exchange, it is also a means of storing wealth (see page 303). Keeping some or all of your wealth as money in a bank account has the advantage of carrying no risk. It earns a relatively small, but safe rate of return. Some assets, such as company shares or bonds, may earn you more on average, but there is a chance that their price will fall. In other words, they are risky.

What determines the size of the demand for money?

What would cause the demand for money to rise? We now turn to examine the various determinants of the size of the demand for money (M_D). In particular, we will look at the role of the rate of interest. First, however, let us identify the other determinants of the demand for money.

Money national income. The more money people earn, the greater will be their expenditure and hence the greater the transactions demand for money. A rise in money ('nominal') incomes in a country can be caused either by a rise in real GDP (i.e. real output) or by a rise in prices, or by some combination of the two.

The frequency with which people are paid. The less frequently people are paid, the greater the level of money balances that will be required to tide them over until the next payment.

Financial innovations. The increased use of credit cards, debit cards and cash machines, plus the advent of interest-paying current accounts, has resulted in changes in the demand for money. The use of credit cards reduces both the transactions and precautionary demands. Paying once a month for goods requires less money on average than paying separately for each item purchased. Moreover, the possession of a credit card reduces or even eliminates the need to hold precautionary balances for many people. On the other hand, the increased availability of cash machines, the convenience of debit cards and the ability to earn interest on current accounts have all encouraged people to hold more money in bank accounts. The net effect has been an increase in the demand for money.

Speculation about future returns on assets. The assets motive for holding money depends on people's expectations. If they believe that share prices are about to fall on the stock market, they will sell shares and hold larger balances of money in the meantime. The assets demand, therefore, can be quite high when the price of securities is considered certain to fall. Some clever (or lucky) individuals anticipated the 2007–8 stock market decline. They sold shares and 'went liquid'.

Generally, the more risky such alternatives to money become, the more will people want to hold their assets as money balances in a bank or building society.

People also speculate about changes in the exchange rate. If businesses believe that the exchange rate is about to appreciate (rise), they will hold greater balances of domestic currency in the meantime, hoping to buy foreign currencies with them when the rate has risen (since they will then get more foreign currency for their money).

The rate of interest. In terms of the operation of money markets, this is the most important determinant. It is related to the opportunity cost of holding money. The

Figure 10.4	The demand for money

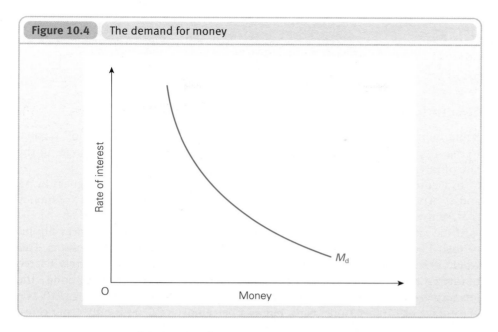

opportunity cost is the interest forgone by not holding higher interest-bearing assets, such as shares, bills or bonds. With most bank accounts today paying interest, this opportunity cost is less than in the past and thus the demand for money for assets purposes has increased.

But what is the relationship between money demand and the rate of interest? Generally, if rates of interest rise, they will rise more on shares, bills and bonds than on bank accounts. The demand for money will thus fall. The demand for money is thus inversely related to the rate of interest.

The demand for money curve

The demand for money curve with respect to interest rates is shown in Figure 10.4. It is downward sloping, showing that lower interest rates will encourage people to hold additional money balances.

A change in interest rates is shown by a movement along the demand for money curve. A change in any other determinant of the demand for money (such as national income or expectations about exchange rate movements) will cause the whole curve to shift: a rightward shift representing an increase in demand; a leftward shift representing a decrease.

> **Pause for thought**
>
> *Which way is the demand for money curve likely to shift in each of the following cases? (a) Prices rise, but real incomes stay the same. (b) Interest rates abroad rise relative to domestic interest rates. (c) People anticipate that share prices are likely to fall in the near future.*

Recap

1. The three motives for holding money are the transactions, precautionary and assets (or speculative) motives.

2. The demand for money will be higher, (a) the higher the level of money national income (i.e. the higher the level of real national income and the higher the price level), (b) the less frequently people are paid, (c) the greater the advantages of holding money in bank accounts, such as the existence of cash machines and the use of debit cards, (d) the more risky alternative assets become and the more likely they are to fall in value, and the more likely the exchange rate is to rise, and (e) the lower the opportunity cost of holding money in terms of interest forgone on alternative assets.

3. The demand for money curve with respect to interest rates is downward sloping.

10.5   EQUILIBRIUM

What effect do the demand and supply of money have on interest rates?

Equilibrium in the money market

Equilibrium in the money market occurs when the demand for money (M_d) is equal to the supply of money (M_s). This equilibrium is achieved through changes in the rate of interest.

In Figure 10.5, assume that the demand and supply of money are given by M_s and M_d. The equilibrium rate of interest is r_e and the equilibrium quantity of money is M_e. But why?

If the rate of interest were above r_e, people would have money balances surplus to their needs. They would use these to buy shares, bonds and other assets. This would drive up the price of these assets. But the price of assets is inversely related to interest rates. The higher the price of an asset (such as a government bond), the less any given interest payment will be as a percentage of its price (e.g. £10 as a percentage of £100 is 10 per cent, but as a percentage of £200 is only 5 per cent). Thus a higher price of assets will correspond to lower interest rates.

As the rate of interest fell, so there would be a contraction of the money supply (a movement down along the M_s curve) and an increase in the demand for money balances, especially speculative balances (a movement down along the M_d curve). The interest rate would go on falling until it reached r_e. Equilibrium would then be achieved.

Similarly, if the rate of interest were below r_e, people would have insufficient money balances. They would sell securities, thus lowering their prices and raising the rate of interest until it reached r_e.

A shift in either the M_s or the M_d curve will lead to a new equilibrium quantity of money and rate of interest at the new intersection of the curves. For example,

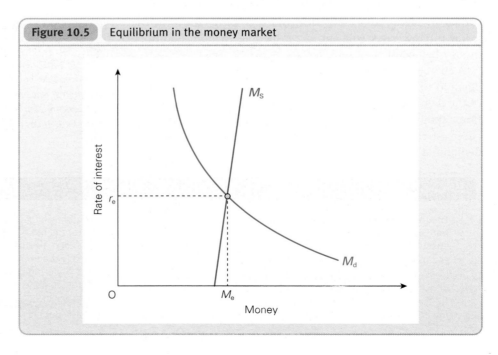

Figure 10.5   Equilibrium in the money market

a rise in the supply of money will cause the rate of interest to fall, whereas a rise in the demand for money will cause the rate of interest to rise.

The link between the money and goods markets

A rise in money supply will cause a rise in aggregate demand. This, in turn will then cause a multiplied rise in national income. The size of the rise in real national income (i.e. output) will depend on the degree of spare capacity in the economy. In this section we see how a rise in money supply causes a rise in aggregate demand. In Chapter 11 we see to what extent this rise in aggregate demand leads to a rise in national output, and to what extent it merely leads to a rise in prices.

There are two ways in which a rise in money supply causes a rise in aggregate demand: the first is via changes in interest rates – known as the **interest-rate transmission mechanism**. The second is via changes in the exchange rate – known as the **exchange-rate transmission mechanism**.

The interest-rate transmission mechanism

The interest-rate transmission mechanism is illustrated in the top part of Figure 10.6.

- A rise in money supply leads to a surplus of money at the current rate of interest. This results in a fall in the equilibrium rate of interest. This would be illustrated by a rightward shift in the M_s line in Figure 10.5, with the rate of interest falling to the point where this new M_s curve crossed the M_d curve.
- This fall in the rate of interest then encourages firms to invest, since it is cheaper to borrow money to finance new buildings, machines, etc. It also encourages consumers to spend, since borrowing through credit cards and personal loans is now cheaper. At the same time, it discourages saving.
- The net effect of these changes in injections and withdrawals is a rise in aggregate demand.

The exchange-rate transmission mechanism

Exchange rates are determined by the demand and supply of currencies. (We will examine this in detail in Chapter 14.) If the supply of sterling on the foreign exchange market (e.g. from importers in the UK wishing to buy foreign currencies

Figure 10.6   Monetary transmission mechanisms

in order to buy foreign goods) exceeds the demand (e.g. from foreign companies wishing to obtain sterling to buy UK exports), the exchange rate will fall ('depreciate'). For example, the pound might depreciate from $1.65 to $1.50, or from €1.30 to €1.20. Conversely, if the demand for sterling exceeds the supply, the exchange rate will rise ('appreciate').

Changes in the money supply will not only affect interest rates, they will also affect the demand and supply of the currency and thus have an effect on exchange rates. The change in the exchange rate will then affect aggregate demand. This exchange-rate transmission mechanism is illustrated in the bottom part of Figure 10.6.

Assume again that the money supply increases. This has the following effects:

■ Part of the excess money balances is used to purchase foreign assets. This therefore leads to an increase in the supply of domestic currency coming on to the foreign exchange markets.

■ As we have already seen, the excess supply of money in the domestic money market pushes down the rate of interest. This reduces the return on domestic assets below that on foreign assets. This, like the first effect, leads to an increased demand for foreign assets and thus an increased supply of domestic currency on the foreign exchange market. It also reduces the demand for domestic assets by those outside the country, and thus reduces the demand for the domestic currency. This causes the exchange rate to fall (depreciate).

■ The fall in the exchange rate (e.g. from €1.50 to €1.40) means that people abroad have to pay less for a pound. This makes UK exports (an injection) cheaper and hence more are sold. People in the UK, by contrast, get less foreign currency for a pound. This makes imports (a withdrawal) more expensive and hence fewer are purchased.

■ Again, the net effect of these changes in injections and withdrawals is a rise in aggregate demand.

With both transmission mechanisms, the resulting rise in aggregate demand then leads to a multiplied rise in national income (GDP). This, however, as we shall see in Section 11.2, may be wholly or partly offset by a rise in prices.

The relationship between the money and goods market is explored in more detail in Web Appendix 10.2, which looks at the 'ISLM' model.

Pause for thought

Before you read on, try to decide what determines the amount that real output rises as a result of a rise in the money supply?

Recap

1. Equilibrium in the money market is where the supply of money is equal to the demand. Equilibrium is achieved through changes in the interest rate.

2. The interest rate mechanism works as follows: a rise in money supply causes money supply to exceed money demand; interest rates fall; this causes investment to rise; this causes a multiplied rise in national income.

3. The exchange rate mechanism works as follows: a rise in money supply causes interest rates to fall; the rise in money supply plus the fall in interest rates causes an increased supply of domestic currency to come on to the foreign exchange market; this causes the exchange rate to depreciate; this will cause increased exports and reduced imports and hence a multiplied rise in national income.

QUESTIONS

1. Imagine that the banking system receives additional deposits of £100 million and that all the individual banks wish to retain their current liquidity ratio of 20 per cent.

    (a) How much will banks choose to lend out initially?
    (b) What will happen to banks' liabilities when the money that is lent out is spent and the recipients of it deposit it in their bank accounts?
    (c) How much of these latest deposits will be lent out by the banks?
    (d) By how much will *total* deposits (liabilities) eventually have risen, assuming that none of the additional liquidity is held outside the banking sector?
    (e) How much of these are matched by (i) liquid assets; (ii) illiquid assets?
    (f) What is the size of the bank deposits multiplier?
    (g) If one half of any additional liquidity is held *outside* the banking sector, by how much less will deposits have risen compared with (d) above?

2. What is meant by the terms *narrow money* and *broad money*? Does broad money fulfil all the functions of money?

3. Which, if any, of the following count as (broad) money? (a) A credit card. (b) A debit card. (c) A cheque book. (d) A bank deposit account pass book. (e) A building society pass book.

4. How does money aid the specialisation and division of labour?

5. What enables banks safely to engage in both maturity transformation and risk transformation?

6. Why do banks hold a range of assets of varying degrees of liquidity and profitability?

7. What is meant by the securitisation of assets? How might this be (a) beneficial and (b) harmful to banks and the economy?

8. What were the causes of the credit crunch and the banking crisis of 2008?

9. If banks choose to operate a 20 per cent liquidity ratio and receive extra cash deposits of £10 million, assuming that the general public does not wish to hold a larger total amount of cash balances outside the banks:

    (a) How much credit will ultimately be created?
    (b) By how much will total deposits have expanded?
    (c) What is the size of the bank deposits multiplier?

10. If the government reduces the size of its budget deficit, why might the money supply nevertheless increase more rapidly?

11. Why might the relationship between the demand for money and the rate of interest be an unstable one?

12. What effects will the following have on the equilibrium rate of interest? (You should consider which way the demand and/or supply curves of money shift.)

    (a) Banks find that they have a higher liquidity ratio than they need.
    (b) A rise in incomes.
    (c) A growing belief that interest rates will rise from their current level.

Log on to MyEconlab and complete the studyplan exercises for this chapter to see how much you have learnt and where you need to revise most. Make sure you access all the supporting textbook resources including the online workbook, newsblog, audio animations, guided solutions and ebook.

Additional case studies in the *Essentials of Economics* MyEconLab (www.pearsoned.co.uk/sloman)

10.1 Barter: its use in Russia in the 1990s. When barter was used as an alternative to money.

10.2 The attributes of money. What makes something, such as metal, paper or electronic records, suitable as money?

10.3 From coins to bank deposit money. This case traces the evolution of modern money.

10.4 Changes in the banking industry. This considers the changing face of the banking industry and asks whether bigger is better.

10.5 Are the days of cash numbered? Does the increased use of credit and debit cards and direct debits mean that cash will become obsolete?

10.6 Gresham's law. Historic examples of 'bad' money driving out 'good' money as people hoard the 'good' money.

10.7 German banking. This case compares the tradition of German banks with that of UK retail banks. Although the banks have become more similar in recent years, German banks have a much closer relationship with industry.

10.8 UK monetary aggregates. This case shows how money supply is measured using both UK measures and eurozone measures.

10.9 Making money grow. A light-hearted illustration of the process of credit creation.

Websites relevant to this chapter

Numbers and sections refer to websites listed in the Web appendix and hotlinked from this book's website at **www.pearsoned.co.uk/sloman**.

■ For news articles relevant to this chapter, see the *Economics News Articles* link from the book's website.

■ For general news on money, banking and prices, see websites in section A, and particularly A1–5, 7–9, 20–22, 25, 26, 31, 36. See also links to economic and financial news in A42.

■ For monetary and financial data (including data for money supply and interest rates), see section F and particularly F2. Note that you can link to central banks worldwide from site F17. See also the links in B1 or 2.

■ For information on the development of ideas, including information on classical, Keynesian, monetarist, new classical and new Keynesian thought, see C12, 18; see also links under *Methodology and History of Economic Thought* in C14, and links to economists in I4 and 17. See also sites I7 and 11 > *Economic Systems and Theories* > *History of Economic Thought*.

■ For links to sites on the role of money in the economy, see the *Financial Economics* sections in I4, 7, 11, 17.

■ For student resources relevant to this chapter, see sites C1–7, 9, 10, 12, 13, 19. See also '2nd floor – economic policy' in site D1. See also site D11 (the virtual bank of Biz/ed).

Web appendices

10.1 The money multiplier. This appendix shows how the money multiplier is calculated.

10.2 *ISLM* analysis. This appendix develops a model that brings together the goods and money markets in one diagram.

CHAPTER MAP

Inflation and unemployment

In the previous chapters we have considered some of the influences on aggregate demand and aggregate supply as well as the importance of money and the financial system. In this chapter we draw on this analysis to consider two major macroeconomic issues: unemployment and inflation.

We have seen that the economy's price level is determined by aggregate demand and supply. In this chapter we will consider what determines the rate of *increase* in prices. In other words, what determines the rate of inflation? For instance, can it be affected by the growth in money supply?

We then turn to unemployment: its nature and causes. We see that it is determined by aggregate demand and supply, but this time for labour rather than for goods and services.

Having looked at inflation and unemployment separately, we then see how they are related. A crucial element in this relationship is people's expectations of inflation. This is the topic for Section 11.5.

In recent years, central banks around the world have set targets for the rate of inflation. This has had a profound effect on people's expectations and also on the relationships between inflation and unemployment. We look at these effects in Section 11.6.

After studying this chapter, you should be able to answer the following questions:

- What are the causes of inflation?
- How do changes in money supply impact on aggregate demand?
- Do changes in aggregate demand affect just prices or both prices and national output?
- What are the causes of unemployment?
- What is the relationship between unemployment and inflation, and is the relationship a stable one?
- How does a policy of targeting a rate of inflation affect the relationship between inflation and unemployment?

11.1 INFLATION

Price levels and inflation rates

Inflation refers to rising price levels; deflation refers to falling price levels. The annual rate of inflation measures the annual percentage *increase* in prices. If the rate of inflation is negative, then prices are falling and we are effectively measuring the rate of deflation.

TC 14 p 266

Typically inflation relates to *consumer* prices. The government publishes a 'consumer prices index' (CPI) each month, and the annual rate of inflation is the percentage increase in that index over the previous 12 months.

A broader measure of inflation relates to the rate at which the prices of all domestically produced goods and services are changing. The price index used in this case is known as the **GDP deflator** or the domestic goods deflator. Figure 11.1 shows the annual rate of changes in the GDP deflator for the USA, Japan, the UK and France. As you can see, inflation was particularly severe in the mid-1970s, but rates have been relatively low in more recent years and indeed Japan has experienced falling prices.

You will find rates of inflation reported for a variety of goods and services. For example, indices are published for commodity prices, for food prices, for house prices (see Box 2.2 on pages 42–3), for import prices, for prices after taking taxes into account and so on. Their respective rates of inflation are simply their annual percentage increases. Likewise it is possible to give the rate of inflation of wage rates ('wage inflation').

Before we proceed, a word of caution: be careful not to confuse a rise or fall in the rate of *inflation* with a rise or fall in *prices*. An increase in the rate of inflation means a *faster* increase in prices. A fall in the rate of inflation means a *slower* increase in prices (but still an increase as long as the rate of inflation is positive).

> **Definition**
>
> **GDP deflator**
> The price index of all final domestically produced goods and services: i.e. all items that contribute towards GDP.

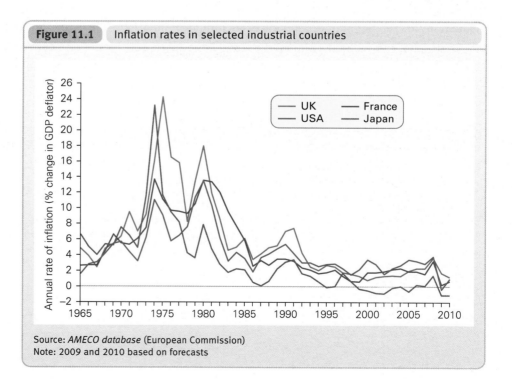

| **Figure 11.1** | Inflation rates in selected industrial countries |

Source: *AMECO database* (European Commission)
Note: 2009 and 2010 based on forecasts

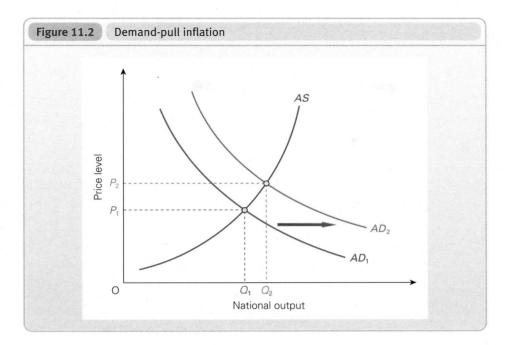

Figure 11.2   Demand-pull inflation

Introduction to the causes of inflation

Demand-pull inflation

Demand-pull inflation is caused by continuing rises in aggregate demand. In Figure 11.2, the *AD* curve shifts to the right (and continues doing so). Firms will respond to the rise in aggregate demand partly by raising prices and partly by increasing output (there is a move up along the *AS* curve). Just how much they raise prices depends on how much their costs rise as a result of increasing output. This in turn depends on how close actual output is to potential output. The less slack there is in the economy, the more will firms respond to a rise in demand by raising their prices. In other words, the steeper is the *AS* curve the larger is the increase in prices. We consider this in more detail in Section 11.2.

Demand-pull inflation is typically associated with a booming economy. Many economists therefore argue that it is the counterpart of demand-deficient unemployment. When the economy is in recession, demand-deficient unemployment will be high, but demand-pull inflation will be low. When, on the other hand, the economy is near the peak of the business cycle, demand-pull inflation will be high, but demand-deficient unemployment will be low.

Cost-push inflation

Cost-push inflation is associated with continuing rises in costs and hence continuing leftward (upward) shifts in the *AS* curve. Such shifts occur when costs of production rise *independently* of aggregate demand. If firms face a rise in costs, they will respond partly by raising prices and passing the costs on to the consumer, and partly by cutting back on production. This is illustrated in Figure 11.3. There is a leftward shift in the aggregate supply curve: from AS_1 to AS_2. This causes the price level to rise to P_2 and the level of output to *fall* to Q_2.

> **Definitions**
>
> **Demand-pull inflation**
> Inflation caused by persistent rises in aggregate demand.
>
> **Cost-push inflation**
> Inflation caused by persistent rises in costs of production (independently of demand).

> **Pause for thought**
>
> *If there is a general rise in costs of production across the country, does this necessarily mean that there is pure cost-push inflation?*

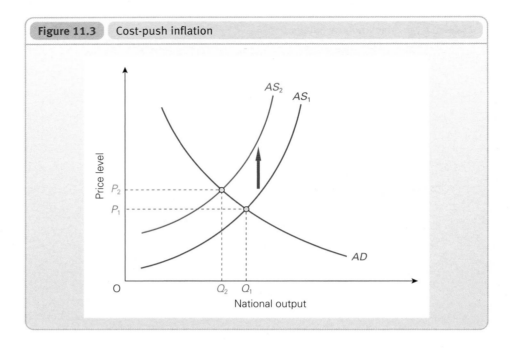

Figure 11.3   Cost-push inflation

Just how much firms raise prices and cut back on production depends on the shape of the aggregate demand curve. The less elastic the *AD* curve, the less sales will fall as a result of any price rise, and hence the more will firms be able to pass on the rise in their costs to consumers as higher prices.

Note that the effect on output and employment is the opposite of demand-pull inflation. With demand-pull inflation, output and hence employment tends to rise. With cost-push inflation, however, output and employment tend to fall.

It is important to distinguish between *single* shifts in the aggregate supply curve (known as 'supply shocks') and *continuing* shifts. If there is a single leftward shift in aggregate supply, there will be a single rise in the price level. For example, if the government raises the excise duty on oil, there will be a single rise in oil prices and hence in industry's fuel costs. This will cause *temporary* inflation while the price rise is passed on through the economy. Once this has occurred, prices will stabilise at the new level and the rate of inflation will fall back to zero again. If cost-push inflation is to continue over a number of years, therefore, the aggregate supply curve must *continually* shift to the left. If cost-push inflation is to *rise*, these shifts must get more rapid.

Rises in costs may originate from a number of different sources, such as trade unions pushing up wages, firms with monopoly power raising prices in order to increase their profits or increases in international commodity prices. With the process of globalisation and increased international competition, cost-push pressures have tended to decrease in recent years. One major exception has been the oil shocks that have occurred from time to time. For example, the near tripling of oil prices from $51 per barrel in January 2007 to $147 per barrel in July 2008 put upward pressure on costs and prices around the world.

The interaction of demand-pull and cost-push inflation

Demand-pull and cost-push inflation can occur together, since wage and price rises can be caused both by increases in aggregate demand and by independent

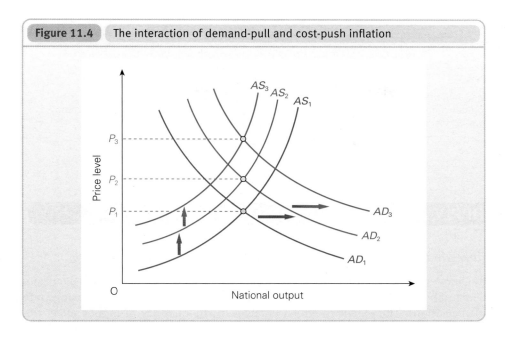

Figure 11.4 The interaction of demand-pull and cost-push inflation

causes pushing up costs. Even when an inflationary process *starts* as either demand-pull or cost-push, it is often difficult to separate the two. An initial cost-push inflation may encourage the government to expand aggregate demand to offset rises in unemployment. Alternatively, an initial demand-pull inflation may strengthen the power of certain groups, who then use this power to drive up costs. Either way, the result is likely to be continuing rightward shifts in the *AD* curve and leftward shifts in the *AS* curve. Prices will carry on rising. This is illustrated in Figure 11.4.

Expectations and inflation

Workers and firms take account of the *expected* rate of inflation when making decisions.

Imagine that a union and an employer are negotiating a wage increase. Let us assume that both sides expect a rate of inflation of 5 per cent. The union will be happy to receive a wage rise somewhat above 5 per cent. That way, the members would be getting a *real* rise in incomes. The employers will be happy to pay a wage rise somewhat below 5 per cent. After all, they can put their price up by approximately 5 per cent, knowing that their rivals will do the same. The actual wage rise that the two sides agree on will thus be somewhere around 5 per cent.

Now let us assume that the expected rate of inflation is 10 per cent. Both sides will now negotiate around this benchmark, with the outcome being somewhere round about 10 per cent.

Thus the higher the expected rate of inflation, the higher will be the level of pay settlements and price rises, and hence the higher will be the resulting actual rate of inflation.

In recent years the importance of expectations in explaining the actual rate of inflation has been increasingly recognised by economists. We examine this in Sections 11.4 and 11.5.

Recap

1. Demand-pull inflation occurs as a result of continuing increases in aggregate demand.

2. Cost-push inflation occurs when there are continuing increases in the costs of production independent of rises in aggregate demand. Single 'supply shocks'

will lead to one-off increases in prices but not to continuing inflation.

3. Expectations play a crucial role in determining the level of inflation. The higher people expect inflation to be, the higher it will be.

11.2 **MONEY SUPPLY, AGGREGATE DEMAND AND INFLATION**

How will changes in money supply affect spending and prices?

In Chapter 10 we saw that increases in the money supply could increase aggregate demand by exerting downward pressure on interest rates and on the exchange rate (depreciation). The extent to which changes in the quantity of money affect the level of aggregate demand is keenly debated, but so too is the impact of any change in aggregate demand on prices and GDP.

In the 1970s and 1980s, many economists were 'monetarists'. The most famous monetarist is Milton Friedman, who argues that inflation can be attributed entirely to increases in the money supply. The faster money supply expands, the higher will be the rate of inflation. New classical economists of today take a similar view. Excessive expansion of the money supply will lead simply to inflation. Keynesians, by contrast, see a much looser association between money and prices.

The debate can best be understood in terms of the **quantity theory of money**. The theory is simply that the level of prices in the economy depends on the quantity of money: the greater the supply of money, the higher will be the level of prices.

A development of the quantity theory is the *equation of exchange*. Focusing on this equation is the best way of understanding the debate over the relationship between money and prices.

The equation of exchange

The **equation of exchange** shows the relationship between the money value of spending and the money value of output (nominal GDP). This identity may be expressed as follows:

$$MV = PY$$

M is the supply of money in the economy (e.g. M4). *V* is its **velocity of circulation**. This is the number of times per year that money is spent on buying goods and services that have been produced in the economy that year (real GDP). *P* is the level of prices of domestically produced goods and services, expressed as an index, where the index is 1 in a chosen base year (e.g. 1990). Thus if prices today are double those in the base year, *P* is 2. *Y* is *real* national income (real GDP): in other words, the quantity of national output produced in that year measured in base-year prices.

PY is thus nominal GDP, i.e. GDP measured at current prices (see the appendix to Chapter 8). For example, if GDP at base-year

Pause for thought

If the money supply is cut by 10 per cent, what must happen to the velocity of circulation if there is no change in GDP at current prices?

prices (Y) is £1 trillion and the price index is 2, then GDP at current prices (PY) is £2 trillion.

MV is the total spending on the goods and services that make up GDP – in other words, (nominal) aggregate demand. For example, if money supply is £250 billion, and money, as it passes from one person to another, is spent on average four times a year on national output, then total spending (MV) is £1 trillion a year. But this too *must* equal GDP at current prices. The reason is that what is spent on output (by consumers, by firms on investment, by the government or by people abroad on our exports) must equal the value of goods produced (PY).

The equation of exchange (or 'quantity equation') is true by definition. MV is *necessarily* equal to PY because of the way the terms are defined. Thus a rise in MV *must* be accompanied by a rise in PY. What a change in M does to P, however, is a matter of debate. The controversy centres on the impact of changes in the money supply on aggregate demand and then on the impact of changes in aggregate demand on output.

Money supply and aggregate demand

The short run

Chapter 10 identified two ways in which changes in the money supply could affect aggregate demand: the interest-rate and exchange-rate transmission mechanisms. Taken together, the impact of an increase in the money supply can be summarised as follows:

1. A rise in money supply will lead to a fall in the rate of interest.
2. The fall in the rate of interest will lead to a rise in investment and other forms of borrowing. It will also lead to a fall in the exchange rate and hence a rise in exports and a fall in imports.
3. The rise in investment, and the rise in exports and fall in imports, will mean a rise in aggregate demand.

However, there is considerable debate over how these transmission mechanisms function.

How interest-rate-sensitive is money demand? The demand for money as a means of storing wealth (the assets motive) can be large and highly responsive to changes in interest rates on alternative assets. Indeed, large sums of money move around the money market as firms and financial institutions respond to and anticipate changes in interest rates. Thus, with an increase in money supply, only a relatively small fall in interest rates on bonds and other assets may be necessary to persuade people to hold all the extra money in bank accounts, thereby greatly slowing down the average speed at which money circulates. The fall in V may virtually offset the rise in M.

In other words, the more sensitive is the demand for money to changes in the rate of interest, the less impact changes in money supply have on aggregate demand.

How stable is the money demand function? Another criticism is that the demand for money is unstable. People hold speculative balances of money when they antici-pate that the prices of other assets, such as shares, bonds and bills, will fall (and hence the rate of return or interest on these assets will rise).

There are many factors that could affect such expectations, such as changes in foreign interest rates, changes in exchange rates, statements of government inten-tions on economic policy, good or bad industrial news, or newly published figures on inflation or money supply. With an unstable demand for money, it is difficult to predict the effect of a change in money supply on interest rates and so aggregate demand.

It is largely for this reason that most central banks today generally prefer to control interest rates directly, rather than indirectly by controlling the money supply. We examine the conduct of monetary policy in Chapter 12.

How interest-rate-sensitive is spending? The problem here is that investment may be insensitive to changes in interest rates. Businesses are more likely to be influenced in their decision to invest by predictions of the future buoyancy of markets. Interest rates do have *some* effect on businesses' investment decisions, but the effect is unpredictable, depending on the confidence of investors.

Where interest rates are likely to have a stronger effect on spending is via mortgages. If interest rates go up, and mortgage rates follow suit, people will suddenly be faced with higher monthly repayments (debt servicing costs) and will therefore have to cut down their expenditure on goods and services (see pages 244–7 for a discussion on the impact of debt servicing on household spending).

How interest-rate-sensitive is the exchange rate? Also the amount that the exchange rate will depreciate is uncertain, since exchange rate movements, as we shall see in Chapter 14, depend crucially on expectations about trade prospects and about future world interest rate movements. Thus the effects on imports and exports are also uncertain.

To summarise: the effects on total spending of a change in the money supply *might* be quite strong, but they could be weak. In other words, the effects are highly unpredictable.

$$M\uparrow \rightarrow V\downarrow \ (?) \rightarrow MV?$$

Keynesians use these arguments to criticise the use of monetary policy as a means of managing aggregate demand.

The long run

In the long run, there is a stronger link between money supply and aggregate demand. In fact, monetarists claim that in the long run V is determined *totally independently* of the money supply (M). Thus an increase in M will leave V unaffected and hence will directly increase expenditure (MV):

$$M\uparrow \rightarrow M\bar{V}\uparrow$$

> **Definition**
>
> **Exogenous variable**
> A variable whose value is determined independently of the model of which it is part.

where the bar over the V term means that it is **exogenously determined**: i.e. determined *independently* of M. But why do they claim this?

If money supply increases over the longer term, people will have more money than they require to hold. They will spend this surplus. Much of this spending will go on goods and services, thereby directly increasing aggregate demand.

The theoretical underpinning for this is given by the *theory of portfolio balance*. People have a number of ways of holding their wealth. They can hold it as money, or as financial assets such as bills, bonds and shares, or as physical assets such as houses, cars and televisions. In other words, people hold a whole portfolio of assets of varying degrees of liquidity – from cash to central heating.

If money supply expands, people will find themselves holding more money than they require: their portfolios are 'unnecessarily liquid'. Some of this money will be used to purchase financial assets and some, possibly after a period of time, to purchase *goods and services*. As more assets are purchased, this will drive up their price. This will effectively reduce their 'yield'. For bonds and other *financial* assets, this means a reduction in their rate of interest. For goods and services, it means an increase in their price relative to their usefulness.

The process will stop when a balance has been restored in people's portfolios. In the meantime, there will have been extra consumption and hence an increase in aggregate demand.

Inflation and changes in aggregate demand

In Section 11.1 we introduced the idea of demand-pull inflation: inflation caused by increases in aggregate demand. But, what impact would we expect changes in aggregate demand to have on prices? Will levels of national output change too?

Assume that there is a rise in aggregate demand. This could be as a result of an increase in money supply as described above (MV rises). The new classical and monetarist position (at least in the long run) is that the result will simply be a rise in prices (P). In contrast, the Keynesian position is that there will also (or even solely) be a rise in national output (Y).

The debate concerning the impact of changes in aggregate demand on prices and output can best be understood in terms of the nature of the aggregate supply (AS) curve. We will start with the short-run AS curve and then look at the long-run curve.

The short-run aggregate supply curve

Most economists argue that aggregate supply is relatively elastic in the short run, except when the economy is operating close to or above potential output (see Figure 11.5(a)). As we saw in Section 9.1, this is because wages and many other input prices tend to be constant, or at least 'sticky', in the short term. In other words, national output (Y) (i.e. real GDP) is variable with respect to changes in aggregate demand.

In other words, national output (Y) (i.e. real GDP) is variable with respect to changes in aggregate demand. A rise in nominal aggregate demand (i.e. a rise in MV) will lead to a rise in Y. Conversely, a policy of restricting aggregate demand is likely to reduce Y as well as P.

Confidence also plays a part. A rise in aggregate demand may encourage firms to produce more in the confidence that they will sell the higher output. A fall in aggregate demand, however, may lead to a decline in confidence. Rather than continuing with current levels of production in the hope that demand will pick up, firms may reduce output and lay off workers.

The long-run aggregate supply curve

A vertical long-run AS curve. Many economists argue that the long-run AS curve is vertical at the potential level of GDP (Y_P): see Figure 11.5(b). New classical and monetarist economists, and some moderate Keynesian economists (the 'new Keynesians') take this position. Any rise in nominal aggregate demand would lead simply to a rise in prices and no long-term increase in output at all. Long-term increases in output could occur only through rightward shifts in this vertical AS curve, in other words through increases in potential output. To achieve this, governments should focus on supply-side policy, such as policies which help foster technological progress (see Chapter 9).

BOX 11.1 ⬛ **HYPERINFLATION**

When prices go crazy: is it the money supply?

In recent years in the UK, along with most other countries of the world, we have come to expect relatively stable prices (see Figure 11.1). If the rate of inflation were to rise to anywhere near the levels reached in the mid-1970s (24 per cent) or the early 1980s (18 per cent), it would be looked upon as a clear sign of economic failure.

But such rates are mild compared with those experienced by many other countries in the past. Inflation in Brazil peaked at 1200 per cent in 1993, in Russia at 2500 per cent in 1992 and in Ukraine at 10 000 per cent in 1993. But even these cases of hyperinflation are mild compared with those experienced by certain European countries in the early 1920s and by Serbia in the 1990s and Zimbabwe in recent years.

Germany 1921–3

Several countries experienced hyperinflation after the First World War. In Austria and Hungary prices were several thousand times their pre-war level. In Poland they were over 2 million times higher, and in the USSR several billion times higher.

But even these staggering rates of inflation seem insignificant beside those of Germany. Following the chaos of the war, the German government resorted to printing money, not only to meet its domestic spending requirements in rebuilding a war-ravaged economy, but also to finance the crippling war reparations imposed on it by the allies in the Treaty of Versailles.

From mid-1921 the rate of monetary increase soared and inflation soared with it. By autumn 1923 the annual rate of inflation had reached a mind-boggling 7 000 000 000 000 per cent! As price increases accelerated, people became reluctant to accept money: before they knew it, the money would be worthless. People thus rushed to spend their money as quickly as possible. But this in turn further drove up prices.

For many Germans the effect was devastating. People's life savings were wiped out. Others whose wages were not quickly adjusted found their real incomes plummeting. Many were thrown out of work as businesses, especially those with money assets, went bankrupt. Poverty and destitution were widespread.

By the end of 1923 the German currency was literally worthless. In 1924, therefore, it was replaced by a new currency – one whose supply was kept tightly controlled by the government.

Serbia and Montenegro 1993–5

After the break-up of Yugoslavia in 1992, the economy of the remaining part of Yugoslavia (Serbia and Montenegro) collapsed. The government relied more and more on printing money to finance public expenditure. Prices soared.

The government attempted to control the inflation by imposing price controls. But these simply made

production unprofitable and output fell further. The economy nosedived. Unemployment exceeded 30 per cent.

In October 1993, the government created a new currency, the new dinar, worth one million old dinars. In other words, six zeros were knocked off the currency. But this did not solve the problem. Between October 1993 and January 1994, prices rose by 5 quadrillion (5×10^{15}) per cent. Normal life could not function. Shops ran out of produce; savings were wiped out; barter replaced normal market activity.

Many Yugoslavian businesses refused to take the Yugoslavian currency, and the German Deutsche Mark effectively became the currency of Yugoslavia. But government organisations, government employees and pensioners still got paid in Yugoslavian dinars so there was still an active exchange in dinars. On November 12, 1993 the exchange rate was 1 DM = 1 million new dinars. . . . By December 15th it was 1 DM = 3.7 billion new dinars. The average *daily* rate of inflation was *nearly 100 percent*. At the end of December the exchange rate was 1 DM = 3 trillion new dinars.[a]

(a) Yugoslavian banknote (1994)

(b) Zimbabwean banknote (2008)

----

[a]   Thayer Watkins *The Worst Episode of Hyperinflation in History: Yugoslavia 1993–94* (www.rogershermansociety.org/ yugoslavia.htm)

At the beginning of January 1994 a 'new new dinar' was introduced, worth 1 billion new dinars. On the 24 January this was replaced by a 'novi dinar' pegged 1 to 1 against the Deutsche Mark. This was worth approximately 13 million new new dinars. The novi dinar remained pegged to the Deutsche Mark and inflation was quickly eliminated.

Zimbabwe 2004–8

The most recent example of hyperinflation is that in Zimbabwe. By mid-2008, the official annual inflation had reached over 11 million per cent (see table). Unofficially, it was closer to 20 million per cent.

Inflation in Zimbabwe

	Official rate of inflation (% annual rate)
2000	57
2001	105
2002	174
2003	585
2004	158
2005	503
2006 Q1	773
2006 Q2	1 147
2006 Q3	1 071
2006 Q4	1 164
2007 Q1	1 883
2007 Q2	5 394
2007 Q3	7 415
2007 Q4	40 911
2008 Q1	165 000
2008 Q2	11 250 000
2008 Q3	231 000 000
2008 Q4	6.5×10^{108}

Sources: *International Financial Statistics* (IMF) and various newspaper sources

The economy had been in turmoil for some time as white-owned farms were seized as part of the policy of land redistribution, squatter settlements in Harare were demolished and many rural homes too were destroyed. As with Serbia, the government printed money to finance its expenditure.

As inflation soared, people rushed to spend their money before inflation made it virtually worthless. Producers, on the other hand, found that the money they received could not cover their costs. Production fell and businesses closed. There was little to buy in the shops. There were chronic shortages of food, medicine and other basics, and electricity and running water were frequently cut. Unemployment was over 80 per cent.

'I just come here to keep my job', said the cashier at a TM supermarket in Harare, where a tin of baked beans cost – at least for the next few hours – a mere 256bn Zimbabwe dollars (worth about US$1 at the current exchange rate). It's just ridiculous. We put the prices up several times a day. The salary I was paid at the start of this month cannot even pay for my bus fare here this morning. I am struggling.'

Harare is fast becoming a city of unemployed, impoverished zillionaires – struggling to spend thick wads of banknotes in empty supermarkets before the cash becomes worthless, and increasingly dependent on funds sent home by the millions of Zimbabweans who have already fled abroad.

In the subdued, seemingly half-empty capital, people wait in long queues outside banks to withdraw a maximum of a 100bn dollars a day. In bars, the price of beer goes up between rounds. Many people are reduced to eating one meal a day. Adults leave hungry children at home and walk for hours to work because they cannot afford the bus fare, while the newspapers advertise lotto prizes of a quadrillion dollars.[b]

Again, as with Serbia, the response of the central bank was to introduce a 'new' currency with fewer zeros. In July 2008, the government had introduced the 100 billion dollar note (with an issue and expiry date, and hence termed a 'cheque' – see picture). On 1 August, 10 zeros were knocked off the currency, making one of the new 100 billion dollar notes worth only 10 new Zimbabwean dollars – initially about I US dollar, but within a few days a tiny fraction of a US cent. In the same month the central bank, the Reserve Bank of Zimbabwe (RBZ), abandoned issuing inflation statistics.

A report released by the Cato Institute in June 2008 – *Zimbabwe, From Hyperinflation to Growth* – said the RBZ's money machine was the source of the hyperinflation. 'The government spends, and the RBZ finances the spending by printing money. The RBZ has no ability, in practice, to resist the government's demands for cash . . . To stop hyperinflation, Zimbabwe needs to immediately adopt a different monetary system', the report said.[c]

In January 2009, the RBZ issued the world's first 100 trillion dollar note. Inflation at the time was estimated to be 6.5 quindecillion novemdecillion per cent – 65 followed by 107 zeros! People, not surprisingly, if they could, were trading in other currencies, such as the US dollar or the South African rand.

---

[b] BBC News
   (http://news.bbc.co.uk/1/hi/world/africa/7528974.stm)
[c] http://allafrica.com/stories/200901220636.html

The RBZ had already endorsed semi-official dollarisation in September 2008 by introducing 'Foreign Exchange Licensed Warehouses and Shops' when some 1000 retail outlets and 250 wholesalers were permitted to trade in foreign currency.

In a statement released earlier in January 2009, the Zimbabwe Congress of Trade Unions (ZCTU) demanded that 'all workers should be paid in foreign currency, given the fact that shops are now selling their goods in foreign currency – even those that have not been licensed to do so'.[d]

With the incoming power-sharing Unity Government in February 2009, the now virtually worthless Zimbabwe dollar was suspended. Instead, multiple currencies were used, including the US dollar, the South African rand and the Botswana pula. Inflation, now measured in US dollar prices, was eliminated, with prices actually falling by 10 per cent between February and May 2009. Later in

the year, prices rose again, but annual inflation was now only in low single figures.

Issuing a new Zimbabwe dollar rigidly pegged to the South African rand would have been an alternative to complete abandonment of the domestic currency. This would be similar to the policy adopted by Serbia in 1994. Also, this policy would not be new to the region; the currencies of Namibia, Lesotho and Swaziland are pegged to the rand.

When confronted by hyperinflation, governments frequently seek to blame anyone but themselves. The Serbian government in 1994 blamed international sanctions against the country. The Zimbabwean government in 2008 did exactly the same.

1. *Would restricting the growth in the money supply be enough to cure hyperinflation?*
2. *Look through the costs of inflation identified in Case Study 11.5 in MyEconLab and assess how serious each of them is likely to be in a period of hyperinflation.*

---

[d] ibid.

But why do these economists argue that the curve is vertical? They justify this by focusing on the *interdependence of markets*. Assume initially that the economy is operating at the potential level of GDP (Y_P). Now assume that there is an increase in demand, such as that following an increase in money supply. The increase in aggregate demand will initially lead firms to raise both prices and output, for the reasons we gave above: the short-run aggregate supply curve is upward sloping. There is a movement from point *a* to point *b* in Figure 11.6. GDP rises to Y_2.

However, as raw material and intermediate goods producers raise their prices, so this will raise the costs of production of firms using these inputs. A rise in the price of steel will raise the costs of producing cars and washing machines. At the same time, workers, seeing the prices of goods rising, will demand higher wages. Firms will be relatively willing to grant these wage demands, given that they are experiencing a buoyant demand from their customers. The effect of all this is to raise firms' *costs*, and hence their prices. As prices rise for any given level of output, so the short-run *AS* curve will shift upward. This is shown by a move to $AS_{2\ (short\ run)}$ in Figure 11.6. The economy moves from point *b* to point *c*. Thus GDP can only temporarily rise above the potential level (Y_P).

The long-run effect, therefore, of a rise in aggregate demand from AD_1 to AD_2 (such as that from an increase in money supply) is a movement from point *a* to point *c*. The long-run aggregate supply curve passes through these two points. It is vertical at the potential level of output. A rise in aggregate demand will therefore have no long-run effect on output. The entire effect will be felt in terms of higher prices.

New classical economists go one step further. They assume that markets are very flexible, and that therefore the effects of higher costs will be passed through into higher prices virtually instantly. What is more, firms will anticipate this and hence take it into account *now*. For them, therefore, the *short*-run aggregate supply curve is vertical also.

An upward-sloping long-run AS curve. Some Keynesian economists, however, argue that the long-run *AS* curve is upward sloping, not vertical. Indeed, it may be even shallower than the short-run curve. For them, potential output is affected by changes in aggregate demand.

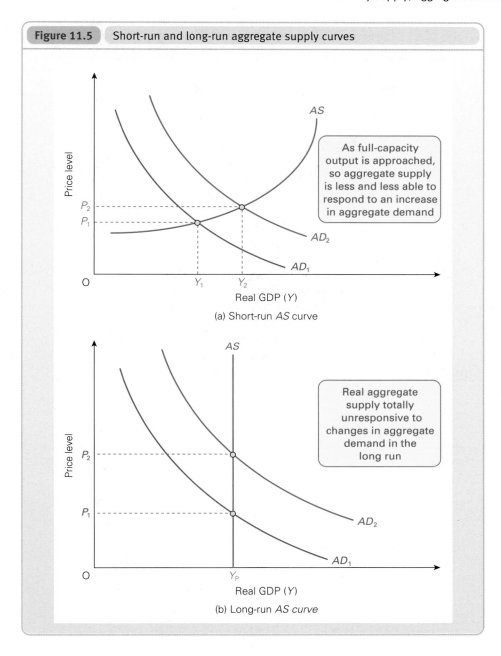

Figure 11.5   Short-run and long-run aggregate supply curves

As full-capacity output is approached, so aggregate supply is less and less able to respond to an increase in aggregate demand

(a) Short-run *AS* curve

Real aggregate supply totally unresponsive to changes in aggregate demand in the long run

(b) Long-run *AS curve*

We saw in Chapter 9 that investment is crucial to long-run economic growth. The argument here is that with a rise in demand, firms may be encouraged to invest in new plant and machinery. This increase in the stock of capital will increase the *capacity* of the economy to produce. In other words, the increase in aggregate demand will increase potential output. The result is that firms may well be able to increase output significantly in the long run with little or no increase in their prices. Their long-run *MC* curves are much flatter than their short-run *MC* curves.

Again assume initially that output is at the potential level. In Figure 11.7 this is shown as Y_{P1}. Aggregate demand then increases to AD_2. Equilibrium moves to point *b* with GDP at Y_2. The resulting increased investment shifts the short-run *AS* curve to the right. Equilibrium moves from point *b* to *d*. Point *d* is now at the new potential level of output, Y_{P2}. The long-run *AS* curve thus joins points *a* and *d*.

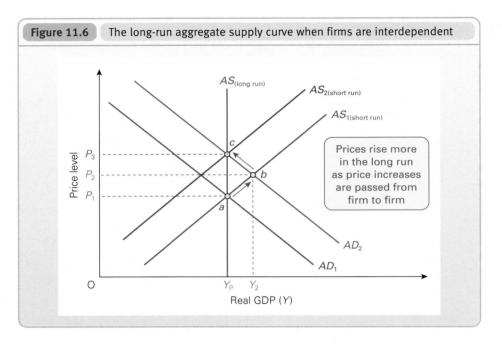

Figure 11.6   The long-run aggregate supply curve when firms are interdependent

Prices rise more in the long run as price increases are passed from firm to firm

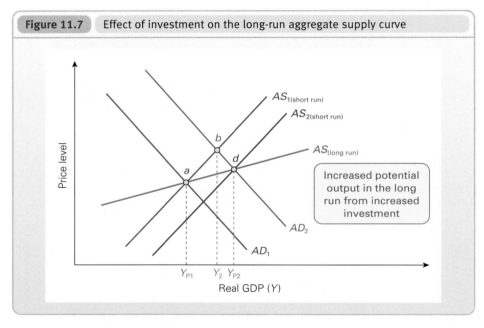

Figure 11.7   Effect of investment on the long-run aggregate supply curve

Increased potential output in the long run from increased investment

Pause for thought

If a shift in the aggregate demand curve from AD₁ to AD₂ in Figure 11.7 causes a movement from point a to point d in the long run, will a shift in the aggregate demand curve from AD₁ to AD₂ cause a movement from point d back to point a in the long run?

The way the diagram is drawn, the long-run *AS* curve is more elastic than the short-run curve. There is a relatively large increase in output and a relatively small increase in price. If the rise in costs had been more substantial, curve $AS_{2(\text{short run})}$ could be above curve $AS_{1(\text{short run})}$. In this case, although the long-run *AS* curve would still be upward sloping, it would be steeper than the short-run curves: point *d* would be above point *b*.

The long-run *AS* curve will be steeper if the extra investment causes significant shortages of materials, machinery or labour.

This is more likely when the economy is already operating near its full-capacity output. It will be flatter, and possibly even downward sloping, if the investment involves the introduction of new cost-reducing technology.

Recap

1. The quantity equation $MV = PY$ can be used to analyse the possible relationships between money and prices.

2. In the short run, the velocity of circulation (V) may vary inversely, but unpredictably, with the money supply (M). The reason is that changes in money supply will have unpredictable and possibly rather weak effects on interest rates, and, similarly, changes in interest rates will have unpredictable and probably rather weak effects on aggregate demand. Thus spending (MV) will change by possibly only a small and rather unpredictable amount.

3. If nominal aggregate demand (MV) does change, then in the short run it is likely to affect real GDP (Y) according to the degree of slack in the economy. The short-run aggregate supply curve tends to be relatively elastic (except when the economy is operating close to or above potential output). This is because both wage rates and prices tend to be relatively sticky.

4. In the long run, according to many economists, the aggregate supply curve is vertical because price increases from any rise in aggregate demand tend to be passed on from one firm to another and feed into wage increases.

5. Some argue, however, that the long-run aggregate supply curve may be upward sloping. If a sustained increase in demand leads to increased investment, this can have the effect of shifting the short-run aggregate supply curve to the right and making the long-run curve upward sloping, not vertical.

UNEMPLOYMENT   11.3

If people want to consume more goods, why are so many people out of work?

Unemployment fluctuates with the business cycle. In recessions, such as those experienced by most countries in the early 1980s, early 1990s and the early and late 2000s, unemployment tends to rise. In boom years, such as the late 1980s, late 1990s and mid-2000s, it tends to fall. Figure 11.8 shows these cyclical movements in unemployment for selected countries.

As well as experiencing fluctuations in unemployment, most countries have experienced long-term changes in average unemployment rates. This is illustrated in Table 11.1, which shows average unemployment rates in the UK, France, the USA and Japan by decade from the 1960s. Average unemployment rates in the 1980s

Table 11.1	Average unemployment by decade (%)				
	1960–9	**1970–9**	**1980–9**	**1990–9**	**2000–9**
UK	1.6	3.5	9.5	8.0	5.4
France	1.7	3.8	8.5	10.5	8.8
USA	4.8	6.2	7.3	5.7	5.4
Japan	1.3	1.7	2.5	3.1	4.6

Source: Based on data in *European Economy* (European Commission)

BOX 11.2   THE COSTS OF UNEMPLOYMENT

Is it just the unemployed who suffer?

The most obvious cost of unemployment is to the *unemployed themselves*. There is the direct financial cost of the loss in their earnings, measured as the difference between their previous wage and their unemployment benefit. Then there are the personal costs of being unemployed. The longer people are unemployed, the more dispirited they may become. Their self-esteem is likely to fall, and they are more likely to succumb to stress-related illness.

Then there are the costs to the *family and friends* of the unemployed. Personal relations can become strained, and there may be an increase in domestic violence and the number of families splitting up.

Then there are the *broader costs to the economy*. Unemployment benefits are a cost borne by taxpayers. There may also have to be extra public spending on benefit offices, social services, health care and the police. What is more, unemployment represents a loss of output. In other words, actual output is below potential output. Apart from the lack of income to the unemployed themselves, this under-utilisation of resources leads to lower incomes for other people too:

■ The government loses tax revenues, since the unemployed pay no income tax and national insurance, and, given that the unemployed spend less, they pay less VAT and excise duties.
■ Firms lose the profits that could have been made, had there been full employment.
■ Other workers lose any additional wages they could have earned from the higher national output.

What is more, the longer people remain unemployed, the more deskilled they tend to become. In other words, their stock of human capital declines. As we saw in Chapter 9, investment in human capital is considered by many as an important influence on an economy's potential output. Therefore, long-term unemployment reduces *potential* as well as actual income.

Finally there is some evidence that higher unemployment leads to increased *crime and vandalism*. This obviously imposes a cost on the sufferers.

The costs of unemployment are to some extent offset by benefits. If workers voluntarily quit their jobs to look for better ones, then they must reckon that the benefits of a better job more than compensate for their temporary loss of income. From the nation's point of view, a workforce that is prepared to quit jobs and spend a short time unemployed will be a more adaptable, more mobile workforce – one that is responsive to changing economic circumstances. Such a workforce will lead to greater allocative efficiency in the short run and more rapid economic growth over the longer run.

Long-term involuntary unemployment is quite another matter. The costs clearly outweigh any benefits, both for the individuals concerned and for the economy as a whole. A demotivated, deskilled pool of long-term unemployed is a serious economic and social problem.

 How might an economist set about measuring the various costs of unemployment to family, friends and society at large?

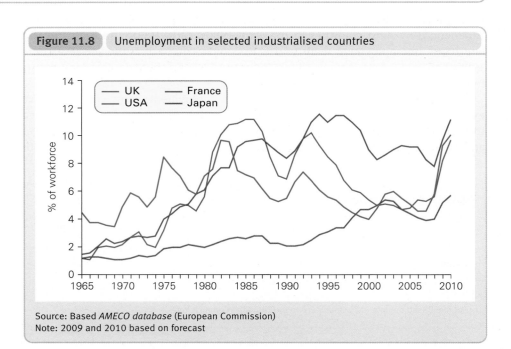

| Figure 11.8 | Unemployment in selected industrialised countries |

Source: Based *AMECO database* (European Commission)
Note: 2009 and 2010 based on forecast

and 1990s were higher than in the 1970s, and average rates in the 1970s were, in turn, higher than in the 1960s. The late 1990s and early 2000s saw a long-term fall in unemployment in many countries, though on the back of very weak economic growth Japan was a notable exception.

The meaning of 'unemployment'

Unemployment can be expressed either as a number (e.g. 2.5 million) or as a percentage (e.g. 10 per cent). But just who should be included in the statistics? Should it be everyone without a job? The answer is clearly no, since we would not want to include children and pensioners. We would probably also want to exclude those who were not looking for work, such as parents choosing to stay at home to look after children.

The most usual definition that economists use for the **number unemployed** is: *those of working age who are without work, but who are available for work at current wage rates*. If the figure is to be expressed as a percentage, then it is a percentage of the total **labour force**. The labour force is defined as: *those in employment (including the self-employed, those in the armed forces and those on government training schemes) plus those unemployed*. Thus if 30 million people were employed and 3 million people were unemployed, the **unemployment rate** would be:

$$\frac{3}{30 + 3} \times 100 = 9.1\%$$

Official measures of unemployment

Claimant unemployment

Two common measures of unemployment are used in official statistics. The first is **claimant unemployment**. This is simply a measure of all those in receipt of unemployment-related benefits. In the UK claimants receive the 'job seeker's allowance'.

Claimant statistics have the advantage of being very easy to collect. However, they exclude all those of working age available for work at current wage rates, but who are *not* eligible for benefits. If the government changes the eligibility conditions so that fewer people are now eligible, this will reduce the number of claimants and hence the official number unemployed, even if there has been no change in the numbers with or without work.

Standardised unemployment rates

Recognising the weaknesses of the claimant statistics, the UK government since 1998 has used the **standardised unemployment rate** as the main measure of unemployment. This is the measure used by the International Labour Organization (ILO) and the Organisation for Economic Co-operation and Development (OECD), two international organisations that publish unemployment statistics for many countries.

In this measure, the unemployed are defined as people of working age who are without work, available to start work within two weeks and *actively seeking employment* or waiting to take up an appointment. The figures are compiled from the results of national labour force surveys. In the UK the labour force survey is conducted quarterly.

But is the standardised unemployment rate likely to be higher or lower than the claimant unemployment rate? The standardised rate is likely to be higher to the

---

Definitions

Number unemployed (economist's definition)
Those of working age who are without work, but who are available for work at current wage rates.

Labour force
The number employed plus the number unemployed.

Unemployment rate
The number unemployed expressed as a percentage of the labour force.

Claimant unemployment
Those in receipt of unemployment-related benefits.

Standardised unemployment rate
The measure of the unemployment rate used by the ILO and OECD. The unemployed are defined as persons of working age who are without work, available for work and actively seeking employment.

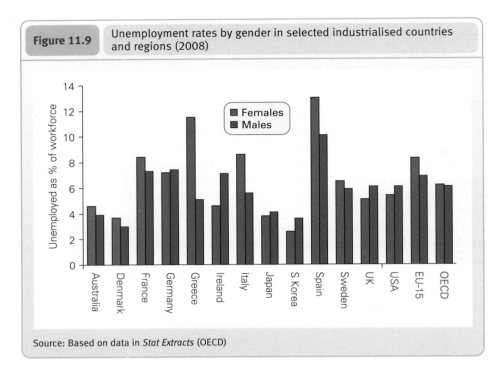

Figure 11.9 Unemployment rates by gender in selected industrialised countries and regions (2008)

Source: Based on data in *Stat Extracts* (OECD)

extent that it includes people seeking work who are nevertheless not entitled to claim benefits, but lower to the extent that it excludes those who are claiming benefits and yet who are not actively seeking work. Clearly, the tougher the benefit regulations, the lower the claimant rate will be relative to the standardised rate. In the three months to July 2009 the standardised unemployment rate in the UK was estimated at 2.47 million (7.9 per cent) while the claimant count rate in August 2009 was measured at 1.61 million (5.0 per cent).

Unemployment rates vary enormously between countries, regions within countries and also by age and gender. Evidence from the EU is examined in Case Study 11.8 in MyEconLab. In most countries, female unemployment is higher than male, as you can see from Figure 11.9. These differences reflect such things as social attitudes, education and unemployment rates in industries employing predominantly women or men. In countries, such as the UK, where male unemployment rates are higher, this is partly due to the decline of various industries, such as mining and heavy manufacturing, which employ mainly men.

Differences by gender have tended to narrow, however, over time. In 1997 the EU-15[1] male unemployment rate was 2½ percentage points higher than the female rate, but by 2008 it was less than 1 percentage point higher than the female rate.

Also, unemployment of those under 25 tends to be higher than those in other age groups. For example, in 2007 the EU-15 unemployment rate for those under 25 was 14.9 per cent compared with a rate of 7.0 per cent average for all ages. Partly this reflects the lack of training opportunities in many countries. In Germany where there is substantial training for school leavers, the rates were 11.7 and 8.6 per cent respectively – a much smaller difference.

---

[1] EU-15 refers to the 15 countries which were members of the EU prior to 2004.

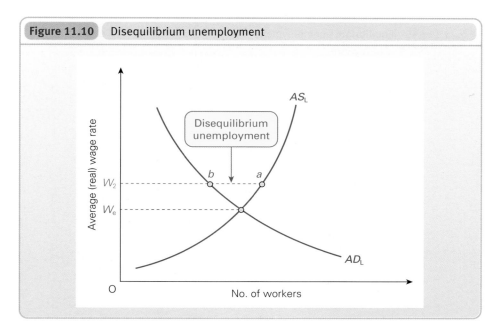

Figure 11.10   Disequilibrium unemployment

Unemployment and the labour market

We now turn to the causes of unemployment. These causes fall into two broad categories: *equilibrium* unemployment and *disequilibrium* unemployment. To make clear the distinction between the two, it is necessary to look at how the labour market works.

Figure 11.10 shows the aggregate demand for labour and the aggregate supply of labour: that is, the total demand and supply of labour in the whole economy. The *real* average wage rate is plotted on the vertical axis. This is the average wage rate expressed in terms of its purchasing power: in other words, after taking prices into account.

The **aggregate supply of labour curve** (AS_L) shows the number of workers *willing to accept jobs* at each real wage rate. This curve is relatively inelastic, since the size of the workforce at any one time cannot change significantly. Nevertheless it is not totally inelastic because (a) a higher wage rate will encourage some people to enter the labour market (e.g. parents raising children), and (b) the unemployed will be more willing to accept job offers rather than continuing to search for a better-paid job.

The **aggregate demand for labour curve** (AD_L) slopes downwards. The higher the real wage rate, the more will firms attempt to economise on labour and to substitute other factors of production for labour.

The labour market is in equilibrium at a wage of W_e, where the demand for labour equals the supply. If the wage rate were above W_e, the labour market would be in a state of disequilibrium. At a wage rate of W_1, there is an excess supply of labour of $a - b$. This is called **disequilibrium unemployment**.

For disequilibrium unemployment to occur, two conditions must hold:

■ The aggregate supply of labour must exceed the aggregate demand.
■ There must be a 'stickiness' in wages. In other words, the wage rate must not immediately fall to W_e.

TC 3
p 11

Definitions

Aggregate supply of labour curve
A curve showing the total number of people willing and able to work at different average real wage rates.

Aggregate demand for labour curve
A curve showing the total demand for labour in the economy at different average real wage rates.

Disequilibrium unemployment
Unemployment resulting from real wages in the economy being above the equilibrium level.

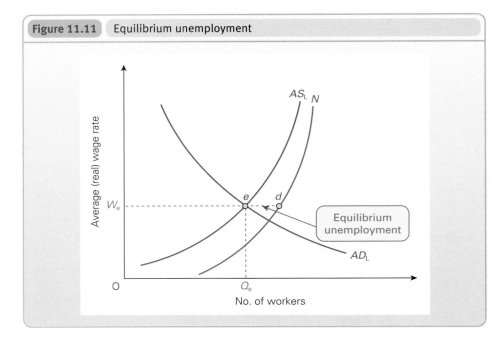

Figure 11.11 Equilibrium unemployment

Even when the labour market *is* in equilibrium, however, not everyone looking for work will be employed. Some people will hold out, hoping to find a better job. The curve N in Figure 11.11 shows the total number in the labour force. The horizontal difference between it and the aggregate supply of labour curve (AS_L) represents the excess of people looking for work over those actually willing to accept jobs. Q_e represents the equilibrium level of employment and the distance $d - e$ represents the **equilibrium level of unemployment**. This is sometimes known as the *natural level of unemployment*.

TC 5
p 40

Types of disequilibrium unemployment

There are three possible causes of disequilibrium unemployment.

Real-wage unemployment

Real-wage unemployment is where trade unions use their monopoly power to drive wages above the market-clearing level. In Figure 11.10, the wage rate is driven up above W_e. Excessive real wage rates were blamed by the Thatcher and Major governments for the high unemployment of the 1980s and 1990s. The possibility of higher real-wage unemployment was also one of the reasons for their rejection of a national minimum wage.

Even though unions have the power to drive up wages in some industries, their power to do so has waned in recent years. Labour markets have become more flexible (see Case Study 6.2 in MyEconLab). What is more, the process of globalisation has meant that many firms face intense competition from rivals in China, India and many other countries. This makes it impossible for them to concede large pay increases. In many cases, they can simply use labour in other countries if domestic labour is too expensive. For example, many firms employ call-centre workers in India, where wages are much lower.

Pause for thought

As far as the national minimum wage is concerned, evidence from the UK suggests that the rate has not been high enough to have significant adverse effects on employment (see Box 6.4 on pages 178–9).

Demand-deficient or cyclical unemployment

Demand-deficient or **cyclical unemployment** is associated with recessions. As the economy moves into recession, consumer demand falls. Firms find that they are unable to sell their current level of output. For a time they may be prepared to build up stocks of unsold goods, but sooner or later they will start to cut back on production and cut back on the amount of labour they employ. In Figure 11.10 the AD_L curve shifts to the left. The deeper the recession becomes and the longer it lasts, the higher will demand-deficient unemployment become.

But if there is surplus labour, why do real wages not fall so as to eliminate the surplus? There are two main reasons, both of which help to explain why real wage rates did not fall during the recessions of the early 1980s and early 1990s.

Efficiency wages. The argument here is that wage rates fulfil two functions. The first is the traditional one of balancing the demand and supply of labour. The second is that of motivating workers. If real wage rates are reduced when there is a surplus of labour, then those workers already in employment may become dispirited and work less hard. If, on the other hand, firms keep wage rates up, then by maintaining a well-motivated workforce, by cutting down on labour turnover and by finding it easier to attract well-qualified labour, firms may find their costs are reduced: a higher real wage is thus more profitable for them. The maximum-profit real wage rate (the **efficiency wage rate**) is likely to be above the market-clearing real wage rate (see page 172). Demand-deficient unemployment is likely to persist.

Insider power. If those still in employment (the insiders) are members of unions, while those out of work (the outsiders) are not, or if the insiders have special skills or knowledge that give them bargaining power with employers, while the outsiders have no influence, then there is no mechanism whereby the surplus labour – the outsiders – can drive down the real wage rate and eliminate the demand-deficient unemployment.

Even if real wages *did* fall, it may not solve the problem of demand-deficient unemployment. In fact, it might even make the problem worse. The reason is that this general cut in wages throughout the economy would reduce workers' incomes and hence reduce their *consumption of goods*. As the aggregate demand for goods fell, there would be a further reduction in demand for labour: the aggregate demand for labour curve would shift further to the left. The fall in wages would be 'chasing' a leftward-shifting AD_L curve. As the wage fell towards equilibrium, so the equilibrium wage itself would be falling and equilibrium would not be reached. There would still be demand-deficient unemployment.

Later, as the economy recovers and begins to grow again, so demand-deficient unemployment will start to fall again. Because demand-deficient unemployment fluctuates with the business cycle, it is sometimes referred to as 'cyclical unemployment'. Figure 11.8 (on page 354) showed such fluctuations in unemployment in various industrial countries.

Growth in the labour supply

If labour supply rises with no corresponding increase in the demand for labour, the equilibrium real wage rate will fall. If the real wage rate is 'sticky' downwards, unemployment will occur. This tends not to be such a serious cause of unemployment

---

Definitions

Demand-deficient or cyclical unemployment
Disequilibrium unemployment caused by a fall in aggregate demand with no corresponding fall in the real wage rate.

Efficiency wage rate
The profit-maximising wage rate for the firm after taking into account the effects of wage rates on worker motivation, turnover and recruitment.

Pause for thought

If this analysis is correct, namely that a reduction in wages will reduce the aggregate demand for goods, what assumption must we make about the relative proportions of wages and profits that are spent (given that a reduction in real wage rates will lead to a corresponding increase in rates of profit)?

as demand deficiency, since the supply of labour changes relatively slowly. Nevertheless there is a problem of providing jobs for school leavers each year with the sudden influx of new workers on to the labour market.

There is also a potential problem over the longer term if social trends lead more women with children to seek employment. In practice, however, with the rapid growth of part-time employment, and the lower average wage rate paid to women, this has not been a major cause of excess labour supply.

Equilibrium unemployment (or natural unemployment)

If you look at Table 11.1 on page 353, you can see how unemployment in the UK was higher in the 1980s and 1990s than in the previous two decades. Part of the reason for this was the growth in equilibrium unemployment.

Although there may be overall *macro*economic equilibrium, with the *aggregate* demand for labour equal to the *aggregate* supply, and thus no disequilibrium unemployment, at a *micro*economic level supply and demand may not match. In other words, there may be vacancies in some parts of the economy, but an excess of labour (unemployment) in others. This is equilibrium unemployment. There are various types of equilibrium unemployment.

Frictional (search) unemployment

Frictional unemployment occurs when people leave their jobs, either voluntarily or because they are sacked or made redundant, and are then unemployed for a period of time while they are looking for a new job. They may not get the first job they apply for, despite a vacancy existing. The employer may continue searching, hoping to find a better-qualified person. Likewise, unemployed people may choose not to take the first job they are offered. Instead, they may continue searching, hoping that a better one will turn up.

The problem is that information is imperfect. Employers are not fully informed about what labour is available; workers are not fully informed about what jobs are available and what they entail. Both employers and workers, therefore, have to search: employers searching for the right labour and workers searching for the right jobs.

One obvious remedy for frictional unemployment is for there to be better job information. This could be provided by government job centres, by private employment agencies, or by local and national newspapers.

Structural unemployment

Structural unemployment is where the structure of the economy changes. Employment in some industries may expand while in others it contracts. There are two main reasons for this.

A change in the pattern of demand. Some industries experience declining demand. This may be due to a change in consumer tastes. Certain goods may go out of fashion. Or it may be due to competition from other industries. For example, consumer demand may shift away from coal and to other fuels. This will lead to structural unemployment in mining areas.

A change in the methods of production (technological unemployment). New techniques of production often allow the same level of output to be produced with fewer workers. This is known as 'labour-saving technical progress'. Unless output expands sufficiently to absorb the surplus labour, people will be made redundant. This creates **technological unemployment**. An example is the job losses in the banking industry

Definitions

Frictional (search) unemployment
Unemployment that occurs as a result of imperfect information in the labour market. It often takes time for workers to find jobs (even though there *are* vacancies) and in the meantime they are unemployed.

Structural unemployment
Unemployment that arises from changes in the pattern of demand or supply in the economy. People made redundant in one part of the economy cannot immediately take up jobs in other parts (even though there are vacancies).

Technological unemployment
Structural unemployment that occurs as a result of the introduction of labour-saving technology.

caused by the increase in the number of cash machines and by the development of telephone and Internet banking.

Structural unemployment often occurs in particular regions of the country. When it does, it is referred to as **regional unemployment**. This is most likely to occur when particular industries are concentrated in particular areas. For example, the decline in the South Wales coal mining industry led to high unemployment in the Welsh valleys.

The level of structural unemployment depends on three factors:

- The degree of regional concentration of industry. The more that industries are concentrated in particular regions, the greater will be the level of structural unemployment if particular industries decline.
- The speed of change of demand and supply in the economy. The more rapid the rate of technological change or the shift in consumer tastes, the more rapid will be the rate of redundancies.
- The immobility of labour. Where workers are less able or less willing to move to a new job, the higher will be the level of structural unemployment.

Seasonal unemployment

Seasonal unemployment occurs when the demand for certain types of labour fluctuates with the seasons of the year. This problem is particularly severe in holiday areas, such as Cornwall, where unemployment can reach very high levels in the winter months.

> **Definitions**
>
> **Regional unemployment**
> Structural unemployment occurring in specific regions of the country.
>
> **Seasonal unemployment**
> Unemployment associated with industries or regions where the demand for labour is lower at certain times of the year.

Recap

1. The two most common measures of unemployment are claimant unemployment (those claiming unemployment-related benefits) and ILO/OECD standardised unemployment (those available for work and actively seeking work or waiting to take up an appointment).

2. Unemployment can be divided into disequilibrium and equilibrium unemployment.

3. Disequilibrium unemployment occurs when the average real wage rate is above the level that will equate the aggregate demand and supply of labour. It can be caused by unions or government pushing up wages (real-wage unemployment), by a fall in

aggregate demand (demand-deficient unemployment), or by an increase in the supply of labour.

4. Equilibrium unemployment occurs when there are people unable or unwilling to fill job vacancies. This may be due to poor information in the labour market and hence a time lag before people find suitable jobs (frictional unemployment), to a changing pattern of demand or supply in the economy and hence a mismatching of labour with jobs (structural unemployment – specific types being technological and regional unemployment), or to seasonal fluctuations in the demand for labour.

THE RELATIONSHIP BETWEEN INFLATION AND UNEMPLOYMENT: THE SHORT RUN

11.4

How will changes in the level of spending affect unemployment and inflation?

In the simple Keynesian theory we developed in Sections 8.5 and 8.6, actual output relative to potential output is determined by aggregate demand. If actual output is below potential output (a negative output gap), there is a deficiency of demand and hence demand-deficient unemployment. If, on the other hand, actual output is temporarily above potential output (a positive output gap), there is a problem of excess demand and hence demand-pull inflation.

Potential output (or real income) in this model is sometimes referred to as the **full-employment level of national income** (Y_F), since there is no disequilibrium unemployment. (In practice, there would still be some unemployment at this level because of the existence of equilibrium unemployment – frictional, structural and seasonal.)

The recessionary gap

If the equilibrium level of national income (Y_e) is below the full-employment level (Y_F), there is what is known as a **recessionary** or **deflationary gap**. This situation is illustrated in Figure 11.12.

The full-employment level of national income (Y_F) (in other words, the potential level of output) is represented by the vertical line. The equilibrium level of national income is Y_e, where $W = J$ and $Y = E$. The recessionary gap is $a - b$: namely, the amount that the E line is below the 45° line at the full-employment level of national income (Y_F). It is also $c - d$: the amount that injections fall short of withdrawals at the full-employment level of income.

If national income is to be raised from Y_e to Y_F, injections will have to be raised and/or withdrawals lowered so as to close the deflationary gap.

Note that the size of the recessionary gap is *less* than the amount by which Y_e falls short of Y_F. This illustrates the multiplier (see section 8.5 on pages 256–9). If injections are raised by $a - b$ (i.e. $c - d$), national income will rise by $Y_F - Y_e$. The multiplier is thus given by:

$$\frac{Y_F - Y_e}{a - b}$$

TC 13
p 253

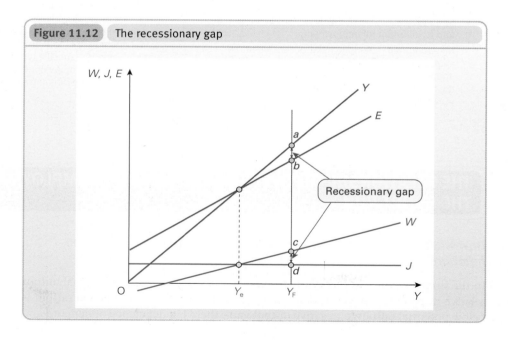

Figure 11.12   The recessionary gap

Figure 11.13   The inflationary gap

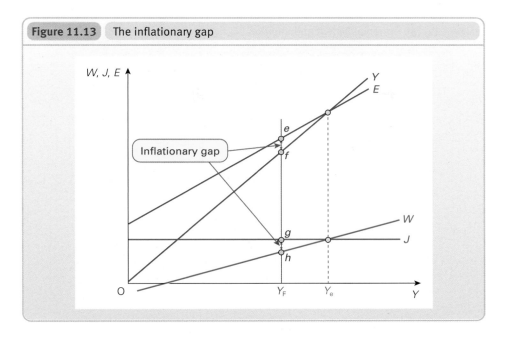

The inflationary gap

If at the full-employment level of income, aggregate expenditure *exceeds* national income, there will be a problem of excess demand. Y_e will be above Y_F. The problem is that Y_F represents a real ceiling to output. In the short run, national income *cannot* expand beyond this point. Y_e cannot be reached. The result will therefore be demand-pull inflation.

This situation involves an **inflationary gap**. This is the amount by which aggregate expenditure exceeds national income, or injections exceed withdrawals, at the full-employment level of national income. This is illustrated by the gaps $e - f$ and $g - h$ in Figure 11.13.

To eliminate this inflation, the inflationary gap must be closed, either by raising withdrawals or by lowering injections.

> **Pause for thought**
>
> *Assume that full-employment national income is £500 billion and that current national income is £450 billion. Assume also that the mpc_d is ⁴/₅.*
> *(a) Is there an inflationary or deflationary gap?*
> *(b) What is the size of this gap?*

Policy implications

Keynesians advocate an active policy of demand management: raising aggregate demand (for example, by raising government expenditure or lowering taxes) to close a deflationary gap, and reducing aggregate demand to close an inflationary gap. We look at various macroeconomic policies in Chapter 12.

Unemployment and inflation at the same time

The simple analysis of recessionary and inflationary gaps implies that the short-run aggregate supply curve looks like AS_1 in Figure 11.14. Up to Y_F, output and employment can rise with no rise in prices at all. The deflationary gap is being closed. At Y_F no further rises in output are possible. Any further rise in aggregate demand is entirely reflected in higher prices. An inflationary gap opens. In other words, this implies that either inflation *or* unemployment can occur, but not both simultaneously.

Two important qualifications need to be made to this analysis to explain the occurrence of both unemployment *and* inflation at the same time.

> **Definition**
>
> **Inflationary gap**
> The excess of aggregate expenditure over income (and injections over withdrawals) at the full-employment level of national income.

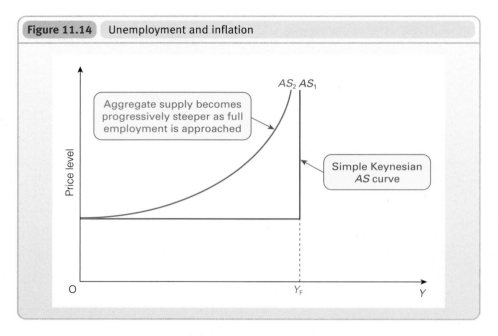

Figure 11.14   Unemployment and inflation

Aggregate supply becomes progressively steeper as full employment is approached

AS_2 AS_1

Simple Keynesian *AS* curve

Price level

O Y_F Y

First, there are *other* types of inflation not caused by an excess of aggregate demand, such as cost-push and expectations-generated inflation. Box 11.3 highlights the mixed empirical relationship between the rate of inflation and the amount of excess or deficient demand (as measured by output gaps) in both the UK and France. Second, there are *other* types of unemployment not caused by the level of aggregate demand, such as frictional and structural unemployment.

Thus, even if a government could manipulate national income so as to get Y_e and Y_F to coincide, this would not eliminate all inflation and unemployment – only demand-pull inflation and demand-deficient unemployment. Keynesians argue, therefore, that governments should use a whole package of policies, each tailored to the specific type of problem. But certainly one of the most important of these policies will be the management of aggregate demand.

Third, not all firms operate with the same degree of slack. A rise in aggregate demand can lead to *both* a reduction in unemployment *and* a rise in prices: some firms responding to the rise in demand by taking up slack and hence increasing output; other firms, having little or no slack, responding by raising prices; others doing both. Similarly, labour markets have different degrees of slack and therefore the rise in demand will lead to various mixes of higher wages and lower unemployment. Thus the short-run *AS* curve will look like AS_2 in Figure 11.14.

KI 27
p 204

The Phillips curve

Definition

Phillips curve

A curve showing the relationship between (price) inflation and unemployment. The original Phillips curve plotted *wage* inflation against unemployment for the years 1861–1957.

The relationship between inflation and unemployment was examined in a famous article by A. W. Phillips back in 1958. He showed the statistical relationship between wage inflation and unemployment in the UK from 1861 to 1957. With wage inflation on the vertical axis and the unemployment rate on the horizontal axis, a scatter of points was obtained. Each point represented the observation for a particular year. The curve that best fitted the scatter has become known as the **Phillips curve**. It is illustrated in Figure 11.15 and shows an inverse relationship between inflation and unemployment.

Given that wage increases over the period were approximately 2 per cent above price increases (made possible because of increases in labour productivity), a

| BOX 11.3 | MIND THE GAP | | EXPLORING ECONOMICS |

Do output gaps explain inflation?

Chapter 9 introduced the concept of output gaps. An output gap measures the difference between an economy's actual level of output and its potential output. A positive output gap shows that the level of actual output is *greater* than the potential level, while a negative output gap shows that the level of output is below the potential level.

The magnitude of the output gap, which is usually expressed as a percentage of potential output, enables us to assess the extent of any demand-deficiency (negative output gap) or the extent of excess demand (positive output gap).

We also saw in Chapter 9 (Section 9.1) that the slope of the short-run aggregate supply may be affected by the amount of slack in the economy. As the economy approaches or exceeds its potential output the aggregate supply curve is likely to get steeper as firms' marginal costs rise faster. Consequently, increases in demand at output levels close to or in excess of an economy's potential output will exert more upward pressure on prices than if the economy has a more significant amount of slack. This suggests that the rate of price inflation is positively related to the size of the output gap.

Charts (a) and (b) plot the output gap (as a percentage of potential output) and the annual rate of economy-wide inflation (rate of increase of the GDP deflator) for the UK and France respectively.

It would appear that for the period from 1965 to the end of the 1980s there was a positive correlation between output gaps and inflation rates, albeit that

turning points in the rates of inflation lag those in the size of output gaps –in other words, it took time for price pressure to fully work through the economy. This reflects, in part, the fact that some prices, such as wage rates, are adjusted relatively infrequently.

Since the 1990s, however, the relationship between output gaps and inflation rates is less clear. Indeed in both the UK and France there is a general reduction in inflation rates regardless of the size of output gaps. This demonstrates that there are several potential influences on rates of inflation.

One explanation is a reduction in cost-push pressures as labour markets became more competitive and flexible, and as firms faced greater competition from the EU, China and many other countries in an increasingly globalised market.

Another explanation is a growing recognition amongst economists and policy-makers of the importance of inflation rate expectations. It is argued that if policy-makers are perceived as making credible (i.e. trusted) low inflation rate announcements by those that enter into discussions on prices, such as unions and firms when negotiating wage rates, then inflation rates will be lower. A good example of this is the adoption of clear inflation targets by the Bank of England and the ECB.

 What factors may have resulted in the lower inflation rates experienced by the UK and France from the 1990s?

(a) UK output gap and inflation;   *(b) French output gap and inflation*

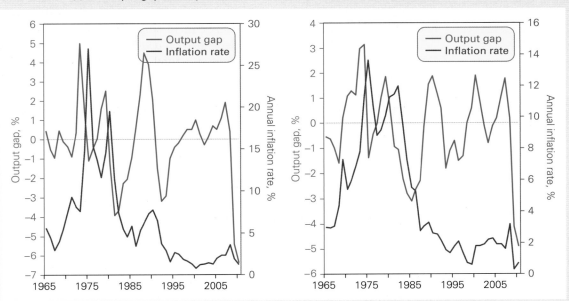

Source: Based on data in *European Economy Statistical Annex* (European Commission, Economic and Financial Affairs)

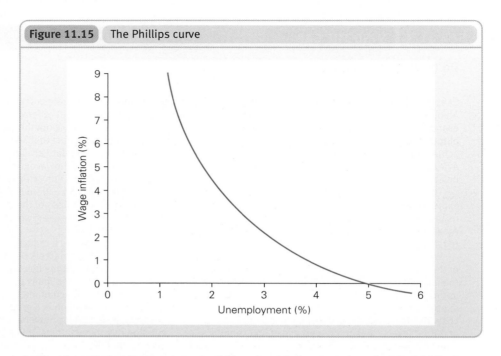

Figure 11.15   The Phillips curve

similar-shaped, but lower curve could be plotted showing the relationship between *price* inflation and unemployment.

The curve has often been used to illustrate the short-run effects of changes in (real) aggregate demand. When aggregate demand rose (relative to potential output), inflation rose and unemployment fell: there was a movement upwards along the curve. When aggregate demand fell, there was a movement downwards along the curve.

The Phillips curve was bowed in to the origin. The usual explanation for this is that as aggregate demand expanded, at first there would be plenty of surplus labour, which could be employed to meet the extra demand without the need to raise wage rates very much. But as labour became increasingly scarce, firms would find that they had to offer increasingly higher wage rates to obtain the labour they required, and the position of trade unions would be increasingly strengthened.

The *position* of the Phillips curve depended on *non*-demand factors causing inflation and unemployment: frictional and structural unemployment; and cost-push and expectations-generated inflation. If any of these non-demand factors changed so as to raise inflation or unemployment, the curve would shift outwards to the right.

The Phillips curve seemed to present governments with a simple policy choice. They could trade off inflation against unemployment. Lower unemployment could be bought at the cost of higher inflation, and vice versa. Unfortunately, the experience since the late 1960s has suggested that no such simple relationship exists beyond the short run.

From about 1966 the Phillips curve relationship seemed to break down. The UK, along with many other countries in the Western world, began to experience growing unemployment *and* higher rates of inflation as well.

Figure 11.16 shows price inflation and unemployment in the UK from 1960 to 2009. From 1960 to 1966 a curve similar to the Phillips curve can be fitted through the data. From 1967 to the early 1990s, however, no simple picture emerges. Certainly the original Phillips curve could no longer fit the data; but whether the curve shifted to the right and then back again somewhat (the broken lines), or whether the relationship broke down completely, or whether there was some quite different relationship between inflation and unemployment, is not clear by simply

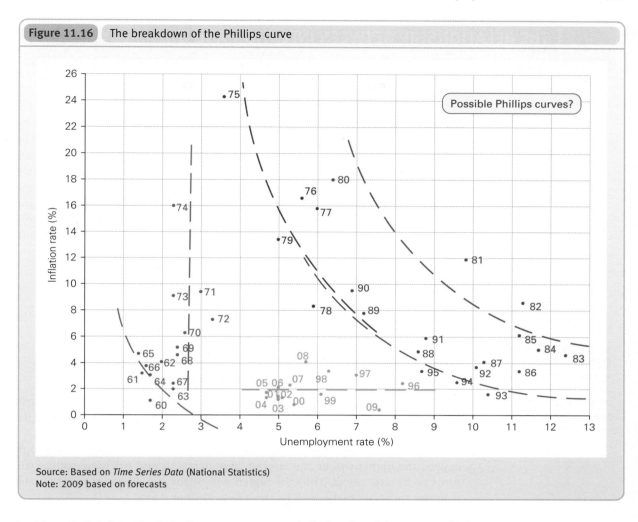

Figure 11.16 The breakdown of the Phillips curve

Source: Based on *Time Series Data* (National Statistics)
Note: 2009 based on forecasts

looking at the data. In fact, in recent years, as inflation has been targeted, the 'curve' would seem to have become a virtually horizontal straight line!

Many economists argue that expectations concerning future inflation rates are an important influence on the inflation–unemployment relationship. We consider this in the next section.

Recap

1. If equilibrium national income (Y_e) is below the full-employment level of national income (Y_F), there will be a recessionary gap. This gap is equal to $Y - E$ or $W - J$ at Y_F. This gap can be closed by increasing injections or reducing withdrawals. This will then cause a multiplied rise in national income (up to a level of Y_F) and will eliminate demand-deficient unemployment.

2. If equilibrium national income exceeds the full-employment level of income, the inability of output to expand to meet this excess demand will lead to demand-pull inflation. This excess demand gives an inflationary gap, which is equal to $E - Y$ or $J - W$ at Y_F.

   This gap can be closed by reducing injections or increasing withdrawals.

3. This simple analysis tends to imply that the short-run AS curve is horizontal up to Y_F and then vertical. If allowance is made for other types of inflation and unemployment, the AS curve will be upward sloping but getting steeper as full employment is approached and as bottlenecks increasingly occur.

4. The Phillips curve showed the trade-off between inflation and unemployment. There seemed to be a simple inverse relationship between the two. After 1966, however, the relationship broke down as inflation *and* unemployment rose.

| 11.5 | **THE RELATIONSHIP BETWEEN INFLATION AND UNEMPLOYMENT: INTRODUCING EXPECTATIONS** |

What happens when people come to expect inflation?

A major contribution to the theory of unemployment and inflation was made by Milton Friedman and others in the late 1960s. They incorporated people's expectations about the future level of prices into the Phillips curve. This can then be used to derive a *vertical* long-run Phillips curve. In other words, it can be used to explain the contention by many economists that there is *no* trade-off between inflation and unemployment in the long run, and that therefore government policy to expand aggregate demand will not create more jobs (except perhaps in the very short term).

This theory of the vertical long-run Phillips curve is known as the *accelerationist theory*.

The expectations-augmented Phillips curve

In its simplest form, the **expectations-augmented Phillips curve** is given by the following:

$$\pi = f(1/U) + \pi^e$$

What this states is that inflation (π) depends on two things:

▪ The inverse of unemployment ($1/U$). This is simply the normal Phillips curve relationship. The higher the rate of (demand-deficient) unemployment, the lower the rate of inflation.
▪ The expected rate of inflation (π^e). The higher the rate of inflation that people expect, the higher will be the level of wage demands and the more willing will firms be to raise prices. Thus the higher will be the actual rate of inflation and thus the vertically higher will be the whole Phillips curve.

Let us assume, for simplicity, that the rate of inflation people expect this year (π_t^e) (where t represents the current time period: i.e. this year) is the same rate that inflation actually was last year (π_{t-1}).

$$\pi_t^e = \pi_{t-1}$$

Thus if unemployment is such as to push up prices by 4 per cent ($f(1/U) = 4\%$) and if last year's inflation was 6 per cent, then inflation this year will be 4 per cent + 6 per cent = 10 per cent.

The accelerationist theory

Let us trace the course of inflation and expectations over a number of years in an imaginary economy. To keep the analysis simple, assume there is no growth in the economy.

Year 1

Assume that at the outset, in year 1, there is no inflation at all; that none is expected; that $AD = AS$; and that equilibrium unemployment is 8 per cent. The economy will be at point *a* in Figure 11.17 and Table 11.2.

TC 9
p 71

Definition

Expectations-augmented Phillips curve
A (short-run) Phillips curve whose position depends on the expected rate of inflation.

Figure 11.17   The accelerationist theory of inflation

Table 11.2   The accelerationist theory of inflation and inflationary expectations

Year	Point on graph	π	=	$f(1/U)$	+	π^e
1	a	0	=	0	+	0
2	b	4	=	4	+	0
3	c	4	=	0	+	4
4	d	8	=	4	+	4
5	e	12	=	4	+	8

Year 2

Now assume that the government expands aggregate demand in order to reduce unemployment. Unemployment falls to 6 per cent. The economy moves to point *b* along curve I. Inflation has risen to 4 per cent, but people, basing their expectations of inflation on year 1, still expect zero inflation. There is therefore no shift as yet in the Phillips curve. Curve I corresponds to an expected rate of inflation of zero.

Year 3

People now revise their expectations of inflation to the level of year 2. The Phillips curve shifts up by 4 percentage points to position II. If *nominal* aggregate demand (i.e. demand purely in money terms, irrespective of the level of prices) continues to rise at the same rate, the whole of the increase will now be absorbed in higher prices. *Real* aggregate demand (i.e. in terms of what it can buy) will fall back to its previous level and the economy will move to point *c*. Unemployment will return to 8 per cent. There is no *demand-pull* inflation now, $(f(1/U) = 0)$, but inflation is still 4 per cent due to expectations $(\pi^e = 4\%)$.

Year 4

Assume now that the government expands *real* aggregate demand again so as to reduce unemployment once more to 6 per cent. This time it must expand *nominal* aggregate demand *more* than it did in year 2, because this time, as well as reducing unemployment, it also has to validate the 4 per cent expected inflation. The economy moves to point *d* along curve II. Inflation is now 8 per cent.

Year 5 onwards

Expected inflation is now 8 per cent (the level of actual inflation in year 4). The Phillips curve shifts up to position III. If at the same time the government tries to keep unemployment at 6 per cent, it must expand nominal aggregate demand 4 per cent faster in order to validate the 8 per cent expected inflation. The economy moves to point *e* along curve III. Inflation is now 12 per cent.

To keep unemployment at 6 per cent, the government must continue to increase nominal aggregate demand by 4 per cent more than the previous year. As the expected inflation rate goes on rising, the Phillips curve will go on shifting up each year.

Thus in order to keep unemployment below the initial equilibrium rate, inflation must go on *accelerating* each year. For this reason, this theory of the Phillips curve is sometimes known as the **accelerationist theory**.

The more the government reduces unemployment, the greater the rise in inflation that year, and the more the rise in expectations the following year and each subsequent year; and hence the more rapidly will price rises accelerate. Thus the true longer-term trade-off is between unemployment and the rate of *increase* in inflation.

TC 13
p 253

The long-run Phillips curve and the equilibrium rate of unemployment

As long as there are demand-pull pressures ($f(1/U) > 0$), inflation will accelerate as the expected rate of inflation (π^e) rises. In the long run, therefore, the Phillips curve will be vertical at the rate of unemployment where *real* aggregate demand equals *real* aggregate supply. This is the *equilibrium* rate of unemployment. Monetarists refer to it as the **natural rate** (U_n). It sometimes also known as the **non-accelerating-inflation rate of unemployment (NAIRU)**. In Figure 11.17 the equilibrium rate of unemployment is 8 per cent.

The implication for government policy is that expanding aggregate demand can reduce unemployment below the equilibrium rate only in the *short* run. In the long run, the effect will be purely inflationary. On the other hand, a policy of restraining aggregate demand, for example by restraining the growth in the money supply will *not*, in the long run, lead to higher unemployment: it will simply lead to lower inflation at the equilibrium rate of unemployment. The implication is that governments should make it a priority to control money supply and thereby nominal aggregate demand and inflation.

Rational expectations

New classical economists go further than the monetarist theory described above. They argue that even the short-run Phillips curve is vertical: that there is *no* trade-off between unemployment and inflation, even in the short run. They base their arguments on two key assumptions:

Pause for thought

What determines how rapidly the short-run Phillips curves in Figure 11.17 shift upwards?

Definitions

Accelerationist theory
The theory that unemployment can only be reduced below the natural rate at the cost of accelerating inflation.

Natural rate of unemployment or **non-accelerating-inflation rate of unemployment (NAIRU)**
The rate of unemployment consistent with a constant rate of inflation: the rate of unemployment at which the vertical long-run Phillips curve cuts the horizontal axis.

- Prices and wage rates are flexible and thus markets clear very rapidly. This means that there will be no disequilibrium unemployment. All unemployment will be equilibrium unemployment, or 'voluntary unemployment' as new classical economists prefer to call it.
- Expectations are 'rational', but are based on imperfect information.

In the accelerationist theory, expectations are based on *past* information and thus take a time to catch up with changes in aggregate demand. Thus for a short time a rise in nominal aggregate demand will raise output, and reduce unemployment below the equilibrium level, while prices and wages are still relatively low.

The new classical analysis is based on **rational expectations**. Rational expectations are not based on past rates of inflation. Instead they are based on the current state of the economy and the current policies being pursued by the government. Workers and firms look at the information available to them – at the various forecasts that are published, at various economic indicators and the assessments of them by various commentators, at government pronouncements, and so on. From this information they predict the rate of inflation as well as they can. It is in this sense that the expectations are 'rational': people use their reason to assess the future on the basis of current information.

But forecasters frequently get it wrong, and so do economic commentators! And the government does not always do what it says it will. Thus workers and firms will be basing expectations on *imperfect information*. The crucial point about the rational expectations theory, however, is that these errors in prediction are *random*. People's predictions of inflation are just as likely to be too high as too low.

If the government raises aggregate demand in an attempt to reduce unemployment, people will anticipate that this will lead to higher prices and wages, and that there will be *no* effect on output and employment. If their expectations of higher inflation are correct, this will *fully* absorb the increase in nominal aggregate demand, such that there will have been no increase in *real* aggregate demand at all. Firms will not produce any more output or employ any more people: after all, why should they? If they anticipate that people will spend 10 per cent more money, but that prices will rise by 10 per cent, their *volume* of sales will remain the same.

Output and employment will only rise, therefore, if people make an error in their predictions (i.e. if they underpredict the rate of inflation and interpret an increase in money spent as an increase in *real* demand). But they are as likely to *overpredict* the rate of inflation, in which case output and employment will fall! Thus there is no systematic trade-off between inflation and unemployment, even in the short run.

> **Definition**
>
> **Rational expectations**
> Expectations based on the *current* situation. These expectations are based on the information people have to hand. While this information may be imperfect and therefore people will make errors, these errors will be random.

> **Pause for thought**
>
> *For what reasons would a new classical economist support the policy of the Bank of England publishing its inflation forecasts and the minutes of the deliberations of the Monetary Policy Committee?*

Keynesian views

Keynesians criticise the monetarist/new classical approach of focusing exclusively on price expectations. Expectations, argue Keynesians, influence *output* and *employment* decisions, not just pricing decisions.

If there is a gradual but sustained expansion of aggregate demand, firms, seeing the economy expanding and seeing their orders growing, will start to invest more and make longer-term plans for expanding their labour force. People will generally *expect* a higher level of output, and this optimism will cause that higher level of output to be produced. In other words, expectations will affect output and employment as well as prices.

Graphically, the increased output and employment from the recovery in investment will shift the *AS* curve to the right and the Phillips curve to the left, offsetting (partially, wholly or more than wholly) the upward shift from higher inflationary expectations.

The lesson here for governments is that a sustained, but moderate, increase in aggregate demand can lead to a sustained growth in aggregate supply. What should be avoided is an excessive and unsustainable expansion of aggregate demand. In turn, this raises questions about the role that governments should play in managing economic stability. This has become especially relevant in light of the financial crisis of the late 2000s. Chapter 12 looks at government policy in more detail.

> **Pause for thought**
>
> *Why is it important in the Keynesian analysis for there to be a* steady *expansion of aggregate demand?*

Recap

1. Expectations can be incorporated into the analysis of the Phillips curve. The effect is to give a vertical long-run curve at the equilibrium rate of unemployment.

2. The simplest analysis of expectations is that the expected rate of inflation this year is what it actually was last year: $\pi_t^e = \pi_{t-1}$

3. If there is excess demand in the economy, producing upward pressure on wages and prices, initially unemployment will fall. But as people's expectations adapt upwards to these higher wages and prices, so ever-increasing rises in nominal aggregate demand will be necessary to maintain unemployment below the equilibrium rate. Price and wage rises will accelerate: i.e. inflation will rise.

4. The new classical theory assumes flexible prices and wages in the short run as well as in the long run. It also assumes that people base their expectations of

inflation on a rational assessment of the *current* situation.

5. People may predict wrongly, but they are equally likely to underpredict or to overpredict. On average over the years they will predict correctly.

6. The rational expectations theory implies that not only the long-run but also the short-run *AS* and Phillips curves will be vertical. If people correctly predict the rate of inflation, they will correctly predict that any increase in nominal aggregate demand will simply be reflected in higher prices. Total output and employment will remain the same: at the equilibrium level.

7. Keynesians argue that if people expect a rise in aggregate demand to be sustained, firms will invest more, thereby increasing potential output (and possibly also reducing unemployment) and not just increasing the rate of inflation.

11.6 INFLATION RATE TARGETING AND UNEMPLOYMENT

Does successful inflation rate targeting produce a horizontal Phillips curve?

The Phillips curve appeared to have shifted to the right in the 1970s and 1980s and then back to the left in the 1990s. It also seems to have changed its shape. Far from being vertical in the long run, it appears now to have become horizontal. Figure 11.18 traces out the path of inflation and unemployment from 1967 to 2010.

What explains the shape of this path? Part of the explanation lies in long-term changes in unemployment. Part lies in the policy of inflation targeting, pursued in the UK since 1992.

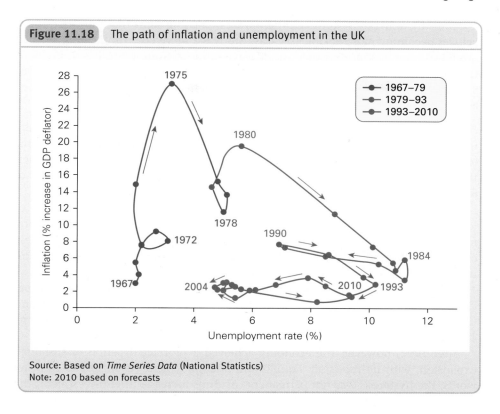

Figure 11.18 The path of inflation and unemployment in the UK

Source: Based on *Time Series Data* (National Statistics)
Note: 2010 based on forecasts

Long-term changes in unemployment

Why was there a substantial rise in unemployment from the early 1970s to the mid-1980s? Why, as a result, was there an apparent rightward shift in the Phillips curve? Why was there then a substantial fall in unemployment for over a decade from the mid-1990s? To answer this, we need to look at the labour market and the determinants of the equilibrium level of unemployment (i.e. the natural rate of unemployment or NAIRU).

The 1970s and 80s was a period of rapid industrial change. The changes included the following:

■ Dramatic changes in technology. The microchip revolution, for example, had led to many traditional jobs becoming obsolete.
■ Competition from abroad. The introduction of new products from abroad, often of superior quality to domestic goods, or produced at lower costs, had led to the decline of many older industries: e.g. the textile industry.
■ Shifts in demand away from the products of older labour-intensive industries to new 'high-tech' capital-intensive products.

The free market simply could not cope with these changes without a large rise in structural/technological unemployment. Labour was not sufficiently mobile – either geographically or occupationally – to move to industries where there were labour shortages or into jobs where there are skill shortages. A particular problem here was the lack of investment in education and training, with the result that the labour force was not sufficiently flexible to respond to changes in demand for labour.

From the mid-1980s, however, there were increasing signs that the labour market was becoming more flexible (see Case Study 6.2 in MyEconLab). People seemed more willing to accept that they would have to move from job to job throughout their career. At the same time, policies were introduced to improve training (see Section 12.4). Another explanation for first the rise of equilibrium unemployment and later the fall is the phenomenon of 'hysteresis'.

Hysteresis. If a recession causes a rise in unemployment which is not then fully reversed when the economy recovers, there is a problem of **hysteresis**. This term, used in physics, refers to the lagging or persistence of an effect, even when the initial cause has been removed. In our context it refers to the persistence of unemployment even when the initial demand deficiency no longer exists.

The recessions of the early 1980s and early 1990s created a growing number of long-term unemployed who were both deskilled and demotivated. What is more, many firms, in an attempt to cut costs, cut down on training programmes. In these circumstances, a rise in aggregate demand would not simply enable the long-term unemployed to be employed again.

The recessions also caused a lack of investment and a reduction in firms' capacity. When demand recovered, many firms were unable to increase output and instead raised prices. Unemployment thus fell only modestly and inflation rose. The NAIRU had increased: the Phillips curve had shifted to the right.

After 1992, however, the economy achieved a protracted period of sustained expansion, with no recession. Equilibrium unemployment began to fall. In other words, the hysteresis was not permanent. As firms increased their investment, the capital stock expanded; firms engaged in more training; the number of long-term unemployed fell.

Inflation targeting

As we have seen, a major determinant of the actual rate of inflation is the rate of inflation that people expect. Since 1992, a policy of inflation targeting has been adopted, and in 1997 the Bank of England was given independence in setting interest rates to achieve the target rate of inflation.

The target was initially set in October 1992 as a range from 1 to 4 per cent for RPIX inflation[2]. With the election of the Labour government in 1997, a single point target of 2.5 per cent was adopted. This was changed to a 2 per cent target for CPI inflation in December 2003.

The public's inflation rate expectations appear to have been affected by inflation rate targeting. Figure 11.19 shows expected inflation and actual inflation from 1990 to 2008. As you can see, for the first few years, expected inflation was between 1 and 2 percentage points above actual inflation, but since 1998 expectations have turned out to be pretty well correct.

So, does this mean that the Phillips curve has now become horizontal, as Figure 11.18 would seem to imply? The answer is that it depends on policy. As long as inflation is successfully kept on target and people believe that it will

---

[2] RPIX is the retail prices index, excluding mortgage interest payments. CPI is the consumer prices index. Differences in how CPI is compiled means that CPI inflation is typically about 0.5 percentage point below RPIX inflation. Thus the current target of 2 per cent CPI inflation is approximately equivalent to the 2.5 per cent RPIX inflation that was used as the target prior to December 2003.

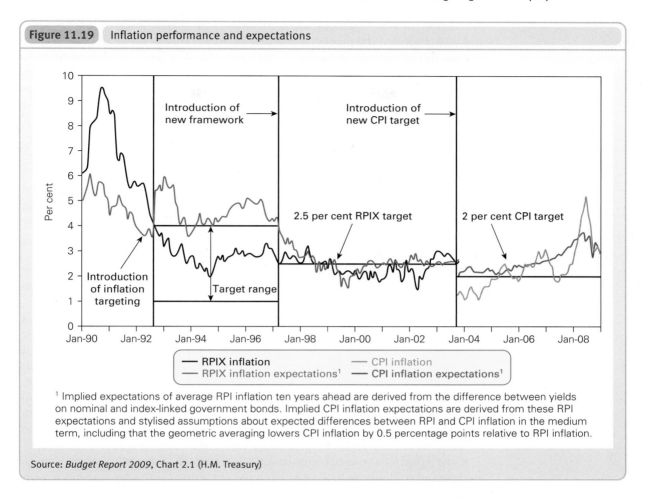

Figure 11.19 Inflation performance and expectations

[1] Implied expectations of average RPI inflation ten years ahead are derived from the difference between yields on nominal and index-linked government bonds. Implied CPI inflation expectations are derived from these RPI expectations and stylised assumptions about expected differences between RPI and CPI inflation in the medium term, including that the geometric averaging lowers CPI inflation by 0.5 percentage points relative to RPI inflation.

Source: *Budget Report 2009*, Chart 2.1 (H.M. Treasury)

remain so, the path of inflation and unemployment will be a horizontal straight line. Movements left and right along the line will depend on what happens to unemployment.

If, however, shocks to the world economy, such as the rapid rises in food, oil and other commodity prices in 2007/8, cause a rise in inflation, then confidence in the central bank's ability to maintain inflation at the target rate may be shaken. Both inflation and unemployment may rise.

Even if the central bank does succeed in achieving the target rate of inflation, in the short term, unemployment will fluctuate with the business cycle. Thus there may be movements left or right from one year to the next depending on the level of economic activity. Such fluctuations in unemployment are consistent with a stable inflation, provided that the fluctuations are mild and are not enough to alter people's expectations of inflation. Thus there was a very slight rise in unemployment, from 5.1 to 5.2 per cent, from 2001 to 2002 as the economic growth slowed slightly and a fall again to 4.8 per cent in 2004 as growth picked up somewhat.

Over the medium term (3 to 6 years), there may a leftward movement if the economy starts in recession and then the output gap is gradually closed through a process of steady economic growth (growth that avoids 'boom and bust'). Demand-deficient unemployment will be gradually eliminated. Thus between 1992 (the trough of the recession) and 2000, the output gap was closed from −3.2 to +1.3 (see the diagram in Box 9.1 on pages 278–9). From 2001 to 2006 it stayed between +0.2 and +0.9. Provided the process is gradual, inflation can stay on target.

Over the longer term, movements left (or right) will depend on what happens to equilibrium unemployment. A reduction in equilibrium unemployment will result in a leftward movement. Evidence suggests that since the mid-1980s, there has been a significant reduction in equilibrium unemployment from around 11 per cent to around 5 per cent. The precise amount, however, is not certain as it is subject to measurement errors.

What if inflation rate targeting were abandoned?

If inflation rate targeting were abandoned and aggregate demand was expanded rapidly, perhaps through tax cuts or a cut in interest rates, the short-run Phillips curve could re-emerge. A rapid expansion of aggregate demand would both reduce unemployment below the equilibrium rate and raise inflation. There would be a positive output gap.

This position could not be sustained, however, as inflationary expectations would rise and the short-run Phillips curve would begin shifting upwards (as in Figure 11.17).

With rising food and commodity prices in 2007/8, combined with a slowing economy, the Bank of England was faced with a dilemma. Should it continue rigidly targeting inflation, which would mean raising interest rates, or should it increase aggregate demand in an attempt to avoid recession, which would mean cutting interest rates? If, as in the USA, it had taken the course of substantially cutting interest rates, it could have undermined its credibility in keeping inflation under control as its over-riding objective. Inflation expectations would have risen. As it was, as Figure 11.19 shows, they were beginning to edge up and were around 3.7 per cent in early 2008 (1.7 percentage points above the target).

If the effect of the credit crunch and rising world commodity prices were to increase the equilibrium level of unemployment, attempts to keep unemployment down by interest rate cuts would have sparked an acceleration of inflation.

As it turned out, inflation fell in late 2008 and the output gap rose substantially (see the figure in Box 9.1 on pages 278–9); inflation was forecast to fall well below the target rate at the 24-month horizon. The Bank of England was thus able to cut interest rates to boost aggregate demand without compromising its inflation target. You will have to see whether it was willing to raise interest rates again once forecasts of inflation rose about 2 per cent.

We examine inflation targeting further in Section 12.3.

Pause for thought

How would you explain the apparent re-emergence of a Phillips loop after 2004?

Recap

1. The Phillips curve shifted to the right in the 1970s and 1980s. Reasons include a growth in equilibrium unemployment caused by rapid technological changes and a persistence of unemployment beyond the recessions of the early 1980s and early 1990s (hysteresis).

2. More recently, equilibrium unemployment has fallen as labour markets have become more flexible and as the lagged effects of the recessions of the early 1980s and early 1990s have faded.

3. Inflation targeting has successfully kept the rate of inflation very close to the target level. Expected inflation has been close to the target too.

4. Evidence shows that the effects of inflation targeting on expectations has made the time-path of the Phillips curve horizontal at the target rate of inflation. This does not mean, however, that a vertical long-run Phillips curve would not soon become apparent if inflation targeting were abandoned.

QUESTIONS

1. Do any groups of people gain from inflation?

2. If everyone's incomes rose in line with inflation, would it matter if inflation were 100 per cent or even 1000 per cent per annum?

3. Imagine that you had to determine whether a particular period of inflation was demand-pull, or cost-push, or a combination of the two. What information would you require in order to conduct your analysis?

4. Trace through the effect of a fall in the supply of money on aggregate demand. What will determine the size of the effect?

5. If V is constant, will (a) a £10 million rise in M give a £10 million rise in MV and (b) a 10 per cent rise in M give a 10 per cent rise in MV? (Test your answer by fitting some numbers to the terms.)

6. If both V and Y are constant, will (a) a £10 million rise in M lead to a £10 million rise in P and (b) a 10 per cent rise in M lead to a 10 per cent rise in P? (Again, try fitting some numbers to the terms.)

7. What would be the implications of different assumptions about the V and Y terms in the quantity equation $MV = PY$ for the effectiveness of monetary policy to control inflation?

8. What determines the shape of the long-run aggregate supply curve?

9. Would it be desirable to have zero unemployment?

10. What major structural changes have taken place in the UK economy in the past 10 years that have increased or decreased structural unemployment?

11. What are the causes of unemployment in the area where you live?

12. What would be the benefits and costs of increasing the rate of unemployment benefit?

13. Consider the most appropriate policy for tackling each of the different types of unemployment.

14. Assume that there is a trade-off between unemployment and inflation, traced out by a 'Phillips curve'. What could cause a leftward shift in this curve?

15. Assume that inflation depends on two things: the level of aggregate demand, indicated by the inverse of unemployment ($1/U$), and the expected rate of inflation (Π_t^e). Assume that the rate of inflation (Π_t) is given by the equation:

$$\Pi_t = (48/U - 6) + \Pi_t^e$$

Assume initially (year 0) that the actual and expected rate of inflation is zero.

(a) Now assume in year 1 that the government wishes to reduce unemployment to 4 per cent and continues to expand aggregate demand by as much as is necessary to achieve this. Fill in the rows for years 0 to 4 in the table. It is assumed for simplicity that the expected rate of inflation in a given year (Π_t^e) is equal to the actual rate of inflation in the previous year (Π_{t-1}).

(b) Now assume in year 5 that the government, worried about rising inflation, reduces aggregate demand sufficiently to reduce inflation by 3 per cent in that year. What must the rate of unemployment be raised to in that year?

(c) Assuming that unemployment stays at this high level, continue the table for years 5 to 7.

Year	U	$48/U - 6$	+	π^e	=	π
0	...	...	+	...	=	...
1	...	...	+	...	=	...
2	...	...	+	...	=	...
3	...	...	+	...	=	...
4	...	...	+	...	=	...
5	...	...	+	...	=	...
6	...	...	+	...	=	...
7	...	...	+	...	=	...

16. In the accelerationist model, if the government tries to maintain unemployment below the natural rate, what will determine the speed at which inflation accelerates?

17. For what reasons may the NAIRU (the equilibrium rate of unemployment) increase?

18. Given the persistence of high levels of unemployment after the recession of the early 1980s, what policies would you advocate to reduce unemployment in such circumstances?

19. Explain each of the following:

   (a) Why there were simultaneously higher rates of inflation *and* unemployment in the 1970s and 1980s than in the 1950s and 1960s.

   (b) Why there were simultaneously lower rates of inflation *and* unemployment in the late 1990s and early 2000s than in the 1970s and 1980s?

20. In what sense is it true to say that the Phillips curve today is horizontal?

Log on to MyEconlab and complete the studyplan exercises for this chapter to see how much you have learnt and where you need to revise most. Make sure you access all the supporting textbook resources including the online workbook, newsblog, audio animations, guided solutions and ebook.

Additional case studies in the *Essentials of Economics* MyEconLab (www.pearsoned.co.uk/sloman)

11.1 **Cost-push illusion.** When rising costs are not a symptom of cost-push inflation.

11.2 **Cost-push inflation and supply shocks.** The distinction between one-off price rises caused by a supply shock, such as an oil price rise or a rise in tax rates, and cost-push inflation.

11.3 **Is inflation dead?** Just because we have low inflation, it does not mean that inflationary forces are dead!

11.4 **Disinflation in Europe and Japan.** What happens when there is negative inflation? Is it a case of survival of the fittest?

11.5 **The costs of inflation.** Is inflation more than a mere inconvenience?

11.6 **Money and inflation in ancient Rome.** A very early case study of the quantity theory of money: how the minting of extra coins by the Romans caused prices to rise.

11.7 **The equation of exchange.** This examines two mere versions that are commonly used: the Fisher version and the Cambridge version.

11.8 **Swimming in the unemployment pool.** The composition and duration of unemployment in the EU

11.9 **Classical 'remedies' for unemployment.** How the policies advocated by the classical economists to cure unemployment would, according to Keynes, make the problem worse.

11.10 **Technology and unemployment.** Does technological progress destroy jobs?

11.11 **A. W. H. Phillips.** A portrait of the shy economist and engineer who invented the famous Phillips curve and Phillips machine.

11.12 **Explaining the shape of the short-run Phillips curve.** This shows how money illusion on the part of workers can explain why the Phillips curve is downward sloping.

11.13 **Milton Friedman (1912–2008).** A profile of the most influential of the monetarist economists.

11.14 **The political business cycle.** This shows how the accelerationist theory and 'clockwise Phillips loops' can be used to analyse the so-called political business cycle.

11.15 **The rational expectations revolution.** A profile of two of the most famous economists of the new classical rational expectations school.

11.16 **Different schools of economic thought.** This examines the range of macroeconomic views that were the basis of macroeconomic debate in the 1970s and 80s.

11.17 **Common ground between economists?** Is there an emerging consensus among economists about the causes of macroeconomic problems?

Websites relevant to this chapter

Numbers and sections refer to websites listed in the Web appendix and hotlinked from this book's website at **www.pearsoned.co.uk/sloman**.

■ For news articles relevant to this chapter, see the *Economics News Articles* link from the book's website.

■ For general news on unemployment, inflation and economic growth, see websites in section A, and particularly A1–5. See also links to newspapers worldwide in A38 and 39, and the news search feature in Google at A41. See also links to economics news in A42.

■ For data on unemployment, inflation and growth, see links in B1 or 2; see also B4 and 12. For UK data, see B3 and 34. For EU data, see G1 > *Publications* > *Publications overview* > *European Economy*. For US data, see Current economic indicators in B5 and the Data section of B17. For international data, see B15, 21, 24, 31, 33. For links to data sets, see B28; I14.

■ For specific data on UK unemployment, see B1, 1. *National Statistics* > the fourth link > *Labour Market* > *Labour Market Trends*. For international data on unemployment, see G1; H3 and 5.

■ For information on the development of ideas, including information on classical, Keynesian, monetarist, new classical and new Keynesian thought, see C12, 18; see also links under Methodology and History of Economic Thought in C14, and links to economists in I4 and 17. See also sites I7 and 11 > *Economic Systems and Theories* > *History of Economic Thought*.

■ For inflation targeting in the UK and the eurozone, see sites F1 and 6.

■ For student resources relevant to this chapter, see sites C1–7, 9, 10, 19.

CHAPTER MAP

Macroeconomic policy

In this chapter we look at various types of policy the government or central bank can use to tackle the macroeconomic problems of low and fluctuating economic growth, unemployment and inflation.

The chapter focuses on the control of aggregate demand and starts by looking at fiscal policy. This involves altering taxes and/or government spending. Cutting taxes or increasing government expenditure will increase aggregate demand, while increasing taxes or cutting government expenditure will reduce aggregate demand.

We then turn to monetary policy. Monetary policy seeks to control aggregate demand by directly controlling the money supply or by altering the rate of interest and then backing this up by any necessary change in money supply. A reduction in interest rates will encourage more borrowing and hence raise aggregate demand. A rise in interest rates will dampen aggregate demand.

Increasingly attention has focused on the longer-term impact of monetary and fiscal policy. In particular we look at the debate about whether the government should actively intervene to manage demand or whether it should merely set fiscal and monetary rules and then stick to them.

The chapter finishes by turning to the supply side. It looks at various policies that aim to increase *potential* output, and hence shift the aggregate supply curve to the right, and to reduce equilibrium unemployment. As we shall see, some of these policies involve 'freeing-up' the market; such policies, not surprisingly, are advocated by the political right. Other supply-side policies involve government investment in training and infrastructure and tend to be more favoured by the political centre and left.

After studying this chapter, you should be able to answer the following questions:

- What are the different types of macroeconomic policy that governments or central banks can use to control the economy?
- How can fiscal policy be used to alter the level of aggregate demand? What are the strengths and drawbacks of using fiscal policy to (a) stabilise the economy; (b) cure fundamental disequilibria?
- How is monetary policy operated by the central bank? How does it alter the money supply? How does it control interest rates?
- How successful is monetary policy likely to be in controlling (a) aggregate demand and (b) inflation?
- Should fiscal and monetary policy be frequently adjusted in an attempt to stabilise the economy? Or should fiscal and monetary rules be set by the government and be then rigidly followed?
- What types of supply-side policy are available to governments? What are their strengths and weaknesses?

12.1 FISCAL POLICY

How can government expenditure and taxation be used to affect the level of economic activity?

TC 13 p 253

Fiscal policy involves the government manipulating the level of government expenditure and/or rates of tax. An *expansionary* fiscal policy will involve raising government expenditure (an injection into the circular flow of income) or reducing taxes (a withdrawal from the circular flow). A *deflationary* (i.e. a contractionary) fiscal policy will involve cutting government expenditure and/or raising taxes.

By changing its fiscal stance government can affect the *level* of aggregate demand. Why might it wish to do this?

TC 7 p 49

First, it can try to remove any severe deflationary or inflationary gaps. For instance, an expansionary fiscal policy could be used to try to prevent an economy experiencing a severe or prolonged recession. This was the approach taken around the world from 2008 when substantial tax cuts and increases in government expenditure were undertaken. Likewise, deflationary fiscal policy could be used to prevent rampant inflation, such as that experienced in the 1970s.

TC 12 p 234

Second, it can try to smooth out the fluctuations in the economy associated with the business cycle. Stabilisation policies involve the government adjusting the level of aggregate demand so as to prevent the economy's actual output level deviating too far from its potential output level – to keep output gaps to a minimum.

Fiscal policy can also be used to influence aggregate *supply*. For example, government can increase its expenditure on infrastructure, or give tax incentives for investment.

Definitions

Fiscal policy
Policy to affect aggregate demand by altering government expenditure and/or taxation.

Budget deficit
The excess of central government's spending over its tax receipts.

Budget surplus
The excess of central government's tax receipts over its spending.

Deficits and surpluses

Central government deficits and surpluses

Since an expansionary fiscal policy involves raising government expenditure and/or lowering taxes, this has the effect of either increasing the budget deficit or reducing the budget surplus. A **budget deficit** in any one year is where central government's expenditure exceeds its revenue from taxation. A **budget surplus** is where tax revenues exceed central government expenditure.

For most of the past 50 years, governments around the world have run budget deficits. In recent years, however, many countries, the UK included, made substantial efforts to reduce their budget deficits, and some achieved budget surpluses for periods of time. The position changed dramatically in 2008/9, however, as many governments increased their expenditure and cut taxes in an attempt to stave off recession.

To finance a deficit, the government will have to borrow (e.g. through the issue of bonds (gilts) or Treasury bills). As we saw in Section 10.3, this will lead to an increase in the money supply to the extent that the borrowing is from the banking sector. The purchase of bonds or Treasury bills by the (non-bank) private sector, however, will not lead to an increase in the money supply.

General government

'General government' includes central and local government. Table 12.1 shows general government deficits/surpluses and debt for selected countries averaged over three recent periods. They are expressed as a proportion of GDP. Deficits refer

KI 29 p 239

Table 12.1 General government deficits/surpluses and debt as percentage of GDP

Country	General government deficits (–) or surpluses (+)			General government debt		
	Average 1991–5	Average 1996–2000	Average 2001–8	Average 1991–5	Average 1996–2000	Average 2001–8
Belgium	−6.5	−1.3	−0.3	139.2	125.2	93.7
France	−4.7	−2.6	−2.9	51.2	68.3	62.6
Germany	−2.9	−1.7	−2.5	46.6	61.6	64.0
Greece	−11.2	−4.0	−4.3	99.3	108.9	97.6
Ireland	−2.5	+2.1	+0.7	90.8	55.8	29.1
Italy	−9.9	−3.1	−3.1	127.6	131.0	105.2
Japan	−1.6	−5.8	−5.0	75.0	113.2	168.2
Netherlands	−3.5	−0.2	−0.6	91.6	79.6	49.2
Sweden	−7.4	+1.1	+1.4	74.9	76.9	47.9
UK	−6.0	−0.3	−2.6	44.7	50.9	41.1
USA	−4.5	0.0	−3.5	73.8	66.9	61.3
Euro area	−5.2	−2.1	−2.0	70.9	80.8	68.2

Source: Based on data in *European Economy Statistical Annex* (European Commission)

to the debt that a government incurs in one year when its spending exceeds its receipts. If the government runs persistent deficits over many years, these debts will accumulate.

As you can see, all of the countries in Table 12.1 experienced deficits in the first period. But, with the exception of Japan, all experienced a reduction of these deficits in the second period and two countries experienced a surplus. Seven of the countries, however, experienced an increase in deficits or a reduction in surpluses in the latest period.

All the countries were forecast to experience a substantial increase in deficits and hence debt from 2008 as governments borrowed more to finance extra spending and/or tax cuts to combat recession.

The whole public sector

To get a more complete view of public finances, we would need to look at the spending and receipts of the entire public sector: namely, central government, local government and public corporations.

Total public expenditure. First we need to distinguish between **current** and **capital expenditures**. Current expenditures include items such as wages and salaries of public-sector staff, administration and the payments of welfare benefits. Capital expenditures give rise to a stream of benefits *over time*. Examples include expenditure on roads, hospitals and schools.

Second we must distinguish between **final expenditure** on goods and services, and **transfers**. This distinction recognises that the public sector directly adds to the economy's aggregate demand through its spending on goods and services, including the wages of public-sector workers, but also that it redistributes incomes between individuals and firms. Transfers include subsidies and benefit payments, such as payments to the unemployed.

Between 2000 and 2008, the UK's public expenditure was typically split 94 to 6 per cent between current and capital expenditure, and 58 to 42 per cent between final expenditure and transfers.

Definitions

Current expenditure
Recurrent spending on goods and factor payments.

Capital expenditure
Investment expenditure; expenditure on assets.

Final expenditure
Expenditure on goods and services. This is included in GDP and is part of aggregate demand.

Transfers
Transfers of money from taxpayers to recipients of benefits and subsidies. They are not an injection into the circular flow but are the equivalent of a negative tax (i.e. a negative withdrawal).

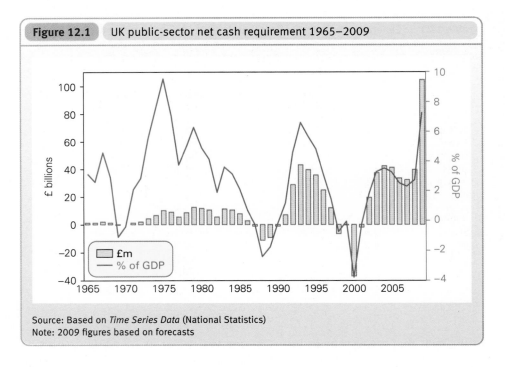

Figure 12.1 UK public-sector net cash requirement 1965–2009

Source: Based on *Time Series Data* (National Statistics)
Note: 2009 figures based on forecasts

Definition

Public-sector net cash requirement (PSNCR)
The (annual) deficit of the public sector, and thus the amount that the public sector must borrow.

Public-sector deficits. If the public sector spends more than it earns (through taxes and the revenues of public corporations, etc.), it runs a deficit. In the UK the principal measure of this deficit is known as the **public-sector net cash requirement (PSNCR)** (previously known as the 'public-sector borrowing requirement'). It is defined as public-sector expenditure minus public-sector receipts and minus its net lending (financial transactions) to other sectors. The reason for the name 'public-sector net cash requirement' is simple. If the public sector runs a deficit in the current year of, say, £1 billion, then it will have to borrow £1 billion in money this year in order to finance it.

If the public sector runs a surplus (a negative PSNCR), it will be able to repay some of the public-sector debts that have accumulated from previous years. Figure 12.1 shows the UK's PSNCR from 1963 expressed in money terms and as a percentage of GDP. It shows that public-sector deficits are the norm: in only 10 of these years did the UK experience public-sector surpluses.

The use of fiscal policy

Automatic fiscal stabilisers

To some extent, government expenditure and taxation will have the effect of *automatically* stabilising the economy. For example, as national income rises, the amount of tax people pay automatically rises. This rise in withdrawals from the circular flow of income helps to dampen down the rise in national income. This effect will be bigger if taxes are progressive (i.e. rise by a bigger percentage than national income). Some government expenditure will have a similar effect. For example, total government expenditure on unemployment benefits will fall, if rises in national income cause a fall in unemployment. This again will have the effect of dampening the rise in national income.

Discretionary fiscal policy

Automatic stabilisers cannot *prevent* fluctuations; they merely reduce their magnitude. If there is a *fundamental* disequilibrium in the economy or substantial fluctuations in national income, these automatic stabilisers will not be enough. The government may thus choose to *alter* the level of government expenditure or the rates of taxation. This is known as **discretionary fiscal policy**. Box 12.1 looks at an example of discretionary fiscal policy in the USA. Web Case 12.8 examines the use of discretionary fiscal policy in Japan from 1991 to the present day.

If government expenditure on goods and services (roads, health care, education, etc.) is raised, this will create a full multiplied rise in national income. The reason is that all the money gets spent and thus all of it goes to boosting aggregate demand.

Cutting taxes (or increasing benefits), however, will have a smaller effect on national income than raising government expenditure on goods and services by the same amount. The reason is that cutting taxes increases people's *disposable*

TC 13
p 253

> **Definition**
>
> **Discretionary fiscal policy**
> Deliberate changes in tax rates or the level of government expenditure in order to influence the level of aggregate demand.

BOX 12.1   BOOSTING THE US ECONOMY   CASE STUDIES & APPLICATIONS

Using fiscal policy to tackle the credit crunch

Measures by the Bush administration

In 2007, the US economy seemed to be heading for recession. As we saw in Box 10.3 on pages 314–15, many large mortgages had been given to people with low credit ratings (sub-prime mortgages) when interest rates had been low. With interest rates rising steeply from 2004 to 2006, many people defaulted on their mortgages and other debt. Banks found themselves in a liquidity crisis as many held large amounts of securitised assets containing sub-prime debt. They cut back on loans in what became known as the 'credit crunch'.

By the end of 2007, the US economy seemed to be heading for recession and by the final quarter or the year, annual economic growth had become negative (−0.2 per cent). In January 2008, President Bush announced an emergency $154 billion stimulus package of tax rebates, worth 1.1 per cent of GDP. The effect was to boost consumer spending, and recession seemed to have been averted. By the second quarter of 2008, the economy was growing at an annual rate of 3.3 per cent.

But the effect was short-lived. Once the tax rebates had been spent, the growth in consumer spending ceased. By the end of 2008, GDP was declining; the country was in recession.

The Obama fiscal stimulus package

Shortly after coming into office in 2009, President Obama signed into law a major fiscal stimulus package, worth $787 billion – the American Recovery and Investment Act. This was in addition to monetary policies designed to increase the flow of credit. The aim of the fiscal stimulus was to create 3.6 million jobs and reverse the collapse in aggregate demand that had followed the credit crunch.

The package included $212 billion in tax cuts for individuals and business, but the main feature was targeted increases in government expenditure to improve infrastructure: doubling the production of renewable energy, modernising some 75 per cent of government buildings to save energy, and large-scale investment in schools, colleges and public universities, in nationwide broadband, in science, research and technology.

The measures would bring the US budget deficit for 2009 to between $1.2 and $1.6 trillion, or between 8 and 11 per cent of GDP. This compared with a forecast 2.9 per cent for Germany, 3.8 per cent for Italy, 6.2 per cent for Spain and 8.8 per cent for the UK.

Whether such measures would work to revive the economy would depend on their effects on consumer behaviour and business confidence. Would the tax cuts, for example, encourage people to go out and spend? Or would people simply save the tax cuts for fear of losing their jobs in the deepening recession? What would be the multiplier and accelerator effects of the increased government expenditure? Would it stimulate further consumer spending and hence increased investment, or would the effects be offset by falling consumer expenditure and thus reduced investment as firms cut back on capacity?

 Which is likely to give a bigger boost to aggregate demand: tax cuts of a given amount targeted to (a) the rich, or (b) the poor?

incomes, of which only *part* will be spent. Part will be withdrawn into extra saving, imports and other taxes. In other words, not all the tax cuts will be passed on round the circular flow of income as extra expenditure. Thus if one-fifth of a cut in taxes is withdrawn and only four-fifths is spent, the tax multiplier will only be four-fifths as big as the government expenditure multiplier.

The effectiveness of fiscal policy

There are two main problem areas with discretionary fiscal policy. The first concerns the *magnitude* of the effects of policy measures. If *G* or *T* is changed, how much will *total* injections and withdrawals change? What will be the size of the resulting multiplier effect? How much will the change in aggregate demand affect output and employment, and how much will it affect prices?

The second concerns the *timing* of the effects. How quickly can policy be changed and how quickly will the changes affect the economy?

Problems of magnitude

Before changing government expenditure or taxation, the government will need to calculate the effect of any such change on national income, employment and inflation. Predicting these effects, however, is often very unreliable for a number of reasons.

Predicting the effect of changes in government expenditure

A rise in government expenditure of £*x* may lead to a rise in total injections (relative to withdrawals) that is smaller than £*x*. This will occur if the rise in government expenditure *replaces* a certain amount of private expenditure. For example, a rise in expenditure on state education may dissuade some parents from sending their children to private schools. Similarly, an improvement in the national health service may lead to fewer people paying for private treatment.

Crowding out. Another reason for the total rise in injections being smaller than the rise in government expenditure is a phenomenon known as **crowding out**. If the government relies on **pure fiscal policy** – that is, if it does not finance an increase in the budget deficit by increasing the money supply – it will have to borrow the money from the non-bank private sector. It will thus be competing with the private sector for finance and will have to offer higher interest rates. This will force the private sector too to offer higher interest rates, which may discourage firms from investing and individuals from buying on credit. Thus government borrowing crowds out private borrowing. In the extreme case, the fall in consumption and investment may completely offset the rise in government expenditure, with the result that aggregate demand does not rise at all.

Definitions

Crowding out
Where increased public expenditure diverts money or resources away from the private sector.

Pure fiscal policy
Fiscal policy that does not involve any change in money supply.

Predicting the effect of changes in taxes

A cut in taxes, by increasing people's real disposable income, increases not only the amount they spend but also the amount they save. The problem is that it is not easy to predict the relative size of these two increases. In part it will depend on whether people feel that the cut in tax is only temporary, in which case they may simply save the extra disposable income, or permanent, in which case they may adjust their consumption upwards.

Predicting the resulting multiplied effect on national income

Even if the government *could* predict the net *initial* effect on injections and withdrawals, the ultimate effect on national income will still be hard to predict for the following reasons:

- The size of the multiplier may be difficult to predict, since it is difficult to predict how much of any rise in income will be withdrawn. In other words, it is difficult to predict the size of the *mpw*. For example, the amount of a rise in income that households save or consume will depend on their expectations about future price and income changes.
- Induced investment through the accelerator (see page 282) is also extremely difficult to predict. It may be that a relatively small fiscal stimulus will be all that is necessary to restore business confidence, and that induced investment will rise substantially. In such a case, fiscal policy can be seen as a 'pump primer'. It is used to start the process of recovery, and then the continuation of the recovery is left to the market. But for pump priming to work, business people must believe that it will work. Business confidence can change very rapidly and in ways that could not have been foreseen a few months earlier.

Random shocks

Forecasts cannot take into account the unpredictable, such as the attack on the World Trade Center in New York in September 2001. Even events that, with hindsight, should have been predicted, such as the banking crisis of 2007–9, often are not. Unfortunately, unpredictable or unpredicted events do occur and may seriously undermine the government's fiscal policy.

> **Pause for thought**
>
> *Give some other examples of 'random shocks' that could undermine the government's fiscal policy.*

The problem of timing

Fiscal policy can involve considerable time lags. It may take time to recognise the nature of the problem before the government is willing to take action; tax or government expenditure changes take time to plan and implement – changes will have to wait until the next Budget to be announced and may come into effect some time later; the effects of such changes take time to work their way through the economy via the multiplier and accelerator.

If time lags are long enough, fiscal policy could even be *de*stabilising. Expansionary policies taken to cure a recession may not come into effect until the economy has *already* recovered and is experiencing a boom. Under these circumstances, expansionary policies are quite inappropriate: they simply worsen the problems of overheating. Similarly, contractionary policies taken to prevent excessive expansion may not take effect until the economy has already peaked and is plunging into recession. The contractionary policies only deepen the recession.

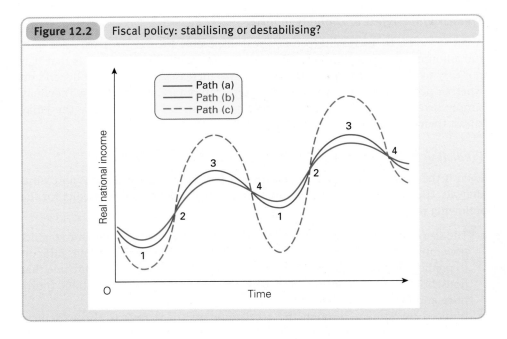

Figure 12.2 Fiscal policy: stabilising or destabilising?

This problem is illustrated in Figure 12.2. Path (a) shows the course of the business cycle without government intervention. Ideally, with no time lags, the economy should be dampened in stage 2 and stimulated in stage 4. This would make the resulting course of the business cycle more like path (b), or even, if the policy were perfectly stabilising, a straight line. With time lags, however, contractionary policies taken in stage 2 may not come into effect until stage 4, and expansionary policies taken in stage 4 may not come into effect until stage 2. In this case the resulting course of the business cycle will be more like path (c). Quite obviously, in these circumstances 'stabilising' fiscal policy actually makes the economy *less* stable.

If the fluctuations in aggregate demand can be forecast, and if the lengths of the time lags are known, then all is not lost. At least the fiscal measures can be taken early and their delayed effects can be taken into account.

Fiscal rules

Given the problems of pursuing active fiscal policy, many governments today take a much more passive approach. Instead of changing the policy as the economy changes, a rule is set for the level of public finances. This rule is then applied year after year, with taxes and government expenditure being planned to meet that rule. For example, a target could be set for public-sector deficits, with government expenditure and taxes being adjusted to keep the deficit at or within its target level. Fiscal (and monetary) rules are examined in more detail in Section 12.3.

The approach to fiscal policy in the UK

From 1998, the UK government set targets for government expenditure, not for just one year, but for a three-year period. Did this mean, therefore, that fiscal policy as a means of adjusting aggregate demand had been abandoned? In one sense, this was the case. The Labour government was committed to following its 'golden rule', whereby public-sector receipts should cover all *current* spending, averaged over the course of the business cycle (see Box 12.2).

But despite this apparent rejection of short-term discretionary fiscal adjustments, there was still a role for automatic fiscal stabilisers: with deficits rising in a recession and falling in a boom. There was also still the possibility, within the golden rule, of financing additional investment by borrowing, thereby providing a stimulus to a sluggish economy.

The golden rule also permitted increased government expenditure (or tax cuts) if there was a budget surplus. Thus in the 2001 Budget the Chancellor announced spending increases of 3.7 per cent per year for three years. The effect was to provide a stimulus to the economy just at a time when the world economy was slowing down. This helped to make the slowdown in UK economic growth in the period 2001–3 much less severe than in many other countries.

But rules can be severely tested by exceptional circumstances such as those that faced the global economy as a result of the credit crunch of the late 2000s. Countries around the world resorted to discretionary fiscal policy to boost aggregate demand. They relaxed or abandoned fiscal rules. In the UK, the golden rule was jettisoned – at least temporarily – and replaced with a 'temporary operating rule' (see Box 12.2). In Section 12.3 we review the debate concerning constraints on a government's discretion over its fiscal and monetary policies.

Recap

1. Fiscal policy affects the size of government budget deficits or surpluses.

2. The size of these alone, such as the PSCNR in the UK, is a poor guide, however, to the government's fiscal stance. A large deficit, for example, may simply be due to the fact that the economy is in recession and therefore tax receipts are low. A better guide is whether the change in the deficit or surplus will be expansionary or contractionary.

3. Automatic fiscal stabilisers are tax revenues that rise, and benefits that fall, as national income rises. They have the effect of reducing the size of the multiplier and thus reducing cyclical upswings and downswings.

4. Automatic stabilisers take effect as soon as aggregate demand fluctuates, but they can never remove fluctuations completely. They also create disincentives and act as a drag on recovery from recession.

5. Discretionary fiscal policy is where the government deliberately changes taxes or government expenditure in order to alter the level of aggregate demand. Changes in government expenditure on goods and services have a full multiplier effect. Changes in taxes and benefits, however, have a smaller multiplier effect as some of the tax/benefit changes will merely affect other withdrawals and thus have a smaller net effect on the consumption of domestic goods.

6. There are problems in predicting the magnitude of the effects of discretionary fiscal policy. Expansionary fiscal policy can act as a pump primer and stimulate increased private expenditure, or it can crowd out private expenditure. The extent to which it acts as a pump primer depends crucially on business confidence – something that is very difficult to predict beyond a few weeks or months. The extent of crowding out depends on monetary conditions and the government's monetary policy.

7. There are various time lags involved with fiscal policy, which makes it difficult to use fiscal policy to 'fine-tune' the economy.

8. In recent years many governments preferred a more passive approach towards fiscal policy. Targets were set for one or more measures of the public-sector finances, and then taxes and government expenditure were adjusted so as to keep to the target.

9. Nevertheless, in extreme circumstances, as occurred in 2008/9, governments were prepared to relax rules and give a fiscal stimulus to their economies.

BOX 12.2   FROM GOLDEN TO TEMPORARY RULES

Putting the discretion back into fiscal policy

If the government persistently runs a budget deficit, the national debt will rise. If it rises faster than GDP, it will account for a growing proportion of GDP. There is then likely to be an increasing problem of 'servicing' this debt: i.e. paying the interest on it. The government could find itself having to borrow more and more to meet the interest payments, and so the national debt could rise faster still. As the government borrows more and more, so it has to pay higher interest rates to attract finances. If it is successful in this, borrowing and hence investment by the private sector could be crowded out (see page 386).

Recognising these problems, many governments in recent years have attempted to reduce their debts.

Preparing for the euro

In signing the Maastricht Treaty in 1992, the EU countries agreed that to be eligible to join the single currency (i.e. the euro), they should have sustainable deficits and debts. This was interpreted as follows: the general government deficit should be no more than 3 per cent of GDP and general government debt should be no more than 60 per cent of GDP, or should at least be falling towards that level at a satisfactory pace.

But in the mid-1990s, several of the countries that were subsequently to join the euro had deficits and debts substantially above these levels (see Table 12.1 on page 383). Getting them down proved a painful business. Government expenditure had to be cut and taxes increased. These fiscal measures, unfortunately, proved to be powerful! Unemployment rose and growth remained low.

The EU Stability and Growth Pact (SGP)

In June 1997, at the European Council in Amsterdam, the EU countries agreed that governments adopting the euro should seek to balance their budgets (or even aim for a surplus) averaged over the course of the business cycle, and that

deficits should not exceed 3 per cent of GDP in any one year. A country's deficit is permitted to exceed 3 per cent only if its GDP has declined by at least 2 per cent (or 0.75 per cent with special permission from the Council of Ministers). Otherwise, countries with deficits exceeding 3 per cent are required to make deposits of money with the European Central Bank. These then become fines if the excessive budget deficit is not eliminated within two years.

There are two main aims of targeting a zero budget deficit over the business cycle. The first is to allow automatic stabilisers to work without 'bumping into' the 3 per cent deficit ceiling in years when economies are slowing. The second is to allow a reduction in government debts as a proportion of GDP (assuming that GDP grows on average at around 2–3 per cent per year).

One criticism levelled at the SGP was whether it was flexible enough. From 2002, Germany, France and Italy breached the 3 per cent ceiling (see Figure (a)). This was partly the result of slow growth and rising unemployment, and hence falling tax revenue and rising benefit payments. Not surprisingly, these countries were reluctant to cut government expenditure to bring the deficit in line for fear of dampening an already sluggish economy. Despite various promises to rein in expenditure, they continued to have deficits in excess of 3 per cent. It is interesting to note that the general government deficits in the USA and Japan in 2003 were 4.8 and 7.9 per cent of GDP respectively, and both countries were adopting *expansionary* fiscal policy.

By 2007, however, after two years of relatively strong growth, deficits had been reduced well below the 3 per cent ceiling. But then the credit crunch hit. As the EU economies slowed, so deficits rose. To combat the recession, in November 2008 the European Commission announced a €200 billion fiscal stimulus plan, mainly in the form of increased public expenditure. €170 billion of the money would come from member governments and €30 billion from the EU, amounting

(a) Keeping budget deficits within the 3% ceiling?

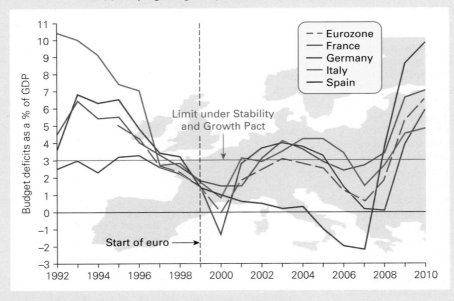

Source: Based on data in *European Economy* (European Commission)
Note: 2009 and 2010 based on forecasts

to a total of 1.2 per cent of EU GDP. The money would be for a range of projects, such as job training, help to small businesses, developing green energy technologies and energy efficiency. Most member governments quickly followed by announcing how their specific plans would accord with the overall plan.

The combination of the recession and the fiscal measures would push most eurozone countries' budget deficits well above the 3 per cent ceiling (see Figure (a)). But since the recession in EU countries was predicted to deepen markedly in 2009, with GDP forecast to decline by 4.0 per cent in the eurozone as a whole, and by 5.4 per cent in Germany, 4.4 per cent in Italy and 3.0 per cent in France, this was not seen to breach SGP rules.

The UK Labour government's golden rule

On being elected in 1997, the Labour government in the UK adopted a similar approach to that of the SGP. It introduced two fiscal rules.

First, under its 'golden rule', the government pledged that over the economic cycle, it would borrow only to invest (e.g. in roads, hospitals and schools) and not to fund current spending (e.g. on wages, administration and benefits). Investment was exempted from the zero borrowing rule because it contributes towards the growth of GDP. To allow the golden rule to operate, government departments were set three-year spending limits and each had separate current and capital (investment) budgets.

Second, under its 'sustainable investment rule', the government also set itself the target of maintaining a stable public-sector debt/GDP ratio below 40 per cent.

As with the Stability and Growth Pact, the argument for the golden rule was that by using an averaging rule over the cycle, automatic stabilisers would be allowed to work. Deficits of receipts over current spending could occur when the economy is in recession or when growth is sluggish (as in 2001–3), helping to stimulate the economy.

However, in the Pre-Budget Report of November 2008, the government argued that its 'immediate priority' was to support the economy by using discretionary fiscal policy. It therefore suspended its golden rule and the sustainable investment rule. These were replaced with a 'temporary operating rule' which meant that once the economy emerged from the downturn the government would use fiscal policies to: (i) improve the 'cyclically adjusted current budget' each year so as to reach balance; and (ii) enable debt to begin falling as a proportion of GDP.

In cyclically adjusting government balances we remove the estimated effects of the economic cycle. For example, during economic downturns we remove the effect of increased welfare payments and lower tax receipts. The government's current budget is the difference between its total receipts and its current expenditures (excluding capital expenditures). Figure (b), shows that the cyclically adjusted current budget balanced across the economic cycle from 1997/8 to 2006/7.

In the Pre-Budget Report of November 2008, amongst other measures the government introduced a 13-month cut in VAT from 17.5 per cent to 15 per cent. It also brought forward from 2010/11 £3 billion of capital spending on projects such as motorways, new social housing, schools and energy efficiency. In addition to the consequences for the current balance, public-sector debt was also set to breach the previous 40 per cent of GDP ceiling. By October 2009, the IMF was forecasting that UK general government debt would be 92 per cent by 2014 (higher than the USA (85%), France (83%) and Germany (82%), but substantially lower than Japan (144%) and Italy (126%)).

The hope, however, was that, as the economy recovered and the government was able to raise taxes again, the golden rule could be resumed once more.

What effects will an increase in government investment expenditure have on public-sector debt (a) in the short run; (b) in the long run?

(b) Output gap and the cyclically adjusted surplus on UK current budget

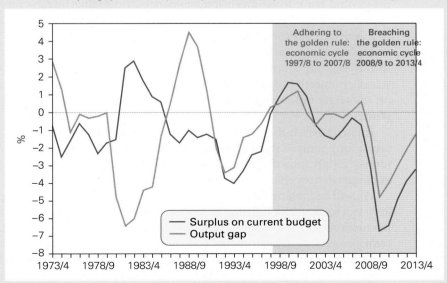

Source: *2009 Budget* (HM Treasury)
Note: 2009/10 onwards based on forecasts

12.2   MONETARY POLICY

How can the supply of money and interest rates be controlled?

Each month in the UK, the Bank of England's Monetary Policy Committee meets to set Bank Rate. The event gets considerable media coverage. Pundits, for two or three days before the meeting, try to predict what the MPC will do and economists give their 'considered' opinions about what the MPC *ought* to do.

The fact is that changes in interest rates have gained a central significance in macroeconomic policy. And it is not just in the UK. Whether it is the European Central Bank setting interest rates for the eurozone countries, or the Federal Reserve Bank setting US interest rates, or any other central bank around the world choosing what the level of interest rates should be, monetary policy is seen as having a major influence on a whole range of macroeconomic indicators.

But is monetary policy simply the setting of interest rates? In reality, it involves the central bank intervening in the money market to ensure that the interest rate that has been announced is also the *equilibrium* interest rate.

The policy setting

In framing its monetary policy, the government must decide on what the goals of the policy are. Is the aim simply to control inflation, or does the government wish also to affect output and employment, or does it want to control the exchange rate?

TC 7
p 49

The government also has to decide the role of the central bank in carrying out monetary policy. There are three possible approaches.

In the first, the government both sets the policy and decides the measures necessary to achieve it. Here the government would set the interest rate, with the central bank simply influencing money markets to achieve this rate. This first approach was used in the UK before 1997.

The second approach is for the government to set the policy *targets*, but for the central bank to be given independence in deciding interest rates. This is the approach adopted in the UK today. The government has set a target rate of inflation of 2 per cent, but then the MPC is free to choose the rate of interest.

The third approach is for the central bank to be given independence not only in carrying out policy, but in setting the policy targets itself. The ECB, within the statutory objective of maintaining price stability over the medium term, has decided on the target of keeping inflation below, but close to, 2 per cent over the medium term.

Finally, there is the question of whether the government or central bank should take a long-term or short-term perspective. Should it adopt a target for inflation or money supply growth and stick to it come what may? Or should it adjust its policy as circumstances change and attempt to 'fine-tune' the economy?

We will be looking primarily at *short-term* monetary policy: that is, policy used to keep to a set target for inflation or money supply growth, or policy used to smooth out fluctuations in the business cycle. It is important first, however, to take a longer-term perspective. Governments generally want to prevent an excessive growth in the money supply over the longer term. Likewise they want to ensure that money supply grows enough and that there is not a shortage of credit, such as that during the credit crunch. If money supply grows too rapidly, then inflation is likely to be high; if money supply grows too slowly, or even falls, then recession is likely to result.

Control of the money supply over the medium and long term

In Section 10.3 we identified two major sources of monetary growth: (a) banks choosing to hold a lower liquidity ratio (probably in response to an increase in the demand for loans); (b) public-sector borrowing financed by borrowing from the banking sector. If the government wishes to restrict monetary growth over the longer term, it could attempt to control either or both of these.

Liquidity of banks

The central bank could impose a statutory **minimum reserve ratio** on the banks, *above* the level that banks would otherwise choose to hold. Such ratios come in various forms. The simplest is where the banks are required to hold a given minimum percentage of deposits in the form of cash or deposits with the central bank.

The effect of a minimum reserve ratio is to prevent banks choosing to reduce their cash or liquidity ratio and creating more credit. This was a popular approach of governments in many countries in the past. Some countries imposed very high ratios indeed in their attempt to slow down the growth in the money supply.

A major problem with imposing restrictions of this kind is that banks may find ways of getting round them. After all, banks would like to lend and customers would like to borrow. It is very difficult to regulate and police every single part of countries' complex financial systems.

Nevertheless, attitudes changed substantially after the excessive lending of the mid-2000s. The expansion of credit had been based on 'liquidity' achieved through secondary marketing between financial institutions and the growth of securitised assets containing sub-prime debt (see Box 10.3 on pages 314–15). After the credit crunch and the need for central banks or governments to rescue ailing banks, such as Northern Rock and later the Royal Bank of Scotland in the UK and many other banks around the world, there were calls for greater regulation of banks to ensure that they had sufficient capital and operated with sufficient liquidity and that they were not exposed to excessive risk of default. As we saw in Box 10.4 on pages 318–20, a number of measures were taken.

Public sector deficits

Section 10.3 showed how government borrowing tends to lead to an increase in money supply. To prevent this, public sector deficits must be financed by selling *bonds* (as opposed to bills, which could well be taken up by the banking sector, thereby increasing money supply). However, to sell extra bonds the government will have to offer higher interest rates. This will have a knock-on effect on private-sector interest rates. The government borrowing will thus crowd out private-sector borrowing and investment. This is known as **financial crowding out**.

If governments wish to reduce monetary growth and yet avoid financial crowding out, they must therefore reduce the size of public-sector deficits.

The less successful a government is in controlling the public-sector deficit, the more it will have to borrow through bond issue, to prevent money supply growing too fast. This will mean high interest rates and the problem of crowding out, and a growing burden of public-sector debt with interest on it that has to be paid from taxation, from further cuts in government expenditure, or from further borrowing.

It is for this reason that, under the Stability and Growth Pact (see Box 12.2), eurozone countries are required to aim for a zero government deficit over the business cycle, so that in times of economic slowdown the deficit will not exceed 3 per cent: the limit set for deficits under the Pact.

KI 13
p 74

> **Definitions**
>
> **Minimum reserve ratio**
> A minimum ratio of cash (or other specified liquid assets) to deposits (either total or selected) that the central bank requires banks to hold.
>
> **Financial crowding out**
> Where an increase in government borrowing diverts money away from the private sector.

Similarly, in the UK, the Labour government adopted the 'golden rule' of fiscal policy. This is that, over the course of the business cycle, the government will borrow only to invest. In other words, leaving investment aside, there is a long-term target for government borrowing of zero.

Short-term monetary measures

Inflation may be off target. Alternatively, the government (or central bank) may wish to alter its monetary policy. What can it do? Various techniques could be used. These can be grouped into three categories: (a) altering the money supply; (b) altering interest rates; (c) rationing credit. These are illustrated in Figure 12.3, which shows the demand for and supply of money. The equilibrium quantity of money is initially Q_1 and the equilibrium interest rate is r_1.

Assume that the central bank wants to tighten monetary policy in order to reduce inflation. It could (a) seek to shift the supply of money curve to the left: e.g. from M_S to M_S' (resulting in the equilibrium rate of interest rising from r_1 to r_2), (b) raise the interest rate directly from r_1 to r_2, and then manipulate the money supply to reduce it to Q_2, or (c) keep interest rates at r_1, but reduce money supply to Q_2 by rationing the amount of credit granted by banks and other institutions.

Credit rationing was widely used in the past, especially during the 1960s. The aim was to keep interest rates low, so as not to discourage investment, but to restrict credit to more risky business customers and/or to consumers. In the UK, the Bank of England could order banks to abide by such a policy, although in practice it always relied on persuasion. The government also, from time to time, imposed restrictions on hire-purchase credit, by specifying minimum deposits or maximum repayment periods.

Such policies were progressively abandoned around the world from the early 1980s. They stifle competition and prevent efficient banks from expanding. Hire-purchase controls may badly hit certain industries (e.g. cars and other consumer durables), whose products are bought largely on hire-purchase credit. What is more,

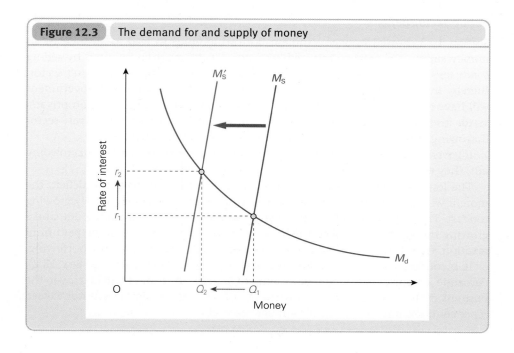

Figure 12.3   The demand for and supply of money

with the deregulation and globalisation of financial markets up to 2007, it had become very difficult to ration credit. If one financial institution was controlled, borrowers could simply go elsewhere.

With the excessive lending in sub-prime markets that had triggered the credit crunch of 2007–9, however, there were calls around the world for tighter controls over bank lending. But this was different from credit rationing as we have defined it. In other words, tighter controls would be used to prevent reckless behaviour by banks, rather than to achieve a particular level of money at a lower rate of interest.

We thus focus on controlling the money supply and controlling interest rates.

Techniques to control the money supply

There are four possible techniques that a central bank could use to control money supply. They have one major feature in common: they involve manipulating the liquid assets of the banking system. The aim is to influence the total money supply by affecting the amount of credit that banks can create.

Open-market operations. **Open-market operations** are the most widely used of the four techniques around the world. They alter the monetary base (cash and reserves in the central bank). This then affects the amount of credit banks can create and hence the level of broad money (M4 in the UK).

Open-market operations involve the sale or purchase by the central bank of government securities (bonds or bills) in the open market. These sales or purchases are *not* in response to changes in the public-sector deficit, and are thus best understood in the context of an unchanged deficit.

If the central bank wishes to *reduce* the money supply, it will sell more securities. When people buy these securities, they pay for them by drawing on their accounts in banks. Thus banks' balances with the central bank are reduced. If this brings bank reserves below their prudent ratio, banks will reduce advances. There will be a multiple contraction of credit and hence of (broad) money supply. (Details of how open-market operations work in the UK are given in Box 12.3.)

Central bank lending to the banks. The central bank in most countries is prepared to provide extra money to banks (through gilt repos, rediscounting bills or straight loans). In some countries, it is the policy of the central bank to keep its interest rate to banks below market rates, thereby encouraging banks to borrow (or sell back securities) whenever such facilities are available. By cutting back the amount it is willing to provide, the central bank can reduce banks' liquid assets and hence the amount of credit they can create.

In other countries, such as the UK and the eurozone countries, it is normally not so much the amount of money made available that is controlled, but rather the rate of interest (or discount). The higher this rate is relative to other market rates, the less will banks be willing to borrow, and the lower, therefore, will be the monetary base. Raising this rate, therefore, has the effect of reducing the money supply.

In response to the credit crunch of 2007–9, central banks in several countries extended their willingness to lend to banks. As we saw in Box 10.4 on pages 318–20, under its 'Special Liquidity Scheme', the Bank of England was willing to swap, on a temporary basis, banks' mortgage and other debt (an illiquid asset) for special 12-month Treasury Bills (a liquid asset). The Bank was effectively lending Treasury Bills against the security of mortgage and other debt. Normally banks could sell these mortgage assets on the money markets as a means of raising finance. With the credit crunch, however, such markets dried up as lenders became more cautious.

Definition

Open market operations
The sale (or purchase) by the authorities of government securities in the open market in order to reduce (or increase) money supply.

Pause for thought

Explain how open-market operations could be used to increase the money supply.

KI 16
p 21

TC 13
p 253

| BOX 12.3 | THE DAILY OPERATION OF MONETARY POLICY | CASE STUDIES & APPLICATIONS |

What goes on at Threadneedle Street?

The Bank of England (the 'Bank') does not normally attempt to control money supply directly. Instead it seeks to control interest rates by conducting open-market operations (OMOs) through short-term and longer-term repos and through the outright purchase of high-quality bonds, These operations, as we shall see, determine short-term interest rates, which then have a knock-on effect on longer-term rates, as returns on different forms of assets must remain competitive with each other.

Let us assume that the Monetary Policy Committee (MPC) of the Bank of England forecasts that inflation will fall below target resulting from a low level of aggregate demand. At its monthly meeting, therefore, it decides to reduce interest rates. What does the Bank do?

The first thing is that it will announce a cut in Bank Rate. But it must do more than this. It must back up the announcement by using OMOs to ensure that its announced interest rate is the equilibrium rate.

Short-term open-market operations

Central to the process is banks' reserves with the Bank of England. Banks are paid at Bank Rate on these reserves. The Bank of England conducts short-term OMOs every week (on a Thursday) at Bank Rate. In other words, if banks start running short of reserves, as they may well do if lower interest rates encourage customers to spend more from their accounts, they can borrow at Bank Rate through short-term repos (with a one-week maturity).

The size of the weekly OMO is adjusted to help banks maintain reserves at the target level and reflect variations in the amount of cash withdrawn or deposited in banks. Fluctuations in banknotes in circulation, and hence in banks' reserves, are accepted *within* the week as the reserve target is a weekly *average*.

Although there is usually a shortage of liquidity in the banking system, in some weeks there may be a surplus. To prevent this driving market interest rates down too far, the Bank will invite banks to bid for outright purchase of short-dated Treasury bills (i.e. ones part-way through their life) at prices set by the Bank to reflect Bank Rate: i.e. in this case, at prices *lower* than the market would otherwise set. At such prices,

the Bank has no difficulty in selling them and hence in 'mopping up' the surplus liquidity.

At the end of the monthly period between MPC interest rate decisions, the Bank of England conducts a 'fine-tuning' OMO. This is conducted on a Wednesday – the day before the MPC decision on interest rates. The idea is to ensure that banks meet their reserve targets as closely as possible. This OMO could expand or contract liquidity as appropriate.

Longer-term open-market operations

Normally once per month – on a Tuesday at 10 a.m. mid-month – the Bank of England conducts longer-term OMOs. This involves repos at 3-, 6-, 9- and 12-month maturities. In other words, the Bank of England lends money to banks to provide longer-term liquidity.

The rate of interest is market determined. Banks bid for the money and the funds are offered to the successful bidders. The bigger the demand for these funds by banks and the lower the supply by the Bank of England, the higher will be the interest rate that banks must pay. By adjusting the supply, therefore, the Bank of England can influence longer-term interest rates.

Since 2006, the Bank of England has also been willing to make outright purchases of gilts and high-quality foreign-currency government bonds. This was used as a means of offsetting the drying up of liquidity in the credit crunch of 2007–9. Such purchases are normally made monthly on a Monday.

In January 2009, as part of a second bank rescue plan (see Box 10.4 on pages 318–20) the Treasury agreed that the Bank of England could purchase up to £75 billion of high-quality assets, such as corporate bonds and assets backed under the Credit Guarantee Scheme. This was extended to £125 billion in May, to £175 billion in August and to £200 billion in November 2009. These open-market purchases would have the effect of injecting extra narrow money into the economy. This massively extended the scope of OMOs to boost liquidity in the economy. This deliberate injection of additional narrow money is known as 'quantitative easing' and is examined in Box 12.5.

 Assume that the Bank of England wants to raise interest rates. Trace through the process by which it achieves this.

Funding. Rather than focusing on controlling the monetary base (as in the case of the above two techniques), an alternative is for the central bank to alter the overall liquidity position of the banks. An example of this approach is a change, by the central bank, in the balance of **funding** government debt To reduce money supply the central bank issues more bonds and fewer bills. Banks' balances with the central bank will be little affected, but to the extent that banks hold fewer bills, there will be a reduction in their liquidity and hence a reduction in the amount of credit created. Funding is thus the conversion of one type of government debt (liquid) into another (illiquid).

Variable minimum reserve ratios. In some countries (such as the USA), banks are required to hold a certain proportion of their assets in liquid form. The assets that count as liquid are known as 'reserve assets'. These include assets such as balances in the central bank, bills of exchange, certificates of deposit and money market loans. The ratio of such assets to total liabilities is known as the **minimum reserve ratio**. If the central bank raises this ratio (in other words, requires the banks to hold a higher proportion of liquid assets), then banks will have to reduce the amount of credit. The money supply will fall.

> ### Definition
>
> **Minimum reserve ratio**
> A minimum ratio of specified liquid assets to deposits (either total or selected) that the central bank requires banks to hold.

Difficulties in controlling money supply

Targets for the growth in broad money were an important part of UK monetary policy from 1976 to 1985. Money targets were then abandoned and have not been used since. The European Central Bank targets the growth of M3 (see Box 12.4), but this is a subsidiary policy to that of setting interest rates in order to keep inflation under control. If, however, a central bank did choose to target money supply as its main monetary policy, how would the policy work?

Assume that money supply is above target and that the central bank wishes to reduce it. It would probably use open-market operations: i.e. it would sell more bonds or bills. The purchasers of the bonds or bills would draw liquidity from the banks. Banks would then supposedly be forced to cut down on the credit they create. But is it as simple as this?

The problem is that banks will normally be unwilling to cut down on loans if people want to borrow – after all, borrowing by customers earns profits for the banks. Banks can always 'top up' their liquidity by borrowing from the central bank and then carry on lending. True, they will have to pay the interest rate charged by the central bank, but they can pass on any rise in the rate to their customers.

The point is that as long as people *want* to borrow, banks and other financial institutions will normally try to find ways of meeting the demand. In other words, in the short run at least, the supply of money is to a large extent demand-determined. It is for this reason that central banks prefer to control the *demand* for money by controlling interest rates (backed up, normally, by open-market operations).

Techniques to control interest rates

The approach to monetary control today in most countries is to focus directly on interest rates. Normally an interest rate change will be announced, and then open-market operations will be conducted by the central bank to ensure that the money supply is adjusted so as to make the announced interest rate the *equilibrium* one. Thus, in Figure 12.3 (on page 394), the central bank might announce a rise in interest rates from r_1 to r_2 and then conduct open-market operations to ensure that the money supply is reduced from Q_1 to Q_2.

Let us assume that the central bank decides to raise interest rates. What does it do? In general, it will seek to keep banks short of liquidity. This will happen automatically on any day when tax payments by banks' customers exceed the money they receive from government expenditure. This excess is effectively withdrawn from banks and ends up in the government's account at the central bank. Even when this does not occur, sales of bills by the central bank will effectively keep the banking system short of liquidity.

BOX 12.4	MONETARY POLICY IN THE EUROZONE

The role of the ECB

The European Central Bank (ECB) is based in Frankfurt and is charged with operating the monetary policy of those EU countries that have adopted the euro. Although the ECB has the overall responsibility for the eurozone's monetary policy, the central banks of the individual countries, such as the Bank of France and Germany's Bundesbank, were not abolished. They are responsible for distributing euros and for carrying out the ECB's policy with respect to institutions in their own countries. The whole system of the ECB and the national central banks is known as the European System of Central Banks (ESCB).

In operating the monetary policy of a 'euro economy' roughly the size of the USA, and in being independent from national governments, the ECB's power is enormous and is equivalent to that of the Fed. So what is the structure of this giant on the European stage, and how does it operate?

The structure of the ECB

The ECB has two major decision-making bodies: the Governing Council and the Executive Board.[a]

The Governing Council consists of the members of the Executive Board and the governors of the central banks of each of the eurozone countries. The Council's role is to set the main targets of monetary policy and to take an oversight of the success (or otherwise) of that policy.

The Executive Board consists of a president, a vice-president and four other members. Each serves for an eight-year, non-renewable term. The Executive Board is responsible for implementing the decisions of the Governing Council and for preparing policies for the Council's consideration. Each member of the Executive Board has a responsibility for some particular aspect of monetary policy.

The targets of monetary policy

The overall responsibility of the ECB is to achieve price stability in the eurozone. The target is a rate of inflation below, but close to, 2 per cent over the medium term. It is a weighted average rate for all the members of the eurozone, not a rate that has to be met by every member individually.

The ECB also sets a reference value for the annual growth of M3, the broad measure of the money supply. This was set at $4\frac{1}{2}$ per cent at the launch of the euro in 1999 and was still the same value in 2008. The reference value is not a rigid target, but is used as a guide to whether monetary policy is consistent with long-run price stability. In setting the reference value, three things are taken into account: the target for inflation, assumptions about the rate of growth of GDP (assumed to have a trend growth rate of 2 to $2\frac{1}{2}$ per cent per year) and the velocity of circulation of M3 (assumed to be declining at a rate of between $\frac{1}{2}$ and 1 per cent per year). The reference value is reviewed in December each year.

---

[a] See www.ecb.int/ecb/orga/decisions/govc/html/index.en.html.

This 'shortage' can then be used as a way of forcing through interest rate changes. Banks will obtain the necessary liquidity from the central bank through repos or by selling it back bills. The central bank can *choose the rate of interest to charge* (i.e. the repo rate or the bill rediscount rate). This will then have a knock-on effect on other interest rates throughout the banking system. (See Box 12.3 for more details on just how the Bank of England manipulates interest rates on a day-to-day basis.)

The effectiveness of changes in interest rates

Even though central bank adjustment of the repo rate is the current preferred method of monetary control in most countries, it is not without its difficulties. The problems centre on the nature of the demand for loans. If this demand is (a) unresponsive to interest rate changes or (b) unstable because it is significantly affected by other determinants (such as anticipated income or foreign interest rates), then it will be very difficult to control by controlling the rate of interest.

Problem of an inelastic demand for loans. If the demand for loans is inelastic, as in Figure 12.4, any attempt to reduce demand (e.g. from Q_1 to Q_2) will involve large rises in interest rates (r_1 to r_2). The problem will be compounded if the demand shifts to the right, due, say, to a consumer-spending boom. High interest rates lead to the following problems:

On the basis of its inflation target and M3 reference value, the ECB then sets the rates of interest. In September 2009, the rates were as follows: 1 per cent for the main 'refinancing operations' of the ESCB (i.e. the minimum rate of interest at which liquidity is offered once per week to 'monetary financial institutions' (MFIs) by the ESCB); a 'marginal lending' rate of 1.75 per cent (for providing overnight support to the MFIs); and a 'deposit rate' of 0.25 per cent (the rate paid to MFIs for depositing overnight surplus liquidity with the ESCB).

Interest rates are set by the Governing Council by simple majority. In the event of a tie, the president has the casting vote.

The operation of monetary policy

The main instrument for keeping the ECB's desired interest rate as the equilibrium rate is open-market operations in government bonds and other recognised assets, mainly in the form of repos. These repo operations are conducted by the national central banks, which must ensure that the repo rate does not rise above the marginal overnight lending rate or below the deposit rate.

The ECB uses four types of open-market operations:

Main refinancing operations.   These are short-term repos with a maturity of one week. They take place weekly and are used to maintain liquidity consistent with the chosen ECB interest rate.

Longer-term refinancing operations.   These take place monthly and have a maturity of three months. They are to provide additional longer-term liquidity to banks as required at rates determined by the market, not the ECB.

Fine-tuning operations.   These can be short-term sales or purchases of short-term assets. They are designed to combat unexpected changes in liquidity and hence to keep money market rates at the ECB's chosen rate.

Structural operations.   These are used as necessary to adjust the amount of liquidity in the eurozone. They can involve either the purchase or sale of various assets.

ECB independence

The ECB is one of the most independent central banks in the world. It has very little formal accountability to elected politicians. Although its president can be called before the European Parliament, the Parliament has virtually no powers to influence the ECB's actions. Also, its deliberations are secret. Unlike meetings of the Bank of England's Monetary Policy Committee, the minutes of the Council meetings are not published.

More details of monetary policy in the eurozone and the role of the ECB are given in Case Study 12.9 in MyEconLab.

 What are the arguments for and against publishing the minutes of the meetings of the ECB's Governing Council and Executive Board?

- They may discourage investment and hence long-term growth.
- They add to the costs of production, to the costs of house purchase and generally to the cost of living. They are thus cost inflationary.
- They are politically unpopular, since the general public do not like paying higher interest rates on overdrafts, credit cards and mortgages.
- The necessary bond issue to restrain liquidity will commit the government to paying high rates on these bonds for the next 20 years or so.
- High interest rates encourage inflows of money from abroad. This drives up the exchange rate. (We examine this in Chapter 14.) A higher exchange rate makes domestic goods expensive relative to goods made abroad. This can be very damaging for export industries and industries competing with imports. Many firms in the UK have suffered badly in recent years from a high exchange rate, caused partly by higher interest rates in the UK than in the eurozone and the USA.

Evidence suggests that the demand for loans may indeed be quite inelastic, especially in the short run. Although investment plans may be curtailed by high interest rates, borrowing to finance current expenditure by many firms cannot easily be curtailed. Similarly, while householders may be discouraged from taking on new mortgages, they may find it difficult to reduce current expenditure as a way of reducing their credit card debt. What is more, although high interest rates may

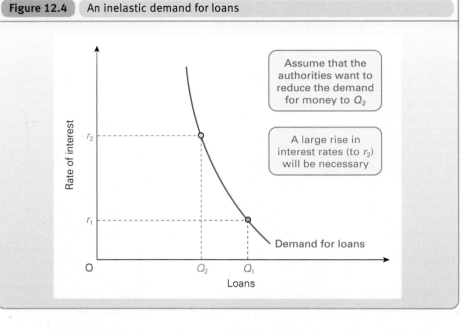

Figure 12.4   An inelastic demand for loans

Assume that the authorities want to reduce the demand for money to Q_2

A large rise in interest rates (to r_2) will be necessary

discourage many firms from taking out long-term fixed-interest loans, some firms may merely switch to shorter-term variable-interest loans.

Problem of an unstable demand.   Accurate monetary control requires the authorities to be able to predict the demand curve for money (in Figure 12.3). Only then can they set the appropriate level of interest rates. Unfortunately, the demand curve may shift unpredictably, making control very difficult. The major reason is *speculation*:

- If people think interest rates will rise and bond prices fall, in the meantime they will demand to hold their assets in liquid form. The demand for money will rise.
- If people think exchange rates will rise, they will hold the domestic currency while it is still relatively cheap. The demand for money will rise.
- If people think the rate of inflation will rise, the transactions demand for money may rise. People plan to spend more while prices are still relatively low.
- If people think the economy is going to grow faster, the demand for loans will increase as firms seek to increase their investment.

It is very difficult for the central bank to predict what people's expectations will be. Speculation depends considerably on world political events, rumour and 'random shocks'.

If the demand curve shifts very much, and if it is inelastic, then monetary control will be very difficult. Furthermore, the central bank will have to make frequent and sizeable adjustments to interest rates. These fluctuations can be very damaging to business confidence and may discourage long-term investment thereby reducing long-run economic growth.

The net result of an inelastic and unstable demand for money is that substantial interest rate changes may be necessary to bring about the required change in aggregate demand. For example, central banks had to cut interest rates to virtually zero in their attempt to tackle the global recession of the late 2000s. Indeed, as we see in Box 12.5, central banks took to other methods as the room for interest rate cuts simply disappeared.

Pause for thought

Assume that the central bank announces a rise in interest rates and backs this up with open-market operations. What determines the size of the resulting fall in aggregate demand?

BOX 12.5   **QUANTITATIVE EASING**

Rethinking monetary policy in hard times

As the economies of the world slid into recession in 2008, central banks became more and more worried that the traditional instrument of monetary policy – controlling interest rates – was insufficient to ward off a slump in demand.

Running out of options?

Interest rates had been cut at an unprecedented rate. Typically central banks have changed interest rates by just a quarter of a percentage point at a time. But in November 2008 the Bank of England cut Bank Rate from 4.5 to 3 per cent and in December to 2 per cent and then by half a percentage point each month to stand at 0.5 per cent by March 2009. The ECB too was making large cuts: from 3.25 to 2.5 per cent in December, to 2 per cent in January. By May it was just 1 per cent.

Central banks were reaching the end of the road for interest rate cuts. The Fed was the first to be in this position. It had cut the target federal funds rate (the overnight rate at which the Fed lends to banks) from 2 to 1.5 per cent in October, to 1 per cent in November and to a range between 0 and 0.25 per cent in December. But you cannot cut nominal rates below zero – otherwise you would be paying people to borrow money, which would be like giving people free money.

The problem was that there was an acute lack of willingness of banks to lend, and firms and consumers to borrow, as people saw the oncoming recession. Banks were more cautious about mortgage lending as the prices of houses fell and unemployment rose, and more cautious about lending to business as the recession deepened. Firms did not want to invest and consumers tried to rein in debt. So the cuts in interest rates were not having enough effect on aggregate demand.

Increasing the money supply

So what were central banks to do? The answer was to increase money supply directly, in a process known as **quantitative easing**. This involves an aggressive version of open-market operations, where the central bank buys up a range of assets, such as securitised mortgage debt and long-term government bonds. The effect is to pump large amounts of additional cash into the economy in the hope of stimulating demand and, through the process of credit creation, to boost broad money too.

In the USA, in December 2008, at the same time as the federal funds rate was cut to a range of 0 to 0.25 per cent, the Fed embarked on large-scale quantitative easing. It began buying hundreds of billions of dollars worth of mortgage-backed securities on the open market

and planned also to buy large quantities of long-term government debt. The Federal Open Market Committee (the interest rate setting body in the USA) said that, 'The focus of the committee's policy going forward will be to support the functioning of financial markets and stimulate the economy through open-market operations and other measures that sustain the size of the Federal Reserve's balance sheet at a high level.'

The result was that considerable quantities of new money were injected into the system. This also had the effect of reducing interest rates on the assets purchased by the Fed, thereby stimulating aggregate demand.

In the UK, in January 2009, the government announced that it was giving the Bank of England authority to purchase a range of high-quality assets to help increase the amount of credit available to business. Initially, this was for the purchase of £50 billion of private-sector assets, including corporate bonds and securitised assets. But, by March 2009 the Chancellor increased the scale and range of assets to be purchased. This allowed for purchases up to £150 billion, including the purchase of government debt on the secondary market, so long as up to £50 billion was the purchase of private-sector assets. By May 2009, the Monetary Policy Committee had announcement that it was looking to purchase up to £125 billion of eligible assets. The extent of the economic downturn along with continuing concerns about banks' balance sheets led the MPC to announce in August that it wanted to increase the size of asset purchases by a further £50 billion to £175 billion. This was extended by a further £25 billion to £200 billion in November 2009.

The aim was directly to increase money supply. In addition, the Monetary Policy Committee was given the power to use asset purchases as an additional means of meeting the inflation target.

The danger of this approach is that in the short run little credit creation may take place. People need to have the confidence to borrow. In the equation $MV = PY$, the rise in (narrow) money supply (M) may be largely offset by a fall in the velocity of circulation (V) (see Chapter 11, pages 345–6). There is also the danger that if this policy is conducted for too long, the growth in money supply may then prove to be excessive, resulting in inflation rising above the target level. It would thus be important for central banks to foresee this and turn the monetary 'tap' off in time.

 Would it be appropriate to define the policy of quantitative easing as 'monetarist'?

Definition

Quantitative easing
A deliberate attempt by the central bank to increase the money supply by buying large quantities of securities through open-market operations. These securities could be securitised mortgage and other private-sector debt or government bonds.

Using monetary policy

It is impossible to use monetary policy as a precise means of controlling aggregate demand. It is especially weak when it is pulling against the expectations of firms and consumers, and when it is implemented too late. However, if the authorities operate a tight monetary policy firmly enough and long enough, they should eventually be able to reduce lending and hence aggregate demand, and with it, inflation. But there will inevitably be time lags and imprecision in the process.

An expansionary monetary policy is even less reliable. If the economy is in recession, no matter how low interest rates are driven, people cannot be forced to borrow if they do not wish to. Firms will not borrow to invest if they predict a continuing recession.

A particular difficulty in using interest rate reductions to expand the economy arises if the repo rate is nearly zero but this is still not enough to stimulate the economy. The problem is that (nominal) interest rates cannot be negative, for clearly nobody would be willing to lend in these circumstances. Japan was in such a situation in the early 2000s. It was caught in what is known as the **liquidity trap**.

Despite these problems, largely of a short-term nature, changing interest rates can be quite effective. After all, they can be changed very rapidly. There are not the time lags of implementation that there are with fiscal policy. Indeed, since the early 1990s, most governments or central banks in OECD countries have used interest rate changes as the major means of keeping aggregate demand and inflation under control.

In the UK, the eurozone and many other countries, a target is set for the rate of inflation. As we have seen, in the UK and the eurozone the target is 2 per cent. If forecasts suggest that inflation is going to be above the target rate, the government or central bank raises interest rates. The advantage of this is that it sends a very clear message to people that inflation *will* be kept under control. People will therefore be more likely to adjust their expectations accordingly and keep their borrowing in check.

Recap

1. Control of the growth in the money supply over the longer term will normally involve governments attempting to restrict the size of their deficits.

2. In the short term, the authorities can use monetary policy to restrict the growth in aggregate demand in one of two major ways: (a) reducing money supply directly, (b) reducing the demand for money by raising interest rates.

3. The money supply can be reduced directly by using open-market operations. This involves the central bank selling more government securities and thereby reducing banks' reserves when their customers pay for them from their bank accounts. Alternatively, the central bank can reduce the amount of lending or rediscounting it is prepared to do (other than as a last-resort measure).

4. Rather than controlling the monetary base in either of these two ways, the central bank could use funding.

This involves increasing the sale of bonds relative to bills, thereby reducing banks' liquid assets. Finally, it could operate a system of variable minimum reserve ratios. Increasing these would force banks to cut back the amount of credit they create.

5. Controlling either the monetary base or broad liquidity in the short term, however, is difficult given that central banks are always prepared to provide liquidity to the banks on demand. Even if the authorities are successful in controlling the money supply, there then arises the problem of severe fluctuations in interest rates if the demand for money fluctuates and is relatively inelastic.

6. The current method of control in the UK and many other countries involves the central bank influencing interest rates by its operations in the gilt repo and discount markets. The central bank keeps banks short of liquidity and then supplies them with liquidity, largely through gilt repos, at its chosen interest rate

(gilt repo rate). This then has a knock-on effect on interest rates throughout the economy.

7. With an inelastic demand for loans, however, changes in interest rates may have to be very large to bring the required changes in monetary growth. High interest rates are politically unpopular and discriminate against those with high borrowing commitments. They also drive up the exchange rate, which can damage exports. Controlling aggregate demand through interest rates is made even more difficult by fluctuations in the demand for money. These fluctuations are made more severe by speculation against changes in interest rates, exchange rates, the rate of inflation, etc.

8. It is impossible to use monetary policy as a precise means of controlling aggregate demand in the short term. Nevertheless, controlling interest rates is a rapid way of responding to changing forecasts, and can be an important signal to markets that inflation will be kept under control, especially when, as in the UK and the eurozone, there is a firm target for the rate of inflation.

DEMAND-SIDE POLICY   12.3

What will be the effect of attempts by the government to control the level of spending in the economy?

Attitudes towards demand management

Debates over the control of demand have shifted ground somewhat in recent years. There is now less debate over the relative merits of fiscal and monetary policy. There is general agreement that a *combination* of fiscal and monetary policies will have a more powerful effect on demand than either used separately.

The debate today is much more concerned with the extent to which governments ought to pursue an active demand management policy or adhere to a set of policy rules.

Those in the Keynesian tradition prefer discretionary policy – changing policy as circumstances change. Those in the monetarist tradition prefer to set firm rules (e.g. targets for inflation, public deficits or growth in the money supply) and then stick to them. The financial crisis of the late 2000s helped to fuel the debate about the *type* and *flexibility* of policy rules and the extent to which governments should have discretion over policy.

The case for rules and policy frameworks

Why should governments commit to rules or design policy frameworks which may involve them giving up control of economic instruments? Well, there are two important arguments against discretionary policy.

Political behaviour. The first concerns the motivation of government. Politicians may attempt to manipulate the economy for their own political purposes – such as the desire to be re-elected. The government, if not constrained by rules, may over-stimulate the economy some time before an election so that growth is strong at election time. After the election, the government strongly dampens the economy to deal with the higher inflation which is now beginning to accelerate, and to create enough slack for another boost in time for the next election.

When politicians behave in this way, they may lose *credibility* for sound economic management. This can lead to higher inflationary expectations, uncertainty and lower long-term investment.

Time lags with discretionary policy. Both fiscal and monetary policies can involve long and variable time lags, which can make the policy at best ineffective and at worst destabilising. Taking the measures *before* the problem arises, and thus lessening the problem of lags, is no answer since forecasting tends to be unreliable.

By contrast, setting and sticking to rules, and then not interfering further, the government can provide a sound monetary framework in which there is maximum freedom for individual initiative and enterprise, and in which firms are not cushioned from market forces and are therefore encouraged to be efficient. By the government setting a target for a steady reduction in the growth of money supply, or a target for the rate of inflation, and then resolutely sticking to it, people's expectations of inflation will be reduced, thereby making the target easier to achieve.

This sound and stable monetary environment, with no likelihood of sudden contractionary or expansionary fiscal or monetary policy, will encourage firms to take a longer-term perspective and to plan ahead. This could then lead to increased capital investment and, as we saw in Chapter 9, raise long-term growth rates.

The optimum situation is for all the major countries to adhere to mutually consistent rules, so that their economies do not get out of line. This will create more stable exchange rates and provide the climate for world growth (we explore these issues in Chapters 13 and 14).

Advocates of this point of view in the 1970s and 1980s were the monetarists, but in recent years support for the setting of targets has become widespread. As we have seen, in both the UK and the eurozone countries, targets are set for both inflation and public-sector deficits.

The case for discretion

Some Keynesians reject the argument that rules provide the environment for high and stable growth. Demand, argue Keynesians, is subject to many and sometimes violent shocks: e.g. changes in expectations, domestic political events (such as an impending election), world economic factors (such as the world economic recession of 2008–9) or world political events (such as a war). The resulting shifts in injections or withdrawals cause the economy to deviate from a stable full-employment growth path.

Any change in injections or withdrawals will lead to a cumulative effect on national income via the multiplier and accelerator and via changing expectations. These effects take time and interact with each other, and so a process of expansion or contraction can last many months before a turning point is eventually reached.

Since shocks to demand occur at irregular intervals and are of different magnitudes, the economy is likely to experience cycles of irregular duration and of varying intensity.

Given that the economy is inherently unstable and is buffeted around by various shocks, Keynesians argue that the government needs actively to intervene to stabilise the economy. Otherwise, the uncertainty caused by unpredictable fluctuations will be very damaging to investment and hence to long-term economic growth (quite apart from the short-term effects of recessions on output and employment).

Difficulties with choice of target under a rules-based policy

Assume that the government or central bank sets an inflation rate target. Should it then stick to that rate, come what may? Might not an extended period of relatively low inflation rates warrant a lower inflation rate target? The government must at least have the discretion to *change* the rules, even if only occasionally.

Then there is the question of whether success in achieving the target will bring success in achieving other macroeconomic objectives, such as low unemployment and stable economic growth. The problem is that something called **Goodhart's law** is likely to apply. The law, named after Charles Goodhart of the LSE and formerly of the Bank of England, states that attempts to control an *indicator* of a problem may, as a result, make it cease to be a good indicator of the problem.

Targeting inflation may make it become a poor indicator of the state of the economy. If people believe that the central bank will be successful in achieving its inflation target, then those expectations will feed into their inflationary expectations, and not surprisingly the target will be met. But that target rate of inflation may now be consistent with both a buoyant and a depressed economy. As we saw for the UK in Figure 11.16 (page 367), it is possible that the Phillips curve may become *horizontal*. An example occurred in 2001/2 when the UK economy slowed down considerably and yet there was virtually no change in the rate of inflation. Thus achieving the inflation target may not tackle the much more serious problem of creating stable economic growth and an environment that will therefore encourage long-term investment.

In extreme cases, as occurred in 2008, the economy may slow down rapidly and yet cost-push factors cause inflation to rise. Targeting inflation in these circumstances will demand *higher* interest rates, which will help to deepen the recession.

> **KEY IDEA 33**
>
> **Goodhart's law.** Controlling a symptom (i.e. an indicator) of a problem will not cure the problem. Instead, the indicator will merely cease to be a good indicator of the problem.

Use of a Taylor rule. For this reason, many economists have advocated the use of a **Taylor rule**[1], rather than a simple inflation target. A Taylor rule takes two objectives into account – (1) inflation and (2) either real national income or unemployment – and seeks to get the optimum degree of stability of the two. The degree of importance attached to each of the two objectives can be decided by the government or central bank. The central bank adjusts interest rates when either the rate of inflation diverges from its target or the level of real national income (or unemployment) diverges from its sustainable (or equilibrium) level.

Take the case where inflation is above its target level. The central bank following a Taylor rule will raise the rate of interest. It knows, however, that this will reduce real national income. This, therefore, limits the amount that the central bank is prepared to raise the rate of interest. The more weight it attaches to stabilising inflation, the more it will raise the rate of interest. The more weight it attaches to stabilising real national income, the less it will raise the rate of interest.

Thus the central bank has to trade off inflation stability against real income stability.

Constrained discretion in the UK

Many countries have, in recent times, been operating economic policy within a framework of rules. This is known as **constrained discretion**.

On being elected in 1997 the UK Labour government set about reforming the frameworks within which fiscal and monetary policies operated.

Fiscal policy. The Labour government set targets for government expenditure, not for just one year, but for a three-year period. It also adopted two operational rules: the

---

[1] Named after John Taylor, from Stanford University, who proposed that for every 1 per cent that GDP rises above sustainable GDP, real interest rates should be raised by 0.5 percentage point and for every 1 per cent that inflation rises above its target level, real interest rates should be raised by 0.5 percentage point (i.e. nominal rates should be raised by 1.5 percentage points).

Definitions

Goodhart's law
Controlling a symptom of a problem, or only part of the problem, will not cure the problem: it will simply mean that the part that is being controlled now becomes a poor indicator of the problem.

Taylor rule
A rule adopted by a central bank for setting the rate of interest. It will raise the interest rate if (a) inflation is above target or (b) real national income is above the sustainable level (or unemployment is below the equilibrium rate). The rule states how much interest rates will be changed in each case.

Constrained discretion
A set of principles or rules within which economic policy operates. These can be informal or enshrined in law.

golden rule and the sustainable investment rule. These were examined in Box 12.2 (on pages 390–1).

Monetary policy. As far as monetary policy is concerned, this involved granting operational independence to the Bank of England.

Operational independence for the Bank of England means that it sets interest rates in order to meet a government-set inflation rate target. Since December 2003, the target has been that CPI inflation should be 2 per cent in 24 months' time.

To achieve this target two years in the future, the Bank of England publishes a quarterly *Inflation Report*, which contains projections for inflation for the next three years. These projections assume that interest rates follow market expectations. They form the basis for the Monetary Policy Committee's monthly deliberations. If the projected inflation in 24 months' time is off target, the MPC will change interest rates accordingly.

Two key projections of the MPC are shown in the Bank of England's *Inflation Report*, which is published each quarter. These are shown in Figure 12.5. They are known as 'fan charts'. The first plots the forecast range of inflation. The second plots the forecast range of real GDP growth. In each case, the darkest central band represents a 10 per cent likelihood, as does each of the eight subsequent pairs of lighter areas out from the central band. Thus inflation or GDP growth are considered to have a 90 per cent probability of being within the fan. The bands get wider as the time horizon is extended, indicating increasing uncertainty about the outcome. Also, the less reliable are considered to be the forecasts by the MPC, the wider will be the fan. The dashed line indicates the two-year target point. Thus in quarter 2 of 2009, the 2 per cent inflation target was for quarter 2 of 2011.

Although projections are made for GDP growth, these are to help inform the forecast for inflation. GDP growth is not itself an explicit target.

Another aim of central bank independence is to enhance transparency in policy-making. In the UK, transparency is enhanced by the publication of the minutes of

Figure 12.5	Fan chart of CPI inflation and GDP growth projections (made in 2009 Q2) based on market interest rate expectations

(a) CPI inflation   (b) Real GDP growth

Source: *Inflation Report May 2009* (Bank of England, with permission)
Note: The projections are based on the assumption that the £125 billion made available under the Asset Purchase Programme will be fully used and remain so throughout the period

the monthly meetings of Bank's Monetary Policy Committee (MPC), at which interest rates are set. One of the main purposes of transparency is to convince people of the seriousness with which the Bank of England will adhere to its targets. This, it is hoped, will keep people's *expectations* of inflation low: the lower expected inflation is, the lower will be the actual rate of inflation.

In both fiscal and monetary policy, therefore, rules appeared to have replaced discretion.

> When there are ever more rapid financial flows across the world that are unpredictable and uncertain, the answer is to ensure stability through establishing the right long-term policy objectives and to build credibility in the policy through well-understood procedural rules that are followed for fiscal and monetary policy.[2]

There was, however, a new form of fine-tuning: the frequent adjustment of interest rates, not to smooth out the business cycle, but to make sure that the inflation rule is adhered to. Nevertheless, with automatic fiscal stabilisers still operating, and with interest rate changes to stabilise inflation also having the effect of stabilising aggregate demand, cyclical fluctuations had become less pronounced – at least until 2007. In the 12 years to 2007, annual economic growth did not fall below 1.8 per cent or rise above 3.8 per cent.

Response to the credit crunch

The global crisis, which started in 2007 with the credit crunch and then developed into the worldwide recession of 2008/9, highlighted differences between countries in their monetary and fiscal frameworks. It also raised the question of whether rules should be abandoned – at least in exceptional circumstances.

Monetary policy responses. In 2007/8, many countries were faced with a possible return of stagflation (low or no growth accompanied by rapidly rising prices). World food and other commodity prices were rising rapidly. This supply-side shock meant that inflation rates rose. For example, in the UK by September 2008, the annual CPI inflation rate had reached 5.2 per cent while general food prices were rising at an annual rate in excess of 10 per cent (see Figure 12.6).

To meet their inflationary target, central banks were under pressure to raise interest rates. But, to avert a recession they were under pressure to cut them.

Eventually, with confidence in the banking system plummeting and inter-bank markets virtually frozen, the Bank of England (along with several other central banks) began cutting interest rates. At least now the rate of inflation was forecast to be below 2 per cent in 24 months' time. The Bank of England reduced the Bank Rate from 4.25 per cent in September 2008 to just 0.5 per cent in March 2009. In addition, as we saw in Box 10.4 on pages 318–20, massive amounts of liquidity and capital were pumped into the banking system to stimulate lending and hence aggregate demand.

But despite general agreement that both inflation and GDP were falling, the extent and speed of the interest rates cuts varied across countries. In part, this reflects differences in the frameworks within which central banks operate. This is explored in Box 12.6.

Pause for thought

If people believe that the central bank will be successful in keeping inflation on target, does it matter whether a simple inflation rule or a Taylor rule is used? Explain.

Pause for thought

Do you agree that 'ever more rapid financial flows across the world that are unpredictable and uncertain' make Keynesian discretionary fiscal (and monetary) policy less suitable? Explain.

---

[2] Extract from the Chancellor's Mansion House speech, 11 June 1998.

BOX 12.6 | INTEREST RATE RESPONSES AND THE FINANCIAL CRISIS OF 2007/8

Passive or aggressive?

The Federal Reserve, the European Central Bank (ECB) and the Bank of England are examples of independent central banks. In each case the responsibility for setting interest rates has been delegated to a decision-making board of the central bank. However, the policy remit of each of these banks is different. We consider here how this may have influenced interest rate decisions in the period from 2005 and, in particular, in the aftermath of the liquidity crisis that hit financial systems across the world from summer 2007.

Remits of the three central banks

In the USA the goals of monetary policy are set down in the Federal Reserve Act, originally proposed in 1913. The Federal Open Market Committee (FOMC) has eight regularly scheduled meetings each year. It is charged with ensuring that there is long-run economic growth so as to achieve the goals of maximum employment, stable prices and moderate long-term interest rates. This, as you can see, is a very broad remit.

The ECB's independence is laid down in the institutional framework for the single monetary policy. Its aim is to promote price stability. For operational purposes the ECB has a target rate of inflation below, but close to 2 per cent over the medium term. It is a weighted average across the eurozone. At the end of the first of two monthly meetings the Governing Council takes its interest rate decision.

The 1998 Bank of England Act made the Bank independent to set interest rates. The Bank's Monetary Policy Committee meets at the beginning of each month to decide on interest rates. The Bank is charged to deliver price stability, but operationally it is a symmetrical target around a 2 per cent inflation rate. Interest rates are set to meet this target 24 months hence. If current inflation exceeds or undershoots this target by more than 1 percentage point then the Governor is forced to write an open letter to the Chancellor of the Exchequer explaining the reasons for it and the Bank's intended response. Subject to delivering price stability, monetary policy should also support the government's economic objectives, including growth and employment.

Different policy responses?

The goals set for the Federal Reserve are broader than those of its two European counterparts. This would be expected to impact on the relationship between interest rates and inflation observed across the three central banks.

Chart (a) displays the annual rates of consumer price inflation for the USA, the eurozone and the UK from 2005. The US rate of inflation is consistently higher than in the UK and eurozone through 2005 and into the autumn of 2006. During much of this period the Federal Reserve was raising interest rates. This can be observed in Chart (b), which plots the interest rates set by the decision-making boards of the three central banks. From 2.25 per cent at the start of 2005 the Fed increased rates to 5.25 per cent by June 2006.

The Fed kept interest rates at 5.25 per cent until the liquidity crisis hit global financial systems in late summer 2007. Interestingly, its broader policy remit appears to have enabled it to respond more

(a) Annual rates of consumer price inflation

(b) Central bank interest rates

aggressively to the impact of financial instability on the macroeconomy.

The responses of the ECB and the Bank of England were constrained by their policy remits and, specifically, their inflation rate targets. This was because inflationary pressures were emerging at around the same time as the liquidity crisis was biting. These emanated largely from the supply side, with increases in the cost of raw materials, energy and fuel. Therefore, the ECB and the Bank of England felt unable to cut rates. They were concerned about easing the brake on aggregate demand and further fuelling inflation, both directly and through raising inflation expectations.

The European Central Bank looks to have been especially concerned about suppressing inflation. It raised its rate from 3.75 to 4 per cent in June 2007 and maintained it at this level to July 2008, when it raised it again to 4.25 per cent. In sharp contrast, the Fed's rate fell from 5.25 per cent in August 2007 to 2 per cent by April 2008.

The Bank of England's interest rate policy from the time of the liquidity crisis was to tread carefully in the presence of inflation rate fears. It eased rates in December 2007 from 5.75 to 5.5 per cent and to 5.25 per cent in February and 5 per cent in April 2008.

Recession and falling inflation rates

From late 2008, inflation rates started to fall as recession around the world took hold; indeed the chart reveals that the US was experiencing deflation in the early months of 2009. The different remits of the central banks now no

longer mattered so much. Whether the remit was to keep inflation to target or to follow a Taylor rule, both required a cut in interest rates.

As you can see from Chart (b), all three banks cut interest rates. The Fed was the earliest and most aggressive cutter and the ECB the least. But by the middle of 2009, all three had made substantial cuts. The Bank of England's rate was 0.5 per cent, the Fed's rate 0.25 per cent and the ECB's 1 per cent.

Our economic commentary demonstrates that different independent central banks can be quite different beasts. Of course, each is reacting to its own economic reality. But, the policy goals of the decision-making boards are very important. On occasions, as in the period mid-2007 to mid-2008, this can result in quite different decisions. While the Fed cut rates aggressively, the Bank of England, and the ECB in particular, were more passive.

Such distinctive responses undoubtedly raise questions about the rights and wrongs of alternative policy rules. Is it better to stick to a firm inflation target, like the ECB? Or is it better to allow central banks to have more discretion to take a number of economic indicators into account, as is the case with the Fed?

 In which of the following circumstances are the three central banks more likely to respond in a similar way: (a) rising demand-pull inflation; (b) rising cost-push inflation? Explain.

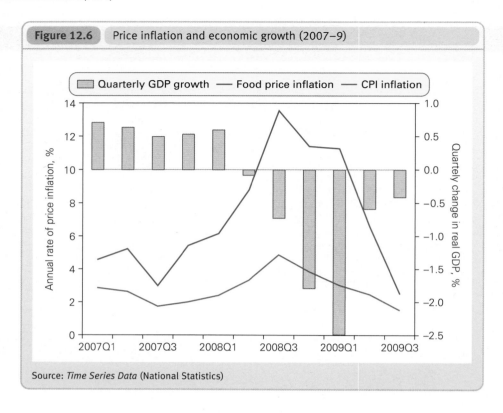

Figure 12.6 Price inflation and economic growth (2007–9)

Source: *Time Series Data* (National Statistics)

Fiscal policy responses. The extent of the downturn put governments under pressure to give their economies a fiscal stimulus (see Box 12.1 on page 385 for the US response). In the UK, with the current budget already in deficit (see Box 12.2 on pages 390–1), the government was in danger of breaching its golden rule and thus would seem to have limited scope for increased expenditure or tax cuts to stimulate aggregate demand.

But the problem was seen to be too serious to stick to rules for rules' sake. The golden rule would have to be abandoned – at least temporarily. As Box 12.2 illustrates, fiscal policy was relaxed with a package of tax cuts and increases in government expenditure, though increases in taxes further down the line were pre-announced. Therefore, the golden and sustainable investments rules were to be temporarily abandoned. They were replaced with more general principles, known as temporary operating rules, for both budget balances and the stock of government debt, which would apply once the economy had emerged from the downturn.

While the economic downturn of the 2008/09 did not lead to the total abandonment of rules, it did lead many countries to soften their implementation of constrained discretion. The debate continues as to how flexible 'constrained' should be!

Recap

1. The case against discretionary policy is that it involves unpredictable time lags that can make the policy destabilising. Also, the government may *ignore* the long-run adverse consequences of policies designed for short-run political gain.

2. The case in favour of rules is that they help to reduce inflationary expectations and thus create a stable environment for investment and growth.

3. The case against sticking to money supply or inflation rules is that they may cause severe fluctuations in interest rates and thus create a less stable economic environment for business planning.

4. Although perfect fine-tuning may not be possible, Keynesians argue that the government must have the discretion to change its policy as circumstances demand.

5. The UK Labour government, elected in 1997, enshrined in law monetary and fiscal frameworks which involved constraining some of its discretion over economic policy. This included making the Bank of England independent. This now targets a 2 per cent rate of inflation, and adjusts interest rates in order to meet that target. To meet its Code for Fiscal Stability, the UK government set a golden rule to balance its current (as opposed to capital) budget over the course of the business cycle.

6. Many countries have pursued a policy of constrained discretion. This came under increasing pressure in 2008 with rising inflation and falling growth. Given the changing economic environment in which we live, rules adopted in the past may no longer be suitable for the present.

SUPPLY-SIDE POLICY   12.4

How might the government attempt to control the level of output and employment directly?

TC 7
p 49

Supply-side policies, as the name suggests, focus on aggregate supply. If successful, they will shift the aggregate supply curve to the right, thus increasing output for any given level of prices (or reducing the price level for any given level of output).

TC 15
p 289

In Chapter 9 we saw that the *AS* curve is fundamentally related to an economy's factors of production, including labour and capital. Therefore, policies which influence the *quantities* of the factors employed, their *effectiveness* in production, including their effectiveness when combined with each other, constitute supply-side policies.

Economists and policy-makers are keen to understand how supply-side policies affect an economy's potential output and, in particular, the rate at which it grows over time. Therefore, supply-side policies can be evaluated on their ability to affect an economy's long-run growth.

But, supply-side policies can impact on other economic variables too. Since labour is an important factor of production, policies may be designed to affect decisions relating to labour supply and the demand for labour. These, of course, impact on employment levels. For instance, policies could be geared to making workers more responsive to changes in job opportunities, such as changes in the skills demanded by employers. Alternatively, they may aim to make employers more adaptable and willing to operate within existing labour constraints.

Inflation rates too might be affected by supply-side policies. For instance, we saw in Chapter 9 how endogenous growth theorists argue that competition amongst firms can increase productivity by encouraging investment in products, processes and people.

TC 4
p 21

Supply-side policies can take various forms. They can be *market-orientated* and focus on ways of 'freeing up' the market, such as encouraging private enterprise, risk taking and competition: policies that provide incentives and reward initiative, hard work and productivity. Alternatively, they can be *interventionist* in nature and focus on means of counteracting the deficiencies of the free market.

First we will examine market-orientated policies. Then we will turn to interventionist policies.

Market-orientated supply-side policies

Radical market-orientated supply-side policies were first adopted in the early 1980s by the Thatcher government in the UK and the Reagan administration in the USA, but were subsequently copied by other right and centre-right governments around the world. The essence of these policies is to encourage and reward individual enterprise and initiative, and to reduce the role of government; to put more reliance on market forces and competition, and less on government intervention and regulation.

Reducing government expenditure

The desire by many governments to cut government expenditure is not just to reduce public-sector deficits and hence reduce the growth of money supply; it is also an essential ingredient of their supply-side strategy.

The public sector is portrayed by some as more bureaucratic and less efficient than the private sector. What is more, it is claimed that a growing proportion of public money has been spent on administration and other 'non-productive' activities, rather than on the direct provision of goods and services.

Two things are needed, it is argued: (a) a more efficient use of resources within the public sector and (b) a reduction in the size of the public sector. This would allow private investment to increase with no overall rise in aggregate demand. Thus the supply-side benefits of higher investment could be achieved without the demand-side costs of higher inflation.

In practice, governments have found it very difficult to cut their expenditure without cutting services and the provision of infrastructure.

Tax cuts

The imposition of taxation can distort a variety of choices that individuals make. Changes to the rates of taxation can lead individuals to substitute one activity for another. Three commonly referred to examples in the context of aggregate supply are:

■ taxation of labour income and its impact on labour supply (including hours worked and choice of occupation).
■ taxation of interest income earned on financial products (savings) and its impact on the funds available for investment.
■ taxation of firms' profits and its impact on capital expenditure by firms.

Over time, the UK has witnessed a decline in the marginal rates of taxation associated with each of these cases. For example, in 1979, the standard rate of income tax in the UK was 33 per cent and the top rate was 83 per cent. In 2009 the standard rate was only 20 per cent and the top rate was only 40 per cent. In 1983 the main rate of corporation tax in the UK stood at 52 per cent. By 2009 this was 28 per cent.

The argument for reducing tax rates on incomes and profits is that it contributes to higher levels of economic output. Specifically, it contributes to there being more labour hours supplied, more moneys invested with financial institutions and more capital expenditure by firms than would otherwise be the case. In other words, there is a substitution effect (see page 182) inducing more of these beneficial activities. In the case of labour, people are encouraged to substitute work for leisure.

However, in each case there is a counteracting incentive: an income effect (see page 182). This is because the higher returns to working, saving and undertaking capital expenditure mean that less of each activity needs to be undertaken to generate the same income flow as before.

Because economic theory offers no firm conclusions as to the benefit of tax cuts, economists and policy-makers often look to empirical evidence for guidance. The evidence on whether people will be prepared to work longer hours, for instance, suggests that the substitution and income effects just about cancel each other out. Anyway, for many people there is no such choice in the short run. There is no chance of doing overtime or working a shorter week. In the long run, there may be some flexibility in that people can change jobs.

Reducing the power of labour

The argument here is that, if labour costs to employers are reduced, their profits will probably rise. This could encourage and enable more investment and hence economic growth. If the monopoly power of labour is reduced, then cost-push inflation will also be reduced.

The Thatcher government took a number of measures to curtail the power of unions. These included the right of employees not to join unions, preventing workers taking action other than against their direct employers and enforced secret ballots on strike proposals. It set a lead in resisting strikes in the public sector.

As labour markets have become more flexible, with increased part-time working and short-term contracts, and as the process of globalisation has exposed more companies to international competition, so this has further eroded the power of labour in many sectors of the economy (see Case Study 6.2 in MyEconLab).

Reducing welfare

New classical economists claim that a major cause of unemployment is the small difference between the welfare benefits of the unemployed and the take-home pay of the employed. This causes voluntary unemployment (i.e. frictional unemployment). People are caught in a 'poverty trap': if they take a job, they lose their benefits (see page 184).

A dramatic solution to this problem would be to cut unemployment benefits. A major problem with this approach, however, is that with changing requirements for labour skills, many of the redundant workers from the older industries are simply not qualified for new jobs that are created. What is more, the longer people are unemployed, the more demoralised they become. Employers would probably be prepared to pay only very low wages to such workers. To persuade these unemployed people to take low-paid jobs, the welfare benefits would have to be slashed. A 'market' solution to the problem, therefore, may be a very cruel solution. A fairer one would be an interventionist policy: a policy of retraining labour.

Another alternative is to make the payment of unemployment benefits conditional on the recipient making a concerted effort to find a job. In the Jobseeker's Allowance introduced in the UK in 1996, claimants must be available for and actively seeking work, and must complete a jobseeker's agreement, which sets out the types of work the person is willing to do, and the plan to find work. Payment can be refused if the claimant refuses to accept the offer of a job.

Policies to encourage competition

If the government can encourage more competition, this should have the effect of increasing national output and reducing inflation. Five major types of policy have been pursued under this heading.

Privatisation. If privatisation simply involves the transfer of a natural monopoly to private hands (e.g. the water companies), the scope for increased competition is limited. However, where there is genuine scope for increased competition (e.g. in the supply of gas and electricity), privatisation can lead to increased efficiency, more consumer choice and lower prices (see Box 7.2 on pages 210–11).

Alternatively, privatisation can involve the introduction of private services into the public sector (e.g. private contractors providing cleaning services in hospitals, or refuse collection for local authorities). Private contractors may compete against each other for the franchise. This may well lower the cost of provision of these services, but the quality of provision may also suffer unless closely monitored. The effects on unemployment are uncertain. Private contractors may offer lower wages and thus may use more labour. But if they are trying to supply the service at minimum cost, they may employ less labour.

Deregulation. This involves the removal of monopoly rights: again, largely in the public sector. The deregulation of the UK bus industry, opening it up to private operators, is a good example of this initiative.

Introducing market relationships into the public sector. This is where the government tries to get different departments or elements within a particular part of the public sector to 'trade' with each other, so as to encourage competition and efficiency.

One example is in the National Health Service. In 2003, the UK government introduced a system of 'foundation trusts'. Hospitals can apply for foundation trust status. If successful, they are given much greater financial autonomy in terms of purchasing, employment and investment decisions. By 2009, there were 120 foundation trusts. Critics argue that funds have been diverted to foundation hospitals away from the less well-performing hospitals where greater funding could help that performance.

The Private Finance Initiative (PFI). This is where a private company, after a competitive tender, is contracted by a government department or local authority to finance and build a project, such as a new road or a prison. The government then pays the company to maintain and/or run it, or simply rents the assets from the company. The public sector thus becomes a purchaser of services rather than a direct provider itself.

The aim of these 'public–private partnerships' (PPPs) is to introduce competition (through the tendering process) and private-sector expertise into the provision of public services (see Web Case 12.7). It is hoped that the extra burden to the taxpayer of the private-sector profits will be more than offset by gains in efficiency. Critics, however, claim that PPPs have resulted in poorer quality of provision and that cost control has often been poor too, resulting in a higher burden for the taxpayer in the long term.

Free trade and capital movements. The opening-up of international trade and investment is central to a market-orientated supply-side policy. One of the first measures of the Thatcher government (in October 1979) was to remove all controls on the purchase and sale of foreign currencies, thereby permitting the free inflow and outflow of capital, both long-term and short-term. Most other industrialised countries also removed or relaxed exchange controls during the 1980s and early 1990s.

The Single European Act of 1987, which came into force in 1993, was another example of international liberalisation. As we shall see in Section 13.6, it created a 'single market' in the EU: a market without barriers to the movement of goods, services, capital and labour.

Interventionist supply-side policies

The basis of the case for government intervention is that the free market is likely to provide too little research and development, training and investment.

There are potentially large external benefits from research and development. Firms investing in developing and improving products, and especially firms engaged in more general scientific research, may produce results that provide benefits to many other firms. Thus the *social* rate of return on investment may be much higher than the private rate of return. Investment that is privately unprofitable for a firm may therefore still be economically desirable for the nation.

Similarly, investment in training may continue yielding benefits to society that are lost to the firms providing the training when the workers leave.

Investment often involves risks. Firms may be unwilling to take those risks, since the costs of possible failure may be too high. When looked at nationally, however, the benefits of investment might well have substantially outweighed the costs, and thus it would have been socially desirable for firms to have taken the risk. Successes would have outweighed failures.

Even when firms do wish to make such investments, they may find difficulties in raising finance. Banks may be unwilling to lend. Alternatively, if firms rely on raising finance by the issue of new shares, this makes them very dependent on the stock market performance of their shares. This depends largely on current profitability and expected profitability in the near future, not on *long-term* profitability.

Types of interventionist supply-side policy

Nationalisation. This is the most extreme form of intervention, and one that most countries had tended to reject, given a worldwide trend for privatisation. The financial crisis of the late 2000s saw the nationalisation of some financial institutions as governments attempted to ensure the stability of the financial system. Indeed, many countries had always stopped short of privatising certain key transport and power industries, such as the railways and electricity generation. Having these industries under public ownership is thought to result in higher investment than if they were under private ownership.

Direct provision. Improvements in infrastructure, such as a better motorway system, can be of direct benefit to industry. Alternatively, the government could provide factories or equipment to specific firms.

Funding research and development. Around about one-third of UK R&D is financed by the government, but around half of this has been concentrated in the fields of defence, aerospace and the nuclear power industry. As a result, there has been little government sponsorship of research in the majority of industry. Since the mid-1970s, however, there have been several government initiatives in the field of information technology. Even so, the amount of government support in this field has been very small compared with Japan, France and the USA. What is more, the amount of support declined between the mid-1980s and the late 1990s.

The UK operates a system of tax credits for small and medium enterprises (SMEs) and for other companies. Companies can claim tax credits on expenditures incurred in carrying out R&D. These credits either take the form of a tax relief, with the credits used to reduce the amount of profit liable for taxation, or for SMEs take the form of a cash sum.

In 2007, the 850 largest UK corporate spenders in R&D invested £21.6 billion, equivalent to around $1^{1}/_{2}$ per cent of GDP. Across the UK's 850 largest firms, the ratio of R&D to sales averaged 1.7 per cent as compared with 4.4 per cent for the largest US investors in R&D. The R&D scorecard is considered in more detail in Case Study 9.9 in MyEconLab.

Training and education. The government may set up training schemes, or encourage educational institutions to make their courses more vocationally relevant, or introduce new vocational qualifications (such as the GNVQs, NVQs and foundation degrees in the UK). Alternatively, the government can provide grants or tax relief to firms which themselves provide training schemes. The UK invests little in training programmes compared with most of its industrial competitors. Alternative approaches to training in the UK, Germany, France and the USA are examined in Case Study 12.18 in MyEconLab.

Assistance to small firms. UK governments in recent years have recognised the importance of small firms to the economy and have introduced various forms of advisory services, grants and tax concessions. For example, in 2009 small firms pay a 21 per cent rate of corporation tax compared with 28 per cent for larger companies. In addition, small firms are subject to fewer planning and other bureaucratic controls than large companies. Support to small firms in the UK is examined in Case Study 12.19 in MyEconLab.

Advice and persuasion. The government may engage in discussions with private firms in order to find ways to improve efficiency and innovation. It may bring firms together to exchange information, so as to co-ordinate their decisions and create a climate of greater certainty. It may bring firms and unions together to try to create greater industrial harmony.

Information. The government may provide various information services to firms: technical assistance, the results of public research, information on markets, etc.

> **Pause for thought**
>
> *How might a new classical economist criticise these various forms of interventionist supply-side policy?*

Recap

1. Market-orientated supply-side policies aim to increase the rate of growth of aggregate supply and reduce the rate of unemployment by encouraging private enterprise and the freer play of market forces.

2. Reducing government expenditure as a proportion of GDP is a major element of such policies.

3. Tax cuts can be used to encourage more people to take up jobs, to work longer hours and to work more enthusiastically. The effects of tax cuts will depend on how people respond to incentives.

4. Reducing the power of trade unions and a reduction in welfare benefits, especially those related to unemployment, may force workers to accept jobs at lower wage rates, thereby decreasing equilibrium unemployment.

5. Other examples of market-orientated supply-side policy include privatisation, competitive tendering for public-sector contracts, deregulation, the Private Finance Initiative and free trade and capital movements.

6. Interventionist supply-side policy can take the form of grants for investment and research and development, advice and persuasion, the direct provision of infrastructure and the provision, funding or encouragement of various training schemes.

QUESTIONS

1. How does the size of (a) the budget deficit and (b) the national debt vary with the course of the business cycle?

2. How would the withdrawals curve shift in each of the following cases? (a) A reduction in the basic rate of tax. (b) An increase in personal allowances.

3. Under what circumstances is a rise in taxes likely to have a disincentive effect?

4. What factors determine the effectiveness of discretionary fiscal policy?

5. Give some examples of changes in one injection or withdrawal that can affect others.

6. Why is it difficult to use fiscal policy to 'fine-tune' the economy?

7. If the government buys back £1 million of maturing bonds from the general public and then, keeping the total amount of its borrowing the same, raises £1 million by selling bills to banks, what will happen to the money supply?

8. Assume that a bank has the simplified balance sheet shown in the table, and is operating at its desired liquidity ratio. Now assume that the central bank repurchases £5 million of government bonds on the open market. Assume that the people who sell the bonds all have their accounts with this bank.

Liabilities	£m	Assets	£m
Deposits	100	Balances with central bank	10
		Advances	90
	100		100

(a) Draw up the new balance sheet directly after the purchase of the bonds.
(b) Now draw up the eventual balance sheet after all credit creation has taken place.
(c) Would there be a similar effect if the central bank rediscounted £5 billion of bills?

(d) How would such open-market operations affect the rate of interest?

9. What effect would a substantial increase in the sale of government bonds and bills have on interest rates?

10. Why would it be difficult for a central bank to predict the precise effect on money supply of open-market operations?

11. Imagine you were called in by the government to advise on whether it should adopt a policy of targeting the money supply. What advice would you give and how would you justify the advice?

12. Imagine you were called in by the government to advise on whether it should attempt to prevent cyclical fluctuations by the use of fiscal policy. What advice would you give and how would you justify the advice?

13. What do you understand by the term 'constrained discretion'? Illustrate your answers with reference to the UK and the eurozone.

14. Is there a compromise between purely discretionary policy and adhering to strict targets?

15. Under what circumstances would adherence to inflation targets lead to (a) more stable interest rates, (b) less stable interest rates than pursuing discretionary demand management policy?

16. Why might market-orientated supply-side policies have undesirable side-effects on aggregate demand?

17. If supply-side measures led to a 'shake-out' of labour and a resulting reduction in overstaffing, but also a resulting rightward shift in the Phillips curve, would you judge the policy a success?

18. What types of tax cut are likely to create the greatest (a) incentives, (b) disincentives to effort?

19. In what ways can interventionist supply-side policy work *with* the market, rather than against it? What are the arguments for and against such policy?

Log on to MyEconlab and complete the studyplan exercises for this chapter to see how much you have learnt and where you need to revise most. Make sure you access all the supporting textbook resources including the online workbook, newsblog, audio animations, guided solutions and ebook.

Additional case studies in the *Essentials of Economics* MyEconLab (www.pearsoned.co.uk/sloman)

12.1   The national debt. This explores the question of whether it matters if a country has a high national debt.

12.2   Fine-tuning in 1959 and 1960. This looks at two Budgets in the era of Keynesian 'fine-tuning'.

12.3   Trends in public expenditure. This case examines attempts to control public expenditure in the UK and relates them to the crowding-out debate.

12.4   The crowding-out effect. The circumstances in which an increase in public expenditure can replace private expenditure.

12.5   Injections against the contagion. The use of discretionary fiscal policy in the late 1990s.

12.6   Any more G and T? Does the Code for Fiscal Stability mean that the UK government balances its books? An examination of the evidence.

12.7   Assessing PFI. Has this been the perfect solution to funding investment for the public sector without raising taxes?

12.8   Discretionary fiscal policy in Japan. Attempts by successive Japanese governments since 1992 to bring the economy out of recession though expansionary fiscal policy.

12.9   Monetary policy in the eurozone. This is a more detailed examination of the role of monetary policy and the ECB than that contained in Box 12.4.

12.10   Central banking and monetary policy in the USA and its response to the credit crunch. This case examines how the Fed conducts monetary policy.

12.11   Goodhart's law. An examination of the difficulty of controlling aggregate demand by setting targets for the money supply.

12.12   Credit and the business cycle. This case traces cycles in the growth of credit and relates them to the business cycle. It also looks at some of the implications of the growth in credit.

12.13   Effective monetary policy versus banking efficiency and stability. This case examines potential conflicts between banking stability, efficiency and the effective operation of monetary policy.

12.14   Should central banks be independent of government? An examination of the arguments for and against independent central banks.

12.15   Managing the macroeconomy. This considers whether there have been conflicts of objectives in recent UK macroeconomic policy.

12.16   Monetary targeting: its use around the world. This examines the types of monetary targets used around the world.

12.17   The supply-side revolution in the USA. 'Reaganomics' and the birth of radical-right supply-side policy in the USA.

12.18   Alternative approaches to training and education. This compares the approaches to training and education – a crucial element in supply-side policy – in the UK, France, Germany and the USA.

12.19   Assistance to small firms in the UK. An examination of current government measures to assist small firms.

12.20   Small-firm policy in the EU. This looks at the range of support available to small and medium-sized firms in the EU.

12.21   Welfare to work. An examination of the policy of the UK Labour government whereby welfare payments are designed to encourage people into employment.

Websites relevant to this chapter

Numbers and sections refer to websites listed in the Web appendix and hotlinked from this book's website at **www.pearsoned.co.uk/sloman**.

- For news articles relevant to this chapter, see the *Economics News Articles* link from the book's website.

- For general news on national economies, the international economy and fiscal policy, see websites in section A, and particularly A1–5. See also links to newspapers worldwide in A38 and 39, and the news search feature in Google at A41. See also links to economics news in A42.

- For data on economic growth, employment and the business cycle, see links in B1 or 2; also see B4 and 12. For UK data, see B3 and 34. For EU data, see G1 > *Publications*. For US data, see B25 and the *Data* section of B17. For international data, see B15, 21, 24, 31, 33. For links to data sets, see B28; I14.

- For information on the development of ideas, see C12, 18; see also links under *Methodology and History of Economic Thought* in C14; and links to economists in I4 and 17. See also sites I7 and 11 > *Economic Systems and Theories > History of Economic Thought.*

- For a model of the economy (based on the Treasury model), see *The Virtual Economy* (site D1). In addition to the model, where you can devise your own Budget, there are worksheets and outlines of theories and the work of famous economists.

- For information on UK fiscal policy and government borrowing, see sites E30, 36; F2. See also sites A1–8 at Budget time. For fiscal policy in the eurozone, see *Public Finances in EMU* in H1.

- For a model of the economy (based on the Treasury model), see *The Virtual Economy* (site D1). In addition to the model, where you can devise your own Budget, there are worksheets and outlines of theories and the work of famous economists.

- Sites I7 and 11 contain links to fiscal policy: go to *Macroeconomics > Macroeconomic Policy > Taxes and Taxation.*

- For monetary policy in the UK, see F1 and E30. For monetary policy in the eurozone, see F6 and 5. For monetary policy in the USA, see F8. For monetary policy in other countries, see the respective central bank site in section F.

- For links to sites on money and monetary policy, see the *Financial Economics* sections in I4, 7, 11, 17.

- For demand-side policy in the UK, see the latest Budget Report (e.g. section on maintaining macroeconomic stability) at site E30.

- For inflation targeting in the UK and eurozone see sites F1 and 6.

- For the current approach to UK supply-side policy, see the latest Budget Report (e.g. sections on productivity and training) at site E30. See also sites E5 and 9.

- For support for a market-orientated approach to supply-side policy see C17.

- For information on training in the UK and Europe, see sites D7; E5; G5, 14. and E34.

- For information on the support for small business in the UK see site E38.

- For student resources relevant to this chapter, see sites C1–7, 9, 10, 19. See also '2nd floor – economic policy' in site D1. Also see sites D10 (*The Virtual Chancellor*) and D11 (*The Virtual Bank of Biz/ed*). See also the *Labour market reforms* simulation in D3.

Web appendix

12.1 *ISLM* **analysis of fiscal and monetary policy.** This appendix uses the *ISLM* model to show the effects of fiscal and monetary policy on national income according to various assumptions about the *IS* and *LM* curves. (For an explanation of *ISLM* analysis, see Web Appendix 10.2.)

International economics

CHAPTER MAP

Globalisation and international trade

In this chapter we begin to explore the increasing interdependencies between countries. We start by considering how economic and financial interdependencies can have important implications for national economies.

We then focus on trade. Trade between nations has the potential to benefit all participating countries (albeit to differing extents). Totally free trade, however, may bring problems to countries or to groups of people within those countries. Many people argue strongly for restrictions on trade. But are people justified in fearing international competition, or are they merely trying to protect some vested interest at the expense of everyone else? Section 13.3 examines the arguments for restricting trade.

If there are conflicting views as to whether we should have more or less trade, what has been happening on the world stage? Section 13.4 looks at the various moves towards making trade freer and at the obstacles that have been met.

A step on the road to freer trade is for countries to enter free-trade agreements with just a limited number of other countries. Examples include the EU and the North American Free Trade Association, NAFTA (the USA, Canada and Mexico). We consider such 'preferential trading systems' in Section 13.5 Then, in Section 13.6 we look at probably the world's most famous preferential trading system, the European Union, and, in particular, at the development of a 'single European market'.

Finally we turn to examine the role of trade for developing countries. Does trade with the rich world help them to develop, or does it merely result in their being dominated by rich countries and giant multinational companies?

After studying this chapter, you should be able to answer the following questions:

- How can economic and financial interdependencies create international business cycles?
- How has international trade grown over the years? Have countries become more or less interdependent?
- What are the benefits from international trade?
- Which goods should a country export and which should it import?
- Why do countries often impose restrictions on trade? Why does the World Trade Organization (WTO) try to get trade restrictions reduced or even eliminated?
- Why do countries form free-trade areas and other types of trading alliance?
- How has the 'single market' in the EU benefited its members?
- What approaches should developing countries adopt towards trade with rich countries?

13.1 GLOBAL INTERDEPENDENCE

How countries are connected through trade and finance

We live in an interdependent world. Countries are affected by the economic health of other countries and by their governments' policies. Problems in one part of the world can spread like a contagion to other parts, with perhaps no country immune. This was clearly illustrated by the credit crunch of 2007/8. A crisis that started in the sub-prime market in the USA soon snowballed into a worldwide recession.

There are two major ways in which this process of 'globalisation' affects individual economies. The first is through trade. The second is through financial markets.

Interdependence through trade

So long as nations trade with one another, the domestic economic actions of one nation will have implications for those which trade with it. For example, if the US administration feels that the US economy is growing too fast, it might adopt various contractionary fiscal and monetary measures, such as higher tax rates or interest rates. US consumers will not only consume fewer domestically produced goods, but also reduce their consumption of imported products. But US imports are other countries' exports. A fall in these other countries' exports will lead to a multiplier effect in these countries. Output and employment will fall.

Changes in aggregate demand in one country thus send ripples throughout the global economy. The process whereby changes in imports into (or exports from) one country affect national income in other countries is known as the **international trade multiplier**.

> **Definition**
>
> **International trade multiplier**
> The effect on national income in country B of a change in exports (or imports) of country A.

The more open an economy, the more vulnerable it will be to changes in the level of economic activity in the rest of the world. This problem will be particularly acute if a nation is heavily dependent on trade with one other nation (e.g. Canada on the USA) or one other region (e.g. Switzerland on the EU).

In 2008, the total value of world exports was $16.3 trillion. This amounted to 26 per cent of world GDP – a percentage that has been growing for many years. This is illustrated in Figure 13.1, which shows the growth in the global volume of exports of goods and in world real GDP. It shows that exports have been growing much more rapidly than GDP. From 1955 to 2010 the average annual growth in world output was 3.6 per cent, whereas the figure for world exports was 5.8 per cent. Interestingly, we can also see how the global financial crisis at the end of the 2000s hit both world output and, in particular, the volume of exports. The fall in total world output in 2009 was the first since the 1930s.

Despite the impact of the global slowdown at the end of the 2000s, it is likely that trade will continue to increase as a percentage of world GDP. This will increase countries' interdependence and their vulnerability to world trade fluctuations.

> **Pause for thought**
>
> *Assume that the US economy expands. What will determine the size of the multiplier effect on other countries?*

> **Pause for thought**
>
> *Are exports likely to continue growing faster than GDP indefinitely? What will determine the outcome?*

Financial interdependence

International trade has grown rapidly, but international financial flows have grown much more rapidly. Over the past 30 years or so, the value of cross-border

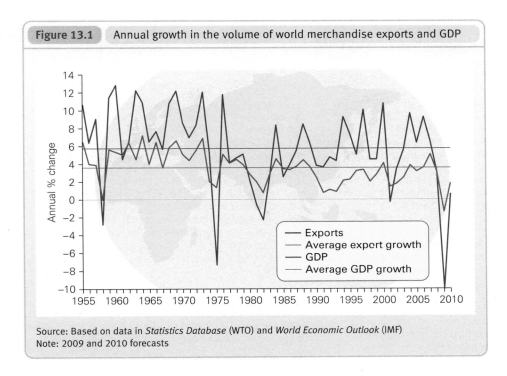

Figure 13.1   Annual growth in the volume of world merchandise exports and GDP

Source: Based on data in *Statistics Database* (WTO) and *World Economic Outlook* (IMF)
Note: 2009 and 2010 forecasts

transactions in bonds and equities (shares) has increased on average by nearly 30 per cent per year. Even after taking inflation into account, this is still a very large real rate of increase.

Each day, trillions of dollars of assets are traded across the foreign exchanges. Many of the transactions are short-term financial flows, moving to where interest rates are most favourable or to currencies where the exchange rate is likely to appreciate. This again makes countries interdependent.

Financial interdependence impacts not only on financial institutions in different countries, but also on national economies. It also illustrates how global responses can be needed. As a result of the credit crunch world leaders were seriously worried that the whole world would plunge into deep recession. A co-ordinated policy response from governments and central banks began in earnest in October 2008 when governments in Britain, Europe, North America and other parts of the world, injected some $2 trillion of extra capital into banks.

Global policy response

As a consequence of both trade and financial interdependence, the world economy, like the economy of any individual country, tends to experience periodic fluctuations in economic activity – an *international* business cycle. The implication of this is that countries will tend to share common problems and concerns at the same time.

This can aid the process of international co-operation between countries. Countries frequently meet in various groupings – from the narrow group of the world's seven richest countries (the G7) to broader groups such as the G20, which, in addition to the G7 and other rich countries also includes larger developing countries, such as China, India and Brazil.

BOX 13.1 DOCTOR, THE WORLD HAS CAUGHT A COLD!

Global answers to global problems?

We don't have to look far to see how much economic and financial interdependence affects our daily lives. As you walk down the street to the supermarket, many of the passing cars originate overseas or perhaps were built here by foreign-owned companies. You look up and the plane flying overhead is taking passengers to some corner of the world. As you enter the supermarket you see an array of goods from all over the world. Clearly, interdependence through trade connects economies. Box 13.2 looks at trade patterns in more detail.

The late 2000s have helped also to demonstrate just how interdependent financial systems and financial institutions have become. In Box 10.3 we saw how secondary marketing allows banks' assets to travel across borders and, for instance, how an American household's mortgage could be bundled up with other debts and sold to investors in any part of the world. Financial products had been given a passport to travel and travel they do!

Increasing economic and financial interdependence mean that problems in one part of the world rapidly spread to other parts. There is an old saying, 'When America sneezes, the rest of the world catches a cold'. The credit crunch was more like flu!

But who should dish out the medicine? How potent can the medicine of national governments be in isolation? What role is there for co-ordinated monetary and fiscal policies and does it require stronger international institutions to deal with world problems?

The chart shows the growth in world output and that in four chosen countries during the 2000s. It is possible to see a coincidence of growth rates across the decade, but it is especially apparent in the period from 2006. This is consistent with the idea of an international business cycle.

Iceland's cold

The decline in output in Iceland in 2009, at nearly 12 per cent, was especially stark. The country had been particularly hit by the global financial crisis.

An aggressive strategy of credit expansion had seen the liabilities of the three largest Icelandic banks rise from 100 per cent of GDP in 2004 to 923 per cent in 2007. Some of the funds from this expansion came from the inter-bank market but also from deposits overseas in subsidiaries of these banks in the Nordic countries and the UK. When the credit crunch hit, they found it increasingly difficult to roll-over loans on the inter-bank market. What is more, the sheer scale of the banks' expansion made it virtually impossible for the Central Bank to guarantee repayments of the loans.

The result was that four of its largest banks were nationalised and run by Iceland's Financial Supervisory Authority.

IMF to the rescue?

In November 2008 the International Monetary Fund's executive board approved a US$2.1 billion loan to Iceland to support an economic recovery programme. An initial payment of US$827 million was made with subsequent payments to be spread over time, subject to IMF quarterly reviews of the recovery programme.

But what is the IMF? And what does it do? Well, it is a 'specialised agency' of the United Nations and is financed by its 185 member countries (as of 2009). The role of the IMF is to ensure macroeconomic stability – such as in the Iceland case – and to foster global growth.

It also works with developing nations to alleviate poverty and to achieve economic stability. To do this it provides countries with loans.

The IMF has not been without controversy, however. Conditions attached to loans have often been very harsh, espcially for some of the most indebted developing countries (see Section 14.7).

The global economic and financial crisis provided the IMF with a challenge: which countries to support with a limited budget? For instance, at the same time as its agreement with Iceland, the IMF was approving a loan

---

Global interdependence also raises important questions about the role of international organisations like the International Monetary Fund (IMF) and the World Trade Organization (WTO).

The IMF's remit is to promote global growth and stability, to help countries through economic difficulty and to help developing economies achieve macroeconomic stability and reduce poverty. In response to the global economic and financial crisis of the late 2000s, the IMF's budget was substantially increased and it became more actively involved with what were previously defined as 'strong performing economies' (see Box 13.1).

The World Trade Organization's role is to encourage freer trade. We consider the WTO in Section 13.4.

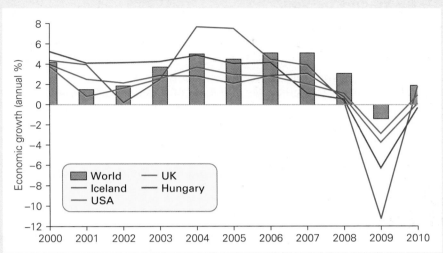

Annual growth in real GDP in the 2000s

Source: Based on data in *European Economy* (European Commission)
Note: 2009 and 2010 forecasts

of US$15.7 billion to Hungary, a member country of the European Union since 2004 (see Section 13.6), which was struggling to meet external debt obligations and finance its general government deficit (3.4 per cent of GDP in 2008). Another country receiving support was Latvia, the EU country with the sharpest rate of economic decline in 2009 (13.1 per cent).

Strengthening the IMF

World leaders meeting as part of the G20 in London in April 2009 announced the need to strengthen global financial institutions. They agreed that the resources available to the IMF should be trebled to US$750 billion.

They also agreed that the IMF would work with a new Financial Stability Board (FSB), made up, amongst others, of the G20 countries and the European Commission, so as to help in identifying potential economic and financial risks. Essentially, the G20 countries were looking for a better 'early warning system' to meet some of the challenges of an increasingly interdependent world.

 Do you see any problems arising from a strengthening of global economic and financial institutions?

Recap

1. Changes in aggregate demand in one country will affect the amount of imports purchased and thus the amount of exports sold by other countries and hence *their* national income. There is thus an international trade multiplier effect.

2. The world is also financially interdependent, with huge flows of finance flowing from one country to another. This makes all countries susceptible to financial shocks, such as the credit crunch of 2007/8.

3. To prevent problems in one country spilling over to other countries and to stabilise the international business cycle will require co-ordinated policies between nations and the intervention of various international agencies, such as the IMF.

13.2 THE ADVANTAGES OF TRADE

Can international trade make all countries better off?

Trading patterns

Developed countries dominate world trade. In 2008, they accounted for 62 per cent of world exports and 66 per cent of world imports. Their share of world trade, however, has declined over time as the exports of many developing countries, such as China and India, have grown rapidly.

The top 10 trading nations account for roughly 50 per cent of world merchandise exports. In 2008, the three countries with the highest shares were Germany (9.3 per cent), China (9.1 per cent) and the USA (8.2 per cent), while the UK was the tenth largest exporter (2.9 per cent).

Box 13.2 considers in more detail the observed patterns and trends in world trade. We then go on to consider why countries actually trade with each other.

Specialisation as the basis for trade

What motivates countries to trade with each other? What do they gain out of it? The reasons for international trade are really only an extension of the reasons for trade *within* a nation. Rather than people trying to be self-sufficient and do everything for themselves, it makes sense to specialise.

Firms specialise in producing certain types of goods. This allows them to gain economies of scale and to exploit their entrepreneurial and management skills and the skills of their labour force. It also allows them to benefit from their particular location and from the ownership of any particular capital equipment or other

KI 1
p 5

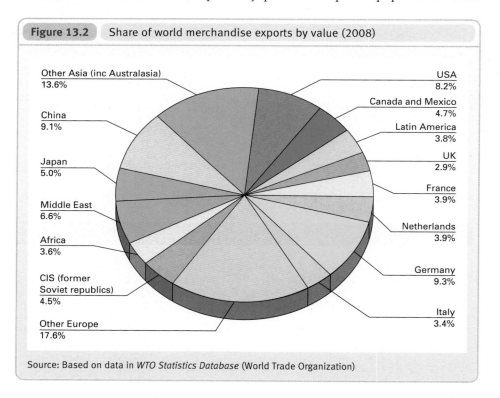

Figure 13.2   Share of world merchandise exports by value (2008)

Other Asia (inc Australasia) 13.6%
China 9.1%
Japan 5.0%
Middle East 6.6%
Africa 3.6%
CIS (former Soviet republics) 4.5%
Other Europe 17.6%

USA 8.2%
Canada and Mexico 4.7%
Latin America 3.8%
UK 2.9%
France 3.9%
Netherlands 3.9%
Germany 9.3%
Italy 3.4%

Source: Based on data in *WTO Statistics Database* (World Trade Organization)

assets they might possess. With the revenues that firms earn, they buy in the inputs that they need from other firms and the labour they require. Firms thus trade with each other.

Countries also specialise. They produce more than they need of certain goods. What is not consumed domestically is exported. The revenues earned from the exports are used to import goods that are not produced in sufficient amounts at home.

But which goods should a country specialise in? What should it export and what should it import? The answer is that it should specialise in those goods in which it has a *comparative advantage*. Let us examine what this means.

The law of comparative advantage

Countries have different endowments of factors of production. They differ in population density, labour skills, climate, raw materials, capital equipment, etc. These differences tend to persist because factors are relatively immobile between countries. Obviously land and climate are totally immobile, but even with labour and capital there tend to be more restrictions (physical, social, cultural or legal) on their international movement than on their movement within countries. Thus the ability to supply goods differs between countries.

What this means is that the relative costs of producing goods will vary from country to country. For example, one country may be able to produce 1 fridge for the same cost as 6 kilos of wheat or 3 Blu-ray players, whereas another country may be able to produce 1 fridge for the same cost as only 3 kilos of wheat but 4 Blu-ray players. It is these differences in relative costs that form the basis of trade.

At this stage we need to distinguish between *absolute advantage* and *comparative advantage*.

Absolute advantage

When one country can produce a good with fewer resources than another country it is said to have an **absolute advantage** in that good. If France can produce wine with fewer resources than the UK, and the UK can produce gin with fewer resources than France, then France has an absolute advantage in wine and the UK an absolute advantage in gin. Production of both wine and gin will be maximised by each country specialising and then trading with the other country. Both will gain.

Comparative advantage

The above seems obvious, but trade between two countries can still be beneficial even if one country could produce all goods with fewer resources than the other, providing the *relative* efficiency with which goods can be produced differs between the two countries.

Take the case of a developed country that is absolutely more efficient than a less developed country at producing both wheat and cloth. Assume that with a given amount of resources (labour, land and capital) the alternatives shown in Table 13.1 can be produced in each country.

> **Definition**
>
> **Absolute advantage**
> A country has an absolute advantage over another in the production of a good if it can produce it with less resources than the other country.

Table 13.1	Production possibilities for two countries				
		Kilos of wheat		**Metres of cloth**	
Less developed country	Either	2	or	1	
Developed country	Either	4	or	8	

TRADING PLACES

Patterns and trends in world trade

In 2008 the total *value* of the world's exports of goods and services was $19.5 trillion. Of this, $15.8 trillion, or 81 per cent, was the export of goods (merchandise exports). The chart shows the *volumes* of total merchandise exports, its subcomponents and world GDP since 1960. Each series is represented as an index with a value of 100 in 1980.

Significantly, total world trade has grown more quickly than world output over this period. While world output in 2008 was roughly 8½ times greater than it was in 1950, world trade has increased by a factor of 32. The growth in the trade of manufactures has been especially marked at around 7.7 per cent per year.

Trade patterns of individual countries

Table (a) shows exports and imports as a proportion of various countries' GDP. As you can see, in all cases the proportions were higher in the 2000s than in the 1960s, and in some cases, notably Ireland, considerably higher.

If we sum the export and imports shares of GDP we obtain a measure of the 'openness' of an economy. Unsurprisingly, we find that economies have become more 'open'. This nicely emphasises the point that

trade has helped to make countries more economically interdependent but, at the same time, increasingly susceptible to changes in economic conditions abroad.

The final three columns of Table (a) show the annual *real* rates of growth in GDP, exports and imports for our selected countries. These data provide further evidence of how trade flows have grown more rapidly than output. They also highlight the importance of not over-interpreting the 'openness' statistic because, while countries like the USA and Japan may appear relatively less open than others, this masks significant growth in trade. Indeed, the USA and Japan were the third and fourth largest exporters of merchandise trade in 2008, accounting between them for 13 per cent of the world's merchandise exports and 18 per cent of the world's merchandise imports.

Trading partners

Finally, who do countries trade with? Table (b) looks at the trading partners of four countries in 2007. The table shows that trading blocs (see Section 13.5) and geography matter. For instance, in the cases of the UK and Germany over one-half of their trade is with other

Volume of world mechandise exports and GDP

Source: Based on data in *WTO Statistics Database* (World Trade Organization)

Table (a) Exports, Imports and GDP in selected industrialised countries

| | Shares of GDP | | | | | | Annual growth rates | | |
| | Exports | | Imports | | Total trade flows (Openness) | | | | |
	1960s	2000s	1960s	2000s	1960s	2000s	GDP	Exports	Imports
Ireland	17.5	98.9	25.4	81.4	42.9	180.3	4.8	9.2	8.0
Netherlands	24.3	77.2	25.2	70.4	49.5	147.6	3.1	6.1	6.0
Germany	14.4	42.9	11.3	38.1	25.7	81.0	2.6	6.2	6.1
Canada	17.8	41.1	16.8	40.5	34.6	81.6	3.4	8.7	5.8
France	8.2	29.3	9.2	30.1	17.3	59.5	3.1	6.1	6.3
UK	12.0	28.8	12.0	32.5	24.0	61.3	2.4	4.5	4.8
Italy	9.3	27.5	10.1	27.5	19.4	55.0	2.9	6.0	5.9
Australia	9.2	20.9	11.8	28.9	21.0	49.8	3.6	5.6	6.4
USA	3.7	11.5	4.5	15.9	8.3	27.4	3.2	6.1	6.3
Japan	3.4	13.5	4.2	10.4	7.7	23.9	4.3	8.3	7.0

Source: Based on data from the AMECO databease managed by the European Commission's Directorate General for Economic and Financial Affairs, with permission

Table (b) Merchandise trade by destination and origin (2007)

UK		Germany		Japan		USA	
Export destinations	%	Export destinations	%	Export destinations	%	Export destinations	%
1 EU 27	57.4	EU 27	64.7	USA	20.4	Canada	21.4
2 USA	14.7	USA	7.6	China	15.3	EU 27	21.3
3 Switzerland	1.8	Switzerland	3.8	EU 27	14.8	Mexico	11.7
4 China	1.7	China	3.1	S Korea	7.6	China	5.6
5 Japan	1.7	Russia	2.9	Taiwan	6.3	Japan	5.4
Import origin	**%**	**Import origin**	**%**	**Import origin**	**%**	**Import origin**	**%**
1 EU 27	55.0	EU 27	59.5	China	20.6	EU 27	18.0
2 USA	8.6	China	7.1	USA	11.6	China	16.9
3 China	7.5	USA	5.9	EU 27	10.5	Canada	15.7
4 Norway	4.6	Switzerland	3.9	Saudi Arabia	5.7	Mexico	10.6
5 Japan	2.5	Russia	3.7	UAE	5.2	Japan	7.4

Source: *WTO Statistics Database* (World Trade Organization)

European Union countries. Similarly, one-third of the value of the USA's exports and one-quarter of its imports can be attributed to Canada and Mexico, members of the North American Free Trade Association (NAFTA).

What do you understand by the term the 'international business cycle'? What factors do you think might influence how much a country's business cycle is dependent on the international business cycle?

Definitions

Comparative advantage
A country has a comparative advantage over another in the production of a good if it can produce it at a lower opportunity cost: i.e. if it has to forgo less of other goods in order to produce it.

Law of comparative advantage
Trade can benefit all countries if they specialise in the goods in which they have a comparative advantage.

Despite the developed country having an absolute advantage in both wheat and cloth, the less developed country (LDC) has a *comparative* advantage in wheat, and the developed country has a *comparative* advantage in cloth. This is because wheat is relatively cheaper in terms of cloth in the LDC: only 1 metre of cloth has to be sacrificed to produce 2 kilos of wheat, whereas 8 metres of cloth would have to be sacrificed in the developed country to produce 4 kilos of wheat. In other words, the opportunity cost of wheat is 4 times higher in the developed country (8/4 compared with 1/2).

On the other hand, cloth is relatively cheaper in the developed country. Here the opportunity cost of producing 8 metres of cloth is only 4 kilos of wheat, whereas in the LDC 1 metre of cloth costs 2 kilos of wheat. Thus the opportunity cost of cloth is 4 times higher in the LDC (2/1 compared with 4/8).

To summarise: countries have a comparative advantage in those goods that can be produced at a lower opportunity cost than in other countries.

If countries are to gain from trade, they should export those goods in which they have a comparative advantage and import those goods in which they have a comparative disadvantage. Given this we can state a **law of comparative advantage**.

> **KEY IDEA 34** *The law of comparative advantage.* Provided opportunity costs of various goods differ in two countries, both of them can gain from mutual trade if they specialise in producing (and exporting) those goods that have relatively low opportunity costs compared with the other country.

But why do they gain if they specialise according to this law? And just what will that gain be? We will consider these questions next.

The gains from trade based on comparative advantage

Before trade, unless markets are very imperfect, the prices of the two goods are likely to reflect their opportunity costs. For example, in Table 13.1, since the less developed country can produce 2 kilos of wheat for 1 metre of cloth, the *price* of 2 kilos of wheat will roughly equal 1 metre of cloth.

Assume, then, that the pre-trade exchange ratios of wheat for cloth are as follows:

LDC:	2 wheat for 1 cloth
Developed country:	1 wheat for 2 cloth (i.e. 4 for 8)

Both countries will now gain from trade, provided the exchange ratio is somewhere between 2:1 and 1:2. Assume, for the sake of argument, that it is 1:1: that 1 wheat trades internationally for 1 cloth. How will each country gain?

The LDC gains by exporting wheat and importing cloth. At an exchange ratio of 1:1, it now only has to give up 1 kilo of wheat to obtain a metre of cloth, whereas before trade it had to give up 2 kilos of wheat.

The developed country gains by exporting cloth and importing wheat. Again at an exchange ratio of 1:1, it now only has to give up 1 metre of cloth to obtain a kilo of wheat, whereas before it had to give up 2 metres of cloth.

Thus both countries have gained from trade.

The actual exchange ratios will depend on the relative prices of wheat and cloth after trade takes place. These prices will depend on total demand for and supply of the two goods. It may be that the trade exchange ratio is nearer to the pre-trade exchange ratio of one country than the other. Thus the gains to the two countries need not be equal.

The limits to specialisation and trade

Does the law of comparative advantage suggest that countries will completely specialise in just a few products? In practice, countries are likely to experience *increasing* opportunity costs. The reason for this is that, as a country increasingly specialises in one good, it will have to use resources that are less and less suited to its production and which were more suited to other goods. Thus ever-increasing amounts of the other goods will have to be sacrificed. For example, as a country specialises more and more in grain production, it will have to use land that is less and less suited to growing grain.

These increasing costs as a country becomes more and more specialised will lead to the disappearance of its comparative cost advantage. When this happens, there will be no point in further specialisation. Thus whereas a country like Germany has a comparative advantage in capital-intensive manufactures, it does not produce only manufactures. It would make no sense not to use its fertile lands to produce food or its forests to produce timber. The opportunity costs of diverting all agricultural labour to industry would be very high.

Other reasons for gains from trade

Decreasing costs. Even if there are no initial comparative cost differences between two countries, it will still benefit both to specialise in industries where economies of scale can be gained, and then to trade. Once the economies of scale begin to appear, comparative cost differences will also appear, and thus the countries will have gained a comparative advantage in these industries.

This reason for trade is particularly relevant for small countries where the domestic market is not large enough to support large-scale industries. Thus exports form a much higher percentage of GDP in small countries such as Singapore than in large countries such as the USA.

Differences in demand. Even with no comparative cost differences and no potential economies of scale, trade can benefit both countries if demand conditions differ.

If people in country A like beef more than lamb, and people in country B like lamb more than beef, then rather than A using resources better suited for lamb to produce beef, and B using resources better suited for producing beef to produce lamb, it will benefit both to produce beef *and* lamb and to export the one they like less in return for the one they like more.

Increased competition. If a country trades, the competition from imports may stimulate greater efficiency at home. This extra competition may prevent domestic monopolies/oligopolies from charging high prices. It may stimulate greater research and development and the more rapid adoption of new technology. It may lead to a greater variety of products being made available to consumers.

Trade as an 'engine of growth'. In a growing world economy, the demand for a country's exports is likely to grow over time, especially when these exports have a high income elasticity of demand. This will provide a stimulus to growth in the exporting country.

Non-economic advantages. There may be political, social and cultural advantages to be gained by fostering trading links between countries.

The terms of trade

What price will our exports fetch abroad? What will we have to pay for imports? The answer to these questions is given by the terms of trade. The **terms of trade** are defined as:

$$\frac{\text{The average price of exports}}{\text{The average price of imports}}$$

expressed as an index, where prices are measured against a base year in which the terms of trade are assumed to be 100. Thus if the average price of exports relative to the average price of imports has risen by 20 per cent since the base year, the terms of trade will now be 120.

If the terms of trade rise (export prices rising relative to import prices), they are said to have 'improved', since fewer exports now have to be sold to purchase any given quantity of imports. Changes in the terms of trade are caused by changes in the demand and supply of imports and exports and by changes in the exchange rate.

Recap

1. Economies have become increasingly interdependent as a result of the increase in world trade and the interdependences of countries' financial systems.

2. Countries can gain from trade if they specialise in producing those goods in which they have a comparative advantage: i.e. those goods that can be produced at relatively low opportunity costs. This is merely an extension of the argument that gains can be made from the specialisation and division of labour.

3. If two countries trade, then, provided that the trade price ratio of exports and imports is somewhere between the pre-trade price ratios of these goods in the two countries, both countries can gain.

4. With increasing opportunity costs there will be a limit to specialisation and trade. As a country increasingly specialises, its (marginal) comparative advantage will eventually disappear.

5. The terms of trade give the price of exports relative to the price of imports expressed as an index, where the base year is 100.

6. Gains from trade also arise from decreasing costs (economies of scale), differences in demand between countries, increased competition from trade and the transmission of growth from one country to another. There may also be non-economic advantages from trade.

13.3 ARGUMENTS FOR RESTRICTING TRADE

If trade can benefit everyone, then why do countries attempt to limit trade?

We have seen how trade can bring benefits to all countries. But when we look around the world we often see countries erecting barriers to trade. Their politicians know that trade involves costs as well as benefits.

Possible barriers to imports include the following:

- *tariffs* (i.e. customs duties) on imports;
- *quotas* (i.e. restrictions on the amount of certain goods that can be imported);
- *subsidies on domestic products* to give them a price advantage over imports;
- *administrative regulations* designed to exclude imports, such as customs delays or excessive paperwork;
- *procurement procedures* whereby governments favour domestic producers when purchasing equipment (e.g. defence equipment).

BOX 13.3   **DO WE EXPLOIT FOREIGN WORKERS BY BUYING CHEAP FOREIGN IMPORTS?**   EXPLORING ECONOMICS

People sometimes question the morality of buying imports from countries where workers are paid 'pittance' wages. 'Is it right', they ask, 'for us to support a system where workers are so exploited?' As is often the case with emotive issues, there is some truth and some misunderstanding in a point of view like this.

First the truth. If a country like the UK trades with a regime that denies human rights and treats its workers very badly, then we may thereby be helping to sustain a corrupt system. We might also be seen to be lending it moral support. In this sense, therefore, trade may not help the cause of the workers in these countries. Arguments like these were used to support the imposition of trade sanctions against South Africa in the days of apartheid.

Now the misunderstanding. If we buy goods from countries that pay low wages, we are *not* as a result contributing to their low-wage problem. Quite the reverse. If countries like India export textiles to the West, this will help to *increase* the wages of Indian workers. If India has a comparative advantage in labour-intensive goods, these goods will earn a better price by being exported than by being sold entirely in the domestic Indian market. Provided *some* of the extra revenues go to the workers (as opposed to their bosses), they will gain from trade.

 Under what circumstances would a gain in revenues by exporting firms not *lead to an increase in wage rates?*

Alternatively, governments may favour domestic producers by subsidising their exports in a process known as **dumping**. The goods are 'dumped' at artificially low prices in the foreign market.

In looking at the costs and benefits of trade, the choice is not the stark one of whether to have free trade or no trade at all. Although countries may sometimes contemplate having completely free trade, typically countries limit their trade. However, they certainly do not ban it altogether.

Arguments in favour of restricting trade

Arguments having some general validity

The infant industry argument. Some industries in a country may be in their infancy but have a potential comparative advantage. This is particularly likely in developing countries. Such industries are too small yet to have gained economies of scale; their workers are inexperienced; there is a lack of back-up facilities – communications networks, specialist research and development, specialist suppliers, etc. – and they may have only limited access to finance for expansion. Without protection, these **infant industries** will not survive competition from abroad.

Protection from foreign competition, however, will allow them to expand and become more efficient. Once they have achieved a comparative advantage, the protection can then be removed to enable them to compete internationally.

To reduce reliance on goods with little dynamic potential. Many developing countries have traditionally exported primaries: foodstuffs and raw materials. The world demand for these, however, is fairly income inelastic, and thus grows relatively slowly (see Section 13.7). In such cases, free trade is not an engine of growth. Instead, if it encourages countries' economies to become locked in to a pattern of primary production, it may prevent them from expanding in sectors like manufacturing which have a higher income elasticity of demand. There may thus be a valid argument for protecting or promoting manufacturing industry.

Definitions

Dumping
When exports are sold at prices below marginal cost – often as a result of government subsidy.

Infant industry
An industry that has a potential comparative advantage, but which is as yet too underdeveloped to be able to realise this potential.

To prevent 'dumping' and other unfair trade practices. A country may engage in dumping by subsidising its exports. The result is that prices may no longer reflect comparative costs. Thus the world would benefit from tariffs being imposed by importers to counteract the subsidy.

It can also be argued that there is a case for retaliating against countries which impose restrictions on your exports. In the short run, both countries are likely to be made worse off by a contraction in trade. But if the retaliation persuades the other country to remove its restrictions, it may have a longer-term benefit. In some cases, the mere threat of retaliation may be enough to get another country to remove its protection.

To prevent the establishment of a foreign-based monopoly. Competition from abroad could drive domestic producers out of business. The foreign company, now having a monopoly of the market, could charge high prices with a resulting misallocation of resources. The problem could be tackled either by restricting imports or by subsidising the domestic producer(s).

All of the above arguments suggest that governments should adopt a 'strategic' approach to trade. **Strategic trade theory** argues that protecting certain industries allows a net gain in the *long* run from increased competition in the market (see Case Study 13.3 in MyEconLab). This argument has been used to justify the huge financial support given to the aircraft manufacturer Airbus, a consortium based in four European countries. The subsidies have allowed it to compete with Boeing, which would otherwise have a monopoly in many types of passenger aircraft. Airlines and their passengers worldwide, it is argued, have benefited from the increased competition.

To spread the risks of fluctuating markets. A highly specialised economy – Zambia with copper, Cuba with sugar – is highly susceptible to world market fluctuations. Greater diversity and greater self-sufficiency can reduce these risks.

To reduce the influence of trade on consumer tastes. The assumption of fixed consumer tastes dictating the pattern of production through trade is false. Multinational companies through their advertising and other forms of sales promotion may influence consumer tastes. Many developing countries object to the insidious influence of Western consumerist values expounded by companies such as Coca-Cola and McDonald's. Thus some restriction on trade may be justified in order to reduce this 'producer sovereignty'.

To prevent the importation of harmful goods. A country may want to ban or severely curtail the importation of things such as drugs, pornographic literature and live animals.

Definitions

Strategic trade theory
The theory that protecting/supporting certain industries can enable them to compete more effectively with large monopolistic rivals abroad. The effect of the protection is to increase long-run competition and may enable the protected firms to exploit a comparative advantage that they could not have done otherwise.

To take account of externalities. Free trade will tend to reflect private costs. Both imports and exports, however, can involve externalities. The mining of many minerals for export may adversely affect the health of miners; the production of chemicals for export may involve pollution; the importation of juggernaut lorries may lead to structural damage to houses; shipping involves large amounts of CO_2 emissions (some 4–5 per cent of total world emissions).

Arguments having some validity for specific groups or countries

The arguments considered so far are of general validity: restricting trade for such reasons could be of net benefit to the world. There are two other arguments, however, that are used by individual governments for restricting trade, where their country will gain, but at the *expense* of other countries, such that there will be a net loss to the world.

The first argument concerns taking advantage of market power in world trade. If a country, or a group of countries, has monopsony power in the purchase of imports (i.e. they are individually or collectively a very large economy, such as the USA or the EU), then they could gain by restricting imports so as to drive down their price. Similarly, if countries have monopoly power in the sale of some export (e.g. OPEC countries with oil), then they could gain by restricting exports, thereby forcing up the price (see Box 5.3).

The second argument concerns giving protection to declining industries. The human costs of sudden industrial closures can be very high. In such circumstances, temporary protection may be justified to allow the industry to decline more slowly, thus avoiding excessive structural unemployment. Such policies will be at the expense of the consumer, however, who will be denied access to cheaper foreign imports.

'Non-economic' arguments for restricting trade. A country may be prepared to forgo the direct economic advantages of free trade in order to achieve objectives that are often described as 'non-economic':

■ It may wish to maintain a degree of self-sufficiency in case trade is cut off in times of war. This may apply particularly to the production of food and armaments.
■ It may decide not to trade with certain countries with which it disagrees politically.
■ It may wish to preserve traditional ways of life. Rural communities or communities built round old traditional industries may be destroyed by foreign competition.
■ It may prefer to retain as diverse a society as possible, rather than one too narrowly based on certain industries.

Pursuing such objectives, however, will involve costs. Preserving a traditional way of life, for example, may mean that consumers are denied access to cheaper goods from abroad. Society must therefore weigh up the benefits against the costs of such policies.

> **Pause for thought**
>
> *If economics is the study of choices of how to use scarce resources, can these other objectives be legitimately described as 'non-economic'?*

Problems with protection

Tariffs and other forms of protection impose a cost on society. This is illustrated in Figure 13.3, which shows the case of a good that is partly home-produced and partly imported. Domestic demand and supply are given by D_{dom} and S_{dom}. It is assumed that firms in the country produce under perfect competition and that therefore the supply curve is the sum of the firms' marginal cost curves.

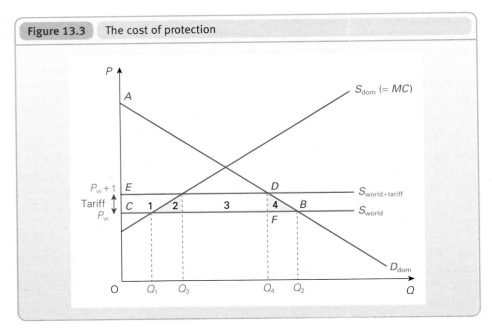

Figure 13.3   The cost of protection

Let us assume that the country is too small to affect world prices: it is a price taker. The world price is given, at P_w. At P_w, Q_2 is demanded, Q_1 is supplied by domestic suppliers and hence $Q_2 - Q_1$ is imported.

Now a tariff is imposed. This increases the price to consumers by the amount of the tariff. Price rises to $P_w + t$. Domestic production increases to Q_3, consumption falls to Q_4, and hence imports fall to $Q_4 - Q_3$.

What are the costs of this tariff to the country? Consumers are having to pay a higher price, and hence consumer surplus falls from area ABC to ADE (see pages 199–200 if you are unsure about consumer surplus). The cost to consumers in lost consumer surplus is thus $EDBC$ (i.e. area $1 + 2 + 3 + 4$). *Part* of this cost, however, is redistributed as a *benefit* to other sections in society. *Firms* get a higher price, and thus gain extra profits (area 1): where profit is given by the area between the price and the *MC* curve. The *government* receives extra revenue from the tariff payments (area 3): i.e. $(Q_4 - Q_3) \times$ tariff. These revenues can be used, for example, to reduce taxes.

But *part* of this cost is not recouped elsewhere. It is a net cost to society (areas 2 and 4).

Area 2 represents the extra costs of producing $Q_3 - Q_1$ at home, rather than importing it. If $Q_3 - Q_1$ were still imported, the country would only be paying P_w. By producing it at home, however, the costs are given by the domestic supply curve (= *MC*). The difference between *MC* and P_w (area 2) is thus the efficiency loss on the production side.

Area 4 represents the loss of consumer surplus by the reduction in consumption from Q_2 to Q_4. Consumers have saved area FBQ_2Q_4 of expenditure, but have sacrificed area DBQ_2Q_4 of utility in so doing – a net loss of area 4.

The government should ideally weigh up such costs against any benefits that are gained from protection.

Apart from these direct costs to the consumer, there are several other problems with protection. Some are a direct effect of the protection; others follow from the reactions of other nations.

Pause for thought

In this model, where the country is a price taker and faces a horizontal supply curve (the small country assumption), is any of the cost of the tariff borne by the overseas suppliers?

Protection as 'second-best'. Many of the arguments for protection amount merely to arguments for some type of government intervention in the economy. Protection, however, may not be the best way of dealing with the problem, since protection may have undesirable side-effects. There may be a more direct form of intervention that has no side-effects. In such a case, protection will be no more than a *second-best* solution.

For example, using tariffs to protect old inefficient industries from foreign competition may help prevent unemployment in those parts of the economy, but the consumer will suffer from higher prices. A better solution would be to subsidise retraining and investment in those areas of the country in *new efficient industries* – industries with a comparative advantage. In this way, unemployment is avoided, but the consumer does not suffer.

Retaliation. If the USA imposes restrictions on, say, imports from the EU, then the EU may impose restrictions on imports from the USA. Any gain to US firms competing with EU imports is offset by a loss to US exporters. What is more, US consumers suffer, since the benefits from comparative advantage have been lost.

The increased use of tariffs and other restrictions can lead to a trade war, with each country cutting back on imports from other countries. In the end, with such beggar-my-neighbour policies, everyone loses.

Protection may allow firms to remain inefficient. By removing or reducing foreign competition, protection may reduce firms' incentive to reduce costs. Thus if protection is being given to an infant industry, the government must ensure that the lack of competition does not prevent it 'growing up'. Protection should not be excessive and should be removed as soon as possible.

Bureaucracy. If a government is to avoid giving excessive protection to firms, it should examine each case carefully. This can lead to large administrative costs. It could also lead to corrupt officials accepting bribes from importers to give them favourable treatment.

> ### Pause for thought
>
> **(a) Protection to allow the exploitation of monopoly/monopsony power can be seen as a 'first-best' policy for the country concerned. Similarly, the use of tariffs to counteract externalities directly involved in the trade process (e.g. the environmental costs of an oil tanker disaster) could be seen to be a first-best policy. Explain why.**
>
> **(b) All the other arguments for tariffs or other forms of protection that we have considered can really be seen as arguments for intervention, with protection being no more than a second-best form of intervention. Go through each of the arguments and consider what would be a 'first-best' form of intervention.**

Recap

1. Countries use various methods to restrict trade, including tariffs, quotas, exchange controls, import licensing, export taxes, and legal and administrative barriers. Countries may also promote their own industries by subsidies.

2. Reasons for restricting trade that have some validity in a world context include the infant industry argument, the problems of relying on exporting goods whose market is growing slowly or even declining, dumping and other unfair trade practices, the danger of the establishment of a foreign-based monopoly, the need to spread the risks of fluctuating export prices, and the problems that free trade may adversely affect consumer tastes, that it may allow the importation of harmful goods and not take account of externalities.

3. Countries may also have other objectives in restricting trade, such as remaining self-sufficient in certain strategic products, not trading with certain countries of which it disapproves, protecting traditional ways of life or simply retaining a non-specialised economy.

4. Protection in the form of tariffs results in higher prices. The resulting loss in consumer surplus is not fully offset by the gain in profits to domestic firms and the tariff revenue for the government. Even if government intervention to protect certain parts of the economy is desirable, restricting trade is unlikely to be a first-best solution to the problem, since it involves side-effect costs. What is more, restricting trade may encourage retaliation; it may allow inefficient firms to remain inefficient; it may involve considerable bureaucracy and possibly even corruption.

13.4 THE WORLD TRADING SYSTEM AND THE WTO

Is trade becoming freer or less free?

After the Wall Street Crash of 1929 (when prices on the US stock exchange plummeted), the world plunged into the Great Depression. Countries found their exports falling dramatically and many suffered severe balance of payments difficulties. The response of many countries was to restrict imports by the use of tariffs and quotas. Of course, this reduced other countries' exports, which encouraged them to resort to even greater protectionism. The net effect of the Depression and the rise in protectionism was a dramatic fall in world trade. The volume of world trade in manufactures fell by more than a third in the three years following the Wall Street Crash. Clearly there was a net economic loss to the world from this decline in trade.

After the Second World War there was a general desire to reduce trade restrictions, so that all countries could gain the maximum benefits from trade. There was no desire to return to the beggar-my-neighbour policies of the 1930s.

In 1947, 23 countries got together and signed the General Agreement on Tariffs and Trade (GATT). By 2009 there were 153 members of its successor organisation, the World Trade Organization, which was formed in 1995. Between them, the members of the WTO account for around 96 per cent of world trade.

The aims of GATT, and now the WTO, have been to liberalise trade. But, whereas GATT focused solely on the trade in goods, the WTO and its agreements also relate to the trade in services and in inventions and designs, sometimes referred to as intellectual property.

WTO rules

The WTO requires its members to operate according to various rules. These include the following:

■ Non-discrimination. Under the 'most favoured nations clause', any trade concession that a country makes to one member must be granted to *all* signatories. The only exception is with free-trade areas and customs unions (such as the EU). Here countries are permitted to abolish tariffs between themselves while still maintaining them with the rest of the world.
■ Reciprocity. Any nation benefiting from a tariff reduction made by another country must reciprocate by making similar tariff reductions itself.
■ The general prohibition of quotas.
■ Fair competition. If unfair barriers are erected against a particular country, the WTO can sanction retaliatory action by that country. The country is not allowed, however, to take such action without permission.
■ Binding tariffs. Countries cannot raise existing tariffs without negotiating with their trading partners.

Unlike the GATT, the WTO has the power to impose sanctions on countries breaking trade agreements. If there are disputes between member nations, these will be settled by the WTO, and if an offending country continues to impose trade restrictions, permission will be granted for other countries to retaliate.

For example, in March 2002, the Bush administration imposed tariffs on steel imports into the USA in order to protect the ailing US steel industry (see Case Study 13.6 in MyEconLab). The EU and other countries referred the case to the WTO, which in December 2003 ruled that they were illegal. This ruling made it legitimate

BOX 13.4   THE DOHA DEVELOPMENT AGENDA

A new direction for the WTO?

Globalisation, based on the free play of comparative advantage, economies of scale and innovation, has produced a genuinely radical force, in the true sense of the word. It essentially amplifies and reinforces the strengths, but also the weaknesses, of market capitalism: its efficiency, its instability, and its inequality. If we want globalisation not only to be efficiency-boosting but also fair, we need more international rules and stronger multilateral institutions.[a]

In November 1999, the members of the World Trade Organization met in Seattle in the USA. What ensued became known as the 'Battle of Seattle' (see Web Case 13.7). Anti-globalisation protesters fought with police; the world's developing economies fell out with the world's developed economies; and the very future of the WTO was called into question. The WTO was accused of being a free trader's charter, in which the objective of free trade was allowed to ride roughshod over anything that might stand in its way. Whatever the issue – the environment, the plight of developing countries, the dominance of trade by multinationals – free trade was king.

As Pascal Lamy, the former EU Trade Commissioner, made clear in the quote above, rules had to be strengthened, and the WTO had to ensure that the gains from trade were fairer and more sustainable.

The rebuilding process of the WTO began in Doha, Qatar, in November 2001. The meeting between the then 142 members of the WTO concluded with the decision to launch a new round of WTO trade talks, to be called the 'Doha Development Agenda'. As with previous trade rounds, the talks were designed to increase the liberalisation of trade. However, this time such a goal was to be tempered by a policy of strengthening assistance to developing economies.

Other areas identified for discussion included: sustainable development and the environment; greater liberalisation of agriculture; rules to govern foreign direct investment; the co-ordination of countries' competition policies; and the use and abuse of patents on medicines.

The talks were originally scheduled for completion by January 2005, but this deadline was extended several times as new talks were arranged and failed to reach agreement. A particular sticking point was the unwillingness of rich countries, and the USA and the EU in particular, to make sufficient reductions in agricultural protection, given the pressure from their domestic farmers. The USA was unwilling to make substantial cuts in agricultural subsidies and the EU in agricultural tariffs.

There was also unwillingness by large developing countries, such as India and Brazil to reduce protection to their industrial and service sectors. What is more, there were large divergences in opinion between developing countries on how much they should reduce their own agricultural protection.

Breakdown of the talks

The talks seemed finally to have broken down at a meeting in Geneva in July 2008. Despite the willingness of developing countries to reduce industrial tariffs by more than 50 per cent, and by the USA and the EU to make deep cuts in agricultural subsidies and tariffs, the talks foundered over the question of agricultural protection for developing countries. This was item 18 on a 'to-do' list of 20 items; items 1 to 17 had already been agreed. China and India wanted to protect poor farmers by retaining the ability to impose temporary tariffs on food imports in the event of a drop in food prices or a surge in imports. The USA objected. When neither side would budge, the talks collapsed.

But even 'success' would not have addressed some thorny issues, such as achieving equal access to rich countries' markets by all banana-producing countries (see Case Study 13.8 in MyEconLab) and protecting cotton producers in developing countries from cheap subsidised cotton grown in the USA. And Africa's interests would not have been properly addressed. In fact, no African country was present in the inner circle of talks at the end.

Many commentators, however, argued that failure was no catastrophe. The gain from total liberalisation of trade would have boosted developing countries' GDP by no more than 1 per cent. And anyway, tariffs were generally falling and were already at an all-time low. But, with the world economy faltering in 2008, there were worries that protectionism would begin to rise again – something that an agreement could have helped. Disillusionment with the WTO could hasten the erection of barriers.

This issue was very much on the minds of the leaders of twenty of the world's largest economies when they met in London in April 2009 to find ways of reforming the financial sector and combating recession. The G20 meeting reaffirmed a commitment not to raise barriers to trade or implement export measures inconsistent with the principles of the WTO.

Further, the world leaders reiterated their desire to see a successful completion to the Doha Round, describing it has 'urgently needed'. But, it remained unclear how long it would take for such a deal to be done. By the time you read this, a final agreement may have been reached – or perhaps not!

---

[a] 'Global policy without democracy', (speech by Pascal Lamy, given in 2001 when he was the EU Trade Commissioner. He later became head of the WTO in 2005).

 Does the process of globalisation mean that the role of the WTO is becoming less and less important?

for the EU and other countries to impose retaliatory tariffs on US products. President Bush consequently announced that the steel tariffs would be abolished.

The greater power of the WTO has persuaded many countries to bring their disputes to it. In the first 14 years of its existence over 400 disputes had been brought (compared with 300 by GATT over the whole of its 48 years).

Trade rounds

Periodically, member countries have met to negotiate reductions in tariffs and other trade restrictions. There have been eight 'rounds' of such negotiations since the signing of GATT in 1947. The last major round to be completed was the Uruguay Round, which began in Uruguay in 1986, continued at meetings around the world and culminated in a deal being signed in April 1994. By that time, the average tariff on manufactured products was 4 per cent and falling. In 1947 the figure was nearly 40 per cent. The Uruguay Round agreement also involved a programme of phasing in substantial reductions in tariffs and other restrictions up to the year 2002 (see Case Study 13.4 in MyEconLab).

Despite the reduction in tariffs, many countries have still tried to restrict trade by various other means, such as quotas and administrative barriers. Also, barriers have been particularly high on certain non-manufactures. Agricultural protection in particular has come in for sustained criticism by developing countries. High fixed prices and subsidies given to farmers in the EU, the USA and other advanced countries means that the industrialised world continues to export food to many developing countries which have a comparative advantage in food production! Farmers in developing countries often find it impossible to compete with subsidised food imports from the rich countries.

The most recent round of trade negotiations began in Doha, Qatar, in 2001 (see Box 13.4). The negotiations have focused on both trade liberalisation and measures to encourage development of poorer countries. In particular, the Doha Development Agenda, as it is called, is concerned with measures to make trade fairer so that its benefits are spread more evenly around the world. This would involve improved access for developing countries to markets in the rich world. The Agenda is also concerned with the environmental impacts of trade and development. The negotiations were originally due to be completed in 2005, but, deadlines continued to be missed and three years later agreement had still not been reached.

What is more, as the world plunged into recession in 2008/9, concerns grew that countries would resort to protectionism to support domestic industries (see Box 13.3). But this is a classic prisoner's dilemma (see page 148). Countries individually use protection to foster their own interests, but the Nash equilibrium is that the world as a whole is worse off as trade declines.

Recap

1. Most countries of the world are members of the WTO and in theory are in favour of moves towards freer trade.

2. In practice, however, countries have been very unwilling to abandon restrictions if they believe that they can gain from them, even though it might be at the expense of other countries.

3. The WTO is more powerful than its predecessor, GATT. It has a disputes procedure and can enforce its rulings.

TRADING BLOCS   13.5

Why do some countries get together and trade more freely between themselves?

The world economy seems to have been increasingly forming into a series of trade blocs, based upon regional groupings of countries: a European region centred on the European Union, an Asian region on Japan and China, a North American region on the USA and a Latin American region. Such trade blocs are examples of **preferential trading arrangements**. These arrangements involve trade restrictions with the rest of the world, and lower or zero restrictions between the members.

Although trade blocs clearly encourage trade between their members, many countries outside these blocs complain that they benefit the members at the expense of the rest of the world. For many developing economies, in need of access to the most prosperous nations in the world, this represents a significant check on their ability to grow and develop.

Types of preferential trading arrangement

There are three possible forms of such trading arrangements.

Free trade areas

A **free trade area** is where member countries remove tariffs and quotas between themselves, but retain whatever restrictions *each member chooses* with non-member countries. Some provision will have to be made to prevent imports from outside coming into the area via the country with the lowest external tariff.

Customs unions

A **customs union** is like a free trade area, but in addition members must adopt *common* external tariffs and quotas with non-member countries.

Common markets

A **common market** is where member countries operate as a *single* market. Like a customs union there are no tariffs and quotas between member countries and there are common external tariffs and quotas. But a common market goes further than this. A full common market includes the following features.

- *A common system of taxation.* In the case of a *perfect* common market, this will involve identical rates of tax in all member countries.
- *A common system of laws and regulations governing production, employment and trade.* For example, in a perfect common market there would be a *single* set of laws governing issues such as product specification (e.g. permissible artificial additives to foods, or levels of exhaust emissions from cars), the employment and dismissal of labour, mergers and takeovers, and monopolies and restrictive practices.
- *Free movement of labour, capital and materials, and of goods and services.* In a perfect common market, this will involve a total absence of border controls between member states, the freedom of workers to work in any member country, and the freedom of firms to expand into any member state.

Definitions

Preferential trading arrangement
A trading arrangement whereby trade between the signatories is freer than trade with the rest of the world.

Free trade area
A group of countries with no trade barriers between themselves.

Customs union
A free trade area with common external tariffs and quotas.

Common market
A customs union where the member countries act as a single market with free movement of labour and capital, common taxes and common trade laws.

■ *The absence of special treatment by member governments of their own domestic industries.* Governments are large purchasers of goods and services. In a perfect common market, they should buy from whichever companies within the market offer the most competitive deal and not show favouritism towards domestic suppliers: they should operate a *common procurement policy*.

The definition of a common market is sometimes extended to include the following two features of *economic and monetary union.*

■ *A fixed exchange rate between the member countries' currencies.* In the extreme case, this would involve a single currency for the whole market.
■ *Common macroeconomic policies.* To some extent this must follow from a fixed exchange rate, but in the extreme case it will involve a single macroeconomic management of the whole market, and hence the abolition of separate fiscal or monetary intervention by individual member states.

We will examine European economic and monetary union in Section 14.6.

The direct effects of a customs union: trade creation and trade diversion

By joining a customs union (or free trade area), a country will find that its trade patterns change. Two such changes can be distinguished: trade creation and trade diversion.

Trade creation

Trade creation is where consumption shifts from a high-cost producer to a low-cost producer. The removal of trade barriers allows greater specialisation according to comparative advantage. Instead of consumers having to pay high prices for domestically produced goods in which the country has a comparative disadvantage, the goods can now be obtained more cheaply from other members of the customs union. In return, the country can export to them goods in which it has a comparative advantage.

Trade diversion

Trade diversion is where consumption shifts from a lower-cost producer outside the customs union to a higher-cost producer within the union.

Assume that the most efficient producer in the world of a particular good is Russia – outside the EU. Assume that before membership, Poland paid a similar tariff on this good from any country, and thus imported the product from Russia rather than from the EU.

After joining the EU, however, the removal of the tariff made the EU product cheaper, since the tariff remained on the Russian product. Consumption thus switched to a higher-cost producer. There was thus a net loss in world efficiency. As far as Poland was concerned, consumers still gained, since they were paying a lower price than before. There was a loss, however, to domestic producers (from the reduction in protection, and hence reduced prices and profits) and to the government (from reduced tariff revenue). These losses may have been smaller or larger than the gain to consumers: in other words, there may still have been a net gain to the Poland, but there could have been a net loss, depending on the circumstances.

KI 34
p 432

Definitions

Trade creation
Where a customs union leads to greater specialisation according to comparative advantage and thus a shift in production from higher-cost to lower-cost sources.

Trade diversion
Where a customs union diverts consumption from goods produced at a lower cost outside the union to goods produced at a higher cost (but tariff free) within the union.

Pause for thought

Is joining a customs union more likely to lead to trade creation or trade diversion in each of the following cases? (a) The union has a very high external tariff. (b) Cost differences are very great between the country and members of the union.

Longer-term effects of a customs union

Over the longer term, there may be other gains and losses from being a member of a customs union.

Longer-term advantages

■ Increased market size may allow a country's firms to exploit (*internal*) *economies of scale*. This argument is more important for small countries, which have therefore more to gain from an enlargement of their markets.

■ *External economies of scale*. Increased trade may lead to improvements in the infrastructure of the members of the customs union (better roads, railways, financial services, etc.). This in turn could bring bigger long-term benefits from trade between members, and from external trade too, by making the transport and handling of imports and exports cheaper.

■ The bargaining power of the whole customs union with the rest of the world may allow member countries to gain *better terms of trade*. This, of course, will necessarily involve a degree of political co-operation between the members.

■ *Increased competition* between member countries may stimulate efficiency, encourage investment and reduce monopoly power. Of course, a similar advantage could be gained by the simple removal of tariffs with any competing country.

■ Integration may encourage a *more rapid spread of technology*.

Longer-term disadvantages

■ *Resources may flow from the country* to more efficient members of the customs union, or to the geographical centre of the union (so as to minimise transport costs). This can be a major problem for a *common market* (where there is free movement of labour and capital). The country could become a depressed 'region' of the community.

■ If integration encourages greater co-operation between firms in member countries, it may also encourage *greater oligopolistic collusion*, thus keeping prices higher to the consumer. It may also encourage mergers and takeovers that would increase monopoly power.

■ *Diseconomies of scale*. If the union leads to the development of very large companies, they may become bureaucratic and inefficient.

■ The *costs of administering* the customs union may be high. This problem is likely to be worse, the more intervention there is in the affairs of individual members.

Preferential trading in practice

Preferential trading has the greatest potential to benefit countries whose domestic market is too small, taken on its own, to enable them to benefit from economies of scale, and where they face substantial barriers to their exports. Most developing countries fall into this category and as a result many have attempted to form preferential trading arrangements.

Examples in Latin America and the Caribbean include the five-member Central American Common Market (CACM) (part of the broader Central American Integration Association), the four-member Andean Community, and the 15-member Caribbean Community (CARICOM). A Southern Common Market (MerCoSur) was formed in 1991, consisting of Argentina, Brazil, Paraguay and Uruguay, and six other South American countries are planning to join. It has a common external tariff and most of its internal trade is free of tariffs.

The image references correspond to margin markers:

KI 23
p 194

KI 16
p 116

In 1993, the six ASEAN nations (Brunei, Indonesia, Malaysia, the Philippines, Singapore and Thailand) agreed to work towards an ASEAN Free Trade Area (AFTA). ASEAN (the Association of South-East Asian Nations) now has ten members (the new ones being Laos, Myanmar, Vietnam and Cambodia) and is dedicated to increased economic co-operation within the region. What progress has been made in achieving AFTA? By 2005 the original six members had reduced internal tariffs to an average of 3.8 per cent and had no tariffs on over 60 per cent of products. Plans are to eliminate all tariffs between these six by 2010 and for the remaining countries by 2015. ASEAN also plans to establish a common market, the ASEAN Economic Community (AEC), by 2020.

In Africa the Economic Community of West African States (ECOWAS) has been attempting to create a common market between its 15 members. The West African franc is used in seven of the countries and another six plan to introduce a common currency, the eco. The ultimate goal is to combine the two currency areas and adopt a single currency for all member states.

North American Free Trade Association (NAFTA)

Along with the EU, NAFTA is one of the two most powerful trading blocs in the world. It came into force in 1994 and consists of the USA, Canada and Mexico. These three countries have agreed to abolish tariffs between themselves in the hope that increased trade and co-operation will follow. Tariffs between the USA and Canada were phased out by 1999 and tariffs between Mexico and the other two countries will be by 2009. New non-tariff restrictions will not be permitted either, but many existing ones can remain in force, thus preventing the development of true free trade between the members. Indeed, some industries, such as textiles and agriculture, will continue to have major non-tariff restrictions.

NAFTA members hope that, with a market similar in size to the EU, they will be able to rival the EU's economic power in world trade. Other countries may join in the future, so NAFTA may eventually develop into a western hemisphere free trade association.

NAFTA is, however, at most only a free trade area and not a common market. Unlike the EU, it does not seek to harmonise laws and regulations, except in very specific areas such as environmental management and labour standards. Member countries are permitted total legal independence, subject to the one proviso that they must treat firms of other member countries equally with their own firms – the principle of 'fair competition'. Nevertheless, NAFTA has encouraged a growth in trade between its members, most of which is trade creation rather than trade diversion.

Case Study 13.9 in MyEconLab looks at the costs and benefits of NAFTA membership to the three countries involved.

Asia–Pacific Economic Cooperation Forum (APEC)

The most significant move towards establishing a more widespread regional economic organisation in east Asia appeared with the creation of the Asia–Pacific Economic Cooperation forum (APEC). APEC links the economies of the Pacific rim, including Asian, Australasian and North and South American countries (19 countries, plus Hong Kong and Taiwan). These countries account for some 60 per cent of the world's total output and 48 per cent of world trade. At the 1994 meeting of APEC leaders, it was resolved to create a free trade area across the Pacific by 2010 for the developed industrial countries, and by 2020 for the rest.

Unlike the EU and NAFTA, APEC is likely to remain solely a free trade area and not to develop into a customs union, let alone a common market. Within the region there exists a wide disparity in GNY per capita, ranging from Japan and the USA at over $34 000 to Vietnam at a mere $500 ($2500 in purchasing-power parity terms – i.e. what goods and services the money can buy). Such disparities create a wide range of national interests and goals. Countries are unlikely to share common economic problems or concerns. In addition, political differences and conflicts within the region are widespread, reducing the likelihood that any organisational agreement beyond a simple economic one would succeed. However, the economic benefits from free trade, and the resulting closer regional ties, could be immense.

In the next section we consider the longest and most comprehensive preferential trading arrangement: the European Union.

Recap

1. Countries may make a partial movement towards free trade by the adoption of a preferential trading system. This involves free trade between the members, but restrictions on trade with the rest of the world. Such a system can be either a simple free trade area, or a customs union (where there are common restrictions with the rest of the world) or a common market (where in addition there is free movement of capital and labour, and common taxes and trade laws).

2. A preferential trading area can lead to trade creation, where production shifts to low-cost producers within the area, or to trade diversion, where trade shifts away from lower-cost producers outside the area to higher-cost producers within the area.

3. Preferential trading may bring longer-term advantages of increased economies of scale (both internal and external), improved terms of trade from increased bargaining power with the rest of the world, increased efficiency from greater competition between member countries and a more rapid spread of technology. On the other hand, it can lead to increased regional problems for members, greater oligopolistic collusion and various diseconomies of scale. There may also be large costs of administering the system.

4. There have been several attempts around the world to form preferential trading systems.

THE EUROPEAN UNION   13.6

What have been the effects of the creation of a 'single market' in the EU?

The European Economic Community (EEC) was formed by the signing of the Treaty of Rome in 1957 and came into operation on 1 January 1958.

The original six member countries of the EEC (Belgium, France, Italy, Luxembourg, Netherlands and West Germany) had already made a move towards integration with the formation of the European Coal and Steel Community in 1952. This had removed all restrictions on trade in coal, steel and iron ore between the six countries. The aim had been to gain economies of scale and allow more effective competition with the USA and other foreign producers.

The EEC extended this principle and aimed eventually to be a full common market with completely free trade between members in all products, and with completely free movement of labour, enterprise and capital.

All internal tariffs between the six members had been abolished and common external tariffs established by 1968. But this still only made the EEC a *customs union*, since a number of restrictions on internal trade remained (legal, administrative, fiscal, etc.). Nevertheless the aim was eventually to create a full common market.

In 1973 the UK, Denmark and Ireland became members. Greece joined in 1981, Spain and Portugal in 1986, and Sweden, Austria and Finland in 1995, Then in May 2004, a further 10 countries joined: Cyprus, the Czech Republic, Estonia, Hungary, Latvia, Lithuania, Malta, Poland, Slovakia and Slovenia. With Bulgaria and Romania joining in 2007, the European Union, as it is now called, has 27 members.

From customs union to common market

The EU is clearly a customs union. It has common external tariffs and no internal tariffs. But is it also a common market? For many years there have been *certain* common economic policies.

Common Agricultural Policy (CAP). The Union has traditionally set common high prices for farm products. This has involved charging variable import duties to bring foreign food imports up to EU prices and intervention to buy up surpluses of food produced within the EU at these above-equilibrium prices (see Box 3.4 on pages 76–7). Although the main method of support has shifted to providing subsidies (or 'income support') unrelated to current output, this still represents a common economic policy agricultural support.

Regional policy. EU regional policy provides grants to firms and local authorities in relatively deprived regions of the Union.

Competition policy. EU policy here has applied primarily to companies operating in more than one member state. For example, Article 81 of the Amsterdam Treaty prohibits agreements between firms (e.g. over pricing or sharing out markets) which adversely affect competition in trade between member states.

Harmonisation of taxation. VAT is the standard form of indirect tax throughout the EU. There are, however, substantial differences in VAT rates between member states, as there are with other tax rates (see Box 13.5).

Social policy. In 1989 the European Commission presented a *social charter* to the EU heads of state. This spelt out a series of worker and social rights that should apply in all member states (see Case Study 13.11 in MyEconLab). These rights were grouped under 12 headings covering areas such as the guarantee of decent levels of income for both the employed and the non-employed, freedom of movement of labour between EU countries, freedom to belong to a trade union and equal treatment of women and men in the labour market. The Social Charter was only a recommendation and each element had to be approved separately by the European Council of Ministers.

The social chapter of the Maastricht Treaty (1991) attempted to move the Community forward in implementing the details of the Social Charter in areas such as maximum hours, minimum working conditions, health and safety protection, information and consultation of workers, and equal opportunities.

The UK Conservative government refused to sign this part of the Maastricht Treaty. It maintained that such measures would increase costs of production and would, therefore, make EU goods less competitive in world trade and increase unemployment. Critics of the UK position argued that the refusal to adopt minimum working conditions (and also a minimum wage rate) would help to make the UK the 'cheap labour sweat-shop' of Europe. One of the first acts of the incoming Labour government in 1997 was to sign up to the Social Chapter.

Despite these various common policies, in other respects the Community of the 1970s and 1980s was far from a true common market: there were all sorts of non-tariff barriers such as high taxes on wine by non-wine-producing countries, special regulations designed to favour domestic producers, governments giving contracts to domestic producers (e.g. for defence equipment), and so on. The Single European Act of 1987, however, sought to remove these barriers and to form a genuine common market by the end of 1992 (see Box 13.5).

BOX 13.5   FEATURES OF THE SINGLE MARKET

Since 1 January 1993 trade within the EU has operated very much like trade within a country. In theory, there should be no more difficulty for a firm in Birmingham to sell its goods in Paris than in London. At the same time, the single market allows free movement of labour and involves the use of common technical standards.

The features of the single market are summed up in two European Commission publications:[a]

- Elimination of border controls on goods within the EU: no more long waits.
- Free movement of people across borders.
- Common security arrangements.
- No import taxes on goods bought in other member states for personal use.
- The right for everyone to live in another member state.
- Recognition of vocational qualifications in other member states: engineers, accountants, medical practitioners, teachers and other professionals able to practise throughout Europe.
- Technical standards brought into line, and product tests and certification agreed across the whole EU.
- Common commercial laws – making it attractive to form Europe-wide companies and to start joint ventures.
- Public contracts to supply equipment and services to state organisations now open to tenders across the EU.

So what does the single market mean for individuals and for businesses?

Individuals

Before 1993, if you were travelling in Europe, you had a 'duty-free allowance'. This meant that you could only take goods up to the value of €600 across borders within the EU without having to pay VAT in the country into which you were importing them. Now you can take as many goods as you like from one EU country to another, provided they are for your own consumption. But to prevent fraud, member states may ask for evidence that the goods have been purchased for the traveller's own consumption if they exceed specified amounts.

Individuals have the right to live and work in any other member state. Qualifications obtained in one member state must be recognised by other member states.

Firms

Before 1993 all goods traded in the EU were subject to VAT at every internal border. This involved some 60 million customs clearance documents at a cost of some €70 per consignment.[b]

This has all now disappeared. Goods can cross from one member state to another without any border controls: in fact, the concepts of 'importing' and 'exporting' within the EU no longer officially exist. All goods sent from one EU country to another will be charged VAT only in the country of destination. They are exempt from VAT in the country where they are produced.

One of the important requirements for fair competition in the single market is the convergence of tax rates. Although income tax rates, corporate tax rates and excise duties still differ between member states, there has been some narrowing in the range of VAT rates. There is now a lower limit of 15 per cent on the standard rate of VAT. Actual rates, however, vary from 15 to 25 per cent.

The member states have also agreed to abolish higher rates of VAT on luxury goods (such rates used to be as high as 38 per cent), and to have no more than two lower rates of at least 5 per cent on 'socially necessary' goods, such as food and water supply.

 In what ways would competition be 'unfair' if VAT rates differed widely between member states?

---

[a] *A Single Market for Goods* (Commission of the European Communities, 1993); *10 Key Points about the Single European Market* (Commission of the European Communities, 1992).

[b] See *A Single Market for Goods* (Commission of the European Communities, 1993).

The benefits and costs of the single market

It is difficult to quantify the benefits and costs of the single market, given that many occur over a long period, and that it is difficult to know to what extent the changes that are taking place are the direct result of the single market. Nevertheless it is possible to identify the *types* of benefit that have resulted, many of which have been substantial.

Trade creation. Costs and prices have fallen as a result of a greater exploitation of comparative advantage. Member countries can now specialise further in those goods and services that they can produce at a comparatively low opportunity cost.

Reduction in the direct costs of barriers. This category includes administrative costs, border delays and technical regulations. Their abolition or harmonisation has led to substantial cost savings.

Economies of scale. With industries based on a Europe-wide scale, many firms can now be large enough, and their plants large enough, to gain the full potential economies of scale (see Box 4.4 on pages 100–1). Yet the whole European market is large enough for there still to be adequate competition. Such gains have varied from industry to industry, depending on the minimum efficient scale of a plant or firm. Economies of scale have also been gained from mergers and other forms of industrial restructuring.

Greater competition. Increased competition between firms has led to lower costs, lower prices and a wider range of products available to consumers. This has been particularly so in newly liberalised service sectors such as transport, financial services, telecommunications and broadcasting. In the long run, greater competition can stimulate greater innovation, the greater flow of technical information and the rationalisation of production.

Despite these gains, the single market has not received a universal welcome within the EU. Its critics argue that, in a Europe of oligopolies, unequal ownership of resources, rapidly changing technologies and industrial practices, and factor immobility, the removal of internal barriers to trade has merely exaggerated the problems of inequality and economic power. More specifically, the following criticisms are made.

Radical economic change is costly. Substantial economic change is necessary to achieve the full economies of scale and efficiency gains from a single European market. These changes necessarily involve redundancies – from bankruptcies, takeovers, rationalisation and the introduction of new technology. The severity of this 'structural' and 'technological' unemployment (see Section 11.3) depends on (a) the pace of economic change and (b) the mobility of labour – both occupational and geographical. Clearly, the more integrated markets become across the EU, the less the costs of future change.

Adverse regional effects. Firms are likely to locate as near as possible to the 'centre of gravity' of their markets and sources of supply. If, before barriers are removed, a firm's prime market was the UK, it might well have located in the Midlands or the north of England. If, however, with barriers now removed, its market has become Europe as a whole, it may choose to locate in the south of England or in France, Germany or one of the Benelux countries instead. The creation of a single European market thus tends to attract capital and jobs away from the edges of the Union and towards its geographical centre.

In an ideal market situation, areas like Cornwall, the south of Italy or Portugal should attract resources from other parts of the Union. Being relatively depressed areas, wage rates and land prices are lower. The resulting lower industrial costs should encourage firms to move into the areas. In practice, however, as capital and labour (and especially young and skilled workers) leave the extremities of the Union, so these regions are likely to become more depressed. If, as a result, their infrastructure is neglected, they then become even less attractive to new investment.

The development of monopoly/oligopoly power. The free movement of capital can encourage the development of giant 'Euro-firms' with substantial economic power. Indeed, recent years have seen some very large European mergers (see Case Study 5.16 in MyEconLab). This can lead to higher, not lower prices, and less choice for the consumer. It all depends on just how effective competition is, and how effective EU competition policy is in preventing monopolistic and collusive practices.

Trade diversion. Just as increased trade creation has been a potential advantage of completing the internal market, so trade diversion has been a possibility too. This is more likely if *external* barriers remain high (or are even increased) and internal barriers are *completely* abolished.

Perhaps the biggest objection raised against the single European market is a political one: the loss of national sovereignty. Governments find it much more difficult to intervene at a microeconomic level in their own economies.

Completing the internal market

Despite the reduction in barriers, the internal market is still not 'complete'. In other words, various barriers to trade between member states still remain. Thus, in June 1997, an Action Plan was adopted by the European Council. Its aim was to ensure that all barriers were dismantled by the launch of the euro in January 1999.

To monitor progress an 'Internal Market Scoreboard' was established. This is published every six months and shows progress towards the total abandonment of any forms of internal trade restrictions (Case Study 13.13 in MyEconLab). It shows the percentage of EU Single Market Directives still to be transposed into national law. In addition to giving each country's 'transposition deficit', the Scoreboard identifies the number of infringements of the internal market that have taken place. The hope is that the 'naming and shaming' of countries will encourage them to make more rapid progress towards totally free trade within the EU.

The Action Plan was largely, but not totally successful. In 1997, the average transposition deficit of member countries was 35 per cent. By 1999, this had fallen to 3.5 per cent and by 2008, to just 1.8 per cent, despite the accession of 12 new members to the EU.

Nevertheless, national governments have continued to introduce *new* technical standards, several of which have had the effect of erecting new barriers to trade. Also, infringements of single market rules by governments have not always been dealt with. The net result is that, although trade is much freer today than in the early 1990s, especially given the transparency of pricing with the euro, there still exist various barriers, especially to the free movement of goods.

To counteract new barriers, the EU periodically issues new Directives. If this process is more rapid than that of the transposition of existing Directives into national law, the transposition deficit increases.

The effect of the new member states

Given the very different nature of the economies of many of the new entrants to the EU, and their lower levels of GDP per head, the potential for gain from membership has been substantial. The gains come through trade creation, increased competition, technological transfer and inward investment, both from other EU countries and from outside the EU.

A study in 2004[3] concluded that Poland's GDP would rise by 3.4 per cent and Hungary's by almost 7 per cent. Real wages would rise, with those of unskilled workers rising faster than those of skilled workers, in accordance with these countries' comparative advantage. There would also be benefits for the 15 pre-2004 members from increased trade and investment, but these would be relatively minor in comparison to the gains to the new members.

> **Pause for thought**
>
> *Why may the new members of the EU have the most to gain from the single market, but also the most to lose?*

In future years, now that the euro is used by at least 16 of the member states, trade within the EU is likely to continue to grow as a proportion of GDP. We examine the benefits and costs of the single currency and the whole process of economic and monetary union in the EU in Section 14.6.

Recap

1. The European Union is a customs union, in that it has common external tariffs and no internal ones. But virtually from the outset it has also had elements of a common market, particularly in the areas of agricultural policy, regional policy, competition policy, and to some extent in the areas of tax harmonisation and social policy.

2. Nevertheless, there were substantial non-tariff barriers to trade within the EU. The Single European Act of 1986 sought to sweep away these restrictions and to establish a genuine free market within the EU: to establish a full common market. Benefits from completing the internal market have included trade creation, cost savings from no longer having to administer barriers, economies of scale for firms now able to operate on a Europe-wide scale, and greater

competition leading to reduced costs and prices, greater flows of technical information and more innovation.

3. Critics of the single market point to the costs of radical changes in industrial structure, the attraction of capital away from the periphery of the EU to its geographical centre, possible problems of market power with the development of giant 'Euro-firms', and the possibilities of trade diversion.

4. The actual costs and benefits of EU membership to the various countries vary with their particular economic circumstances. These costs and benefits in the future will depend on just how completely the barriers to trade are removed, on the extent of monetary union and on the effects of enlarging the Union.

13.7 TRADE AND DEVELOPING COUNTRIES

The importance of international trade to developing countries

The role of international trade is one of the most contentious for developing countries. Should they adopt an open trading policy with few if any barriers to imports? Should they go further and actively promote trade by subsidising their export sector? Or should they restrict trade and pursue a policy of greater self-sufficiency? These are issues we shall be examining in this section.

---

[3] M. Maliszewska, *Benefits of the Single Market expansion for current and new member states* (Centrum Analiz Społeczno-Ekonomicznych).

Whether it is desirable that developing countries should adopt policies of more trade or less, trade is still vital. Certain raw materials, capital equipment and intermediate products that are necessary for development can be obtained only from abroad. Others *could* be produced domestically but only at much higher cost.

Trade strategies

As they develop, countries' policies towards trade typically go through various stages.

Primary outward-looking stage. Traditionally, developing countries have exported primaries – minerals such as copper, cash crops such as coffee, and non-foodstuffs such as cotton – in exchange for manufactured consumer goods. In their early phase of development, countries have little in the way of an industrial base and thus if they want to consume manufactured goods they have to import them.

Secondary inward-looking stage. In seeking rapid economic development, most developing countries drew lessons from the experience of the advanced countries. The main conclusion was that industrialisation was the key to economic success.

But industrialisation required foreign exchange to purchase capital equipment. This led to a policy of **import-substituting industrialisation**, which involved cutting back on non-essential imports and thereby releasing foreign exchange. Tariffs and other restrictions were imposed on those imports for which a domestic substitute existed or which were regarded as unimportant.

Secondary outward-looking stage. Once an industry had satisfied domestic demand, it had to seek markets abroad if expansion was to continue. What is more, as we shall see, import substitution brought a number of serious problems for developing countries. The answer seemed to be to look outward again, this time to the export of manufactured goods. Many of the most economically successful developing countries (especially Hong Kong, Singapore, South Korea, Taiwan and, more recently, China) have owed their high growth rates to a rapid expansion of manufactured exports.

We will now examine the three stages in more detail.

Approach 1: Exporting primaries – exploiting comparative advantage

The justification for exporting primaries

Despite moves towards import substitution and secondary export promotion, many developing countries still rely heavily on primary exports. Three major arguments have been traditionally used for pursuing a policy of exporting primaries. In each case the arguments have also been used to justify a policy of free or virtually free trade.

Exporting primaries exploits comparative advantage. Traditional trade theory implies that countries should specialise in producing those items in which they have a comparative advantage: i.e. those goods that can be produced at relatively low opportunity costs. For most developing countries this means that a large proportion of their exports should be primaries.

Exporting primaries provides a 'vent for surplus'. Trade offers a vent for surplus: i.e. a means of putting to use resources that would otherwise not be used. These surpluses occur where the domestic market is simply not big enough to consume all the available output of a particular good. There is far too little demand within Zambia

KI 34
p 432

> **Definition**
>
> **Import-substituting industrialisation (ISI)**
> A strategy of restricting imports of manufactured goods and using the foreign exchange saved to build up domestic industries.

to consume its potential output of copper. The same applies to Namibian uranium and Peruvian tin.

Exporting primaries provides an 'engine for economic growth'. According to this argument, developing countries benefit from the growth of the economies of the developed world. As industrial expansion takes place in the rich North, this will create additional demand for primaries from the poor South.

Traditional trade theory in the context of development

There are several reasons for questioning whether the above arguments justify a policy of relying on primary exports as the means to development.

Comparative costs change over time. Over time, with the acquisition of new skills and an increase in the capital stock, a developing country that once had a comparative advantage in primaries may find that it now has a comparative advantage in certain *manufactured* products, especially those which are more labour-intensive and use raw materials of which the country has a plentiful supply. The market, however, cannot necessarily be relied upon to bring about a smooth transition to producing such products.

Concentrating on primary production may hinder growth. A country may gain in the short run by exporting primaries and using the money earned to buy imports. But primary production may have little potential for expansion and thus growth may be slower.

The benefits from trade may not accrue to the nationals of the country. If a mine or plantation is owned by a foreign company, it will be the foreign shareholders who get the profits from the sale of exports. In addition, these companies may bring in their own capital and skilled labour from abroad. The benefits gained by the local people will probably be confined to the additional wages they earn. With these companies being in a position of monopsony power, these wages are often very low.

Trade may lead to greater inequality. Trade shifts income distribution in favour of those factors of production employed intensively in the export sector. If exports are labour-intensive, greater equality will tend to result. But if they are land- or raw-material-intensive then trade will redistribute income in favour of large landowners or mine owners.

Exporting primary exports may involve external costs. Mining can lead to huge external costs, such as the despoiling of the countryside and damage to the health of miners. Mines and plantations can lead to the destruction of traditional communities and their values.

These arguments cast doubt on whether a policy of relying on free trade in primary exports is the best way of achieving economic development. Various trends in the international economy have also worked against primary exporters.

Problems for primary exporters: long term

Long-term trends in international trade have caused problems for primary exporting countries in a number of ways.

Low income elasticity of demand for primary products. As world incomes grow, so a smaller proportion of these incomes is spent on primaries. But why? Since food is a necessity of life, consumers, especially in rich countries, already consume virtually all they require. A rise in incomes, therefore, tends to be spent more on luxury goods and services, and only slightly more on basic foodstuffs.

Agricultural protection in advanced countries. Faced with the problem of a slowly growing demand for food produced by their own farmers, advanced countries increasingly imposed restrictions on imported food. Reducing these restrictions has been one of the main aims of the Doha Development Agenda (the latest round of WTO trade negotiations: see Box 13.4).

Technological developments. Synthetic substitutes have in many cases replaced primaries in the making of consumer durables (such as furniture and household appliances), clothing and industrial equipment. Also, the process of miniaturisation, as micro-chips have replaced machines, has meant that less and less raw materials have been required to produce any given amount of output.

Rapid growth in imports. There tends to be a high income elasticity of demand for imported manufactures. This is the result partly of the better-off in developing countries increasingly being able to afford luxury goods, and partly of the development of new tastes as people are exposed to the products of the developed world – products such as Coca-Cola, Levi jeans, mobile phones and iPods. In fact, the whole process has been dubbed 'Coca-Colanisation'.

The terms of trade. Between 1980 and 2000, non-fuel primary product prices fell by 47 per cent (see Table 13.2). This reflected the slow growth in demand for primaries and led to a decline in the terms of trade for primary exporters. This is because they were having to export more and more in order to buy any given quantity of imports, such as manufactured goods. A quite different picture emerged in the 2000s. As the demand for food and raw materials grew rapidly, reflecting the rapid growth of China and various other emerging economies, so primary commodity prices rose sharply. This is shown in the final column of Table 13.2.

Approach 2: Import-substituting industrialisation (ISI)

Dissatisfaction with relying on primary exporting has led most countries to embark on a process of industrialisation. The newly industrialised countries (NICs), such as Malaysia and Brazil, are already well advanced along the industrialisation road. Other developing countries have not yet progressed very far, especially the poorest African countries.

The most obvious way for countries to industrialise was to cut back on the import of manufactures and substitute them with home-produced manufactures. This could not be done overnight: it had to be done in stages, beginning with

Table 13.2   World primary commodity prices (2000 = 100)

	1960	1970	1980	1990	2000	2007	2008
Food	254	199	214	122	100	169	236
Metals and minerals	174	183	152	127	100	313	332
All non-fuel commodities	221	184	188	118	100	177	190
Oil	27	15	122	86	100	252	344

Source: Data drawn from *World Development Indicators 2005* (World Bank); *Handbook of Statistics 2008* (UNCTAD)

Definition

Tariff escalation
The system whereby tariff rates increase the closer a product is to the finished stage of production.

assembly, then making some of the components, and finally making all, or nearly all, of the inputs into production. Most developing countries have at least started on the first stage. Several of the more advanced developing countries have component manufacturing industries. Only a few of the larger NICs, such as India, Brazil and South Korea, have built extensive capital goods industries.

The method most favoured by policy makers is **tariff escalation**. Here tariff rates (or other restrictions) increase as one moves from the raw materials to the intermediate product to the finished product stage. Thus finished goods have higher tariffs than intermediate products. This encourages assembly plants, which are protected by high tariffs from imported finished products, and are able to obtain components at a lower tariff rate.

One of the problems with ISI is that countries are desperately short of resources to invest in industry. As a result, a policy of ISI has usually involved encouraging investment by multinational companies. But even without specific 'perks' (e.g. tax concessions, cheap sites, the cutting of red tape), multinationals will still probably be attracted by the protection afforded by the tariffs or quotas.

Adverse effects of import substitution

Some countries, such as South Korea and Taiwan, pursued an inward-looking ISI policy for only a few years. For them it was merely a stage in development, rapidly to be followed by a secondary outward-looking policy. Infant industries were initially given protection, but when they had achieved sufficient economies of scale, the barriers to imports were gradually removed.

The countries that have continued to pursue protectionist ISI policies have generally had a poorer growth record. They have also tended to suffer from other problems, such as a deepening of inequality. The development of the modern industrial sector has often been to the detriment of the traditional sectors and also of the export sector.

The criticisms of ISI are numerous, and include the following.

It has run directly counter to the principle of comparative advantage. Rather than confining ISI to genuine infant industries and then gradually removing the protection, ISI has been applied indiscriminately to a whole range of industries. Countries are producing goods in which they have a comparative *disadvantage*.

KI 34
p 432

It has cushioned inefficient practices and encouraged the establishment of monopolies. Without the competition from imports, many of the industries are highly inefficient and wasteful of resources. What is more, in all but the largest or most developed of the developing countries the domestic market for manufactures is small. If a newly established industry is to be large enough to gain the full potential economies of scale, it will necessarily be large relative to the market. This means that it will have considerable monopoly power.

KI 16
p 116

It has involved artificially low real interest rates. In order to encourage capital investment in the import-substituting industries, governments have often intervened to keep interest rates low. This has encouraged the use of capital-intensive technology with a consequent lack of jobs. It has also starved other sectors (such as agriculture) of much needed finance, and it has discouraged saving.

It has led to urban wages above the market-clearing level. Wages in the industrial sector, although still low compared with advanced countries, are often considerably higher than in the traditional sectors.

- They are pushed up by firms seeking to retain labour in which they have invested training.
- Governments, seeking to appease the politically powerful urban industrial working class, have often passed minimum wage laws.
- Trade unions, although less widespread in developing than in advanced countries, are mainly confined to the new industries.

Higher industrial wages again encourage firms to use capital-intensive techniques.

It has involved overvalued exchange rates. Restricting imports tends to lead to an appreciation of the exchange rate. This makes non-restricted imports cheaper, which then discourages the production of domestic goods, such as food and component parts, which compete with those imports. Also, a higher exchange rate discourages exports. Exports tend to be priced in dollars. If the exchange rate appreciates, domestic currency will buy more dollars; or put another way, a dollar will exchange for less domestic currency. Thus exporters will earn less domestic currency as the exchange rate appreciates.

It does not necessarily save on foreign exchange. Many of the new industries are highly dependent on the importation of raw materials, capital equipment and component parts. Foreign inputs, unlike foreign finished goods, are often supplied by a single firm, which can thus charge monopoly prices. What is more, a large proportion of the extra incomes generated by these industries tends to be spent on imports by the new urban élites.

Protection has not been applied evenly. Many different tariff rates have often been used in one country: in fact, a policy of tariff escalation demands this. In addition, governments have often used a whole range of other protectionist instruments – such as the licensing of importers, physical and value quotas and foreign exchange rationing. These have often been applied in a haphazard way. The result is that protection has been highly uneven.

Income distribution is made less equal. Additional incomes generated by the modern sector tend to be spent on modern-sector goods and imported goods. Thus there is a multiplier effect *within* the modern sector, but virtually none between the modern sector and the traditional sectors. Also as we saw above, an overvalued exchange rate leads to a bias against agriculture and thus further deepens the divide between rich and poor. Finally, the relatively high wages of the modern sector encourage workers to migrate to the towns, where many, failing to get a job, live in dire poverty.

Social, cultural and environmental problems. A policy of ISI often involves imposing an alien set of values. Urban life can be harsh, competitive and materialistic. Moreover, the drive for industrialisation may involve major costs to the environment, as a result of waste products from new industries, often with low environmental standards.

Finally, import substitution is necessarily limited by the size of the domestic market. Once that is saturated, ISI can come to an abrupt halt. At that stage, further expansion can only come from exporting; but if these industries have been over-protected, they will be unable to compete in world markets.

Approach 3: Exporting manufactures – a possible way forward?

The countries with the highest rates of economic growth have been those that have successfully made the transition to being exporters of manufactures. Table 13.3 gives some examples.

Table 13.3	Growth rates and export performance of selected secondary outward-looking countries					
	Average annual growth in real GDP (%)		Share of manufactures in merchandise exports (%)		Average annual growth rate of merchandise exports (%)	
	1960–90	1991–2009	1970	2008	1960–90	1991–2008
Brazil	5.5	3.0	13	44	14.1	8.0
Malaysia	6.8	6.2	7	65	13.4	10.0
South Korea	8.4	5.4	77	87	30.4	13.9
Singapore	9.2	6.4	28	70	16.3	7.4
Hong Kong	7.9	4.4	96	94	18.3	8.8
China	8.1	10.2	35	93	13.4	17.9
All developing countries	4.3	4.9	27	60	13.6	8.7

Sources: Data drawn from *Handbook of Statistics* (UNCTAD) and *World Development Indicators* (World Bank)

The transition from inward-looking to outward-looking industrialisation

How is a country to move from import substituting to being outward looking? One approach is to take it industry by industry. When an industry has saturated the home market and there is no further scope for import substitution, it should then be encouraged to seek markets overseas. The trouble with this approach is that if the country is still protecting other industries, there will probably still be an overvalued exchange rate. Thus specific subsidies, tax concessions or other 'perks' would have to be given to this industry to enable it to compete. The country would still be highly interventionist, with all the distortions and misallocation of resources this tends to bring.

The alternative is to wean the whole economy off protection. Three major things will need doing. There will need to be a devaluation of the currency (see Section 14.4) in order to restore the potential profitability of the export sector. There will also need to be a dismantling of the various protective measures that had biased production towards the home market. Finally there will probably need to be a removal or relaxing of price controls. But these are things that cannot be done 'at a stroke'. Firms may have to be introduced gradually to the greater forces of competition that an outward-looking trade policy brings. Otherwise there may be massive bankruptcies and a corresponding massive rise in unemployment.

The benefits from a secondary outward-looking policy

The advocates of outward-looking industrialisation make a number of points in its favour.

It conforms more closely to comparative advantage. Countries pursuing an open trade regime will only be able to export goods in which they have a comparative advantage. The resources used in earning a unit of foreign exchange from exports will be less than those used in saving a unit of foreign exchange by replacing imports with home-produced goods. In other words, resources will be used more efficiently.

Economies of scale. If the home market is too small to allow a firm to gain all the potential economies of scale, these can be gained by expanding into the export market.

Increased competition. By having to compete with foreign companies, exporters will be under a greater competitive pressure than industries sheltering behind protective barriers. This will encourage (a) resource saving in the short run through reductions in inefficiency, and (b) innovation and investment, as firms attempt to adopt the latest technology, often obtained from developed countries.

Increased investment. To the extent that outward-looking policies lead to a greater potential for economic growth, they may attract more foreign capital. To the extent that they involve an increase in interest rates, they will tend to encourage saving. To the extent that they lead to increased incomes, additional saving will be generated, especially given that the *marginal* propensity to save may be quite high. The extra savings can be used to finance extra investment.

It can lead to more employment and a more equal distribution of income. The manufactured goods in which a country has a comparative advantage will be those produced by labour-intensive techniques (since wage rates are comparatively low in developing countries). Export expansion will thus increase the demand for labour relative to capital and thus create more employment. The increased demand for labour will tend to lead to a rise in wages relative to profits.

It removes many of the costs associated with ISI. Under a policy of ISI, managers may spend a lot of their time lobbying politicians and officials, seeking licences (and sometimes paying bribes to obtain them), adhering to norms and regulations or trying to find ways round them. If an outward-looking policy involves removing all this, managers can turn their attention to producing goods more efficiently.

Drawbacks of an export-orientated industrialisation strategy

The export of manufactures is seen by many developed countries as very threatening to their own industries. Their response has often been to erect trade barriers. These barriers have tended to be highest in the very industries (such as textiles, footwear and processed food) where developing countries have the greatest comparative advantage. Even if the barriers are *currently* low, developing countries may feel that it is too risky to expand their exports of these products for fear of a future rise in barriers. Recognising this problem, the WTO is very keen to ensure fair access for developing countries to the markets of the rich world (see Box 13.4).

The success of developing countries such as China, Malaysia and South Korea in exporting manufactures does not imply that other developing countries will have similar success. As additional developing countries attempt to export their manufactures, they will be facing more and more competition from each other.

Another problem is that, if a more open trade policy involves removing or reducing exchange and capital controls, the country may become more vulnerable to speculative attack. This was one of the major factors contributing to the East Asian crisis of the late 1990s. Gripped by currency and stock market speculation, and by banking and company insolvency, many countries of the region found that economic growth had turned into a major recession. The 'miracle' seemed to be

| BOX 13.6 | THE CHINESE 'ECONOMIC MIRACLE' |

Riding the dragon

'China is amazing. It is capitalism, but at an unprecedented speed.' 'The talent of Chinese software engineers is unbelievable. I can't believe how effective they are.' (Bill Gates, Chairman, Microsoft)

'If your business isn't making money in China, it probably wouldn't make money anywhere else.' (Carlos Ghosn, President, Nissan Motor Company)[a]

On the basis of several indicators, China's economic performance is extraordinary. From 1990 to 2008 annual economic growth averaged 9.9 per cent. Its exports grew by an average of 19.5 per cent (see chart). In 2004 it overtook Japan to become the world's third largest exporter (after Germany and the USA). In Purchasing Power Parity (PPP) terms (after adjusting for differences in the average price of goods between countries which are not accurately reflected in exchange rates), China is the world's second biggest economy after the USA, or third if the eurozone is taken as a single economy.

And as China's economy and exports have boomed, so foreign investment has flooded into the country. In 1990 foreign direct investment (FDI) into China was $3.5 billion. By 2007 the figure had risen to $71.8 billion.

Chinese export-orientated growth has been based on three key factors: specialising in goods in which it has a comparative advantage; having an economy that is favourable to both domestic and inward investment; and having an exchange rate that is undervalued in PPT terms (a higher exchange rate would 'equalise' the power of different currencies to purchase a given basket of goods in China).

Specialisation

China has been industrialising rapidly. With the huge size of the domestic market and with an open policy towards exporting, China has specialised in goods that exploit its diverse but relatively well-trained labour force. Huge industrial complexes have sprung up along the coast from where it is easy to export.

Chinese firms have adapted to changing world markets and to their own changing comparative advantage. Twenty years ago, textiles and clothing were China's main export industry. These relatively labour-intensive industries were ideally suited to exploit the abilities of China's abundant labour. Today textiles and clothing account for a sixth of China's exports. Electronic goods, by contrast, account for more than a third and are growing at a rate three times as fast as textiles. Electronic goods exploit China's increasingly well-trained and well-educated workforce.

Investment

But why are foreign investors attracted to China? Is it simply that the economy is growing rapidly? Clearly that is part of the attraction, but it is more than that. For a start, the Chinese economy is huge. With a population of 1.33 billion and a GDP of $3.9 trillion in 2008, China represents a massive potential market. The government has also invested heavily in improving the country's transport, power and communications infrastructure.

What is more, much of the growth in income in the Chinese economy is concentrated in the hands of the middle class, which now constitutes over 20 per cent of the population and 50 per cent of the urban population. The demand for consumer goods by these middle-class Chinese is very income elastic. As a result, sales of electrical goods, furniture, cars and fashion clothing are growing rapidly. Not only foreign manufacturers, but foreign retailers too are taking advantage of this. For example, Wal-Mart entered China in 1996 and by 2008 had 77 Supercenters in China, sourcing 95 per cent of its merchandise from local suppliers. Carrefour, the French supermarket chain, entered China in 1995 and by 2008 had 118 stores.

But foreign investors are attracted not only by the growing domestic Chinese market. They are also attracted by the opportunity to manufacture high-tech products with a highly skilled workforce.

---

[a] 'Is China a goldmine or minefield?' *BBC News Online*, 19 February 2004 (**http://news.bbc.co.uk/1/hi/business/ 3494069.stm**).

| **Pause for thought** |

Why may small developing countries have more to gain than large ones from a policy of becoming exporters of manufactured products?

over. Nevertheless, the countries with the least distortions fared the best during the crisis. Thus Singapore and Taiwan, which are open and relatively flexible, experienced only a slowdown, rather than a recession.

Exporting manufactures can be a very risky strategy for developing countries. Perhaps the best hope for the future for

Growth in Chinese exports and GDP (%)

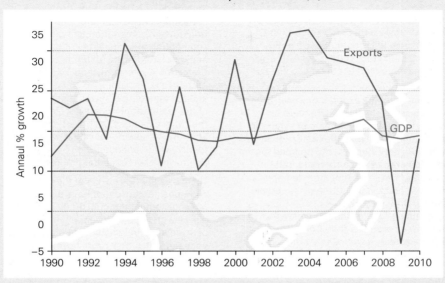

Source: Data drawn from *World Development Indicators* (World Bank) and *Outlook 2009*
(Asian Development Bank)

More and more companies become cutting edge and
leapfrog foreign rivals. Whether games consoles, DVD
recorders or flat-screen monitors, Chinese factories are
grabbing high-tech market share.

'Ten years ago, China was about low cost', says
Infineon's Ulrich Schumacher. 'Now it is at the forefront
of technical development. Infineon can develop twice
as fast in China as anywhere else.'

'Engineers are working in three shifts, seven days
a week', enthuses Mr Schumacher. 'In Germany that
would not be possible: there, engineers don't work
on weekends.'

Bill Gates is similarly impressed after his latest visit
to Microsoft's research lab in Beijing, one of four in
China and Hong Kong. 'The talent of the people there
is unbelievable, I can't believe how effective they are',
he says.

All this is worrying news for high-tech workers in
industrialised countries, who hoped their skills would
give them a competitive advantage in the globalised
economy.[b]

1 *In what ways does a booming Chinese economy
   benefit the rest of the world?*
2 *Why may the Chinese be reluctant to adopt a
   freely floating exchange rate?*

---

[b] *ibid.*

the poorer nations lies in increased manufacturing trade *between* themselves. That
way they can gain the benefits of specialisation and economies of scale that trade
brings, while at the same time producing for a growing market. The feasibility of
this approach depends on whether developing countries can agree to free trade
areas or even customs unions (see Section 13.5). There does, however, seem to be a
strong movement in this direction.

Recap

1. Trade is of vital importance for the vast majority of developing countries, and yet most developing countries suffer from chronic balance of trade deficits.

2. Developing countries have traditionally been primary exporters. This has allowed them to exploit their comparative advantage in labour-intensive goods and has provided a market for certain goods that would otherwise have no market at home.

3. There are reasons for questioning the wisdom of relying on traditional primary exports, however. With a low world income elasticity of demand for primary products, with the development of synthetic substitutes for minerals and with the protection of agriculture in developed countries, the demand for primary exports from the developing world has grown only slowly. At the same time, the demand for manufactured imports into developing countries has grown rapidly. Until recently, the result was a decline in the terms of trade. The rapid growth in demand for primary products from China and India has, to some extent, reversed this trend and terms of trade have improved for many primary exporters.

4. Import-substituting industrialisation (ISI) was seen to be the answer to the problems of primary exporting. ISI was normally achieved in stages, beginning with the finished goods stage and then working back towards the capital goods stage. ISI, it was hoped, would allow countries to benefit from the various long-term advantages associated with manufacturing.

5. For many countries, however, ISI brought as many, if not more, problems than it solved. It often led to the establishment of inefficient industries, protected from foreign competition and facing little or no competition at home either. It led to considerable market distortions, with tariffs and other forms of protection haphazardly applied; to overvalued exchange rates, with a resulting bias against exports and the agricultural sector generally; to a deepening of inequalities and to large-scale social problems as the cities expanded, as poverty and unemployment grew and as traditional values were undermined; to increased dependency on imported inputs; and to growing environmental problems.

6. The most rapidly growing of the developing countries are those that have pursued a policy of export-orientated industrialisation. This has allowed them to achieve the benefits of economies of scale and foreign competition, and to specialise in goods in which they have a comparative advantage (i.e. labour-intensive goods) and yet which have a relatively high income elasticity of demand. Whether countries that have pursued ISI can successfully turn to an open, export-orientated approach will depend to a large extent on the degree of competition they face not only from advanced countries but also from other developing countries.

QUESTIONS

1. How might the interdependence of economies through trade affect an economy's business cycle? Could other forms of interdependence could also affect an economy's business cycle?

2. Referring to Table 13.1 on page 429, show how each country could gain from trade if the LDC could produce (before trade) 3 wheat for 1 cloth and the developed country could produce (before trade) 2 wheat for 5 cloth, and if the exchange ratio (with trade) was 1 wheat for 2 cloth. Would they both still gain if the exchange ratio was (a) 1 wheat for 1 cloth and (b) 1 wheat for 3 cloth?

3. Imagine that two countries, Richland and Poorland, can produce just two goods, computers and coal. Assume that for a given amount of land and capital, the output of these two products requires the following constant amounts of labour:

	Richland	Poorland
1 computer	2	4
100 tonnes of coal	4	5

Assume that each country has 20 million workers.

(a) If there is no trade, and in each country 12 million workers produce computers and 8 million workers produce coal, how many computers and tonnes of coal will each country produce? What will be the total production of each product?

(b) What is the opportunity cost of a computer in (i) Richland; (ii) Poorland?

(c) What is the opportunity cost of 100 tonnes of coal in (i) Richland; (ii) Poorland?

(d) Which country has a comparative advantage in which product?

(e) Assuming that price equals marginal cost, which of the following would represent possible exchange ratios? (i) 1 computer for

40 tonnes of coal; (ii) 2 computers for 140 tonnes of coal; (iii) 1 computer for 100 tonnes of coal; (iv) 1 computer for 60 tonnes of coal; (v) 4 computers for 360 tonnes of coal.

(f) Assume that trade now takes place and that 1 computer exchanges for 65 tonnes of coal. Both countries specialise completely in the product in which they have a comparative advantage. How much does each country produce of its respective product?

(g) The country producing computers sells 6 million domestically. How many does it export to the other country?

(h) How much coal does the other country consume?

4. Why doesn't the USA specialise as much as General Motors or Texaco? Why doesn't the UK specialise as much as Unilever? Is the answer to these questions similar to the answer to the questions, 'Why doesn't the USA specialise as much as Luxembourg?' and 'Why doesn't Unilever specialise as much as the local florist?'

5. To what extent are the arguments for countries specialising and then trading with each other the same as those for individuals specialising in doing the jobs to which they are relatively well suited?

6. The following are four items that are traded internationally: wheat; computers; textiles; insurance. In which one of the four is each of the following most likely to have a comparative advantage: India; the UK; Canada; Japan? Give reasons for your answer.

7. Would it be possible for a country with a comparative disadvantage in a given product at *pre*-trade levels of output to obtain a comparative advantage in it by specialising in its production and exporting it?

8. Go through each of the arguments for restricting trade and provide a counter-argument for not restricting trade.

9. It is often argued that if the market fails to develop infant industries, then this is an argument for government intervention, but not necessarily in the form of restricting imports. What *other* ways could infant industries be given government support?

10. How would you set about judging whether an industry had a genuine case for infant/senile industry protection?

11. Does the consumer in the importing country gain or lose from dumping? (Consider both the short run and the long run.)

12. What is fallacious about the following two arguments? Is there any truth in either?

(a) 'Imports should be reduced because money is going abroad which would be better spent at home.'

(b) 'We should protect our industries from being undercut by imports produced using cheap labour.'

13. Make out a case for restricting trade between the UK and Japan. Are there any arguments here that could not equally apply to a case for restricting trade between Scotland and England or between Liverpool and Manchester?

14. In what ways may free trade result in harmful environmental effects? Is the best solution to these problems to impose restrictions on trade?

15. If countries are so keen to reduce the barriers to trade, why do many countries frequently attempt to erect barriers?

16. What factors will determine whether a country's joining a customs union will lead to trade creation or trade diversion?

17. How would you set about assessing whether or not a country had made a net dynamic gain by joining a customs union? What sort of evidence would you look for?

18. What would be the economic effects of (a) different rates of VAT; (b) different rates of personal income tax; (c) different rates of company taxation between member states, if in all other respects there were no barriers to trade or factor movements between the members of a customs union?

19. Is trade diversion in the EU more likely or less likely in the following cases?

(a) European producers gain monopoly power in world trade.

(b) Modern developments in technology and communications reduce the differences in production costs associated with different locations.

(c) The development of the internal market produces substantial economies of scale in many industries.

20. Why is it difficult to estimate the magnitude of the benefits of completing the internal market of the EU?

21. Look through the costs and benefits that we identified from the single European market. Do the same costs and benefits arise from a substantially enlarged EU?

22. If there have been clear benefits from the single market programme, why do individual member governments still try to erect barriers, such as new technical standards?

23. If a developing country has a comparative advantage in primary products, should the government allow market forces to dictate the pattern of trade?

24. Why will a high exchange rate harm the agricultural sector in a developing country?

25. In what ways may free trade have harmful cultural effects on a developing country?

26. If a developing country has a comparative advantage in the production of wheat, should it specialise as much as possible in the production of wheat and export what is not consumed domestically?

27. What are the advantages and disadvantages for a developing country of pursuing a policy of ISI?

28. Will the production of labour-intensive manufactures for export lead to more or less inequality in a developing country?

29. Would the use of import controls help or hinder a policy of export-orientated industrialisation?

30. Should all developing countries aim over the long term to become *exporters* of manufactured products?

Log on to MyEconlab and complete the studyplan exercises for this chapter to see how much you have learnt and where you need to revise most. Make sure you access all the supporting textbook resources including the online workbook, newsblog, audio animations, guided solutions and ebook.

Additional case studies in the *Essentials of Economics* MyEconLab (www.pearsoned.co.uk/sloman)

13.1   David Ricardo and the law of comparative advantage. The first clear statement of the law of comparative advantage (in 1817).

13.2   Fallacious arguments for restricting trade. Some of the more common mistaken arguments for protection.

13.3   Strategic trade theory. The case of Airbus is used to illustrate the arguments that trade restrictions can be to the strategic advantage of countries in developing certain industries and preventing the establishment of foreign monopolies.

13.4   The Uruguay Round. An examination of the negotiations that led to substantial cuts in trade barriers.

13.5   The World Trade Organization. This looks at the various opportunities and threats posed by this major international organisation.

13.6   Steel barriers. This case considers the US administration's imposition of tariffs on imported steel in 2002, and the reactions of other countries to these tariffs.

13.7   The Battle of Seattle. This looks at the protests against the WTO at Seattle in November 1999 and considers the arguments for and against the free trade policies of the WTO.

13.8   Banana, banana. The dispute between the USA and the EU over banana imports.

13.9   Assessing NAFTA. Who are the winners and losers from NAFTA?

13.10 **Free trade and the environment.** Do whales, the rainforests and the atmosphere gain from free trade?

13.11 **The social dimension of the EU.** The principles of the Social Charter.

13.12 **The benefits of the single market.** Evidence of achievements and the Single Market Action Plan of 1997.

13.13 **The Internal Market Scoreboard.** Keeping a tally on progress to a true single market.

13.14 **Multinational corporations and developing economies.** Do MNCs benefit developing economies?

Websites relevant to this chapter

Numbers and sections refer to websites listed in the Web appendix and hotlinked from this book's website at **www.pearsoned.co.uk/sloman**.

- For news articles relevant to this chapter, see the *Economics News Articles* link from the book's website.

- For general news on international trade, see websites in section A, and particularly A1–5, 7–9, 24, 25, 31. For articles on various aspects of trade and developing countries, see A27, 28; I9. See also links to newspapers worldwide in A38 and 39, and the news search feature in Google at A41. See also links to economics news in A42.

- For international data on imports and exports, see site H16 > *Resources > Trade statistics*. See also *World Economic Outlook* in H4 and trade data in B23. See also the trade topic in I14.

- For details of individual countries' structure of imports and exports, see B32.

- For UK data, see B1, *1. National Statistics* > the fourth link > *Compendia and Reference > Annual Abstract > External trade and investment.* See also B3 and 34. For EU data, see G1 > *Publications > Publications overview > European Economy.*

- For discussion papers on trade, see H4 and 7.

- For trade disputes, see H16.

- For various pressure groups critical of the effects of free trade and globalisation, see H12–14.

- For information on various preferential trading arrangements, see H20–22.

- For EU sites, see G1, 3, 7–14, 16–18.

- For information on trade and developing countries, see H4, 7, 9, 10, 16, 17. See also links to development sites in I9.

- Sites I7 and 11 contain links to various topics in *International Economics* (*International trade*, *International agreements*, *Economic co-operation* and *EU Economics*) and to *Trade and trade policy* in *Economic Development*. Site I4 has links to *International economics*, *Development economics* and *Economic development*. Site I17 has links to *International economics*, *Trade policy* and *Development economics*.

- For student resources relevant to this chapter, see sites C1–7, 9, 10, 19.

Web appendices

13.1 **The gains from trade.** This appendix uses general equilibrium analysis (see Web Appendix 7.1) to analyse the gains from trade and the limits to specialisation under increasing opportunity costs.

13.2 **Trade creation and trade diversion.** A graphical analysis of the welfare gains and losses from joining a customs union.

CHAPTER MAP

Balance of payments and exchange rates

In this chapter we will first explain what is meant by the balance of payments. In doing so we will see just how the various monetary transactions between the domestic economy and the rest of the world are recorded.

Then (in Sections 14.2 and 14.3) we will examine how rates of exchange are determined, and how they are related to the balance of payments. We will see what causes exchange rate fluctuations, and how the government can attempt to prevent these fluctuations.

A government could decide to leave its country's exchange rates entirely to market forces (a free-floating exchange rate). Alternatively, it could attempt to fix its currency's exchange rate to some other currency (e.g. the US dollar). Or it could simply try to reduce the degree to which its currency fluctuates. In Section 14.4, we look at the relative merits of different degrees of government intervention in the foreign exchange market: of different 'exchange rate regimes'.

We then turn to look at attempts to achieve greater currency stability between the members of the EU. Section 14.5 looks at the European exchange rate mechanism, which sought in the 1980s and 1990s to limit the amount that member currencies were allowed to fluctuate against each other. Then Section 14.6 examines the euro. Has the adoption of a single currency by 12 EU countries been of benefit to them? Would it benefit the UK to join?

Finally, as with Chapter 13, we look at the position of developing countries, and this time focus on the issue of debt. Why are so many developing countries facing severe debt problems and what can be done about it?

After studying this chapter, you should be able to answer the following questions:

- What is meant by 'the balance of payments' and how do trade and financial movements affect it?
- How are exchange rates determined and what effects do changes in the exchange rate have on the economy?
- How do governments and/or central banks seek to influence the exchange rate and what are the advantages and disadvantages of such intervention?
- What are the advantages and disadvantages of the euro for member countries?
- What are the origins of the severe debt problem faced by many developing countries? What can be done about the problem?

14.1 THE BALANCE OF PAYMENTS ACCOUNT

What is meant by a balance of payments deficit or surplus?

In Chapter 8 we identified balance of payments deficits as one of the main macroeconomic problems that governments face. But what precisely do we mean by 'balance of payments deficits' (or surpluses), and what is their significance?

A country's balance of payments account records all the flows of money between residents of that country and the rest of the world. *Receipts* of money from abroad are regarded as credits and are entered in the accounts with a positive sign. *Outflows* of money from the country are regarded as debits and are entered with a negative sign.

There are three main parts of the balance of payments account: the *current account*, the *capital account* and the *financial account*. Each part is then subdivided. We shall look at each part in turn, and take the UK as an example. Table 14.1 gives a summary of the UK balance of payments for 2008.

The current account

The **current account** records payments for imports and exports of goods and services, plus incomes flowing into and out of the country, plus net transfers of money into and out of the country. It is normally divided into four subdivisions.

The trade in goods account. This records imports and exports of physical goods (previously known as 'visibles'). Exports result in an inflow of money and are therefore a credit item. Imports result in an outflow of money and are therefore a debit item. The balance of these is called the **balance on trade in goods** or **balance of visible trade** or **merchandise balance**. A *surplus* is when exports exceed imports. A deficit is when imports exceed exports.

KI 21
p 239

Definitions

Current account of the balance of payments

The record of a country's imports and exports of goods and services, plus incomes and transfers of money to and from abroad.

Balance on trade in goods or **balance of visible trade** or **merchandise balance**

Exports of goods minus imports of goods.

Table 14.1 UK balance of payments, 2008

	2008		Average 1993–2008
	£m	% of GDP	% of GDP
Current account:			
Balance on trade in goods	−92 876	−6.4	−3.7
Balance on trade in services	48 878	3.4	2.0
Balance of trade	**−43 998**	**−3.0**	**−1.7**
Income balance	33 129	2.3	0.8
Net current transfers	−13 624	−0.9	−0.8
Current account balance	**−24 493**	**−1.7**	**−1.8**
Capital account:			
Capital account balance	**3 505**	**0.2**	**0.1**
Financial account:			
Net direct investment	−7 885	−0.5	−1.8
Portfolio investment balance	389 529	27.0	3.1
Other investment balance	−381 468	−26.4	0.3
Balance of financial derivatives	18 143	1.3	0.1
Reserve assets	1 338	0.1	0.0
Financial account balance	**19 657**	**1.4**	**1.6**
Net errors and omissions	**1 331**	**0.1**	**0.0**
Balance	*0*	*0*	*0*

Source: *The Pink Book* and *United Kingdom Economic Accounts* (National Statistics)

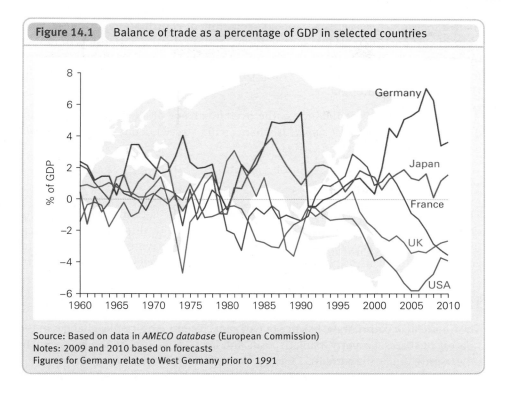

Figure 14.1   Balance of trade as a percentage of GDP in selected countries

Source: Based on data in *AMECO database* (European Commission)
Notes: 2009 and 2010 based on forecasts
Figures for Germany relate to West Germany prior to 1991

The trade in services account. This records imports and exports of services (such as transport, tourism and insurance). Thus the purchase of a foreign holiday would be a debit, since it represents an outflow of money, whereas the purchase by an overseas resident of a UK insurance policy would be a credit to the UK services account. The balance of these is called the **services balance**.

The balance of both the goods and services accounts together is known as the **balance on trade in goods and services** or simply the **balance of trade**. Figure 14.1 shows the balance of trade for selected countries as a proportion of their GDP (national output). Over the period shown, Japan and Germany have typically run balance of trade surpluses, while the USA and the UK have run deficits. The French balance of trade averages close to zero.

We can relate the balance of trade to our circular flow model in Chapter 8. A balance of trade deficit represents a net leakage from the circular flow because imports (a withdrawal) are greater than exports (an injection). Conversely, a balance of trade surplus is a net injection for an economy.

In equilibrium, injections must equal withdrawals. Thus a net withdrawal on the balance of trade, must be offset by a net injection elsewhere: either investment exceeding saving and/or government expenditure exceeding tax revenue. This is why we often see countries with trade deficits running government budget deficits. If we revisit Table 12.1 on page 383, this appears to be the case for the USA and the UK. Countries which run both trade deficits and government budget deficits are said to experience *twin deficits*. Case Study 14.1 in MyEconLab considers the evidence for twin deficits.

Income flows. These consist of wages, interest and profits flowing into and out of the country. For example, dividends earned by a foreign resident from shares in a UK company would be an outflow of money (a debit item).

> **Definitions**
>
> **Services balance**
> Exports of services minus imports of services.
>
> **Balance on trade in goods and services** or **balance of trade**
> Exports of goods and services minus imports of goods and services.

> **Pause for thought**
>
> *Can countries run twin surpluses with both a budget surplus and a balance of trade surplus?*

Current transfers of money. These include government contributions to and receipts from the EU and international organisations, and international transfers of money by private individuals and firms. Transfers out of the country are debits. Transfers into the country (e.g. money sent from Greece to a Greek student studying in the UK) would be a credit item.

The **current account balance** is the overall balance of all the above four subdivisions. A *current account surplus* is where credits exceed debits. A *current account deficit* is where debits exceed credits.

The capital account

The **capital account** records the flows of funds, into the country (credits) and out of the country (debits), associated with the acquisition or disposal of fixed assets (e.g. land), the transfer of funds by migrants, and the payment of grants by the government for overseas projects and the receipt of EU money for capital projects.

The financial account[1]

The **financial account** of the balance of payments records cross-border changes in the holding of shares, property, bank deposits and loans, government securities, etc. In other words, unlike the current account, which is concerned with money incomes, the financial account is concerned with the purchase and sale of assets. Case Study 14.2 in MyEconLab considers some of the statistics behind the UK's financial account.

Direct investment. If a foreign company invests money from abroad in one of its branches or associated companies in the UK, this represents an inflow of money when the investment is made and is thus a credit item. (Any subsequent profit from this investment that flows abroad will be recorded as an investment income outflow on the current account.) Investment abroad by UK companies represents an outflow of money when the investment is made. It is thus a debit item. Direct investment flows will be affected by 'waves' in merger and acquisition (M&A) activity, such as that around the turn of millennium.

Note that what we are talking about here is the acquisition or sale of assets: e.g. a factory or farm, or the takeover of a whole firm, not the imports or exports of equipment.

Portfolio investment. This is changes in the holding of paper assets, such as company shares. Thus if a UK resident buys shares in an overseas company, this is an outflow of funds and is hence a debit item. Portfolio investment is likely to be affected by relative interest rates. For instance, there was an increase in the demand for UK bonds in the middle part of the 2000s reflecting relatively higher interest rates in the UK compared to other economies, such as the USA and the eurozone (see Box 12.6 on pages 408–9).

Other investment and financial flows. While direct and portfolio investments are concerned primarily with long-term investment, these consist primarily of various types of short-term monetary movement between the UK and the rest of the world. Deposits by overseas residents in banks in the UK and loans to the UK from abroad are credit

---

[1] Prior to October 1998, this account was called the 'capital account'. The account that is *now* called the capital account used to be included in the transfers section of the current account. This potentially confusing change of names was adopted in order to bring the UK accounts in line with the system used by the International Monetary Fund (IMF), the EU and most individual countries.

items, since they represent an inflow of money. Deposits by UK residents in overseas banks and loans by UK banks to overseas residents are debit items. They represent an outflow of money.

Short-term monetary flows are common between international financial centres to take advantage of differences in countries' interest rates and changes in exchange rates. The late 2000s also highlighted the importance of confidence in financial institutions as a driver of financial flows. The UK's balance of 'other investment' went from a deficit of around £13 billion in 2006 to a deficit of over £380 billion in 2008 partly because of a large disinvestment of financial assets with UK financial institutions by non-residents.

Flows to and from the reserves. The UK, like all other countries, holds reserves of gold and foreign currencies. From time to time the Bank of England (acting as the government's agent) will sell some of these reserves to purchase sterling on the foreign exchange market. It does this normally as a means of supporting the rate of exchange (as we shall see below). Drawing on reserves represents a *credit* item in the balance of payments accounts: money drawn from the reserves represents an *inflow* to the balance of payments (albeit an outflow from the reserves account). The reserves can thus be used to support a deficit elsewhere in the balance of payments.

Conversely, if there is a surplus elsewhere in the balance of payments, the Bank of England can use it to build up the reserves. Building up the reserves counts as a debit item in the balance of payments, since it represents an outflow from it (to the reserves).

When all the components of the balance of payments account are taken together, the balance of payments should exactly balance: credits should equal debits. As we shall see below, if they were not equal, the rate of exchange would have to adjust until they were, or the government would have to intervene to make them equal.

When the statistics are compiled, however, a number of errors are likely to occur. As a result there will not be a balance. To 'correct' for this, a **net errors and omissions item** is included in the accounts. This ensures that there will be an exact balance. The main reason for the errors is that the statistics are obtained from a number of sources, and there are often delays before items are recorded and sometimes omissions too.

Figure 14.2 summarises the main accounts of the UK's balance payments: current, capital and financial accounts. It presents each as a percentage of national income. In conjunction with the net error and omissions item, which averages close to zero over the long run, we can see how the accounts combine to give a zero overall balance. For much of the period since the late 1980s, current account deficits have been offset by surpluses on the financial account.

Definition

Net errors and omissions item
A statistical adjustment to ensure that the two sides of the balance of payments account balance. It is necessary because of errors in compiling the statistics.

1. The balance of payments account records all payments to and receipts from foreign countries.

2. The current account records payments for the imports and exports of goods and services, plus incomes and transfers of money to and from abroad.

3. The capital account records all transfers of capital to and from abroad.

4. The financial account records inflows and outflows of money for investment and as deposits in banks and other financial institutions. It also includes dealings in the country's foreign exchange reserves.

5. The whole account must balance, but surpluses or deficits can be recorded on any specific part of the account. Thus the current account could be in deficit, but it would have to be matched by an equal and opposite capital plus financial account surplus.

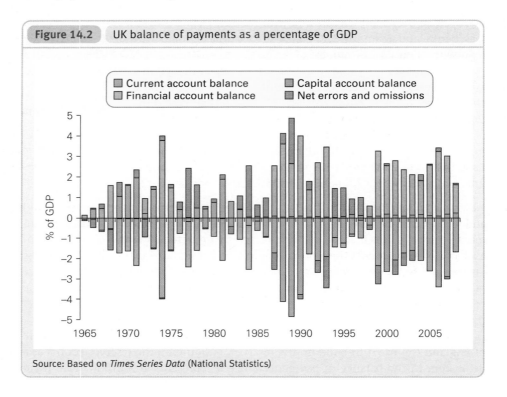

Figure 14.2   UK balance of payments as a percentage of GDP

Source: Based on *Times Series Data* (National Statistics)

14.2   EXCHANGE RATES

What causes exchange rates to change?

An exchange rate is the rate at which one currency trades for another on the foreign exchange market.

If you want to go abroad, you will need to exchange your pounds into euros, dollars, Swiss francs or whatever. To do this you will go to a bank. The bank will quote you that day's exchange rates: for example, €1.45 to the pound, or $1.50 to the pound. It is similar for firms. If an importer wants to buy, say, some machinery from Japan, it will require yen to pay the Japanese supplier. It will thus ask the foreign exchange section of a bank to quote it a rate of exchange of the pound into yen. Similarly, if you want to buy some foreign stocks and shares, or if companies based in the UK want to invest abroad, sterling will have to be exchanged into the appropriate foreign currency.

Likewise, if Americans want to come on holiday to the UK or to buy UK assets, or American firms want to import UK goods or to invest in the UK, they will require sterling. They will be quoted an exchange rate for the pound in the USA: say, £1 = $1.54. This means that they will have to pay $1.54 to obtain £1 worth of UK goods or assets.

Exchange rates are quoted between each of the major currencies of the world. These exchange rates are constantly changing. Minute by minute, dealers in the foreign exchange dealing rooms of the banks are adjusting the rates of exchange. They charge commission when they exchange currencies. It is important for them, therefore, to ensure that they are not left

Pause for thought

How did the pound 'fare' compared with the US dollar, Australian dollar and the yen from 1985 to 2009? What conclusions can be drawn about the relative movements of these three currencies?

| Figure 14.3 | Sterling exchange rates against selected currencies |

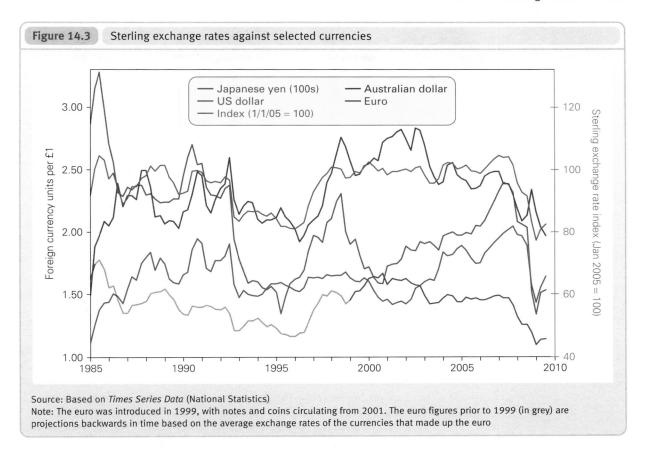

Source: Based on *Times Series Data* (National Statistics)
Note: The euro was introduced in 1999, with notes and coins circulating from 2001. The euro figures prior to 1999 (in grey) are projections backwards in time based on the average exchange rates of the currencies that made up the euro

with a large amount of any currency unsold. What they need to do is to balance the supply and demand of each currency: to balance the amount they purchase to the amount they sell. To do this they will need to adjust the price of each currency – namely, the exchange rate – in line with changes in supply and demand.

Not only are there day-to-day fluctuations in exchange rates, but also there are long-term changes in them. Figure 14.3 shows the average quarterly exchange rates between the pound and various currencies for selected years from 1985.

One of the problems in assessing what is happening to a particular currency is that its rate of exchange may rise against some currencies (weak currencies) and fall against others (strong currencies). In order to gain an overall picture of its fluctuations, therefore, it is best to look at a weighted average exchange rate against all other currencies. This is known as the **exchange rate index** or the **effective exchange rate**. The weight given to each currency in the index depends on the proportion of trade done with that country. Figure 14.3 also shows the sterling exchange rate index based on January 2005 = 100.

Determination of the rate of exchange in a free market

In a free foreign exchange market, the rate of exchange is determined by demand and supply. This is known as a **floating exchange rate**, and is illustrated in Figure 14.4.

For simplicity, assume that there are just two countries: the UK and the USA. When UK importers wish to buy goods from the USA, or when UK residents wish to invest in the USA, they *supply* pounds on the foreign exchange market in order to obtain

Definitions

Exchange rate index or **effective exchange rate**
A weighted average exchange rate expressed as an index, where the value of the index is 100 in a given base year. The weights of the different currencies in the index add up to 1.

Floating exchange rate
When the government does not intervene in the foreign exchange markets, but simply allows the exchange rate to be freely determined by demand and supply.

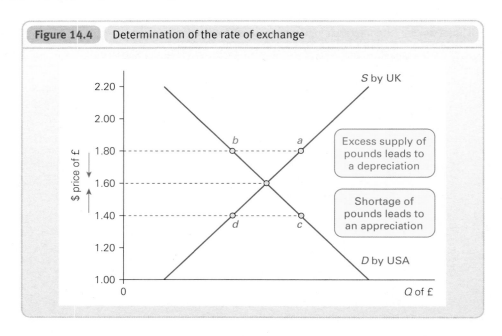

Figure 14.4   Determination of the rate of exchange

dollars. In other words, they go to banks or other foreign exchange dealers to buy dollars in exchange for pounds. The higher the exchange rate, the more dollars they obtain for their pounds. This effectively makes American goods cheaper to buy, and investment more profitable. Thus the *higher* the exchange rate, the *more* pounds are supplied. The supply curve of pounds therefore typically slopes upwards.

When US residents wish to purchase UK goods or to invest in the UK, they require pounds. They *demand* pounds by selling dollars on the foreign exchange market. In other words, they go to banks or other foreign exchange dealers to buy pounds in exchange for dollars. The lower the dollar price of the pound (the exchange rate), the cheaper it is for them to obtain UK goods and assets, and hence the more pounds they are likely to demand. The demand curve for pounds, therefore, typically slopes downwards.

The equilibrium exchange rate is where the demand for pounds equals the supply. In Figure 14.4 this is at an exchange rate of £1 = $1.60. But what is the mechanism that equates demand and supply?

TC 5
p 40

If the current exchange rate were above the equilibrium, the supply of pounds being offered to the banks would exceed the demand. For example, in Figure 14.4 if the exchange rate were $1.80, there would be an excess supply of pounds of *a* – *b*. Banks would not have enough dollars to exchange for all these pounds. But the banks make money by *exchanging* currency, not by holding on to it. They would thus lower the exchange rate in order to encourage a greater demand for pounds and reduce the excessive supply. They would continue lowering the rate until demand equalled supply.

Similarly, if the rate were below the equilibrium, say at $1.40, there would be a shortage of pounds of *c* – *d*. The banks would find themselves with too few pounds to meet all the demand. At the same time they would have an excess supply of dollars. The banks would thus raise the exchange rate until demand equalled supply.

In practice, the process of reaching equilibrium is extremely rapid. The foreign exchange dealers in the banks are continually adjusting the rate as new customers make new demands for currencies. What is more, the banks have to watch closely what each other is doing. They are constantly in competition with each other and

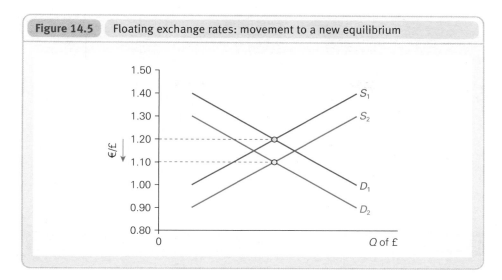

Figure 14.5   Floating exchange rates: movement to a new equilibrium

thus have to keep their rates in line. The dealers receive minute-by-minute updates on their computer screens of the rates being offered round the world.

Shifts in the currency demand and supply curves

Any shift in the demand or supply curves will cause the exchange rate to change. This is illustrated in Figure 14.5. If the demand and supply curves shift from D_1 and S_1 to D_2 and S_2 respectively, the exchange rate will fall from €1.20 to €1.10. A fall in the exchange rate is called a **depreciation**. A rise in the exchange rate is called an **appreciation**.

But why should the demand and supply curves shift? The following are the major possible causes of a depreciation:

- *A fall in domestic interest rates*. UK rates would now be less competitive for savers and other depositors. More UK residents would be likely to deposit their money abroad (the supply of sterling would rise), and fewer people abroad would deposit their money in the UK (the demand for sterling would fall).
- *Higher rates of inflation in the domestic economy than abroad*. UK exports will become less competitive. The demand for sterling will fall. At the same time, imports will become relatively cheaper for UK consumers. The supply of sterling will rise. To the extent, however, that a higher rate of inflation causes the central bank to raise interest rates, this could have the opposite effect.
- *A rise in domestic incomes relative to incomes abroad*. If UK incomes rise, the demand for imports, and hence the supply of sterling, will rise. If incomes in other countries fall, the demand for UK exports, and hence the demand for sterling will fall.
- *Relative investment prospects improving abroad*. If investment prospects become brighter abroad than in the UK, perhaps because of better incentives abroad, or because of worries about an impending recession in the UK, again the demand for sterling will fall and the supply of sterling will rise.
- *Speculation that the exchange rate will fall*. If businesses involved in importing and exporting, and also banks and other foreign exchange dealers, think that the exchange rate is about to fall, they will sell pounds now before the rate does fall. The supply of sterling will thus rise.

Definitions

Depreciation
A fall in the free-market exchange rate of the domestic currency with foreign currencies.

Appreciation
A rise in the free-market exchange rate of the domestic currency with foreign currencies.

Pause for thought

Go through each of the above reasons for shifts in the demand for and supply of sterling and consider what would cause an appreciation of the pound.

Recap

1. The rate of exchange is the rate at which one currency exchanges for another. Rates of exchange are determined by demand and supply in the foreign exchange market. Demand for the domestic currency consists of all the credit items in the balance of payments account. Supply consists of all the debit items.

2. The exchange rate will depreciate (fall) if the demand for the domestic currency falls or the supply increases. These shifts can be caused by a fall in the domestic interest rates, higher inflation in the domestic economy than abroad, a rise in domestic incomes relative to incomes abroad, relative investment prospects improving abroad or the belief by speculators that the exchange rate will fall.

3. The opposite in each case would cause an appreciation (rise).

14.3 EXCHANGE RATES AND THE BALANCE OF PAYMENTS

How does the balance of payments affect the exchange rate?

Exchange rates and the balance of payments: no government or central bank intervention

In a free foreign exchange market, the balance of payments will *automatically* balance. But why?

KI 6
p 21

The credit side of the balance of payments constitutes the demand for sterling. For example, when people abroad buy UK exports or assets they demand sterling in order to pay for them. The debit side constitutes the supply of sterling. For example, when UK residents buy foreign goods or assets, the importers of them require

BOX 14.1   DEALING IN FOREIGN CURRENCIES

CASE STUDIES & APPLICATIONS

A daily juggling act

Imagine that a large car importer in the UK wants to import 5000 cars from Japan costing ¥15 billion. What does it do?

It will probably contact a number of banks' foreign exchange dealing rooms in London and ask them for exchange rate quotes. It thus puts all the banks in competition with each other. Each bank will want to get the business and thereby obtain the commission on the deal. To do this it must offer a higher rate than the other banks, since the higher the ¥/£ exchange rate, the more yen the firm will get for its money. (For an importer a rate of, say, ¥200 to £1 is better than a rate of, say, ¥180.)

Now it is highly unlikely that any of the banks will have a spare ¥15 billion. But a bank cannot say to the importer 'Sorry, you will have to wait before we can agree to sell them to you.' Instead the bank will offer a deal and then, if the firm agrees, the bank will have to set about obtaining the ¥15 billion. To do this it must offer Japanese who are supplying yen to obtain pounds at a sufficiently *low* ¥/£ exchange rate. (The lower the ¥/£ exchange rate, the fewer yen the Japanese will have to pay to obtain pounds.)

The banks' dealers thus find themselves in the delicate position of wanting to offer a *high* enough exchange rate to the car importer in order to gain its business, but a *low* enough exchange rate in order to obtain the required amount of yen. The dealers are thus constantly having to adjust the rates of exchange in order to balance the demand and supply of each currency.

In general, the more of any foreign currency that dealers are asked to supply (by being offered sterling), the lower will be the exchange rate they will offer. In other words, a higher supply of sterling pushes down the foreign currency price of sterling.

 Assume that an American firm wants to import Scotch whisky from the UK. Describe how foreign exchange dealers will respond.

foreign currency to pay for them. They thus supply pounds. A floating exchange rate ensures that the demand for pounds is equal to the supply. It thus also ensures that the credits on the balance of payments are equal to the debits: that the balance of payments balances.

This does not mean that each part of the balance of payments account separately balances, but simply that any current account deficit must be matched by a capital plus financial account surplus and vice versa.

For example, suppose initially that each part of the balance of payments *did* separately balance. Then let us assume that interest rates rise. This encourages larger short-term financial inflows as people abroad are attracted to deposit money in the UK: the demand for sterling would shift to the right (e.g. from D_2 to D_1 in Figure 14.5). It will also cause smaller short-term financial outflows as UK residents keep more of their money in the country: the supply of sterling shifts to the left (e.g. from S_2 to S_1 in Figure 14.5). The financial account will go into surplus. The exchange rate will appreciate.

As the exchange rate rises, this will cause imports to be cheaper and exports to be more expensive. The current account will move into deficit. There is a movement up along the new demand and supply curves until a new equilibrium is reached. At this point, any financial account surplus is matched by an equal current (plus capital) account deficit.

Exchange rates and the balance of payments: with government or central bank intervention

The government or central bank may be unwilling to let the country's currency float freely. Frequent shifts in the demand and supply curves would cause frequent changes in the exchange rate. This, in turn, might cause uncertainty for businesses, which might curtail their trade and investment.

The central bank may thus intervene in the foreign exchange market. But what can it do? The answer to this depends on its objectives. It may simply want to reduce the day-to-day fluctuations in the exchange rate, or it may want to prevent longer-term, more fundamental shifts in the rate.

Reducing short-term fluctuations

Assume that the UK government believes that an exchange rate of €1.20 to the pound is approximately the long-term equilibrium rate. Short-term leftward shifts in the demand for sterling and rightward shifts in the supply, however, are causing the exchange rate to fall below this level (see Figure 14.5). What can the government do to keep the rate at €1.20?

Using reserves. The Bank of England can sell gold and foreign currencies from the reserves to buy pounds. This will shift the demand for sterling back to the right.

Borrowing from abroad. The government can negotiate a foreign currency loan from other countries or from an international agency such as the International Monetary Fund. It can then use these moneys to buy pounds on the foreign exchange market, thus again shifting the demand for sterling back to the right.

Raising interest rates. If the Bank of England raises interest rates, it will encourage people to deposit money in the UK and encourage UK residents to keep their money in the country. The demand for sterling will increase and the supply of sterling will decrease.

Maintaining a fixed rate of exchange over the longer term

Governments may choose to maintain a fixed rate over a number of months or even years. The following are possible methods it can use to achieve this (we are assuming that there are downward pressures on the exchange rate: e.g. as a result of higher aggregate demand and higher inflation).

Contractionary policies. This is where the government deliberately curtails aggregate demand by either *fiscal policy or monetary policy* or both.

Contractionary fiscal policy involves raising taxes and/or reducing government expenditure. Contractionary monetary policy involves reducing the supply of money and raising interest rates. Note that in this case we are talking about not just the temporary raising of interest rates to prevent a short-term outflow of money from the country, but the use of higher interest rates to reduce borrowing and hence dampen aggregate demand.

A reduction in aggregate demand works in two ways:

■ It reduces the level of consumer spending. This directly cuts imports, since there will be reduced spending on Japanese Blu-ray players, German cars, Spanish holidays and so on. The supply of sterling coming on to the foreign exchange market thus decreases.

■ It reduces the rate of inflation. This makes UK goods more competitive abroad, thus increasing the demand for sterling. It will also cut back on imports as UK consumers switch to the now more competitive home-produced goods. The supply of sterling falls.

Supply-side policies. This is where the government attempts to increase the long-term competitiveness of UK goods by encouraging reductions in the costs of production and/or improvements in the quality of UK goods. For example, the government may attempt to improve the quantity and quality of training and research and development (see Chapter 9).

Controls on imports and/or foreign exchange dealing. This is where the government restricts the outflow of money, either by restricting people's access to foreign exchange, or by the use of tariffs (customs duties) and quotas. For instance, the Icelandic government put in place controls on foreign currency exchanges in the aftermath of the collapse of its largest banks (see Box 13.1) in order to bolster the krona and to build up foreign reserves.

> **Pause for thought**
>
> *What problems might arise if the government were to adopt this third method of maintaining a fixed exchange rate?*

Recap

1. In a free foreign exchange market, the balance of payments will automatically balance, since changes in the exchange rate will balance the demand for the currency (credits on the balance of payments) with the supply (debits on the balance of payments).

2. There is no guarantee, however, that there will be a balance on each of the separate parts of the balance of payments account.

3. The government can attempt to prevent the rate of exchange falling by central bank purchases of the domestic currency in the foreign exchange market, either by selling foreign currency reserves or by using foreign loans. Alternatively, the government can raise interest rates. The reverse actions can be taken if it wants to prevent the rate from rising.

4. In the longer term, it can attempt to prevent the rate from falling by pursuing contractionary policies, protectionist policies or supply-side policies to increase the competitiveness of the country's exports.

FIXED VERSUS FLOATING EXCHANGE RATES
14.4

Should exchange rates be 'left to the market'?

Are exchange rates best left free to fluctuate and be determined purely by market forces, or should the government or central bank intervene to fix exchange rates, either rigidly or within bands? Unfortunately, the answer is not clear-cut. Both floating and fixed exchange rates have their advantages and disadvantages.

Advantages of fixed exchange rates

Surveys reveal that most business people prefer relatively rigid exchange rates: if not totally fixed, then at least pegged for periods of time. The following arguments are used to justify this preference.

Certainty. With fixed exchange rates, international trade and investment become much less risky, since profits are not affected by movements in the exchange rate.

Assume that a firm correctly forecasts that its product will sell in the USA for $1.50. It costs 80p to produce. If the rate of exchange is fixed at £1 = $1.50, each unit will earn £1 and hence make a 20p profit. If, however, the rate of exchange were not fixed, exchange fluctuations could wipe out this profit. If, say, the rate appreciated to £1 = $2, and if units continued to sell for $1.50, they would now earn only 75p each, and hence make a 5p loss.

Little or no speculation. Provided the rate is *absolutely* fixed – and people believe that it will remain so – there is no point in speculating. For example, between 1999 and 2001, when the old currencies of the eurozone countries were still used, but were totally fixed to the euro, there was no speculation that the German mark, say, would change in value against the French franc or the Dutch guilder.

Prevents governments pursuing 'irresponsible' macroeconomic policies. If a government deliberately and excessively expands aggregate demand – perhaps in an attempt to gain short-term popularity with the electorate – the resulting balance of payments deficit will force it to constrain demand again (unless it resorts to import controls).

Governments cannot allow their economies to have a persistently higher inflation rate than competitor countries without running into balance of payments crises, and hence a depletion of reserves. Fixed rates thus force governments (in the absence of trade restrictions) to keep the rate of inflation roughly to world levels.

Disadvantages of fixed exchange rates

Exchange rate policy may conflict with the interests of domestic business and the economy as a whole. A balance of payments deficit can occur even if the economy is not 'overheating'. For example, there can be a fall in the demand for the country's exports as a result of an external shock (such as a recession in other countries) or because of increased foreign competition. If protectionism is to be avoided, and if supply-side policies work only over the long run, the government will be forced to raise interest rates. This is likely to have two adverse effects on the domestic economy:

■ Higher interest rates may discourage long-term business investment. This in turn will lower firms' profits in the long term and reduce the country's long-term rate of economic growth. The country's capacity to produce will be restricted and businesses are likely to fall behind in the competitive race with their international rivals to develop new products and improve existing ones.

■ Higher interest rates will have a dampening effect on the economy by making borrowing more expensive and thereby cutting back on both consumer demand and investment. This can result in a recession with rising unemployment. It will, however, improve the balance of payments. There will be an improvement not only on the financial account, as money flows into the country to take advantage of the higher rates of interest, but also on the current account. The recession will lead to reduced demand for imports, and lower inflation is likely to make exports more competitive and imports relatively more expensive.

The problem is that, with fixed exchange rates, domestic policy is entirely constrained by the balance of payments. Any attempt to reflate and cure unemployment will simply lead to a balance of payments deficit and thus force governments to deflate again.

Competitive contractionary policies leading to world depression. If deficit countries pursued contractionary policies, but surplus countries pursued expansionary policies, there would be no overall world contraction or expansion. Countries may be quite happy, however, to run a balance of payments surplus and build up reserves. Countries may thus competitively deflate – all trying to achieve a balance of payments surplus. But this is a beggar-my-neighbour policy. Not all countries can have a surplus! Overall the world must be in balance. The result of these policies is to lead to general world recession and a restriction in growth.

Problems of international liquidity. If trade is to expand, there must be an expansion in the supply of currencies acceptable for world trade (dollars, euros, gold, etc.): there must be adequate **international liquidity**. Countries' reserves of these currencies must grow if they are to be sufficient to maintain a fixed rate at times of balance of payments disequilibrium. Conversely, there must not be excessive international liquidity. Otherwise the extra demand that would result would lead to world inflation. It is important under fixed exchange rates, therefore, to avoid too much or too little international liquidity.

The problem is how to maintain adequate control of international liquidity. The supply of dollars, for example, depends largely on US policy, which may be dominated by its internal economic situation rather than by any concern for the well-being of the international community. Similarly, the supply of euros depends on the policy of the European Central Bank, which is governed by the internal situation in the eurozone countries.

Inability to adjust to shocks. With sticky prices and wage rates, there is no swift mechanism for dealing with sudden balance of payments crises – like that caused by a sudden increase in oil prices. In the short run, countries will need huge reserves or loan facilities to support their currencies. There may be insufficient international liquidity to permit this. In the longer run, countries may be forced into a depression by having to deflate. The alternative may be to resort to protectionism, or to abandon the fixed rate and **devalue**.

Speculation. If speculators believe that a fixed rate simply cannot be maintained, speculation is likely to be massive. If, for example, there is a large balance of payments deficit, speculative selling will worsen the deficit and may itself force a devaluation. Speculation of this sort had disastrous effects on some south-east Asian currencies in 1997 (see Case Study 14.9 in MyEconLab) and on the Argentinean peso in 2002 (see Case Study 14.10).

Definitions

International liquidity
The supply of currencies in the world acceptable for financing international trade and investment.

Devaluation
Where the government refixes the exchange rate at a lower level.

Advantages of a free-floating exchange rate

The advantages and disadvantages of free-floating rates are to a large extent the opposite of fixed rates.

Automatic correction. The government simply lets the exchange rate move freely to the equilibrium. In this way, balance of payments disequilibria are automatically and instantaneously corrected without the need for specific government policies.

No problem of international liquidity and reserves. Since there is no central bank intervention in the foreign exchange market, there is no need to hold reserves. A currency is automatically convertible at the current market exchange rate.

Insulation from external economic events. A country is not tied to a possibly unacceptably high world inflation rate, as it could be under a fixed exchange rate. It is also to some extent protected against world economic fluctuations and shocks.

Governments are free to choose their domestic policy. Under a floating rate the government can choose whatever level of domestic demand it considers appropriate, and simply leave exchange rate movements to take care of any balance of payments effect. Similarly, the central bank can choose whatever rate of interest is necessary to meet domestic objectives, such as achieving a target rate of inflation. The exchange rate will simply adjust to the new rate of interest – a rise in interest rates causing an appreciation, a fall causing a depreciation. This freedom for the government and central bank is a major advantage, especially when the effectiveness of contractionary policies under fixed exchange rates is reduced by downward wage and price rigidity, and when competitive contractionary policies between countries may end up causing a world recession.

Disadvantages of a free-floating exchange rate

Despite these advantages there are still a number of serious problems with free-floating exchange rates.

Unstable exchange rates. The less elastic are the demand and supply curves for the currency in Figure 14.5, the greater the change in exchange rate that will be necessary to restore equilibrium following a shift in either demand or supply. In the long run, in a competitive world with domestic substitutes for imports and foreign substitutes for exports, demand and supply curves are relatively elastic. Nevertheless, in the short run, given that many firms have contracts with specific overseas suppliers or distributors, the demands for imports and exports are less elastic.

Speculation. Short-run instability can be lessened by stabilising speculation, thus making speculation advantageous. If, due to short-run inelasticity of demand, a deficit causes a very large depreciation, speculators will *buy* pounds, knowing that in the long run the exchange rate will appreciate again. Their action therefore helps to lessen the short-run fall in the exchange rate.

Nevertheless, in an uncertain world where there are few restrictions on currency speculation, where the fortunes and policies of governments can change rapidly, and where large amounts of short-term deposits are internationally 'footloose', speculation can be highly destabilising in the short run. Considerable exchange rate overshooting can occur.

An example of such overshooting occurred between August 2008 and January 2009 when the pound depreciated 18 per cent against the euro, 27 per cent against

Figure 14.6 Depreciating sterling in 2008

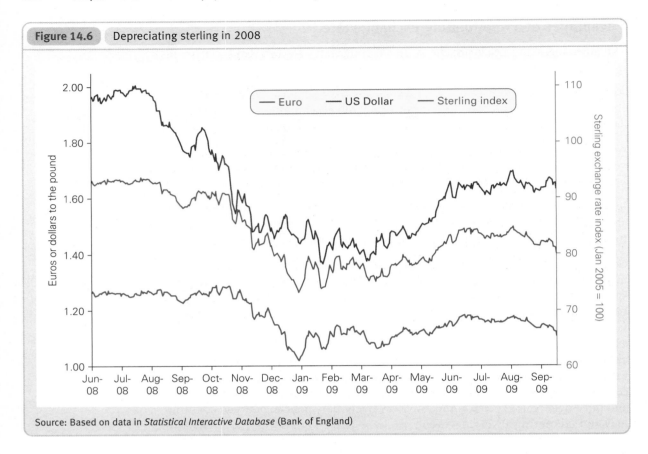

Source: Based on data in *Statistical Interactive Database* (Bank of England)

the US dollar, 38 per cent against the yen and the exchange rate index fell 20 per cent (see Figure 14.6). Speculators were predicting that interest rates in the UK would fall further than in other countries and stay lower for longer. This was because recession was likely to be deeper in the UK, with inflation undershooting the Bank of England's 2 per cent target and perhaps even becoming negative. But the fall in the exchange rate represented considerable overshooting and, after reaching a low of £1 = €1.02 at the end of December 2008, was trading between €1.10 and €1.15 during the first half of 2009.

This is just one example of the violent swings in exchange rates that have occurred in recent years. They even occur under managed floating exchange rate systems where governments have attempted to dampen such fluctuations!

The continuance of exchange rate fluctuations over a number of years is likely to encourage the growth of speculative holdings of currency. This can then cause even larger and more rapid swings in exchange rates.

Uncertainty for traders and investors. The uncertainty caused by currency fluctuations can discourage international trade and investment. To some extent the problem can be overcome by using the **forward exchange market**. Here traders agree with a bank *today* the rate of exchange for some point in the *future* (say, six months' time). This allows traders to plan future purchases of imports or sales of exports at a known rate of exchange. Of course, banks charge for this service, since they are taking on the risks themselves of adverse exchange rate fluctuations.

Definition

Forward exchange market
Where contracts are made today for the price at which a currency will be exchanged at some specified future date.

Pause for thought

If speculators on average gain from their speculation, who loses?

KI 13
p 74

How a current account deficit can coincide with an appreciating exchange rate

Since the early 1970s, most of the major economies of the world have operated with floating exchange rates. The opportunities that this gives for speculative gain has led to a huge increase in short-term international financial movements. Vast amounts of moneys transfer from country to country in search of higher interest rates or a currency that is likely to appreciate. This can have a bizarre effect on exchange rates.

If a country pursues an expansionary fiscal policy, the current account will tend to go into deficit as extra imports are 'sucked in'. What effect will this have on exchange rates? You might think that the answer is obvious: the higher demand for imports will create an extra supply of domestic currency on the foreign exchange market and hence drive down the exchange rate.

In fact the opposite is likely. The higher interest rates resulting from the higher domestic demand can lead to a massive inflow of short-term finance. The financial account can thus move sharply into surplus. This is likely to outweigh the current account deficit and cause an *appreciation* of the exchange rate.

Exchange rate movements, especially in the short term, are largely brought about by changes on the financial rather than the current account.

 Why do high international financial mobility and an absence of exchange controls severely limit a country's ability to choose its interest rate?

But dealing in the futures market only takes care of short-run uncertainty. Banks will not be prepared to take on the risks of offering forward contracts for several years hence. Thus firms simply have to live with the uncertainty over exchange rates in future years. This will discourage long-term investment. For example, the possibility of exchange rate appreciation may well discourage firms from investing abroad, since a higher exchange rate means that foreign exchange earnings will be worth less in the domestic currency.

As Figure 14.3 showed (see page 473) there have been large changes in exchange rates. Such changes make it difficult not only for exporters. Importers too will be hesitant about making long-term deals. For example, a UK manufacturing firm signing a contract to buy US components in 1980, when $2.40 worth of components could be purchased for £1, would find a struggle to make a profit some four years later when only just over $1.00 worth of US components could be purchased for £1!

Lack of discipline on the domestic economy. Governments may pursue irresponsibly inflationary policies (for short-term political gain, say). This will have adverse effects over the longer term as the government will at some point have to deflate the economy again, with a resulting fall in output and rise in unemployment.

Exchange rates in practice

Exchange rates have become extremely volatile. Currencies can gain or lose several percentage points in the space of a few days. These changes can then make all the difference between profit and loss for trading companies. There are a number of reasons for this volatility:

- Inflation or money supply targets. Central banks may have to make considerable changes to interest rates in order to keep to their targets. These in turn cause exchange rate fluctuations.
- A huge growth in international financial markets. This has encouraged the international transfer of money and capital.

BOX 14.3 THE EURO/DOLLAR SEESAW

Ups and downs in the currency market

For periods of time, world currency markets can be quite peaceful, with only modest changes in exchange rates. But with the ability to move vast sums of money very rapidly from one part of the world to another and from one currency to another, speculators can suddenly turn this relatively peaceful world into one of extreme turmoil.

In this box we examine the huge swings of the euro against the dollar since the euro's launch in 1999. In Case Studies 14.7 and 14.8 in MyEconLab we examine other examples of currency turmoil.

First the down . . .

On 1 January 1999, the euro was launched and exchanged for $1.16. By October 2000 the euro had fallen to $0.85. What was the cause of this 27 per cent depreciation? The main cause was the growing fear that inflationary pressures were increasing in the USA and that, therefore, the Federal Reserve Bank would have to raise interest rates. At the same time, the eurozone economy was growing only slowly and inflation was well below the 2 per cent ceiling set by the ECB. There was thus pressure on the ECB to cut interest rates.

The speculators were not wrong. As the diagram shows, US interest rates rose, and ECB interest rates initially fell, and when eventually they did rise (in October 1999), the gap between US and ECB interest rates soon widened again.

In addition to the differences in interest rates, a lack of confidence in the recovery of the eurozone economy and a continuing confidence in the US economy encouraged investment to flow to the USA. This inflow of finance (and lack of inflow to the eurozone) further pushed up the dollar relative to the euro.

The low value of the euro meant a high value of the pound relative to the euro. This made it very difficult for UK companies exporting to eurozone countries and also for those competing with imports from the eurozone (which had been made cheaper by the fall in the euro).

In October 2000, with the euro trading at around 85¢, the ECB plus the US Federal Reserve Bank, the Bank of England and the Japanese central bank all intervened on the foreign exchange market to buy euros. This arrested the fall, and helped to restore confidence in the currency. People were more willing to hold euros, knowing that central banks would support it.

Fluctuations between the euro and the dollar

Sources: Federal Reserve, ECB and Bank of England. Data is freely available from European Central Bank, Frankfurt am Main, Germany (www.ecb.europa.eu/home/html/disclaimer.en.html)
Note: Federal Funds Rate (US) Main Refinancing Operations Rate (Eurozone)

... then the up

The position changed completely in 2001. With the US economy slowing rapidly and fears of an impending recession, the Federal Reserve Bank reduced interest rates 11 times during the year: from 6.5 per cent at the beginning of the year to 1.75 per cent at the end (see the chart). Although the ECB also cut interest rates, the cuts were relatively modest: from 4.75 at the beginning of the year to 3.25 at the end. With eurozone interest rates now considerably above US rates, the euro began to rise.

In addition, a massive deficit on the US current account, and a budget deficit nearing 4 per cent of GDP, made foreign investors reluctant to invest in the US economy. In fact, investors were pulling out of the USA. One estimate suggests that European investors alone sold $70 billion of US assets during 2002. The result of all this was a massive depreciation of the dollar and appreciation of the euro, so that by December 2004 the euro had risen to $1.36: a 60 per cent appreciation since July 2001!

In 2004–5, the US economy began to experience strong economic growth once more (an annual average of 3.4 per cent) and consequently the Fed raised interest rates several times, from 1 per cent in early 2004 to 5.25 by June 2006. With growth in the eurozone averaging just 1.8 per cent in 2004–5, the ECB kept interest rates constant at 2 per cent until early 2006. The result was that the euro depreciated against the dollar in 2005. But then the rise of the euro began again as the US growth slowed and eurozone growth rose and people anticipated a narrowing of the gap between US and eurozone interest rates.

In 2007 and 2008, worries about the credit crunch in the USA led the Fed to make substantial cuts in interest rates to stave off recession. In August 2007 the US federal funds rate was 5.25 per cent. It was then reduced on several occasions to stand at between 0 and 0.25 per cent by December 2008. The ECB, in contrast, kept the eurozone rate constant at 4 per cent for the first part of this period and even raised it to 4.25 temporarily in the face of rapidly rising commodity prices. As a result, short-term finance flooded into the eurozone and the euro appreciated again, from $1.37 in mid-2007 to $1.58 in mid-2008.

Eventually, in September 2008, with the eurozone on the edge of recession and predictions that eurozone rates would fall, the euro at last began to fall. It continued to do so as the ECB cut rates, to stand at 1 per cent by May 2009.

What is clear from the 10 years of the euro, is that interest-rate volatility and divergences in interest rates between the USA and the eurozone have been a major factor in exchange-rate volatility between the euro and the dollar – itself a cause of uncertainty in international trade and finance.

The effects on business in the eurozone

From 2002 to 2008 the euro appreciated by a massive 82 per cent against the dollar. So has a strong euro been bad for European business? With over 22 per cent of the eurozone's GDP determined by export sales (to non-eurozone countries), and a large part of those exports going to the USA, the dollar/euro exchange rate will invariably be significant. The question is, how significant? The investment bank Morgan Stanley estimated that for every 10 per cent rise in the value of the euro against the dollar, European corporate profits fall by 3 per cent.

And it was not just the fact that the euro has been strong. What also worried European businesses was the *speed* at which the euro strengthened against the dollar. The question was whether they could adjust quickly enough to accommodate the rise.

However, the impact of the euro's rise on eurozone business was tempered by a number of factors:

- Companies are increasingly using sophisticated management and operational systems, in which value creation is spread throughout a global value chain. Often procurement systems are priced in dollars.
- Firms hedge their currency risks. Companies typically use forward exchange markets to agree to buy or sell currencies in the future at a price quoted *today* (this, of course, costs them a premium).
- Many European companies (BMW is an example) have located some of their production facilities in the USA and use them to help meet demand in the US market. This helps to insulate them from the effects of the rise in the value of the euro.

The result is that most businesses in the eurozone seem to have accommodated the euro's large and rapid rise.

 *Find out what has happened to the euro/dollar exchange rate over the past 12 months. (You can find the data from the Bank of England's Statistical Interactive Database at **www.bankofengland.co.uk/ statistics/index.htm**). Explain why the exchange rate has moved the way it has.*

- The abolition of exchange controls in most industrialised countries.
- The growth in information technology. The simple use of a computer can transfer capital and finance internationally in a matter of seconds.
- The preference for liquidity. With the danger of currency fluctuations, companies prefer to keep their financial capital as liquid as possible. They do not want to be locked into assets denominated in a declining currency.
- The growing speculative activities of trading companies. Many large companies have a team of dealers to help manage their liquid assets: to switch them from currency to currency in order to take advantage of market movements.
- The growing speculative activities of banks and other financial institutions.
- The growing belief that rumour and 'jumping on the bandwagon' are more important determinants of currency buying or selling than cool long-term appraisal. If people believe that speculation is likely to be destabilising, their actions will ensure that it is. Many companies involved in international trade and finance have developed a 'speculative mentality'.
- The growing belief that governments are powerless to prevent currency movements. As short-term capital (or 'hot money') grows relative to official reserves, it is increasingly difficult for central banks to stabilise currencies through exchange market intervention.

Recap

1. Completely fixed exchange rates bring the advantage of certainty for the business community, which encourages trade and foreign investment. They also help to prevent governments from pursuing irresponsible macroeconomic policies.

2. However, with fixed rates domestic policy is entirely constrained by the balance of payments. What is more, they can lead to competitive contractionary policies worldwide; there may be problems of excessive or insufficient international liquidity; there may be difficulty in adjusting to external shocks; and speculation could be very severe if people came to believe that a fixed rate was about to break down.

3. The advantages of free-floating exchange rates are that they automatically correct balance of payments disequilibria; they eliminate the need for reserves; and they give governments a greater independence to pursue their chosen domestic policy.

4. On the other hand, a completely free exchange rate can be highly unstable, especially when the elasticities of demand for imports and exports are low and there are shifts in currency demand and supply; in addition, speculation may be destabilising. This may discourage firms from trading and investing abroad. What is more, a flexible exchange rate, by removing the balance of payments constraint on domestic policy, may encourage governments to pursue irresponsible domestic policies for short-term political gain.

14.5   THE ORIGINS OF THE EURO

Definition

Adjustable peg
A system whereby exchange rates are fixed for a period of time, but may be devalued (or revalued) if a deficit (or surplus) becomes substantial.

How did the majority of the EU countries arrive at a single currency?

There have been many attempts to regulate exchange rates since 1945. By far the most successful was the Bretton Woods system, which was adopted worldwide from the end of the Second World War until 1971. This was a form of **adjustable peg** exchange rate, where countries pegged (i.e. fixed) their exchange rate to the US dollar, but could re-peg it at a lower or higher level ('devalue' or 'revalue' their exchange rate) if there was a persistent and substantial balance of payments deficit or surplus.

With growing world inflation and instability from the mid-1960s, it became more and more difficult to maintain fixed exchange rates, and the growing likelihood of devaluations and revaluations fuelled speculation. The system was abandoned in the early 1970s. What followed was a period of exchange rate management known as **managed floating**. Under this system, exchange rates were not pegged but allowed to float. However, central banks intervened from time to time to prevent excessive exchange rate fluctuations. This system largely continues to this day.

However, on a regional basis, especially within Europe, there were attempts to create greater exchange rate stability. The European system involved establishing exchange rate bands: upper and lower limits within which exchange rates were allowed to fluctuate. The name given to the EU system was the **exchange rate mechanism (ERM)**.

The ERM

The ERM came into existence in March 1979 and the majority of the EU countries were members. The UK, however, chose not to join at that time. Spain joined in 1989, the UK in 1990 and Portugal in April 1992. Then in September 1992, the UK and Italy indefinitely suspended their membership of the ERM, but Italy rejoined in November 1996 as part of its bid to join the single European currency (see Section 14.6). Austria joined in 1995, Finland in 1996 and Greece in 1998. By the time the ERM was replaced by the single currency in 1999, only Sweden and the UK were outside the ERM.

Features of the ERM

Under the system, each currency was given a central exchange rate with each of the other ERM currencies in a grid. However, fluctuations were allowed from the central rate within specified bands. For most countries these bands were set at $\pm 2\frac{1}{4}$ per cent. The central rates could be adjusted from time to time by agreement, thus making the ERM an 'adjustable peg' system. All the currencies floated jointly with currencies outside the ERM.

If a currency approached the upper or lower limit against *any* other ERM currency, intervention would take place to maintain the currencies within the band. This would take the form of central banks in the ERM selling the strong currency and buying the weak one. It could also involve the weak currency countries raising interest rates and the strong currency countries lowering them.

The ERM in practice

In a system of pegged exchange rates, countries should harmonise their policies to avoid excessive currency misalignments and hence the need for large devaluations or revaluations. There should be a convergence of their economies: they should be at a similar point on the business cycle and have similar inflation rates and interest rates.

The ERM in the 1980s. In the early 1980s, however, French and Italian inflation rates were persistently higher than German rates. This meant that there had to be several realignments (devaluations and revaluations). After 1983 realignments became less frequent, and then from 1987 to 1992 they ceased altogether. This was due to a growing convergence of members' internal policies.

By the time the UK joined the ERM in 1990, it was generally seen by its existing members as being a great success. It had created a zone of currency stability in a world of highly unstable exchange rates, and had provided the necessary environment for the establishment of a truly common market by the end of 1992.

Definitions

Managed floating
A system of flexible exchange rates, but where the government intervenes to prevent excessive fluctuations or even to achieve an unofficial target exchange rate.

The exchange rate mechanism (ERM)
A semi-fixed system whereby participating EU countries allow fluctuations against each other's currencies only within agreed bands. Collectively they float freely against all other currencies.

Crisis in the ERM. Shortly after the UK joined the ERM, strains began to show. The reunification of Germany involved considerable reconstruction in the eastern part of the country. Financing this reconstruction was causing a growing budget deficit. The Bundesbank (the German central bank) thus felt obliged to maintain high interest rates in order to keep inflation in check. At the same time, the UK was experiencing a massive current account deficit (partly the result of entering the ERM at what many commentators argued was too high an exchange rate). It was thus obliged to raise interest rates in order to protect the pound, despite the fact that the economy was sliding rapidly into recession. The French franc and Italian lira were also perceived to be overvalued, and there were the first signs of worries as to whether their exchange rates within the ERM could be retained.

TC 9
p 71

At the same time, the US economy was moving into recession and, as a result, US interest rates were cut. This led to a large outflow of capital from the USA. With high German interest rates, much of this capital flowed to Germany. This pushed up the value of the German mark and with it the other ERM currencies. In September 1992, things reached crisis point. First the lira was devalued. Then two days later, on 'Black Wednesday' (16 September), the UK and Italy were forced to suspend their membership of the ERM: the pound and the lira were floated. At the same time, the Spanish peseta was devalued by 5 per cent.

Turmoil returned in the summer of 1993. The French economy was moving into recession and there were calls for cuts in French interest rates. But this was only possible if Germany was prepared to cut its rates too, and it was not. Speculators began to sell francs and it became obvious that the existing franc/mark parity could not be maintained. In an attempt to rescue the ERM, the EU finance ministers agreed to adopt very wide ±15 per cent bands. The result was that the franc and the Danish krone depreciated against the mark.

> **Pause for thought**
>
> *Under what circumstances may a currency bloc like the ERM (a) help to prevent speculation; (b) aggravate the problem of speculation?*

A return of calm. The old ERM appeared to be at an end. The new ±15 per cent bands hardly seemed like a 'pegged' system at all. However, the ERM did not die. Within months, the members were again managing to keep fluctuations within a very narrow range (for most of the time, within ±2$\frac{1}{4}$ per cent!). The scene was being set for the abandonment of separate currencies and the adoption of a single currency: the euro.

The Maastricht Treaty and the road to the single currency

The ERM was conceived as a stage on the road to complete economic and monetary union (EMU) of member states. Details of the path towards EMU were finalised in the Maastricht Treaty, which was signed in February 1992. The timetable for EMU involved the adoption of a single currency by 1999 at the latest.

One of the first moves was to establish a European Monetary Institute (EMI). Its role was to co-ordinate monetary policy and encourage greater co-operation between EU central banks. It also monitored the operation of the ERM and prepared the ground for the establishment of a European central bank in time for the launch of the single currency.

Before they could join the single currency, member states were obliged to achieve convergence of their economies. Each country had to meet five convergence criteria:

■ Inflation: should be no more than 1$\frac{1}{2}$ per cent above the average inflation rate of the three countries in the EU with the lowest inflation.

■ Interest rates: the rate on long-term government bonds should be no more than 2 per cent above the average of the three countries with the lowest inflation.
■ Budget deficit: should be no more than 3 per cent of GDP.
■ National debt: should be no more than 60 per cent of GDP.
■ Exchange rates: the currency should have been within the normal ERM bands for at least two years with no realignments or excessive intervention.

> **Definition**
>
> **Currency union**
> A group of countries (or regions) using a common currency.

Before the launch of the single currency, the Council of Ministers had to decide which countries had met the convergence criteria and would thus be eligible to form a **currency union** by fixing their currencies permanently to the euro. Their national currencies would effectively disappear.

At the same time a European System of Central Banks (ESCB) would be created, consisting of a European Central Bank (ECB) and the central banks of the participating member states. The ECB would be independent, both from governments and from EU political institutions. It would operate the monetary policy on behalf of the countries that had adopted the single currency.

Recap

1. One means of achieving greater currency stability is for a group of countries to peg their internal exchange rates and yet float jointly with the rest of the world. The exchange rate mechanism of the EU (ERM) was an example. Members' currencies were allowed to fluctuate against other member currencies within a band. The band was $\pm 2\frac{1}{4}$ per cent for the majority of the ERM countries until 1993.

2. The need for realignments seemed to have diminished in the late 1980s as greater convergence was achieved between the members' economies. However, growing strains in the system in the early 1990s led to a crisis in September 1992. The UK and Italy left the ERM. There was a further crisis in July 1993 and the bands were widened to ± 15 per cent.

3. Thereafter, as convergence of the economies of ERM members increased, fluctuations decreased and remained largely within $\pm 2\frac{1}{4}$ per cent.

4. The ERM was seen as an important first stage on the road to complete economic and monetary union (EMU) in the EU.

5. The Maastricht Treaty set out a timetable for achieving EMU. This would culminate in the creation of a currency union: a single European currency with a common monetary policy operated by an independent European Central Bank.

ECONOMIC AND MONETARY UNION (EMU) IN EUROPE 14.6

Do countries benefit from using the euro?

Birth of the euro

In March 1998, the European Commission ruled that 11 of the 15 member states were eligible to proceed to EMU in January 1999. The UK and Denmark were to exercise an opt-out negotiated at Maastricht, and Sweden and Greece failed to meet one or more of the convergence criteria. (Greece joined the euro in 2001.)

The euro came into being on 1 January 1999, but euro banknotes and coins were not introduced until 1 January 2002. In the meantime, national currencies continued to exist alongside the euro, but at irrevocably fixed rates. The old notes and coins were withdrawn a few weeks after the introduction of euro notes and coins.

In May 2004, 10 new members joined the EU and in January 2007 another two. Under the Maastricht Treaty, they should all make preparations for joining the euro by meeting the convergence criteria. Estonia, Lithuania and Slovenia were the first to join ERM2 in June 2004 with Latvia, Cyprus, Malta and Slovakia following in 2005. They adopted the wide band of ±15 per cent against the euro. Slovenia adopted the euro in 2007, Malta and Cyprus in 2008 and Slovakia in 2009.

How desirable is EMU?

Advantages of the single currency

Elimination of the costs of converting currencies. With separate currencies in each of the EU countries, costs were incurred each time one currency was exchanged into another. The elimination of these costs, however, was probably the least important benefit from the single currency. The European Commission estimated that the effect was to increase the GDP of the countries concerned by an average of only 0.4 per cent. The gains to countries like the UK, which have well-developed financial markets, would be even smaller.

Increased competition and efficiency. Despite the advent of the single market, large price differences remained between member states. Not only has the single currency eliminated the need to convert one currency into another (a barrier to competition), but it has brought more transparency in pricing, and has put greater downward pressure on prices in high-cost firms and countries.

Elimination of exchange rate uncertainty (between the members). Removal of exchange rate uncertainty has helped to encourage trade between the eurozone countries. Perhaps more importantly, it has encouraged investment by firms that trade between these countries, given the greater certainty in calculating costs and revenues from such trade. In times of economic uncertainty, exchange rate volatility between currencies can be high, as the experience of sterling showed during the credit crunch of 2008. The associated uncertainty for the UK in its trade with eurozone countries would have been eliminated had it adopted the euro. Without the euro, countries throughout Europe could have suffered considerably during the banking turmoil from wildly diverging exchange rates and interest rates.

Increased inward investment. Investment from the rest of the world is attracted to a eurozone of some 326 million inhabitants, where there is no fear of internal currency movements. By contrast, the UK, by not joining, has typically found that inward investment has been diverted away to those countries within the eurozone. From 1990 to 1998, the UK's share of inward investment to EU countries (including from other EU countries) was 21.0 per cent. From 1999 to 2003, it was 12.5 per cent, and it fell throughout this period, from 17.5 per cent in 1999 to 6.5 per cent in 2003. However, from 2003 to 2005, its share did increase substantially as the UK economy grew more strongly than other major economies in the EU. But, this was relatively short-lived and since then it has fallen again, with the volatility of sterling acting as a deterrent to investment.

Lower inflation and interest rates. A single monetary policy forces convergence in inflation rates (just as inflation rates are very similar between the different regions within a country). With the ECB being independent from short-term political manipulation, this has resulted in a low average inflation rate in the eurozone countries. This, in turn, has helped to convince markets that the euro will be strong relative to other currencies. The result is lower long-term rates of interest. This, in turn, further encourages investment in the eurozone countries, both by member states and by the rest of the world.

Opposition to EMU

Monetary union has been bitterly opposed, however, by certain groups. Many 'Eurosceptics' see within it a surrender of national political and economic sovereignty.

The lack of an independent monetary and exchange rate policy. This is a serious problem, they argue, if an economy is at all out of harmony with the rest of the Union. For example, if countries such as Italy and Greece have higher rates of inflation (due, say, to greater cost-push pressures), then how are they to make their goods competitive with the rest of the Union? With separate currencies these countries could allow their currencies to depreciate. For example, the depreciation of sterling in 2008 helped to soften the oncoming recession by making exports more competitive and dampening the demand for imports.

With a single currency, countries with higher endemic inflation or slower growth in productivity could become depressed 'regions' of Europe, with rising unemployment and all the other regional problems of depressed regions *within* a country. This might then require significant regional policies – policies that might not be in place or, if they were, would be seen as too interventionist by the political right.

The reply given by proponents of EMU is that it is better to tackle the problem of high inflation or low productivity in such countries by the disciplines of competition from other EU countries, than merely to feed that inflation by keeping separate currencies and allowing periodic depreciations, with all the uncertainty that they bring.

> **Pause for thought**
>
> *How might multiplier effects (the principle of cumulative causation) lead to prosperous regions becoming more prosperous and less prosperous regions falling even further behind?*

What is more, the high-inflation countries tend to be the poorer ones with lower wage levels (albeit faster wage *increases*). With higher mobility of labour and capital as the single market develops, resources are likely to be attracted to such countries. This could help to narrow the gap between the richer and poorer member states.

The critics of EMU counter this by arguing that labour is relatively immobile, given cultural and language barriers. Thus an unemployed worker in Wales could not easily move to a job in Turin or Helsinki. What the critics are arguing here is that the EU is not an **optimal currency area** (see Box 14.4).

Perhaps the most serious criticism is that the same rate of interest must apply to all eurozone countries: the 'one-size-fits-all' problem. The trouble is that while one country might require a lower rate of interest in order to ward off recession (such as Germany in 2003–5), another might require a higher one to prevent inflation. As convergence between the member economies increases, however, this problem is likely to lessen.

Asymmetric shocks. Another problem for members of a single currency occurs in adjusting to a shock when that shock affects members to different degrees. These are known as **asymmetric shocks**. For example, a sudden change in the price of oil would affect an oil-producing country like the UK differently from oil-importing countries. This problem is more serious, the less the factor mobility between member countries and the less the price flexibility within member countries.

This problem, however, should not be overstated. The divergences between economies are often the result of a lack of harmony between countries in their demand-management policies: something that is impossible in the case of monetary policy, and more difficult in the case of fiscal policy, for countries in the eurozone. Also, many of the shocks that face economies today are global and have similar (albeit not identical) effects on all countries. Adjustment to such shocks would often be better with a single co-ordinated policy, something that is much easier with a single currency and a single central bank.

> **Definitions**
>
> **Optimal currency area**
> The optimal size of a currency area is one that maximises the benefits from having a single currency relative to the costs. If the area were to be increased or decreased in size, the costs would rise relative to the benefits.
>
> **Asymmetric shocks**
> Shocks (such as an oil price increase or a recession in another part of the world) that have different-sized effects on different industries, regions or countries.

BOX 14.4 | OPTIMAL CURRENCY AREAS

When it pays to pay in the same currency

Imagine that each town and village used a different currency. Think how inconvenient it would be having to keep exchanging one currency into another, and how difficult it would be working out the relative value of items in different parts of the country.

Clearly there are benefits of using a common currency, not only within a country but across different countries. The benefits include greater transparency in pricing, more open competition, greater certainty for investors and the avoidance of having to pay commission when you change one currency into another. There are also the benefits from having a single monetary policy if that is delivered in a more consistent and effective way than by individual countries.

So why not have a single currency for the whole world? The problem is that the bigger a single-currency area gets, the more likely the conditions are to diverge in the different parts of the area. Some parts may have high unemployment and require expansionary policies. Others may have low unemployment and suffer from inflationary pressures. They may require *contractionary* policies.

What is more, different members of the currency area may experience quite different shocks to their economies, whether from outside the union (e.g. a fall in the price of one of their major exports) or from inside (e.g. a prolonged strike). These 'asymmetric shocks' would imply that different parts of the currency area should adopt different policies. But with a common monetary policy and hence common interest rates, and with no possibility of devaluation/revaluation of the currency of individual members, the scope for separate economic policies is reduced.

The costs of asymmetric shocks (and hence the costs of a single-currency area) will be greater, the less the mobility of labour and capital, the less the flexibility of prices and wage rates, and the fewer the alternative policies there are that can be turned to (such as fiscal and regional policies).

So is the eurozone an optimal currency area? Certainly strong doubts have been raised by many economists.

- Labour is relatively immobile.
- There are structural differences between the member states.
- The transmission effects of interest rate changes are different between the member countries. This arises partly because countries have different proportions of debt relative to GDP. For instance, in 2007, the Netherlands had a mortgage debt to GDP ratio of 100 per cent, while in Italy it was 20 per cent. But, as well as differences in the amount of accumulated debt, there are also differences between countries in the proportion of debt subject to variable interest rates.
- Exports to countries outside the eurozone account for different proportions of the members' GDP (see Box 13.2 on pages 430–1). During the 2000s, the value of exports was equivalent to about 100 per cent of Irish GDP, in Greece the figure was less than 25 per cent. Therefore, economies are affected differently by a change in the rate of exchange of the euro against other currencies.
- Wage rates are relatively inflexible.
- Under the Stability and Growth Pact (see Box 12.2 on pages 390–1), the scope for using discretionary fiscal policy is curtailed, except in times of severe economic difficulty (as in 2009).

This does not necessarily mean, however, that the costs of having a single European currency outweigh the benefits. Also, the problems outlined above should decline over time as the single market develops. Finally, the problem of asymmetric shocks can be exaggerated. European economies are highly diversified; there are often more differences *within* economies than between them. Thus shocks are more likely to affect different industries or localities than whole countries. Changing the exchange rate, if that were still possible, would hardly be an appropriate policy in these circumstances.

 Why is a single currency area likely to move towards becoming an optimal currency area over time?

Even when shocks are uniformly felt in the member states, however, there is still the problem that policies adopted centrally will have different impacts on each country. For example, in the UK, a large proportion of borrowing is at variable interest rates. In Germany, by contrast, much is at fixed rates. Thus if the ECB were to raise interest rates, the contractionary effects would be felt disproportionately in the UK. Of course, were this balance to change – and there is some evidence that types of borrowing are becoming more uniform across the EU – this problem would diminish.

The problem for economists is that the issue of monetary union is a very emotive one. 'Europhiles' often see monetary union as a vital element in their vision of a united Europe. Many Eurosceptics, however, see EMU as a surrender of sovereignty and a threat to nationhood. In such an environment, a calm assessment of the arguments and evidence is very difficult.

Recap

1. The euro was born on 1 January 1999. Twelve countries adopted it, having at least nominally met the Maastricht convergence criteria. Euro notes and coins were introduced on 1 January 2002, with the notes and coins of the old currencies withdrawn a few weeks later.

2. The advantages claimed for EMU are that it eliminates the costs of converting currencies and the uncertainties associated with possible changes in exchange rates between the member states of the EU. This encourages more investment, both inward and by domestic firms. What is more, a common central bank, independent from domestic governments, provides the stable monetary environment necessary for a convergence of the EU economies and the encouragement of investment and trade within the Union.

3. Critics claim, however, that it might make adjustment to domestic economic problems more difficult. The loss of independence in policy making is seen by such people to be a major issue, not only because of the loss of political sovereignty, but also because domestic economic concerns may be at variance with those of the Union as a whole. A single monetary policy is claimed to be inappropriate for dealing with asymmetric shocks. What is more, countries and regions at the periphery of the Union may become depressed unless there is an effective regional policy.

DEBT AND DEVELOPING COUNTRIES   14.7

Can their debt burden be lifted?

Perhaps the most serious of all balance of payments problems in the world today is that faced by some of the poorest developing countries. Many of them experience massive financial outflows year after year as a result of having to 'service' debts that they have incurred in their attempts to finance development (see Table 14.2). This debt problem has its origins back in the 1970s.

The oil shocks of the 1970s

In 1973–4, oil prices quadrupled and the world went into recession. Oil imports cost more and export demand was sluggish. The current account deficit of oil-importing developing countries rose from 1.1 per cent of GDP in 1973 to 4.3 per cent in 1975.

It was not difficult to finance these deficits, however. The oil surpluses deposited in commercial banks in the industrialised world provided an important additional

Table 14.2   Debt ratios: average of all developing countries in selected years

	1974	1980	1984	1986	1988	1990	1994	1998	2000	2002	2004	2006	2007
Ratio of debt to GNY (%)	11	21	31	35	36	35	39	41	38	38	33	26	25
Ratio of debt to exports (%)	80	86	166	231	201	182	170	157	123	120	91	65	66
Ratio of debt service to exports (%)	12	14	22	28	26	20	17	20	20	18	14	12	10

Source: *Global Development Finance* (World Bank, 2009)

source of finance. The banks, flush with money and faced with slack demand in the industrialised world, were very willing to lend to developing countries to help them finance continued expansion. The world recession was short-lived, and with a recovery in the demand for their exports and with their debts being eroded by high world inflation, developing countries found it relatively easy to service these increased debts (i.e. pay interest and make the necessary capital repayments).

In 1979/80 world oil prices rose again (from $15 to $38 per barrel). This second oil shock, like the first one, caused a large increase in the import bills of developing countries. But the full effects on their economies this time were very much worse, given the debts that had been accumulated in the 1970s and given the policies adopted by the industrialised world after 1979. But why were things so much worse this time?

■ The world recession was deeper and lasted longer (1980–3) and, when recovery came, it came very slowly. Developing countries' current account balance of payments deteriorated sharply. This was due both to a marked slowing down in the growth of their exports and to a fall in their export prices.
■ The tight monetary policies pursued by the industrialised countries led to a sharp increase in interest rates. This greatly increased developing countries' costs of servicing their debts. It also led to a sharp fall in inflation, which meant that the debts were not being eroded so rapidly.
■ The problem was made worse by the growing proportion of debt that was at variable interest rates. This was largely due to the increasing proportion of debt that was in the form of loans from commercial banks.

After 1979, many developing countries found it increasingly difficult to service their debts. Then in 1982 Mexico, followed by several other countries such as Brazil, Bolivia, Zaire and Sudan, declared that it would have to suspend payments. There was now a debt crisis, which threatened not only the debtor countries, but also the world banking system.

Coping with debt: rescheduling

There are two dimensions to dealing with debt problems of developing countries. The first is to cope with difficulties in servicing their debt. This usually involves some form of rescheduling of the repayments. The second dimension is to deal with the underlying causes of the problem. Here we will focus on rescheduling.

Rescheduling official loans

Official loans are renegotiated through the 'Paris Club'. Industrialised countries are members of the club, which arranges terms for the rescheduling of their loans to developing countries. Agreements normally involve delaying the date for repayment of loans currently maturing, or spreading the repayments over a longer period of time. Paris Club agreements are often made in consultation with the International Monetary Fund (IMF), which works out a programme for the debtor country to tackle its underlying economic problems.

Several attempts have been made since the mid-1980s to make rescheduling terms more generous, with longer periods before repayments start, longer to repay when they do start, and lower interest rates. In return, the developing countries have had to undertake various 'structural adjustment programmes' supervised by the IMF (see below).

But despite apparent advances made by the Paris Club in making its terms more generous, the majority of low-income countries failed to meet the required IMF conditions, and thus failed to have their debts reduced. What is more, individual Paris Club members were often reluctant to reduce debts unless they were first convinced that other members were 'paying their share'. Nevertheless some creditor countries have unilaterally introduced more generous terms and even cancelled some debts.

The net effect of rescheduling, but only very modest debt forgiveness, can be seen in Table 14.2. By the mid-1990s average debt service ratios had fallen from the levels of the mid-1980s and yet the ratio of total debt to GNY was higher. There were thus growing calls for the cancellation of debts (see below).

Rescheduling commercial bank loans

After the declarations by Mexico and other countries of their inability to service their debts, there was fear of an imminent collapse of the world banking system. Banks realised that disaster could only be averted by collective action of the banks to reschedule debts. Banks were prepared to reschedule some of the debts and to provide some additional loans in return for debtor countries undertaking structural adjustment (as described below). Additional loans, however, fell well short of the amount that was needed. Banks were unwilling to supply extra money to deal with current debt-servicing problems when they saw the problem as a long-term one of countries' inability to pay. Nevertheless, banks were increasingly setting aside funds to cover bad debt, and thus the crisis for the banks began to recede.

As banks felt less exposed to default, so they became less worried about it and less concerned to negotiate deals with debtor countries. Many of the more severely indebted countries, however, found their position still deteriorating rapidly. What is more, many of them were finding that the IMF adjustment programmes were too painful (often involving deep cuts in government expenditure) and were therefore abandoning them. Thus in 1989 US Treasury Secretary Nicholas Brady proposed measures to *reduce* debt.

> **Pause for thought**
>
> *What are the relative advantages and disadvantages to a developing country of rescheduling its debts compared with simply defaulting on them (either temporarily or permanently)?*

The *Brady Plan* involved the IMF and the World Bank lending funds to debtor countries to enable them to repay debts to banks. In return for this instant source of liquidity, the banks would have to be prepared to accept repayment of less than the full sum (i.e. they would sell the debt back to the country at a discount). To benefit from such deals, the debtor countries would have to agree to structural adjustment programmes. Several such agreements were negotiated; much of the debt reduction has involved 'debt swaps' of one sort or another (see Case Study 14.17 in MyEconLab).

Dealing with the debt

Structural reforms

The severe structural adjustment programmes frequently demanded by the IMF before it is prepared to sanction the rescheduling of debts include:

- Tight fiscal and monetary policies to reduce government deficits, reduce interest rates and reduce inflation.
- Supply-side reforms to encourage greater use of the market mechanism and greater incentives for investment.
- A more open trade policy and devaluation of the currency in order to encourage more exports and more competition.

These policies, however, often brought extreme hardship as countries are forced to deflate. Unemployment and poverty increase and growth slows down or becomes negative. Even though in the long run developing countries may emerge as more efficient and better able to compete in international trade, in the short run the suffering may be too great to bear. Popular unrest and resentment against the IMF and the country's government may lead to riots and the breakdown of law and order, and even to the overthrow of the government.

A more 'complete' structural adjustment would extend beyond simple market liberalisation and tough monetary policies to much more open access to the markets of the rich countries, to more aid and debt relief being channelled into health and education, and to greater research and development in areas that will benefit the poor (e.g. into efficient labour-intensive technology and into new strains of crops that are suitable for countries' specific climate and soil conditions and which do not require large amounts of chemicals).

Debt forgiveness

By the end of the 1990s, the debt burden of many of the poorest countries had become intolerable. Despite portions of their debt being written off under Paris Club terms, the debts of many countries were still rising. Between 1980 and 2000, the debt of sub-Saharan Africa had increased some $3^{1}/_{2}$ times, from $61 billion to $212 billion. Some countries, such as Ethiopia and Mozambique, were spending nearly half their export earnings on merely servicing their debt.

Even with substantial debt rescheduling and some debt cancellation, highly indebted countries were being forced to make savage cuts in government expenditure, much of it on health, education and transport. The consequence was a growth in poverty, hunger, disease and illiteracy. African countries on average were paying four times more to rich countries in debt servicing than they were spending on health and education: it was like a patient giving a blood transfusion to a doctor! The majority of these countries had no chance of 'growing their way out of debt'. The only solution for them was for a more substantial proportion of their debt to be written off.

The heavily indebted poor countries (HIPC) initiative. In 1996 the World Bank and the IMF launched the HIPC initiative. A total of 42 countries, mainly in Africa, were identified as being in need of substantial debt relief. This number was subsequently reduced to 41. The object of the initiative was to reduce the debts of such countries to 'sustainable' levels by cancelling debts above 200 to 250 per cent of GDP (this was reduced to 150 per cent in 1999 and to a lower level for five countries).

The HIPC process involves countries passing through two stages. In the first stage, eligible countries must demonstrate a track record of 'good performance'. This means that they must satisfy the IMF, World Bank and Paris Club that they are undertaking adjustment measures, such as cutting government expenditure and liberalising their markets. It also involves the countries preparing a Poverty Reduction Strategy Paper (PRSP) to show how they will use debt relief to tackle poverty, and especially how they will improve health and education. Once the IMF and World Bank are satisfied that the country is making sufficient progress, the 'decision point' is reached and the country enters the second stage

During this second stage, some interim debt relief is provided. Meanwhile the country must establish a 'sound track record' by implementing policies established at the decision point and based on the PRSP. The length of this stage depends on how long it takes the country to implement the policies. At the end of the second stage, the country reaches the 'completion point' and debts are cancelled by the various creditors, on a pro rata basis, to bring the debt to the sustainable threshold.

Despite the initial welcome given to the HIPC initiative, it has been heavily criticised:

- The qualifying period is too long. By 2008, only 23 countries had reached the completion point, with another 10 having reached the decision point, with the remaining 8 yet to get even to the decision point. The total amount of relief committed by the end of 2007 was $49 billion. By 2004, total debt of the HIPC countries had reached $145 billion. By 2006, this had fallen to $101 billion. Despite having a previous 'good track record', many countries still had to adhere to the full two-stage process, which could be very lengthy.
- The thresholds have been set too high, with the resulting reduction in debt servicing being quite modest, or in many cases zero. In response to this criticism and calls for creditor countries to do more, the G8 countries agreed at the Gleneagles summit in July 2005 to cancel all remaining debt owed to the World Bank, IMF and African Development Bank by HIPC countries once they reached the completion point. For the 23 countries that had reached the completion point by 2008, this amounted to a further $21 billion beyond that agreed at the decision point.
- Countries in arrears to multilateral agencies, such as the World Bank and IMF, have first to meet any back payments due. For some of the poorest countries, particularly those which have suffered civil wars (such as the Republic of Congo), such a requirement is virtually impossible to meet. Individual donor countries have sometimes agreed to partial forgiveness of arrears, but this has generally been insufficient to allow enough funds to be diverted to clear arrears with multilateral agencies.
- The IMF reform programmes have been too harsh. The required reductions in government expenditure lead to deep cuts in basic health and education, and deflationary policies lead to reductions in investment.
- Many of the non-HIPCs are also suffering debts which divert a large percentage of their income from poverty relief. Just because non-HIPCs can manage to service their debts, it does not make it desirable that they should be forced to do so.

According to many charities, such as Oxfam, a much better approach would be to target debt relief directly at poverty reduction, with the resources released being used for investment in fields such as health, education, rural development and basic infrastructure. The focus, they argue, should be on what countries can afford to pay *after* essential spending on poverty relief and human development.

Should all debt be cancelled and aid increased?

In recent years there have been growing calls for the cancellation of debts and a significant increase in aid, especially for the poorest developing countries, many ravaged by war, drought or AIDS. The United Nations has for many years called on wealthy countries to give 0.7 per cent of their GDP in aid. In practice they give only a little over 0.2 per cent.

HIPC relief plus the cancellation of debts agreed at the Gleneagles summit (see above) amounted to some $60 billion. This is still, however, only a tiny proportion of the $400 billion of debt owed by low-income countries and some $3.4 trillion owed by developing countries as a whole. Then there is the plight of many non-HIPC countries, such as Kenya, which could be argued to be in greater need of debt relief than some HIPC countries.

At the summit France, Germany, Italy and the UK also committed themselves to meeting the 0.7 per cent of GDP aid target by 2015. The G8 as a whole agreed to increase aid to Africa by $25 billion a year by 2010 – a more than doubling of aid compared to 2004. But agreeing is not doing. In 2005, total aid from developed countries amounted to 0.33 per cent of their GDP. By 2007, this had fallen to 0.28 per cent. Nonetheless, at the G20 meeting in London in April 2009, countries reaffirmed their 'Gleneagles commitments' and agreed to review the flexibility of the World Bank's and IMF's Debt Sustainability Framework which assesses the grant eligibility of low income countries (LICs).

The argument against debt cancellation and a substantial increase in aid is that this could represent a 'moral hazard'. Once the burden of debt had been lifted and aid had been increased, countries might be tempted to squander the money. It might also encourage them to seek further loans, which might again be squandered.

If, however, moneys were paid into national 'Poverty Funds', which could be monitored by civil society, Parliament and possibly multilateral agencies, this might help to ensure that the money would be used to fund key poverty-reducing projects, such as health, education, clean water and other basic infrastructure projects. (Web Case Study 14.18 examines some of the issues surrounding aid.)

> **Pause for thought**
>
> *Should rich countries cancel all debts owed to them by developing countries?*

Recap

1. After the 1973 oil crisis, many developing countries borrowed heavily in order to finance their balance of trade deficits and to maintain a programme of investment. After the 1979 oil price rises, the debt problem became much more serious. There was a world recession and real interest rates were much higher. Debt increased dramatically, and much of it at variable interest rates.

2. Rescheduling can help developing countries cope with increased debt in the short run and various schemes have been adopted by creditor countries and the banks.

3. If the problem of developing countries' debt is to be tackled then simple rescheduling is not enough. The IMF favours 'structural adjustment' programmes, involving tight fiscal and monetary policies and market-orientated supply-side policies. A more 'complete' structural adjustment, however, would involve more open access to the markets of the rich countries, more aid and debt relief being channelled into health and education, and greater research and development in areas that will benefit the poor.

4. In 1996 the World Bank and the IMF launched the HIPC initiative to help reduce the debts of heavily indebted poor countries to sustainable levels. HIPC relief has been criticised, however, for being made conditional on the debtor countries pursuing excessively tough IMF adjustment programmes, for being too modest in the amount of debts cancelled, for having an excessively long qualifying period and for delays in its implementation. A better approach might be to target debt relief directly at programmes to help the poor.

QUESTIONS

1. Which of the following items are credits on the UK balance of payments and which are debits?

   (a) The expenditure by UK tourists on holidays in Greece.
   (b) The payment of dividends by foreign companies to investors resident in the UK.
   (c) Foreign residents taking out insurance policies with UK companies.
   (d) Drawing on reserves.
   (e) Investment by UK companies overseas.

2. The table shows the items in the UK's 2007 balance of payments.

   (a) Fill in the missing totals for (a) the balance of trade, (b) the current account balance, (c) the portfolio investment balance; and (d) for net errors and omissions.
   (b) UK's GDP in 2007 was estimated at £1,402,218 million. Calculate each item on the balance of payments as a percentage of GDP.
   (c) Compare the value of each item in £ millions and as percentages of GDP with those for 2008 in Table 14.1.

	£ millions
Current account:	
Balance on trade in goods	−89 754
Balance on trade in services	42 457
Balance of trade	
Income balance	20 572
Net current transfers	−13 602
Current account balance	
Capital account:	
Capital account balance	2 566
Financial account:	
Net direct investment	−37 980
Portfolio investment balance	
Other investment balance	−18 806
Balance of financial derivatives	−19 001
Reserve assets	−1 191
Financial account net flows	39 712
Net errors and omissions	

3. What is the relationship between the balance of trade and the circular flow model?

4. Explain how the current account of the balance of payments is likely to vary with the course of the business cycle.

5. Is it a 'bad thing' to have a deficit on the direct and portfolio investment part of the financial account?

6. Why may credits on a country's short-term financial account create problems for its economy in the future?

7. List some factors that could cause an increase in the credit items of the balance of payments and a decrease in the debit items. What would be the effect on the exchange rate (assuming that it is freely floating)? What effect would these exchange rate movements have on the balance of payments?

8. What policy measures could the government adopt to prevent the exchange rate movements in question 7?

9. What are the major advantages and disadvantages of fixing the exchange rate with a majority currency such as the US dollar?

10. What adverse effects on the domestic economy may follow from (a) a depreciation of the exchange rate and (b) an appreciation of the exchange rate?

11. What will be the effects on the domestic economy under free-floating exchange rates if there is a rapid expansion in world economic activity? What will determine the size of these effects?

12. Why would banks not be prepared to offer a forward exchange rate to a firm for, say, five years' time?

13. Under what circumstances would the demand for imports be likely to be inelastic? How would an inelastic demand for imports affect the magnitude of fluctuations in the exchange rate?

14. Why are the price elasticities of demand for imports and exports likely to be lower in the short run than in the long run?

15. Assume that the government pursued an expansionary fiscal policy and that the resulting budget deficit led to higher interest rates. What would happen to (a) the current account and (b) the financial account of the balance of payments? What would be the likely effect on the exchange rate, given a high degree of international financial mobility?

16. Consider the argument that in the modern world of large-scale short-term international financial movements, the ability of individual countries to affect their exchange rate is very limited.

17. Why does high international financial mobility and an absence of exchange controls severely limit a country's ability to choose its interest rate?

18. What practical problems are there in achieving a general harmonisation of economic policies between (a) EU countries; (b) the major industrialised countries?

19. What are the causes of exchange rate volatility? Have these problems become greater or less in the past ten years? Explain why.

20. Why did the ERM with narrow bands collapse in 1993? Could this have been avoided?

21. Did the exchange rate difficulties experienced by countries under the ERM strengthen or weaken the arguments for progressing to a single European currency?

22. Under what circumstances may a pegged exchange rate system like the ERM (a) help to prevent speculation; (b) aggravate the problem of speculation?

23. By what means would a depressed country in an Economic Union with a single currency be able to recover? Would the market provide a satisfactory solution or would (Union) government intervention be necessary, and if so, what form would the intervention take?

24. Assume that just some of the members of a common market like the EU adopt full economic and monetary union, including a common currency. What are the advantages and disadvantages to those members joining the full EMU and to those not joining?

25. Is the eurozone likely to be an optimal currency area? Is it more or less likely to be so over time? Explain your answer.

26. It is often argued that international convergence of economic indicators is a desirable objective. Does this mean that countries should seek to achieve the same rate of economic growth, monetary growth, interest rates, budget deficits as a percentage of their GDP, etc?

27. Why is it difficult to achieve international harmonisation of economic policies?

28. To what extent was the debt crisis of the early 1980s caused by inappropriate policies that had been pursued by the debtor countries?

29. Imagine that you are an ambassador of a developing country at an international conference. What would you try to persuade the rich countries to do in order to help you and other poor countries overcome the debt problem? How would you set about persuading them that it was in their own interests to help you?

30. Has increased globalisation been a good thing for national economies?

Log on to MyEconlab and complete the studyplan exercises for this chapter to see how much you have learnt and where you need to revise most. Make sure you access all the supporting textbook resources including the online workbook, newsblog, audio animations, guided solutions and ebook.

Additional case studies in the *Essentials of Economics* MyEconLab (www.pearsoned.co.uk/sloman)

14.1   **Balance of trade and the public finances.** An examination of countries' budget and balance of trade balances

14.2   **Making sense of the financial balances on the balance of payments.** An examination of the three main components of the financial account.

14.3   **The UK's balance of payments deficit.** An examination of the UK's persistent trade and current account deficits.

14.4   **Does PPP hold in the long run?** This considers the relationship between inflation rate differentials and movements in sterling.

14.5   **The Gold Standard.** A historical example of fixed exchange rates.

14.6   **A high exchange rate.** This case looks at whether a high exchange rate is necessarily bad news for exporters.

14.7   **The sterling crisis of early 1985.** When the pound fell almost to $1.00.

14.8   **Currency turmoil in the 1990s.** A crisis in Mexico; a rising yen and German mark; a falling US dollar – why did this all happen?

14.9   **The 1997/8 crisis in Asia.** The role played by the IMF.

14.10   **Argentina in crisis.** An examination of the collapse of the Argentinean economy in 2001/2.

14.11   **The Tobin tax.** An examination of the possible use of small taxes on foreign exchange transactions. The purpose is to reduce currency fluctuations.

14.12   **The euro, the US dollar and world currency markets.** An analysis of the relationship between the euro and the dollar.

14.13   **Using interest rates to control both aggregate demand and the exchange rate.** A problem of one instrument and two targets.

14.14   **The UK Labour government's convergence criteria for euro membership.** An examination of the five tests set by the UK government that would have to be passed before the question of euro membership would be put to the electorate in a referendum.

14.15   **Debt and the environment.** How high levels of debt can encourage developing countries to damage their environment in an attempt to increase export earnings.

14.16   **The great escape.** This case examines the problem of capital flight from developing countries to rich countries.

14.17   **Swapping debt.** Schemes to convert a developing country's debt into other forms, such as shares in its industries.

14.18   **Economic aid.** Does aid provide a solution to the debt problem?

Websites relevant to this chapter

Numbers and sections refer to websites listed in the Web appendix and hotlinked from this book's website at **www.pearsoned.co.uk/sloman**.

■ For news articles relevant to this chapter, see the *Economics News Articles* link from the book's website.

■ For general news on countries' balance of payments and exchange rates, see websites in section A, and particularly A1–5, 7–9, 20–25, 31. For articles on various aspects of economic development, see A27, 28; I9. See also links to newspapers worldwide in A38 and 39, and the news search feature in Google at A41. See also links to economics news in A42.

■ For international data on balance of payments and exchange rates, see *World Economic Outlook* in H4 and *OECD Economic Outlook* in B21 (also in section 6 of B1). See also the trade topic in I14.

■ For details of individual countries' balance of payments, see B32.

■ For UK data on balance of payments, see B1, 1. *National Statistics* > the fourth link > *Economy* > *United Kingdom Balance of Payments* – the *Pink Book*. See also B3, 34; F2. For EU data, see G1 > *Publications* > *Publications overview* > *European Economy*.

■ For exchange rates, see A3; B34; F2, 6, 8.

■ For data on debt and development, see B24 (*Global Development Finance*) and B31. Also see the debt section in I14.

■ For discussion papers on the balance of payments and exchange rates, see H4 and 7.

■ For information on debt and developing countries, see H4, 7, 9, 10, 12–14, 17–19. See also links to development sites in I9.

■ Sites I7 and 11 contain links to *Balance of payments and exchange rates in International economics* and to *Capital flows and aid in Economic Development*.

■ For student resources relevant to this chapter, see sites C1–7, 9, 10, 19. See also *Virtual Developing Country* in *Virtual Worlds* in site C2.

Web appendix

14.1 The effectiveness of fiscal and monetary policies. A comparison of the effectiveness of fiscal and monetary policies under fixed and floating exchange rates.

Web appendix

All the following websites can be accessed from MyEconLab (**www.pearsoned. co.uk/sloman**) at **Hot Links**. You will find all the following sites listed. Click on the one you want and the 'hot link' will take you straight to it.

The sections and numbers below refer to the ones used in the Web references at the end of each chapter of the text. Thus if the reference were to number A21, this would refer to the Moneyextra site.

GENERAL NEWS SOURCES   A

As the title of this section implies, the websites here can be used for finding material on current news issues or tapping into news archives. Most archives are offered free of charge. However, some do require you to register. As well as key UK and American sources, you will also notice some slightly different places from where you can get your news, such as the St Petersburg Times and Kyodo News (from Japan). Check out sites number 38 Refdesk, 43 Guardian World News Guide and 44 Online Newspapers for links to newspapers across the world. Try searching for an article on a particular topic by using site number 41 Google News Search.

1. BBC news
2. The Economist
3. The Financial Times
4. The Guardian
5. The Independent
6. ITN
7. The Observer
8. The Telegraph
9. The Times, Sunday Times
10. The New York Times
11. Fortune
12. Time Magazine
13. The Washington Post
14. Moscow Times (English)
15. St Petersburg Times (English)
16. Straits Times
17. New Straits Times
18. The Scotsman
19. The Herald
20. Euromoney
21. Moneyextra
22. Market News International
23. BusinessWeek online
24. Ananova
25. CNN Money
26. Wall Street Journal
27. Asia related news
28. allAfrica.com
29. Greek News Sources (English)
30. Kyodo News: Japan (English)
31. Euronews
32. The Australian
33. Sydney Morning Herald
34. Japan Times
35. Reuters
36. Bloomberg
37. David Smith's Economics UK.com
38. Refdesk (links to a whole range of news sources)
39. Newspapers on World Wide Web

40. Yahoo News Search
41. Google News Search
42. Moreover RSS feeds

43. Guardian World News Guide
44. Online Newspapers

B SOURCES OF ECONOMIC AND BUSINESS DATA

Using websites to find up-to-date data is of immense value to the economist. The data sources below offer you a range of specialist and non-specialist data information. Universities have free access to the MIMAS and ESDS sites, which are huge databases of statistics. Site 34, the Treasury Pocket Data Bank, is a very useful source of key UK and world statistics, and is updated monthly. It downloads as an Excel file.

1. Economics Network gateway to economic data
2. Biz/ed Gateway to economic and company data
3. National Statistics
4. Data Archive (Essex)
5. Bank of England Statistical Database
6. Economic Resources (About)
7. Nationwide House Prices
8. House Web (data on housing market)
9. Telegraph shares and markets
10. Halifax House Price Index
11. Land Registry (house prices, etc.)
12. Manchester Information and Associated Services (MIMAS)
13. Economist economic and financial indicators
14. FT market data
15. Economagic
16. Groningen Growth and Development Centre
17. Resources for economists on the Internet
18. Joseph Rowntree Foundation
19. Intute: Social Sciences (Economics)
20. Energy Information Administration
21. OECD statistics
22. CIA world statistics site
23. UN Millennium Country Profiles
24. World Bank statistics
25. Federal Reserve Bank of St. Louis, US Economic Data sets (FRED)
26. Ministry of International Trade and Industry (Japan)
27. Financial data from Yahoo
28. Nanyang Technological University, Singapore: Statistical Data Locators
29. Davidson Data Center and Network (DDCN)
30. Oanda Currency Converter
31. World Economic Outlook Database (IMF)
32. Economist Country Briefings
33. OFFSTATS links to data sets
34. Treasury Pocket Data Bank (source of UK and world economic data)
35. Economic and Social Data Service (ESDS)
36. The Official Yearbook of the United Kingdom of Great Britain and Northern Ireland
37. NationMaster
38. European Economy Statistical Annex
39. Business and Comsumer Surveys (all EU countries)
40. Gapminder (via Google)
41. WebEc Economics Data
42. WTO International Trade Statistics database
43. UNCTAD trade, investment and development statistics
44. London Metal Exchange

SITES FOR STUDENTS AND TEACHERS OF ECONOMICS   C

The following websites offer useful ideas and resources to those who are studying or teaching economics. It is worth browsing through some just to see what is on offer. Try out the first four sites, for starters. The Internet Economist is a very helpful tutorial for economics students on using the Internet.

1. Economics Network of the UK's Higher Education Academy
2. Biz/ed
3. Ecedweb
4. Studying Economics
5. Economics and Business Education Association
6. Tutor2U
7. Council for Economic Education
8. Internet for Economics
9. Oxford School of Learning
10. Teaching resources for economists
11. METAL – Mathematics for Economics: enhancing Teaching And Learning
12. Federal Reserve Bank of San Francisco: Economics Education
13. Excel in Economics Teaching
14. WebEc resources
15. BibEc papers
16. Online Opinion (Economics)
17. The Idea Channel
18. History of Economic Thought
19. Resources For Economists on the Internet (RFE)
20. Classroom Expernomics
21. VCE Economics (Economics teaching resources – Australian)
22. Why Study Economics?
23. Economic Classroom Experiments
24. Veconlab: Charles Holt's classroom experiments
25. Embedding Threshold Concepts

ECONOMIC MODELS AND SIMULATIONS   D

Economic modelling is an important aspect of economic analysis. There are a number of sites that offer access to a model for you to use, e.g. Virtual economy (where you can play being Chancellor of the Exchequer). Using such models can be a useful way of finding out how economic theory works within an environment that claims to reflect reality.

1. Virtual economy
2. Virtual factory
3. Virtual Learning Arcade
4. About.com Economics
5. Classic Economic Models
6. Economics Network Handbook, Chapter on Simulations, Games and Role-play
7. Estima (statistical analysis)
8. SPSS (statistical analysis)
9. National Institute of Economic and Social Research
10. Software available on the Economics Network site
11. RFE Software
12. Virtual Chancellor
13. Veconlab: Charles Holt's classroom experiments
14. EconPort
15. Denise Hazlett's Classroom Experiments in Macroeconomics
16. Games Economists Play
17. Finance and Economics Experimental Laboratory at Exeter (FEELE)
18. Classroom Expernomics
19. The Economics Network's Guide to Classroom Experiments and Games

E UK GOVERNMENT AND UK ORGANISATIONS' SITES

If you want to see what a government department is up to, then look no further than the list below. Government departments' websites are an excellent source of information and data. They are particularly good at offering information on current legislation and policy initiatives.

1. Gateway site (DirectGov)
2. Department for Communities and Local Government
3. Central Office of Information
4. Competition Commission
5. Department for Children Schools and Families
6. Department for International Development
7. Department for Transport
8. Department of Health
9. Department for Work and Pensions
10. Department for Business, Innovation and Skills
11. Environment Agency
12. UK euro information site
13. Low Pay Commission
14. Department for Environment, Food and Rural Affairs (DEFRA)
15. Office of Communications (Ofcom)
16. Office of Gas and Electricity Markets (Ofgem)
17. Official Documents OnLine
18. Office of Fair Trading (OFT)
19. Office of Rail Regulation (ORR)
20. The Takeover Panel
21. Sustainable Development Commission
22. OFWAT
23. National statistics (ONS)
24. National Statistics Time Series Data
25. HM Revenue and Customs
26. UK Intellectual Property Office
27. Parliament website
28. Scottish Government
29. Scottish Environment Protection Agency
30. HM Treasury
31. Equality and Human Rights Commission
32. Trades Union Congress (TUC)
33. Confederation of British Industry
34. Adam Smith Institute
35. Chatham House
36. Institute for Fiscal Studies
37. Advertising Standards Authority
38. Business Link
39. Campaign for Better Transport

F SOURCES OF MONETARY AND FINANCIAL DATA

As the title suggests, here are listed useful websites for finding information on financial matters. You will see that the list comprises mainly central banks, both within Europe and further afield.

1. Bank of England
2. Bank of England Monetary and Financial Statistics
3. Banque de France (in English)
4. Bundesbank (German central bank – in English)
5. Central Bank of Ireland
6. European Central Bank
7. Eurostat
8. US Federal Reserve Bank
9. Netherlands Central Bank (in English)
10. Bank of Japan (in English)
11. Reserve Bank of Austalia
12. Bank Negara Malaysia (in English)
13. Monetary Authority of Singapore

14. National Bank of Canada
15. National Bank of Denmark (English)
16. Reserve Bank of India

17. Links to central bank websites from the Bank for International Settlements
18. The London Stock Exchange

EUROPEAN UNION AND RELATED SOURCES   G

For information on European issues, the following is a wide range of useful sites. The sites maintained by the European Union are an excellent source of information and are provided free of charge.

1. Economic and Financial Affairs: (EC DG)
2. European Central Bank
3. EU official website
4. Eurostat
5. Employment and Social Affairs (EC DG)
6. Booklets on the EU
7. Enterprise and Industry: (EC DG)
8. Competition: (EC DG)
9. Agriculture and Rural Development: (EC DG)
10. Energy and Transport: (EC DG)
11. Environment: (EC DG)
12. Regional Policy: (EC DG)
13. Taxation and Customs Union: (EC DG)
14. Education and Culture: (EC DG)
15. European Patent Office
16. European Commission
17. European Parliament
18. European Council

INTERNATIONAL ORGANISATIONS   H

This section casts its net beyond Europe and lists the Web addresses of the main international organisations in the global economy. You will notice that some sites are run by pressure groups, such as Jubilee Research, while others represent organisations set up to manage international affairs, such as the International Monetary Fund and the United Nations.

1. Food and Agriculture Organization
2. International Air Transport Association (IATA)
3. International Labour Organization (ILO)
4. International Monetary Fund (IMF)
5. Organisation for Economic Co-operation and Development (OECD)
6. OPEC
7. World Bank
8. World Health Organization
9. United Nations
10. United Nations Industrial Development Organization
11. Friends of the Earth
12. Jubilee Research
13. Oxfam
14. Christian Aid (reports on development issues)
15. European Bank for Reconstruction and Development (EBRD)
16. World Trade Organization (WTO)
17. United Nations Development Program
18. UNICEF
19. EURODAD – European Network on Debt and Development
20. NAFTA
21. South American free trade areas
22. ASEAN
23. APEC

I ECONOMICS SEARCH AND LINK SITES

If you are having difficulty finding what you want from the list of sites above, the following sites offer links to other sites and are a very useful resource when you are looking for something a little bit more specialist. Once again, it is worth having a look at what these sites have to offer in order to judge their usefulness.

1. Gateway for UK official sites
2. Alta Plana
3. Data Archive Search
4. Inomics (search engine for economics information)
5. RePEc bibliographic database
6. Links to economics resources sites
7. Intute: Social Sciences (Economics)
8. WebEc
9. One World (link to economic development sites)
10. Economic development sites (list) from OneWorld.net
11. Biz/ed Internet catalogue
12. Web links for economists from the Economics Network
13. Yahoo's links to economic data
14. OFFSTATS links to data sets
15. Excite Economics links
16. Internet Resources for Economists
17. Google Web Directory: Economics
18. Resources for Economists on the Internet
19. UK University Economics Departments
20. Economics education links
21. Development Gateway

J INTERNET SEARCH ENGINES

The following search engines have been found to be useful.

1. Google
2. Altavista
3. Whoosh UK
4. Excite
5. Go.com
6. Search.com
7. MSN
8. UK Plus
9. Yahoo!
10. Ask
11. Kartoo
12. Blinkx (for videos and audio podcasts)

Key ideas and glossary

1. **Scarcity** is the excess of human wants over what can actually be produced. Because of scarcity, various choices have to be made between alternatives (page 5).

2. **Opportunity cost.** The cost of something measured in terms of what you give up to get it/do it. The best alternative forgone (page 7). **(Threshold concept 1)**

3. **Rational decision making** involves weighing up the marginal benefit and marginal cost of any activity. If the marginal benefit exceeds the marginal cost, it is rational to do the activity (or to do more of it). If the marginal cost exceeds the marginal benefit, it is rational not to do it (or to do less of it) (page 10). **(Threshold concept 2)**

4. **Modelling in economics** involves specifying how one variable (the 'dependent variable') depends on one or more other variables ('independent variables'). It involves 'holding constant' all other variables that might influence the outcome (the *ceteris paribus* assumption). A model can be expressed in words, as a graph, or mathematically in terms of one or more equations. In this book we use mainly verbal descriptions and graphs (page 11). **(Threshold Concept 3)**

5. **People respond to incentives.** It is important, therefore, that incentives are appropriate and have the desired effect (page 21). **(Threshold Concept 4)**

6. **Changes in demand or supply cause markets to adjust.** Whenever such changes occur, the resulting 'disequilibrium' will bring an automatic change in prices, thereby restoring equilibrium (i.e. a balance of demand and supply) (page 21).

7. **The principle of diminishing marginal utility.** The more of a product a person consumes over a given period of time, the less will be the additional utility gained from one more unit (page 34).

8. **Equilibrium is the point where conflicting interests are balanced.** Only at this point is the amount that demanders are willing to purchase the same as the amount that suppliers are willing to supply. It is a point that will be automatically reached in a free market through the operation of the price mechanism (page 40). **(Threshold Concept 5)**

9. **People gain from voluntary interaction.** When people buy from or sell to other people, or when they are employed by or employ other people, both parties will gain from the interaction (page 47). **(Threshold Concept 6)**

10. **Government intervention may be able to rectify various failings of the market.** Government intervention in the market can be used to achieve various economic objectives which may not be best achieved by the market. Governments, however, are not perfect and their actions may bring adverse as well as beneficial consequences (page 49). **(Threshold Concept 7)**

11. **Elasticity.** The responsiveness of one variable (e.g. demand) to a change in another (e.g. price). This concept is fundamental to understanding how markets work. The more elastic variables are, the more responsive is the market to changing circumstances (page 67). **(Threshold Concept 8)**

12. **People's actions are influenced by their expectations.** People respond not just to what is happening now (such as a change in price), but to what they anticipate will happen in the future (page 71). **(Threshold Concept 9)**

13. **People's actions are influenced by their attitudes towards risk.** Many decisions are taken under conditions of risk or uncertainty. Generally, the lower the probability of (or the more uncertain) the desired outcome of an action, the less likely it is that people will undertake the action (page 74).

14. **Output depends on the amount of resources and how they are used.** Different amounts and combinations of inputs will lead to different amounts of output. If output is to be produced efficiently, then inputs should be combined in the optimum proportions (page 86).

15. **The law of diminishing marginal returns.** When increasing amounts of a variable factor are used with a given amount of a fixed factor, there will come a point when each extra unit of the variable factor will produce less extra output than the previous unit (page 87).

16. **Market power benefits the powerful at the expense of others.** When firms have market power over prices, they can use this to raise prices and profits above the perfectly competitive level. Other things being equal, the firm will gain at the expense of the consumer. Similarly, if consumers or workers have market power, they can use this to their own benefit (page 116).

17. **Economic efficiency** is achieved when each good is produced at the minimum cost and where consumers get maximum benefit from their income (page 122).

18. **People often think and behave strategically.** How you think others will respond to your actions is likely to influence your own behaviour. Firms, for example, when considering a price or product change will often take into account the likely reactions of their rivals (page 136).

19. **Equity** is where income is distributed in a way that is considered to be fair or just. Note that an equitable distribution is not the same as a totally equal distribution and that different people have different views on what is equitable (page 181).

20. **Allocative efficiency in any activity is achieved where any reallocation would lead to a decline in net benefit.** It is achieved where marginal benefit equals marginal cost. Private efficiency is achieved where marginal private benefit equals marginal private cost ($MB = MC$). Social efficiency is achieved where marginal social benefit equals marginal social cost ($MSB = MSC$) (page 192). **(Threshold Concept 10)**

21. **Markets generally fail to achieve social efficiency.** There are various types of market failure. Market failures provide one of the major justifications for government intervention in the economy (page 193).

22. **General equilibrium.** A situation where all markets are in equilibrium. This situation can be assessed as to whether or not allocative efficiency is achieved. This will depend on whether or not markets are perfect (page 193). (**Threshold Concept 11**)

23. **Externalities are spillover costs or benefits.** Where these exist, even an otherwise perfect market will fail to achieve social efficiency (page 194).

24. **The free-rider problem.** People are often unwilling to pay for things if they can make use of things other people have bought. This problem can lead to people not purchasing things which would be to the benefit of themselves and other members of society to have (page 197).

25. **The principal-agent problem.** Where people (principals), as a result of a lack of knowledge, cannot ensure that their best interests are served by their agents. Agents may take advantage of this situation to the disadvantage of the principals (page 202).

26. **The problem of time lags.** Many economic actions can take a long time to take effect. This can cause problems of instability and an inability of the economy to achieve social efficiency (page 203).

27. **Societies face trade-offs between economic objectives.** For example, the goal of faster growth may conflict with that of greater equality; the goal of lower unemployment may conflict with that of lower inflation (at least in the short run). This is an example of opportunity cost: the cost of achieving more of one objective may be achieving less of another. The existence of trade-offs means that policy-makers must make choices (page 204).

28. **Economies suffer from inherent instability.** As a result, economic growth and other macroeconomic indicators tend to fluctuate (page 234). (**Threshold Concept 12**)

29. **Stocks and flows.** A stock is a quantity of something at a given point in time. A flow is an increase or decrease in something over a specified period of time. This is an important distinction and a common cause of confusion (page 239).

30. **The principle of cumulative causation.** An initial event can cause an ultimate effect that is much larger (page 253). (**Threshold Concept 13**)

31. **The distinction between nominal and real figures.** Nominal figures are those using current prices, interest rates, etc. Real figures are figures corrected for inflation (page 266). (**Threshold Concept 14**)

32. **Long-term growth in a country's output depends on growth in the quantity and/or productivity of its resources.** Potential economic growth depends on the country's resources, technology and productivity. This is crucial to understanding what underlies the wealth of nations and why some countries have faster growth rates than others (page 289). (**Threshold Concept 15**)

33. **Goodhart's law.** Controlling a symptom (i.e. an indicator) of a problem will not cure the problem. Instead, the indicator will merely cease to be a good indicator of the problem (page 405).

34. **The law of comparative advantage.** Provided opportunity costs of various goods differ in two countries, both of them can gain from mutual trade if they specialise in producing (and exporting) those goods that have relatively low opportunity costs compared with the other country (page 432).

Absolute advantage A country has an absolute advantage over another in the production of a good if it can produce it with less resources than the other country can.

Accelerationist theory The theory that unemployment can only be reduced below the natural level at the cost of accelerating inflation.

Accelerator theory The *level* of investment depends on the *rate of change* of national income, and as a result tends to be subject to substantial fluctuations.

Active balances Money held for transactions and precautionary purposes.

Actual growth The percentage annual increase in national output actually produced.

Ad valorem tariffs Tariffs levied as a percentage of the price of the import.

Ad valorem tax A tax on a good levied as a percentage of its value. It can be a single-stage tax or a multi-stage tax (such as VAT).

Adaptive expectations hypothesis The theory that people base their expectations of inflation on past inflation rates.

Adjustable peg A system whereby exchange rates are fixed for a period of time, but may be devalued (or revalued) if a deficit (or surplus) becomes substantial.

Aggregate demand Total spending on goods and services made in the economy. It consists of four elements, consumer spending (C), investment (I), government spending (G) and the expenditure on exports (X), less any expenditure on imports of goods and services (M): $AD = C + I + G + X - M$.

Aggregate demand for labour curve A curve showing the total demand for labour in the economy at different levels of real wage rates.

Aggregate supply The total amount of output in the economy.

Aggregate supply of labour curve A curve showing the total number of people willing and able to work at different average real wage rates.

Allocative efficiency A situation where the current combination of goods produced and sold gives the maximum satisfaction for each consumer at their current levels of income. Note that a redistribution of income would lead to a different combination of goods that was allocatively efficient.

Appreciation A rise in the free-market exchange rate of the domestic currency with foreign currencies.

Arc elasticity The measurement of elasticity between two points on a curve.

Assets Possessions, or claims held on others.

Asymmetric information Where one party in an economic relationship (e.g. an agent) has more information than another (e.g. the principal).

Asymmetric shocks Shocks (such as an oil price increase or a recession in another part of the world) that have different-sized effects on different industries, regions or countries.

Automatic fiscal stabilisers Tax revenues that rise and government expenditure that falls as national income rises. The more they change with income, the bigger the stabilising effect on national income.

Average (total) cost Total cost (fixed plus variable) per unit of output: $AC = TC/Q = AFC + AVC$.

Average cost pricing or **mark-up pricing** Where firms set the price by adding a profit mark-up to average cost.

Average fixed cost Total fixed cost per unit of output: $AFC = TFC/Q$.

Average (or 'mid-point') formula for price elasticity of demand ΔQ_D/average $Q_D \div \Delta P$/average P.

Average physical product Total output (TPP) per unit of the variable factor in question: $APP = TPP/Q_v$.

Average rate of income tax Income taxes as a proportion of a person's total (gross) income: T/Y.

Average revenue Total revenue per unit of output. When all output is sold at the same price, average revenue will be the same as price: $AR = TR/Q = P$.

Average variable cost Total variable cost per unit of output: $AVC = TVC/Q$.

Balance of payments account A record of the country's transactions with the rest of the world. It shows the country's payments to or deposits in other countries (debits) and its receipts or deposits from other countries (credits). It also shows the balance between these debits and credits under various headings.

Balance of payments on current account The balance on trade in goods and services plus net investment income and current transfers.

Balance on trade in goods Exports of goods minus imports of goods.

Balance on trade in goods and services (or balance of trade) Exports of goods and services minus imports of goods and services.

Balance on trade in services Exports of services minus imports of services.

Balancing item (in the balance of payments) A statistical adjustment to ensure that the two sides of the balance of payments account balance.

It is necessary because of errors in compiling the statistics.

Bank bills Bills that have been accepted by another institution and hence insured against default.

Bank (or deposits) multiplier The number of times greater the expansion of bank deposits is than the additional liquidity in banks that causes it: $1/L$ (the inverse of the liquidity ratio).

Barometric firm price leadership Where the price leader is the one whose prices are believed to reflect market conditions in the most satisfactory way.

Barriers to entry Anything that prevents or impedes the entry of firms into an industry and thereby limits the amount of competition faced by existing firms.

Barter economy An economy where people exchange goods and services directly with one another without any payment of money. Workers would be paid with bundles of goods.

Base year (for index numbers) The year whose index number is set at 100.

Basic rate of tax The main marginal rate of tax, applying to most people's incomes.

Benefits in kind Goods or services which the state provides directly to the recipient at no charge or at a subsidised price. Alternatively, the state can subsidise the private sector to provide them.

Bilateral monopoly Where a monopsony buyer faces a monopoly seller.

Bill of exchange A certificate promising to repay a stated amount on a certain date, typically three months from the issue of the bill. Bills pay no interest as such, but are sold at a discount and redeemed at face value, thereby earning a rate of discount for the purchaser.

Bretton Woods system An adjustable peg system whereby currencies were pegged to the US dollar. The USA maintained convertibility of the dollar into gold at the rate of $35 to an ounce.

Broad definitions of money Items in narrow definitions plus other items that can be readily converted into cash.

Broad money in UK (M4) Cash in circulation plus retail and wholesale bank and building society deposits.

Budget deficit The excess of central government's spending over its tax receipts.

Budget surplus The excess of central government's tax receipts over its spending.

Business cycle or trade cycle The periodic fluctuations of national output round its long-term trend.

Capital All inputs into production that have themselves been produced: e.g. factories, machines and tools.

Capital account of the balance of payments The record of the transfers of capital to and from abroad.

Capital adequacy ratio (CAR) The ratio of a bank's capital (reserves and shares) to its risk weighted assets. Under the Basel II Accord, a bank's CAR should be a minimum of 8 per cent.

Capital expenditure Investment expenditure; expenditure on assets.

Cartel A formal collusive agreement.

Central bank Banker to the banks and the government.

Centrally planned or command economy An economy where all economic decisions are taken by the central authorities.

Certificates of deposit (CDs) Certificates issued by banks for fixed-term interest-bearing deposits. They can be resold by the owner to another party.

Ceteris paribus Latin for 'other things being equal'. This assumption has to be made when making deductions from theories.

Change in demand This is the term used for a shift in the demand curve. It occurs when a determinant of demand *other* than price changes.

Change in supply The term used for a shift in the supply curve. It occurs when a determinant *other* than price changes.

Change in the quantity demanded The term used for a movement along the demand curve to a new point. It occurs when there is a change in price.

Change in the quantity supplied The term used for a movement along the supply curve to a new point. It occurs when there is a change in price.

Claimant unemployment Those in receipt of unemployment-related benefits.

Clearing system A system whereby inter-bank debts are settled.

Closed shop Where a firm agrees to employ only union members.

Coase theorem By sufferers from externalities doing deals with perpetrators (by levying charges or offering bribes), the externality will be 'internalised' and the socially efficient level of output will be achieved.

Collateralised debt obligations (CDOs) These are a type of security consisting of a bundle of fixed-income assets, such as corporate bonds, mortgage debt and credit-card debt.

Collusive oligopoly Where oligopolists agree (formally or informally) to limit competition between themselves. They may set output quotas, fix prices, limit product promotion or development, or agree not to 'poach' each other's markets.

Collusive tendering Where two or more firms secretly agree on the prices they will tender for a contract. These prices will be above those which would be put in under a genuinely competitive tendering process.

Command-and-control (CAC) systems The use of laws or regulations backed up by inspections and penalties (such as fines) for non-compliance.

Commercial bills Bills of exchange issued by firms.

Common market A customs union where the member countries act as a single market with free movement of labour and capital, common taxes and common trade laws.

Comparative advantage A country has a comparative advantage over another in the production of a good if it can produce it at a lower opportunity cost: i.e. if it has to forgo less of other goods in order to produce it.

Competition for corporate control The competition for the control of companies through takeovers.

Complementary goods A pair of goods consumed together. As the price of one goes up, the demand for both goods will fall.

Compounding The process of adding interest each year to an initial capital sum.

Compromise strategy One whose worst outcome is better than the maximax strategy and whose best outcome is better than the maximin strategy.

Conglomerate merger When two firms in different industries merge.

Constrained discretion A set of principles or rules within which economic policy operates. These can be informal or enshrined in law.

Consumer durable A consumer good that lasts a period of time, during which the consumer can continue gaining utility from it.

Consumer sovereignty A situation where firms respond to changes in consumer demand without being in a position in the long run to charge a price above average cost.

Consumer surplus The excess of what a person would have been prepared to pay for a good (i.e. the utility) over what that person actually pays.

Consumption The act of using goods and services to satisfy wants. This will normally involve purchasing the goods and services.

Consumption function The relationship between consumption and national income. It can be expressed algebraically or graphically.

Consumption of domestically produced goods and services (C_d) The direct flow of money payments from households to firms.

Consumption smoothing The act by households of smoothing their levels of consumption over time despite facing volatile incomes.

Convergence of economies When countries achieve similar levels of growth, inflation, budget deficits as a percentage of GDP, balance of payments, etc.

Core workers Workers, normally with specific skills, who are employed on a permanent or long-term basis.

Cost-benefit analysis The identification, measurement and weighing up of the costs and benefits of a project in order to decide whether or not it should go ahead.

Cost-plus pricing (full-cost pricing) When firms price their product by adding a certain profit 'mark-up' to average cost.

Cost-push inflation Inflation caused by persistent rises in costs of production (independently of demand).

Countervailing power When the power of a monopolistic/oligopolistic seller is offset by powerful buyers who can prevent the price from being pushed up.

Cournot model A model of duopoly where each firm makes its price and output decisions on the assumption that its rival will produce a particular quantity.

Credible threat (or promise) One that is believable to rivals because it is in the threatener's interests to carry it out.

Cross-price elasticity of demand The percentage (or proportionate) change in quantity demanded of one good divided by the percentage (or proportionate) change in the price of another.

Cross-price elasticity of demand (arc formula) ΔQ_{Da}/average $Q_{Da} \div \Delta P_b$/average P_b.

Cross-subsidise To use profits in one market to subsidise prices in another.

Crowding out Where increased public expenditure diverts money or resources away from the private sector.

Currency union A group of countries (or regions) using a common currency.

Current account balance of payments Exports of goods and services minus imports of goods and services plus net incomes and current transfers from abroad. If inflows of money (from the sale of exports, etc.) exceed outflows of money (from the purchase of imports, etc.), there is a 'current account surplus' (a positive figure). If outflows exceed inflows, there is a 'current account deficit' (a negative figure).

Current expenditure Recurrent spending on goods and factor payments.

Customs union A free trade area with common external tariffs and quotas.

Cyclical or demand-deficient unemployment Disequilibrium unemployment caused by a fall in aggregate demand with no corresponding fall in the real wage rate.

Deadweight loss of an indirect tax The loss of consumer plus producer surplus from the imposition of an indirect tax.

Deadweight welfare loss The loss of consumer plus producer surplus in imperfect markets (when compared with perfect competition).

Debit card A card that has the same use as a cheque. Its use directly debits the person's current account.

Debt-servicing costs The costs incurred when repaying debt, including debt interest payments.

Decision tree (or game tree) A diagram showing the sequence of possible decisions by competitor firms and the outcome of each combination of decisions.

Deflationary gap The shortfall of national expenditure below national income (and injections below withdrawals) at the full-employment level of national income.

Deflationary policy Fiscal or monetary policy designed to reduce the rate of growth of aggregate demand.

Demand curve A graph showing the relationship between the price of a good and the quantity of the good demanded over a given time period. Price is measured on the vertical axis; quantity demanded is measured on the horizontal axis. A demand curve can be for an individual consumer or group of consumers, or more usually for the whole market.

Demand management policies Demand-side policies (fiscal and/or monetary) designed to smooth out the fluctuations in the business cycle.

Demand schedule (market) A table showing the different total quantities of a good that consumers are willing and able to buy at various prices over a given period of time.

Demand schedule for an individual A table showing the different quantities of a good that a person is willing and able to buy at various prices over a given period of time.

Demand-deficient or cyclical unemployment Disequilibrium unemployment caused by a fall in aggregate demand with no corresponding fall in the real wage rate.

Demand-pull inflation Inflation caused by persistent rises in aggregate demand.

Demand-side policies Policies designed to affect aggregate demand: fiscal policy and monetary policy.

Dependency Where the development of a developing country is hampered by its relationships with the industrialised world.

Depreciation (of a currency) A fall in the free-market exchange rate of the domestic currency with foreign currencies.

Depreciation (of capital) The decline in value of capital equipment due to age, or wear and tear.

Deregulation Where the government removes official barriers to competition (e.g. licences and minimum quality standards).

Derived demand The demand for a factor of production depends on the demand for the good that uses it.

Destabilising speculation Where the actions of speculators tend to make price movements larger.

Devaluation Where the government re-pegs the exchange rate at a lower level.

Diminishing marginal utility As more units of a good are consumed, additional units will provide less additional satisfaction than previous units.

Diminishing marginal utility of income Where each additional pound earned yields less additional utility.

Direct taxes Taxes on income and wealth. Paid directly to the tax authorities on that income or wealth.

Discounting The process of reducing the value of future flows to give them a present valuation.

Discretionary fiscal policy Deliberate changes in tax rates or the level of government expenditure in order to influence the level of aggregate demand.

Diseconomies of scale Where costs per unit of output increase as the scale of production increases.

Disequilibrium unemployment Unemployment resulting from real wage rates in the economy being above the equilibrium level.

Disguised unemployment Where the same work could be done by fewer people.

Disposable income Income after tax and other deductions and after the receipt of benefits.

Diversification Where a firm expands into new types of business.

Dominant firm price leadership When firms (the followers) choose the same price as that set by a dominant firm in the industry (the leader).

Dominant strategy game Where the *same* policy is suggested by different strategies.

Dumping When exports are sold at prices below marginal cost – often as a result of government subsidy.

Economic efficiency A situation where each good is produced at the minimum cost and where individual people and firms get the maximum benefit from their resources.

Economic model The representation, graphically, mathematically or in words, of the relationship between two or more variables. A model is a simplification of reality designed to explain just part of a complex process of economic relationships. It is thus based on various simplifying assumptions.

Economies of scale When increasing the scale of production leads to a lower cost per unit of output.

Economies of scope When increasing the range of products produced by a firm reduces the cost of producing each one.

ECU (European Currency Unit) The predecessor to the euro: a weighted average of EU currencies. It was used as a reserve currency and for the operation of the exchange rate mechanism (ERM).

Efficiency wage hypothesis The hypothesis that the productivity of workers is affected by the wage rate that they receive.

Efficiency wage rate The profit-maximising wage rate for the firm after taking into account the effects of wage rates on worker motivation, turnover and recruitment.

Elastic demand (with respect to price) Where quantity demanded changes by a larger percentage than price. Ignoring the negative sign, it will have a value greater than 1.

Elasticity A measure of the responsiveness of a variable (e.g. quantity demanded or quantity supplied) to a change in one of its determinants (e.g. price or income).

Endogenous growth theory A theory that the rate of economic growth depends on the rate of technological progress and diffusion, both of which depend on size of the capital stock and the capital goods industries, and also on institutions, incentives and the role of government.

Endogenous money supply Money supply that is determined (at least in part) by the demand for money.

Entrepreneurship The initiating and organising of the production of new goods, or the introduction of new techniques, and the risk taking associated with it.

Envelope curve A long-run average cost curve drawn as the tangency points of a series of short-run average cost curves.

Environmental charges Charges for using natural resources (e.g. water or national parks), or for using the environment as a dump for waste (e.g. factory emissions or sewage).

Equation of exchange $MV = PQ$. The total level of spending on GDP (MV) equals the total value of goods and services produced (PQ) that go to make up GDP.

Equilibrium A position of balance. A position from which there is no inherent tendency to move away.

Equilibrium price The price where the quantity demanded equals the quantity supplied: the price where there is no shortage or surplus.

Equilibrium ('natural') unemployment The difference between those who would like employment at the current wage rate and those willing and able to take a job.

Equities Company shares. Holders of equities are owners of the company and share in its profits by receiving dividends.

Equity A distribution of income that is considered to be fair or just. Note that an equitable distribution is not the same as an equal distribution and that different people have different views on what is equitable.

ERM (exchange rate mechanism) A system of semi-fixed exchange rates used by most of the EU countries prior to adoption of the euro. Members' currencies were allowed to fluctuate against each other only within agreed bands. Collectively they floated against all other currencies.

Excess capacity (under monopolistic competition) In the long run, firms under monopolistic competition will produce at an output below their minimum-cost point.

Exchange equalisation account The gold and foreign exchange reserves account in the Bank of England.

Exchange rate The rate at which one national currency exchanges for another. The rate is expressed as the amount of one currency that is necessary to purchase *one unit* of another currency (e.g. $1.60 = £1).

Exchange rate band Where a currency is allowed to float between an upper and lower exchange rate, but is not allowed to move outside this band.

Exchange rate index or effective exchange rate A weighted average exchange rate expressed as an index where the value of the index is 100 in a given base year. The weights of the different currencies in the index add up to 1.

Exchange rate overshooting Where a fall (or rise) in the long-run equilibrium exchange rate causes the actual exchange rate to fall (or rise) by a greater amount before eventually moving back to the new long-run equilibrium level.

Exchange rate regime The system under which the government allows the exchange rate to be determined.

Exchange-rate transmission mechanism How a change in money supply affects aggregate demand via a change in exchange rates.

Exogenous money supply Money supply that does not depend on the demand for money but is set by the authorities.

Exogenous variable A variable whose value is determined independently of the model of which it is part.

Expectations-augmented Phillips curve A (short-run) Phillips curve whose position depends on the expected rate of inflation.

Explicit costs The payments to outside suppliers of inputs.

External benefits Benefits from production (or consumption) experienced by people *other* than the producer (or consumer).

External costs Costs of production (or consumption) borne by people *other* than the producer (or consumer).

External diseconomies of scale Where a firm's costs per unit of output increase as the size of the whole industry increases.

External economies of scale Where a firm's costs per unit of output decrease as the size of the whole *industry* grows.

Externalities Costs or benefits of production or consumption experienced by society but not by the producers or consumers themselves. Sometimes referred to as 'spillover' or 'third-party' costs or benefits.

Factors of production (or resources) The inputs into the production of goods and services: labour, land and raw materials, and capital.

Final expenditure Expenditure on goods and services. This is included in GDP and is part of aggregate demand.

Financial account of the balance of payments The record of the flows of money into and out of the country for the purposes of investment or as deposits in banks and other financial institutions.

Financial crowding out When an increase in government borrowing diverts money away from the private sector.

Financial deregulation The removal of or reduction in legal rules and regulations governing the activities of financial institutions.

Financial flexibility Where employers can vary their wage costs by changing the composition of their workforce or the terms on which workers are employed.

Financial intermediaries The general name for financial institutions (banks, building societies, etc.) which act as a means of channelling funds from depositors to borrowers.

Fine-tuning The use of demand management policy (fiscal or monetary) to smooth out cyclical fluctuations in the economy.

First-mover advantage When a firm gains from being the first one to take action.

Fiscal drag The tendency of automatic fiscal stabilisers to reduce the recovery of an economy from recession.

Fiscal policy Policy to affect aggregate demand by altering the balance between government expenditure and taxation.

Fiscal stance How deflationary or reflationary the Budget is.

Fixed costs Total costs that do not vary with the amount of output produced.

Fixed exchange rate (totally) Where the government takes whatever measures are necessary to maintain the exchange rate at some stated level.

Fixed factor An input that cannot be increased in supply within a given time period.

Flexible firm A firm that has the flexibility to respond to changing market conditions by changing the composition of its workforce.

Floating exchange rate When the government does not intervene in the foreign exchange markets, but simply allows the exchange rate to be freely determined by demand and supply.

Forward exchange market Where contracts are made today for the price at which currency will be exchanged at some specified future date.

Franchising Where a firm is given the licence to operate a given part of an industry for a specified length of time.

Free trade area A group of countries with no trade barriers between them.

Freely floating exchange rate Where the exchange rate is determined entirely by the forces of demand and supply in the foreign exchange market with no government intervention whatsoever.

Free-market economy An economy where all economic decisions are taken by individual households and firms and with no government intervention.

Free-rider problem When it is not possible to exclude other people from consuming a good that someone has bought.

Frictional (search) unemployment Unemployment that occurs as a result of imperfect information in the labour market. It often takes time for workers to find jobs (even though there are vacancies) and in the meantime they are unemployed.

Full-employment level of national income The level of national income at which there is no deficiency of demand.

Functional flexibility Where employers can switch workers from job to job as requirements change.

Funding Where the authorities alter the balance of bills and bonds for any given level of government borrowing.

Future price A price agreed today at which an item (e.g. commodities) will be exchanged at some set date in the future.

Futures or forward market A market in which contracts are made to buy or sell at some future date at a price agreed today.

Gaia philosophy The respect for the rights of the environment to remain unharmed by human activity. Humans should live in harmony with the planet and other species. We have a duty to be stewards of the natural environment, so that it can continue to be a self-maintaining and self-regulating system.

Game theory (or the theory of games) The study of alternative strategies oligopolists may choose to adopt, depending on their assumptions about their rivals' behaviour.

GDP (gross domestic product at market prices) The value of output (or income or expenditure) in terms of the prices actually paid. GDP = GVA + taxes on products – subsidies on products.

GDP deflator The price index of all final domestically produced goods and services: i.e. all items that contribute towards GDP.

General equilibrium A situation where all the millions of markets throughout the economy are in a simultaneous state of equilibrium.

General government debt The combined accumulated debt of central and local government.

General government deficit (or surplus) The combined deficit (or surplus) of central and local government.

Geographical immobility The lack of ability or willingness of people to move to jobs in other parts of the country.

GNY (gross national income) GDP plus net income from abroad.

Goodhart's law Controlling a symptom of a problem, or only part of the problem, will not cure the problem: it will simply mean that the part that is being controlled now becomes a poor indicator of the problem.

Government bonds or 'gilt-edged securities' A government security paying a fixed sum of money each year. It is redeemed by the government on its maturity date at its face value.

Government surplus (from a tax on a good) The total tax revenue earned by the government from sales of a good.

Green tax A tax on output designed to charge for the adverse effects of production on the environment. The socially efficient level of a green tax is equal to the marginal environmental cost of production.

Gross domestic final expenditure Total expenditure by a country's residents on final goods and services. It thus includes expenditure on imports and excludes expenditure on exports.

Gross domestic product (GDP) The value of output produced within the country over a 12-month period.

Gross national income (GNY) GDP plus net income from abroad.

Gross value added at basic prices (GVA) The sum of all the values added by all industries in the economy over a year. The figures exclude taxes on products (such as VAT) and include subsidies on products.

Historic costs The original amount a firm paid for factors it now owns.

Hit-and-run competition When a firm enters an industry to take advantage of temporarily high profits and then leaves again as soon as the high profits have been exhausted.

Horizontal merger When two firms in the same industry at the same stage in the production process merge.

Households' disposable income The income available for households to spend: i.e. personal incomes after deducting taxes on incomes and adding benefits.

Human capital The qualifications, skills and expertise that contribute to a worker's productivity.

Human Development Index (HDI) A composite index made up of three elements: an index for life expectancy, an index for school enrolment and adult literacy, and an index for GDP per capita (in PPP$).

Hysteresis The persistence of an effect even when the initial cause has ceased to operate. In economics, it refers to the persistence of unemployment even when the demand deficiency that caused it no longer exists.

Idle balances Money held for speculative purposes: money held in anticipation of a fall in asset prices.

Imperfect competition The collective name for monopolistic competition and oligopoly.

Implicit costs Costs which do not involve a direct payment of money to a third party, but which nevertheless involve a sacrifice of some alternative.

Import-substituting industrialisation (ISI) A strategy of restricting imports of manufactured goods and using the foreign exchange saved to build up domestic substitute industries.

Income effect (of a price change) The effect of a change in price on quantity demanded arising from the consumer becoming better or worse off as a result of the price change.

Income effect of a rise in wage rates Workers get a higher income for a given number of hours worked and may thus feel they need to work *fewer* hours as wage rates rise.

Income effect of a tax rise Tax increases reduce people's incomes and thus encourage people to work more.

Income elasticity of demand The percentage (or proportionate) change in quantity demanded divided by the percentage (or proportionate) change in income.

Income elasticity of demand (arc formula) ΔQ_{D}/average $Q_{D} \div \Delta Y$/average Y.

Increasing opportunity costs of production When additional production of one good involves ever-increasing sacrifices of another.

Independence (of firms in a market) Where the decisions of one firm in a market will not have any significant effect on the demand curves of its rivals.

Independent risks Where two risky events are unconnected. The occurrence of one will not affect the likelihood of the occurrence of the other.

Index number The value of a variable expressed as 100 plus or minus its percentage deviation from a base year.

Indirect taxes Taxes on expenditure (e.g. VAT). Paid to the tax authorities, not by the consumer, but indirectly by the suppliers of the goods or services.

Indivisibilities The impossibility of dividing a factor into smaller units.

Induced investment Investment that firms make to enable them to meet extra consumer demand.

Industrial policies Policies to encourage industrial investment and greater industrial efficiency.

Industry's infrastructure The network of supply agents, communications, skills, training facilities, distribution channels, specialised financial services, etc. that supports a particular industry.

Inelastic demand Where quantity demanded changes by a smaller percentage than price. Ignoring the negative sign, it will have a value less than 1.

Infant industry An industry that has a potential comparative advantage, but which is as yet too underdeveloped to be able to realise this potential.

Inferior goods Goods whose demand *decreases* as consumer incomes increase. Such goods have a negative income elasticity of demand.

Inflation rate (annual) The percentage increase in prices over a 12-month period.

Inflationary gap The excess of national expenditure over income (and injections over withdrawals) at the full-employment level of national income.

Infrastructure (industry's) The network of supply agents, communications, skills, training facilities, distribution channels, specialised financial services, etc. that supports a particular industry.

Injections (J) Expenditure on the production of domestic firms coming from outside the inner flow of the circular flow of income. Injections equal investment (I_{d}) plus government expenditure (G_{d}) plus expenditure on exports (X).

Input–output analysis This involves dividing the economy into sectors where each sector is a user of inputs from and a supplier of outputs to other sectors. The technique examines how these inputs and outputs can be matched to the total resources available in the economy.

Insiders Those in employment who can use their privileged position (either as members of unions or because of specific skills) to secure pay rises despite an excess supply of labour (unemployment).

Inter-temporal substitution effect Higher prices may lead to higher interest rates and thus less borrowing and more saving.

Interdependence (under oligopoly) One of the two key features of oligopoly. Each firm will be affected by its rivals' decisions. Likewise its decisions will affect its rivals. Firms recognise this interdependence. This recognition will affect their decisions.

Interest-rate transmission mechanism How a change in money supply affects aggregate demand via a change in interest rates.

International harmonisation of economic policies Where countries attempt to co-ordinate their macroeconomic policies so as to achieve common goals.

International liquidity The supply of currencies in the world acceptable for financing international trade and investment.

International substitution effect As prices rise, people at home and abroad buy less of this country's products and more of products from abroad.

International trade multiplier The effect on national income in country B of a change in exports (or imports) of country A.

Intervention price (in the CAP) The price at which the EU is prepared to buy a foodstuff if the market price were to be below it.

Interventionist supply-side policies Policies to increase aggregate supply by government intervention to counteract the deficiencies of the market.

Investment The production of items that are not for immediate consumption.

Joint float Where a group of currencies pegged to each other jointly float against other currencies.

Joint supply Where the production of more of one good leads to the production of more of another.

Kinked demand theory The theory that oligopolists face a demand curve that is kinked at the current price, demand being significantly more elastic above the current price than below. The effect of this is to create a situation of price stability.

Labour All forms of human input, both physical and mental, into current production.

Labour force The number employed plus the number unemployed.

Land (and raw materials) Inputs into production that are provided by nature: e.g. unimproved land and mineral deposits in the ground.

Law of comparative advantage Trade can benefit all countries if they specialise in the goods in which they have a comparative advantage.

Law of demand The quantity of a good demanded per period of time will fall as price rises and will rise as price falls, other things being equal (*ceteris paribus*).

Law of diminishing (marginal) returns When one or more factors are held fixed, there will come a point beyond which the extra output from additional units of the variable factor will diminish.

Lender of last resort The role of the Bank of England as the guarantor of sufficient liquidity in the monetary system.

Liabilities All legal claims for payment that outsiders have on an institution.

LIBOR The London inter-bank offered rate – the rate at which banks lend to each other. The LIBOR varies with the length of loan.

Liquidity The ease with which an asset can be converted into cash without loss.

Liquidity preference The demand for holding assets in the form of money.

Liquidity ratio The proportion of a bank's total assets held in liquid form.

Liquidity trap When interest rates are at their floor and thus any further increases in money supply will not be spent but merely be held in idle balances as people wait for the economy to recover and/or interest rates to rise.

Lock-outs Union members are temporarily laid off until they are prepared to agree to the firm's conditions.

Long run The period of time long enough for *all* factors to be varied.

Long run under perfect competition The period of time that is long enough for new firms to enter the industry.

Long-run average cost curve A curve that shows how average cost varies with output on the assumption that *all* factors are variable. (It is assumed that the least-cost method of production will be chosen for each output.)

Long-run marginal cost The extra cost of producing one more unit of output assuming that all factors are variable. (It is assumed that the least-cost method of production will be chosen for this extra output.)

Long-run profit maximisation An alternative theory of the firm which assumes that managers aim to shift cost and revenue curves so as to maximise profits over some longer time period.

Long-run shut-down point This is where the *AR* curve is tangential to the *LRAC* curve. The firm can just make normal profits. Any fall in revenue below this level will cause a profit-maximising firm to shut down once all costs have become variable.

Lorenz curve A curve showing the proportion of national income earned by any given percentage of the population (measured from the poorest upwards).

Macroeconomics The branch of economics that studies economic aggregates (grand totals): e.g. the overall level of prices, output and employment in the economy.

Managed floating A system of flexible exchange rates but where the government intervenes to prevent excessive fluctuations or even to achieve an unofficial target exchange rate.

Marginal benefit The additional benefit of doing a little bit more (or 1 unit more if a unit can be measured) of an activity.

Marginal consumer surplus The excess of utility from the consumption of one more unit of a good (*MU*) over the price paid: $MCS = MU - P$.

Marginal cost (of an activity) The additional cost of doing a little bit more (or 1 unit more if a unit can be measured) of an activity.

Marginal cost (of production) The cost of producing one more unit of output: $MC = \Delta TC/\Delta Q$.

Marginal disutility of work The extra sacrifice/hardship to a worker of working an extra unit of time in any given time period (e.g. an extra hour per day).

Marginal physical product The extra output gained by the employment of one more unit of the variable factor: $MPP = \Delta TPP/\Delta Q_v$.

Marginal productivity theory The theory that the demand for a factor depends on its marginal revenue product.

Marginal propensity to consume The proportion of a rise in national income that goes on consumption: $mpc = \Delta C/\Delta Y$.

Marginal propensity to consume domestically produced goods (mpc_d) The proportion of a rise in national income that is spent on goods and services produced within the country.

Marginal propensity to import The proportion of an increase in national income that is spent on imports: $mpm = \Delta M/\Delta Y$.

Marginal propensity to save The proportion of an increase in national income saved: $mps = \Delta S/\Delta Y$.

Marginal propensity to withdraw The proportion of an increase in national income that is withdrawn from the circular flow: $mpw = \Delta W/\Delta Y$, where $mpw = mps + mpt + mpm$.

Marginal rate of income tax The income tax rate. The rate paid on each *additional* pound earned: $\Delta T/\Delta Y$.

Marginal revenue The extra revenue gained by selling one more unit per time period: $MR = \Delta TR/\Delta Q$.

Marginal revenue product (of a factor) The extra revenue a firm earns from employing one more unit of a variable factor: $MRP_{factor} = MPP_{factor} \times MR_{good}$.

Marginal tax propensity The proportion of an increase in national income paid in tax: $mpt = \Delta T/\Delta Y$.

Marginal utility The extra satisfaction gained from consuming one extra unit of a good within a given time period.

Market The interaction between buyers and sellers.

Market clearing A market clears when supply matches demand, leaving no shortage or surplus.

Market for loanable funds The market for loans from and deposits into the banking system.

Market loans Short-term loans (e.g. money at call and short notice).

Market-orientated supply-side policies Policies to increase aggregate supply by freeing up the market.

Mark-up A profit margin added to average cost to arrive at price.

Maturity gap The difference in the average maturity of loans and deposits.

Maximax The strategy of choosing the policy that has the best possible outcome.

Maximin The strategy of choosing the policy whose worst possible outcome is the least bad.

Maximum price A price ceiling set by the government or some other agency. The price is not allowed to rise above this level (although it is allowed to fall below it).

Mean (or arithmetic mean) The sum of the values of each of the members of the sample divided by the total number in the sample.

Means-tested benefits Benefits whose amount depends on the recipient's income or assets.

Median The value of the middle member of the sample.

Medium of exchange Something that is acceptable in exchange for goods and services.

Menu costs of inflation The costs associated with having to adjust price lists or labels.

Merit goods Goods which the government feels that people will underconsume and which therefore ought to be subsidised or provided free.

Microeconomics The branch of economics that studies individual units: e.g. households, firms and industries. It studies the interrelationships between these units in determining the pattern of production and distribution of goods and services.

Minimum price A price floor set by the government or some other agency. The price is not allowed to fall below this level (although it is allowed to rise above it).

Minimum reserve ratio A minimum ratio of cash (or other specified liquid assets) to deposits (either total or selected) that the central bank requires banks to hold.

Mixed economy An economy where economic decisions are made partly by the government and partly through the market.

Mixed market economy A market economy where there is some government intervention.

Mobility of labour The willingness and ability of labour to move to another job.

Monetarists Those who attribute inflation solely to rises in money supply.

Monetary base Notes and coin outside the central bank.

Monetary policy Policy to affect aggregate demand by altering the supply or cost of money (rate of interest).

Money illusion When people believe that a money wage or price increase represents a *real* increase: in other words, they ignore or underestimate inflation.

Money market The market for short-term loans and deposits.

Money multiplier The number of times greater the expansion of money supply is than the expansion of the monetary base that caused it: $\Delta Ms/\Delta Mb$.

Monopolistic competition A market structure where, like perfect competition, there are many firms and freedom of entry into the industry, but where each firm produces a differentiated product and thus has some control over its price.

Monopoly A market structure where there is only one firm in the industry.

Monopsony A market with a single buyer or employer.

Moral hazard The temptation to take more risks when you know that someone else will cover the risks if you get into difficulties. In the case of banks taking risks, the 'someone else' may be another bank, the central bank or the government.

Multiplier (injections multiplier) The number of times a rise in income exceeds the rise in injections that caused it: $k = \Delta Y/\Delta J$.

Multiplier effect An initial increase in aggregate demand of £xm leads to an eventual rise in national income that is greater than £xm.

Multiplier formula (injections multiplier) The formula for the multiplier is $k = 1/mpw$ or $1/(1 - mpc_d)$.

Narrow definitions of money Items of money that can be spent directly (cash and money in chequebook/debit-card accounts).

Nash equilibrium The position resulting from everyone making their optimal decision based on their assumptions about their rivals' decisions. Without collusion, there is no incentive for any firm to move from this position.

National debt The accumulated budget deficits (less surpluses) over the years: the total amount of government borrowing.

National expenditure on domestic product (E) Aggregate demand in the Keynesian model: i.e. $C_d + J$.

Nationalised industries State-owned industries that produce goods or services that are sold in the market.

Natural level of output The level of output in monetarist analysis where the vertical long-run aggregate supply curve cuts the horizontal axis.

Natural level of unemployment The level of equilibrium unemployment in monetarist analysis measured as the difference between the (vertical) long-run gross labour supply curve (N) and the (vertical) long-run effective labour supply curve (AS_L).

Natural monopoly A situation where long-run average costs would be lower if an industry were under monopoly than if it were shared between two or more competitors.

Natural rate of unemployment The rate of unemployment at which there is no excess or deficiency of demand for labour.

Natural wastage When a firm wishing to reduce its workforce does so by not replacing those who leave or retire.

Near money Highly liquid assets (other than cash).

Negative income tax A combined system of tax and benefits. As people earn more, they gradually lose their benefits until beyond a certain level they begin paying taxes.

Net errors and omissions A statistical adjustment to ensure that the two sides of the balance of payments account balance. It is necessary because of errors in compiling the statistics.

Net investment Total investment minus depreciation.

Net national product (NNY) GNY minus depreciation.

Network economies The benefits to consumers of having a network of other people using the same product or service.

New classical school The school of economists which believes that markets clear virtually instantaneously and that expectations are formed 'rationally'.

New Keynesians Economists who seek to explain the downward stickiness of real wages and the resulting persistence of unemployment.

Nominal GDP GDP measured in current prices. These figures take no account of inflation.

Nominal values Money values measured at *current* prices.

Non-accelerating-inflation rate of unemployment (NAIRU) The rate of unemployment consistent with a constant rate of inflation. (In monetarist analysis, this is the same as the natural rate of unemployment: the rate of unemployment at which the vertical long-run Phillips curve cuts the horizontal axis.)

Non-bank private sector Households and non-bank firms. In other words, everyone in the country other than banks and the government (central and local).

Non-collusive oligopoly Where oligopolists have no agreement between themselves, formal, informal or tacit.

Non-excludability Where it is not possible to provide a good or service to one person without it thereby being available for others to enjoy.

Non-price competition Competition in terms of product promotion (advertising, packaging, etc.) or product development.

Non-rivalry Where the consumption of a good or service by one person will not prevent others from enjoying it.

Normal goods Goods whose demand increases as consumer incomes increase. They have a positive income elasticity of demand. Luxury goods will have a higher income elasticity of demand than more basic goods.

Normal profit The opportunity cost of being in business: the profit that could have been earned in the next best alternative business. It is counted as a cost of production.

Normal rate of return The rate of return (after taking risks into account) that could be earned elsewhere.

Normative statement A value judgement.

Numerical flexibility Where employers can change the size of their workforce as their labour requirements change.

Occupational immobility The lack of ability or willingness of people to move to other jobs irrespective of location.

Oligopoly A market structure where there are few enough firms to enable barriers to be erected against the entry of new firms.

Oligopsony A market with just a few buyers or employers.

Open economy One that trades with and has financial dealings with other countries.

Open-market operations The sale (or purchase) by the authorities of government securities in the open market in order to reduce (or increase) money supply or influence interest rates.

Opportunity cost Cost measured in terms of the best alternative forgone.

Optimal currency area The optimal size of a currency area is the one that maximises the benefits from having a single currency relative to the costs. If the area were increased or decreased in size, the costs would rise relative to the benefits.

Outsiders Those out of work or employed on a casual, part-time or short-term basis, who have little or no power to influence wages or employment.

Overheads Costs arising from the general running of an organisation, and only indirectly related to the level of output.

Participation rate The percentage of the working-age population that is part of the workforce.

Perfect competition A market structure where there are many firms; where there is freedom of entry into the industry; where all firms produce an identical product; and where all firms are price takers.

Perfectly contestable market A market where there is free and costless entry and exit.

Phillips curve A curve showing the relationship between (price) inflation and unemployment. The original Phillips curve plotted *wage* inflation against unemployment for the years 1861–1957.

Picketing When people on strike gather at the entrance to the firm and attempt to dissuade workers or delivery vehicles from entering.

Plant economies of scale Economies of scale that arise because of the large size of the factory.

Poll tax A lump-sum tax per head of the population. Since it is a fixed *amount*, it has a marginal rate of zero with respect to both income and wealth.

Portfolio balance The balance of assets, according to their liquidity, that people choose to hold in their portfolios.

Positive statement A value-free statement that can be tested by an appeal to the facts.

Potential growth The percentage annual increase in the capacity of the economy to produce.

Potential output The output that could be produced in the economy if there were a full employment of resources (including labour).

Poverty trap Where poor people are discouraged from working or getting a better job because any extra income they earn will be largely taken away in taxes and lost benefits.

Predatory pricing Where a firm sets its prices below average cost in order to drive competitors out of business.

Preferential trading arrangements A trade agreement whereby trade between the signatories is freer than trade with the rest of the world.

Price benchmark A price that is typically used. Firms, when raising prices, will usually raise them from one benchmark to another.

Price discrimination Where a firm sells the same product at different prices in different markets or different parts of the market or to different customers.

Price elasticity of demand ($P\varepsilon_D$) The percentage (or proportionate) change in quantity demanded divided by the percentage (or proportionate) change in price: $\%\Delta Q_D \div \%\Delta P$.

Price elasticity of demand (arc formula) ΔQ/average $Q \div \Delta P$/average P. The average in each case is the average between the two points being measured.

Price elasticity of supply The percentage (or proportionate) change in quantity supplied divided by the percentage (or proportionate) change in price: $\%\Delta Q_S \div \%\Delta P$.

Price elasticity of supply (arc formula) ΔQ_S/average $Q_S \div \Delta P$/average P.

Price mechanism The system in a market economy whereby changes in price in response to changes in demand and supply have the effect of making demand equal to supply.

Price taker A person or firm with no power to be able to influence the market price.

Primary labour market The market for permanent full-time core workers.

Principal–agent problem Where people (principals), as a result of lack of knowledge, cannot ensure that their best interests are served by their agents.

Prisoners' dilemma Where two or more firms (or people), by attempting independently to choose the best strategy for whatever the other(s) are likely to do, end up in a worse position than if they had co-operated in the first place.

Private efficiency Where a person's marginal benefit from a given activity equals the marginal cost.

Private limited company A company owned by its shareholders. Shareholders' liability is limited to the value of their shares. Shares can only be bought and sold privately.

Producer surplus The excess of total revenue over total cost: i.e. profit.

Product differentiation When one firm's product is sufficiently different from its rivals' to allow it to raise the price of the product without customers all switching to the rivals' products. A situation where a firm faces a downward-sloping demand curve.

Production The transformation of inputs into outputs by firms in order to earn profit (or meet some other objective).

Production possibility curve A curve showing all the possible combinations of two goods that a country can produce within a specified time period with all its resources fully and efficiently employed.

Productive efficiency A situation where firms are producing the maximum output for a given amount of inputs, or producing a given output at the least cost.

Productivity deal When, in return for a wage increase, a union agrees to changes in working practices that will increase output per worker.

Profit (rate of) Total profit ($T\Pi$) as a proportion of the total capital employed (K): $r = T\Pi/K$.

Profit-maximising rule Profit is maximised where marginal revenue equals marginal cost.

Progressive tax A tax whose average rate with respect to income rises as income rises.

Proportional tax A tax whose average rate with respect to income stays the same as income rises.

Prudential control The insistence by the Bank of England that banks maintain adequate liquidity.

Public good A good or service that has the features of non-rivalry and non-excludability and as a result would not be provided by the free market.

Public limited company A company owned by its shareholders. Shareholders' liability is limited to the value of their shares. Shares may be bought and sold publicly – on the Stock Exchange.

Public-sector borrowing requirement The old name for the public-sector net cash requirement.

Public-sector debt repayment (PSDR) or **Public-sector surplus** The old name for a negative public-sector net cash requirement. The (annual) surplus of the public sector, and thus the amount of debt that can be repaid.

Public-sector net cash requirement The (annual) deficit of the public sector, and thus the amount that the public sector must borrow. In the UK the principal measure, which takes into account financial transactions by the public sector, is known as the public sector net cash requirement.

Purchasing-power parity exchange rate The rate of exchange of a country's currency into the US dollar that would allow a given amount of that currency to buy the same amount of goods in the USA as within the country concerned.

Pure fiscal policy Fiscal policy that does not involve any change in money supply.

Quantitative easing A deliberate attempt by the central bank to increase the money supply by buying large quantities of securities through open-market operations. These securities could be securitised mortgage and other private sector debt or government bonds.

Quantity demanded The amount of a good a consumer is willing and able to buy at a given price over a given period of time.

Quantity theory of money The price level (P) is directly related to the quantity of money in the economy (M).

Quota (set by a cartel) The output that a given member of a cartel is allowed to produce (production quota) or sell (sales quota).

Rate of economic growth The percentage increase in output between two moments of time, typically over a 12-month period.

Rate of profit Total profit ($T\Pi$) as a proportion of the capital employed (K): $r = T\Pi/K$.

Rational choices Choices that involve weighing up the benefit of any activity against its opportunity cost.

Rational consumer A person who weighs up the costs and benefits to him or her of each additional unit of a good purchased.

Rational consumer behaviour The attempt to maximise total consumer surplus.

Rational economic behaviour Doing more of activities whose marginal benefit exceeds their marginal cost and doing less of those activities whose marginal cost exceeds their marginal benefit.

Rational expectations Expectations based on the *current* situation. These expectations are based on the information people have to hand. Whilst this information may be imperfect and therefore people will make errors, these errors will be random.

Rational producer behaviour When a firm weighs up the costs and benefits of alternative courses of action and then seeks to maximise its net benefit.

Rationalisation The reorganising of production (often after a merger) so as to cut out waste and duplication and generally to reduce costs.

Rationing Where the government restricts the amount of a good that people are allowed to buy.

Real balance effect As the price level rises, the value of people's money assets falls. They therefore spend less in their attempt to protect the real value of their savings.

Real business cycle theory The new classical theory that explains cyclical fluctuations in terms of shifts in aggregate supply, rather than aggregate demand.

Real GDP GDP measured in constant prices that ruled in a chosen base year, such as 2000 or 2005. These figures *do* take account of inflation. When inflation is positive, real GDP figures will grow more slowly than nominal GDP figures.

Real growth values Values of the rate of growth of GDP or any other variable after taking inflation into account. The real value of the growth in a variable equals its growth in money (or 'nominal') value minus the rate of inflation.

Real income Income measured in terms of how much it can buy. If your *money* income rises by 10 per cent, but prices rise by 8 per cent, you can only buy 2 per cent more goods than before. Your *real* income has risen by 2 per cent.

Real values Money values corrected for inflation.

Real-wage unemployment Disequilibrium unemployment caused by real wages being driven up above the market-clearing level.

Recession A period where national output falls for six months or more.

Recognised banks Banks licensed by the Bank of England. All financial institutions using the word 'bank' in their title have to be recognised by the Bank of England. This requires them to have paid-up capital of at least £5 million and to meet other requirements about their asset structure and range of services.

Rediscounting bills of exchange Buying bills before they reach maturity.

Reflationary policy Fiscal or monetary policy designed to increase the rate of growth of aggregate demand.

Regional multiplier effects When a change in injections into or withdrawals from a particular region causes a multiplied change in income in that region.

Regional unemployment Structural unemployment occurring in specific regions of the country.

Regressive tax A tax whose average rate with respect to income falls as income rises.

Regulatory capture Where the regulator is persuaded to operate in the industry's interests rather than those of the consumer.

Relative price The price of one good compared with another (e.g. good X is twice the price of good Y).

Repos Sale and repurchase agreements. An agreement between two financial institutions whereby one in effect borrows from another by selling it assets, agreeing to buy them back (repurchase them) at a fixed price and on a fixed date.

Restrictive practice Where two or more firms agree to adopt common practices to restrict competition.

Retail banks 'High-street banks'. Banks operating extensive branch networks and dealing directly with the general public, with published interest rates and charges.

Retail deposits and loans Deposits and loans made through bank/building society branches at published interest rates.

Retail prices index (RPI) An index of the prices of goods bought by a typical household.

Revaluation Where the government re-pegs the exchange rate at a higher level.

Reverse repos When gilts or other assets are *purchased* under a sale and repurchase agreement. They become an asset to the purchaser.

Risk When an outcome may or may not occur, but its probability of occurring is known.

Sale and repurchase agreement (repo) An agreement between two financial institutions whereby one in effect borrows from another by selling it assets, agreeing to buy them back (repurchase them) at a fixed price and on a fixed date.

Scarcity The excess of human wants over what can actually be produced to fulfil these wants.

Search theory This examines people's behaviour under conditions of ignorance where it takes time to search for information.

Seasonal unemployment Unemployment associated with industries or regions where the demand for labour is lower at certain times of the year.

Secondary action Industrial action taken against a company not directly involved in a dispute (e.g. a supplier of raw materials to a firm whose employees are on strike).

Secondary labour market The market for peripheral workers, usually employed on a temporary or part-time basis, or a less secure 'permanent' basis.

Secondary marketing Where assets are sold before maturity to another institution or individual.

Securitisation Where future cash flows (e.g. from interest rate or mortgage payments) are turned into marketable securities, such as bonds.

Self-fulfilling speculation The actions of speculators tend to cause the very effect that they had anticipated.

Set-aside A system in the EU of paying farmers not to use a certain proportion of their land.

Short run (in production) The period of time over which at least one factor is fixed.

Short-run shut-down point This is where the *AR* curve is tangential to the *AVC* curve. The firm can only just cover its variable costs. Any fall in revenue below this level will cause a profit-maximising firm to shut down immediately.

Short run under perfect competition The period during which there is too little time for new firms to enter the industry.

Sight deposits Deposits that can be withdrawn on demand without penalty.

Social benefit Private benefit plus externalities in consumption.

Social cost Private cost plus externalities in production.

Social efficiency Production and consumption at the point where marginal social benefit equals marginal social cost ($MSB = MSC$).

Special deposits A system used up to 1980. Deposits that the banks could be required to make in the Bank of England. They remained frozen there until the Bank of England chose to release them.

Special-purpose vehicles (SPVs) Legal entities created by financial institutions for conducting specific financial functions, such as bundling assets together into fixed interest bonds and selling them.

Specialisation and division of labour Where production is broken down into a number of simpler, more specialised tasks, thus allowing workers to acquire a high degree of efficiency.

Specific tax A tax on a good levied at a fixed amount per unit of the good, irrespective of the price of that unit.

Speculation Where people make buying or selling decisions based on their anticipations of future prices.

Speculators People who buy (or sell) commodities or financial assets with the intention of profiting by selling them (or buying them back) at a later date at a higher (lower) price.

Spot price The current market price.

Stabilising speculation Where the actions of speculators tend to reduce price fluctuations.

Stakeholders (in a company) People who are affected by a company's activities and/or performance (customers, employees, owners, creditors, people living in the neighbourhood, etc.). They may or may not be in a position to take decisions, or influence decision taking, in the firm.

Standardised unemployment rate The measure of the unemployment rate used by the ILO and OECD. The unemployed are defined as persons of working age who are without work, available to start work within two weeks and either have actively looked for work in the last four weeks or are waiting to take up an appointment.

Steady-state national income The long-run equilibrium level of national income. The level at which all investment is used to maintain the existing capital stock at its current level.

Strategic trade theory The theory that protecting/supporting certain industries can enable them to compete more effectively with large monopolistic rivals abroad. The effect of the protection is to increase long-run competition and may enable the protected firms to exploit a comparative advantage that they could not have done otherwise.

Structural unemployment Unemployment that arises from changes in the pattern of demand or supply in the economy. People made redundant in one part of the economy cannot immediately take up jobs in other parts (even though there are vacancies).

Sub-prime debt Debt where there is a high risk of default by the borrower (e.g. mortgage holders who are on low incomes facing higher interest rates and falling house prices).

Substitute goods A pair of goods that are considered by consumers to be alternatives to each other. As the price of one goes up, the demand for the other rises.

Substitutes in supply These are two goods where an increased production of one means diverting resources away from producing the other.

Substitution effect of a price change The effect of a change in price on quantity demanded arising from the consumer switching to or from alternative (substitute) products.

Substitution effect of a rise in wage rates Workers will tend to substitute income for leisure as leisure now has a higher opportunity cost. This effect leads to *more* hours being worked as wage rates rise.

Substitution effect of a tax rise Tax increases reduce the opportunity cost of leisure and thus encourage people to work less.

Sunk costs Costs that cannot be recouped (e.g. by transferring assets to other uses).

Supernormal profit (also known as **pure profit**, **economic profit**, **abnormal profit**, or simply **profit**). The excess of total profit above normal profit.

Supply curve A graph showing the relationship between the price of a good and the quantity of the good supplied over a given period of time.

Supply schedule A table showing the different quantities of a good that producers are willing and able to supply at various prices over a given time period. A supply schedule can be for an individual producer or group of producers, or for all producers (the market supply schedule).

Supply-side economics An approach that focuses directly on aggregate supply and how to shift the aggregate supply curve outwards.

Supply-side policy Government policy that attempts to alter the level of aggregate supply directly (rather than through changes in aggregate demand).

Sustainability (environmental) The ability of the environment to survive its use for economic activity.

Sustainable output The level of national output corresponding to no excess or deficiency of aggregate demand.

Tacit collusion Where oligopolists take care not to engage in price cutting, excessive advertising or other forms of competition. There may be unwritten 'rules' of collusive behaviour such as price leadership.

Takeover bid Where one firm attempts to purchase another by offering to buy the shares of that company from its shareholders.

Tariff escalation The system whereby tariff rates increase the closer a product is to the finished stage of production.

Tariffs (or import levies) Taxes on imported products: i.e. customs duties.

Tax allowance An amount of income that can be earned tax-free. Tax allowances vary according to a person's circumstances.

Taylor rule A rule adopted by a central bank for setting the rate of interest. It will raise the interest rate if (a) inflation is above target or (b) real national income is above the sustainable level (or unemployment is below the equilibrium rate). The rule states how much interest rates will be changed in each case.

Technological unemployment Structural unemployment that occurs as a result of the introduction of labour-saving technology.

Terms of trade The price index of exports divided by the price index of imports and then expressed as a percentage. This means that the terms of trade will be 100 in the base year.

Third-degree price discrimination When a firm divides consumers into different groups and charges a different price to consumers in different groups, but the same price to all the consumers within a group.

Time deposits Deposits that require notice of withdrawal or where a penalty is charged for withdrawals on demand.

Total consumer expenditure on a product (*TE*) (per period of time) The price of the product multiplied by the quantity purchased: $TE = P \times Q$.

Total consumer surplus The excess of a person's total utility from the consumption of a good (*TU*) over the amount that person spends on it (*TE*): $TCS = TU - TE$.

Total cost The sum of total fixed costs and total variable costs: $TC = TFC + TVC$.

Total physical product The total output of a product per period of time that is obtained from a given amount of inputs.

Total (private) surplus Total consumer surplus (*TU – TE*) plus total producer surplus (*TR – TVC*).

Total producer surplus (*TPS*) Total revenue minus total variable cost (*TR – TVC*): in other words, total profit plus total fixed cost (*TΠ + TFC*).

Total revenue (*TR*) (per period of time) The total amount received by firms from the sale of a product, before the deduction of taxes or any other costs. The price multiplied by the quantity sold: $TR = P \times Q$.

Total social surplus Total benefits to society from consuming a good minus total costs to society from producing it. In the absence of externalities, total social surplus is the same as total (private) surplus.

Total utility The total satisfaction a consumer gets from the consumption of all the units of a good consumed within a given time period.

Tradable permits Each firm is given a permit to produce a given level of pollution. If less than the permitted amount is produced, the firm is given a credit. This can then be sold to another firm, allowing it to exceed its original limit.

Trade creation Where a customs union leads to greater specialisation according to comparative advantage and thus a shift in production from higher-cost to lower-cost sources.

Trade cycle or business cycle The periodic fluctuations of national output round its long-term trend.

Trade diversion Where a customs union diverts consumption from goods produced at a lower cost outside the union to goods produced at a higher cost (but tariff free) within the union.

Traditional theory of the firm The analysis of pricing and output decisions of the firm under various market conditions, assuming that the firm wishes to maximise profit.

Transfer payments Moneys transferred from one person or group to another (e.g. from the government to individuals) without production taking place.

Treasury bills Bills of exchange issued by the Bank of England on behalf of the government. They are a means whereby the government raises short-term finance.

Uncertainty When an outcome may or may not occur and its probability of occurring is not known.

Underemployment Where people who want full-time work are only able to find part-time work.

Unemployed (economist's definition) Those of working age who are without work, but who are available for work at current wage rates.

Unemployment rate The number unemployed expressed as a percentage of the labour force.

Unit elastic demand Where quantity demanded changes by the same percentage as price. Ignoring the negative sign, it will have a value equal to 1.

Universal benefits Benefits paid to everyone in a certain category irrespective of their income or assets.

Value added tax (VAT) A tax on goods and services, charged at each stage of production as a percentage of the value added at that stage.

Variable costs Total costs that vary with the amount of output produced.

Variable factor An input that can be increased in supply within a given time period.

Velocity of circulation The number of times annually that money on average is spent on goods and services that make up GDP.

Vent for surplus When international trade enables a country to exploit resources that would otherwise be unused.

Wage–price spiral Wages and prices chasing each other as the aggregate demand curve continually shifts to the right and the aggregate supply curve continually shifts upwards.

Wage taker An employer (or employee) who is unable to influence the wage rate.

Weighted average The average of several items, where each item is ascribed a weight according to its importance. The weights must add up to 1.

Wholesale banks Banks specialising in large-scale deposits and loans and dealing mainly with companies. Interest rates and charges may be negotiable.

Wholesale deposits and loans Large-scale deposits and loans made by and to firms at negotiated interest rates.

Wide monetary base (M0) Notes and coin outside the central bank plus banks' operational deposits with the central bank.

Withdrawals (W) (or leakages) Incomes of households or firms that are not passed on round the inner flow. Withdrawals equal net saving (S) plus net taxes (T) plus expenditure on imports (M): $W = S + T + M$.

Working to rule Workers do the bare minimum they have to, as set out in their job descriptions.

Index

Page numbers in **bold** indicate definitions